NO GREATER LOVE: THE TRUE STORY OF FATHER JOHN P. WESSEL

NO GREATER LOVE:
THE TRUE STORY OF
FATHER JOHN P. WESSEL

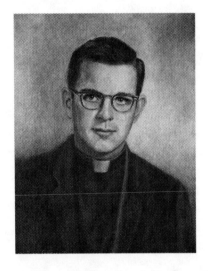

A Biography of Father John P. Wessel

Karin M. Burke

with

Foreword by Father Andrew Apostoli, C.F.R.

Introduction by Monsignor Joseph C. Shenrock, P.A.

This book was printed in the United States of America.

To order additional copies of this book, contact:
Xlibris Corporation
1-888-795-4274
www.Xlibris.com
Orders@Xlibris.com
23304

CONTENTS

Dedication

To the Sacred Heart of Jesus and the Immaculate Heart of Mary

To my Mother and Father

with my eternal love and gratitude

*   *   *

To all our priests, and especially to Monsignor Joseph C. Shenrock
for his friendship and support

To all mothers and fathers of priests, and especially to
Mrs. Kathleen Hogan Wessel for her gracious example and strong faith

To our Holy Fathers, Pope John Paul II
Pope Benedict XVI

FOREWORD

by Father Andrew Apostoli, C.F.R.

Father John Patrick Wessel was ordained a "priest forever" on May 22, 1965. That was right during the time of the Second Vatican Council, which held its final session in the Fall of that year. The Council was convoked by Pope John XXIII, who prayed it would bring about a "New Pentecost" for the Catholic Church, with a new outpouring of the Holy Spirit upon the Church and on each of her members. As we know from Catholic theology, the Ordination of a priest involves a generous outpouring of the Holy Spirit, transforming the man who receives the Gift of God into an "alter Christus," or "another Christ." As a result, when he carries out his priestly office, he will speak and act "in persona Christi," or "in the person of Christ."

Archbishop Fulton J. Sheen was a noted participant at the Second Vatican Council. He deeply loved the Priesthood! He saw the importance of priestly holiness in the mission of the Church. So important was it that he remarked shortly after the Council, "If there is any key to the reform of the Church and the salvation of the world, it lies in the renewal of the Priesthood." How prophetic he was!

He also spoke in terms of a "Sanctified Priesthood" as a fruit of the Council. Priests can and will be holy if they submit themselves to the light of truth and the fire of love being poured forth within them by the Holy Spirit they received on the day of their Ordination. In St. Paul's words to his young disciple Timothy, "I remind you to stir into flame the Gift of God bestowed when my hands were laid on you. The Spirit God has given us is no cowardly spirit, but rather one that makes us strong, loving and wise." (2 Tim. 1:6-7).

Fr. John Wessel was, without doubt, an outstanding example of the "Sanctified Priesthood!" Though he was a priest for only six years (1965-1971), he gathered a great harvest of souls for the Kingdom of God. He touched countless lives as a dedicated parish priest through his inspiring sermons in the pulpit, and his ministry of mercy in the confessional or at the bedside of the sick, and as an excellent teacher of Sacred Scripture and Religion. But it was, above all, the youth through the Catholic Youth Organization (CYO) that he loved most and ministered to so well! They, in turn, flocked to his Masses, retreats and service projects. He was a humble and holy priest, faithful to the Magisterium of the Church. At a time when many priests and religious were leaving their consecrated vocations, he wanted to be a good priestly example, especially for the sake of his youth. As he once wrote while a seminarian, "The eyes of the world are on a priest!"

Archbishop Fulton J. Sheen, in speaking of Jesus, would always stress that He was both Priest and Victim. Pagan priests and even the priests of the Old Testament, he would say, always offered a victim separate from themselves. But Jesus offered Himself, thus making Himself, the Victim offered as well as the Priest offerer. Archbishop Sheen said that every Catholic Priest then must, like Jesus, be both a priest and a victim. Like Jesus, Fr. Wessel was both a priest and a victim. As a priest, he ministered the Sacraments and offered spiritual help to the people. As a victim, he offered himself daily in the fulfillment of his priestly responsibilities. He could say like St. Paul, whom he admired so much as a tireless worker-priest, his life was being poured forth as a libation. (Cf. 2 Tim. 4:6). For the overwhelming majority of priests, being a "victim" with Jesus means the "white martyrdom" of daily giving in service to the people of God. But to Fr. John Patrick Wessel, God also gave the crown of "red martyrdom" so that he became a victim of that supreme love which Jesus described as "laying down your life for your friends!" (Cf. Jn 15:13).

No doubt, as Fr. Wessel offered what would be his last Mass on the morning of Friday, December 17, 1971, when he said the words of consecration over the bread, "This is My Body which will be given up for you," he had no idea that by that night, he would join Jesus in offering up his own body and the life it held. Nor did he realize as he consecrated the chalice filled with wine that morning with the words, "This is my Blood . . . It will be shed for you and for all," that he would shed his own blood. He was attempting to help a young distraught Vietnam War veteran who in his confusion and distress, shot the young priest who had come to offer him counsel and comfort. Jesus the Eternal Priest-Victim had offered Himself as priest-victim for souls. Fr. John Patrick Wessel united himself fully to Jesus when he offered himself with a victimal love like that of Jesus!

Fr. Andrew Apostoli, C.F.R.
Mercy Sunday, 2004

INTRODUCTION

by Rev. Msgr. Joseph C. Shenrock, P.A.

It is with great joy and pleasure that I write this introduction to the new book on Father John P. Wessel. I have known the Wessel family for over 50 years. My first assignment as a newly ordained priest was at Sacred Heart Church in Mount Holly, New Jersey, where I met the Wessel family. Through the years I have built a close friendship with them.

John Wessel was in the eighth grade when I arrived in Mount Holly and he was preparing to enter St. Charles College to begin his studies for the priesthood. In an age when the priesthood is being damaged by the press, it is a wonder to remember a good and saintly priest, who gave his life in the service of the Church.

I hope and pray that readers of this book will realize that there are many good and dedicated priests in the world like Father John Wessel.

Rev. Msgr. Joseph C. Shenrock, P.A.

In using the word "saint" or other similar terms, and in describing reports of favors apparently received from Divine Providence, the author in no way intends to anticipate the judgment of the Holy See whose decision is respectfully awaited. In all matters, the author wishes to conform completely to the decree of Pope Urban VIII "Coelestis Jerusalem" of July 5, 1634 and all other ecclesiastical legislation pertinent to this subject.

∗ ∗ ∗

Although the quotations in this text are faithful to the actual statements and manner of expression of the persons who are quoted, in some instances the quotations have been edited slightly to correct grammatical errors.

The Author

INTRODUCTION

"The time has come to speak courageously about priestly life as a priceless gift and a splendid and privileged form of Christian living."

Pope John Paul II

It is the kind of story that tends to stay with you, even if you didn't know the man.

The bare outlines of his life, briefly summarized, appear at first glance quite ordinary:

> Father John P. Wessel was born on September 20, 1939 in Mount Holly, New Jersey. He was ordained to the priesthood in St. Mary's Cathedral, Trenton, on May 22, 1965. His first assignment was Blessed Sacrament Church, Trenton, where he remained until September 23, 1971, when he was transferred to St. Joseph's Church, Toms River.

But for those of us who were privileged to know him, if only briefly, we have long remembered the story of the young, dedicated, energetic, humble parish priest, who suddenly one day, while assisting another human being in a routine act of kindness, offered a very great sacrifice. For those of us who lived through those days, in December of 1971, the memory of his heroic witness for Christ remains with us and inspires us, even now.

I myself was a student at the last parish school where he served. He came among us like a breath of fresh air, and quickly earned the love and respect of all those around him. All too soon—for we had just started to really know him—he was gone from our midst. The title of the Irish ballad, *Johnny We Hardly Knew Ye*, seems almost fitting.

Yet, we did know him, and through these pages will hopefully come to know him better in a deeper way. And for those who never knew him, it is my hope that you too will come to know and love him.

His life was a gift to us; his life is now a gift to *you*.

*   *   *

Father John Patrick Wessel's story begins over thirty years ago. He embarked upon his priesthood in the middle of the decade of the sixties, one of the most turbulent, rebellious, and yet idealistic eras in American history—

The sixties had started out brightly. Hope was in the air, and despite the omnipresent specter of communism, a new spirit of optimism was sweeping America and igniting the whole world. In 1961, a new, young, Catholic President, John Fitzgerald Kennedy, was at the helm of the Republic, while a new, innovative, and young at heart Italian cardinal, Angelo Giuseppe Roncalli, had in 1958 been elevated to the papacy of the Roman Catholic Church. As the spiritual head of the world's 430 million Roman Catholics,[2] the Pontiff's first official act was to choose the name John.

And so it was that these two men who shared a common name and faith presided over the beginning of the sixties, a decade that began in hope and ended in turbulence, in ways that neither could have foreseen nor would live to see.

But at the dawn of the decade, it was a great time to be an American, and a great time to be a Catholic. John F. Kennedy, a mere forty-three years old, seemed to embody everything that the young and vigorous nation thought best about itself. Gone were the days when, several generations ago, a Catholic could not hold public office, nor engage in certain occupations, much less aspire to the presidency. "Here on earth," Kennedy exhorted the nation in his inaugural address, "God's work must truly be our own."

The Roman Catholic Church too was growing and changing—not in substance or dogma, for the eternal truth of Jesus Christ and His Church was constant—but in format and approach, in finding new ways of reaching out to people, meeting the challenges of new philosophies, addressing new problems which confronted the modern world. In order to do this, Pope John XXIII promptly convened the Second Vatican Council, a gathering of all the Bishops of the Church.

In 1962, the Pope confidently proclaimed that we must open a new window and allow the Holy Spirit to renew the Church like a fresh breeze. "Come Holy Spirit. Fill the hearts of your faithful and enkindle in them the fire of your love" was his prayer. The Second Vatican Council was an invitation to the Holy Spirit to breathe new life into the Church. But the end of the Council and the implementation of its inspired deliberations, as well as the end of the decade itself, would be presided over by another, Pope Paul VI, for John XXIII died in 1963.

The Council was remarkable, not simply because the last worldwide gathering of its kind took place in 1870. More importantly, the convocation of the Bishops of the Church (and observers from other Christian faiths) would change much of the outward manifestation of Catholicism, so much so that the Catholic Church is today described by reference to pre- and post-Vatican II in much the same way that the birth of Jesus Christ divided the measurement of civilization into B.C. and A.D.

Within the Church, many would embrace the changes of Vatican II with ease and enthusiasm, while others would find it difficult or even impossible to adjust. To some, the Church was not changing fast enough; to others it was changing much too quickly.

Either way, in the words of Bob Dylan, the generation's troubadour—the times they were a changin'.

The young Catholic President no doubt had great plans to lead his country bravely into the "New Frontier" he frequently alluded to, but all that was silenced on November 22, 1963, with an assassin's bullet. The assassination of the young President was in many ways symbolic of the country's loss of innocence. The vulnerability of an American President to the power of evil served to remind the nation of its own frailty and mortality. By the end of the decade, the murders of his brother Robert F. Kennedy, and Dr. Martin Luther King, Jr., two other revered leaders, would leave the country reeling and grieving.

The conflict between democracy and communism, manifested most ominously in the nuclear arms race, continued throughout the 1960s. This reality was brought to America's doorstep with communist Cuba less than ninety miles from our southern shores. Emboldened by the failed 1961 Bay of Pigs invasion, then-communist Russia (U.S.S.R.), under Khrushchev, tested American resolve by placing nuclear missiles in Cuba aimed at the U.S. mainland. For two perilous weeks in October 1962, the world teetered on the brink of nuclear annihilation, while confused schoolchildren practiced air raid drills and frantic parents built bomb shelters in backyards, until October 28th (the Feast of St. Jude, patron saint of hopeless cases) brought deliverance and respite from the immediate threat of nuclear war.

America soon became embroiled in South Vietnam, thought to be the last stand of resistance to communism, and the Vietnam War became one of the defining events of the decade. U.S. involvement in the war was the legacy of his predecessor, but under President Kennedy our commitments in Southeast Asia became intractable. During subsequent American presidencies of Johnson and Nixon, the Vietnam War became an increasingly massive and seemingly hopeless conflict which drained more and more young American lives and resources. By 1965, the United States was fully engaged in the combat, as young men coming of age contended with the military draft and the prospect of losing their lives in a far-off land. By the end of this conflict, 45,997 Americans had been killed in combat; 10,928 died of non-combat causes; 303,640 wounded; nearly 600 captured; and over 1,300 missing.[3]

A decade that began with such hope would end with war and violence, turmoil, rebellion, and social unrest, as America struggled to define who we were and what we believed. For the remainder of the decade, America was often divided over issues such as Vietnam, race relations, poverty, and civil rights. Protests and demonstrations, particularly anti-war protests, could often be found in the streets. Rebellion against the "system"—the "establishment"—anything that represented law and order, authority, and the status quo, was the mood of the country, particularly among the young.

Yet it was also a study in contrasts, for there were many positive aspects in the thinking of that era: the high idealism of youth; an emphasis on peace, love and brotherhood; an abhorrence of war; social concern for the poor and less fortunate; a disdain of greed and material possessions; the rejection of discrimination and prejudice in favor of racial harmony and equality; the Civil Rights movement, founded by Dr. Martin Luther King on Christian principles; the desire for a simple and natural way of life; and an emphasis on genuineness in social and interpersonal relationships.

Perhaps because of the war, and some of the ugliness of life in the 1960s, the young, more so than in most generations, began to question and reject the values and conventions their parents held dear. The term "generation gap" was created to describe the void between parents and children who almost could not communicate.

The traditional morals and values of the older generation were, more often than not, eschewed in favor of a hedonistic, morally ambiguous, "live for today" mentality. "If it feels good, do it" and "free love" were common slogans. Pleasure and the gratification of the senses became paramount.

Mind-altering drugs became prevalent as well, and many a young person was seduced into the lifestyle of "tune in, turn on, drop out." Drugs were exalted in the lyrics of popular songs and in the lives of youthful role models. Musicians, actors, entertainers, and athletes became gurus to the young, replacing parents, teachers and religious leaders as authority figures.

In the trend toward personal and social liberation, it was inevitable that some would seek to liberate themselves from Almighty God as well. The influence of traditional religious faith began to decline as the judicial branch of government, under novel interpretations of the U.S. Constitution, sharply limited the role of religion in public life: The so-called "separation" of Church and State soon became a "divorce." In 1963, simple prayer was forbidden in public schools. By the end of the decade, Pope Paul VI would note with alarm an increasing sentiment against the child and the family taking root in Western civilization, which revolved more and more around personal gratification and self-centered individualism.

To some, God and religion were no longer relevant, and traditional religious structures and institutions, just another facet of the despised "establishment," came under attack. "God is dead," they said. Or was He?

By the close of the decade of the 1960s, profound changes had taken place in American life. On the surface level, all seemed as it was—yet on a deeper level, America was no longer sure of who we were and what we believed. Too much had changed. The old beliefs and value systems had been tossed aside. Living through the sixties was as if one had taken up residence on the edge of an active volcano. And the seeds that had been sown in the turbulent sixties would be ready for the harvest in the not-too-distant future.

*   *   *

It was around this time that a young, twenty-five-year-old John P. Wessel hopefully embarked upon his chosen vocation, the Roman Catholic priesthood.

The Catholic Church was also affected by the spirit of rebellion and confusion of the times; those for whom the Church was a vocation—priests, sisters, religious—were not immune to the turbulence around them. They sought to remain true to their beliefs and calling in an increasingly anti-religious and despairing world and to combat the heresies of modernism and selfish individualism. In particular, they struggled to reach out to the next generation with the immutable truth of Christian doctrine, even as the world questioned God's existence and His love for humanity.

As secular society became more and more inhospitable to religious life, some priests and religious were unable to persist in their vocations and left quietly to find their own path; others left publicly with great commotion and fanfare. Yet others, like Father John Wessel, stayed on and persevered, convinced that what he had to offer, the Gospel of Jesus Christ, was infinitely more valuable than man-made philosophies or social trends.

Father John Wessel, like the vast majority of priests and religious, went about his duties quietly, faithfully and devotedly, without attracting attention. His daily task was ministering the sacraments, sharing the love of Christ with others, transforming lives and winning souls, especially of the young. He labored in a world that was increasingly skeptical and unwilling to listen to God's message, yet so willing to listen to anyone else's—the charming, the popular, even the bizarre. Like a "voice crying in the wilderness," he persevered, he succeeded, he cared—through the sixties, and into the new decade filled with hope, as all new decades are, and the promise of better days ahead.

One person at a time, one soul at a time, Father John "fought the good fight" quietly and largely unnoticed. Until one day—when his humble and unassuming life was dramatically thrust beyond the confines of his small parish community onto a much wider stage.

That Father John Wessel would expend himself trying to help a troubled soul, and achieve renown in doing so, was a witness of his fidelity to Christ's own words that perfectly suited those turbulent times: "Whatever you did for one of these least brothers of mine, you did it for me" (Matthew 25:40).

Father John Wessel's Christian witness still speaks to us today.

*   *   *

I must confess that his story has fascinated me during these long years. What kind of man would become a priest during one of the most rebellious, anti-establishment, and anti-religious eras of this century? What kind of man would forego the pleasures and allurements of this world for a life of quiet dedication, continual and often thankless self-service, and perpetual chastity? And what kind of man would go to the aid of someone in a situation that was by all accounts hopeless, even to the point of risking his own life?

It has been my privilege to prepare this biography of this great yet unassuming man. What emerges in these pages is a portrait of a complex human being, which hopes to provide answers to these questions, while chronicling the true story of one dedicated life. It is a life which provides rich lessons for us today by the example of his courage, faith and love; by his zealous and joyful dedication to his priesthood; and in the manner in which he fully embraced his own humanity.

One need not be a Roman Catholic or even a Christian to appreciate Father Wessel's story, nor is it necessary to have any particular faith at all to be inspired by his example. This is, first and foremost, the story of a man, a real human being, who became a role model and a hero. His story should resonate with all persons who admire the qualities of bravery, perseverance, goodness and self-sacrifice; his example transcends barriers of time and place, culture and creed. May the telling of his story uplift and edify you, no matter what your walk in life, your circumstances, your religious beliefs or lack of them.

At the same time, this is a story of a man who was also a priest, and Father Wessel's joy in his priesthood was as apparent as his commitment to it. Thus, this work hopefully may serve a second benefit, through his example, to encourage religious vocations, in particular, to the priesthood—"a priceless gift and a splendid and privileged form of Christian living," in the words of our Holy Father.[4]

My thoughts and prayers are with the young (or not-so-young) man who may be holding this book in his hands. Perhaps, like John Wessel, you may feel Christ's call to the priesthood. Do not be afraid to answer *Yes* to Him, because you are needed: Christ needs you and His people need you. Do not be deterred if you think yourself unworthy, for John Wessel never thought himself worthy. And do not be afraid that you are not holy enough, or smart enough, for John Wessel never thought he was either. Those whom the Lord calls are often not the most obvious choices—one need only to contemplate the lives of the Apostles—and neither was young Johnny Wessel the most obvious choice. All that is necessary is the grace and courage to, like Father Wessel, give a generous and open-hearted response to Jesus Christ.

A few years after his death, those who knew him in life began a process that may one day result in Father John Wessel's canonization as a modern day saint.

Finally, it is my hope that this work may serve to bolster the cause for Father Wessel's sanctity and holiness and evidence his exercise of heroic virtues. In doing so, I am reminded of what a priest friend of mine, Monsignor Anthony Dalla Villa, once said about sainthood: "The greatest saints the Church has produced have been, first and foremost, the most human."

*   *   *

The world today is badly in need of saints and heroes, and just as badly is it in need of priests. Perhaps it is time to tell Father John P. Wessel's story. It is a story that is worth knowing, and it has been a story worth telling.

Not unlike the times in which Father John Wessel carried out his ministry, the present days are also tumultuous and confusing: Our society is yet again in the midst of "wars and rumors of wars." For the Roman Catholic Church too, it is a time of confusion and internal scandal. While such scandal is the work of but a few, it has caused pain and sorrow for many in the Body of Christ—to her priests, religious, and lay people alike. For those who love the Church, and for those who have made Her their vocation, it is a particularly difficult time.

And yet, it is especially during these trying times that we can learn from Father Wessel's example. His life instructs us on the true meaning and value of priesthood and what a difference a priest can make in the lives of others. Father Wessel's response to the turmoils of his day inspires us to do likewise: By being faithful to the small tasks that God gave him to do; by believing in the love of God and the power of the Holy Spirit to protect and guide the Church and to heal the Body of Christ; by never giving up through rough times, never ceasing to give of himself to others, and above all, never losing faith in people.

Far from being discouraged, Father's response to the turbulence of *his* times, both literally and in a spiritual sense—build a boat named *Eucharist* and invite everyone aboard!

*   *   *

Father Wessel had a wonderful way of looking at the world, grounded in his firm faith and authentic Christianity. He was able to distill the essence of life, focusing on the important things and letting go of the little things that so distract us but really don't matter. He once said, "You'll be a success in life if you have a positive influence on at least one person."

It is in this spirit that I hope and pray this endeavor has such an effect: If, through reading the story of Father John P. Wessel's life, one man is inspired to enter the priesthood; if one woman is inspired to enter the religious life; or if just one person is inspired to love and care for another through his example—then I hope that I will have been that success of which Father spoke.

This is the story of John Patrick Wessel, the man, the priest—and perhaps, future American saint.

Karin M. Burke

December 26, 2003
Feast of St. Stephen

CHAPTER 1

ONE FRIDAY IN DECEMBER

Friday, the 17th of December. When the day began, it was as normal as any other day at St. Joseph Rectory: the daily Masses; school was in session; the daily chores; appointments; visits to the sick and shut-in; telephone calls and doorbell ringing.

But it was not to end as a "normal" day.[1]

The year was 1971. It was the time of President Nixon and Vietnam. Young people listened to the music of Lennon and Dylan; their parents to Sinatra and Bennett. It was a time of idealism and passion, disorder and chaos, civil unrest and protest songs; love beads, tie-dyed clothes, bell bottoms and long hair; slogans and peace signs; innocence and disillusionment. It was a time of love and a time of war.

St. Joseph was a busy, large, Roman Catholic parish church in Toms River, New Jersey, a suburban town with a sizeable population of families and children. The church, situated on Hooper Avenue near the center of town, was both geographically and spiritually at the heart of community life. Most of the town's nearly 44,000 residents were Christian; close to half of these were Roman Catholics.[2]

Toms River was the county seat of Ocean County, on the eastern coast of New Jersey, a short distance from the shores of the Atlantic. It had perhaps more than its share of business and commerce than its neighboring shore towns. Stately offices of lawyers, doctors and realtors lined Hooper Avenue and Washington Street, the main thoroughfares of town. At the intersection stood the old, white-framed, 1850s era courthouse. All day long, busy attorneys transacted their business at this legal hub on tree-lined Washington Street. Restaurants and shops dotted the small business district around Washington and Main Streets. A large hospital, Community Memorial, was located slightly beyond the town proper on nearby Route 37.

The town was clean, decent and peaceful; the housing affordable. While most residents were young, growing families, an increasing number were elderly, having been attracted by the pleasant, sedate senior citizens' tracts that were beginning to sprout up all over the county. While containing a mix of both affluence and poverty, most of the area's population was solidly middle class, middle American.

Years ago, anticipating the needs of the growing population of Catholic families in Ocean County, Father (later Monsignor) Lawrence Donovan, St. Joseph's far-sighted pastor, built the area's first Catholic high school, and under his direction the existing parish grade school was expanded.[3] St. Joseph also attended to the spiritual needs of the Catholic sick at the local hospital, the residents of three area nursing homes, and the inmates at the county jail.

Parish life started early in the morning at St. Joseph Rectory, and that Friday in December was no different. With the schools, the hospital, and other daily duties, there was more than enough work for the four priests at St. Joseph, in addition to the ever-present requests from parishioners with an endless range of temporal and spiritual needs.

It was a cold, gray day. A dreary, dark, rainy Friday. Thick clouds hung overhead, and with the wind chilling the already cold temperatures, it looked as if the pouring rain would soon give way to snow. Perhaps the ominous clouds and dark, dreary weather were portents of things to come.

There was, however, a special excitement in the air for soon it would be Christmas, time to celebrate the most joyous of events in the Christian calendar, the birth of the Savior, Jesus Christ. The church and schools were full of activity, planning their Christmas pageantry. Students and teachers were anxiously looking forward to a long Christmas vacation and the round of Christmas parties. Christmas decorations adorned the altar of St. Joseph Church; the beautiful red and green colors of poinsettia, holly, and fir boughs added to the gaiety of the season. A little straw crèche with its replica of that first stable in Bethlehem was already in place on the altar, the humble manger empty until the first Mass of Christmas when the statue of the Infant Jesus would be given its rightful place.

John Wessel was looking forward to Christmas. He was young, handsome, thirty-two years old, with black hair and clear blue eyes, the beauty and intensity of which were obscured by his thick black-framed glasses. At five-ten, he was of medium height and medium build. When in repose or lost in thought, he could appear quiet and serious, almost ethereal, but he was most always on the move, active and animated. He had a good sense of humor and laughed easily. His ready smile was memorable, although he sometimes appeared a bit shy because of a habit of ducking his head when he smiled. In many ways he was boyish, but he also possessed wisdom and maturity beyond his years. His personality and physique attested to his strength and masculinity.

John Wessel was the kind of person who was everyone's friend. He loved and accepted each person, no matter what their station or occupation in life, or social skills, or lack thereof. In fact, he was most often drawn to the outcast, the down and out, the rejected, the troubled. Because of his great compassion, he hated to see anyone in pain, and wanted only to relieve the suffering of others, be it psychological, physical, emotional or spiritual. This trait was not so much the result of his vocation as it was the reason for it.

Father John Wessel, the associate pastor of St. Joseph's Church, had been a priest for six and a half years. He shared his duties with the older, florid and gregarious pastor, Father Donovan, and two young Irish priests-in-residence, Father Brendan Gallagher and Father Sean Maguire* [1], the latter just newly ordained and newly arrived from Ireland. A nearby convent housed the Sisters of St. Dominic who taught in the parish schools. Completing the parish "family" were Mrs. Mary Moser, the housekeeper, and Jeanne, a high school girl who worked part-time at the rectory after school.

Father John Wessel was neither introspective nor self-absorbed, but had he paused that day to reflect on the past few months, he might have felt great satisfaction at the path which God had set before him. He had come to Toms River only three months ago from his first assignment, Blessed Sacrament Church in Trenton. It had been difficult for him to leave the

---

[1] For this and all future references, an asterisk (*) indicates the name has been changed.

people and places he had come to know and love for a new and unknown station, and he came with all the usual trepidation that accompanies such a major change. There was the inevitable loneliness and period of adjustment. Yet, he prayed for the Lord's help and guidance as he tried to do some good for the people of his new parish. His fervent prayers were more than answered each day.

He liked his pastor, Father Donovan. They got along well. The parishioners and his fellow priests had welcomed him. He was enthusiastic and challenged at the opportunity to work with youth, and found special fulfillment in his role as chaplain of the high school. In three short months, he had already begun to form the high school teens into a real Christian community—with a youth retreat, a morning prayer group—and he had great plans for the future. There was so much more he hoped to do, and God willing, he would do it.

Father Wessel had awakened early and celebrated Mass in the morning of December 17th. Saying Mass and receiving the Holy Eucharist strengthened and prepared him for the day ahead. It was, as he often said, the high point of his day. Afterward, he went about the daily assignments, meetings and chores that he had planned.

At lunchtime, when the grade school children were playing football in the parking lot, Father Wessel could be found among them. The students tossed the football to him a few times, and he returned it; the inclement weather could not dampen the children's enthusiasm for a game of football with the young priest. Father Gallagher, walking past the schoolyard on his way to church, looked over and took in the scene of John Wessel playing catch with the students for a few moments.

Father Wessel made a point to be a visible presence in the high school. He visited the classrooms, celebrated Mass for them regularly, heard their confessions, and participated in their recreational and leisure activities. He wanted the young people to know that he was informal and approachable, not stuffy, and that he was there if they needed someone to talk with. Many a youngster could approach him with ease over a game of sports or other casual activity.

By mid-afternoon on Friday, school had ended. A practice which fast became a daily ritual in the rectory was "coffee-and-tea time" in the kitchen after school. It was a time to unwind, to enjoy each other's company, and shoot the breeze about everything and anything. "Coffee-and-tea time" was for anyone in the rectory who wanted to drop by.

This day, Father Wessel, Father Maguire and Jeanne were sitting in the kitchen indulging in this newly acquired habit. It was about 2:30 in the afternoon, and the lively conversation may have encompassed everything from the day's events to the weather to preparations for Christmas.

Father Wessel was ahead of schedule that Christmas, and proud of it. He had finished his Christmas shopping that week, and all his presents were wrapped. Several boxes of unopened Christmas cards were waiting to be sent to his many friends and loved ones.

"That whole afternoon tea group felt very harmonious," Father Maguire recalled of that day. "We all had good feelings about each other." Not that this was unusual—they often felt that way—but it would stand out in his memory because of events that were soon to unfold.[4]

Strangely enough, death became part of the conversation that afternoon, and Father Wessel said, very seriously, that if he died no one would care.

Jeanne, surprised, didn't know what to say. "Sure, sure," she countered. "You know darn well people would care."

I just don't want people to be crying over me when I die, he remarked.[5]

Adding to the conversation, and as if to follow his earlier train of thought, Father Wessel mentioned that he had been asked to visit a troubled young man who was in need of counseling. Father Maguire recognized the man's name.

"I really don't want to go," Father Wessel confided to the younger priest, referring to the request to visit the troubled young man.[6] Father Maguire recalled questioning him but that John Wessel seemed as if he wanted to just drop the subject, and so it was dropped.

Father Maguire remembered the Christmas party for the grade school faculty scheduled for three o'clock that afternoon. Sister Juliana Naulty, the grade school principal, and her faculty had worked hard on the preparations. All the priests had been invited and were expected to attend.

Assuming that Father Wessel was also going, as he had planned to, Father Maguire went up to his room to get his coat, thinking that Father Wessel would wait for him and that they would go together.

When he came back downstairs a few minutes later, Father Wessel was already gone. It was about 2:50 in the afternoon. John Wessel must have left for the grade school, Father Maguire thought, and he hurried over to meet him there.[7]

Father Wessel's mood was "ponderous when I last left him," Maguire would later recall, like "a man who had to make a choice"—whether to enjoy the conviviality of a Christmas party with friends, or to answer a call for help that he would have much preferred to have ignored.[8]

Christmas was just a week away. A tree in the rectory still had to be trimmed. Before he left, Jeanne asked Father Wessel to help her trim the tree that night. If he wasn't too tired, he'd be happy to help her, he said.

Father Wessel put on his black trench coat over his black clerical suit and stepped out into the cold, blustery, December afternoon.

*   *   *

A short time later, a short distance away, a young mother suddenly heard a sound like a strong blast from outside the window of her small apartment. She instinctively gathered up her infant son, bolted the front door, closed the curtains, and ran upstairs. Cautiously, she looked out the window. There was a man lying motionless on the sidewalk outside, face down. Frightened, she called the police.[9]

Surely no one at St. Joseph's Rectory nor at the festive Christmas party at the grade school that afternoon paid much attention to the sound of sirens wailing past the rectory and down Hooper Avenue.

It wasn't too long after Father Wessel had left that a call came in to the rectory. It was the local hospital. There was noise and confusion in the background, Jeanne remembered, and an excited nurse said she had to talk to one of the priests. Jeanne rang Father Gallagher's room.

"A young priest from St. Joseph has been shot," said the nurse. "He's in the Emergency Room. We need you to identify him."

"A young priest? Who?" he thought. It was about four o'clock.[10]

Father Gallagher ran out of his room and at the same time the pastor, Father Donovan, was coming out of his. Father Gallagher repeated what he had just been told. The pastor's reaction was the same—"Who?" It couldn't be one of our priests, he thought. All were accounted for. Father Wessel and Father Maguire were at the faculty party; the two of them were there in the rectory.

"I'll go over and give you a call from there," Father Gallagher assured the pastor. He left at once for Community Memorial Hospital to answer the emergency call.

When Father Gallagher first saw him, the injured man was lying on a stretcher surrounded by several physicians. One doctor was in charge and seemed to be directing the others in whatever had to be done. They appeared to be doing everything they possibly could for the injured man, Gallagher recalled.

There was blood pouring out from the man's wounds, blood pouring off the stretcher and spilling onto the Emergency Room floor. "I remember blood coming off that stretcher onto the floor," said Gallagher. "It was really a difficult sight."

Father Gallagher made the identification at the hospital.

It was Father Wessel.[11]

*　　*　　*

Father Wessel was not moving at all. Fleetingly, Gallagher may have thought back to the last time he saw John Wessel animated and active just a few hours before, tossing a football to the children on the playground at lunchtime.

Father Gallagher stayed with Father Wessel as he was wheeled out of the Emergency Room and up to the Intensive Care Unit. He anointed him and gave him the Last Rites of the Church.[12]

Gallagher called the rectory to tell the pastor. "Oh my God, no!" the pastor said. Father Donovan and another priest, a good friend of the pastor's who happened to be visiting that day, left for the hospital immediately.

Father John Wessel, only thirty-two years old, lay gravely wounded and clinging to life in a hospital ward. It was, ironically, the same hospital where he himself had often visited the sick and anointed the dying.

So many unanswered questions—

What had happened in the space of a few hours that Friday afternoon that so dramatically altered the course of events on that seemingly ordinary day?

What had happened to Father Wessel between the three and four o'clock hours to place him in harm's way?

And who in that small, peaceful, suburban town would want to shoot the beloved young priest—and why?

Many lives would be changed forever, many more would be affected, by the events of that one Friday in December.

At the rectory, it was recalled in the midst of all the turmoil that Father Wessel had a family—a widowed mother, a sister and a brother. As he rushed to the hospital, an emotional and upset Father Donovan told Jeanne to call Mrs. Wessel. It remained for the young girl to complete the daunting task of telephoning the young priest's mother with the awful news. Her son had been shot. That was all they knew.[13]

CHAPTER 2

A CHILD IS BORN

John Patrick Wessel was born on September 20, 1939 in Mount Holly, New Jersey. The birth of the infant was awaited with great joy and anticipation by his young parents, Dr. Edward J. Wessel, a well-known Mount Holly dentist, and his wife, Kathleen, a former schoolteacher. John's mother was the former Kathleen Hogan, daughter of Mr. and Mrs. Patrick Hogan of Burlington Road in Mount Holly.[1] John's father was the son of the late Julian Wessel, Sr., a Philadelphia banker, and his wife Rosalie. Little John was welcomed into the bosom of the young family which already included two older children, Edward, Jr., then seven years old, and Maryann, aged five.

The child had come into the world at the beginning of World War II. The news from Europe had been distressing in the fall of that year. On September 1, 1939, Germany had invaded Poland. On September 3, Britain and France declared war on Germany, but there was little they could do to help the beleaguered Poles, who were no match for the German war machine.

Germany and Russia had secretly agreed to divide Poland, and so, on September 17, with the Polish armies ready to collapse, Russia invaded Poland from the east. Most Polish resistance ended in a matter of days, but in Warsaw, the people fought on without food or supplies until September 27, when the city surrendered. Thus Poland began its long suffering under Nazi occupation, to be followed by decades of communist oppression. The atrocities of the Holocaust and the concentration camps would soon become evident. And somewhere in Poland, a young student-actor and future Pope would shortly begin clandestine studies for the priesthood in Kraków even as the Nazis overran his native land.

As the year 1939 drew to a close, Hitler was preparing for even greater conquests, together with his allies in Italy and Japan. It was the calm before a great storm that would soon involve even the United States.[2]

But closer to home, in quaint, picturesque Mount Holly in the southern part of New Jersey, the Wessels' new baby John was baptized at Sacred Heart Church by the pastor, Father J. Arthur Hayes. His godparents were Dr. Julian Wessel, his father's younger brother, and Miss Clare Hogan, his mother's older sister.

If it is true that one's name foreshadows destiny, then the name "John Patrick" which the baby's parents had carefully chosen for him certainly provided an indication of his future life. He was named in honor of his maternal great-uncle, Father John Duggan, a Catholic priest of the Diocese of Newark, and his maternal grandfather, Patrick Hogan.

The chubby, dark-haired, blue-eyed baby John was a mild-tempered, wonderful child, and a source of immense joy to his parents, as indeed, were all their children. Two years earlier, a baby boy named James had been born to Edward and Kathleen Wessel but had died in infancy of pneumonia. The birth of baby John two years later must have seemed to his parents like an answer to prayer.

During the first year of John's life, Father Hayes often visited the Wessels to look in on the new baby and his mother. Always Father Hayes reassured the parents that the child would be fine.

"He'll grow up all right, Mrs. Wessel," the pastor said confidently. "Don't you worry."

Father Hayes had a booming, forceful manner and a jaunty self-confidence that made his prophecy for the child seem not mere wishful thinking but a promise, a guarantee, to the anxious mother.

One day, in fact, Father Hayes made an amazingly accurate prediction about the baby's destiny.

"He'll live. He'll live," Hayes said to John Wessel's mother, "and some day he'll be a priest."[3]

For the moment, at least, the prediction of the child's future vocation was completely forgotten by his worried mother, who was only too glad to hear the priest's pronouncement that her son would be fine.

*   *   *

It was not surprising that John Wessel would become a priest, since a strong Catholic faith was a part of his heritage. His family had been blessed with an abundance of religious vocations. There were several nuns and a monk on his father's side, and a number of nuns and priests among his mother's Irish ancestors. But above all else, the family into which young John Patrick was born knew well—and perhaps better than most—the incomparable joys of answering a call to the priesthood, as well as its sacrifices and sorrows.

The Duggans and the Hogans

John Wessel's maternal grandmother, Mary Duggan, immigrated to America from her native Ireland in the early 1880s. Here she met and married Patrick Hogan, a farmer from Salem, New Jersey.

Since the mid-seventeenth century, many generations of the Duggan family have made their ancestral home on a tract of land called "Shandangan" in County Cork in the southwesterly part of Ireland, just outside the great port city of Cork.

John's grandmother, Mary Duggan, was born at Shandangan in 1863, the second youngest of nine children of a devoutly religious couple, Cornelius and Mary Murphy Duggan.

Prayer and the sacraments were a vital part of life for the Duggans of Shandangan. As was the custom, the Angelus would be said three times during the day, with workers pausing in the fields or in their homes to recite the prayer that commemorates the visitation of the Archangel Gabriel to the Blessed Virgin Mary. After dinner, the family would gather by the stone hearth to recite the Rosary. In fact, one of Mary Duggan's earliest memories was of sitting on a three-cornered stool at her mother's feet, as her mother, rocking peacefully in a rocking chair by the fireplace, taught her to recite the Acts of Faith, Hope and Charity.

Among Mary's eight siblings was her oldest brother, Denis, born in 1848. He had also learned the prayers and devotions at his mother's knee and inspired perhaps by his parents' deep faith, Denis had decided to enter the priesthood. After the years of required study had been completed, he was ready to become a priest, and his family was preparing to celebrate his ordination.

The story is told in Duggan family lore that on a day shortly before the ordination of her oldest son Denis, his mother Mary hitched up the horse and wagon and rode into town to get the clothing to be worn by her son at his ordination. On her way home, the horse bolted, and Mary Murphy Duggan was thrown from the wagon. Severely injured, she died a short time later.

One can only imagine how great the Duggan family's shock and sorrow, not only at the sudden death of their beloved mother, but for the incomparably tragic timing of the accident on the eve of their son's commencement of his priesthood. The happiness and joy that should have accompanied the ordination was mixed with great and unanticipated sadness, for the newly ordained priest, Father Denis J. Duggan, and his family were in mourning. The eight remaining Duggan children, including John Wessel's grandmother Mary, still a small girl, were now motherless.

Father Denis J. Duggan was the first of his immediate family to emigrate to America. He became a priest in the Diocese of Trenton, New Jersey, and enjoyed many years of dedicated service in Mount Holly, Salem, and then Bordentown where in 1899 he celebrated his twenty-fifth anniversary as a priest. He was elevated to the rank of Monsignor.

While at Salem, Father Denis was instrumental in establishing the Catholic Church of St. Anne's in nearby Elmer, New Jersey. The ground was broken for the church in 1894. A program prepared for the church's one hundredth anniversary in 1994 described him and his efforts:

> The mission of Elmer was formerly attached to the parish of Salem and it was the Rev. Denis J. Duggan who purchased the first church site. The first Mass at Elmer was celebrated in 1892 by Rev. Father Duggan in a large room of the old farmhouse of Anthony Kitsinger which stood near the Deerfield Road close to the present railroad station called Harding. Rev. Denis Duggan was born in Macroom, County Cork, Ireland in October 1848. He studied the classics at St. Vincent's College in that city and Theology at the renowned Seminary of Maynooth. In 1874 he was ordained and worked in his native diocese and coming to America, he was accepted into the Diocese of Trenton and appointed assistant to Fr. Fitzsimmons of Camden. Father [Duggan] was a learned theologian, a great friend to the parochial school system and a singer well versed in the art of music.

*   *   *

Meanwhile, little Mary Duggan grew up on Shandangan and learned to be an excellent seamstress.

In the early 1880s, Mary Duggan, now a vivacious, pretty and headstrong Irish lass, decided she would go to America to visit her brother, Father Denis, who was then stationed in the small town of Salem, in the County of Salem, on the Delaware River in southwestern New Jersey. She had intended to come alone, but her brother John, the youngest of the Duggan clan, insisted on tagging along. He would not be dissuaded.

So they sailed across the Atlantic Ocean to America in 1882 or 1883[4], twenty-year-old Mary Duggan, and her brother John, about eighteen, ending up in Salem to visit Father Denis. They were only supposed to stay for a certain time and had plans to return to Ireland, but fate mysteriously intervened.

Young John Duggan was enamored of the new country. What's more, he'd become interested in the priesthood. His sister Mary and brother Denis wanted to send him back to Cork, but it was no use, he wouldn't go. So Mary Duggan, perhaps sensing the hand of God in these altered plans, moved herself and John to Jersey City, New Jersey to live with their cousin, Julia.

Mary Duggan went to work as a seamstress in New York City to support John's education. An excellent seamstress, she began to run a profitable business working in all the large stores in the city, where the fine skills she acquired in Ireland—sewing, knitting, crocheting, needlepoint and embroidery—were always in great demand. When John graduated from Pratt Institute in Brooklyn, he resolved to continue his education and become a Marist priest, and Mary continued her work as a seamstress to pay the tuition for his education.

John Duggan attended a seminary in Maine, and then went to Catholic University, in Washington, D.C., where he was ordained a priest of the Marist Order. John had hoped to join the Diocese of Trenton, where his brother and family were, but to his great disappointment there were no openings. But he was able to join the Newark diocese, and was assigned as a young priest to St. Patrick's Cathedral in Newark. He then returned to his alma mater, Catholic University, where he taught for many years, and eventually went to Paterson, New Jersey, where he became a pastor. Father John Duggan spent his remaining years at a parish in Sterling, New Jersey.

*　　*　　*

Perhaps there was another reason why Mary Duggan was in no hurry to return to her native land. During her frequent visits to her brother in Salem, New Jersey, Mary Duggan had made the acquaintance of the man who would be John Wessel's grandfather. Young and handsome, Patrick Hogan was a tall, wiry, and gentle farmer. Born in Salem in 1863, Patrick was one of thirteen children of a well-known Salem farming family. Acquaintance soon turned into love, and eventually into a proposal of marriage.

In 1898, Mary Duggan, at the age of thirty-five, was married to Patrick Hogan at St. Michael's Church in Jersey City. The young couple began their married life together in Salem, New Jersey.

When Mary decided to marry Patrick Hogan, her brother, Father Denis, was not enthused to put it mildly. While he liked the Hogans, he didn't think the young couple well suited each other because the Hogans were farmers and, as he said to his sister, "What do you know about farming? You'll be of no help." He anticipated a catastrophe as the newly immigrated New York City seamstress tried to fit herself into the mold of a South Jersey farmer's wife.

Fortunately, despite the sage counsel of her brother, Mary and Patrick Hogan enjoyed a long and happy marriage. For a while, they lived in Salem where John Wessel's godmother, Clare, the oldest of their six children, was born in 1899. But it was difficult for Patrick Hogan to make a living in Salem and there were better opportunities for him to buy his own farm elsewhere. When Clare was less than a year old, the Hogans decided to move a little farther north, to Mount Holly, in Burlington County.

That John's Grandmother and Grandfather Hogan settled in Mount Holly in the first place was because Father Denis Duggan had been a priest there. When they were looking for a place to live, he said, "Well, there's a town called Mount Holly, and there's a lot of good farming there."

Somewhere around the turn of the century, Mary and Patrick Hogan bought a large farm of several hundred acres out on Burlington Road, about a mile and a half from the center of town in Mount Holly. It was a wonderful place, with a great white clapboard house, a barn and a stable. A vast expanse of farmland that the Hogans would cultivate for grain stretched out in all directions. There were plenty of woods, meadows, marshes and fields, where they would hunt wild game and raise animals—horses, cows, sheep, ducks, and turkeys. The land also held wild fruit trees and berries, lush flowering trees and, true to its name, an abundance of holly trees that would be cut and used as festive Christmas decorations. Five more Hogan children—Cornelius, Carlton, Michael, Kathleen, and James—were born on the wild and beautiful stretch of land that forever became known to them simply as "the Farm."

* * *

Yet another religious vocation flowered in the devout Duggan family, that of Mary Hogan's older sister, Kathleen.

As a young girl of about twenty, Kathleen Duggan had traveled to America with a religious community of Sisters called the Order of the Incarnate Word. She was stationed at a novitiate in San Antonio, Texas, where she prepared to take her final vows. Her letters addressed to her sister, whom she referred to by her nickname "Molly"—still single and living with her cousin in Jersey City—from 1884 to 1886, attest to her spiritual progress and her deep desire to become a nun.

"I knew very little about Kathleen when I was growing up except that my Grandmother had a picture of her at the Farm," said John Wessel's sister, Maryann (Wessel) Beitel. Kathleen was a beautiful lady who resembled St. Theresa, "The Little Flower." Grandmother Hogan would always say, "That was my sister Kathleen who died in San Antonio, Texas, and she was such a saint."

Training for the religious life was rigorous and the novices really had to prove they were worthy. "We are here now more than a year and have not got the habit yet," Kathleen wrote to Mary in 1884, "and as to the time we will, if that will ever be, we are as much in the dark as you are. There is only one thing I know. That is if I wait until I deserve it, I'll never get it; however, Bishop is away at the [First Vatican] Council at present and perhaps when he comes back in about a month we may get it then. But this last year was not half the length of that month so it seems to us."

Kathleen wrote that at one time she thought herself accepted into the Order of nuns until she laughed out of turn. "There I was when I was supposed to be praying and have my thoughts totally on my prayers and something came to my mind and I giggled." She was punished by having her final vows delayed for another month or so, because her superiors wanted to make sure that she was mature enough and would take her life more seriously.

In a letter written in 1885, Kathleen talks about her great happiness in finally being professed as a nun.

> Dearest Molly,
>
> It is time I should let you know of my great joy as you were the one to whom I wrote in my trouble. I feel certain it is owing in a great measure to your prayers in that I enjoy my present great happiness. On the tenth of March I've had the great honor of changing my name from Kathleen to Sister Mary St. Leonide of the Annunciation. They call me Sister St. Leonide. I must leave you to imagine my happiness and how I counted the days till lest it would be over that I may write to you but though it is more than a week gone by, I have to ask to be allowed to remain up after all the sisters to write this.

In 1886, Kathleen, now Sister Mary St. Leonide of the Annunciation, wrote again to her sister:

> I received your letter of July 10th on the 18th and am glad to find you continue strongly. Now I am going to tell you something very, very nice so you can make a sweet little present to the Sacred Heart of *my* Spouse and our Savior. Take care you offer it to Him now before you read farther. Well, Molly darling, the fact is that I am afraid you will be disappointed in your expectation of seeing me in the spring for by that time I expect to be in Heaven.
>
> When I was very bad some time ago, I didn't wish to scare you telling you I had many hemorrhages from my lungs but lately they have come on again and on Tuesday night last I had a very strong one. I coughed up so very great [a] quantity [of blood].

Kathleen was dying of tuberculosis, but her letter revealed that she was ecstatic about going home to Jesus. She was given about six months to live. In 1887, there came a letter from Kathleen's Superior to Mary Duggan informing her that her sister had died. "I would guess that she was probably about twenty-eight years old, but these letters indicate such a spiritual person of such great faith and total trust in the Lord," said Maryann Beitel.

*   *   *

Life on the Farm was not all idyllic and free of trials for Mary and Patrick Hogan. One of the first trials was the painful realization for Mary Hogan that the role she had chosen for herself would involve many sacrifices as well as joys.

When her beloved younger brother, John Duggan, was ordained to the priesthood in Washington, D.C., his sister Mary, who had worked so hard to help him achieve his religious vocation, could not be there. She was married with two little children at the time, and recently moved to Mount Holly. With her responsibilities to her family and the Farm to help manage, she was not able to make the long trip to Washington, D.C., by rail. Mary must have prayed for her brother even though she was far away, and no doubt her mind and soul were united with him on that day. But one can only imagine her sadness, and that of her brother. On the most momentous occasion of John Duggan's life, none of his family was present to share the joy of his ordination.

Another trial that the Hogans experienced in full measure was the initial ostracism by their Mount Holly neighbors because of their Catholic faith. In those early days, there was great and palpable discrimination toward Catholics in that predominantly Protestant part of New Jersey. When the Hogans first moved to Mount Holly and bought their large farm, their Protestant neighbors would have little to do with them. Eventually, however, they began to realize that the Catholic family was nice, decent, and hard-working, and the Hogans thenceforth enjoyed good relations with their neighbors. Yet for the rest of her life, Mary Hogan stressed to her children the importance of setting a good example. What they did and how they behaved, she often reminded them, would be a reflection on their faith.

Mary Hogan's lessons were quite effective. All the children in her large and motivated family distinguished themselves in some way: Both Carlton and James Hogan became medical doctors, and for many years, Dr. James Hogan practiced medicine in an office on High Street in Mount Holly. Michael Hogan became a businessman, settled in Westfield, New Jersey, and founded an electronics company. Clare and Kathleen Hogan graduated college and became teachers. Cornelius became a dentist and settled in Burlington.

Mary and Patrick Hogan were also very religious people. They communicated their Catholicism by their quiet faith and fervent example. The Rosary was always said at night at the Hogans' Farm, and the Angelus was recited three times daily. Praying was very much a part of their lives.

Mary Hogan was not just content to live her religion. Faith was a family affair, and everybody around her lived it too. She insisted that her six children get on their knees each night and say the Rosary with her, as she herself had done as a child. She taught the treasured prayers of her faith to her four boys and two girls, just as her own mother had done with her by the great stone fireplace at Shandangan. The importance of the family Rosary was never lessened, even as the wild Hogan boys got older and, being boys, tried to disappear in the woods around the Farm after dinner in search of more interesting boyhood diversions. Mary Hogan, a prayerful and devout woman, insisted on the observance of faith, and imparted this example to her children and grandchildren.

In no small way the gracious example and living faith of Mary Hogan played a part in the religious vocation of yet another young boy named John—her grandson John Patrick Wessel.

*   *   *

Grandfather Patrick Hogan died in 1945, as did Father John Duggan. He had lived long enough to see the arrival of his grand-nephew who shared his name and would carry on his vocation.

For the Duggans and the Hogans, "hardship was very common, but they were such survivors, and it was all because they had such faith," reflected Maryann Beitel. They felt that "whatever happened, they were being guided by the Lord, and they took it in that manner. And certainly there were many, many tragedies but it was not as if it overwhelmed them. They still went on with their lives."[5]

The Wessels

That observation is equally true for John's paternal ancestors, the Wessels.

John's father, Dr. Edward J. Wessel, was born and raised in Philadelphia. His own father, Julian Wessel, Sr., had died when he was only three years old. Edward Wessel was the second youngest of seven children, only five of whom survived to adulthood.

Both of John's paternal grandparents were from an area which was then called East Prussia. John's paternal grandmother, Rosalie Wessel, born in 1872 in the town of Suwalki, was of Polish descent. Her husband, John's grandfather, Julian Wessel, Sr., was of German ancestry. His ancestors were small landowners in eastern Germany and in what is now Poland. He was born in 1869 in East Prussia, came to America, and founded a bank in Philadelphia, where he and his wife had settled.

Grandmother Rosalie Wessel was "a profile of courage," according to Maryann Beitel. At a young age, she suffered the loss of her husband and two children, raised five children alone after she was widowed, and died at the age of ninety-five. Moreover, she had a difficult time with English and was a very shy person.

Five Wessel children survived to adulthood: Wanda, an accountant, never married and lived with her mother. Walter, who lived in California with his wife, Lillian, was a career Naval officer and veteran of four wars. Matthew, a physician, died very suddenly in his early thirties of septicemia contracted while performing an operation. (This was just a few years before life-saving penicillin was invented). Edward, John Wessel's father, born in 1905, became a dentist in Mount Holly. Finally, Julian, Jr., who also became a dentist, lived with his wife, Helen, and their children in Philadelphia. Known as "Uncle Jule" to his nieces and nephews, he was John Wessel's godfather.

Brothers Edward and Julian Wessel, two years apart, were close not only in age but in temperament, outlook, and profession. They lived near to each other all their lives and spent a great deal of time together. They both studied dentistry at Temple University Dental School in Philadelphia, and were godfathers to each other's children. "They were brothers and best friends," said John's cousin, Julian Wessel.

The family of John's paternal grandfather, Julian Wessel, was known as "Baltic Germans"—ethnic Germans who journeyed eastward and settled around the Baltic region in what is now Russia and Poland. During the reign of Tzar Peter the Great of Russia, Germans, especially those skilled in certain trades or professions, such as farmers, craftsmen, merchants, and physicians, were sought out and welcomed into Russia in the eighteenth and early nineteenth century. Encouraged with grants of land, the Wessels were part of that movement in the late eighteenth century that spread out the German people into Eastern Europe. Some ethnic Germans intermarried with their Russian and Polish neighbors, as was the case with Julian and Rosalie Wessel.

The area of East Prussia where the Wessel family had resided is now Poland. The land was at times claimed by both Germany and Poland. It was, in fact, a catalyst in the start of the Second World War: The Nazis invaded the land ostensibly to "liberate" the so-called ethnic or Baltic Germans, whom they considered German under German law. By this time, however, John Wessel's ancestors had long since emigrated to the United States.

John's Grandfather and Grandmother Wessel knew each other in Europe—they were from the same region though not the same town—but they did not marry until they arrived in Philadelphia within a couple of months of each other around the mid-1880s. Seeking to establish himself in Philadelphia, Julian, an educated man who spoke several languages, including English, started a small bank with two other investors. The bank, called the Polish Beneficial Association, was situated in the Bridesburg section of the city and still exists today.

Julian Wessel, Sr., was also a founding parishioner of St. John Cantius Church at Thompson and Almond Streets in Philadelphia. He was "a very, very religious person, a devout Roman Catholic, very devoted to the parish," said his grandson Julian.[6]

In 1910, he died of tuberculosis at about forty or forty-one years of age, leaving his widow to raise their children. At the time, his youngest child, Julian, Jr., was only nine months old. It was a struggle for all. Thankfully, the children all turned out very well; they too were all highly motivated people who accomplished a great deal with their lives.

In this respect, John's Grandmother Wessel was a very strong influence. Her whole life was devoted to her family and the education of her children, and then, caring for their families and children as well. "She was an excellent cook, very friendly, kindly, and compassionate, and never raised her voice," recalled her grandson Julian.

Like Mary Hogan, Grandma Rosalie Wessel was also an extremely devout Catholic. She was very pleased when her grandson John became a priest and lived to see him ordained. Remarking upon her death, Father John Wessel once said that due to her incredible devotion as a Roman Catholic, he was sure that she had secured a place in Heaven.

When Grandma Wessel was very sick, she feared that she would not go to Heaven. "It's a funny thing," Father Wessel said to his cousin, Julian Wessel, after their grandmother's death. "It's the people that really deserve to go to Heaven the most, and probably will go, who are the ones that are scared the most that they won't. And the people that have lived horrible lives and have many transgressions and sins either don't care or know they're not going. It's amazing and paradoxical that Grandma Wessel was so good you'd have to look so hard for a sin, and yet she was so scared of being separated from God."[7]

The legacy of a religious vocation is evident in John Wessel's father's side of the family as well. One of Grandfather Julian Wessel's uncles had been a Capuchin Franciscan in Europe in the early 1800s. He was an abbot in a monastery, and his pectoral cross, with a relic imbedded inside it, has been handed down for generations within the Wessel family.[8]

From both sides of young John Wessel's family, the child received a priceless gift—the heritage of faith and service.

CHAPTER 3

BOYHOOD YEARS

Mount Holly and its environs was a wonderful place for a boy to grow to maturity. In many ways, John's boyhood years in Mount Holly were idyllic, despite the fact that during the first five years of his life the country was at war in Europe and in the Pacific. The little town pitched in and contributed its share to the war effort. As everywhere else across America, its citizens grew victory gardens, helped out at Red Cross bandage drives, donated blood, invested in war bonds, and sent its native sons to fight and die for global freedom. Yet in many ways, except for the ever-present ration cards which rationed gasoline, sugar, food and the like, life continued apace. Even in the height of war, there was some semblance of normalcy in Mount Holly, New Jersey.

There was a certain poetry in the ebb and flow of life, the cyclical rhythm of life in a small American town—the changes of the season, the births and deaths, marriages, anniversaries and funerals, the Christmases, the Easters, the Sunday Masses. Day in, day out, year in, year out, people found meaning in those small moments of grace, reveling in the value of friendship, the joys of married life, a child's achievement in school, a long quiet walk at sunset, the crisp smell of autumn leaves, a barbecue or a garden party, the satisfaction of a life well lived at the end of the day.

John Wessel grew up in a devout Roman Catholic family. His father, Dr. Edward J. Wessel, was a well-known local dentist. He was a gentle, loving man with a dignified bearing and cultured manner—handsome and impeccably dressed. He was a confidant of the priests of Sacred Heart Parish, the only Catholic Church in the town of Mount Holly. Master of ceremonies at many parish functions, Dr. Wessel served as a liaison between the priests and the town fathers, and was respected as a wise and able businessman and as a leader in the community. His self-giving participation in church functions and evident devotion to his faith set an outstanding example of masculine spirituality and Christian fatherhood for his children.

John's mother, Kathleen Hogan Wessel, was a refined, gracious and attractive, blue-eyed brunette. She appeared perfectly suited to her husband in temperament and interests, and like her husband, her Roman Catholic faith was a central aspect of her life. She was, after all, the daughter of Mary and Patrick Hogan.

Personally close to the priests and the nuns of the parish, Kathleen Wessel worked tirelessly in every phase of the Sacred Heart PTA, from fund-raising to curriculum planning, including a term as the PTA's first president. She also served as a member of the board of several charities in and around Mount Holly.

Mrs. Kathleen Wessel was one of that rare breed of Great Ladies that are seen all too infrequently today. Although educated to be a schoolteacher, she relinquished her own career, stayed at home, and devoted herself to motherhood and to the happiness of her husband. With great dignity and style, she made their home into a peaceful, inviting and well-ordered oasis for family and friends. Spare time was reserved, not for herself, but for charity. The Wessels' home was a happy one, and together they enjoyed the richness of family life.

John Wessel's parents had met through the intervention of the Hogan brothers. Kathleen Hogan's two brothers, James and Carl, attended Hahneman Medical School in Philadelphia. Another brother, Cornelius, was studying dentistry in Philadelphia. At the same time, Edward Wessel was studying at Temple in Philadelphia, and through classes and such he met the Hogan brothers. They brought him home to the Farm and introduced him to their sister—his future wife.[1]

The Edward Wessels were married on August 22, 1931 in Sacred Heart Church in Mount Holly.

By the time baby John came along, Dr. Wessel had achieved a certain level of professional success. What is remarkable is the manner in which the Wessel family responded to any material blessings that came their way.

To them, financial prosperity and abundance were gifts from God to be received humbly and thankfully and to be used wisely. Prayerful and devout Catholics, they looked for opportunities to be of service to others and to give out of their bounty, especially to their Church. "Give back what you have been given" might have been Dr. Wessel's creed.

For years, Dr. Wessel donated his dental services without charge to all the priests and nuns of the parish. He also volunteered his dentistry services for two institutions in New Lisbon—one a sanitarium for the tubercular; another a nursing home. In his position as Rotarian president, he found time to involve himself in even more charitable works.

The Wessel parents' example of volunteering their skills and time to the church and community functions left an impression with all of their children, and instilled the idea of charitable public service. "Material things were definitely unimportant all of my life," recalled Maryann Beitel. "It was not important as to what you had materially . . . Your gift of life came from the Lord and so it was to be used accordingly." The Wessel children learned that "there's not anything more important than serving other people, helping other people," she said.

> Numerous times, without us really knowing what they were doing, my parents were out helping other people, be it through helping the sick or just in compassion. They were very, very sensitive to the needs of others . . . and as a result we were all very in tune to other people's feelings.

Spiritual life was always a family affair. "It was always all of us going to Mass together. My parents were very involved with Sacred Heart Church. . . . It wasn't just a woman's sort of thing; it was husband and wife together, Forty Hour Devotions, it was all a part of our family. And I think the fact that it was always together that had its effect on John."[2]

The family lived in a three-story, red brick and white trim house on 38 Garden Street, near the center of town, on a row street with other professional residences of doctors and lawyers. It was a beautiful house—comfortable and spacious—with more than enough room so that Johnny, brother Eddie, and sister Maryann had their own bedrooms. The Wessel home served the varied purposes of being the family home, the dentist's office, and in the basement the dental workshop.

He was "a crackerjack dentist," recalled his daughter, Maryann. For years after he died, people used to say, "There was never a dentist like Dr. Wessel." He was renowned for being one of the few dentists in the area who gave gas. "People came from all over to have gas" because most people hated to have their teeth ground without any painkillers.

Dr. Wessel's practice was a family affair. He did everything for his patients without the assistance of a nurse. Mrs. Wessel answered the phone and typed the bills; as Maryann got older and learned typing, she too prepared the bills and answered the phone. "It was a one-family operation," she said.

John Wessel's older sister and brother were very much like their parents in temperament and interests. Both were refined, gentle, quietly intelligent and gifted in music and the arts.

Young Edward, Jr., called Eddie, tall and slender like his Grandfather Hogan, was an excellent student and a gifted musician. He graduated high school at the age of sixteen, studied medicine and became a brilliant surgeon. He was cultured and intelligent, and possessed a lively and witty sense of humor.

Maryann, a pretty and poised young lady, greatly resembled her mother in her attractive and delicate features. Although she too was musically inclined, Maryann studied English and education in college and graduate school and became a teacher like her mother. Closer to her brother John in age, Maryann's most enduring memory of childhood is that of her dear but "bratty little brother" Johnny constantly tagging along and playing pranks on her and her girlfriends.

While Johnny Wessel had elements of both his parents' personalities and temperament, he was clearly something else altogether. He was uniquely himself, and perhaps a throwback to some wild Irish or German-Polish ancestor of a generation or two ago. Although mature and sensitive in his inner life and in relation to others, his exterior was rough and rugged, at times disheveled, down-to-earth and ready for adventure, the very antithesis of his gentle and refined family.

He was a lively, very noisy, and sometimes mischievous boy. He loved the outdoors—swimming, fishing, canoeing, playing cowboys and Indians, feeding the animals on his grandparents' farm, hunting with bow and arrow, collecting Indian arrowheads. He never lost his love for the rough physical contact of football.

Growing up during World War II brought a strong military influence on John's formative years. There were ever-present reminders that the country was at war. Dr. Wessel, exempt from military service because of his age and family, served as a local air raid warden in town. Two of John Wessel's maternal uncles, James and Carlton Hogan, entered military service during the war.

Like his Hogan uncles in the service, John's paternal uncle, Walter Wessel, was a career Naval officer and veteran of four wars. He was a fascinating man—respected and admired—whose adventurous travels and military exploits were recounted in the family.[3]

Surplus military goods were the best toys available for a young boy. Johnny's favorite toy, his mother recalled later, was an Army back pack, and he loved to play "soldier" in backyard sandbox "forts."

When Johnny was six, his letter to "Santa Clause" requested presents that would hardly serve a future priest:

"I want for Christmas a hearing telephone, a ring with the letters J.P.W., a parachute with a soldier on it, goggles, Army suit, camouflage helmet, and a gun."[4]

Young Johnny built model tanks and airplanes, and was interested in military things. His vocation was hanging in the balance for a while as a youngster since it looked like he could have gone into the military as easily as the priesthood.

Little Johnny always used to march around with a knapsack and a little stick for a gun, which prompted his Aunt Helen Wessel to say, "That boy's going in the Army. I can see it!" Later she was quite surprised that he became a priest.[5]

For the rest of his life, John would retain a keen interest in World War II. A box containing his books was discovered in the basement of Blessed Sacrament Church after he had left. In it were more than thirty different paperback copies of Ballantine's *Illustrated History of World War II.*

The war years also touched John and his family in other ways. John's beloved uncles, Carl and Jim Hogan, who had joined different branches of military service, were frequent visitors to the Wessel home. Young John, who was entranced with the allure of all things military, would delight in their company. A portrait taken at one family gathering at the Farm in 1943 shows a four-year-old John, dressed in a sailor suit, proudly saluting his two uncles in uniform, Jim in his Navy blues and Carl in his dark green Army colors.[6]

A few months later, tragedy struck. The family received word that Uncle Carl was missing in action. On November 26, 1943, a German plane released a radio-controlled air-to-surface missile hitting his troopship. The British troopship, *H.M.T. Rohna*, was part of a 24-ship convoy in the Mediterranean Sea sailing from Oran, North Africa on its way to India. Carl Hogan, an Army captain and medical officer, was being transported with his unit aboard the *Rohna* for duty in the China-Burma-India Theater. Approximately 1050 American soldiers lost their lives. Presumed dead, Dr. Carlton P. Hogan was posthumously awarded the Purple Heart. His body was never recovered.

After the enemy missile hit, the *Rohna* sank rapidly at night in rough seas. According to eyewitnesses, Captain Hogan gave his life belt to a wounded enlisted man who had lost his in the attack, although this unselfish act meant his own almost certain death. A survivor recalled seeing Captain Hogan on deck, performing his duties amid the chaos. "The last I saw of him before I abandoned ship was him attending to the wounded."[7]

When John learned that his beloved Uncle Carl had been killed, the youngster was devastated. He was only four years old. It was the first time the little boy had ever experienced the deep and often inexplicable sorrow that is part of life. For a time, not even his mother was able to console him. Young John "cried for hours," his mother recalled.

"Why?" the little boy sobbed through his tears. "Why?"

His mother's gently soothing words—that Uncle Carl was a hero, that he had given his life for his country, that he was now in Heaven and that God would take care of him—seemed to fall on deaf ears. All Johnny could comprehend was that his beloved Uncle Carl was gone, and the little boy just didn't see why.

In the end, there was nothing his mother could do except to grieve with her son. She, too, had lost a beloved brother.

Despite the times of sadness, John Wessel's early family life was a pleasant and happy one.

John and his little playmates were frequently engaged in games of "cops-and-robbers" and "cowboys-and-Indians." Once Dr. Wessel bought his three children a large circus tent. When it was pitched, it took up most of the backyard. To their mother's joy, a misguided arrow shot during a "shoot 'em up" with the neighborhood "Indians" deflated the tent forever.

In addition to their happy home life on Garden Street, the Wessel children spent much of their time at another family homestead—their grandparents' Farm. Mary and Patrick Hogan still lived on the Farm, not too far from the Wessel home on Garden Street. The elder Hogans, and Grandma Hogan in particular, had a great influence on the lives of all the children, especially on young John.

The Wessel children were always at the Farm, weekends and summertimes. It was a beautiful way to grow up. The Hogan farm was still a real working farm with all the animals that a child could imagine—horses, cows, sheep, ducks, turkeys, chickens. How joyful it must have been to the young Wessel children to go out to the barn and see the little animals, to watch them grow, and to see them bear offspring. The Farm always seemed to be filled with baby animals—little lambs, calves, fuzzy chicks and ducklings, and a foal or two. The children loved to help feed and groom the animals and follow them around. Many a time, a mother duck and her tame little ducklings would trail around the Farm after one of the children. Not surprisingly, each of the Wessel children developed a lifelong love of animals.

Young John loved the Farm, and he loved the outdoor life. As a child, he would always find some activity that would take him outdoors, and this pattern continued throughout his adult life. He wanted nothing to do with quieter, indoor pursuits, and camping would always be his favorite vacation.

Fall brought with it hunting season, and the annual family tradition of a Thanksgiving Day hunt on the Farm. When Johnny was old enough, he would be permitted to join his father and the older men, Uncle Jim and Uncle Michael and their friends, as they trekked across the marshy lands with rifles in tow looking for wild game early on Thanksgiving morning.

In addition to its evident joys, there was also a practical reason for exposing the children to life on the Farm. John's father often had office hours in the evening for the convenience of his patients. In order to get the children out of the house in the evening, their mother would pile the youngsters into the family car after dinner and drive the short distance to the Farm. This became their routine every day in all but the worst of weather.

After hours of playing on the Farm, or listening to Grandmother Hogan's stories, the children would come home exhausted and ready for bed.

Their father would join his wife and children on the Farm whenever he could, sharing in their fun-filled activities. To this day there are the remains of a tree hut that was built by Dr. Wessel and his sons Ed and John in one of the Farm woods.

By this time, Mary Hogan was the picture of a kindly, white-haired Irish grandmother, with the same sweet smile and gentle Irish brogue that she'd brought from County Cork. During those many visits to the Farm, Mary Hogan would impart the example of faith to her grandchildren, as she had done with her own children. The youngsters said the Rosary with their grandparents in the evenings, and recited the Angelus when the clock struck six. Grandmother Hogan remained a very religious woman all her life, and young John was keenly aware of that.

Being Irish, and a grandmother besides, another thing always ready on Mary Hogan's lips was her stories. Following in the great tradition of wonderful Irish *seanchai*, who would travel from town to town spinning tales for a living, Grandma Hogan was a wonderful storyteller, with a whole new generation of eager listeners who would beg for her stories. Many an evening, Grandma Hogan would sit by the hearth and spellbind the children with her tales, all true, of the exploits of one branch of her family that went to the Midwest and settled in Nebraska.

The lives of these pioneering ancestors demonstrate great faith, courage, and perseverance.

Property in Ireland generally passed to the eldest son. While the eldest, Cornelius Duggan (who was the father of Mary Duggan Hogan), stayed on at the family home at Shandangan, County Cork, three other of his siblings—his brother, Daniel, and two sisters, Catherine and Margaret—emigrated to America. These three could see that there was no future for them in Ireland. The two girls, Catherine and Margaret, came to America first in 1849, landing in New York City.

Daniel came several years later, bringing with him a wife, also named Catherine, and settled in Massachusetts. They had left Ireland because they wanted to own their own land, and to have the freedom to live their lives as they wished. But they soon realized that there was such anti-Catholic bigotry in Massachusetts that this would not be possible for them as Catholics. As luck would have it, they heard about a colony being organized by Father Jeremiah Trecy, a native of Drogheda, County Louth, Ireland. Here they would have an opportunity to become homesteaders and acquire land, and also to serve as lay missionaries by bringing their Catholic faith to the Indians indigenous to the Midwest.

The saga of the immigrant Irish Duggan family in America is recounted in an article in the journal, *Nebraska History*. It was written by one of John Wessel's Nebraska cousins, Dr. Thomas Ashford Kuhlman, in 1981:

> The future of these three Duggans [Daniel and Catherine, his wife, and sister Margaret] was determined once and for all when Daniel read in an advertisement in the Boston Pilot, a Catholic newspaper in the winter of 1855-56. It was the time of no-nothingism and "No Irish Need Apply" signs, and Father Trecy, encouraged by the Irish Immigrant Aid Convention organized in Buffalo, New York, by the brilliant Irish journalist Thomas Magee, was advertising for a group of Gaels (Irish) to "go where no one lives." Here, for Daniel, was the opportunity to gain land. In the American West there would be neither the near-feudalism of Shandangan nor the humiliations offered by Yankee prejudice. Daniel, his wife, and sister Margaret quickly decided to join the Trecy adventure.

Dr. Thomas A. Kuhlman, "The Capt. Cornelius O'Connor House in Homer: A Symbol for the Dakota County Irish," 63 *Nebraska History* 1, 16 (1981).[7]

Meanwhile, Catherine Duggan had married a man named Cornelius O'Connor, who was known as "Captain O'Connor." When he settled in Nebraska, he was given the title of Captain and was entrusted to organize troops to help protect the pioneers from the Indians. Continues the *Nebraska History* article:

> The Cornelius O'Connors would remain in the East to join the Colony in another [year] if Daniel sent back favorable reports.

The Duggans, then, were among the approximately two dozen families who gathered near Gary Owen outside of Dubuque, Iowa in the spring of 1856 and traveled by ox-drawn covered wagons across the state, arriving at their Dakota County destination on June 2nd. [They arrived in a place which they named the St. John's Colony.] On that day, the men of the Colony erected a forty foot cross to symbolize the religious significance of their settlement.[8]

The children and grandchildren of these three pioneers learned the saga of their ancestors' western migration—the wearisome, tedious traveling in ox-drawn carriages; the hardships incurred from the Indians—and as they began to homestead their acreage, how they toiled to build their homes and plant their crops. They survived both a siege of locusts which ate everything they planted, and the extreme winter of 1856-1857 which was one of the coldest winters on record. Most of the pioneers went back East because it was too difficult to survive, if in fact they did survive at all. The Duggans stayed.

Their descendants passed these stories down through written and oral history. It was through stories like those in the *Nebraska History* that Grandmother Hogan would enthrall her young grandson Johnny with tales of the Indians, based upon the true adventures of her two aunts and her uncle, and their children—her cousins—who settled in St. John's Colony (Jackson), Nebraska, where to this day their great-grandchildren and great-great-grandchildren live.

Catherine and Captain O'Connor went West in 1857. The O'Connor branch of the family settled in Homer, Nebraska. Many of the stories, too, that Grandmother Hogan used to share with her young grandchildren came from the letters and memoirs from her Aunt Catherine O'Connor.

The O'Connors of Homer, Nebraska had ten children. Seven out of the ten died in their twenties of tuberculosis, or what they then called consumption. Captain Cornelius O'Connor, who died in 1902, helped to build St. Cornelius Catholic Church, which was named after him.

Homer and St. John's Colony were little outposts near the Iowa border, just due south of Sioux City, Iowa, a few miles east of the mighty Missouri

River, and about eighty miles north of a town named Omaha, which had just been founded by settlers in 1854 as a "jumping off" point for pioneers traveling westward. As Roman Catholic missionaries, the Duggan family built the churches and evangelized the Indians in that area, tending to their temporal and spiritual needs. The Duggans befriended the Indians, and remained very much involved with missionary work to the several indigenous tribes. Some of the family even ran the Indian reservations in that part of the Midwest.

Grandmother Hogan was a good writer and she communicated with her cousins out West, and then shared their letters with her family. This memoir, written in 1969 by one of Catherine's granddaughters, Charlotte, is of her grandparents, Catherine and Captain O'Connor, who raised her:

> So many times I have thought of putting down things that happened when I was a youngster in school, but days and years slip by and I didn't do it. Now that I am older, eighty years, in September 12, 1969, I'd like my children and grandchildren to know of some of the things of years gone by. I remember my grandmother, Catherine Duggan O'Connor, telling me of the Indians when she and Grandfather came West in 1857. She told me of Indians sitting outside their little home with feathers in their hair and full Indian dress, shawls, etc. Grandmother was not afraid of them but they would often come into the house and help themselves to bread or any food she had and then would leave. A great many of the pioneers could not stand the strain of Indians and left for their former homes in the East.
>
> . . .
>
> When I was only a little more than two years old when my parents, John and Margaret Kelly died [presumably of consumption], my grandmother and grandfather raised me. And such wonderful grandparents they were.
>
> Grandmother had an Indian squaw who walked from the reservation to Homer to wash for Grandma. She had a small daughter called Mehong who always came with her, and Mehong was a pretty little girl and loved to play with my Aunt Katey who was about the same age. They played as all little girls played

and never quarreled. Then, when evening came, the mother and daughter went home together.

Further on in Charlotte's memoir is an interesting story which shows the wonderful faith of these pioneering people:

> One time when the Civil War was going on, Grandma was alone and an Army officer came to the house and asked Grandma if she saw a deserter. There had been a soldier come to the door and said to Grandma, "For God's sakes, save me!" There was only one room in the house and there was a closet where Grandfather kept his tools, as he was a carpenter, and was away building government buildings in Omaha. Grandma said she had no place for the deserter to hide except the closet, and Grandma showed him the place.
>
> Shortly afterward the officer came and asked if there was a soldier in the house and Grandma said, "See for yourself," and the officer pushed the curtain to the closet back and found no one there. The officer went away and came back in a short time and swore he saw a deserter come toward the little house, but he couldn't find him, and went away cursing Grandma. Grandma told me she said a prayer to our Blessed Mother to help her do the right thing and when the officer looked in the closet and couldn't find the deserter, Grandma said she thought it was a miracle because the deserter pleaded "for God's sakes" save him, and He did. Grandma said she didn't tell a lie, but simply said for the officer to look for himself and there was no other place for anyone to hide. After a couple of hours, the man came out of the closet, and Grandma gave him some of Grandpa's washed clothes, and he went in the shrubbery and changed from his Army uniform and left and Grandma never saw or heard of him. She was always sorry she didn't ask about his family or his name or where he was from but she was so excited, she forgot to ask him anything.
>
> Why didn't the officer find the deserter? Grandma always had such faith in our Blessed Mother that I think God answered

her prayer. More things are wrought by prayer than this world knows.

At another point, Charlotte's memoir continues with a glimpse of the pioneers' relationships with each other and with the Indians:

> When I was quite small, Uncle Tim [O'Connor] had Indians pick corn for him in the fall. They camped on the ground west of the brick house and they had several tents and were good workers. They were harmless but I never went near them after dark. Grandma told me of the many times Indians did harm people but they never harmed us. Uncle Tim and Uncle C.J. had the government store near the Winnebago agency and both could speak Indian very well.[9]
>
> There was one elderly Indian who always came to visit Grandfather in the fall. His name was White Breast. He couldn't speak English but Grandfather could speak some Indian and they ate dinner together and spent a few hours at Grandpa and Grandma's home. Then he would walk back to the reservation. He came every year until Grandpa died and then he came no more. He told Uncle C.J. in Homer that it made him too lonesome to come after Grandfather had passed away. He was a fine-looking Indian, tall, straight and had white hair. . . .
>
> All the Indians knew Uncle C.J. O'Connor and Uncle Tim O'Connor very well and always got along with them. Some squaws would come each year selling gooseberries, five cents a quart. They would pick the wild berries and peddle them around. We had a squaw who died who did our washing. She was a real sweet Indian and I liked her very much. One day when Katherine was about four years old, she said to the squaw, "My, your hands are dirty." I felt embarrassed but the squaw said to Katherine, "No dearie, that is the way God made me," and that was all.
>
> Uncle Tim and Aunt Lottie had many friends who worked for the government at the agency at Winnebago. They often had parties in the old brick house and friends from Sioux City would come too. Aunt Mary was a great musician and would

play for the dancers and I would sit on the stairway and watch them dance. Grandma always had lovely cakes and pies and refreshments for the crowd and Grandfather would enjoy visiting with them all. No liquor was ever served, I remember that. Although Grandfather always had it in the house and would fix a toddy with sugar and water when he went to bed.

The house of Charlotte's memory is now designated a historical house called the O'Connor Mansion. That was the home that Captain O'Connor and his wife, Catherine Duggan O'Connor, Grandmother Hogan's aunt, built after they were settled in Homer. It was sold by a grandson to Dakota County and is now the Dakota County Historical Society Museum.

Catherine's sister, Margaret Duggan, had married Thomas Ashford several years after she came out West. Thomas Ashford was an entrepreneur. He joined the Colorado Gold Rush in 1859 and built a brick house not too far away from the O'Connor Mansion.

Daniel Duggan, the brother who went out with the Trecy Colony and settled in Jackson (originally St. John's), Nebraska, and his wife Catherine had seven children. Daniel Duggan, records the *Nebraska History* article, "established schools, churches and roads and he established the first Catholic church in St. John's, which was called St. Patrick's."[10]

Before John Wessel's grandmother, Mary Duggan, was married, she made a trip to the Midwest to visit the Nebraska branch of her family. She had seen firsthand the prairie settlements where they lived, the rugged churches that they had built, and the American Indians who lived peacefully in that part of Nebraska with the White and immigrant settlers. As evident from the family letters and memoirs, the Irish missionaries enjoyed good relations with their Indian neighbors.

Evenings after supper, and after prayers were said, while dusk turned to darkness, these wonderful stories rolled off Mary Hogan's lips and were passed on to young Johnny and his brother and sister. Sometimes Grandma Hogan would recount the tales from memory in her lilting Irish brogue. At other times, she would read the fascinating accounts from the faded journals and letters of her pioneer family as they settled in the Midwest, pausing to add her own commentary along the way.

Young John just loved his grandmother's stories. He would sit in awe for hours while Grandma Hogan would enrapture him with stories of the

Indians and the settlement of the Midwest. Through her mesmerizing tales, the child's mind and imagination were opened to worlds beyond the time and space of the little South Jersey town where he was born. She filled him with a fervent interest in Indian lore and life, and a great love for the Indians. As he listened enraptured to his grandmother's stories, the young boy began to feel the first faint stirring of a desire to be a missionary someday himself, and to go to far-flung lands and teach and preach to native tribes who had never heard the Gospel and who did not know how much God loved them.

As she looked into the bright, expectant, smiling face of her young grandson, Mary Hogan might have been reminded of yet another young boy named Johnny a long, long time ago. Grandma Hogan shared a common bond with the family priest, Father J. Arthur Hayes, as to the destiny of the young boy, for she always felt sure that someday, her grandson Johnny would be a priest.[11]

CHAPTER 4

ON CHIPPEWA TRAIL

Several months after John's Uncle Carl was reported missing in action and presumed dead, his grandfather Patrick Hogan died. Shortly after Grandpa Hogan's death, Grandma Hogan moved into the family's Garden Street home, and the Farm was put up for rent for a time, but was never entirely relinquished by the family.[1]

In 1945, the Second World War was over. The Wessel family rejoiced and thanked God, along with the rest of America, when Germany surrendered unconditionally at Allied headquarters in Reims, France, on May 7, 1945, and Victory in Europe ("V-E") Day was celebrated the following day.

Japan would be defeated shortly thereafter. On August 6, 1945, the first atomic bomb used in warfare leveled Hiroshima, Japan; a second atomic weapon destroyed Nagasaki three days later. Immediately, Tokyo pressed for peace, and on September 2, 1945, Japan formally surrendered to the Allies under the command of General Douglas MacArthur aboard the *U.S.S. Missouri* in Tokyo Bay. Victory Over Japan ("V-J") Day was proclaimed on that day, and once again, a war weary nation gave thanks to God for the hard-won victory and the end of hostilities.[2]

The Wessels had cause to rejoice in the safe return of their Uncles James Hogan and Walter Wessel. This family, like the rest of the country, began to look expectantly to the future and, hopefully, to a new era of peace and prosperity.

In 1945, when John was five, his family acquired a summer home in nearby Medford Lakes, New Jersey, which became for the next twelve years the center of hiking, swimming, canoeing, camping, and the other outdoors activities he loved. Before acquiring the Medford Lakes property, the family would drive to the Jersey shore and back for respite from the long, hot summers to enjoy a day at the beach. Fortunately, through one of his patients, Dr. Wessel had the opportunity to purchase the home in Medford Lakes, about ten miles south of Mount Holly. It would provide a perfect summertime getaway for the family and hours of wholesome warm weather activity for the children. And like his grandparents' Farm, the summers spent at Medford Lakes would have a significant influence on John's life.

Medford Lakes was a privately owned community in the township of greater Medford, situated on a huge wooded tract with three large lakes and many smaller ones meandering through it. It was an entire community of log cabins, although the "cabins" were actually great lodges rather than the small log huts of Abe Lincoln's day. There was a quiet, casual elegance to summers at the Lakes. It was a peaceful refuge and resort.[3]

By the time John's family had settled in Medford Lakes, a small log cabin style country church, St. Mary of the Lakes, had been established for the town's Catholic population. Before that, St. Mary was a mission church of Mount Holly, and the priests of Sacred Heart Church came to St. Mary during the summer to offer Sunday Mass. Winterizing in 1943 provided year round service for Catholic families over an extended area, and in the same year St. Mary became an independent parish and was assigned its first pastor.

In the early days, an Indian chief named Strongwolf taught beadwork in the craft shop, a small building on Tecumseh Trail behind the Pavilion. The Chief lived in a tepee on the Horse Desert, in an area which later became a school.

The Indian influence was very much a part of life at the Lakes, from the ever-present totem poles, to the wooden Indian at the town hotel, the Log Cabin Lodge, to the fascinating names given to the local lakes and trails—Mudjekeewis, Shingowack, Chickagami, Mishe Mokwa, Wauwauskaske, and Mushkodasa—in honor of the first inhabitants.

The family's home was on Chippewa Trail, one of many roads that were named after Indian tribes. It was just the thing for a young boy already enamored with Indian lore and life. In keeping with the rustic wooden architecture in the community, the Wessel home was a great two-story log cabin style house which bordered on Lake Aetna, one of the several finger lakes that dotted the area of Medford.

Johnny could walk out of his back door, take a running dive off the dock in his backyard, and splash into the cool water. Each summer day, he could spend long hours swimming and diving in the lake, or wile away the day canoeing, or trek through the unexplored woodlands looking for Indian arrowheads or unusual stones with his faithful dog "Topper" at his side—all the while imagining that he was living the life of a brave Indian or a missionary explorer of long ago.

"All Wessels are animal lovers," said John's cousin, Julian Wessel. John dearly loved dogs and he always had his favorite canine companion with him to share in outdoor adventures. The Wessels' favorite breed of dog was the English Springer Spaniel.[4] Topper the First was a liver and white English Springer Spaniel. When he died, they immediately purchased Topper the Second, a black and white English Springer Spaniel.

Years later John would fondly recall memories of the Wessels' first dog, a black Scottish terrier. Scotty loved to dive off the dock. Once at the end of the summer, when the lake was drained, the 14-year-old, nearly blind dog leapt high off the dock and landed, much confused, smack into the muddy bottom of what had been Lake Aetna.[5]

The high point of social activity for the residents was membership in the Colony Club, which together with its auxiliary organizations, conducted most all social, athletic and recreational activities, including bazaars, card parties, festivals, dances, and the annual water pageant and canoe carnival on Lower Aetna Lake, a popular event which began when the early colonists lashed two canoes together and vied to see who could create the most original float. The moonlight procession of illuminated floats on the water has remained a magical and thrilling tradition attracting crowds from miles around.

Popular at the Lakes was a summer day camp for children which provided wholesome organized activities in a supervised environment. John participated in the day camp each summer, as did the rest of the colonists' children, under the watchful eye of the camp director and his youth counselors. The young boys went on overnight camp outs, shot bows and arrows, ran track and field, went biking and hiking, sailing, and canoeing, took part in Sunday swim races, learned arts and crafts, and enjoyed good friendship and camaraderie.

At five years of age, John went on his first supper hike with his preschool group of friends. One could see the development of a young boy who would someday possess an unquenchable love for the outdoors and for all of nature.

A portrait of the young campers taken one summer shows a tanned, healthy, chubby young John Wessel at about seven or eight years of age pictured with a dozen or more boys and their adult counselor. In the photograph, John's dark hair is almost blonde from long hours in the summer sun. John continued on at the camp each summer, eventually becoming a counselor himself to the younger boys.

The goal of the young campers like John was to obtain the bronze shield, which represented nine years of successful achievement in camp work. A wooden plaque, fashioned after the Medford Lakes' traditional "arrowhead" emblem, was presented to the child at the completion of the first camp year. Each succeeding year, accomplishment insignias were painted on it covering one-eighth of the space. When completely covered, the coveted shield was awarded to the proud recipient.[6]

But the real value of the camp was measured in terms of the physical benefits, association with others, acquired techniques and skills, and lessons in good sportsmanship that each boy acquired for life. By this unit of measurement, its value was priceless.[7]

Summer camp was traditionally marked at the end of the season with the popular Annual Mile Swim, in which all the youngsters could participate. John loved to swim, but he never kidded himself that he was a fantastic swimmer. What he possessed in strength and endurance he lacked in speed and style. Without anyone pushing him, John decided to enter the mile race. He was eleven years old.

The day of the race arrived. There were at least thirty participants at the start, though not all of them would finish. The entire Lakes community turned out to cheer them on, including John's parents, brother and sister.

At the sound of the starter's pistol, the racers plunged into the water and began the arduous course around the lake and back. One by one, the swimmers began to cross the finish line, amidst the excited sounds of cheering, yelling, and splashing water. John was not among them.

Soon other racers began to drop out, exhausted, muscles cramped, unable to complete the course, only to be rescued by canoes posted along the lake and brought back to shore.

Still no sign of John. Minutes passed.

Finally, off in the distance was a lone figure—a boy, tired but swimming steadily home. He could not win, nor even come close, and he surely knew it. But he would not give up either. He was determined to finish. With more heart and guts than skillful strokes, the boy forced himself onward to the cheers of the approving crowd.

John came in dead last, long after the other thirty participants had either crossed the finish line or dropped out. When he splashed into the docks, he got a rousing hand from the grandstand spectators for his perseverance.

Looking half sheepish and slightly embarrassed, John said to his friend, who had been following him in a canoe, "Come on, Tommy. Let's get out of here." Without sitting down for a moment's rest, he and his friend paddled off in the canoe.

In time, John would excel at long distance swimming which he loved. He would work hard at whatever he did, even though many things, from academic subjects to sports, did not come easily to him. But John was not a quitter, and he was not afraid to try. He might not always come in first, but he would always finish the race.

CHAPTER 5

SCHOOL DAYS

The only thing apparently lacking in John's idyllic early life was the opportunity for formal religious education to reinforce the faith which he learned at home.

Since the early beginnings of Roman Catholic parochial school education, in the Spanish colonies of the Southwest United States in the seventeenth century,[1] the parochial school system has been renowned for its academic excellence, religious training, and disciplined and moral environment.

To his devout parents, a solidly Catholic education was surely desired for their son John, as indeed, it had been for their older children as well. But that was quite impossible since there was no Catholic school in the area around Mount Holly. Both Eddie and Maryann attended the public school, where they had done quite well in their secular studies, while taking religious instruction privately. So, it seemed, would John.

But all that was about to change. Whether by accident or design, every opportunity was suddenly provided for the spiritual formation of a future priest.

The Congregation of the Sisters, Servants of the Immaculate Heart of Mary was an Order of religious Sisters headquartered at the Marian Convent at Marywood College in Scranton, Pennsylvania. They first came to the attention of the Most Reverend William A. Griffin, D.D., then Bishop of the Diocese of Trenton, through their fine teaching work in Asbury Park, New Jersey. As a result, Bishop Griffin applied to their community to ask for some Sisters to come to Mount Holly and do catechetical work in the area.

Sister M. Christina Murphy, I.H.M., and another young nun, Sister Stella, were summoned by their Reverend Mother, who explained that the Bishop of Trenton wanted Sisters to teach in the area of Sacred Heart Parish, and perhaps in due time, God willing, to open a grammar school. The Reverend Mother asked the two Sisters if they would mind coming to Mount Holly with her and doing catechetical work in the parish. Without a moment's hesitation, both Sisters said, "Well, it's God's work, and if that's what they want, that's what we'll do."

Throughout their first year in Mount Holly, the Sisters with Mother Alphonsus as their Superior, conducted catechetical classes in the mission homes—mostly farm homes—located near the school bus stops of the far-flung parish which were convenient for the greatest numbers of children.

As their work progressed, the Sisters formed a real community—with each other, with the parish priests, and with the families in town, whom they were slowly getting to know. They experienced the friendship and assistance of the kindly Catholic parishioners, among them the Hogans and the Wessels, who pitched in to help in their work. The Sisters' material needs were taken care of while they devoted themselves to the more important business. It was hard work, indeed, but they loved it.

Meanwhile, the Bishop, whose watchful eye discerned that the time had come to centralize the location of catechetical instruction, felt it was time to announce the opening of a regional Catholic school. Fortunately, a mansion situated on a five-acre site on High Street near the center of Mount Holly became available that would provide just the perfect location. The property was purchased from the John D. Johnson family in 1943, and the building was renovated to serve as a combined school and convent.[2]

By September of 1944, the first Mount Holly Regional Catholic Grade School on High Street was open and ready for business, the very year that young John Wessel started kindergarten. It would be formally dedicated by Bishop Griffin a month later. The school consisted of a kindergarten and the first four grades, with a new grade to be added over each of the succeeding four years. Eighty students were expected on the opening day but, much to the surprise and consternation of the pastor, Father George E. Duff, and the faculty (now numbering seven Sisters), 144 pupils arrived! Provisions were quickly made to accommodate the extra students.

Father Duff, who was the school's guiding light and first pastor, would not remain more than a year after its opening to see the results of his efforts. In 1946, Monsignor James S. Foley replaced him as pastor of Sacred Heart Church, where he would serve until 1950. About the same time, there came to the parish a young, newly ordained curate, Father J. Morgan Kelly, whom the Immaculate Heart of Mary Sisters affectionately called "our little brother." Monsignor Foley would then be succeeded as pastor by Father (later Monsignor) Joseph V. Kozak, who in the early 1940s had been a young curate at Sacred Heart under the tutelage of Father J. Arthur Hayes.

In 1946, Mother M. Brigida Strome, I.H.M., replaced Mother Alphonsus as the new principal of the school. By 1948, the enrollment of the school had grown to 427 students, who were by then being taught by ten Sisters. Expecting a further increase in enrollment with the addition of the eighth grade, the construction of a new, six-room school was commenced.

The new school building was once again dedicated by Bishop Griffin in October 1948, almost four years to the day from the dedication of the first ediface.

On June 17, 1949, the first graduating class of thirty-six students from Mount Holly Regional Catholic Grade School received their diplomas from His Excellency, Bishop Griffin.

The dream of building a Catholic grammar school could not have been realized without the active involvement of the town's many parishioners, particularly those who were the parents of school-age children.

Dr. Edward and Kathleen Wessel were involved in every aspect of the school's operations, ready to do anything they could to make the endeavor a success.

Dr. Edward Wessel was instrumental in helping obtain the grounds for the new Catholic school. It was quite an uphill battle, because Mount Holly, a predominantly Presbyterian community, was not well disposed toward Catholics at that time. Dr. Wessel was one of the leaders in the church involved in purchasing and refurbishing the Johnson Estate that became Mount Holly School.

Kathleen Wessel was asked to be the first president of the PTA, a challenge she accepted despite her own doubts about the adequacy of her abilities and experience. It was a surprise to no one that Mrs. Wessel did an excellent job.

On a balmy Sunday afternoon, the 15th of October 1944, Bishop William Griffin dedicated the first Mount Holly Regional Catholic Grade School. The dedication ceremony was an impressive affair; in addition to His Excellency the Bishop, all the priests of the diocese were in attendance, as well as assorted dignitaries, parents, students, and town fathers. Fifteen years later, the name of the school would be changed to Sacred Heart School.

That October day was an especially memorable one for John Wessel and his family, too. In recognition of his work on behalf of the school and his leadership in the church community, Dr. Edward Wessel was selected to give the address at the dedication ceremony. Dr. Wessel spoke to the crowds on the lawn of the new convent and school, as Bishop Griffin and the other dignitaries looked on. The Bishop was distantly related to the Hogan family, and the Hogans and the Wessels in the audience that day must have been proud of their families' contribution to bringing a quality Catholic education to their little community.

Like many little boys, Johnny didn't relish school. Many mornings, he was firmly pushed out the door on his way to Mount Holly School, where he entered kindergarten in September 1944, just a few days shy of his fifth birthday. During his first years in school, John was remembered by his sister as "a balking little boy who intensely disliked furthering his education at all."

The Wessel home was about six blocks from the school. To get there, John had to walk west on Garden Street, turn north at the corner of Garden and High Streets and walk the few blocks to the school, situated just past the old courthouse and jail in the center of town.

Kathleen Wessel vividly recalled her friends up on High Street telling her that John would walk by on his way to school every morning swinging on every tree that he passed.

They'd yell, "John! You'll be late for school!" And he'd say, "No, I won't." But his mother knew he would be. Somehow, the warnings of family and friends that he would be late for school never seemed to deter John from swinging on every tree along the way.

The grammar school that John Wessel so reluctantly attended as a young kindergartner would eventually provide him with two benefits of incalculable value in life: first, the certainty of his religious vocation; second, a true and lasting friendship.

CHAPTER 6

I CALL YOU FRIENDS

Among John Wessel's classmates in kindergarten class in the fall of 1944 was a young boy named James Dubell. He was among those students in the audience who watched Bishop Griffin dedicate the new Catholic grade school, and was duly impressed that the father of his classmate Johnny was giving the address. James Dubell lived on Buttonwood Street, three short blocks from John's house on Garden Street.[1]

Soon Johnny and Jimmy, or "Wess" and "Dube" as they nicknamed each other, were fast friends, spending time with each other's families and visiting back and forth at each other's homes. In time, neither would remember precisely when they first became friends, since it seemed as though they'd known each other all their lives.

John and Jim would prove to be good companions along life's journey. In school, both would be altar boys. Years later, both would be priests. Always, they would remain friends.

"My relationship with John goes back to grammar school, the primary grades," Monsignor James H. Dubell began. "I cannot . . . remember, really, first being with him or being close friends . . . but it was a primary grade." Among his earliest memories of John:

> I went to his house—I spent much more time at his house than he spent at my house because his house was bigger, his house had a lot of places to hide and play, his house had three floors and a basement—so I spent an awful lot of time at his house. I felt like a member of the family, I was so close to them.

The earliest recollection I have is that John and I would play and hide in the cabinets underneath the counter tops in the kitchen. That's how small we were that we could fit in there! . . . I was always frightened that we wouldn't be able to get out, because we would get in and we would lock the door . . . and then we would have to call somebody, like his mother, to open the door and let us out . . . But he was never frightened. He would laugh and joke, and was not afraid of anything. One of the characteristics of John's life is that he was a courageous person, and little things like that would not frighten him.

Edward and Kathleen Wessel welcomed all of their children's friends, and so their home became a friendly, active place centered on the activities of young people—Eddie and his older high school friends, Maryann and her girlfriends, and John and his buddy Jim were frequently all together at the Wessel home in Mount Holly or Medford Lakes, or gathered around the noisy and crowded dinner table.

"Wess" and "Dube" were total opposites in many ways—such as personalities, habits, and personal characteristics—and both came from different social and economic worlds. So different, in fact, that had they not gone to the same school together they may never even have met. Yet somehow, these two kindred spirits managed to negotiate their differences with ease to become the best of friends. The areas where they differed were really just external and peripheral. At the core of it, they had much more in common than apart. As James Dubell recalled, "We were like night and day—opposites. But we were very close friends."

A few undeniable facts shaped John's early life: The first, that he was the youngest in his family. The fact that John had a brother and a sister who were much older than he was an important part of his life. To John and his school friend Jim, these older siblings seemed like "giants"—really big and bright and so far above the much younger boys. So John always had to live up to the fact that he had an older brother and sister, both of whom were above average students.

As a typical youngest child, little Johnny was always pestering and bothering his sister Maryann. She, in turn, was always screaming and hollering at him. To her, he was the pest of a little brother who was always upsetting her plans.

John's brother Eddie lived upstairs on the third floor with John, but Ed was off in another world populated by "big guys." He was involved in more mature activities, his friends were older, and he was advancing academically at a fast pace. To Ed, his little brother would always remain affectionately, "Johnny," no matter how old.

But it was always a very significant part of John's life that he had an older brother and sister. John never felt neglected in any way, though. If anything, he was probably given special attention by his parents simply because he was the youngest. But as a youngster, John was always doing impish things with his older siblings, like a typical little brother who was always messing up their plans. When they had company, he would always be around to disturb things somehow. And naturally, they didn't always appreciate him being around.

Dubell vividly recalled John's summer home in Medford Lakes, where John and his mother, sister and brother would stay for the entire summer. The thing that John loved most, and in which he excelled, was swimming—long distance swimming.

"I would go and visit," Dubell remembered. "But when I went to visit, it was like I was out of touch with all that was going on. I came from the city, Mount Holly, and when I went down there I was like a city slicker . . . These kids had been living in their bathing suits all summer, running around in their bare feet, and here comes this guy from the city who's getting into a bathing suit for the first time and its already July 15th or something!"

"John would make fun of you in a nice sort of way, and he would tell you to get out of your street clothes and into your bathing suit and take the canoe out and ride out on the lake."

Then, in the middle of the lake, he would upset the canoe and its passengers. A good swimmer, John was so full of adventure, he seemed never to be afraid of anything, and he would encourage his city slicker friend to join him in his daring activities.

Another of John's favorite activities was hiking. John and Jim would often take walks in the woods. Frequently, Jim's compass told him that they were going in the wrong direction, and he would say to John, "We're lost!" John would say, "No, we're not." John was never worried or anxious, and somehow they always found their way home.

Jim wondered at times where John's fearlessness came from. Once he even asked him about it. The boys would ride their bikes all around in Mount Holly or Medford Lakes. On one occasion, they were far away from home when a storm was coming up and it began to get very dark and windy. John wasn't afraid at all.

"Why aren't you afraid?" Jim asked him. John didn't say anything, but he answered it with a kind of expression on his face that said, "What makes you think I'm not afraid! I'm just not showing it!"

"He was this rough-and-ready type of a guy, courageous, not afraid of almost anything," Dubell recalled.

But for all John's courage, he was not superhuman, and he certainly experienced his moments of fear. On one occasion, he let Jim know his true feelings, much to his friend's surprise.

When they were old enough, John and Jim became altar boys at Sacred Heart Church. They used to ride their bikes to church to serve at Mass. At that time, Sacred Heart Church was located on Washington Street, somewhat beyond the center of town, a good mile and a quarter trip. Early one morning, John was pedaling his bike to church for the 6:30 a.m. Mass. He had on the uniform of the Catholic schoolboy—jacket, white shirt, and necktie—and a kid from the public school began to follow John and chase him. John made a point of telling Jim about the incident. John felt sure that the kid was going to beat him up, and he was scared. Jim thought it funny that his friend would be scared of the public school kid, because he didn't think John was afraid of anybody. But John was indeed concerned, so much so that he began to take a different route to the church and solicitously advised his friend to do the same. "Oh, they'll beat you up because they don't like us Catholic schoolers being in uniforms," John warned him. He wanted to protect his friend from a similar encounter with a public school bully.

A second important factor in John's early life was that he came from a family of means. Yet, paradoxically, John was totally unconcerned about wealth and material possessions. Not only was he an unspoiled, unaffected boy, but in later years, he would consciously embrace the virtue of poverty with an almost zealous devotion.

John's family never flaunted money, and never did frivolous things with it. They were not social climbers, and didn't buy material things to impress others. As a matter of fact, John's family never talked about those things. They just lived on a different level that their means and good taste made possible. Their lifestyle was genuine and sincere.

Jim Dubell was very much a part of John's family, and very warmly accepted by them, but at the same time he was keenly aware his middle class family was not a part of the same social set as the Wessels. It didn't bother him, and certainly didn't affect his friendship with John, but as a youth, Jim always found it fascinating and impressive to enter into such a different world than his own. It was a world of elegance and style and seemingly effortless grace.

And what a world it was! One thing that guests invariably noticed was that the Wessels ate very well. "Ma, they had steak, and it was an inch thick!" Jim would tell his mother excitedly after dinner at his friend's house. "Ma, they had rye bread, and *real* butter!" And for dessert, there was always fresh fruit—blueberries, strawberries—desserts that working class folks would have but occasionally as a special treat.

Another notable feature was the beauty and elegance of the Wessels' home, which made most others modest by comparison. "I remember their house being not only beautifully appointed, and different from any other house that I was ever in, but I remember it being peaceful and homey," Dubell recalled.

John's family had a cleaning lady whose name was Pearl. "Nobody that I knew had a cleaning lady," Dubell observed. Wearing a crisp white uniform, she came to the Wessel home two or three times a week, and was quite a steady presence during John's growing up years. The Wessels treated Pearl like one of their family, and cared for her for many years.

"It's not like we were poor," he explained, "but it's like there was Johnny Wessel's level—and then there was everybody else's level."

Everybody else bought secondhand cars; John's family would have a shiny, brand-new Buick. Everybody else bought a television set ten years after it came on the market and paid it off on time; John's family would order a new RCA TV from a Sears and Roebuck catalogue and have it delivered straight away.

John had a new bicycle when everyone else had hand-me-downs. But by the same token, if anyone needed a bike, John would be the first one to lend you his, and it didn't matter much to him when, if ever, he got it back.

John was always well liked and respected by his classmates, a measure of just how unspoiled and down-to-earth he really was. "It's not like anybody ever threw stones at Johnny Wessel," James Dubell recalled. "We never sat around and said, 'He's really rich and we're really poor.' Never! Because he didn't give that impression when he was around. As a matter of fact, John would look more tattered than any of us!"

John's pants were always ripped. "He was a rough-and-tumble, outdoors kind of a person. And therefore, he always kept his clothes that way," said Dubell. "He had a pair of Bostonian wing tips as a young kid, and he'd walk through the woods in them, in the water, and the briars. And the rest of us would be walking so that we wouldn't get our feet wet, but he didn't care!" That's the kind of person Johnny Wessel was.

Here, again, it made for some interesting contrasts between the two boys. Jim was neat, well groomed, and a good dresser. "I was the kind of guy who, if I were going somewhere, would comb my hair ten times," Dubell laughed, "but John was the kind of guy who would wash his face and run his fingers through his hair and he was ready to go out." John's mother used to chide him sometimes, "Why don't you shine your shoes like Jimmy does? Why don't you comb your hair like Jimmy does?" But to no avail. John would always remain a rough-and-ready type of a guy, physical, outdoorsy, courageous, unafraid—but definitely not neat as a pin.

Another important factor in John Wessel's life was the intellectual and cultural atmosphere in which he grew up. That environment was attributable to the influence of John's parents, and the fact that his older brother and sister were fine students. John's brother, Eddie, entered college at the University of Notre Dame when he was sixteen years old. In this kind of academic and cultured world that was very much in evidence in the Wessel household, the conversation was always enlightening and uplifting.

Memorable were the family conversations around the dinner table, or on the long car rides back and forth to Medford Lakes or Philadelphia. Their conversations were always interesting, always about something significant that was happening in the country or in the world. It was an intelligent, informed type of conversation.

"I would always come away feeling that I'd learned something, as young as I was," Dubell recalled. "It might be something mechanical, it might be something political, it might be something historical," but it was "always an elevated type of conversation."

Music was also very prevalent in the household. All the Wessel children played the piano. Evenings, the family gathered 'round the piano in the living room and took turns playing and singing along. Music was a big part of John's early life, particularly classical music.

John was not sufficiently musically inclined, however, to pursue piano lessons beyond childhood, although years later as an adult he taught himself to play the guitar. But through these early influences, John developed a great love and appreciation for music, all kinds of music—from contemporary to classical—particularly sacred and liturgical music.

Finally, John grew up in a very religious environment—one in which the Roman Catholic Church was very important and the priest was a significant person. "The family looked upon the priest as an educated man, as an honest man, and as a helpful person in the community, as a person that you would turn to," said Dubell.

Such was the kind of an environment John Wessel grew up in, as recalled by John's first and most enduring friend.

In grammar school, John was not a great student. He was only an average student who did best in the subjects that he loved. He worked very hard at whatever he did, because some subjects did not come easily to him. But he was persevering and was an enthusiastic student nonetheless.

John was keenly interested in history and did very well in that subject. In fact, James Dubell traces John's early love of Indians and Indian lore to his larger love of history: "I always understood that Indians were just a part of history" and it was history that he liked. "The Indian was also an outdoorsman, a rough-and-ready guy who wasn't afraid, and also an underdog, so the Indian kind of matched his own personality . . . Being in Medford Lakes, that was part of the Indian lore, the Colony Club, totem poles and things like that. John rode in a canoe and Indians rode in canoes."

John loved bows and arrows. He used to shoot them in his basement, where they would ricochet off the stone wall. He loved collecting arrowheads and picking up stones around Medford Lakes. John "liked hunting because it was out-of-doors, in the woods, reminded him of Indians, reminded him of the colonial days, and he would just like that sort of thing," said Dubell.

"He was always the best history student in his class, all through school, no matter what period of history it was," said Dubell.

John Wessel was drawn to many different periods in history. His curiosity was not limited to any one particular historical phase. He was fascinated principally with significant eras of military history, as befitting a young and inquisitive boy who was born and raised during World War II.

Sometimes his attention would be drawn to the Civil War; sometimes the Revolutionary War or the Crusades. At another time, it would be the First and Second World Wars, and at that point he became very interested in the combat airplanes used in those wars and built his own model airplanes—his favorite plane was the German Messerschmitt. He could tell his friends all about the characteristics of each plane.

Like many boys his age, John was an avid "collector." He had a collection of guns which his father bought him—including an old rifle and a Revolutionary War musket—and a collection of swords. John also had a great stamp collection. He and Jim used to work for hours on the floor in John's room sorting through all the stamps and putting them in a book. "We really had a lot of fun with that. The places reminded him of history. Everything in his life . . . related to history."

However, as much as John excelled in history, he was recalled as "the worst speller." This said a lot about John as a person, because "it doesn't mean that he was not bright, just that he was not given to details," said James Dubell.

> I think the reason why he was a good history student was that he didn't get bogged down in details. He could see a whole picture and he could appreciate it, while those of us who are into details never did learn history. We were always interested in memorizing this date or this man, whereas John was always interested in the bigger picture. He would fill in the details as best he could.

Actually, John was not just a poor speller; his spelling was atrocious. It was, recalled his friend, "a thing of humor" all through his life. John would guess at "some of the craziest spellings, and it wouldn't even be close." Even years later in his priestly ministry, Father John Wessel would send out a pastoral letter with more than a few misspelled words, because he was not a particular person, and he was not into detail.

"Also, he was the kind of person that, whatever impression he made on you, that was fine with him. You either took him or you left him," said Dubell. "He wasn't out to win anybody's affection, or attention, or anything like that. At least, that was the perception I had. If you liked him, you liked him. If you didn't like him, he wasn't going to hurt himself to make you like him. . . . He was not a politician. There was nothing false about him at all."

"He certainly had respect for himself and a good self-image, but he was devoid of any airs at all. He used to get very impatient with me when he felt that I was trying to pull something by studying extra hard, by working on something," Dubell recalled. John would ask his friend, "What are you trying to prove, Dube? You don't have to prove anything."

John was not considered a good athlete as a youngster. He was a little clumsy. Although he did play basketball, it didn't really appeal to him. All summer long, John would be in Medford Lakes engaging in one of his favorite activities, swimming. In addition to swimming, the two sports that he liked most were tennis and football—especially football, because football is a rough, physical sport which complimented John's rough nature.

He was happy to play the line. He didn't need to be the quarterback, or run the ball, or catch the ball—he just wanted to play. He just wanted to be out there in the middle of the action on the field. To James Dubell, that "says a lot about his personality. Some people would say, if I don't carry the ball or catch the ball, I'm not going to play, but not him."

Among his peers in grammar school, John was always the leader, and was very well liked and respected. He was perceived by his classmates "as a good boy, yet also as a hell raiser!" If you wanted to do something crazy, Johnny Wessel was your man. "He'd go along with you, and he would enjoy it and he would have fun at it," said Dubell. "He loved horseplay."

He was thought to be a little shy around girls, certainly not a ladies' man, or girl crazy. He would shy away from adolescent "spin the bottle" type party games—but of course, this was elementary school. Johnny was just a real all-American boy.

Yet there was one girl in his class with whom he shared a close friendship. She was a pretty, sweet little girl named Eileen Egan. Like John, she was a religious child, and perhaps that's what drew them to befriend each other. Today, she is a religious Sister.

Eileen and John were classmates from kindergarten through eighth grade. Her mother was a nurse who cared for John's grandfather, Patrick Hogan, during his last illness. Sometimes, Eileen and her younger brother would join John on hikes, exploring the terrain of the Hogan farm. But

Eileen quickly learned that a hike for John could easily turn into an organized expedition! "He was an intense sort of guy who enjoyed the adventures of outdoors," she recalled.

Eileen thought John was one of the "best boys" when they were kids. "At our seventh and eighth grade dances, he could be coerced into one big two-step for old time's sake," she remembers. "It was most evident at these times that he was meant for hiking not waltzing."

James Dubell related an incident that was so typical of John's personality and sense of humor:

> Somebody had a Halloween party and John decided that he and I were going to get together and we were going to go as a horse. So he made this horse's head out of papier-mâché. He loved to work with papier-mâché and plaster of Paris, because that's what his father worked with as a dentist. His father made teeth, so John would have all the plaster of Paris he wanted. His father had a workshop down in the basement and that's where he did his dental work. There were teeth all over the place, and he had little buffing machines and different things down there. John would melt the wax like his father did, and he would put it in a mold and fill a mold with plaster of Paris. And when it would dry he would take it off, and there would be a little Indian and he would paint it. For his train set, he would make mountains out of papier-mâché.
>
> So anyway, he made this horse's head out of papier-mâché and he got a green-and-brown Army blanket. And he was the horse's head and I was the horse's backside—and we had a great time at it! He would really enjoy those kinds of things.

Just a real all-American boy.

CHAPTER 7

FILLED WITH WISDOM AND GRACE

"We had a good school experience," said one of Johnny Wessel's classmates at Mount Holly Regional Catholic School. "The Immaculate Heart of Mary Sisters were great teachers and had a way of affirming the best in each of us." The young pupils learned the "three R's", the arts and humanities, and were trained in the fundamentals of their faith. Their religious experience embodied all the richness of the traditional Roman Catholic Church: First Friday Mass, Forty Hours Devotion, Benediction, May Processions, and mission club. John Wessel, an altar boy, was one of the "old faithfuls," this classmate recalled—always on call and ready to serve.[1]

While John pursued his elementary education, the domestic calm of post-war America, under the helm of the Baptist businessman from Missouri, President Harry S Truman, provided a sharp contrast to the communism that was spreading abroad, particularly in the newly liberated Eastern European nations.

The world had entered the nuclear age with a vengeance—and with it, the ideological and strategic conflict between democracy and communism. The threat of communism, with its godless atheism, espoused in its most lethal form by the former Soviet Union, was very much on the minds of Americans. In 1953, thirteen-year-old John Wessel's concern about the world situation prompted him to pen a zealous, idealistic letter to Russian Premier Joseph Stalin:

"Dear Joe Stalin," John began familiarly in his rounded schoolboy script on composition paper. He dated his letter February 18, 1953.

We Americans are on the edge of our seats awaiting your decision about the control of atomic weapons. Your people have the idea that we want war and we want to destroy the world. You know that is not true. You planted that thought in their minds. That was a grave mistake on your part. Your people will discover the truth and will distrust you and your fellow fascists who want to rule this world. All the arms you have produced and all the lives you have taken with them will matter little when the free world has a strength more powerful than all the A bombs, H bombs and all other man-made weapons. We have God on our side.

John appears not to have finished his passionate defense of God and country, much less mailed it. A few weeks later Joe Stalin was dead.

In 1944, however, John's school years at Mount Holly Regional Catholic School were off to an inauspicious start.

In Sister M. Carina's kindergarten class, he was an enthusiastic, outgoing child. Even at that early age, he spoke about the priesthood. After morning prayers were said, little Johnny would pick up the American flag and announce, "I'm going to march to the Star-Spangled Banner." And then he would declare to Sister Carina, "I'm going to the country sometime. I'm going to be a priest for all the people in the country. I'm going to teach all the people in the mountains about God," he'd say.[2] (Why the mountains, in particular, is a mystery.)

In the kindergarten Christmas Nativity play, John was cast as Saint Joseph. Sister Carina hoped that her outgoing young student would be able to carry off the indispensable role of the Chaste Spouse of the Blessed Virgin and Foster Father of the Infant Jesus. For his role as the saintly carpenter, John was costumed in a white robe, with a censure around his waist and a scarf tied around his head. With great majesty, he carried a staff.

The play was late in starting because the would-be Saint Joseph got a sudden case of stage fright. John ran off the stage and vehemently declared before Mother Alphonsus and the anxious Sisters that he wasn't going to be in the play. After some prodding, he confessed the problem to Sister Carina: He didn't believe he was worthy to be Saint Joseph. "Give the part to somebody else," he implored. Eventually John was calmed down and returned to his spot on the stage to complete the play. In time, none in the audience would remember the bout of stage fright, only what a wonderful Saint Joseph they had that day.[3]

Despite this wobbly start, John would always be assigned a leading part in school programs at the end of each year because he was both a natural leader and an outstanding speaker.

Sister M. Raymond Rafferty, John's sixth grade teacher and later principal, recalled John as a very outgoing child and a leader among his peers. "I always remember that when you were instructing him, if he had any thoughts about what you were talking about, he always expressed himself very well. He would tell you what he was going to do about that particular question." His favorite expression was, "Sister, wait till I tell you this!" And whatever story he had to tell his teacher would be related with great enthusiasm, and at the end of his story the class would all give him a round of applause. That would encourage the other children to be more outgoing.

"All the way through life he was that way," said Sister Raymond, who knew John Wessel until his graduation. "He was very brave, in other words. When you were instructing him, he always had his hand up for something he was going to do in reference to what you were talking about."

Sister M. Lucy, John's first grade teacher, remembered that John and his best friend, Jimmy Dubell, were real boys. "They always did their work, sometimes after a little prodding."

During first grade, John developed a serious blood condition causing him to miss many weeks of school. The boy got very much behind in his studies, and as a result, had difficulty mastering his primary reading skills. By the end of his first grade, he had developed a serious reading problem, and the summer following first grade he was tutored in reading. There were moments of great frustration as he forced himself, oftentimes without outside intervention, to go over phonics rules.[4] But the same spirit of determination which later inspired John to finish the mile swim race at Medford Lakes also enabled him to gradually overcome his reading difficulties.

John made his First Holy Communion on May 25, 1947. What a momentous and memorable day it was for John, and what a proud day for his parents and family.

John is pictured in the official First Holy Communion photograph with his second grade classmates at the altar of Sacred Heart Church. Flanking the class are the pastor, Monsignor James Foley, his young curate, Father Morgan Kelly, and Sister M. Lucy and Sister M. Patricia, the first and second grade teachers.[5]

Both Monsignor Foley and Father Kelly were regarded as outstanding priests whose interest extended to everyone in the parish. Monsignor Foley loved children and was a constant presence in the school. Young Father Kelly was also, and the children idolized him so much that, no matter where he went, they always followed him around. These priests surely were inspirational models for young boys like John and Jim, and their evident joy in their vocation bore witness to the priesthood as a happy, holy, and fulfilling life.

A few incidents come to mind that show John's early love for Jesus Christ. Carving a cross in the headboard of his Cushman bed, he wove a crucifix of palm and glued it there.[6]

When he was eight, John built a prie-dieu (a bench upon which to kneel and pray) out of an orange crate. Painstakingly, he covered the kneeler with red and blue plaid cloth in a colorful Scottish Royal Stewart tartan design, over which he had affixed a red cross; on the front (where his hands rested), a plain red cloth with a cross and chalice in the middle in vivid blue.

As John's mother recalled, "Things like this pointed the way."[7]

At an early age, John showed an intense concern for the feelings of others. As their youngest child matured, John's mother and father marveled at his great sensitivity. John always tried to be positive and charitable toward others in his speech and actions. "He would never allow you to say anything that wasn't nice about anybody," his mother said.

His sister Maryann also recalled how "if ever our dinner conversation hinged on any unkind remarks, we were quickly reminded of our lack of charity."[8]

In fact, one evening at the dinner table, when Dr. Wessel was saying something about a person that John didn't think was kind, the young boy gently rebuked his father, "Oh, Dad, you shouldn't say that about him!"

John's third grade teacher, Sister M. Ignatia Murphy, also observed this trait and related the following story:

> John disclosed a thoughtfulness for the feelings of others,
> most unusual in a child of eight years. For example, when we
> had a project on Indian life, John brought in some arrowheads

from his own collection to show to the class. The next day, another member of the class, having a vivid imagination, brought arrowheads, also.

As the youngsters crowded around my desk before the class bell rang, fingering and admiring the arrowheads, this child explained he had found his arrowhead the previous day in a brook which ran through the farm. He claimed that the arrowhead was still covered with blood and hair when he discovered it. Of course it was at this point the bell rang for class.

John had been taking all of this in, but didn't say anything. Later in the morning when the opportunity presented itself, John sidled up to me and whispered that I shouldn't believe what the other child had told me about the arrowhead because it couldn't be true and explained why. When I had assured him that I agreed with his explanation he went back to his place satisfied. He had prevented hard feelings and embarrassment for the other child. This was so characteristic of him.[9]

*   *   *

In one sense, everyone John encountered along the way during his formative school years had some impact on his life: The energetic, engaging priests in the parish, the gentle, radiant Sisters of the Immaculate Heart of Mary, and other teachers and friends, all helped form the boy's sense of himself and his chosen destiny. Yet, a few of John's early instructors stand out as having a particularly strong and positive influence on the young boy's choice of vocation.

One such person was Sister Mary Christina Murphy, the same young nun who was among the first to come to Mount Holly to teach catechism lessons in rural farm homes. The young, diminutive nun, not much taller than some of her strapping students, was John's fourth grade teacher. That year, she said, there were eighty children in the classroom, and miraculously, no discipline problems whatsoever!

"I would say he was a very unusual child," Sister Christina recalled about young John Wessel. "He came from a very good Catholic background, his family and his grandparents. He was the type of boy that loved. He had great compassion and love for everyone. And at the same time, he was a real boy."

"He was just different—different than any child I have ever taught." While John was still very much a little boy, "when it came to the big things he was mature and he knew what was right."

Among the "big things" was John's sense of compassion and concern for others.

"We had a lot of poor children at Mount Holly School at one time, and they were the ones that he reached out to. He had compassion for the poor," said Sister Christina.

There were two little girls who came to school from way out in the country. They were from a good family, but they were very poor. Their parents were probably rural farmers who, lacking modern conveniences and utilities, did the best they could. But when the two little girls came to school, they looked so unkempt and dirty that nobody wanted to sit near them. One child was in John's fourth grade class.

Every time John saw somebody avoiding the girl or treating her rudely, he would purposefully get up and sit next to her. "One day, we saw him moving his seat," Sister Christina recalled. "He never said anything, but he always made it a point to move next to this one girl and he would help her with the math" or whatever subject they happened to be studying. "And I used to laugh when he would try to help her with the math because I thought, 'John, you can't do it yourself!' But it was just to show her she was needed, too."

Young John provided his classmates with a lesson in love and acceptance of this little girl. And through his example, he brought others around to it, too.

John was an encouragement to his friends and "never had anything but a good word." About some difficult subject they were trying to learn in school, he would often say to them, "If I can do it, you can. Don't worry about it. You'll get it," he'd encourage them. "If I can do it, you can."

"John was close to anybody who needed him," said Sister M. Espiritu Dempsey, I.H.M., his eighth grade teacher. "I think that even his friendship with Jim [Dubell] was more that they both had the same desire"—to be priests—and they were "both traveling the same spiritual road."[10]

Sister Christina became convinced that John made a promise never to hurt anyone. "His love for people and his fear of hurting anyone was his greatest concern."[11] One time, in fact, she thought she was going to be disowned by Johnny Wessel because she had corrected his buddy, Jimmy Dubell, during class.

When John sensed that his friend was hurt by Sister's correction, he waited until the lesson was over and approached her. "Sister, why did you do that to Jimmy?" he asked. John was very open, she recalled. He had no pretense. There was nothing secretive about him. He came out with everything that was on his mind.

"Well, John, I thought it necessary," she replied patiently, and proceeded to explain why. Her explanation seemed to satisfy him, and he said, "Oh, I think I understand."

Sister Christina quoted John after he had a chance to think the incident over, "I'm sorry. I know it isn't proper to hold something against a person and especially when the person is a teacher."[12]

John himself once provided a clue as to the origins of a lifelong quality of genuine concern for others. While recuperating from a serious bout of whooping cough at age four, his dad bought John a scooter as a get-well present. John didn't like the scooter and made a point of telling his father so.

Years later, John confided to his sister, "When Dad took that scooter away from me and gave it to a poor child, I could see that I had really hurt him, and I felt terrible. I vowed then that I would never be so ungrateful."[13]

It was a vow that John would keep for the rest of his life.

John was a prayerful child. Each morning, from her office the principal would recite prayers over the loudspeaker before classes began. Morning prayers usually consisted of the Our Father, the Hail Mary, and the Apostles' Creed.

John loved the opportunity to lead the class in saying the morning prayers along with the principal. "If I wasn't in the classroom when the bell rang at that time, he'd get up and lead them," said Sister Christina.

During the month of May, the children recited the Rosary each day in honor of the Blessed Mother Mary. Not surprisingly, John was one who was always ready to lead the prayers.

He was the kind of child who would give his parents a "spiritual bouquet" on important feast days. One Easter, when John was quite young, he sent a card to "Mother and Daddy" itemizing all the spiritual works and prayers that he had offered for them: "Hail Mary's—10; visits to the Blessed Sacrament—1; Ejaculations—100."

John Wessel displayed an evident devotion to Mary, the Blessed Mother, because she was the mother of Christ. "He really compared every mother to her," Sister Christina recalled. He would often say "how lucky mothers were to have little boys like our Blessed Mother." And Sister Christina would reply, "Well, thank you, John. What about the little girls?" "Oh, they're all right too," he conceded.

A typical fourth grade curriculum included subjects such as English, Religion, mathematics and history. "In the beginning, he didn't like math, but he really became a whiz in his older years," said Sister Christina. By the time he graduated from elementary school, John had acquired a love of mathematics that rivaled, but never quite eclipsed, his love of history.

"John's favorite school subjects were mathematics and history," his sister Maryann recalled. "He had a love for both and thus they came easily to him. Languages were his nemesis."[14]

"Now as a student, he didn't like English," Sister Christina recalled about fourth grader John. "That was my pet subject. He would often say to me, 'Why do I have to study subjects and predicates?' And I'd say, 'John, that's English grammar. You can't write anything and you can't speak well unless you know English grammar.' And he would say, 'Well, I think I'm doing okay.' . . . I would say 'Yes, you are John, but when it comes to writing, now that's a different story.'"

It was during his year in Sister Christina's fourth grade, at nine years of age, that John Wessel made known to her his desire to become a priest. That was the year that Sister said she learned more Indian history than she ever hoped to learn. "John's great desire was to become a priest and work among the Indians, and maybe someday, a martyr for them."[15]

It so happened that in history class, they were studying Saint Isaac Jogues and the North American Martyrs. The Saint's biography may be briefly summarized:

St. Isaac Jogues, born in 1607 at Orleans, France, and his companions "were the first martyrs of the North American continent."[16]

As a young Jesuit, Isaac Jogues, a man of learning and culture, taught literature in France. He gave up that career to work among the Huron Indians in the New World, and in 1636 he and his companions, under the leadership of Jean de Brébeuf, arrived in Quebec. The Hurons were constantly warred upon by the Iroquois, and in a few years Father Jogues was captured by the Iroquois and imprisoned for 13 months. His letters and journals tell how he and his companions were led from village to village, how they were beaten, tortured and forced to watch as their Huron converts were mangled and killed.[17]

"Isaac managed to escape and eventually got back to France, his body and features so changed from all he had undergone, that he was not recognized when he arrived at the Jesuit College of Rennes."[18]

Isaac Jogues . . . returned to France, bearing the marks of his sufferings. Several fingers had been cut, chewed or burnt off. Pope Urban VII gave him permission to offer Mass with his mutilated hands: "It would be shameful that a martyr of Christ be not allowed to drink the Blood of Christ." Welcomed home as a hero, Father Jogues might have sat back, thanked God for his safe return, and died peacefully in his homeland. But his zeal led him back once more to the fulfillment of his dreams. In a few months he sailed for his missions among the Hurons.

In 1646 he and Jean de Lalande, who had offered his services to the missioners, set out for Iroquois country in the belief that a recently signed peace treaty would be observed. They were captured by a Mohawk war party, and on October 18 Father Jogues was tomahawked and beheaded. Jean de Lalande was killed the next day at Ossernenon, a village near Albany, New York.[19]

Within a few years, six more of Saint Isaac Jogues' fellow missionaries received their martyrdom at the hands of the Iroquois and the Mohawks: Rene Goupil, an oblate; Father Jean de Brébeuf, a Jesuit; Father Anthony Daniel; Father Gabriel Lalemant; Father Charles Garnier; and Father Noel Chabanel.

"These eight Jesuit martyrs of North America were canonized in 1930."[20]

In the math class that followed, John said to Sister Christina, "You know, Sister, I *loved* that history lesson today."

"Well, fine, John," she said. "Let's talk about it tomorrow in history class. Let's get to the math." And so they did.

The next time Sister Christina sat with John to work on the math lesson, the story of Saint Isaac Jogues that he learned in history class was still very much on his mind.

Once again, he began to speak about it. "You know, that Isaac Jogues was a great man," he said thoughtfully.

"Yes, John, he was," the young Sister agreed. Then the boy confided to her, "You know, someday *I'd* like to be a missionary and teach the Indians."

"Fine, John," she replied.

"But I have to be a priest first," John continued.

"Yes, well, I'll tell you what, John," she said. "You say three Hail Marys every night; I'll say three for you, and then we'll ask our Blessed Mother to guide you. If it's your vocation to be a priest, you will be it."

Eileen Egan sat across from John. She had been writing at her desk, but was taking in the conversation between John and Sister Christina. Raising her eyes from the paper, she looked over at Sister Christina. "Can that go for me, too?" she asked.

"Yes, Eileen, that can go for you, too," the nun assured her.

"And you'll say the Hail Marys for me, too?"

"Yes," Sister Christina said. "You say three Hail Marys every night, and I'll say the three."

John continued talking to Sister Christina. "You know, I think I'm going—I *know* I'm going to be a priest." And she said, "Well, fine, John," and reminded him to tell it to her during history class. But it always amused her that John would never speak up during history even though he was good in that subject. Instead, he just sat there, mystified, hanging on to every word she had to say about the North American Martyrs.

John spoke with her almost every day about his desire to be a missionary priest like Saint Isaac Jogues, even after the history lessons had long since passed the section on North American Martyrs.

As time went on, John became more and more certain that he wanted above all else to become a priest and work among the Indians. Maybe someday, he said, he would become a martyr for them. Always, her response would be the same. "Well, John, if that's what God wants, then that's what's going to happen."

His desire for martyrdom was no fleeting fancy. In Sister Raymond's sixth grade class, Eileen Egan recalled: "One time the Supervisor came and we were asked what we wanted to be when we grew up. I'd always wanted to be a teacher so that was no problem. John promptly said, 'Martyr.'"[21]

In Sister Christina's Religion class, the children were taught the fundamentals of their faith, and here too were plenty of heroic saints for John to want to emulate. Their studies included inspiring tales about the lives of the first Apostles and martyrs of the early Christian Church: Saint Peter, Saint Stephen, Saint Paul, Saint John the Baptist, and so many others. "Anything we studied of a martyr interested and intrigued him," Sister Christina recalled. "It added to his desire to be a martyr, which was most unusual, I would say, for a young boy."

One such martyr they studied was Saint Stephen, the first disciple to give his life for Jesus Christ.[22]

> Acts [6:1-5] says that Stephen was a man filled with grace and power, who worked great wonders among the people. Certain Jews, members of the Synagogue of Roman Freedmen, debated with Stephen but proved no match for the wisdom and spirit with which he spoke. They persuaded others to make the charge of blasphemy against him. He was seized and carried before the Sanhedrin.
>
> In his speech, Stephen recalled God's guidance through Israel's history, as well as Israel's idolatry and disobedience. He then claimed that his persecutors were showing this same spirit. "[Y]ou always oppose the holy Spirit; you are just like your ancestors." (Acts 7:5-51b).
>
> His speech brought anger from the crowd. "But [Stephen], filled with the holy Spirit, looked up intently to heaven and saw the glory of God and Jesus standing at the right hand of God, and he said, 'Behold, I see the heavens opened and the Son of Man standing at the right hand of God.' . . . They threw him out of the city, and began to stone him. . . . As they were stoning Stephen, he called out, 'Lord Jesus, receive my spirit. . . .

Lord, do not hold this sin against them.'" (Acts 7:55-56, 58a, 59, 60b).[23]

Such was the death of Stephen, the First Martyr of the Christian faith, the "Proto-Martyr" as he is called. His Feast Day is celebrated by the Church on December 26th.[24]

The students also studied about Saint Paul who, before his conversion, persecuted the followers of Jesus. Scripture has it that Saint Paul (then called Saul) was present at the martyrdom of Saint Stephen.

According to legend, Sister Christina told the class, it was Saint Paul who threw the first stone that struck Stephen. Later Saint Paul was temporarily blinded by God because of it.

John was intrigued to learn that Saint Paul was believed to have thrown the first stone at Saint Stephen. He often talked about it with Sister Christina. "But he wasn't Saint Paul then?" John asked.

"No, John, he wasn't," she replied. "He was Saul. He became Paul later, and that's when he became the Saint."

"You know, he was a rough guy, wasn't he?" John asked about Saint Paul.

"Yes, he was John," she replied. "Remember, in those days a lot of Christ's followers were just rough men. They were fishermen. They did the hard work that an everyday man does."

"But he was a great follower of God's," John said. Sister agreed and reminded him, "But he wasn't always. Remember, John, he was one who persecuted." And she recounted the story of Saint Paul's early persecution of Saint Stephen and the Jews who believed that Jesus was the Messiah, and his dramatic conversion on the road to Damascus, making the story simple yet imaginative for her audience of nine- and ten-year-olds. "Then when Paul was struck blind, he looked up and said, 'Oh, God give me my sight'," she finished with a flourish. And John, clearly impressed, could only exclaim, "Oh, boy!"

John was taken with Saint Paul, perhaps because the personal characteristics of the rough and rugged Saint, who traveled and preached far and wide all over the civilized world, were ones that he could relate to. He would also become quite impressed with Saint Francis of Assisi, who had such love for nature and animals.

John greatly enjoyed the stories of these ordinary people who, by the grace of God, were able to do extraordinary things; no doubt the stories of their lives encouraged him to consider his own vocation.

His grandmother Mary Hogan always said that she felt sure her grandson Johnny was going to grow up to be a priest, even before he ever breathed a word of it to her. In fact, Mary Hogan told a group of I.H.M. Sisters that she knew that her grandson was destined for the priesthood.[25]

John's mother also had the same feeling. "They must've been studying Indians and he felt that they were so poorly treated," said Mrs. Wessel, that "he decided that he wanted to be a missionary, and he was going to take care of the Indians."[26]

"He wasn't one who was looking for attention," Sister Christina explained. Rather, his conversations with his teacher when he was nine years old marked the beginning of a serious vocation.

John was so intelligent, she recalled, that as far as any conversation was concerned, he usually understood things with great depth and maturity even as a young boy. And if he didn't understand, he would make sure he did. "Explain it to me," he'd ask.

One remarkable incident, in particular, serves to illustrate John Wessel's early desire to enter the priesthood.

Every first Friday of the month, Mass was celebrated at Sacred Heart Church, followed by Forty Hours Devotion, a beautiful and reverent devotion of the Church where Christ in the Blessed Sacrament is exposed on the altar in a beautiful gold monstrance for public worship, prayer and adoration. The grade school would participate in First Friday Mass, and during the day, each class would take their turn visiting the Blessed Sacrament for prayer and adoration. Altar boys were assigned to keep vigil before the Blessed Sacrament at various times.

John wanted to become an altar boy, like his older brother, but as a fourth grader he was considered too young to serve at Mass. After seeing his strong desire to serve, Sister Christina, who had charge of the altar boys, told him, "We will work with you, but you can't go on the altar until fifth or sixth grade." So she trained a group of boys, including John, to be altar boys and, one day, to assist the priest at Mass. Edward, a senior altar boy, helped him too, and John easily learned the required Latin responses. But

Johnny had such a burning desire to be a priest on the altar that he almost couldn't help what occurred next.

One day, Forty Hours Devotion was being held at the church on Washington Street. John was one of the altar boys who was keeping vigil before the Blessed Sacrament, along with his friend, James Dubell. They had walked from the school to the church, about a half mile away, to fulfill their altar boy assignment.

Sister Christina also walked to the church that day, and as she entered Sacred Heart Church, she was greeted by a most unusual sight. John Wessel was kneeling on the altar, praying before the Blessed Sacrament. But something more—"I looked at him and I thought, 'What has he got on!'" Her surprise was matched by that of the principal, Mother Brigida, who came in right behind her with a group of children.

Sister Christina turned to the principal and said in amazement, "Look at John Wessel up there!" Mother Brigida started to laugh. "He's in Monsignor's clothes!" she said.

John had put on Monsignor Foley's red cassock and over it, the Monsignor's white-and-red-trimmed surplice. Thus dressed, he was kneeling up straight, right in front of the Blessed Sacrament, deeply lost in prayer. The Monsignor's garments hung in folds like a tent around the small boy, and the red cassock trailed way down over his feet onto the sanctuary floor. A closer look revealed that there were two boys on the altar, one on either side of the Blessed Sacrament. His friend Jimmy was kneeling on the other side, but wearing his own black cassock and white surplice, the usual garments for altar boys.

The principal went up to John and called to him. "John," she exclaimed, "What are you doing with Monsignor's things?"

"Well," he said calmly, "I just wanted to see what it felt like to be a priest so that when I'm a priest, I'll know."

"What are you praying for?" Mother Brigida asked the boy.

"Well," he said, "I'm asking God that, when I grow up, if he really wants me, then I will be that priest." Then he paused and added, "I think I'm going to be that priest."

It was impossible for Mother Brigida to be angry with a child as sincere as John Wessel, nor was Monsignor Foley when she told him later about the incident. "Monsignor Foley just laughed at that," Sister Raymond recalled. "He enjoyed it so much!"[27]

*　　*　　*

These early incidents serve to illustrate John's serious interest in the priesthood, beginning in kindergarten, and his desire to offer his life, however God may choose to dispose of it, in some way for the good of others. Although he was "all boy" in many ways, as his friends and teachers readily attest, it was equally evident that John's vocation and his spiritual sense remained strong, constant, and continually increasing. Thus, his spiritual life, marked by a maturity surpassing his years, can only be attributed to the action of Divine Grace.

As Sister Christina summed up, regarding John's desire to become a priest, "That never left his mind."

By 1950, both Monsignor Foley and Father Kelly had left and Sacred Heart Church had a new pastor, Father (later Monsignor) Joseph V. Kozak. In 1952, Sister Raymond Rafferty replaced Mother Brigida Strome as principal of the grade school. That same year, Sister Christina Murphy moved on to another assignment, just as Johnny Wessel was about to enter eighth grade.

Sister Christina went on to teach in Oregon, and later in Coeur d'Alene, Idaho, where among her students were some Nez Perce Indian children from the neighboring reservations. All the while she thought about the young fourth grade boy who once confided to her that he wanted to be a priest and martyr for the Indians. She wondered if he would really follow through with his vocation.

CHAPTER 8

VOCATION

When John was twelve or thirteen years old, he must have been deeply touched by the sight of a crucifix in a store window.[1] The cross inspired him to write this poem:

The Cross in the Store Window

Cross of gold, cross of ivory
What do I see nailed to thee?
A God of gold, a God of ivory?
No, a God of Sympathy.

Cross of gold, cross of ivory
With what did they pierce thee?
Nails of gold, nails of ivory?
No, nails of cruelty.

Plaque of gold, plaque of ivory
What did they write on thee?
Words of gold, words of ivory?
No, words of oddity.

If this be error and upon me proved,
I never wrote, nor no God ever loved.[2]

John Wessel's commitment to the priesthood deepened over his grammar school years. In 1952, he entered eighth grade with a burning desire to be a priest, and a missionary priest at that.

John did not immediately inform his parents about his plans. Privately, he worried that he was lacking in some way for the vocation that he'd set his heart upon.

It was the last year of elementary school—a time to look forward to secondary education and to begin to make plans to enter the adult world a few years hence. Most of John's fellow classmates in the class of '53 would be attending the public high school in Mount Holly.

The dream of entering the priesthood which John shared in common with his friend James Dubell was really always present, but it really began to blossom for both young men around seventh and eighth grades.

Jim was the first to decide to study for the priesthood. Upon his graduation, he resolved, he would attend St. Charles College, the minor seminary in Catonsville, Maryland, a suburb of Baltimore, where boys from the Trenton diocese went to train to become diocesan priests. St. Charles was actually a six-year institution, comprising four years of high school and the first two years of college.

As Jim and John began to talk about their plans early on in eighth grade, they discovered that both had made the same choice of vocation. Each had arrived at it independently, but the fact that they had a shared desire lent great support to both of them.

John's only reservation was whether or not he would attend the minor seminary with Jim, because to do so was to become a diocesan priest and work within the confines of the Diocese of Trenton, or to become a priest of a missionary religious order where he could go anywhere at all.

John had pretty much made up his mind—he would join the Maryknolls.

"Well, maybe I'd go to St. Charles," John said to Jim one day after hearing of his friend's plans, "but . . . I've been writing to this guy, see—." Excitedly he began to tell Jim about the Maryknolls. He had sent away for some information about the Order, and he showed his friend the book he was reading. It was entitled *Men of Maryknoll*, and it detailed the inspiring, true life stories of the early Maryknoll missionaries.

"I got this information about the Maryknolls, and I'm going to write to them," John said enthusiastically. Jim thought his friend's idea sounded pretty complicated, and besides, he'd never even heard of the Maryknolls. But, he thought, it was so typical of his friend John that not only had he heard of them, he was already making plans to join them!

John was an adventurer at heart. He wanted not only to see the world but to conquer it for Christ. The outdoor life of the missionary was inviting to him, and the idea of roughing it in faraway places appealed to his youthful imagination.

"He did want to be a missionary priest," Dubell recalled. "He had a dream of going off to a foreign country and living among the natives in a primitive situation, and all the while bringing Jesus Christ to those people."

Early in his eighth grade year, John decided it was now time to speak to the pastor of Sacred Heart Church, Father Joseph V. Kozak, about his plans to become a Maryknoll priest.

Father Joseph Kozak was a strong, tall, stocky man. Were it not for his cleric's garb and collar, his physical appearance, at least, would more closely suggest a Marine charging up Iwo Jima to plant the American flag, rather than a parish priest. Yet, his fearsome appearance was softened by twinkling blue eyes and a friendly smile, which made his countenance seem at once open and inviting of trust. To those who knew him, Father Kozak was considered a very good priest.

Father Kozak listened intently to the earnest, idealistic young man sitting before him. He wanted to be a missionary priest, John Wessel was telling him, go someplace where people had never heard of Jesus Christ, and bring the knowledge of Christ to them. He wanted to help those in the greatest need, so maybe he would work among the poor, among the Indians. He'd read this book about the Maryknolls, he told the pastor, and he thought that was what he wanted to be.

Father Kozak encouraged John in his choice of vocation, but urged the boy to consider studying to become a diocesan priest, at least initially. "Now, listen, young man," Father Kozak began gently. "The diocese needs priests. You don't have to go running off to some foreign country. You stay right here in this country. We need you, right here in our own diocese." In this way, the pastor tried to show John that all God's work is missionary work, whether near or far, and that the spiritual needs right in one's own community can be just as great, if not greater, as those in far-off places.

John was convinced.

Shortly after speaking with Father Kozak, John sought out Jim and recounted the details of his visit with the pastor. "Father Kozak said that I should go to the diocesan seminary, and later on, if I want to change, I can join the Maryknolls," he said.

With the persuasive encouragement of the pastor, then, John's path was set on a different course than the one he'd planned, but, as time would prove, the right course after all.

The knowledge that the two friends would at least have each other to begin their studies for the priesthood was an encouragement to both. As James Dubell recalled:

> We didn't know how it was going to turn out but . . . we knew that we would still be together, so this was a part of our past that we could take with us. Our backgrounds were similar in terms of church anyway. We grew up together as altar boys and we were like partners as altar boys. So we influenced each other in that sense.

During the course of their last year at Mount Holly School, both young men made plans to enter the minor seminary. This included making arrangements to take the entrance examinations. And they began to study as never before.

Father Kozak went to John Wessel's parents and informed them of their son's desire to begin studying for the priesthood after eighth grade. Edward and Kathleen Wessel were—to put it mildly—surprised! Until that time, there had been no talk of a vocation that they could recall, although in retrospect, there had been little signs along the way.

Kathleen Wessel recalled: "We weren't for it at all! He was only in eighth grade, and he was the youngest, and we didn't want to part with him. After high school, maybe we could see it."

It wasn't that his parents were distressed to learn that John was considering the priesthood. On the contrary, as devoutly religious people, they were undoubtedly pleased and proud. Rather, it was his choice of vocation and contemplated departure from home at such a young age that disturbed and worried them.

His mother wisely didn't say much to John to discourage him, but she kept after Father Kozak like a guided missile honing in on a target. "He's too young," she persisted, hoping to convince the pastor to her point of view. "He shouldn't do it."

But as much as Father Kozak may have dreaded his encounters with the anxious mother, it was John's father, Edward Wessel, who was even more strongly opposed to his son's entering the seminary after eighth grade.

Dr. Edward Wessel was upset. He did not think it was a good idea, and he was not in favor of it. He dearly loved all his children, but he especially didn't want to see his youngest son go away. He would miss the boy terribly, and he didn't want to lose him. John's father felt that a boy that age was too young to really know what he wanted to do. Moreover, he thought the seminary was too far away from home, and that his son needed parental influence and guidance. But again, Edward Wessel, like his wife, prudently did not openly discourage John.

With infinite tact and patience, Father Kozak convinced his mother first, and then finally, his father, to allow John to attend the diocesan seminary. The pastor was assured of the sincerity of the boy's desire. The fact that John's best friend would be with him also helped reassure his concerned parents. If this was just a childish fantasy, then John would soon outgrow it, and the worst that could happen would be that he would receive an excellent high school education at the minor seminary. But if it was not—

"We never discouraged him from going into the seminary at that time, but we never encouraged him either," Kathleen Wessel quite distinctly remembered.

In the end, it was John who really wanted to go of his own volition—and how could his parents stand in his way?

John's only concern: How to go about it?

"What are we going to do?" John asked Jim forlornly. He was momentarily crestfallen as he contemplated the requirements for admission to St. Charles College that he and Jim had just received by mail. It looked pretty tough.

Admission to the seminary hinged, among other things, on satisfactory performance on the entrance examinations in four subjects: Religion, English, arithmetic, and spelling. John figured that he'd do well enough in the Religion and math, but English and spelling were his nemesis. John knew right away that he was in trouble.

It was at this point that Divine Providence came to his rescue in the form of Sister Mary Espiritu Dempsey, I.H.M., John's eighth grade teacher at Mount Holly School that year. (By this time, their eighth grade classroom was located in the modern building that Bishop Griffin had dedicated in 1948.)

She was a young Sister, in her late twenties, and like all the other teaching Sisters, a member of the Servants of the Immaculate Heart of Mary. She was fairly new, having come to the school only in 1950. Her name "Espiritu" was Spanish for Holy Spirit.

Her coming to Mount Holly was almost accidental; she knew it was a temporary sojourn and she would not stay long. John Wessel was about to meet the second Sister who was most instrumental in securing his vocation, and that of his friend James Dubell, at a critical moment in their lives.

That fall, Sister Espiritu endeared herself to her eighth grade students, and John Wessel in particular, because sometimes as a special treat, she would let the class listen to the World Series on the radio for an hour in the afternoon if they were very, very good. That year pitted the New York Yankees against the Brooklyn Dodgers, and Sister Espiritu's eighth grade class avidly followed the play-by-play radio broadcast, live from Ebbets Field, as the Yankees captured their third Series in a row, defeating the Dodgers 4 to 2 in the final game.

The whole class just loved her for that.

John and Jim decided to talk to Sister Espiritu about their problem with the entrance examinations. She would know what they ought to do.

Both of them wanted to be priests, they explained to her one day after class. They brought in and shared with her the letters they had received from the minor seminary saying that they would have to pass the entrance examinations in order to be admitted. Both young men said that "they didn't feel that they could pass them," she recalled.

In an instant, she sorted through jumbled thoughts in search of an appropriate response. Both young men wanted to be priests so badly, she could tell. But then again, she didn't believe in their going off to the seminary after eighth grade. They're too young, one side of her seemed to say. But another side pulled in the opposite direction as she remembered there was no Catholic high school in the area for these boys. "Who am I," she thought, finally, "to make this judgment if these two young men feel that they are called?"

Sister Espiritu looked up, smiled at them and said, "Are you willing to work for it?"

"Oh yeah!" they jumped, unable to get the words out fast enough. "We'll do whatever you ask us to do, Sister," they eagerly told her.

"Well," she said, "why don't we have this little project together, and the three of us will work on this after school every afternoon." The young Sister was impressed that two young eighth grade boys could be full of such gratitude. They were all smiles, and constantly thanked her for offering to help, she recalled.

And so each day after school for a whole year, Sister Espiritu helped John and James prepare for their seminary entrance exams. While Sister Espiritu went out to assist with the dismissal of the students at the end of the school day, the two young men busied themselves in the classroom, helping with the clean-up and other chores. When Sister Espiritu finally returned, the blackboards would be washed, the chalk and erasers put away, the waste baskets emptied. And Johnny and Jimmy would be sitting there waiting.

She would give them little assignments, concentrating on the subjects that they would have to know for the exam—English, math, and spelling—and they worked together for an hour or two every day. After these hours of explaining, encouraging, motivating, pushing and prodding on the part of their gentle tutor, the two young men would walk home, engaged in animated conversation along the way, discussing what they'd learned that afternoon, and making tentative, hopeful plans about the seminary they both fervently wanted to attend.

To Sister Espiritu, it was amazing! Neither was the type of young man who would want to spend their after school hours studying, but they did, and they were eager and happy to do it.

"What a privilege for me to participate even in a small way," Sister Espiritu once wrote about those days. "Through these daily meetings I grew into an even deeper knowledge and love of them and a deeper appreciation of the beauty and peace of Christ's goodness as reflected in two of His priests-to-be."

Then, a wonderful rapport began to develop at the same time between the two young students and their young teacher. The few occasions when one boy had to miss an evening's study with Sister Espiritu provided a rare opportunity for the other to share a secret or a problem in confidence, or to seek her wise counsel. And John Wessel had a special admiration for his eighth grade teacher, recalled his sister Maryann.

After school one day, John stayed to see if he could help. As usual, he cleaned the blackboards, emptied the baskets, and then just stayed around to talk some more to his teacher. This day they were alone.

John began talking to Sister Espiritu about being an altar boy. He loved serving at Mass, he told her, and he loved going to Mass in the convent chapel in the morning. But, unknown to Sister Espiritu, there was just one thing that was bothering him.

"His only concern," Sister Espiritu recalled about John, "was his unworthiness to approach Christ."

Suddenly, John looked at her and said, "You're so lucky."

Sister Espiritu was amused and perplexed. "Why?" she asked.

"Well," he said, matter-of-factly, "you can receive Holy Communion every morning of your life." His words, so unexpected, took her completely by surprise.

"Well, so can you, Johnny," she said.

"Oh, no," he said quietly, as if he were sharing a sacred confidence. "I'm not worthy to do that."

"But Johnny, you made your First Communion," she insisted. "You can receive."

Again he demurred and shook his head. "No, I'm not really worthy to receive God every day like that." John was so humble, and so aware of his own human imperfections, that it was unthinkable to him to receive the Lord daily. Communion was reserved for Sunday Mass, and only after a good confession. But how he wished he could receive the Lord every day like Sister Espiritu!

"John," she said with gentle conviction, "we don't receive God because we're worthy, or I wouldn't be walking up there either. *None* of us are worthy," she said emphatically. John was listening, and the truth of her words began to resonate in his soul. "It's to get to know Him more, and to love Him, and to let Him love you."

John seemed to accept the explanation that his teacher gave him. At that moment, God must have given him the increase in wisdom and grace, and as she spoke to him, John began to understand that no one could approach Christ for any reason except to become more like Him in every way—simply because of love for Him.

A peaceful expression came over his boyish countenance as he reflected on her words: To know Him, to love Him, and become more like Him in every way. "That's what I want," he said firmly.[3]

Many mornings from then on, John would come to the 6:30 a.m. Mass in the convent chapel to receive the Lord.[4]

It seemed like such a private and sacred confidence that John had shared with her that Sister Espiritu never revealed it to anyone at the time. She answered his questions as best she could, but she couldn't bring herself to press him further or even to discuss it with him again. "I just thought it was one of the most beautiful experiences in my life, to have a young man, as full of life as he was, have this depth of a relationship with God. It was wonderful, and I think I was privileged to share in it."

What a contradiction was this child! When Sister Espiritu thought of John Wessel, she decided that he was "extraordinary in his ordinariness." He was first "a very ordinary boy." The only way he was any different from other boys was that he was "more of a boy" and "very mannish." He was honest, down-to-earth, very well liked, outgoing, friendly, and laughed freely. Always playing on the playground, he enjoyed life, sports, and fooling around.

Yet, there was an inner depth to him that not everyone would see. John had both a great desire for a relationship with the Lord and a great desire to be a priest. He frequently shared this desire with his eighth grade teacher. "I want to be a priest more than anything. That's what I want to do with my life."

Yet there were times he thought it would never happen.

One day, John confessed to Sister Espiritu that he didn't think he was worthy to be a priest. "That's not up to you, Johnny, that's up to the Lord," the young nun told him. "You can't determine that. If that's what you want to be, that's how the Lord talks to us. He doesn't come down and give us a message or write us a letter," she said. "That desire that you have is your call."

After that, John would occasionally be plagued with doubts about his perceived unworthiness to be a priest. On those occasions, Sister Espiritu was there to remind him of his own potential: "But John, that's not for you to judge. There is something there. And everything that's good in you is the influence of God, and that's how God's presence is within us, in the good that's in us."

She was a young Sister, still growing spiritually herself. Sometimes, she "wasn't even sure about what I was talking about, to tell the truth" but she prayed for the right words and somehow they came. "He would just pull out of you things from the depths of your being, because you wanted to respond to him and you wanted to convince him of the potential he had," she recalled. He was very humble, very sincere. Both boys were, in fact. And, she thought, God must love them very much for children of that age to have such a sincere desire to serve Him.

Not only did John have misgivings that he was not worthy enough to become a priest; he feared he was not bright enough, either.

"John was not the best student," Sister Espiritu continued. He had some background reading problems that were evident to her.

> But then, when you talked to him, you'd think, he's a very
> intelligent young man . . . I don't know that book knowledge was
> that important to him. I think . . . that he wanted to be a priest
> so badly that he would have paid whatever price there was—and
> that's when he got really serious about his work.

Sister Espiritu was not the only person concerned about John's reading abilities. John's mother, Kathleen Wessel, was also very well aware that her son was not a particularly good student and had a reading impediment which made learning difficult. When John decided to go to the minor seminary, she wanted him to be aware that his chosen vocation would constantly involve him in the subjects he found most difficult.

His mother took him aside one day and patiently explained, "John, if you enter the seminary, you must understand that from that day forward, your whole life will be reading. Now, are you sure that's what you want?" she questioned.

"Yes, Mom. That's what I want," John replied without a moment's hesitation.

"Well, all right then," she said.

Having been assured that John was fully aware of the challenges that lay ahead, his parents enrolled him in a special reading clinic offered at

Temple University in Philadelphia during the summer between his eighth and ninth grades.

Every day, while his friends were enjoying summer sports and outdoors fun, thirteen-year-old John would rise up early and take the bus into Philadelphia to attend his reading classes. "It helped him tremendously," his mother said.

Fortunately, John did very well with the abilities he had been given. Through dint of hard work, both in Sister Espiritu's eighth grade class and in the summer reading clinic at Temple University, he eventually developed his reading skills to their full potential.

"It did not come easy to him," John's sister Maryann recalled. "It was through sheer grit and determination that John overcame this and eventually became a vociferous reader."

Even as he prepared to leave home, John was well aware that there would be some suffering to his family due to his going away to the seminary at a young age. With a maturity beyond his years, he was sensitive to the fact that his leaving would be heartbreaking to his parents. He didn't want to hurt them, yet he felt he had to follow his calling and hoped that they understood. He was confident that if he was doing God's will, then God would take care of his family.

Again, he would often confide in Sister Espiritu. "Well, if I do pass those tests," John would begin, "it's going to be tough, I think, on my family if I go. But they're going to want it in the end. They're going to want what makes me happy, what I need to do."

In June 1953, Father Joseph V. Kozak recommended John Wessel as a candidate for priesthood with these words: "He stems of good Catholic stock—is a faithful altar boy—is possessed of good health and is certainly no less than average in his school studies. Morally, I feel, he leaves little to be desired."

"I cannot help but feel," Father Kozak continued, "that John is not only sincere in his desire to become a priest but that he has the wherewithal physically, mentally and spiritually to realize that desire and eventually make a good priest."[5]

And why did thirteen-year-old John want to become a priest? He answered this question himself in an essay on the seminary entrance examination:

My first reason is that by being God's representative on earth I can get closer to Him and His Blessed Mother. In this way I can get to love Them so much that I will never sin against Jesus in any way. By this love which I already have and all the love I hope to attain by knowing God better I hope to win the bliss of heaven for my parents, my many associates and myself.

My second reason is that by my good works on earth I can try to help other people to meet our heavenly Father and Mother in heaven and contribute just a little comfort to some of the weary servicemen who have fought to keep Our Lord and God in the churches of our homeland and other free countries. Some day, if God will it, they will free the enslaved countries and then all the countries of the world will be God loving, God fearing and free.

Each day it will be my privilege "to go unto the altar of God" as his personal emissary.[6]

*   *   *

One day that summer, a letter arrived at 38 Garden Street addressed to John Wessel from St. Charles College in Catonsville. John had passed all of his exams. He was accepted into St. Charles College. He was on his way to the seminary!

Perhaps John rushed to tell his family, and then immediately sought out his friend "Dube" and shared the news with him as well. The immense joy and happiness that he must have felt upon learning of his own acceptance into the seminary was surpassed only by the knowledge that his friend had also passed his exams. Both of them were going to the seminary together!

One person who was not there to share the good news was Sister Espiritu. She had been transferred back to Scranton, Pennsylvania at the end of the school year, just as suddenly as she had come to Mount Holly.

It was almost as if this young Sister was meant to be there during that one period of time and no longer, because she had such a wonderful impact on the vocations of the two young priests-to-be. Like a guardian angel, she encouraged them, helped them study, and inspired them with the confidence to go forward and achieve their goals.

"Of all the students I've taught, those were the two young men I feel closer to. And I remember, just as if it was yesterday, that I taught them."

That year spent with eighth graders John and Jim as they prepared for the seminary was "one of the most memorable experiences," said Sister Espiritu. The two boys "made a very great impression" on the young Sister. "I just know they were real boys, and full of fun, and had this driving desire to be priests. It was just the most important thing in their lives."

That summer of '53, John said goodbye to his classmates and goodbye to the big old school on High Street that had been a second home to him for the past nine years. It was a summer for hearty farewells and graduation parties, where he bid goodbye to school friends.

John was leaving Mount Holly School a mature young man with a mission in life that he could hardly wait to begin. Chances are he never bothered much looking back. Nostalgia wasn't his style.

John was only looking forward.

Family

Mrs. Kathleen H. Wessel and her children (l-r) Maryann, infant John Patrick, and Edward, Jr., 1940. (Photo from Wessel family album)

The Garden Street home in Mount Holly where John Wessel grew up. (Photo from Wessel family album)

"Shandangan"—the Duggan family ancestral home in County Cork, Ireland. (Photo from Wessel family album)

"The Farm"—John loved to visit the Mount Holly farm of his maternal grandparents, Patrick and Mary Duggan Hogan. (Photo by author)

The Catholic grammar school John Wessel attended in Mount Holly. (Inset) Young John in Kindergarten. (Photo from Wessel family album)

Eighth grader John Wessel had already decided on a vocation to the priesthood when this portrait was taken. (Photo from Wessel family album)

Medford Lakes/Later Family

The Wessel family's summer home in Medford Lakes. (Photo from Wessel family album)

John captured the serenity of Medford Lakes from the dock of his summer home. (Photo by Fr. John Wessel from his album)

John's snapshot of his father, Dr. Edward J. Wessel, at Medford Lakes, which he captioned "Pop's vacation?" (Photo by Fr. John Wessel from his album)

Music was an important part of family life. (L-r) John Wessel's father, mother, sister Maryann, and John, gather 'round the piano. (Photo from Fr. John Wessel's album)

John Wessel was a rugged outdoorsman who loved all of nature.
(Photo from Fr. John Wessel's album)

Wessel family portrait. (Standing, l-r) Maryann, Edward, Jr. and
his fiancée Pat, Mrs. Kathleen H. Wessel, Dr. Edward J. Wessel.
(Seated) Seminarian John Wessel with his grandmother, Mary
Duggan Hogan. This photograph, taken by John in 1956, was
his favorite. (Photo by Fr. John Wessel from his album)

CHAPTER 9

ST. CHARLES, CATONSVILLE:

THE EARLY YEARS

St. Charles College was situated on the crest of a ridge, overlooking the city of Baltimore, in the pleasant suburb of Catonsville, Maryland.[1] The spacious campus, over two hundred acres, consisted of several large, imposing and interconnecting structures which comprised the minor seminary—the Chapel of Our Lady of the Angels, an administration building, a dormitory building, a refectory and infirmary building, a science building, and a powerhouse.[2]

The historical beginnings of St. Charles can be attributed to the generosity of Charles Carroll of Carrollton, the only Catholic signer of the Declaration of Independence. He liberally donated property as well as funds for the establishment of the first preparatory school in the United States that would prepare young men in their pursuit of higher studies for the priesthood. He accounted the establishment of this school as one of the most important services of his long and useful career.[3] In his bequest, Charles Carroll expressed the wish that the foundation should "remain under the charge of the Sulpicians," a French Catholic Order of teaching priests dedicated exclusively to the formation of parish priests.[4]

> The Sulpician method, which originated in Paris with its founder, Jean-Jacques Olier, emphasizes the community life of faculty and students and includes a daily rhythm of liturgy, study and social life. The soul of the Sulpician method, however,

is the presence of faculty mentors and spiritual directors who personally guide seminarians through their years of priestly formation, an approach that since 1791 has spread to many other seminaries in our country.[5]

Father Olier, in his *Pietas Seminarii*, outlined the purpose of seminary training:

> The first and ultimate end of this institute is to live supremely for God, in Christ Jesus our Lord, in order that the interior dispositions of His Son may so penetrate the very depths of our heart, that each one may say what St. Paul confidently affirmed of himself, "Christ is my life," and elsewhere: "I live, no it is not I who live, but it is Christ who lives in me." Such shall be the sole hope of all, their sole meditation, their sole exercise: to live the life of Christ interiorly, and to manifest it exteriorly in their mortal body.[6]

The ideals of Father Olier's Society were of tremendous influence in nurturing and forming the American priesthood.[7]

St. Charles was a combination six-year preparatory high school and junior college known as the minor seminary. While not all of its graduates would become ordained clergy, a St. Charles education was designed to prepare those young men, academically, spiritually and morally, who were seriously inclined to the priesthood. Admittance standards were rigorous, as was the course of study.

Many students attended all six years, although some enrolled after high school for the first two college years, while others transferred in at various grade levels. Upon graduation from St. Charles, the seminary student received an Associate Degree. From there, the student went on to a major seminary for the completion of the last two years of college, followed by a four-year graduate level theology program, leading to a post-graduate degree and eventual ordination. At each level, the seminarian was granted progressively more and more freedom, privacy, and responsibility, as he moved closer and closer to becoming a priest.

Most, but not all, St. Charles graduates finished their last two years of college at St. Mary's Seminary, School of Philosophy, on North Paca

Street in downtown Baltimore, followed by four years of graduate studies at St. Mary's Seminary, School of Theology, in the Roland Park suburb of Baltimore. While some St. Charles graduates attended other major seminaries, both in America and overseas, so frequently was this educational route taken by diocesan clergy that, even today, it is not uncommon to hear these institutions referred to familiarly as simply "Paca Street" or "Roland Park." Like St. Charles, both St. Mary's institutions were conducted under the auspices of the Sulpician Fathers.[8]

Like all academic institutions, the students at St. Charles had developed their own informal and unofficial traditions which they passed down year after year. Class names were one such tradition. The first year high students were called "Crustos" by the upperclassmen—a term having some connection to the belly of a snake, or in other words, the lowest of the low. It was a bit of a put-down to the newcomers, but one which was taken in good humor.

Second year high students were known as "Termites"—still lowly, but progressing along; not quite so lowly as a Crusto.

Upon high school graduation, the seminary student looked forward to returning as a "Poet." Studying the Latin poets in the first year of college was a required subject. Hence, the birth of the "Poets."

Finally, in the last year of St. Charles, the second year of college, one had arrived. The seminarian was a "Rhet" for Rhetorician. That year they studied the Latin orators. Graduation was preceded by the annual "Rhet Week" at the end of each year. The Rhets were excused from their classes to play sports outdoors while their younger colleagues were in class.

The style of life at St. Charles in the 1950s was like a military regimen, more closely akin to a strict private prep school than a contemporary seminary.

In reminiscences about St. Charles by her alumni, the word that tends to crop up in conversation is "Spartan." Except for the beautiful chapel, the physical appearance of the cavernous old stone structures was austere. Dormitories were cold in winter, and students had to walk to the end of the hall for a drink of water or for the lavatory.

Nevertheless, generations of young Catholic men and future priests seemed to thrive on the structure and routine of the minor seminary, and recall their alma mater with a fond mixture of love, loyalty, camaraderie and friendship.

The seminarians' day was very regimented; everything was done according to a fixed schedule. Weekdays, the young men arose promptly at 5:40 a.m. to begin the long day, which did not end until "lights out" at 10:30 at night. Bells rang constantly throughout the day to call the seminarian to the next scheduled activity. There was time set aside for studying, class instruction, prayer, meals, and recreation, and the students were required to comply with the schedule. There were no exceptions.

All the young men boarded on campus, even those whose families lived nearby. Students could not leave the seminary grounds except on a few occasions. At all other times, special permission was required to leave the property, and then only for a serious medical problem or a family emergency.

There were times built in to the schedule, however, when everybody was allowed to leave: on a "free day," an official walk, or on scheduled vacations. On Columbus Day, the students were granted a "walk afternoon," meaning that the seminarians could leave campus for a few hours to walk into town in a group. But on an official walk, the seminarian could not visit a home, even if he lived in Baltimore and passed by his own house.

On other holidays, such as Washington's Birthday or Thanksgiving, "free days" with designated hours were given, from 9:00 a.m. to 9:00 p.m. or 12 noon to 12 midnight. Usually two weeks vacation were granted at Christmas and one week at Easter.

Regimen was observed even off campus. No alcohol was allowed, of course, and the young men had to be sure to be back by the time their leave ended. The rule that they had to report to the rector's office upon their return was very strictly enforced.

The dress code allowed for regular clothing for class, but on Sundays the seminarians dressed in black or dark blue suits, white shirts and dark ties. Similarly, on an official walk, the seminarians wore a suit and a suit coat.

The Chapel of Our Lady of the Angels, the site of magnificent liturgies at St. Charles College, was the focus of the young men's spiritual life each day.

The chapel had a marble floor throughout. The coat of arms of St. Charles College, which is actually the coat of arms of Charles Carrollton, was imbedded in mosaic tiles in the sanctuary floor. An interlocking A-M, for *Auspice Maria*, Latin for "under Mary's protection," was also in mosaic on the floor.

A painting in the top of the dome directly over the altar illustrates the chapel's patron, Our Lady of the Angels. Against a majestic gold background, the Blessed Virgin Mary is pictured as being crowned Queen of Heaven by two angels, while two other angels kneel in adoration, and the Heavenly Father extends his hands in blessing.

Along the narrow ceiling arch which borders the sanctuary dome, a globe-shaped mosaic depicts a white-bearded God the Father holding His Son Jesus Christ on the cross as two angels appear to support the globe.

The first few rows of wooden pews surrounding the altar were monastery style—facing each other. The remaining pews faced the altar.

The entire chapel served to remind the seminarian of his journey from layman to priest. Ornate stained glass windows decorate the upper and lower levels of the chapel. Each window appears to depict two figures each. The stained glass windows of the lower level depict the candidate in the various steps along the way to priestly life at that time, and the Old Testament equivalent: seminarian, tonsure, porter, lector, exorcist, acolyte, subdeacon, deacon, priest and bishop. The windows of the upper level depict two patron saints who represent the virtues of each step.[9]

Behind the chapel was a statue of Our Lady of Lourdes. Stones from the first St. Charles seminary, which was destroyed by fire in 1911, surrounded the statue. Another statue of the Sacred Heart of Jesus kept vigil over St. Charles at the entrance to the administration building. (Both statues were later moved to the grounds of St. Mary's Seminary at Roland Park.)

Every morning, there was Mass and meditation. In the afternoon, there was the examination of conscience. After meals, a visit was made to the chapel before the Blessed Sacrament. In the evening, Night Prayers, called Compline, were recited in English at the end of each day. On Sundays and Holy Days, High Mass was celebrated, and in place of Compline, there was evening Vespers. The seminarians would assemble in community and chant the Psalms in Latin.

After the Night Prayers, silence was the rule. The seminarians marched single file from the chapel to their dormitories in silence, and were not permitted to talk until after Mass the next morning. This was called the Grand Silence.

The dormitories were large open spaces with roughly seventy beds to a room, with a chair beside each bed. It also contained a common room with sinks, mirrors, and lockers. There were about three floors of dormitories to house all the students.

In the huge dining room, called the refectory, the young men sat in assigned seats. Throughout the six years at St. Charles, there were eight to a table, and the seat assignments were rotated a few times a year, but always the seminarian sat in his assigned seat at every meal.

The priests and professors (for most were priests) sat at a long table at the head of the refectory while the seminarians took turns waiting on the tables.

At St. Charles (and at Paca Street, too), books were read aloud at certain meals. At breakfast the young men could talk to one another, but at lunch and dinner, usually there was a Silent Meal, as a spiritual book or meditation was read to them.

The presence of a visiting priest or dignitary who was invited to stay for dinner provided an occasion to cancel the Silent Meal, and then all were allowed to speak freely at the table.

Early in September 1953, Edward and Kathleen Wessel made the long drive from Mount Holly, New Jersey to Catonsville, Maryland, to deliver their son Johnny into the capable hands of the Sulpician Fathers at St. Charles College. It was to be the first of many journeys the Wessel family would make to Maryland. It was a bittersweet time for the family, to be sure, as his parents dropped Johnny off at the massive front door with his little trunk and bid him goodbye. They probably reminded him to "just do your best, and remember, you always have a place to come home to."

St. Charles was a world of regimen and routine, structure and conformity, a world populated by over four hundred young boys gathered from most every state east of the Mississippi, boys from just about every conceivable walk of life, culture and heritage.

John Wessel, thirteen years old, had now entered this world. He was looking forward to it perhaps with some trepidation, but mostly with optimism and faith and hope. A few weeks after his arrival in the minor seminary, John turned fourteen on September 20, 1953.

Studies in the minor seminary were very strict and rigorous. It was basically a liberal arts education, heavy in English, Latin and Greek, with a good amount of mathematics and science, but mainly it was the humanities that were stressed. As a matter of fact, there was really very little formal

Religion class in first high. Latin classes were held seven periods a week, whereas Religion class was only two periods a week.

There were over one hundred young seminarians with John Wessel and James Dubell in their freshmen class, and they were from all over the East Coast—from as far south as Florida, as far north as Maine, as far west as Illinois. There was the usual anxiety about studying and academic pressure. Six days a week were spent in the classroom studying Latin, algebra, general science, history and English, among others. The incoming class was broken up into three different tracks for studies—an A class, a B class and a C class—a system to separate the young men into manageable groups. John Wessel was in the C class.

John began to apply himself as a student. Overall, he did well academically—better in some classes (history, science, math, music) than in others. Predictably, the languages still gave him problems and he had to work very hard.

But John began to carve out a place for himself solidly "in the middle to upper part of the class. He wasn't in the top ten percent," James Dubell recalled, "but you could see his understanding of things was very good."

In addition to the regime of classes, the seminarians had a regular routine of athletic events in which all had to participate. Each young man was assigned to a team and a schedule of various sports competitions was held during the year.

The St. Charles men did not play against outside high school or college teams, just intramural sports among themselves. Still, it provided a good level of competition and fun, and everybody got a chance to play. Popular biannual athletic events were the October and May Games, in which all six of the St. Charles grades competed against each other in track and field.

There were also organized extracurricular activities of a social or spiritual nature that were available to the seminarians—choir, drama, yearbook, Mission Society, and many more.

So it was a very regimented combination of academic and spiritual studies and a minimum of social and athletic programs.

The second Sunday of the month was "visiting Sunday."[10] It was a joy and a high point for the lonely young men and their families. On that day, families came in droves. John's parents would come to the seminary and visit him regularly once a month (sometimes joined by Maryann or Eddie if they weren't away at college). In the best and worst of weather, in all twelve years, the family never failed to visit Johnny in the seminary on visiting Sunday. The seminarians weren't allowed off campus, and their families weren't allowed inside (except for the first floor of the administration building), so they would park their cars on the lower campus, where they would visit and walk around the manicured grounds.

As much as it could be said that there was camaraderie among the seminarians, then certainly the same esprit de corps was evident among their families on visiting Sundays. Motivated by their common belief in the worthiness of their child's vocation, there was a cheerful, good-natured willingness on the part of these families to accept hardships and meet obstacles to support the dream of the young man who was preparing to enter religious life.

On those Sundays, the Wessels would rise at five in the morning to attend the early six o'clock Mass in Mount Holly before leaving for Baltimore. Visiting hours were from one o'clock to 4:15 p.m., and so as not to lose precious time, they'd pack their lunch to eat in the car on the way down. It was all worthwhile just to visit their son for a few hours one Sunday a month.

In between visits, John's mother maintained a steady stream of correspondence with him, keeping him abreast of little news from home and encouraging him in his studies. These little chatty notes provided a welcome contact with home and reminded John of his family's love and support.

As John slowly settled in at St. Charles, he began to feel comfortable and realized that he had plenty of company. He saw a mass of young thirteen- or fourteen-year-old boys like himself, all similarly turned out neatly in suit and tie. Young men who would soon become his buddies for the next six, eight, or twelve years—guys who answered to monikers like Tex, Winnie, Tillie, Lexy, Smitty, Sammy, Jody and Mouse. Like soldiers at boot camp, friendships would emerge out of the common experience they shared. Close bonds would be forged as the young men studied, worked and prayed together. And further along, as their ranks were trimmed and the less promising candidates weeded out, only the "best and the brightest" remained.

As a consequence, friendships were formed in predictable ways. Once they began to know each other, fellows tended to gravitate toward those from their own state and diocese. There was a shared recognition, a welcome familiarity in the sea of strangeness.

Throughout the seminary, John Wessel and James Dubell were in the same classes and remained good friends, within the confines of their structured environment. They would walk and talk together, help each other with studies, and encourage each other as best they could.

"John was not an outgoing youth, but he did make friends readily. He enjoyed boyish pranks and slapstick horseplay," James Dubell recalled. John made several new friends in the seminary. "He had two very close friends, Carl Wingate and Michael Choma, with whom he enjoyed the out-of-doors. John was affable and approachable toward his peers."[11]

In St. Charles, there was a large study hall for the first year high school class in the dormitory building, where the students were seated alphabetically. The tall, lanky boy who had the seat next to John in study hall that first year was Carl Wingate, but everyone called him Winnie. In a short time, he and John became good friends. "One of the reasons we were close is he's 'W-e' and I'm 'W-i', so he ended up next to me," recalled Carl Wingate, who was from Baltimore.

Wingate was an extrovert, a great conversationalist, and the more outgoing of the two. His friendly, easygoing, laconic manner and good sense of humor were qualities that John could appreciate. But he also shared John's sense of adventure (or at least, was willing to go along with it) and so the two complemented each other.

Study hall was silent, and a priest walked up and down the aisles to make sure the silence was observed. But when the proctor wasn't looking it was not too difficult to ask the fellow next to you if you needed help with an assignment.

After class, and after the official recreation period when the young men had to be outdoors, the study hall could be used for their projects or hobbies. There was not much room for personal effects in the dormitory lockers, but the study hall desk was large and had a shared bookcase, and it became the repository for personal belongings and hobbies and crafts—in John's case, model airplanes.

John liked his model airplanes, and on his desk, he had his favorite plastic model—a Messerschmitt. Also on his desk was a classic statue of *The Wrestlers*. John spent a great deal of time building model airplanes and Carl, although not a model airplane enthusiast, would help John build and glue them.

"Then he got into the ones you take outside with the wires and fly around," Wingate recalled. And the first flight "usually hit the ground" and John would come in to the study hall with all the pieces and start putting them back together again. He liked doing that kind of thing.

John Wessel was good about sharing his hobbies and activities with his friends. Fencing was a hobby that John enjoyed at St. Charles, and one day, he decided to teach his friend Carl how to fence.

"He got swords somewhere and he was going to become the great fencer," Wingate recalled. John kept several masks and épées in his locker at the high school seminary. "We put these masks on and we'd go down to the basement and hack away at each other. We didn't know what we were doing. He said he did but—."

The young men started out having fun, but then "we'd get whacking those things and we got aggressive . . . I remember he was trying to teach me how to stand and I'd just whack around and try and stab him." John was "really into '*Touche!*' and all the French terms and how to do it right," said Wingate, but since the object of the game is to stick the other guy, that's what his friend went for.

"I'd get him pretty good," he recalled. "He'd get mad, because he had all the terms and techniques—but I think I was a little quicker!"[12]

Another seminary friend, Michael Choma, credits John Wessel with introducing him to a lifelong love of archery and bow hunting. John had an old bow that he'd brought from home. "I told him I hadn't shot a bow in my life. So he was going to teach me," Choma recalled. They went outside and John showed him how to use the bow, and from then on, Mike became interested in the sport.[13]

Another favorite activity was hiking. John was memorable for his love of it. "He'd hike you to death!" recalled Wingate. In high school, the young men could go for walks in the woods of the huge campus if they got permission. "He liked to do that. We would go out on nice afternoons—he loved nature—and we'd study together."

John was "a good student, and he really studied," Wingate recalled. This is confirmed by the recollections of James Dubell, who wrote:

> He was a good student—except for spelling and public reading . . . As a student, John excelled in no subject but

history—he had a vivid grasp of all history—he studied it on his own in his youth and would continue to enjoy it as a hobby for the rest of his life. His next favorite subjects were math and science.

He disliked English, however, because of the exactitude required by way of spelling, grammar, and punctuation. Such preciseness and care were not part of his rough, careless, mannish, out-of-door personality. He would become impatient at the insistence for such precision, and thought of such things as picayune and insignificant.

This same carelessness held true for oral recitation and reading in public. He would often mispronounce words and stumble while reading in public, but he was always good natured about the amusement it created among his peers and the corrections he would receive from his teacher.[14]

Academically, John had an edge in history. Carl Wingate was better at Greek, which they began to study in third year high, so he would help John in the subject. "Usually we went to the chapel, sat in the last row and we'd just study Greek together for tests, and say forms and walk around the grounds."

John was actually quite good in Greek, but he didn't feel comfortable with the subject and always wanted to study more. "I'd be more inclined to say, 'Let's do it later' and he'd say, 'No, we've got that test tomorrow'," Wingate recalled. "I wasn't really worried about it, but he had to be real thorough . . . He wanted to be real sure early."

These qualities of perfectionism and precision were carried over into John's public reading of Greek.

Greek is a language that sounds rather choppy and fast, and John would hesitate when he read it aloud. He'd hold a vowel quite long until he was sure he was right. To his classmates, he sounded like a Southerner. "It was like somebody from Florida speaking Greek, rather than a Greek" speaking Greek, and Wingate used to tease John good-naturedly that he read his Greek with "a Southern drawl." Thus was born a joke which found its way into the class yearbook: "Address his mail to Southern Greece."

"John was memorable in class 'cause he could usually be depended on to hold the class up for a little while," W. Michael Mueller, his classmate in Greek, recalled.

Latin was studied every year in the seminary. Knowledge of Latin was tremendously important for the seminarian because at that time (and for the foreseeable future, so they thought) all Catholic liturgical celebrations throughout the world were conducted in Latin. Even today, Latin is still the official language of the Roman Catholic Church.

"We had to learn Latin and Greek, and really know it," a former St. Charles seminarian recalled. "And if you didn't know it—out you went!"

John struggled mightily with Latin, although he always managed to obtain passing grades. It was, with the possible exception of French, his most difficult subject in the seminary. The usual pressures to learn a difficult, complicated, and archaic foreign language were compounded, in John's case, because of his inherent reading difficulties that he'd taken such great pains to overcome.

One of John's professors, Father Raymond E. Brown, S.S., helped him with his Latin in high school. John liked Father Brown, who was scholarly and, in the words of a former student, "one of the most brilliant people that ever went through the seminary."

In later years, Father Brown would distinguish himself as an eminent author and Scripture scholar. A graduate of St. Charles College, Father Brown came back in 1953 to teach at his alma mater. After teaching a few years, Father Brown left to pursue graduate studies, and to begin to earn his many doctorates. Their paths would cross again at Roland Park when Father Brown returned to teach Scripture at the major seminary.

Father Brown remembered his former student John Wessel as a very nice, sincere young man, an ordinary student, bright enough but not brilliant. John was boyish and tousled, neither polished nor sophisticated, and had a fine character.

"He wasn't a problem seminarian at all," Father Brown said about John Wessel. "Whatever he was interested in, he was very enthusiastic about."

John was well liked by his peers and teachers, but like most everyone, he had his share of embarrassing moments and personal mortifications, principally in the area of languages, where he was the most vulnerable. On one occasion, a National Latin Exam was given to the seminarians, and the Latin teacher convinced the class that they should really study hard and do well. Everybody studied. Afterward the teacher came into the classroom and said, "Some of you didn't do as well as I thought on that exam."

Now, *bonus* is an adjective meaning "good" in Latin, and it's just about the first adjective taught in Latin class. "Somebody," the teacher said pointedly, "put that *bonus* means 'bone' on that test!" John started laughing out loud. It was so absurd!

With that, the teacher shot back, "What are you laughing at, Wessel? You're the one that did it!"

He had to take a lot of ribbing from his classmates after that. Often he was asked, "What does *bonus* mean, John?"

John also had to endure a celebrated reading gaffe or two in English class during public recitations.

Once during a reading of the archaic prose of a Shakespearean drama, it was John's turn to read aloud. His pronunciation of unfamiliar words was so bad that the whole class exploded with laughter, causing the teacher to get a little upset because what was supposed to be a dramatic reading had now become a comedy.

John just shook his head, looked down and turned beet red until the laughter subsided. And then he was fine. He was sensitive, but not to a fault.

Privately, it bothered and embarrassed him, but publicly he maintained good cheer and the ability to laugh at himself.[15]

John "was very thorough and wanted to do it right. He had a good sense of humor, but he didn't like to make a mistake," Wingate offered. But if he did, he'd be "just slightly embarrassed for the moment, but then he'd kick right back in and it didn't deter him from trying anything again."

"John took it good-naturedly," recalled James Dubell about his classmates' teasing of his pronunciations. Everyone genuinely respected his intelligence, integrity and good naturedness.[16]

One time though, John's good nature was stretched to its limit.

In his college years at St. Charles, John was paired up with a fellow named Howard Rawlings* for study hall, so that they had seats next to each other and shared a common bookcase. John had to work hard at his studies. Rawlings, by contrast, was a terribly bright fellow who never had to study, and he usually earned A's and high B's on everything he did. But he also had a very quick wit and a satirical way, and he wasted no time in poking fun at John.

Most of the time, John took it with the best of humor, which made it all the funnier. But on occasion, John would run out of patience with Howard, particularly after he got a poor grade in some test or examination, and Howard would say something like, "Well, John, if you'd only study, if you'd only work harder, John, you wouldn't have all these troubles."

Well, one day John Wessel lost it. "In the middle of this rather quiet study hall there was a commotion and all we heard were books hitting the floor," recalled Michael Mueller. Everyone turned around in their seats to see what in the world was going on. "John was pushing all of Howard's books onto the floor out of his desk!"

Howard was just sitting at his desk, momentarily at a loss for words. "I think Howard's life was actually in danger at that time," Mueller half joked. John had enough of Howard's teasing this particular day.

Everybody knew Howard, and while nobody had any hostility toward him, they all knew that he was really being rough on John and lording it over him, so they were just waiting for John to get back at him. And he finally did. John and Howard made up after the incident and remained friends, but "we all remember John for at least finally having given Howard his comeuppance," Mueller recalled.[17]

And what a fine moment in comeuppance it was!

St. Charles offered many extracurricular activities for a young man to choose from, and John Wessel was involved in many things—tennis and football, in particular. He played on the tennis team, and did well enough to be the team co-captain in his Rhet year, sharing the honor along with James Dubell. But John's favorite sport was football. Here he was noted for his bravado, lack of fear, and aggressive play.[18]

Intramural football at St. Charles was "supposed" to be touch football instead of tackle, but when John played the game—well, it often became a tough, bruising, mud-splattered event.

He always played A class football, and always wound up playing on the championship football teams.[19]

John was a tackle. He played defensive lineman on the left side. "He did just about everything and took it, I think, a little more seriously than I took most of it," recalled Wingate, his teammate, who played left end, "but he was a real good athlete."

As a football player, John Wessel was "like a tank," added Michael Choma. He was "very aggressive when it came to football" and "he played his heart out."

"He always played a difficult, unattractive position like a guard or a tackle," James Dubell also recalled. "He never caught the ball or threw the pass. He was always one of the guys in the trench, always came out of the game all muddy and bruised." Again, that was his style: When he played, he played hard.

John Wessel loved Notre Dame. First, because both were Irish—so naturally he would love "the Fighting Irish." When John wrote Paul Horning a fan letter and Horning sent back an autographed picture of himself, John was so excited about that, Carl Wingate recalled.

Then, too, John's older brother, Edward, was a student at Notre Dame University. One day, Eddie picked up a blue practice sweatshirt from Notre Dame, with the university logo and a white number 35 on it, and sent it to John as a gift.

Well, that was like God's gift to John! He would wear it everywhere—even to bed. John is pictured in the school yearbook, wearing that old blue jersey in a football game, while lunging forward to block a pass. When Notre Dame played football, "we always had to know what happened," said Wingate. One year around 1957, John and his friend Winnie even went to South Bend, Indiana and visited the famous University.

Another of John's favorite activities was the Mission Society, under the direction of its moderator, Father Edwin J. Schneider—"Pop" Schneider, as the students affectionately called him—himself a graduate of Notre Dame.

The Mission Society was a natural for John, who was still intensely drawn to the idea of missionary work. It brought the seminarians into contact with missionaries from all over the world who visited the college. John liked the Mission Society moderator, "Pop" Schneider. He was a chemist, and John was good at the sciences—physics and chemistry—so they had a good rapport. In his last two years at St. Charles, John served as an officer in the Mission Society: first as vice president, and then as president.

John also worked in the Mission Store on campus, which sold a variety of religious articles that the students could buy. There were four students who operated the Mission Store, and John was "the main man" there.

At St. Charles, too, John discovered a surprising flair for drama and the arts.

John loved choral singing. He sang second bass in the choir all through the seminary. It was an honor to be selected, because not everyone had the vocal ability to pass the choirmaster's high standards, but John evidently did. Singing in the choir was a form of worshiping God. It brought him in touch with the liturgy and the sacraments, and he thought it was a grand way of participating in the sacramental life of the Church.

In addition to singing in the official choir, John joined the more informal choral groups in school, like the glee club and barbershop quartets. At Christmas time, some of the guys would get together and walk around the campus singing Christmas carols. John could always be found right in the middle of it. He just loved to sing his heart out.

"And he couldn't tell you one note from another," James Dubell recalled, "but yet he could belt out a song. He didn't care if you liked it or not. He was having a good time . . . just expressing himself."

Drama and comedy productions were a staple of campus life and an outlet for creative talents. John became involved in dramatics. The students put on some humorous skits, as well as more serious plays.

John helped built props for the plays, and in his last year had a role in the school production of the Donald Bevan/Edmund Trzcinski play, later a Billy Wilder film, *Stalag 17*. John was cast as Witherspoon, one of the POWs being held by the Nazis, and his pal Mike Mueller played Joey, a shell-shocked mute. Mueller's acting role, as he recalled, consisted in just sitting there and keeping his mouth shut, but Witherspoon was a speaking part. Away from the strictures and precision of Shakespearean recitation in English class, John's engaging and charismatic persona began to shine through in these theatrical productions.

John also became interested in photography. He dabbled a little in photography in his early years, but photography really became his forte later on. Self-taught and extremely creative, John was an avid "shutter bug." He joined the photography staff of *The Carolite*, the school yearbook, and eventually became its head photographer. Classmates remember that John could be found in either one of two places—"always in the dark room or on the grid iron."

As a high school student, John was mature in that he was docile, obedient, and he adjusted to change without great difficulty. He never talked back to his superiors; instead, he took correction as a way of acting out his desire for an almost militaristic type of formation. He never questioned the wisdom of directions given to him.[20]

At times, the rules of seminary life could appear to be arbitrary and unfair, but John never complained. One Thanksgiving Day, John came home by train from Baltimore for a rare and brief visit with his family. He had to be back in his dormitory at St. Charles that same evening, in time for the nine o'clock curfew. After a sumptuous dinner, John's mother drove him back to Philadelphia to catch the train to Baltimore.

It was dark and pouring rain that night. Kathleen Wessel took a wrong turn—in the torrent of rain, she was barely able to see out the window in front of her—and the loss of valuable time resulted in John's missing his train. Knowing he would be late, John called ahead to St. Charles, but still got in trouble for coming back after curfew and received some sort of punishment.

Maryann was steamed when she heard about John's punishment. "It wasn't fair!" she thought, and said as much to her younger brother.

John's only response was to defend his superior's decision. Patiently, he explained, "That's the rule, Maryann. That's the way it is. There's no reason to criticize it, because it won't hurt me to be punished."

In line with John's sense of obedience and maturity was his deep, devout spiritual life. His prayer life was sincere and steady, manly and matter-of-fact. He participated in daily Mass, Communion, and prayers. During the Lenten season, friends recall John saying the Stations of the Cross daily and making extra penances.[21]

"He was a person that, back in the seminary you would find in the chapel, just praying and meditating," said James Dubell. "Not for anyone to see him, but just because he felt a need to do that."

John's spiritual life was an inspiration to all in his college years at the seminary. His faith in God was recognized and respected by all.[22]

In the seminary, John continued to have a keen sense of others' feelings. He would often "take aside" a classmate whom he sensed had a problem or was feeling low, and try to cheer him up.[23]

A seminary, loosely translated, is a "greenhouse." It comes from the Latin *seminarium*, a seed plot, a nursery—a place where something develops, grows, or is bred. A seminary is a seed plot for the seed of a vocation.

The seed of John's spiritual life seemed to take root and grow in the environment of the minor seminary. Spiritually, he flourished and acquired depth "like a plant in a pot," recalled classmate Wingate. From the first day he arrived, John was "on track" and sure of his desire to be a priest. The only concern he ever expressed to friends was whether he had sufficient talent or was holy enough.

Each of the seminarians had a "confessor," a priest who was available to provide individual spiritual direction to the young "penitent," as he was called. The seminarian picked out his own confessor and met with him once a week. John Wessel's confessor in the minor seminary was Father William T. O'Keefe, S.S., who was also the Infirmarian and taught German, Latin and Religion. John liked his confessor, and their good rapport probably helped John overcome any difficulties and doubts regarding his worthiness.

John responded well to the routine and schedule of daily spiritual life built into the typical French school spirituality that was the Sulpician model designed by Father Olier.

"He didn't gripe about all the scheduled stuff we had," Wingate recalled. John's approach was to read the directions to be sure he understood exactly what was expected of him, and do his best. John never questioned the schedule of spiritual life that was laid out for him, because he knew the priests were there to help him and they knew what they were doing.

"We would roll out of bed onto the floor and say the Morning Offering," Wingate recalled. Then they went down to chapel for meditation. One of the priests would read while the seminarians listened, or at least tried to stay awake. After the meditation, Mass would be celebrated. After Mass, they went back upstairs and made their beds, then came down for breakfast—it was now 7:30 a.m. There were short little prayers before and after meals. Classes began promptly at 8:15 a.m., and prayers were said before and after every class.

"Just before lunch, we'd all pile in the study hall and there would be what they called Particular Examen," an examination of conscience. A reading would be selected from a little green book, and for each day of the year, there were things in your life that you were supposed to look at, Wingate recalled.

There was time for private recitation of the Rosary and for private spiritual reading. John liked to sit and read his New Testament when it was time to do so. Everyone did during the day, but John "really enjoyed it," said Wingate.

Devotion to Mary, the Mother of God, figured prominently in the student's spiritual life. They prayed to Mary before and after every class with the *Ave Maria* and the *Sub tuum praesidium*; as Our Lady of Victory before games on the playing field; and in the Rosary, the Little Office, and in private devotions.[24]

The seminarian's spiritual life was also a very private matter. There was not a great deal of group faith sharing, or Scripture discussion, as there is today. Much of the time was spent in quiet and in silence, reflecting on the meditations, reading Scripture alone. "Most of our spirituality was private. . . . It was you and God," said Wingate. It was difficult to tell that much about the spiritual life of another classmate—that is, whether he was spiritually maturing, or just going through the motions—except that John Wessel is remembered for his serious approach to sacramental and spiritual life. He did everything that was asked of him and more.

John took the routine of spiritual life seriously, and the routines became habits for him, Wingate recalled. "We'd walk to chapel together, then we'd go in and both kneel there and pray. During Lent, we'd drift in and . . . said the stations on our own." John strictly observed the spiritual disciplines, even when some others did not.

On Good Friday, for instance, the seminarians were asked to be silent out of respect for the solemnity of the day. And some guys would hide behind the handball courts and talk. "He wouldn't, and I didn't either," said Wingate. "We took those things seriously."

One incident serves to illustrate the extent of John Wessel's seriousness and piety.

One day in high school, John Wessel and Carl Wingate were out walking around—one of John's many endless hikes on the grounds of St. Charles. They were just walking, and talking as they went about this and that. Then John said to Wingate, "I want to tell you a joke."

"All right," Wingate said, "Is it clean, or is it funny?"

John laughed. "It's funny."

"Okay, what's the joke?"

They walked a little farther, and John began to tell the joke. It was the mildest off-color little joke. He laughed, and so did Wingate, at the silly punch line. It was so innocent that Wingate gave it no further thought.

"The next morning we went down for meditation and John was all worried," said Wingate. "He was sitting next to me and said, 'You know that joke I told you? I can't go to Communion.'"

"I asked, 'Why not?' He said, 'I don't think that joke was proper.'"

"I'd always think of that," said Wingate. To him, the incident said a lot about the kind of fellow John Wessel was. Carl Wingate didn't think it was such a big deal. But John had uttered an improper word, or so he thought, and "he couldn't receive Eucharist on that same tongue till he went to confession."

"So we both got up and got in the confession line!" Wingate recalled.

Retreats were an important element of spiritual life at St. Charles and were given for the seminarians throughout the year. Sometimes, there would be a Recollection Weekend. A priest would give a meditation Saturday night and then would say Mass on Sunday. But there was always one special retreat, the Annual Retreat, at the beginning of each school year, which lasted almost a week, from Monday to Friday. For the Annual Retreat, the seminary would bring in a visiting priest to serve as Retreat Master.

Usually, during the Annual Retreat, there would be morning Mass and then a talk; in the afternoon another talk, and some hours for spiritual reading. This went on each day. There was always ample time to pray, to slow down and reflect, and to get some new and refreshing input.

Not surprisingly, John Wessel greatly enjoyed the retreats and took them quite seriously.

As a young boy in grammar school, Johnny had expressed the desire to be a "martyr" for the Christian faith. Yet, as his knowledge progressed in the seminary, he began to have a different understanding of what it really meant to be a martyr.

In Latin and Greek classes, he studied the origin of the word, and learned that to be a martyr actually meant to be a living witness, *martyr* being derived from the Greek word for *witness*.

Wingate well remembered the day they learned the word in class. He and John talked about it afterward. John liked the term "martyr," but his perspective of what it meant began to evolve after that.

John's ideal of being a martyr was "a key concept in his life," Wingate recalled, but "the idea of it was more of the basic meaning of the word, as a *witness*, rather than the popular meaning of the word"—a gruesome and violent death.

"We lived with the concept of martyrs, but I think that, as we got older, we didn't think so much of the gory stuff as we did of the living witness—the long term."

As he grew to adulthood, John's concept of "martyrdom" was more as a daily living witness of Christ than the idea of dying violently or tragically. "Being a witness was very important to him" but in the true sense of the word—as a witness to the faith.

"We almost got the idea that *living* the faith as a witness is actually a more difficult job" than in being killed for the faith, Wingate recalled. "As a long term witness, it can be a much longer martyrdom in a sense."

CHAPTER 10

TRIAL BY FIRE

Throughout high school, John Wessel had a predictable routine every summer: He'd come home to Mount Holly, bringing with him his trunk full of clothes, and head off to Medford Lakes. There he would enjoy helping his dad around the house and yard, and working as a youth counselor at the local summer camp. He plunged into the social and athletic activities at the Lakes from June to September, and he especially enjoyed the annual canoe carnival.[1]

Kathleen Wessel well remembered those summer vacations, not only for the fun they had together as a family, but because John's father still secretly hoped his youngest son would remain at home at the end of the summer. "His father really was hoping, against hope" that John would decide to stay and not return to the seminary, his mother recalled. "He just missed him so much."

"So all summer long we had a wonderful summer," said Mrs. Wessel. "He went camping, he went fishing, boating. Nothing was said until a week before he was to go back, then John would start getting his clothes together . . ."

John would pack his trunk and get ready to go back to Baltimore after Labor Day. Seeing his preparations, and realizing that he was intent on returning to the seminary, his parents stifled any sense of disappointment. They deliberately tried to remain neutral about his choice of vocation. "We never really encouraged, but we never discouraged," his mother emphasized. "He always knew that he had a place to come to if he changed his mind."

Most of the seminarians were intent on earning money for their tuition, and they were grateful for any summer job they could find. Tuition was about $700 per year and, while not prohibitively expensive, it was still a big commitment for working-class parents, who could have sent their sons to the free public high schools—even though, in some dioceses, part of the tuition was picked up by the good people of the church.

John did not have the same financial concerns as most of his peers in the seminary, at least not in the early years. He was always very mindful, however, to invite his seminary friends to visit him over the summer. Together they would enjoy the activities at Medford Lakes.

James Dubell worked on a farm near home for the summer. He picked peaches and cut corn in the morning, and then sold the produce at a roadside market in the afternoon. It was hard work, but it paid well. Whenever he had the chance and a day off, Jim would visit John and his family at the Lakes. Carl Wingate and other seminary friends also came to visit.

Carl Wingate recalled his first visit to John Wessel's hometown:

> We got to be close friends sitting next to each other in the seminary. We did a lot of stuff—we played handball together, we played tennis together—and so one summer he said, 'You want to come up to Medford Lakes, out to Mount Holly?' And then we went. His parents wanted to take us to the movies, so we went to see *Moby Dick* in Camden, New Jersey. Then we went back to Mount Holly, and then we went up to Medford Lakes for a few days . . .
>
> He had a canoe there, and he said, 'I want to teach you how to be safe in a canoe.' So we went out in the lake and he'd say, 'All right, we're going to sink it.' So he'd fill it with water and it would go down. He said, 'Now, what would you do?' So we had to get it turned over and then it would float back up, then you hang on to it, then you kind of learn how to flip it over and get it over with most of the water out of it. We had a lot of fun learning all that. I don't know if he was setting me up, but I got to where I felt pretty comfortable in a canoe.

During the time that John was in high school, his father suffered several heart attacks. Dr. Wessel recuperated at Medford Lakes. "I remember visiting there," James Dubell recalled, "and it was just a slower pace. But his father recovered and he went back to work."

The family was changing in other ways as well. Edward, Jr. had graduated from the University of Notre Dame and was attending medical school at the University of Pennsylvania in Philadelphia. While there, he met a pretty, gentle brunette named Patricia, who soon became a frequent visitor to the Wessel home in Mount Holly. In 1956, Ed and Pat became engaged to wed the following summer, in August 1957, the year before Ed was to graduate from medical school.

During the summer, Pat was introduced to Ed's younger brother "Johnny." He was much younger than Ed, she thought, but he was "a joker and we always clowned around a lot. We sprayed hoses and watered people down and danced" in the backyard on Garden Street. But as much as he was "a fun person" he was always "a little proper," recalled Pat Wessel of her first impressions of John.

John's sister Maryann also graduated from college in 1956 and began her career as a teacher.

In the summer of 1956, Edward and Kathleen Wessel celebrated their twenty-fifth wedding anniversary. The three Wessel children joined together to throw their parents a surprise anniversary party in honor of the momentous occasion. It was held in their Medford Lakes home, and it truly was a great surprise to the parents. All their friends from Medford Lakes and Mount Holly were present, along with their Hogan and Wessel relatives. Even the priests of Sacred Heart parish, Father Kozak, Father Edward Strano, and the new curate, Father (later Monsignor) Joseph C. Shenrock, attended the festivities.

Looking back, it was perhaps fortunate that the children were able to do this for their parents at that time. Within a year, everything would change.

Despite his earlier heart problems, Dr. Edward Wessel still was the picture of a healthy and virile man—he was only fifty-one years of age. It took everyone by surprise when suddenly, in April of 1957, during John's last year of high school, Dr. Wessel was not feeling well. He grew progressively worse, but the cause of his sickness was undetermined. Uncle Jim Hogan, a medical doctor, suspected it was his heart. In May, Dr. Wessel went into the hospital for exploratory surgery.

His family received a diagnosis for which they were completely unprepared. It was cancer of the stomach. Barring a miracle, the illness was incurable and fatal. "I remember we were all in total shock," Maryann recalled. "It was the first tragedy in our family, and we all kind of clung to one another . . . all the family and all the uncles and aunts."

After a brief hospitalization Dr. Wessel came home and, for the duration of his illness, was cared for by his family. Initially, he was well enough to make frequent visits to his brother, Julian, in Philadelphia, with whom he enjoyed a very close relationship.[2]

As he weakened physically, his spiritual life, which had always been strong and intense, became even more prominent and radiant. Dr. Wessel insisted on going to the sacraments of the Church as often as he could. Despite their ultimate faith in God, it was, nonetheless, a time of great sadness for John and his family.

As the cancer progressed, John's father was eventually confined to his bed upstairs in the Garden Street home where the family had spent so many happy years. Dr. Wessel was in great pain, for which he was given morphine by his son, Edward, on the recommendation of his doctors.[3] But almost to the last, Dr. Edward Wessel was fully conscious and talking, even as his strength and vitality slipped away.[4]

What passed between John and his father during this time is not known. John returned home at the end of his school year knowing of his father's terminal condition. He would often slip into his father's bedroom and just sit with him and hold his hand. He prayed with him and prayed for him quietly at his bedside.[5] Perhaps he may have talked to his father about God's love for him, and his own deep love for him as well. At other times, perhaps he just kept a silent vigil while his father slept.

One thing can be certain: Witnessing the intense suffering and death of his once strong, healthy father from the painful cancer must have been a deep and life-altering experience for the young seminarian John Wessel.

On July 22, 1957, after receiving the Last Rites of the Church, Dr. Edward Wessel passed away quietly after a short but intensely painful illness. During this time, John's maturity and spiritual stamina showed its strength. When death came, John showed little emotion. He said that he "wanted to be strong for his mother, brother, and sister," and that he "knew God would help them and unite them in love." He had great faith and showed unusual strength based on that faith in God.[6]

Since the age of fourteen, John had been deprived of daily contact with his father except during summer vacations. It is possible that John may have realized that he hadn't much of a chance to get to know his father better and to spend more time with him while he was alive. Perhaps this explains why, in later years, John Wessel often remarked, referring to his own father, that you could continue to love someone who had died, and said that he felt he had grown closer to his father even after his death.[7]

Friends, family and clergy quickly gathered at the Garden Street home to comfort the Wessels on the night of July 22nd. The family was still numb from the shock of Dr. Wessel's untimely death, comforted solely by the knowledge that his agony was over.

John was "very consoling to his mother and his brother and sister," recalled Monsignor Joseph Shenrock, who hastened to the Wessel house the night John's father died. "And he always did say that he was closer to his dad in death than he had been in life."

James Dubell spent quite a bit of time with John during that painful summer, and was also with John on the day his father died. "He took it very well," recalled Dubell about John. "I never remember seeing him cry" over his father's death, although "I'm sure he did" privately.

Maryann also attested to her brother's strength. "I remember he would try to control his emotions, because he felt as if that helped us, and he didn't want to upset us. I often felt that he went up to his room and cried his eyes out, but nevertheless, he never, ever showed us."

Dr. Wessel's funeral Mass was celebrated at Sacred Heart Church by the new pastor, Father Francis P. Gunner. Dr. Wessel's numerous friends in the community, including many distinguished Protestants, were among those in attendance at the Catholic funeral Mass. Dr. Edward Wessel was laid to rest in St. Mary's Cemetery in Mount Holly.

Somehow, John and his family pulled through the ritual of death and burial. John was briefly reunited with his old grade school classmate, Eileen Egan, who came to pay her respects at his father's wake. She managed to speak a few words of condolence to John, and then whispered that she had decided to enter the convent. Eileen had been thinking about it for many years—John probably knew as much—but she had finally made up her mind after high school to become a Sister, Servant of the Immaculate Heart of Mary.

John brightened at the happy news. "Good for you!" he said, and gave her a playful punch on the arm by way of congratulations.

"I just remember him standing there, so valiant," Eileen Egan recalled about John Wessel at his father's wake. "I think that was very painful for him," but he was "like a soldier, so disciplined." His composure was a tower of strength for the rest of his family.

In addition to coping with their grief, this was also the time for the surviving family to confront some harsh economic realities: There would no longer be any income. The household had depended on Dr. Wessel's earnings and now that was gone. Meanwhile, Eddie had his bills from medical school, and was about to be married and leave home. John had his seminary tuition. The house still needed to be kept up; the living expenses met.

James Dubell was John's confidant during these times. "I remember more than anything there seemed to be the uncertainty about—where do we go from here?" he recalled. "So I'm sure that the focus of their discussions at that time, although I was not in on it, was survival." John very definitely felt a responsibility to stay home and support the family instead of returning to the seminary in the fall. "I know we talked about whether he would go back or not."

To those who knew him, the death of his father had a profound and maturing influence on young John Wessel. With his older brother about to leave home, John was, for all practical purposes, the man of the house.

But Kathleen Wessel acted quickly and decisively to provide for her family's financial needs. Her late husband had acquired a number of valuable properties over the years, and she sold them all right away—including the beloved summer home on Chippewa Trail in Medford Lakes. She then returned to work as a school teacher the year after her husband died.

Through the experience, said Dubell, John "probably decided once and for all that he was going to become a priest" and that "he would continue to study for the priesthood, and that this was going to be his life." John grew up in that sense. Although John never stated directly that this was the "turning point" for him, "I just had that feeling," said his friend.

Kathleen Wessel also wondered whether John would elect to return to the seminary in the fall. At the end of each previous summer, and without any prompting, John would pack his trunk to go back to the seminary. But this summer was different. After his father died, his mother found herself thinking, "Oh, now he'll stay. He won't go back again."

"So we said nothing all that summer," Mrs. Wessel recalled. As always, they neither encouraged nor discouraged him. The Wessels tried to maintain a semblance of normalcy and did things together as a family.

John's mother thought to herself, "Well, if he goes back now, he's got it"—meaning, his vocation was assured.

When the summer was over and it came time to return to the seminary . . . John went upstairs and packed his clothes.

"He never faltered," Maryann recalled about her brother's commitment to the priesthood. Once John turned his face toward the altar, he never wavered from his course.

CHAPTER 11

MOURNING

John Wessel returned to St. Charles in September of 1957 to start his first year of college, and he brought with him the many profound changes that had occurred in his family and in his personal life. The previous spring, John had graduated from St. Charles College High School. With everything that had happened since, it must have seemed like such a long time ago.[1]

John had done very well in his junior and senior years. In his senior year, he earned an 84.5 grade average. John had excelled in Religion and history, and had done quite well in Greek, English, and elocution. Latin continued to be his most difficult subject, but French was not far behind.

In addition to proficiency in Latin and Greek, the seminarian was required to select an additional foreign language to study for the last two years of high school and the first year of college. John's choices had been between German and French. Although of German ancestry, he chose the latter, and passed with a 77.5 average grade in senior year French.

John was now a college student—a Poet, and he could see the light at the end of the tunnel. He was beginning to get closer to the prize.

In his first year of college, John Wessel lived in a house on campus known as the Frederick House. Because of the overcrowded conditions in the dormitories, the seminary allowed certain students to occupy that residence: "Frederick Manor" men, as they were called by their slightly jealous classmates. There were three men to a room in Frederick House, and they were just simple rooms, used for sleeping and nothing else.

One of John Wessel's roommates that year was a seminarian named Eugene Rebeck, from Perth Amboy, New Jersey. Although they didn't know it at the time, many years later, after their ordination to the priesthood, they would work together in Catholic youth ministry.

John kept up with his studies and activities. His grades dipped slightly in college—74.8 overall in first year—which given the death of his father was understandable. With dint of hard work, however, he would attain a much improved 81.2 grade average in his second college year.

John began college with a new resolve to pursue his goal of becoming a priest in the Diocese of Trenton. And now, he was not doing what Father Kozak or anybody else expected of him, but he was doing what he wanted for himself.

"I think the death of his father convinced him that he wanted to work in the [Trenton] diocese," Dubell recalled. Perhaps now it all started to make sense to John—God's will was not for him to go to some far-off continent as a Maryknoll missionary, but to stay in his community and be of service to it, all the while remaining close to his widowed mother and family. "All of that fell into place after the death of his father. I think that he just examined himself and his own life and he put himself on track and he said, 'This is what I'm going to do.'" After his father died, "I don't think John ever had a doubt about his vocation."

To his friend, John's personality seemed to undergo a noticeable change when he returned to the seminary. He became a little quieter and seemed to acquire a greater depth.

"During this freshman year of college, John showed signs of greater maturity—he was more involved in his studies, more concerned about the welfare of his mother, and more sympathetic to the feelings and problems of others," wrote James Dubell. At this time, too, John even seemed to his friend to "increase his interest in football" and to "take up an avid interest in photography." He became even more involved in the college yearbook staff as a photographer.[2]

"You could just sense a difference that came over him. He wasn't the freewheeling, crazy guy that he had been before. All of a sudden he seemed to take on a manliness about him. He grew up real fast," Dubell recalled. Before that, there had been "a lot of little boy in him."

But no longer.

John took his father's death quietly and stoically, other seminary friends observed. His bereavement was not showy nor self-pitying. "It was a kind of quiet, respectful type of attachment. I think he just took it," Wingate recalled. "He changed a little. . . . It was just a close-knit family; somebody was gone." But John was sure that his father was in Heaven.

After his father died, John's mother came alone to visit him in Catonsville each visiting Sunday—a heart-wrenching reunion for mother and son, since the absence of the father was made even more obvious to both. Dubell recalled how hard that was for John. "But he took it like a man. He talked about it a little. We would discuss it, but it wasn't like, 'Feel sorry for me.' He resisted any kind of attention to himself. He never felt sorry for himself. He was manly that way—he wouldn't want to upset you. He was real grown up," Dubell added about eighteen-year-old John. "It was amazing."

Maryann at times accompanied her mother on these trips to visit John. Later on, William Beitel would also join them. In 1957, Maryann had met William ("Bill") Beitel, the man she would later marry.

At first, Bill met John only briefly on holidays when he came home. "We got to know each other a little bit that way, and then later when his mother or Maryann wanted to go down and visit, I was a handy driver for them so I was happy to drive them down."

Bill's arrival on the scene was fortuitous. He came into Maryann's life around the time her father became gravely ill. His quiet, reliable presence was a blessing to both Maryann and her mother, especially during their difficult period of mourning.

John impressed Bill Beitel because he was "such a down-to-earth guy, and he had absolutely no time for the trappings of formality. He was a very informal person, and his clothes under his little cassock were always rugged clothes, Army boots, and he'd always be stomping around in the woods."

Bill had difficulty, at first, visualizing John as a priest. "If this kid makes it," he thought to himself, "it's going to be unusual." But as he got to know John, he realized it wasn't so unusual after all: John was just a very unique individual, and he would make a very unique kind of priest.

The aftermath of Dr. Wessel's death was a very difficult time emotionally for his surviving family. Going to the cemetery to visit his grave in Mount

Holly was especially painful. "Those were the tough years," Maryann said, without exaggeration.

Father Joseph C. Shenrock, the new young curate at Sacred Heart Church, was a great help and support to Maryann during this time. To distract her from her grief, he persuaded her to become involved in directing a comedy for the parish drama club. She was an English major in college, and it was a natural outlet for her talents. Before too long, she found herself enjoying the theatrical effort in spite of herself.

But there would be yet another sadness. John's beloved grandmother, Mary Hogan, passed away in October of 1957. All of the wounds of John's fresh grief, and that of his family, must have been opened anew at the loss of the gentle Irish woman of his childhood who inspired him with daring stories and encouraged his early dreams of missionary zeal.

Would there ever be another year like this one?

One bright event as the year 1957 drew to a close was the wedding of young Dr. Edward Wessel and his bride, Pat. The young couple exchanged their vows in a small, quiet church wedding in Philadelphia on November 30, 1957. Almost immediately, they went overseas to Germany, where Ed, who had joined the Army as a medical doctor, performed his residency as an Army captain. While there, their first two children were born.

They planned their wedding for the Saturday after Thanksgiving to accommodate John's schedule. He was to be the best man.

"Eddie and Johnny were really close as brothers," recalled a cousin. Their relationship was similar to that enjoyed by their late father, Edward, Sr., and his younger brother, their Uncle Jule. They were "not only brothers but they were buddies."[3]

On the day of the wedding, it was pouring rain. John and Ed gathered their cutaway suits and formal accessories to bring to the church for the big event. Then the brothers took a detour and drove all around town looking for umbrellas. They hastily bought one and then hurried to the church.

An unintended moment of levity presented itself, attributable to the last minute rush and the groom's pre-wedding jitters. The groom and his best man got to the sacristy and were changing into their formal clothes, when Ed dropped his gloves in the toilet. "So he made John wear the wet gloves, and John never let him forget it!" recalled the bride.

"I think John thought we were crazy, but he was a good sport," Pat said. "He went along with the whole thing" for his big brother's sake.

*   *   *

Throughout this most difficult year, John's faith and stamina had been tested as never before. He had experienced the pain of his own grief and the weight of the emotional and physical suffering of those he loved.

John learned to accept the "crosses" of life with patient endurance. He grew in maturity, faith and compassion for all who were suffering and in pain.

CHAPTER 12

THE PILGRIMS

Kathleen Wessel sat down one day and realized that the first anniversary of her husband's death was not far off. How, she wondered, would she and her family ever get through it.[1]

Suddenly, an opportunity presented itself. A pilgrimage tour of Europe had been arranged by the Archbishop of San Francisco and was still open to travelers. Kathleen Wessel heard of the tour and, on the spur of the moment, decided to take the trip with the San Francisco group in the summer of 1958.

"I don't know why I did it," Mrs. Wessel said years later. All she knew was that she badly needed to get away, and didn't want to go alone. She and John would go to Europe together.[2]

The tour would visit the Catholic shrines and churches throughout Europe, including stops in Paris, Assisi, Rome, and Lourdes—the latter the sight of miraculous apparitions of the Blessed Virgin Mary.

As long as they were in Europe, the Wessels decided they might as well visit Ireland and see their Irish relatives, of which there were quite a few.

John was eighteen years old, and it would be his first trip overseas. He was excited. He concentrated on his goal of getting ready for this momentous event and happily plunged into making thorough preparations: applying for his passport, getting his inoculations, choosing suitable clothing, and buying last minute items. In early June, John wrote to the Office of the Bishop of Trenton asking for assistance in arranging an audience with the Pope while he and his mother were in Rome. A few days later, he received a reply instructing him to contact the Superior of the Graduate House of Studies for American Priests at the North American College at Via dell' Umilta upon his arrival in the Eternal City.[3]

John and his mother joined up with the San Francisco group on the East Coast for the seven-hour transcontinental flight across the Atlantic. They landed at Orly Airport in Paris on June 23, 1958.

Paris! The exciting, beautiful, City of Light. Home of the Eiffel Tower and the Champs Élysées, the Cathedral of Notre Dame and the Church of St. Sulpice, where Father Jean-Jacques Olier began his seminary for the training of parish priests in 1642.

Yet, the first stop on the journey for the two weary travelers from New Jersey was not everything they had hoped for—at least, not initially.

First, there was a mix-up with the luggage. The suitcase containing all of Mrs. Wessel's shoes had been misplaced en route. It would not catch up with them again until they reached Rome. For the moment, the only shoes Kathleen Wessel had to wear were the dress pumps on her feet.

Then homesickness set in. Jet-lagged and tired, John and his mother dragged themselves to their Parisian hotel. A world away, they were still grief stricken over the death of their father and husband. In a few weeks it would be the first year anniversary of his death. They began to wonder why they had ever left Mount Holly.

"We were both so homesick" at first, John later said, that "we just looked at each other, and said—'What are we doing here?' 'Why did we come here?'"[4]

Fortunately, their dejection proved to be only transitory. Many of their fellow travelers soon befriended the Wessels. Traveling makes for good companionship, and barriers among people dropped quickly. Before too long, mother and son met a number of nice people who became their friends on the tour.

John made a big hit with the travelers. He was the "youngest person on the tour, and they all loved him," said his mother. "He was always carrying the bags. I think that's why they loved him!"

There were two young priests traveling with the group who also befriended the young seminarian and his mother.[5] Kathleen Wessel distinctly recalled how kind and hospitable the two young priests were to John and her. They made sure the Wessels were included in their activities, sensing perhaps the family's unspoken needs.

The priests offered Mass each morning at the various shrines they visited on the tour through Europe, and would always invite John and his mother to come along. "It was so nice," Kathleen Wessel recalled. "They would go out in the morning to say Mass, and John and I would go with them. And they were so kind to us and kind to John. He just had nice experiences."

One of the first stops on the pilgrimage was Lourdes, a little village in the far southwesterly corner of France nestled in the foothills of the Pyrenees, which separate France from Spain. To reach it, John and his mother had to travel by rail and motor coach across the picturesque and wild terrain to reach the Gascony region where Lourdes is situated.

Lourdes is one of the most beloved pilgrimage shrines of the Roman Catholic faith. It was here that the Blessed Virgin Mary miraculously appeared to a poor, humble peasant girl named Bernadette Soubirous in 1858, and here that miracles and cures continue to this day, particularly through bathing in the waters of the miraculous spring that emerged on the site of the apparitions.

A beautiful church, called the Rosary, and a statue of the Virgin stand at the grotto where the visions occurred. Thousands of persons visit these shrines every year, all year long. Some leave gifts; some leave their crutches as evidence of a cure. Others bathe in the sacred waters of the grotto spring, in hope that a miracle will restore them to health of mind, body and soul. The underground Basilica of Pius X, the second largest in the world, opened in 1958 in honor of the one hundredth year anniversary of the apparitions.[6]

It was an interesting coincidence that the young priest-to-be, John Wessel, was drawn to Lourdes for the centennial of the apparitions of the Blessed Virgin Mary—the same Lady of Lourdes whose statue watched protectively over the young seminarians on the grounds of St. Charles College. Interesting, and fitting that he was to share this experience with his mother.

"At Lourdes, it was just awesome, and John was very impressed because he was just eighteen at the time, and he didn't miss a thing," his mother recalled. Mother and son would attend the daily Mass at the grotto each morning, and John even served as an altar boy a few times.

He loved to wander all through the area and surrounding countryside. It was breathtakingly beautiful. "I'd go back to the hotel, exhausted," Kathleen Wessel recalled, "and he'd go off to the mountains and roam around."

Fortunately, John had a basic knowledge of French from his studies at St. Charles, and was able to communicate in a rudimentary way with the French people.

John had always had a strong devotion to the Blessed Mother and a reverence for the Rosary. But on this visit, he developed a particular devotion to Mary as Our Lady of Lourdes. And since John and his mother had shared this pilgrimage together, their mutual devotion to Our Lady of Lourdes grew to be a very special bond between mother and son.

At Lourdes, the Stations of the Cross are arranged on the side of a mountain, and pilgrims are invited to make the stations. Each station depicts a scene from the passion and death of Jesus Christ. Prayers and devotions are said at each station as the pilgrim meditates on each event of Christ's suffering. The pilgrims walk from station to station in commemoration of the Way of the Cross that Christ walked—from the Agony in the Garden on the Mount of Olives, to the site of the Crucifixion on the hill at Calvary, to the tomb of Christ's burial.

Kathleen Wessel was able to make the Stations of the Cross with John on the hilly terrain, without any pain whatsoever, even in her uncomfortable dress shoes. She later accounted this as a small miracle.

At night, Mrs. Wessel retired to the hotel, but John would return again to the grotto to participate in the beautiful candlelight processions in honor of the Blessed Mother. While his mother rested, he with youthful enthusiasm wanted to absorb so much, do so much, and be in the heart of things.

John was greatly impressed with the faith and the beauty of Lourdes. His mother could sense that he was profoundly moved by the experience, even though he didn't talk about it much. There was no need to, for there were few words to describe the interior feelings of awe and reverence that the holy shrine invoked. Both mother and son were overwhelmed by their pilgrimage.

Much as John may have wanted to linger at Lourdes, it was on to Italy for the next leg of the tour.

The little hill town of Assisi is about ninety miles north of Rome, one of many towns carved out of the Apennine Mountains in the Umbrian region of Italy. It is famous as the birthplace of one of the Roman Catholic Church's greatest saints—Francis of Assisi.

The life of this Saint was quite influential on the spirituality of John Wessel.

St. Francis was born at Assisi in 1182 of a rich merchant family.[7] Francis's father, Peter Bernardone, was reputed to be one of the richest cloth merchants in Assisi and traveled extensively to buy and sell fine fabrics. In this regard, he made many trips to France, frequenting the fairs of Provence and Champagne where Europe, Asia, and Africa exchanged their products.[8] It was during one of these business trips that his son was born.

Dame Pica, Francis's mother, had her child christened *Giovanni*—John. However, upon Peter Bernardone's return, he joyfully re-named him Francis.[9]

In his young manhood, Francis was far from the saint he was destined to become. Quite the contrary. He loved the "dolce vita" of the times. By today's standards, he would be known as a gang leader, a party animal, a spendthrift—in fact, a ne'er do well.[10] But "[s]erious illness brought the young Francis to see the emptiness of his frolicking life as leader of Assisi's youth."[11]

"One day, about the year 1206, Francis entered the neglected chapel of Saint Peter Damian, and poured out his soul before the crucifix."[12] Three times a voice from the crucifix called him. The third time, he heard these words: "Go, Francis, restore my house which is falling into ruins as you see."[13]

> Francis's soul was filled with ineffable joy as he realized that it was God Who spoke to him . . . As he thought that Our Lord wished him to repair the church of Saint Damian, he . . . begged alms door to door to repair the church. When the work was completed he restored another church near Assisi, dedicated to Saint Peter. He then commenced the restoration of Saint Mary of the Angels, which belonged to the Benedictines, about one mile from the city.
>
> While attending Mass in the restored chapel of Our Lady of the Angels (also known as *Portiuncula*, i.e., smallest portion) . . . destined to be the cradle of the Franciscan Order, Francis heard the words as read in the Gospel: "Do not possess gold nor silver, nor money in your purse, nor scrip for your journey, nor two coats, nor shoes, nor a staff". Francis was overjoyed as he felt these words were addressed to himself . . . [and] cried out, "That is what I want . . . that is the object of all my ambition."[14]

People began to realize that this man was actually trying to be Christian and faithfully live the Gospel, and they became St. Francis's loyal followers. "The Franciscan Order spread rapidly throughout Christendom, as may be judged by the fact that in 1219 five thousand Friars attended its General Chapter."[15]

Francis's "devotion and loyalty to the Church were absolute and highly exemplary at a time when various movements of reform tended to break the Church's unity."[16]

> He was torn between a life devoted entirely to prayer and a life of active preaching of the Good News. He decided in favor of the latter, but always returned to solitude when he could. He wanted to be a missionary in Syria or in Africa, but was prevented by shipwreck and illness in both cases.[17]

"In 1224, on the Feast of the Exaltation of the Holy Cross, as St. Francis was praying on Mount Alvernia, he received the Sacred Stigmata, the Impression on his flesh of Our Lord's Five Most Sacred Wounds."[18] In this manner, Francis was "chosen by God to be a living manifestation to the world of Christ's life on earth, a life of poverty and suffering."[19]

> Two years later, on October 4, 1226, at the age of forty-four St. Francis died at Assisi; and on June 16, 1228, he was canonized by Pope Gregory IX.
>
> It was St. Francis's deep love for the Christ Child that inspired him to build the first Christmas crib, which is the joy and inspiration of young and old in all Catholic churches.
>
> St. Francis also directed St. Clare in the founding of the Poor Clares at Saint Damian's in Assisi. The Sisters are known as the Second Order of St. Francis. In addition to these two Orders, St. Francis founded the Third Order, for persons living in the world and desirous of sharing the privileges and graces of the religious state.[20]

Saint Francis of Assisi died as dramatically as he had lived. He "asked his superior to have his clothes removed when the last hour came and for permission to expire lying naked on the earth, in imitation of his Lord."[21] And so he died as he desired, devoid of all worldly goods, while singing the 141st Psalm.[22]

One sensed that the presence of St. Francis still infused the town of Assisi with peace, joy, and holiness in a way that was almost tangible. Here too, John was quite taken with Assisi and its patron saint. He had loved St. Francis before his trip, but visiting the birthplace of the Saint, and walking where he walked, must have moved him all the more.

"St. Francis of Assisi made a very big impression," his mother once again recalled. John threw himself into the spiritual devotions that were a part of the town's rich heritage.

John attended daily Mass and was able to serve a few times at the Basilica of San Giorgio, the site of the tomb of St. Francis. How moving an experience it was to celebrate Mass in the same church where the Saint had once stood and preached and prayed.

Again, John didn't talk openly about what he was experiencing, but his mother could just feel it. "Everything pertaining to St. Francis he loved so—the medals, everything he could get his hands on."

The young seminarian, who coincidentally shared Francis's baptismal name, also shared the Saint's love for nature and the beauty of God's creation. "John was an outdoor person. He was better off outdoors than anybody I've known," his mother said. "He loved to climb mountains and go camping." *The Canticle of the Sun*, a song which St. Francis composed in praise of all of God's creation, must have struck a responsive chord in John's heart.

As in Lourdes, John roamed around the village and surrounding Umbrian countryside while in Assisi. "Oh, he traveled! He walked that ground! In his mind, he *was* Saint Francis," his mother exclaimed.

John was attracted to St. Francis's devotion to poverty, and in later life, tried to embrace and emulate it. He admired Francis's devotion to Christ crucified. And he loved the Saint's spirituality, which was summed up in the magnificent *Prayer of Saint Francis of Assisi*.

> Lord, make me an instrument of your peace:
> where there is hatred, let me sow love;
> where there is injury, pardon;
> where there is doubt, faith;

where there is despair, hope;
where there is darkness, light;
where there is sadness, joy.

O Divine Master,
grant that I may not so much seek
to be consoled as to console,
to be understood as to understand,
to be loved as to love.
For it is in giving that we receive,
it is in pardoning that we are pardoned,
it is in dying that we are born to eternal life.

It was John Wessel's favorite prayer, and it would always remain so.

Their visit to Rome, the Eternal City, was highlighted by an audience with Pope Pius XII. When John arrived in Rome, he called upon the Superior at the North American College at Via dell' Umilta, and he and his mother were granted what was called a "private audience" with the Pontiff. They arrived at St. Peter's Basilica in Vatican City and were ushered into a huge room where quite a few people had gathered, waiting to see the Pope.

Imagine what John Wessel must have felt during his encounter with the Pontiff:

Suddenly, the Holy Father entered. He addressed the crowd in his native Italian and gave them his blessing. Then the Pope personally greeted each person, including Kathleen and John, and said a few words to them. As the Holy Father came closer, John's sense of awe and excitement must have mounted as the distance between himself and the Pontiff grew ever smaller. Perhaps he mentally practiced the greeting he'd prepared for Pope Pius XII.

John was deeply impressed with his meeting with Pope Pius XII, but he did not express it outwardly. It was just something that was felt and experienced, but hard to put into words.

John went exploring the Coliseum and other famous Roman sites with the two young priests he'd met on the tour, new friends who shared his youthful sense of adventure. They marveled at the grandeur of that ancient, timeless city.

On the tour through Europe, Kathleen Wessel reckoned that they visited just about every major church and shrine. After a few weeks, the Wessels left the tour and went off on their own to Ireland.

After landing at Shannon Airport near Limerick, John and his mother made their way the short distance down to Cork, in the southern part of Ireland, to visit their Duggan relatives.

John and his mother arrived at the family homestead, "Shandangan," and were warmly embraced by their Irish relatives. The reunion was a festive occasion, as befitting an Irish homecoming. Although they were meeting for the very first time, there was a definite feeling of family.

Shandangan was then occupied by the descendants of William Duggan, Grandmother Hogan's elder brother, who inherited the estate after their oldest brother Denis became a priest. No doubt many more extended family members, relatives or descendants of Cornelius and Mary Murphy Duggan could be located in the vicinity of County Cork.

As they were shown around by their hosts, the American cousins were quite impressed by all the property and land that their Irish relatives owned, as generations of the Duggan clan had made their home at Shandangan.

Here too, they were quite moved by the experience, for John and his mother were able to see the home that Grandmother Hogan loved so well and spoke of so often. They could see and touch the great stone fireplace of Grandmother Hogan's memory where she, as a little girl, learned the Acts of Faith, Hope and Charity at her mother's knee. They could see the bustling harbor of Cork, presumably the place from which Daniel, Catherine and Margaret Duggan emigrated to America in the mid-1800s; where Mary's sister, Kathleen, departed for her brief life as a nun in Texas; and where the feisty, twentyish Mary Duggan, with her young brother Johnny in tow, set sail for America in the 1880s.

It was fitting then that the latter generations of those Irish forebears should return again to their roots in the land of Erin.

John made quite a big hit with his Irish relatives. "They just loved him," his mother recalled. He too loved them, and Ireland. All too quickly, it seemed, it was time to leave. With some reluctance, John and his mother bid their Duggan cousins goodbye and flew home to America, arriving in Boston on August 22, 1958.

Despite its shaky start, both mother and son had a wonderful time on their European trip. And John, of course, took numerous pictures.

James Dubell was one of the first to see John's pictures of his trip. "I think it had a big influence on him . . . in terms of spirituality, and in terms of seeing Europe and the places that he had studied about. Again, it's part of history, and he loved history." And, he added, John "enjoyed being with his mother and being close with her."

John's 1958 pilgrimage trip to Europe came at a very influential moment in his life.

Perhaps, his mother thought, it even clinched his vocation.

CHAPTER 13

ST. CHARLES, CATONSVILLE:

THE LATER YEARS

Shortly after John Wessel returned to St. Charles in September 1958 for his second year of college, it was time for the Annual Retreat. For the "Rhet Retreat," a young, energetic, visiting priest named Father John Ritzius, a Paulist alumnus of St. Charles, was Retreat Master. At the start of the Annual Retreat, the seminarians repaired to the chapel to celebrate Mass and to listen to the talks that the Retreat Master had prepared for them.[1]

The retreat was "a time of self-examination, a withdrawing for a few days with Christ that He might increase and we might decrease," Father Ritzius told the men. The aim of the retreat conferences was to give the seminarians helpful and practical suggestions for "supernaturalizing" their lives. In the course of his talks, many of the "do's and don't's" of the spiritual life were outlined. Father Ritzius gave them a plan for sanctity by offering a simple definition of a saint: "A saint is a gentleman who supernaturalizes his manners."[2]

There was time for reflection on the Retreat Master's words, as well as for contemplation on the particular message or meaning that God, through the grace of the Holy Spirit, wished to impart to each individual retreatant. It was important to find a quiet place to be alone with God. In peace and silence, one could move closer to the Lord and be more aware of His presence and love. Often one discovered a surprising insight, or a new inspiration, as the Spirit of God prompted; for others, merely a calm certainty of being on the right track.

The notes from John Wessel's "Rhet Retreat," dated September 19, 1958, appear to be private reflections or exhortations to himself, probably written in solitude, perhaps at the end of the retreat or at the end of each day's talks, to remember important points. In any event, they provide an intimate glimpse into John's spiritual life as a nineteen-year-old seminarian, and reveal a young man desiring to know and love God as much as humanly possible.

"Retreat," he penned in his distinctive script. "What can I say—all trouble disappears when God is close. Vocations are all too strong when He is close. Who can run from Him? But how can one stay close to Him?"[3]

"You get so tired of trying to be the best but you are so angry when you aren't the best," John continued, as if addressing himself. "So much grace is needed to keep one on his feet."

"How to stay on one's feet.

1) do little things for God's sake only—kneel in a hard place, forget insults right away, don't always get your own way.
2) use your head—be grown up about problems. Decide and do things immediately. Remember the example of St. Theresa—ask her to pray for you. Love, love, love someone = God."

St. Theresa of the Child Jesus, a humble French cloistered Carmelite nun known as "The Little Flower," would appeal to John. Like him, she dreamed of going off to a foreign mission field; like him, the circumstances of her life required her to stay at home and find joy and fulfillment in the ordinary duties of daily life. Instead she devoted her cloistered religious life "to save souls and pray for priests."[4]

"Love his saints and love his Mother," John continued with his list. "St. Joseph, St. Anthony, St. Michael, St. Patrick, St. Joan of Arc, St. Theresa, St. Francis. Pray for souls."

"Remember God always subjects those he loves to great trials of tunnel darkness. Prayer conquers all—prayer, love, time. Grace does all. Virtue is grace acting in the soul of man. Be mindful of the poor—be brave about them."

Later, John wrote down some quotations:

"God asks only self-surrender and for gratitude," St. Martin.

"To love you, striking deeds are forbidden me."

"Oh Jesus, Jesus, if the desire of love brings such delight,
what must it be really to possess it and enjoy it for eternity."

The latter two quotations appear to be taken from St. Theresa's autobiography, *Story of a Soul*—but perfectly expressed John's thoughts as well.[5]

Lastly, John added, "St. Theresa, teach me your little way."

On the final page of his retreat notes, John pencils a biting self-criticism. During or shortly after the retreat, he became painfully aware that, in some unspecified way, he had fallen short of the spiritual perfection he was seeking. He was hard on himself. (Was this perhaps the infamous book-throwing incident in study hall, or some other?)

> Boy! Have I goofed already. I showed uncharity, impiety, disrespect and disobedience. God has been so good, and I've failed already. I wish I could start again.
>
> Please God, teach me your love. Please give me prudence.

John resolved that the key to his growth in holiness was the daily visit to the Blessed Sacrament—prayer and meditation before the Lord Jesus in the tabernacle of the chapel. "Visit—most important religious duty of the day as regards to me now," he wrote. His own personal failure, as he saw it, was not without gain; if nothing else, it reminded him that he was weak, as are we all, and showed him the means to grow in holiness.

The significance of this retreat to John Wessel is amply demonstrated by the fact that, for the rest of his life, he kept the retreat notes he made in 1958. What he learned that week must have provided a lifetime of inspiration.

As he had done in high school, John remained active in college extracurricular activities during his Rhet year: He was an officer of the Mission Society, a co-captain of the tennis team, and on the defensive line of the football team. He participated in the choir, the glee club, and the Sodality, a society devoted to the Blessed Virgin Mary.

Football competition was tough that year, but John and his teammates enjoyed their second consecutive undefeated season, finishing the year with an 8-0 win-loss record.

But of all his activities, John was best known and most remembered for photography. That last year, as in years past, he worked as the head photographer on the committee which produced *The Carolite*, the St. Charles yearbook. John, together with his team of men, had the responsibility for taking and assembling virtually all of the photos that were used in *The Carolite*. He loved the work and relished the responsibility.

James Dubell recalled how much John liked his photography, "not only just taking pictures, but even more so the developing of them. He liked working with the chemicals in the darkroom. I can still remember that stinky, smelly darkroom. He would spend hours and hours there. He really enjoyed that sort of thing."

John's official team in the photo lab consisted of fellow classmates Carl Wingate, Michael Choma, and several other men. John's friend from the Trenton diocese, James Roche, also worked on the yearbook as assistant editor.

John was a whiz at trick photography—double exposures, interesting angles, variations in lighting, delayed photography, superimposing one or more pictures onto another. He often thought up unusual shots. Carl Wingate assisted him in the darkroom, and John tried to instruct him in the fine art of developing prints.

Prior to his college years, John had practiced his photography on his family, who became his willing subjects. In fact, one of John's best loved photographs—the one he always kept on his desk wherever he went—was a beloved family portrait which he took in the backyard garden at home in Mount Holly one warm, pleasant day in 1956.

John had set the camera on a tripod and, using a delayed exposure, was able to get into the picture himself. Pictured were John's sister Maryann, his brother, Ed, Ed's fiancée Pat, and his mother and father. John is seated next to his grandmother, Mary Hogan.

John treasured the picture, because it was the last group portrait of his family before that difficult year when two of those he loved were suddenly gone. It was a reminder of happier days.

John wanted the class of '59 yearbook to be something special. In addition to the standard pictures and group shots, he decided he would also create an interesting montage of still life and portraits of seminarians, positioned in such as way as to appear that the men were part of the still life background. He had two themes for the background, academics and sports, and superimposed upon these would be full length pictures of his classmates. Thus, using trick photography and a lot of glue, a guy would appear to be leaning against a ruler, for example, or hanging off a basketball net, or carrying a pencil upon which another fellow sat, or reclining in a baseball mit, and so on.

John would decide which shots he wanted, and Carl would schedule the appointments for portraits of the various individuals, clubs, teams, and groups. "He'd say, 'Schedule this, schedule this, schedule this'," Wingate recalled, "and then he'd say, 'You be there.'" When the time came to take the picture, John would turn to his friend Winnie and say, "Well, get in it."

"He appreciated my making all the arrangements so he put me in the picture. So then everybody said, 'Wessel, you've got Wingate in all those pictures. He's all over the yearbook.' And he liked that, but he'd say, 'Oh, I couldn't keep him out.'"

That became one of their running jokes: John would say, in mock surprise, "Can't keep Wingate out of those pictures!" And Wingate would say, also in mock surprise, "How did I get in so many pictures?"

Wess and Winnie worked together on the academic and sports montages. They had to get all the people together and have them pose—this was Wingate's job—all the while trying to imagine the tennis nets and baseball bats that would be in the background.

"I had everybody stand," Wingate recalled, "then we took all the pictures. Then I had to cut them out with a razor blade. Then we glued them all in there." Painstakingly, each figure was glued onto the still life background, and when it was completed, the final pictures had to be taken. So realistic were the montages that one can actually see the "shadows" of the fellows as they appear to interact with and move against the still life background.

The end result was quite novel and creative, considering that this was the 1950s, way before modern artists started doing such avant-garde things.[6]

The head photographer also had to be on hand and ready for informal shots and athletic events. John was there to capture the activities, and also thought up the captions that went beneath the pictures. Most of the captions were wry and humorous, but among the most humorous were those that never made it into the yearbook. One picture taken at an athletic competition shows a group of men in gym shorts marching in formation, wearing strange-looking, pointy hats and carrying pennants—this was apparently some sort of solemn procession. John's pithy caption: "Don't we look like goons!"

But since John couldn't be in all places at once, he often would send his friend, Mike Choma, out to take pictures, sometimes with comical results.

"One day he sent me out," Choma recalled. "He wanted pictures of the baseball team, somebody sliding into home or first base or second or third base." John was looking for pictures of general baseball—pitching, hitting, catching, and so forth—one or two slides into a base, perhaps, but other things, too. But all Choma heard was that John wanted a slide, so Mike did just that.

"So I came back within a couple hours, and he developed the negatives. And it turned out, out of twenty-four pictures, there were twenty-four slides. They were all the same!" It wasn't exactly what John wanted. John raised a little Cain and immediately grabbed the camera and film and went out and got what he wanted. Choma just had to laugh.[7]

On a more serious note, each yearbook had a theme that ran throughout and tied it together as a cohesive element. John Wessel picked the theme of the *Carolite* that year—"The Cross." The cross of Christ, the cross of priestly life. It was a reflection of what was important to him in his own spirituality, where his heart was, so to speak.

Pictures of a wooden cross in three different seasons—autumn, winter, and spring—exemplified the theme throughout the yearbook. In John's photographs, the cross was life-sized, and apparently spattered in blood to simulate the wounds of Christ. A Roman centurion stands watch on the side of the cross in full military regalia, as if to suggest that Christ has just died and has been taken down from the cross; yet the soldier also appears to be awaiting His return.

Here too, the end result was quite impressive: three dreamy, reflective portraits of the cross in three seasons.

But what a joint project it was!

For the portraits of the cross, John Wessel and Carl Wingate recruited two of their fellow seminarians, Sam Lupico and John "Lexy" Morrisey. Together the four of them, John and Winnie and Sammy and Lexy, worked on the theme pictures during the year. Each man had something important to do.

Lexy had to get the wood. His father borrowed some wood from the Gas and Electric Company, so that Lexy and his friends could make the realistic, life-sized cross. It was easily eight or ten feet high. So concerned was John

Wessel for realism that they even tacked on a little wooden sign at the top inscribed, "Jesus of Nazareth, King of the Jews" in Latin, Greek, and Hebrew, just as Pontius Pilate had done almost two thousand years before.

Winnie had to get himself painted. John wanted the cross to look just right, so therefore, there had to be blood stains on the cross precisely where Christ's bleeding body would have lain. "I had to put paint on the back of my hands and feet," Wingate recalled, "and Wess said, 'Lay on this thing 'cause we have to make it real.' So all the red paint on that cross is my hand prints . . ."

They found a place in the woods on the grounds of St. Charles and set the huge cross upright in the ground.

Sammy had to dress up as a Roman centurion and stand there by the cross. He and the others went to a costume store in downtown Baltimore and rented a suit of armor. "Sammy was the only one it fit," as Wingate recalled—the costume store having a limited range of sizes—so the distinction fell to him. Sammy was small and skinny "and those little shin guards wouldn't go around anybody else's legs," said Wingate. But in costume, he looked every inch the imposing Roman centurion, in a soldier's tunic covered with a metal breastplate, metal shin guards and sandals, a regal cloak over his shoulders, a plumed helmet on his head, and a sword and spear in hand.

And John? Well, he took the pictures, of course.

"We did it in the winter," said Wingate. The autumn shot was no problem. To distinguish autumn from winter, they simply waited for a snowfall, and the sight of the snow-covered cross was beautiful and ethereal (although poor Sammy must have been freezing in his Roman sandals).

Spring posed a bit of a dilemma. There had to be the suggestion of new life and springtime in the photograph, but there were no flowering trees or bushes at the site where they'd planted the cross. It was too difficult to move it, and so for a while it appeared as though spring might end up looking a lot like autumn. That would never do!

An expedient solution presented itself. There were a great number of flowering dogwoods on the grounds of St. Charles, and as they began to sprout their delicate pink and white blossoms in early spring, they caught the attention of the photography crew. The men decided to cut down one of the dogwood trees, with the full knowledge that Father Chudzinski, the high school principal, who also had charge of the grounds, would have killed them for it. They then dug a hole behind the cross and stuck some of the purloined dogwood branches in it, making it look like a flowering tree in springtime. Some other flowering branches were placed around the cross and in the nearby woods. The overall effect was quite beautiful, even pious—but most important, spring-like.

Shortly before graduation, the yearbook came out. John Wessel received well-deserved accolades from his classmates for his photography. As was typical, he modestly deflected the compliments away from himself and onto the friends who helped him. Many of those who signed his yearbook nonetheless praised his photography.

The final results of John Wessel's photographic artistry and determination can still be seen in the 1959 *Carolite*: Three meditative photographs of the cross of Christ in different seasons perfectly exemplified the yearbook theme. In fact, it is hard to imagine how it could have been done any better.

Here is how the 1959 *Carolite* described their theme, "The Cross, The Seminarian." It provides a good summary of seminary life as well:

> The pictures of a cross that you see throughout this yearbook attempt to duplicate symbolically a scene that took place in Our Lord's life nineteen hundred years ago. The three pictures dramatize that scene on Golgotha when Christ offered His life on a cross. During His life, however, Our Lord carried another cross, the unseen one that He wants us to share. Now that we are graduating from St. Charles', we look back at the cross we carried in common as students here.
>
> One of the most fundamental elements in our life at St. Charles' is prayer. The cross that we all shared here was made up of faithfulness to Jesus the Savior. Spiritual guidance from our confessors often steadied us in this most important aspect of spiritual growth.
>
> Study presented a series of difficulties and formed, naturally, the heavy crosspiece in our community life. Constant application to our work was a daily task, but acquiring the right attitude towards our studies was itself a hard lesson to learn.
>
> The lighter side of school life undoubtedly came in recreation, but again the seminarian's cross lay just under the

surface. Charity was the byword on every playing field if we were to apply the lessons we learned in the spiritual field of action. These three aspects of our life at St. Charles' show the cross as we found it in common. Now our last year at St. Charles' has ended; and we are a little anxious about the future, the major seminary. We know that the life ahead of us will not become any easier, but with our training here we hope that soon we will readily take up the cross of a priestly life.[8]

In the end, it was such a beautiful and well-done endeavor that even Father Chudzinski probably would have approved and donated the dogwood tree himself.

John's last year at St. Charles had been an interesting one in the realm of world affairs. It was a year of many changes, possibly a foretaste of things to come.

In October of their fall semester, Pope Pius XII had died. Pius XII was remembered by the Church and the world for his emphasis on the celebration of the Mass and the Blessed Virgin Mary. John Wessel had a far more personal reason for remembering Pope Pius: He had met the frail, elderly Pontiff in Rome that previous summer. By month's end, a new Pope had been elected—Pope John XXIII. In January 1959, the new Pope had called for an Ecumenical Council, the first since 1870.

The new year brought other changes as well. Headlines captured the main events: "Revolutionary Fidel Castro's forces conquer Cuba"; "Soviets send rocket hurtling past the moon"; "Three rock and rollers die in small plane"; "Alaska becomes the 49th and largest state." Hawaii would not be far behind.[9]

Still, the outside world imposed little on seminary life. The seminarians had more immediate concerns—classes, studies, and grades. Soon it was spring, and time for the Easter holiday, the May Games and final examinations. The May Games were particularly satisfying that year. In the two-day track and field competitions, once again the Rhet team carried the day, and the class of '59 became the first class to win both the October and May Games for three consecutive years.

At long last, graduation day had arrived. After six years at St. Charles, it was on to the "major seminary"—St. Mary's School of Philosophy on North Paca Street in downtown Baltimore.

But before that happened, it was time for the annual tradition known as "Rhet Week," which was pure fun.

"That's when you felt like something was happening," said Wingate. "A week before the seminary closed, we didn't have to go to classes. All the other kids were sitting in study hall, and you were out playing tennis, handball, and softball. You could go downtown, and you could go to movies."

John Wessel and his friends did a lot that week. They played sports, went into town, hung out together. Although they were aware they would all see each other again next year at Paca Street, the young men also realized that it would never again be quite the same. As Wingate explained, "We kind of knew—it's the end of a cycle."

"So, near the end of Rhet Week, the tailor comes in from Baltimore and measures you," Wingate continued, "and you buy your cassocks and your collars, and your black suit, your black hat and your biretta [a square cap with three projections on top, worn by the clergy] . . . And so you bought all that stuff. So this was big time. Now you felt like you were becoming something . . ."

The feeling was justified because, as John and his classmates approached graduation, they were indeed becoming something.

The night before graduation, by long-standing tradition, the seminarians gathered together at the statue of Our Lady of Lourdes behind the chapel and sang hymns in honor of the Blessed Mother. It was a fitting way to thank the Mother of God for her heavenly intercession and protection over her future priests. After the hymns, the seminarians repaired to the chapel for evening Mass, the last they would celebrate together as a class at St. Charles.

At the completion of his time at St. Charles College, John ranked 36th in a class of 52, with a general average of 79.3 for his two college years.

The rector, Father John F. Linn, S.S., wrote of John Wessel:

> He has only average talent, but he is industrious and applies himself well. He worries over his work, and this tends to discourage him. He is a likeable and cheerful character who gives good promise as a candidate for the priesthood. . . . Mr. Wessel is recommended for the major seminary.[10]

"We had good teams, good spirit, good unity," recalled Carl Wingate about his St. Charles class. The class of '59 worked hard, played hard, and won more athletic events than any team in recent memory. When they left, Father Linn told them, with just a hint of admiration, "You broke more rules than anybody!"

From their early beginnings as an assortment of apprehensive, homesick young boys, they had become at the end of six years, through the wisdom and guidance of the Sulpician Fathers, a cohesive and unified group of mature, devout and dedicated men, ready to be Christ's witnesses—martyrs in the truest sense.

CHAPTER 14

LAST OF THE MOHICANS

No understanding of John Wessel would be complete without mention of the annual canoe-and-camping trips. This yearly tradition began just after John finished high school and continued well into his years at the major seminary, and beyond.[1]

One fine spring day in the minor seminary, John leaned over to Wingate, who sat across from him in class, and said, "Hey, Winnie. Remember all that fun we had with the canoe?"

"Yeah?" Wingate looked at him dubiously. He wasn't that thrilled with the canoe, but he knew John liked it.

"Let's go up to Lake George."

John got out a map and showed it to his friend. He explained that Lake George was the northern New York lake made famous in *The Last of the Mohicans* (the second of James Fenimore Cooper's classic novels called *Leather-Stocking Tales*). Lake George had also figured prominently in early American history: Battles were fought along its shores in both the French and Indian War and the Revolutionary War. John had mapped out a nine-day canoe trip along the 36-mile lake.

"You want to go canoeing? Let's go up and canoe Lake George!" John said, with unbridled enthusiasm.

Carl Wingate recalled that he and John did have a lot of fun learning how to paddle a canoe during the summer in Medford Lakes. Thanks to John, Wingate felt pretty comfortable in a canoe—but again, he began to wonder if John hadn't been setting him up for something big all along.

But he and John were good friends. They did things together. "He did a lot of things for me," Wingate thought, and so he agreed for his friend's sake.

"All right," he said, "I'll talk to my parents."

Carl Wingate's parents liked the Wessels, whom they had met on numerous visiting Sundays at St. Charles. The Wingates gave their blessing for their son to go on the canoe trip. They knew that "it was probably all right if I was doing something with the Wessels."

"When I think back now, we were crazy" to do it, Wingate reflected, "but you know, it was just an adventure to him." John had read all the books on American history and Fort Ticonderoga, which was up around there, and he wanted to go see it. As Wingate wryly put it, they had to be Hawkeye and Chingachgook "and sail or paddle our way up and have the same adventure."

John was elated when Winnie agreed to the trip. "We need a couple of other guys," he said. "Who do you think would go?"

Eventually, they recruited two fellow classmates from the seminary, Mike Choma and Mike Mueller, also rugged outdoorsmen. "I picked two guys who would be the same type, so we usually ended up with four," Wingate explained, "because you need two canoes, really, to carry all the stuff. So we went, and the first time was kind of fun."

Interestingly, the other fellows thought that Carl Wingate had initiated these trips. He was perceived as the organizer because, of the two, John was not the dominant personality. Carl was the more extroverted.[2] But it was actually John Wessel who was the idea man and Carl Wingate who helped him carry it out. The two friends made a good team in that way, each balancing the other's individual strengths and weaknesses.

As best as can be recalled, John Wessel, Carl Wingate, Mike Choma and Mike Mueller went on that first canoe trip to Lake George during the summer of 1958.

The camping trips were "therapeutic" for John, said his sister. In the seminary, the young men had no luxuries. Their fun was the outdoors and sports and camaraderie with each other. Why did John choose Lake

George? Perhaps a reason can be found in the fact that Lake George was one of the last places that the Wessels visited as a family in the summer of 1956—Father, Mother and Maryann—but for some reason, John did not go with them.[3]

The first Lake George canoe trip occurred the year after John's father passed away, and after the family's summer home at Medford Lakes had been sold. Was the camping trip a way to ease his grief at his father's death? Or to test his own endurance? Or to recapture the outdoors life he enjoyed every summer at the Lakes? All these factors could have played a part, but more probably "he just loved the outdoors and he wanted to do something to get away from studies," said Maryann.[4]

Lake George in northeastern New York is a popular summer vacation spot. The lake is 36 miles long and from one to three miles wide, and empties into Lake Champlain, which lies to the north on the New York-Vermont border and stretches into Canada.[5]

The men rented canoes in New Jersey, loaded them onto two cars and drove up to northern New York. John had everything organized—food, menu, equipment, pup tents, first aid kit. John was "a make-do guy" in the words of a friend:

> Not alone, but certainly, without him it wouldn't have happened. And he just made guys fall into line, and made plans and [took care of] the details. Somebody had to do grocery shopping. Well, John didn't delegate. He just said, "Whaddaya like?" and we went and bought beef stew in a can. We liked to eat beef stew and canned spaghetti and all kinds of other delights. But he would make it happen.[6]

At their starting point at the northernmost part of the lake, they put the canoes in the water, unloaded all the gear, and set up camp for the night. Then, taking two cars, a couple of men drove down to the southern tip of the lake. After dropping a car off to pick them up at the end of the journey, they drove back up again in one car to rejoin the others at the camp site.

It was a great experience for the men. Each morning they would break camp, load their gear into the canoes and paddle until evening. At night, they would set up camp again, John having calculated how much distance they could expect to cover in a day.

Food was primitive, mostly canned goods heated over a campfire, and plenty of jugs of fresh water, although Lake George was so clean and crystal clear they could drink the water right out of the lake.[7] They'd say grace at meals, and a prayer every day, but mostly it was a social adventure. The men enjoyed each other's company and the natural beauty of the countryside.

There in the wilderness, surrounded by the incredible beauty of God's creation, John's thoughts may have hearkened back to his boyhood days paddling around Medford Lakes, or perhaps to the Umbrian hills of Italy, to the very places where he had roamed about in the footsteps of Saint Francis.

It was not just that John was able to see God in His creation. It was more than that. Just like Saint Francis, John experienced a special closeness with God when he was close to nature.

To Mike Mueller, "the trip to Lake George was one of the defining moments in my life—having just finished seminary high school, being on a camping trip with some friends. It was a bonding experience, I guess, when I look back on it," he explained, although "I certainly didn't think of it as that at the time. It was just another good thing to do with some good friends."

Several other summer canoe trips followed. Usually around the spring of each year, John would get out the map and start looking at it. Before long, he'd say to Wingate, "Well, *this* year, why don't we go to . . ."

Each summer John thought up a different and more challenging trip. In 1959, they canoed the Fulton Chain of the beautiful Finger Lakes in northwestern New York. In 1960, they canoed Moosehead Lake, the largest lake in Maine. They subsequently returned to Lake George once more.

After that, John became interested in white water canoeing on the rivers of Maine: The East Branch of the Penobscot River and the West Branch of the Allagash River became the subject of future expeditions. "Then, he gets into shooting rapids up in Baxter State Park—which wasn't even on the map!" exclaimed Wingate.

Baxter State Park was nearly two hundred thousand acres of virgin forest land in Maine, abounding with moose, deer, and other wild animals. A number of rivers and lakes ran through it. They weren't actually in the park, but nearby, on private land owned by a lumber company which allowed canoers access to it.[8] "It was a big empty spot. They hadn't even surveyed it yet," Wingate recalled. "But that was John's sense of adventure."

Some of the participants switched around on these camping trips. Carl Wingate and Mike Choma went on every single one. Mike Mueller went on the first three, but lost touch with John after college. Classmate James Roche, his younger brother Bill, and Mike Choma's younger brother Dick, also joined them on several of the trips. John's brother-in-law Bill Beitel went on the trip to the Allagash one summer. Usually, there were at least four men but sometimes seven or eight.

John was always looking for new recruits to join in the outdoors adventure. He took dozens of pictures on all the camping trips, Wingate recalled, and had them made into a set of slides. "I remember one time in the seminary, trying to drum up business one night when we had a free night. He did a slide show to try and get other guys interested in this, but I don't think we ever got any takers. They enjoyed seeing them, but they said, no way were they going to go!"

For those who went, however, the summer canoe trips were occasions for excitement and adventure.

Carl Wingate related the following story about the first Lake George trip:

"One time we went up the lake, and John and I were in an aluminum canoe, and Mike Mueller and Mike Choma—it was just the four of us that time—were in wood. And we left upper Lake George . . . They took off! Well, you know, wood floats, so you'd take a stroke and you go ten feet. Aluminum, you take a stroke, you go two feet."[9]

"Well, they were way ahead of us down the lake. And I said, 'John, this is ridiculous. We're never going to catch them or keep up with them.' So I said, 'Let's pull over and think this over.' So we pulled over. And then we cut down a couple little trees and made a mast, and we took the tent and made a sail."

The men had a small transistor radio and listened to the broadcast of the weather forecast as they made camp for the night. "I remember the news was in French, because it came from Canada up there, and we both had studied French. And it said the winds were going to be coming down the lake" from north to south, Wingate recalled. "I said, 'John, we can catch this wind tomorrow and just fly down this lake!'" The next morning, the two men put into action their plan to catch up with the two others in the wooden canoe.

"Well, they were way down there—this little teeny speck—and all of a sudden we came flying down the lake right past them! They couldn't believe it! We put sticks across like a catamaran from our canoe to theirs so we wouldn't blow over, and they put up a sail. And gee, what took us four or five days to paddle, we came down in four or five hours or something!"

Along the way, they passed a paddle-wheeled steamboat that took tourists up the lake "and they were all running over taking pictures of us coming back." The tourists had never seen anything like a makeshift catamaran made out of two canoes, some saplings and a pup tent. "We were like the big attraction on the lake!"

The Moosehead Lake trip in 1960 was another memorable adventure.

There were five men on that trip. They got out on Moosehead Lake, and "the lake was like an ocean. We never realized how big it really was," said Mike Choma. They had their campsite set up, but had decided to paddle out to an island. "But we got out on the lake and we were sailing, and the wind came up and just blew us across the lake, so we were sort of marooned" on an island in the middle of Moosehead Lake "for about two or three days."[10] When the men finally returned to their warm and well-stocked campsite, they were so starved that they couldn't be bothered with the niceties of setting up, starting a fire and cooking food.

"That lake is big!" John Wessel later told James Roche about being stranded on the island. "It turns into an ocean. You wouldn't believe it but we could not get back. And when we got back to camp, we were so hungry, I remember we just opened jars of peanut butter and jelly. One guy grabbed a jar of peanut butter, one guy grabbed a jar of jelly, and we just stuck spoons in it and were jamming peanut butter and jelly down our faces."[11]

The group had canoed about halfway down the huge lake when they came to what looked like a high cliff or mountain. (Perhaps it was Mount Kineo, 1,958 feet high, in the middle of Moosehead Lake.) They stopped for the day and set up camp, and John decided that he wanted to climb to the top of the mountain, so they did.

"That was John," Wingate recalled. "If there's a mountain there, he's going to go up and see what it looks like from the top."

"Everything John did had to have a goal," Choma confirmed. If there was a river, he wanted to shoot it, or a mountain, he wanted to climb it. "It was the challenge. If somebody said, you couldn't do it, we did it."

The view from the mountaintop was breathtaking.

Returning to the canoes, they paddled on further and came to the southerly tip of Moosehead Lake, where once again they set up camp for the night. They were on the outskirts of a little town called Greenville.

"There was a dance in town, a street dance," Wingate recounted. "Well, we had real strict rules" in the seminary. "When we left in the summer, you couldn't get near girls, or even work a job where a lot of girls were working, so they really read us the riot act."

"Well, we get up there—it was Mike Mueller . . . Mike Choma, Dick Choma, Wessel and myself. I don't remember if there was anybody else. I think it was just the five of us. But I said to Wess, 'Let's go into town for this dance.'"

"And so he and I slept in the same tent. So, everybody got to sleep. Well, we sneaked out of the tent and we get in the canoe and we paddle across the lake to some railroad tracks, because we knew they went to town. We wouldn't be able to paddle in at night. So we walked those tracks and went all the way into town. Then we got at the dance, and it was a small town. I forget what day it was—some big holiday up there—but they had the streets marked off and it was just a big street festival!"

There were a few hundred people at the street festival, parents, grandparents, kids. The whole town must have turned out for the dance. The townsfolk were friendly, and welcomed the two out-of-town campers. A number of young ladies were especially interested in the handsome strangers.

"We had a good time, and John said, 'Should we dance? Is it a serious sin?'

"I said, 'John, just dance! I mean, it's with somebody we don't even know. We're just street dancing.' I think we danced twice. I don't know if John ever danced in his life, but he asked this girl, or the girl asked him, and it was hilarious to watch them go down the street!"

"Anyway, after it was over, we had to walk back" to camp. "We got back at three or four in the morning. John always felt bad about that. Then we went to town, and all these girls would see John and me that we had met at the dance. We talked a lot, and spent a lot of time socializing. And the other guys were with us, and we're walking down the street, and these girls are saying, 'Hi, John!' 'Hi, Carl!' And these guys are going, 'How do they know your name?'

"I said, 'I don't know. Maybe they think we're somebody they know.'"

"And then we went to Mass, and all these girls were waiting for us after Mass to say hello!"

Wingate always remembered that incident, not only because they had such a great time at the street dance, but because John was so worried that the other guys would somehow find out about their escapade, and the two of them would be thrown out of the seminary.

A number of hilarious moments fondly recalled by the participants on these camping trips centered around food.[12]

One favorite "funny food story" was of an eggs-and-pine needles breakfast on the Moosehead Lake trip.

Their menu was very basic, but every now and then, they'd have eggs for breakfast as a special treat. "We walked down the railroad tracks and we went into town and got these eggs, because we'd been eating peanut butter and jelly, and Spam, and that kind of stuff," recalled Carl Wingate. Each of the men had their allotted number of eggs, and they were cooking them over the fire in those little metal fold-up cups that come in camping kits. "One of the guys—I think it was Wessel but can't swear to it—had his eggs in the cup, and we were all just cooking them and eating them. And whoever it was, was going to really relish this and was making a big deal out of it." He wanted to cherish this special moment and make the most of it, waving his egg cup around with a great flourish. "And messing around, his cup fell over and he saw the eggs hit the pine needles" on the ground.

"And it looked like the pine needles just sucked 'em up!" The prized soft-boiled eggs lay there on the pine needles for a moment before oozing down through the prickly needles. In an instant, the eggs had disappeared into the pine needles. "And we started laughing, because if he would've done it quick and eaten it, he would've had his eggs."

Another time, the men were intent on having fish for breakfast. "We were catching bass and had a whole stringer full of them. We were going to have fresh fish for breakfast, so we left them on the string [in the water]. We caught them in the evening before—they bite best in the evening—and we were going to get up in the morning and have fresh fish," recalled Wingate.

The next morning "we went down and pulled the stringer out, and the heads were there but everything was gone!" Raccoons had come in the night and "ate all the fish—the good parts. They left the parts we didn't want to eat!"

But the canoe trips were far more than pure fun. They were also arduous and occasionally dangerous. They challenged a man's endurance, resourcefulness, intelligence and survival skills.

Once on the Moosehead Lake trip, the men almost burnt a forest down. They had been camping in a pine forest, and their campfire was a pit that had been burning for two or three days. While trying to extinguish the fire as they broke camp, they found that it had spread underground.

"When we went to put the fire out, we sort of dug around the pit and smoke came up where the shovel went in," Mike Choma recalled. "So we dug a little further, and smoke came up there. The farther we got away, there was still more smoke coming up." The tree roots had caught fire and were smoldering underneath the ground. "So we began digging all the way around. We dug a twenty-foot diameter circle, hitting all the roots, till we got it all out."

On another occasion, it got dark out on Lake George, and so they went on the mainland and made camp. "They told you not to because of bears," said Wingate. Bears inhabited the mainland, not the islands, around Lake George. But it was dark and they were tired.

The men took precautions. They wrapped up their food provisions in a sack of netting, tied it up with a rope, flung it over a tree branch, and tied the rope at the other end to a peg about ten feet high so bears couldn't reach it. Next, they buried their garbage and empty food containers so the scent of food wouldn't attract wild animals. Carl Wingate picked up the story:

> Wess had a .22 rifle, I think, that we always took. And so we all were going to take turns watching in case the bear came and started bothering people. So we were sleeping.
>
> . . . I don't know whose watch it was . . . I think Wess was up, because I went to sleep. He might've had the .22. Lot of good that would've done! But anyway, we woke up the next morning and . . . there were bear prints all over the ground! I can't remember if it tore open that sack—I don't think it did, but you could see bear prints underneath it—but it had dug up the garbage pit and just crunched those cans that we threw away. Now, they had honey and jam and stuff in 'em, and the bear cleaned all that out and left. But the poor bear must've been stepping over us, walking around there. It's a good thing

that we were asleep, because if we'd have shot at that thing with a .22, that's even worse off than being asleep!

John Wessel was a great navigator. As seminary friend and fellow camper Mike Mueller noted:

> John was the kind of guy you would not want to go on a canoe trip without, because of his reliability and his good sense, his good judgment. I am a sailor at this point, and I still cherish those characteristics in a lot of my crew people . . . stamina, good judgment and reliability. And that certainly describes John in many ways.

"He was the navigator," Wingate said of John, "and he had the map, and he'd say, 'Well, we're gonna be here.'" John would calculate the distance to their next campsite, and usually it turned out fine. But occasionally, John would miscalculate the distance they would be able to travel on the water.

"Well, one night, it got a little spooky," Wingate recounted, "because we were supposed to be somewhere while it was daylight, and we weren't anywhere near there—and it's pitch black!" The men were portaging between lakes on the Fulton Chain trip, walking along a tiny stream in the mud, carrying the canoes and equipment because the water was so shallow, only about four inches deep.

"I remember we saw a porcupine. We all froze. He looked at us and we looked at him, and he just kept going," said Wingate.

Finally, they hit deeper water, which enabled them to sit in the canoe and row. It was still pitch black, but they were in a swamp and couldn't stop anyplace to camp. "So we just kept figuring we were going to get to the lake soon. And it kept getting darker."

"I'm sitting on the front," Wingate continued, "and John's paddling guide, and he said, 'Now, if you hear anything, let me know.' Well, I can hear water, and it sounds like it's going over a fall. I said, 'John, I think something's up ahead there that I don't want to go over in the dark!' And he goes, 'Well, listen to it. How does it sound?'"

The sound of rushing water seemed to be getting louder and closer. "I said, 'It sounds pretty far down.' And he said, 'Okay.'"

Suddenly, their canoe was jolted by a thud. They hit a beaver dam in the river which, in the dark, they could barely see. "Then we weren't sure how deep it was between the beaver dam and the water that continued on the other side. So we climbed out on the beaver dam and started dropping rocks, and trying to remember the physics—how fast the sound travels per second to figure out how far down it was."

John had read books that told him how to calculate the distance by the number of seconds it took for the sound to bounce back. He was really into it, recalled Wingate.

Carl was not inclined to wait for this method to work. "I said, 'I'm walking around and going down and seeing where this is.' Well, it was about nine feet"—straight down. They had to take everything out of the canoes. Stumbling around in the dark, and covered with mosquito bites, the men carried their canoes and supplies down the nine-foot drop and got back into the water again. They started out onto a lake.

"Then we got out on this lake, but we didn't have any light, and these boats are out . . . speeding around!" Wingate continued. "Well, you know, we're sitting out there in the pitch dark! . . . They could have cut us in half!" The men were afraid that without a lantern they just looked like another floating log on the lake and somebody might hit them. "So that was a little spooky. But we'd scream and yell and go 'nutso' if a boat came anywhere near us," said Wingate.

The men quickly got off the water and headed to the first island they found to spend the night.[13]

Canoeing on the rivers of Maine, full of rapids, was as exciting as it was strenuous, recalled Bill Beitel. John and Bill had done some camping together over the years. So when John invited his brother-in-law to come along on the annual canoe trip to the Allagash one year, Bill eagerly took a week's vacation and went up with John and his friends to Maine.[14]

"It's a thing you do once in your life unless you're in the business of doing it" because it really was a lot of work, Beitel recalled. But it was also "a very wonderful thing to do."

> We would ride the river each day, but there were no signs of people. We didn't see a human the whole time. We heard people lumbering with chain saws up on the mountain, but we didn't see a soul. Never passed a soul for all that time—which is unusual today.

> We were in the wilderness, and if we'd had a problem of any
> kind, there was nothing we could do but continue on, so it was
> kind of challenging. We had a first aid kit, but it was humble.
> We never thought who would break an arm or a leg or anything
> like that . . . We were too young to worry about that!

The men were miles from nowhere. Anything could have happened. The woods were populated with bears, wild animals, snakes, poisonous plants. They easily could have become injured or sick, or suffered some emergency. But John had great faith. "God will take care of us," he would always say. And somehow they always were taken care of.

Riding the rapids was both exhilarating and dangerous. Frequently, the canoes were upset, and men and supplies went tumbling into the white water rapids. Tossed into the rushing, pounding water and sharp, jutting rocks, there was always the possibility of serious injury or drowning.

The West Branch of the Allagash was full of rapids. So naturally, John loved it. "We sank, and our sleeping bags and paddles would be floating down the river," Wingate recalled. "And then you had to try and get down and find all this stuff because you can't do anything in a canoe without a paddle."

Everyone got their turn to be thrown overboard. Wingate would get sick of it after a while, as the canoe capsized yet again, but it did not bother John. "To him, this was fun. This was adventure. This was the real thing. This isn't paddling around Medford Lakes! This is just like the pioneers, and that was his thing. He loved all that stuff!"

"We were upset a couple of times" in the white water rapids, Beitel also recalled. "Near the end of the trip, we lost a lot of things, especially food, so we had one more day to come out or be really hungry. We found cans of things, so we salvaged enough to get through the next day."

But they came closest by far to a near tragedy on the trip to the East Branch of the Penobscot in 1963, when John Wessel and James Roche nearly drowned. Several other campers came along that year, including Roche's younger brother, Bill, about fourteen. John was very solicitous of the youth and took him under his wing, Roche recalled.

James Roche picked up the story of their close call:

> Wess and I were canoe mates on that one. We just had a
> very good time. It was just a good "let your hair down from the

studies in the seminary" time and get out there and just not shave, relax and be with people who were doing exactly the same thing as yourself, just relaxing . . . But in that moment of rugged, male stuff, we hit the last day of the trip, I remember, because we were coming up on the town of Millinocket where we were going to stop and get out of the river and go home. John and I were in the first canoe as we parked and looked at this section of the river. It was a real drop that you just don't see in a river, but there was enough of a straight line view to see how it just dropped away. So there was a very rapid section, and we were just overconfident and kind of feeling this experience.

Now, we knew the river and we knew how to canoe . . . but didn't take normal precautions, and the end result was that we almost drowned. We lost three-quarters of the gear that we had in the canoe and we almost lost the canoe as well. But the bad thing was the drowning part . . .

They had come to a place called Grindstone Falls. John and Jim were in an aluminum canoe. Mike and Dick Choma were in canvas. Carl Wingate and Jim's younger brother, Bill, were with them, too.

Grindstone Falls was so long that you couldn't see the end of it. "Our habit had been whenever we came to a set of rapids, we would walk down beside it, study it and figure out which way we would go and then shoot it. But when we got to Grindstone, it was near the end of the trip, and the river was very wide at that point and they just didn't want to take the time to walk down and look it over," Mike Choma recalled. Also, a couple of canoers came by who had just shot the falls. There was nothing but high pitches down there, but it was fine, they said.

John Wessel said to Mike Choma, "Jimmy and I are going to do it. What do you suggest?" And Choma said, "Well, I would suggest go straight down the middle. If you run into trouble, you can go left or right."

So John and Jim took off. "We got out there on the river and it became very treacherous, and we had a very heavy canoe, full of gear plus ourselves," recalled James Roche.

The others waited and watched to see how they did. The agreement was that if they made it, then the other men would come down also. "And

I had my little brother, thankfully, in the other canoe back with the other guys," said Roche, who continued:

> We came down the river and the canoe filled up with water. We both got knocked out at different times . . . and so we were hanging on and trying to get some of the water out, hold on to some of the equipment, get back in, get the canoe off of a rock or two or three. I was just amazed at all of it because the force of the river was very impressive once you get out there in it, and the rocks were enormous.

From his vantage point high up on the riverbank, Mike Choma recalled what happened next. "They got part way down, and the front of the canoe would go up in the air straight up, and you couldn't see the guy in the back. And then it would go straight down and you couldn't see the guy in front. You just saw the guy in back . . . and then, they turned broadside." Mike and his brother Dick just turned and looked at each other, incredulous, and said, "They better turn, point downstream again, 'cause they're going to hit a boulder."

But John and Jim stayed broadside too long. "They're in trouble," Mike said as he watched them struggle.

All of a sudden, John and Jim's canoe slammed broadside into a boulder. The force of the impact bent the canoe into a horseshoe. Mike and Dick began to paddle down the side of the river until they got to them. "It took us about an hour or so to get down there and it was very rough. The pitches were about ten feet high," Mike recalled.

Somehow, John and Jim got themselves loose from the rocks and boulders in the middle of the river. They were too far out for anyone to even toss them a rope and pull them to shore. They headed the canoe toward the opposite shore and began paddling. And just as it "finally looked like we were getting free of the worst of it," said Roche, the canoe capsized, nearly drowning the men.

James Roche continued:

> This time I was in the back, because we had switched places at least once or twice in the course of this long moment.

John was in the front, and we were paddling like crazy to get to the . . . other side of the river, which was a very broad section. The canoe was full of water and some equipment, and we're paddling just to make it over there. And the boat became a submarine—just went under. But we were paddling and with the force of the river's current also, as the canoe went down, the lashing rope at the end of the canoe wrapped itself around my leg, right up high around the thigh. The canoe weighed a ton. It was full of water and going down to the bottom. Not too deep a bottom but deep enough. And I thought to myself, 'This is how you drown.' I remember having that very calm thought as I went underwater.

And then the thing just ripped off. I was still almost like paddling in a slow motion type of moment in my mind, and then I popped up to the surface . . . We got the canoe back. I don't know how we did it, but we got it back up and then we got over to the side.

Most of the gear was gone. There were a few items floating in a small calm section on the side of the river. John and Jim had one paddle between them now and were trying to maneuver the canoe with it, but not doing too well, in the calm section at the side of the river. Jim was now in the front of the canoe again.

I remember coming under a log, and overhead was a hanging branch and it knocked me down in the canoe. So I got up again but I was all right . . . and I said, "Watch out for that branch!" and I tried to push it aside with the paddle. And it's much bigger than me and it pushed me back into the canoe, so I got back up and I was now under it. John hit it, and I felt this tug on the canoe, but I was more intent on finding gear before it sank. And I looked back and here I had lost John! He was hanging on the branch, out of the canoe. It was a humorous moment following on a very scary moment.

Roche pulled the canoe around and came back to retrieve John, who was stuck in the tree branch, hanging over the water. From their close encounter, the two men managed to save the canoe and themselves and several pieces of gear and equipment. They got whatever they could find back in their canoe, jumped on it somewhat to straighten it out, and started to go down the opposite side to a point where they could come across, rejoin with the others, and continue on the way down.

Said Mike Choma, "The canoe looked as if somebody had taken a cannonball and hit it all over the place. It wasn't broken, but it had been bent right at the keel, just like a horseshoe." All Jim Roche could say was, "Holy smokes! I was glad my little brother was not in the canoe with me. That would have been the worst."[15]

Eventually, the men took more precautions while riding the white water rapids. "We tied ropes around the guys in case we lost them, we could pull them out of the water," Wingate recalled.

John, when he wasn't riding the rapids, would be busy taking snapshots or motion pictures of it for posterity.

A wonderful photograph captured John Wessel and James Roche shooting the rapids of the Penobscot on the last trip the seminarians took together in 1964, the year before graduation and ordination.

"We had done our stint of coming down river for one day of the week trip and we had come through this rapids section," said James Roche, recalling how the photo came about. After they got through it, someone said, "We ought to run it again and take pictures of ourselves running it." So John said, "Come on, Rochie. We're gonna do it!"

Jim was reluctant. This is playing with fire for no good reason, he thought. We've come through it well and it wasn't a snap. But John prevailed. "So we got in the canoe. He was the better canoeist and stronger physically . . . so he got the back. That's the key position in the canoe. And what you see in that picture is me getting ready to say, 'Oh, my God!'"

"We tipped over seconds later."

But not before they snapped a memorable picture.[16]

*   *   *

All too soon, the adventures would be over, and it was back to civilization. The men would load up the cars and return to New Jersey, physically tired, but inwardly refreshed and invigorated.

The last thing to do was to return the rented canoes. Wingate recalled an amusing story after one of the trips to Maine:

We'd rent these canoes in New Jersey, at Medford Lakes, because the guy knew John. Then we would throw them on top of our cars and go to Maine and shoot rapids. This guy thinks we're going to paddle around a lake! Took us a whole day with a rubber mallet to bang out all the dents and make those canoes look like canoes again.

We brought them back to the guy and he said, "My God! What did you guys do?"

John said, "Oh, we went to Maine."

He said, "You rented the canoes for a week in New Jersey and took them to *Maine*!!"

"Well," John replied, in all innocence, "you didn't say we couldn't take them anywhere."

CHAPTER 15

ST. MARY'S, PACA STREET

St. Mary's Seminary, School of Philosophy, was situated on North Paca Street in the heart of Baltimore. It was there at "old" St. Mary's that John Wessel completed his last two years of college, majoring in philosophy. By all accounts, John's years at Paca Street, from September of 1959 to June 1961, were among the happiest of his life.[1]

By that time, St. Mary's Seminary had progressed far beyond its humble beginnings in 1791 in the former One Mile Tavern, where "one room of the inn was used as a chapel. Later a small brick chapel was built known as *La Petite Chapelle*."[2]

Enrollment in the seminary for training for the priesthood was small at first. To help boost seminary enrollment, the Sulpicians founded and staffed St. Mary's College, the first college chartered in the State of Maryland, in 1799. St. Mary's College opened its doors to Americans of all creeds in 1803, and was accorded the rank of university in 1805. The University and Seminary thus were conjoined.[3]

The college's first president, Father William DuBourg, later became Bishop of New Orleans. "He built St. Mary's chapel, and added buildings to the campus which were in use until the 1890s."[4]

St. Mary's College soon became "a victim of its own success." Increased attention to non-clerical students and liberal arts subjects only served to divert the resources of the seminary and the faculty from their primary mission of preparing candidates for the priesthood. In 1850, St. Mary's College was closed. The Sulpicians' Superior General ordered that its members in America "withdraw from any activities not directly associated with seminary education."[5] The secular influence thus removed, the Suplicians were free to get on with the business of training priests.

> Even though St. Mary's became more monastic in character during this period, the seminary continued to expand. A cornerstone for a new building was laid in 1876. Until then, most of the seminary had faced Pennsylvania Avenue. The new site would soon become St. Mary's second name: Paca Street.[6]

In 1929, the seminary expanded to a new campus when the Theology department moved north to a large tract on Roland Avenue.

The original Paca Street seminary, once a mile outside the city, was now in the central business district of Baltimore, and continued to be the locus of the Philosophy department.[7]

The seminary John Wessel attended was located at 600 North Paca Street in what was at that time a poor neighborhood adjacent to the bustling Baltimore business district. It was reached by traveling along Franklin Street, a main thoroughfare, and turning right for a short distance on North Paca. A long, high brick wall on the left side of the street informs that one has reached the seminary grounds, yet simultaneously serves to enclose the seminary grounds from the rest of the neighborhood, whose poor residents crowded into narrow brick row houses along quaint and colonial-looking Paca Street.

A visitor once described it thus:

> The great walled yard . . . was not trimmed to a nicety; that would have been to destroy its serene and natural air. There was room for a baseball diamond, also courts for tennis and basket-ball. The plot is of an irregular shape, providing unexpected corners here and there. At one end is the convent for the sisters who keep house for the seminary, with a little hidden flower garden, the prettiest thing imaginable. Here also stands the house of Mother Seton . . . The house, which dates from about 1808, though small, has a spacious air with its graceful stairway and well-proportioned rooms. . . .
>
> The most secluded corner of the plot is also the noisiest, for it lies behind the wall at the point where the Paca Street trolley-

cars turn into Druid Hill Avenue. This is the burial ground where
the priests of the seminary lie in peace, though not in quiet. One
or two laymen have found a sanctuary here also.[8]

The antiquated seminary building dated back to the time the French
Sulpicians had arrived and settled there almost two hundred years ago.

Today, that area of Paca Street appears refurbished and charming. At
the time John Wessel studied there, however, it was recalled as being one of
the worst areas of the city—panhandlers and derelicts were always present
on the streets around the seminary.

A different world, a city within a city, awaited on the other side of the
wall.

Because of its smaller size, more intimate atmosphere, and obvious
historical roots in the old inner city, the seminary could be described as
homey by comparison to the large, imposing campus at Catonsville.

Most Paca Street alumni will attest that there was progressively more
freedom and privacy at the major seminary. "I think it was a little freer than
St. Charles because by that time you were able to have two in a room,"
rather than sixty other guys, recalled Monsignor Eugene Rebeck. "You were
able to study in your room rather than in the study hall of St. Charles." Not
that the seminarians were free to come and go as they pleased, but within
the whole system "there seemed to be a little bit of letting go."[9]

The focal point of John's spiritual life was the beautiful and dignified
Chapel of the Presentation of the Virgin Mary in the Temple, ensconced
behind seminary walls. The interior of the chapel, which represents the
first neo-Gothic ecclesiastical building in America, was lean, classical and
austere, in stark contrast with the ornate late Italian Renaissance style chapel
of the minor seminary.[10]

On the facade of the simple red brick chapel, above the main entrance,
a chiseled legend from the prophet Habakkuk proclaimed: "The Lord is in
his Holy Temple. Let all the Earth keep Silence before him."

The chapel had a long and distinguished history, and figured
prominently in the life of St. Elizabeth Ann Bayley Seton, a widowed mother
of five children and a convert to Catholicism, who founded the Daughters
of Charity and was canonized a saint in 1975.[11]

Archbishop John Carroll dedicated the chapel on the Feast
of Corpus Christi, June 16, 1808. Just as the mass began, Mrs.

> Elizabeth A. Seton and her three daughters . . . arrived at St.
> Mary's Chapel after a seven day voyage from New York, having
> landed in Fell's Point the night before. She had been urged by
> Archbishop Carroll and . . . [Father] DuBourg . . . to come to
> Baltimore and establish a Catholic school for girls. After the
> mass, Mrs. Seton went to inspect the new house which was to
> be her home for one very important year.[12]

On March 25, 1809, the Feast of the Annunciation of Our Lady, a "momentous event" took place in the newly blessed chapel. Elizabeth Ann Seton privately took her first vows of chastity, poverty, and obedience, binding for one year, before Archbishop Carroll. The Archbishop conferred the title of "Mother" upon her and granted her permission to receive Communion daily.

Four young ladies, who were to form the nucleus of the Sisters of Charity of Saint Joseph's (later uniting with the Daughters of Charity), also took their vows in the lower chapel.[13]

The chapel was used by Mother Seton as a school until June of 1809, when she and her fledgling community of Sisters moved to Emmitsburg, Maryland.

While living in Baltimore, the Chapel of the Presentation was the focal point of Mother Seton's daily life, as for successive generations of seminarians. The future Saint once referred to it as "the most elegant chapel in America open from daylight till nine at night."[14]

The Chapel of the Presentation thus boasts an interesting spiritual and historical heritage: Three of the most important religious communities for women trace their roots back to this little chapel. In addition to Mother Seton's Daughters of Charity, the chapel was instrumental in the founding of the Oblate Sisters of Providence and the Sisters, Servants of the Immaculate Heart of Mary.[15]

Because of John Wessel's love for history, he may well have found a special joy in living in the place that sheltered the first French Sulpicians when they arrived in America, and later served as home to Mother Seton over a century ago as she took her first religious vows and prepared for her vocation of teaching young Catholic girls.

It was at Paca Street that the seminarians first began to dress in the clerical garb of priests. From then on, the long black cassock and Roman collar were worn at all times—to class, to meals, to the chapel—the only exception being for engaging in athletics.

Sulpician archivist Father John W. Bowen, S.S., wrote, "The students' version of the rule specified that the cassock was the first thing to go on in the morning and the last thing to be taken off at night; how this was accomplished was never very clear."[16]

On the street the dress code consisted of a black suit with Roman collar and a black hat, although from a certain date in spring through the summer months, a straw hat rather than a black hat was required.

The only time cassocks were worn on the street was on formal occasions when the seminarians would walk to the Basilica of the Assumption, a distance of roughly a half mile, for Mass on all the major feast days and pontifical celebrations. Row upon row, in black cassocks and black birettas, the men made an impressive sight as they walked as a group through the streets of Baltimore. Yet it wasn't always easy to walk that half mile in a cassock. "We would be criticized by people going by, mostly guys driving by," James Dubell recalled. "They would scream out something like, 'Get a job!' or 'Go to work!' or something like that."

The street people would constantly beg money from the seminarians, continued James Dubell. Out for walks in their black suits and Roman collars, panhandlers would come up to them and ask for a dime.

John Wessel was not bothered by the "down and out" of Paca Street. Always "concerned for the poor people who begged on the streets of Baltimore, he went out of his way to give his money and time" to the panhandlers who congregated all over the neighborhood around the seminary.[17]

Although the physical surroundings of St. Mary's School of Philosophy were as different from the rolling hills of St. Charles, Catonsville as night from day, the routine of academic life and spiritual formation at Paca Street remained the same in most respects: classes, study time, daily Mass in the chapel, Silent Meals, athletic competitions, private devotions, spiritual reading, Night Prayers, the Grand Silence, Wednesday afternoon "walk days," and visits from family on the second Sunday of the month.

John's genuine interest in the various departments of philosophy grew during his two years at Paca Street. In addition to philosophy, he studied liberal arts subjects—logic, biology, sociology, psychology, education, English, public speaking, Gregorian chant, cosmology, ethics, economics, and rational theology. John was an average to above average student, and his grades showed steady improvement each semester in senior college.

John was chosen to sing in the choir at Paca Street—a group carefully selected for their interest and capability in voice and Church music. In his choir director, Father Eugene Walsh, S.S., John may have found a kindred spirit, for Walsh, according to his biographer, "considered camping, canoeing, or hiking in the woods to be as helpful to the development of the spirit as a whole series of retreats."[18]

"At St. Mary's Seminary, Paca Street, John Wessel continued to practice his prayer life with devotion, sincerity, and success," wrote his friend James Dubell. "John's faith in God was a personal conviction that demonstrated itself in his speech and actions. In addition to daily Mass and communion, he made daily visits to the Blessed Sacrament. He was gentle and generous and charitable toward his fellow seminarians and the professors."[19]

One of John's professors, Father William J. Lee, S.S., wrote of his former pupil:

> I knew John as a student . . . when I was teaching at our old seminary on Paca Street. While still in college he was a person with a clear and serious commitment to his future ministry. He avoided drawing attention to himself and tended to be quiet and reserved, and at the same time he was always pleasant, gentlemanly, and a good mixer. I felt that he was a person who exerted a strong influence for good on the Seminary community.[20]

"I remember seeing a lot of maturity in John" during his last two years of college, his sister Maryann recalled. "And he loved St. Mary's Paca Street. He was very, very happy there."

The pace was also different at the major seminary. The individual was given more responsibility and became involved in more varied activities. "Once we got to the major seminary, philosophy and theology, then we were kind of spread out more," said Carl Wingate. He and John Wessel were still close, "but it was just a lot more people and a lot more activities. You didn't have as much free time. You went through the day, morning till night, and you were in your own room. . . . We were still close but we just didn't do as much together then."

John and Carl did share the same priest, Father Haycock, for their confessor at Paca Street. This situation gave rise to a humorous incident that neither would ever forget.

The seminarians conferred with their confessor once a week. They were called, in alphabetical order, out of the study hall, and usually the confessor would send for two or three men at once.

"So, Wessel and I would be waiting outside the priest's room," recalled Wingate. "Wess would go in, and then he would come out and I would go in." Father Haycock was on a crusade of sorts to get his penitents to memorize the Bible. "He would flip the Bible open and say, 'What's it say in Job 3:7?' or something. Well, who knows," Wingate exclaimed. "John would say, 'I don't know' and he'd give him a lecture . . . 'Don't you read your Bible? You *should* know!'" John would come out of the priest's room, soundly chastened, and then it was Wingate's turn.

"I'd go in," Wingate continued, "and he'd say, 'What's in Job 3:7?' And I didn't know either, so I'd get a lecture."

After a while, Wingate realized that their confessor always told them what the verse was while he was lecturing them—"You should read that because it says such and such."

"Well, I knew he looked at it about ten minutes before we got there, 'cause he didn't know it either. So, one week, John goes in and comes out.

"I said, 'Hey, John, what's the Bible verse?' He said, 'It's Malachi 1:11.'"

"I said, 'What's that say?' He said, 'Sacrifice will be offered to the Lord from sunrise to sunset.'"

"I said, 'Okay, thanks.' Well, he leaves."

Then, Wingate went in to see Father Haycock. "All right, Mr. Wingate, tell me what it says in Malachi 1:11," the priest asked.

"Malachi 1:11, let me think," said Wingate, appearing to be thinking for a while. "And then I said, 'A Mass will be offered, a Sacrifice will be offered to the Lord from sunrise to sunset.'"

Father Haycock "almost dropped dead," Wingate recalled. The priest jumped up and exclaimed, "You got it! You're the first one ever that got the Scripture! You read the Bible!" He was so excited, almost crying, because one of his penitents finally knew the Scripture verse.

The next week, Wessel and Wingate went up to see Father Haycock as usual. "John goes in, and he's in there a long time, and he comes walking out. And I said, 'Hey, John, what's the verse?'" Perhaps Carl had failed to notice the dark scowl on John's face as he left his confessor's room.

"Go to hell!" John replied—which "wasn't typical of John."

"And I said, 'Is *that* the verse?'"

"No," John admitted to the dumbfounded Wingate. "I went in there, and I was mad. He's always screaming at me about knowing the Bible, and I told him it's impossible for anybody to be able to open the Bible and just, you pick a verse, and they know it. And Father Haycock says, 'Oh, no it's not. Wingate got it last week!'"

"I'm never telling you again," John said adamantly. "I kept hearing how good you were that you knew the Bible!"

That was the only time Wingate ever saw John Wessel mad, but it was soon over and their friendship continued intact. They could laugh about it later on. In the end, it probably taught them both valuable lessons. Ironically, as Carl Wingate admitted, John probably knew "ten times more of the Bible" than he did.

To Wingate, the incident demonstrated John's loyalty. Rather than expose his friend's subterfuge and lack of Scripture knowledge, John simply accepted the scolding from his confessor. "Most people would have said, 'I told him what it was,'" Wingate ruefully admitted, "but John would take the punishment and let him think I knew. That was John." It wasn't necessary for John to defend himself or to needlessly embarrass his friend. Neither his obedience nor his sense of loyalty would permit it.[21]

Once they were at St. Mary's, Paca Street, and continuing each year through graduation from the School of Theology at Roland Park, the seminarians were assigned a certain portion of the summer to go out and work in a parish in their own diocese. Here at last was the chance to live and work as a diocesan priest and get some hands-on experience tending to the spiritual and temporal needs of a parish population.

John Wessel's first summer assignment in 1960 was at Our Lady of the Mount Church in the tiny town of Mount Bethel, in the Watchung Mountains of Somerset County, New Jersey. The young pastor, Father (later Monsignor) Amedeo L. Morello, was favorably impressed with his young seminarian who, he noted, was very interested in history and well regarded by the people of his parish.

Father Morello wrote the Bishop of Trenton in August 1960:

John Wessel impressed me as being a completely interested seminarian—interested in the development of his own character as he prepares for the priesthood and interested in the work and activities of the priesthood.

One quality which particularly struck me is John's adaptability. While music is not his forte, he obtained excellent results by dint of industrious work with the children, teaching them appropriate hymns and giving them a simple introduction to Gregorian chant. In this and other phases of the Vacation School program, John demonstrated a spirit of ready, willing and eager co-operation. This spirit should stand him in good stead as he proceeds along the path to the priesthood.[22]

John's steady routine of life at Paca Street as a student and future priest was occasionally interrupted by the happenings of his family back at home. In 1960, his sister, Maryann, and William Beitel were married in Mount Holly. Father Joseph Shenrock officiated the nuptials at Sacred Heart Church. Brother Edward came home from Germany to give his sister away, and John served on the altar along with his friend, James Dubell. Maryann recalled John's supportive and calming presence throughout.

John was serene and serious on the altar as he helped his sister with whispered cues during the wedding ceremony. "All of a sudden, he became my mentor," Maryann said. A change was taking place: Their relationship had evolved from combative young siblings to loving, supportive adults where John, although the younger, was a protective and strong influence for his sister. Many times after that "he was always around to calm me down."[23]

The spring of John's last year at Paca Street was a time of intense preparation and pressure. In addition to the usual anxiety about final exams and college graduation, in the major seminary there began the screening process known as "calls to orders." The first call was to tonsure, the first transition from the lay to the clerical state, followed by the four minor orders.

During calls to orders, the seminarian would sit in his dormitory room and wait to be "called" to the various clerical states that existed in the pre-Vatican II Church: tonsure, porter, lector, exorcist, acolyte, subdeacon,

deacon, until finally, one became a priest. Calls to orders were held each year, usually in the spring. Beforehand, the faculty would have assembled to evaluate each candidate. The priests would then make the rounds on the night of the "call" to communicate their decision to the candidates.

The night of the call, the seminarian would sit in his room with his door open, listening for the footsteps of the approaching faculty and praying, no doubt. If they thought he was ready for the next phase, they'd come and knock on his door and say, "You've been called." The seminarian would respond, in Latin, *Deo gratias*, meaning "Thanks be to God."

"But sometimes guys didn't get the call, and they just walked past their door," Wingate recalled. Great was the disappointment of the seminarian who missed the call on that important night. A missed call to orders wasn't necessarily the end of a vocation. The rector would tell the student why he didn't make it—whether due to grades or something else—and give him an opportunity to improve himself. "It wasn't like you were done or anything," continued Wingate, just that "there was something they wanted you to work on." The next time around, in many cases, the man who had applied himself got the call.

"If anybody got called, it would be John, but he wasn't always sure." John would become anxious around calls to orders, because it was "just so important to him," Wingate recalled.

"Aw, geez," John would always ask him, "you think I'm going to get called?" John was concerned every time that he wouldn't make it. He worried that "something was wrong, or it was going to be studies, or he wasn't holy enough." The further along John went, though, the more comfortable he felt about calls to orders.

"I would say, 'You don't have anything to worry about!'" Wingate recalled. "But he always was a little anxious."

Despite a hectic year-end schedule, in May 1961, John found the time to write a congratulatory note to his brother and sister-in-law, Edward and Pat, on the birth of the couple's first son, Carlton. John had just become an uncle for the second time. Carlton was the Edward Wessels' second child; their daughter, Anne Marie, had been born the previous year.

"Congratulations on the new member of the family," John began. "I guess the Wessels will live on for another generation. I wonder what his future holds. God Bless him and you . . ."

"School has been a rat race this last month," he added. "Last week I handed in my final copy of the dissertation and the week before that, we had comprehensives in Philosophy and then the graduate record exam. Now I must catch up on my fourth quarter matter to get ready to review for finals. It will be over soon, thank God."

John also had some good news of his own to share:

> We had calls to orders (minor orders) last Thursday evening, and I made the grade. The whole class was a bit on edge for the last week wondering if they would make it or get "clipped". About fifteen percent didn't make it but no one is telling who. Now I have to see if I should "clip" myself. The whole mess is about receiving tonsure at the beginning of next year.[24]

And next year, John would be advanced to tonsure in a ceremony presided over by the Bishop of the Archdiocese of Baltimore in St. Mary's Chapel, Roland Park. As he would kneel before the Bishop, a lock of John's hair would be clipped as a symbolic reminder that he had entered into the clerical state. In olden times, the seminarian's hair was shaved off at the top.

"The weather over here is muggy as hell," John's letter continued. "You can't keep anything dry and it's been raining for the past week off and on all day long. Shows you aren't a pure intellect when weather can get you down!" he joked.

The remainder of John's letter was devoted to family news and world events. "Mom is fine and quite anxious to see you and her grandchildren this summer," he wrote. "She gets all upset, though, about the world situation. I think she's turning into an existentialist."

The Berlin Wall, communism, the Bay of Pigs invasion, Fidel Castro: World affairs in the summer of 1961 were tense indeed, and within a short time, destined to become much worse.

On June 5, 1961, John Wessel was awarded a Bachelor of Arts degree from St. Mary's Seminary, School of Philosophy.

At the end of his two years of philosophy studies, he was an average student having a general average of 81.36 and ranking 51st in a class of 105. The rector of St. Mary's, Paca Street, Father J. Carroll McHugh, wrote of John Wessel: "He seemed to have a good character. He is very manly, sincere, interested and earnest."

John's years at Paca Street were capped off with a second overseas trip with his mother to visit his brother, Edward, and his family in Germany. Kathleen Wessel had asked her youngest son to accompany her abroad, and John, having first sought the advice of his confessor, wrote to the Bishop of Trenton and obtained a release from his summer parish assignment.

John and his mother arrived in Le Havre, France on July 13, 1961, and made their way to visit Ed and Pat Wessel in what was then West Germany. The highlight of their visit was a camping odyssey of about two weeks duration through Scandinavia.[25]

They packed up the entire family—Kathleen Wessel and John, Ed and Pat, little Anne Marie and two-month-old infant "Carl"—in a Volkswagen Beetle, loaded up with a camping tent and equipment. Somehow, the four adults and two youngsters all managed to cram inside the tiny foreign car. "We brought a carrier for the back of the Volkswagen and a carrier for the top, and we put all the equipment up on the top or in the back," recalled Pat Wessel. The huge tent piled on top of the car had the comical effect of being almost as big and round as the Volkswagen itself.

Their camping itinerary took them up through northern Germany, into Denmark, Sweden, and Norway. Once in Norway, they went to Oslo and camped there for about a week, because "we wanted to be around the *fjords*." Norway is known as the "Land of the Midnight Sun" for good reason: From May through July, "the sun shines there at night as well as in the day." Deep blue *fjords*, or narrow bays, reach like arms of the sea to embrace the land and "reflect the majestic mountains that tower at their sides."[26]

"We took off and we did fine," continued Pat. "We had a few little minor incidents where we stopped short in Hamburg and the tent slid off the top of the Volkswagen and landed on the front of the car downtown at a red light. And all the Germans stood around and watched as Ed and Johnny got this back up on top."

They stopped at a number of lovely campsites along the way. Invariably, the accommodations were clean and comfortable. "Camping was the vacation of choice in Europe at that time," Pat explained. Camp sites were very beautiful and very well kept. "People of means camped. They brought their vases and their flowers and their clocks, their tablecloths and linens. That was camping for them."

Denmark was pouring rain. As Ed and John pitched the tent in pouring rain, they said it reminded them of "Hamlet country" because it was so "eerie and foggy."

John "liked being around the kids." He hadn't been around babies very much, but he would pitch right in and change their diapers and take care of them. Sometimes John would feign protest when he was asked to dispose of yet another baby's diaper. "Hey, I'm not going to get married. I'm going to be a priest!" he'd say, in mock horror.

The Scandinavian countryside was breathtakingly beautiful. Huge cliffs and mountains, icy clear lakes, waterfalls, greenery and forests dotted the landscape. John must have been entranced with the Scandinavian scenery. He captured it on film every chance he could.

Having enjoyed a happy family reunion and an exciting, breathtaking camping trip for most of the summer, John and his mother said their goodbyes to Ed and Pat and their children and flew to Paris on the 22nd of August. At the French coast, they boarded the *U.S.S. America* for the voyage across the Atlantic. They arrived at the port of New York on August 29, 1961, just in time for John to return to Baltimore and graduate school.

Before that happened, however, John had an interesting encounter during the ocean voyage. He met an attractive young woman who took a liking to him. Her name was Laura* and, like John, she was from the East Coast and had been traveling to Europe with her family.[27]

Their meeting had all the ingredients for a shipboard romance—a handsome young man, an attractive young woman, an exciting location. Such a chance encounter in a romantic setting could have turned into an eventful relationship. But since the handsome young man was a seminarian and a priest-to-be, there would be complications.

John, for his part, probably told her straight away that he was studying for the priesthood, since he was totally sincere and above reproach. Yet, he also felt an attraction to the young woman. During the long ocean crossing, the two young people had ample time to become friends, talk about their overseas travels, and share their youthful hopes and dreams for the future. John probably enjoyed his first mature friendship with a woman outside of his own family. It may have added a dimension to his emotional growth to know that a pretty young woman found him interesting and attractive, and that he could experience those feelings for her as well.

Their friendship continued after the voyage. The young woman would write to John and he would write back to her, like an older brother, giving her sage counsel in various matters. "She was always appreciating his advice," John's mother recalled.

Sometimes we receive things in life, not necessarily because we are destined to choose them, or even that we should do so, but simply to let us know that we could have done so, and that nothing has been denied us.

It was at this juncture that John Wessel unwittingly came to a crossroads in his life. Would he choose to continue this relationship, and all the possibilities it could bring—the love of one woman, marriage, and family life? Or would he choose to become a priest instead to love and serve all people with Christ-like charity?

CHAPTER 16

ST. MARY'S, ROLAND PARK

In September of 1961, John Wessel entered St. Mary's Seminary, School of Theology, in the Roland Park section of Baltimore to study theology for four years. Roland Park, as the School of Theology was called, was a grand and beautiful campus situated on a large tract at the southwest corner of Northern Highway and Roland Avenue, the latter a well-to-do, tree-lined street of stately homes.[1]

In keeping with its seriousness of purpose was the physical appearance of Roland Park's huge, imposing, museum-like four-story Italian Renaissance seminary building. High above six massive columns at the building's main entrance was a bas-relief sculpture of Jesus Christ and His Apostles with the command, "Go Teach All Nations," etched in stone. In their comings and goings, the seminarians merely had to look up to be reminded with these words of the sole purpose of their graduate studies.

The seminary's patron was the Blessed Mother under the title of *Sedes Sapientiae*, "Our Lady, Seat of Wisdom." A delicate and beautiful alabaster statue of Our Lady, Seat of Wisdom holding the Infant Jesus graced the marble foyer outside the seminary chapel, which was built in 1954 and dedicated to the Presentation of the Blessed Virgin Mary.[2] A small-scale version of the same statue, *Sedes Sapientiae*, could be found in every dormitory room, along with a crucifix on each wall.[3]

Roland Park, being at once a post-graduate institution of learning and a serious training ground for priests, was a highly academic establishment conducted at a more rigorous level of scholarship than the seminarians had previously encountered. John Wessel's course work during those four years heavily emphasized dogmatic and moral theology, Sacred Scripture, Church history, canon law, and sacred eloquence or homiletics. Forty-hour weeks of classes were the norm. In this environment, the seminarians were intensely absorbed in critical thinking and theology. They read the scholarly periodicals, and studied the writings of all the major theologians of the time.

"During those six years of philosophical and theological studies at Paca Street and Roland Park, John Wessel's scholastic efforts deepened and his interests broadened."[4]

In the School of Theology, John quickly "took a special interest in the study of Sacred Scripture, especially the life and work of St. Paul, with whom he identified as a rough, outdoors, fearless, Spartan, crusading, Christ-like man."[5] In later years, John would be remembered as a man who had a great love for all of Scripture, but most of all the New Testament Gospels, Epistles and Acts of the Apostles.

His professor for Sacred Scripture was Father Raymond Brown, whom John also chose as his confessor for the next four years. John was one of about twenty-five other students whom the priest was directing at Roland Park. Typically, John would meet with Father Brown each week for confession, and at least once monthly for spiritual direction concerning his religious, psychological and intellectual life.[6]

In Roland Park, as a result of the penitent-confessor relationship, John became closer to Father Brown, whom he knew from St. Charles and greatly admired. On occasion they could be found playing a game of handball together.[7]

"John Wessel's academic performance improved markedly over the years. In the bottom half in his high school, and only middling in college, John received his Bachelor of Sacred Theology degree (S.T.B.) cum laude in 1963 and, by the time his seminary studies were finished, had moved comfortably into the top 30 percent of his class."[8]

Because of his early reading and language problems, these subjects would never be John's forte. But once he no longer had to struggle through English, Latin and Greek, he discovered his aptitude for subjects that called for critical thinking and reasoning—philosophy and theology—and began to do well. He realized that he had other gifts, and was able to excel in other things and be recognized for it.

He even developed the confidence to laugh at himself. "Once I stopped trying to be a scholar in Latin and Greek, fortune smiled," John said.[9]

Written scholarship was quite important at Roland Park, with two term papers per semester being the norm. John had developed an ingenious solution to his lifelong reading and spelling problems: He would give his papers to classmate James Roche to edit for minor points of spelling and punctuation. "Here Rochie, just read that over," he'd say, and that is how John's friend "Rochie" became his unofficial proofreader toward the end of high school and in the major seminary.

To James Roche, John Wessel struck him as "an interesting guy and a combination of quality in a rough package. I found that intriguing, and more so as I would find things out that just, at the time, totally left me speechless."

John had "a level of broadness and exposure to things" that gave him "a richness of experience"—his family background, his trips abroad, for example—and yet, he would keep it on the inside, and "you would find it out in little surprise moments." As he grew to know him better, Jim Roche would learn about John "that what you see is not all that's there. He's not just a rough cut person who spits and smokes and likes to play football. He's a guy with other experiences and other talents."

As he proofread John's papers, James Roche was impressed with his friend's intellectual abilities. "I would describe it as more the scientific mind than the literary mind. He had the brains to do his own work, for sure, but he didn't bother about spelling," Roche said of John's scholarship.[10]

John's grades climbed steadily into the 80's and 90's during his four years of graduate theology. Interestingly, he took Biblical Hebrew as an elective and did extremely well. Still, the young man had to work quite hard at his studies. And he did so gladly for one reason only: Being a priest was so important that he was willing to discipline himself and make whatever sacrifices were necessary.

His activities outside the classroom and library began to show a greater range. He was again chosen to sing in a select choir, remained active in the Mission Society, and engaged in athletics and dramatics. In addition, John participated in the Catholic Evidence Guild (a group whose aim was to better understand and effectively communicate Catholic teaching among non-Catholics), and in several other study and discussion groups. He did pastoral and catechetical work in the schools, hospitals and correctional institutions in the city of Baltimore. He continued his interest in photography and became the photographer for the school magazine, *The Voice*. All of these experiences prepared him for parish work ahead.[11]

At Roland Park, John Wessel and Mike Choma roomed together for several years. They first met in freshman Latin class at St. Charles and became good friends through common interests and common struggles with languages. As roommates, however, they were like characters out of Neil Simon's comedy, *The Odd Couple*. John was messy, and Mike was neat as a pin—until John succeeded in teaching him to be messy.

"Everything had to be in its place," Mike recalled about himself back then. "Doors had to be closed. The closet door had to be shut. Things had to be hung up." John would come in like a hurricane, throw things about, and leave them where they landed. "He'd open the closet door, take stuff out, leave the closet door open, throw stuff on the desk, open a drawer, leave the drawer open . . . God, this would really get to me!"

At first the two tried studying together. "We'd try to help each other out," Mike recalled, "but it got to a point where we just got on each other's nerves, and he would go down and study in the library and I would study up in the room for a week, and then we'd switch. So that worked out. Then when it came time for exams, that's where I just gave in and said 'All right, I'll do it your way, John.' And what we did is we both sat at our desks in the room, and we just took a course and just went through it. We had all our notes, and as we finished the notes, they just went overhead to the back of us on the floor. Where they landed, that's where they stayed for a week. And for a whole week we would have a pile of trash in the room almost knee deep. And after the last exam, then we both came up and cleaned up the place. But that's the way we lived!"[12]

In many respects, the routine of seminary life was still the same at Roland Park: rising at 6 a.m., Mass and meditation, the Rosary, the Grand Silence and Night Prayers, class and study time, and lights out at 10:30 p.m. While it was still a very regimented life, the students felt a sense of greater freedom, and at the same time, a sense of greater responsibility in that more was expected of them.[13]

Months were still punctuated by visits from loved ones on the second Sunday. John's mother and family continued to visit him without fail for the next four years on visiting Sunday and attended all the important ceremonies as he progressed through the minor and major clerical orders. John's sister recalled his happiness:

> I could see a lot of joy with John and his friends . . . They had such a good time in the seminary. They were into drama. I never knew John could act but there he was! . . . I remember his friends coming home and they just had such a good time together.[14]

At Roland Park, the seminarians were allowed off the grounds so infrequently that they became providers of their own entertainment in all sorts of ways. One winter John and his friends built a toboggan slide in the snow down a high hill near the handball court. At the bottom of the run they made a curve which banked all the way up about ninety degrees, so that the men were turned almost upside down as they went around it. Avoiding the trees along the run was also a challenge. The fellows would slide down the hill on plastic trays or little squares of cardboard, whatever they could get their hands on. "It was daring," recalled Mike Choma. "The icier it got, the faster it went."[15]

John Wessel had a good sense of humor and genuinely enjoyed life, as illustrated by a little story for which he is still remembered. On one occasion, a number of men had gathered at the slide and were taking their turns down the hill in the snow. John went down on a piece of cardboard, and he didn't know it but the cardboard had slipped out from under him. But he just kept going down anyway, having a grand time—all to the amusement of his classmates. "They loved John," Father Ronald Bacovin recalled. He was "good to be with" and "a lot of laughter."[16] Another classmate also recalled John's "wonderful sense of humor." He was "always with a smile" and had "a very warm temperament."[17]

During those few times that John Wessel had a free day in the seminary, one of his favorite activities was to visit his cousin Julian Wessel in Philadelphia, and spend the day at I. Goldberg, a camping, sporting goods and military store in the city. A few times a year, John would call up his teenage cousin and say, "Meet me at I. Goldberg." They would get together for lunch in downtown Philadelphia and just "hang out" at the store for the afternoon, looking at all the equipment and talking about sports.

"We never took public transportation," Julian recalled, because his cousin loved to walk around the city, even on the coldest days. The outing was usually capped off by seeing a movie, and the action-oriented James Bond films were among their favorites.[18]

While enjoying these diversions, however, John Wessel never lost sight of the most important reasons for his being in the seminary, that of spiritual preparation for his vocation.

"Throughout the seminary years, John Wessel's spiritual life was steady, devout and growing deeper. He made daily visits to the Blessed Sacrament and demonstrated by his speech and actions a faith in God that won the respect of his fellow seminarians and his teachers," said James Dubell.[19] John possessed a "genuine piety" and was considered to be "religious in a way that was acceptable to everyone," recalled other classmates.[20]

While at Roland Park, John worked seriously on the development of his inner life in Christ. He was not afraid to be candidly self-critical, and always seemed to be striving in a quiet way for perfection and "holiness" in the authentic sense of the word. He had a mature awareness that a priest must, first and foremost, be holy—not just superficially so but from the inside out. Among John's notes from his seminary days are these random quotes which illustrate the essence of the young seminarian:

> Rise with the Lord. Live always in his presence. Be conscious of his *grace*.
>
> Remember John, always what you are and how small you really are. If you feel no one can take your place—get out. Pride kills, and you are already proud. Truth is not pride, but the eyes of the *world* are upon a priest.
>
> Learn how to meditate. If you don't you will never do it on your own. *Remember that.*
>
> Don't blame—do. It is easy and even easier to follow a "saintly" priest to hell. Always be a little different. Don't follow too closely, and always listen to those who are able to speak from outside the world.
>
> What is love? Kindness when you are bearing your own cross. Doing little things for others without them knowing.
>
> Save for the missions and give something worthwhile in a humble manner.

Virtue is not your ultimate, *Christ is*. Difficult, but read the New Testament more, looking for the mind of Christ. You must be in love: 1) giving, 2) knowing, 3) interested, 4) sacrificing.

And from notes entitled, "Retreat 1962," he wrote:

John, you have reached a certain level of natural virtue—you will make a good priest but as you stand not an especially holy one. Holy means apart, but not just apart from things but close to other things. You must learn to live in God's sphere, not the good material world—you are a Christian, not a good pagan. Pray constantly.

Christ's interests should [and] shall motivate your actions. Love of God—*vele bonum*. When you love a human, as you are starting to do more often, love them for the good of God, not yourself. When you love the beauties of this world, love them as the reflection of God's goodness and for His goodness. You do not as yet "live" a supernatural life but you have good potential for it. It breaks out into its true beauty in crisis.[21]

John Wessel developed the habit of making an annual retreat for one week at the end of each summer at the Benedictine monastery of Mount Savior in Pine City, a little town outside of Elmira, New York. James Roche often accompanied him. At the monastery, they shared the rugged and humble lifestyle of the Benedictine monks, rising early, eating simply, keeping the Divine Office, and devoting themselves to prayer, spiritual reading, and peaceful, quiet reflection.[22]

Each year, as before, John was assigned a certain portion of the summer months to work at a parish in the Diocese of Trenton. The comments of his pastors during his summer assignments uniformly attest to his suitability for the priesthood and his fine character.[23]

Father Alfred D. Smith wrote in 1962:

Mr. Wessel showed himself to be a fine candidate for the priesthood during his stay in St. Joseph's, Keyport. He was very diligent and earnest in carrying out all of the tasks that were assigned to him. He was a source of edification both to the children and the adults with whom he came in contact.

Mr. Wessel proved himself to be very capable and dependable in every way. We would be happy to welcome him back at any time.

And in 1964, Father Vincent A. Lloyd, pastor of St. Gabriel's Church, Bradevelt, New Jersey, said, "I find John Wessel to be courteous and circumspect. He had good character and is highly thought of by the children and adults who have associated with him."

John's spiritual development now had an added dimension—namely, getting out into the field via apostolates organized by the seminary.[24] Although the seminarian's main focus was to study and do well academically, it was at this point that the men were allowed to do some pastoral work one day a week on Wednesday afternoon "walk days," when everyone had to be off the seminary grounds. In the large city of Baltimore, there were plenty of opportunities to venture forth and put their theoretical knowledge of ministry into practical application at schools, hospitals, and other institutions in the area through a voluntary program called the Camillus Society. Through it, the seminarians could visit places like city hospitals, tubercular wards, and orphanages, or work with the deaf and mentally retarded, or engage in street preaching.[25]

John Wessel joined the Camillus Society during his four years at Roland Park, and seemed to thrive on the new opportunities for pastoral work. It was at this time that he began his public evangelization. "They could go out and talk with people, and there was a lot of contact with people. He would go to the prisons," his sister Maryann recalled. "I remember he was enjoying this newfound freedom that he could go and talk to criminals, and into hospitals."[26]

The places that John Wessel chose to go with the Camillus Society foreshadowed with amazing accuracy his future priestly ministry. Although the seminarian often would choose one apostolate and stick with it,[27] John became involved in a number of institutions.[28] One almost gets the sense of a young man trying to prepare himself, through practical experience, for the many varied situations he would encounter as a priest. He visited local nursing homes and an institute for the mentally ill.[29] For two years, he taught catechism at Bryn Mawr, a high school in the neighborhood of Roland Park, and was "walk head" or leader of the group who went to the high school each Wednesday afternoon. But perhaps he is best remembered for his apostolate of visiting prisoners.

John chose to go with a group of seminarians to the Maryland State Penitentiary once a week for a two- to three-hour visit. There he was a source of spiritual comfort to many.[30] Ministry to prisoners and the mentally ill were considered to be challenging apostolates, but John, a fellow seminarian recalled, "took the more difficult ones."[31]

John loved the trips to the Maryland State Penitentiary, recalled Carl Wingate, who accompanied John on a few occasions.[32]

"Usually, you'd go there in the afternoon," Wingate recalled. "They had recreation and the guys would be in the yard, and you'd just go out and kind of talk to them. It was more a visit." There was nothing formal about it. Preaching was done not so much by words as by example. "They'd be glad to see you, and you'd ask them how they were."

Most of the inmates were "lifers" serving terms for serious capital offenses: murder, assault, rape, robbery. This was "the Pen," not the city jail. These inmates were grateful that the seminarians came to visit and listen to them. Their appreciation was genuine and touching. "You'd go at Christmas," Wingate continued, "and they'd get some little thing they got from somewhere and they'd want to give it to you as a Christmas present. It was a real moving experience, and I know John loved that."

John Wessel seems to have been drawn to those who were especially difficult to love, the forgotten, the rejected, the "outcasts" of society. "He was drawn towards anything down and out," said Wingate. This trait would continue for the rest of John's life.

John had a unique ability to relate to people. Although on the shy side, his classmates thought of him as warm, engaging, and affable.[33] He was not gregarious but was "good with people," said James Roche.[34]

The seminarian's involvement with prison ministry gave rise to a highly unorthodox tradition: The State Pen Annual Football Game. Each year, the seminarians would choose an All-Star Team of their best players, and the inmates at the Maryland State Penitentiary would do the same. On an afternoon shortly before graduation, one would find the incongruous sight of deacons about to be priests facing off at the line of scrimmage with hard core lifers for a serious game of football.

John Wessel played on the All-Star seminary team against the inmates during his last year at Roland Park. The game that year was tough and hard fought. The seminarians came back elated that they were able to hold their own against the prisoners, who initially had underestimated their abilities. The Roland Park men matched up well and gave their opponents a good fight.[35]

At Roland Park, "meals were often in silence to give students a chance to display homiletical talents (or lack of them)."[36] There was an actual pulpit in the dining room, and two students were assigned per Silent Meal to deliver a practice sermon in lieu of books being read aloud, as in earlier years. One of the professors from the year before would have assigned a topic to the student, who had to write a sermon over the summer and hand it in to the Homiletics professor within forty-eight hours of returning from vacation. The professor would have a copy of the text, and the student would have to memorize it and deliver it verbatim from the podium. The would-be homilist was graded on both content and delivery. Even if the student subsequently learned that he made a mistake in the text, or that he was preaching heresy even, he still had to deliver the sermon as written—the presumption being that he should have known better than to write it in the first place.[37]

The practice sermons were somewhat of a "baptism of fire" for many a young seminarian. On the assigned day, the student donned a white surplice over his cassock, was given a glass of water at the pulpit, and stood and preached his memorized text to four hundred hungry men eating, all the while trying to act and sound as if he were addressing a church congregation.[38] "From the preacher's point of view," Father Bowen observed, "it was a real challenge to capture the attention of a community more interested in food than in the food for thought being offered from the pulpit."[39] If the student changed the text or made a mistake, Father O'Connor, the Homiletics professor, would ring a buzzer which was concealed under the table "loud enough to make you jump out of your skin" and he would call out something like, "You're corrupting the text!" or "That word is pronounced such and such." If the student had memory failure, the professor would call out the next line to help him along.[40]

The ritual of the practice sermon, according to seminary "lore," also provided an occasion for some high jinx and practical jokes. Sometimes a few men would sneak in early and fill the water glass at the pulpit with salt. "You're giving your speech and you take a little drink and you think you're going to die but you can't show it!" said a classmate. "So there was some fun and games. But I don't think that happened to John, and I don't think John did it to anybody else."[41]

John did well with his homilies, Carl Wingate observed. "You'd practice it with somebody. I remember practicing with John," he said. "I'm sure John didn't get buzzed or anything."

In his fourth year of theology, John Wessel, along with the other deacons, went on the "preaching circuit." Each Sunday they went out to deliver sermons in nearby churches, at the seminaries of St. Charles and Paca Street, or at the Cathedral in Baltimore. But this time, it wasn't just a talk before a bunch of hungry guys eating dinner, but a real church with a real congregation listening attentively to the young deacons.[42]

John took the preparation of his sermons seriously. His seminary notes included the following reminder: "Sermons: You have learned that you cannot speak without full preparation. That means writing your talk out—from beginning, body, and conclusion. . . . When you prepare you do well, otherwise you make a fool of yourself."[43]

Contemporary events intruded little on life behind seminary walls. "We were really isolated in a way. We knew what was happening but even in the major seminary, we were pretty restricted," a classmate recalled.[44] But occasionally the outside world intruded in dramatic fashion.

One Friday afternoon in November of their third year of theology, John Wessel and James Roche went for a walk in the woods behind the seminary. They hadn't gone too far when suddenly, an urgent voice yelled out from the seminary window, "Hey, the President's been shot!"

Stunned, the two men froze for an instant, and then John said, "Come on, I've got a radio up in my lab." The photography lab on the fourth floor of the building was where John developed his pictures for the seminary publications. The two men quickly ran up the stairs to the top floor, turned on the radio and, like the rest of the country, listened to the incomprehensible news out of Dallas. John F. Kennedy, the first Roman Catholic President of the United States, was dead.[45]

"That moment would stick in memory," recalled James Roche.

*   *   *

"John always had that combination of not just a scientific mind but . . . he was a 'doer' kind of a person," said seminary friend Roche.[46] The observation that John Wessel was a "doer" is apt; he was a man of action. John "would dismiss details or problems, little sticking points or something like that, that would discourage me. John was not that way. Little things did not hinder him" from doing something important that he wanted to do. "And that impressed me." John "wasn't afraid of things. . . . He was confident and he would try things" like football or camping in the wilderness.

But at the same, John could be "careless about other things." For instance, he would smoke cigarettes. "Even back then, we knew better," said Roche, who attributes it to "that inner energy and drive that was a part of him." John's drive and energy showed itself "in all the physical things he did. He was not just a man of education or ideas or words, but he was also a man of action, and producing things, and hands-on activities."

John did all the photography for *The Voice*, a magazine for students and alumni which the seminarians at Roland Park published quarterly. Consequently, the photography room became his home away from home. Once again, Carl Wingate served as photographer's assistant and helped John develop the pictures. Carl shared these memories:

> If I didn't have to work in the sacristy, I'd usually go up to the darkroom with him and we'd talk . . . just about God and how neat He was. Nothing real dramatic. The photography room was all the way up on the top of the building. Now, we were allowed to go up there. It was out of bounds to other students. There was this spiral staircase and you could go up on the roof of the school, and there was a little . . . patio . . . up there. You could look out over the whole city. And we'd go up there a lot at night and pray, or just look out at the city and talk.[47]

In the seminary there were some men of limited means who couldn't afford a portrait from a professional photographer to hand out to family and friends on important occasions, such as ordination to the major clerical states. John very quietly and tactfully put his photographic talents at the service of his fellow seminarians of lesser means.

> We'd have them come up there to the photography room and pin a sheet on the wall and take their picture, then make a hundred copies they could give to Grandma or whoever. We had a budget for it. John was always thinking that way. He'd spend hours up there running these prints off for guys who couldn't pay. You know, professional photographers cost a fortune. So he'd make two 8 x 10's, five 5 x 7's and 20 wallet size. Sometimes we'd charge them. It might cost John and me $20 to $30 to do it. But we knew who the kid was and . . . just so he didn't feel like charity, we'd say, "Well, it runs about five bucks." So they'd give us the five bucks and we'd give them the picture package.[48]

Ironically, it was precisely because of his photography that John suffered a minor criticism of sorts, although not with any lasting impact on his academic career. In the second semester of every year, the rector and faculty at Roland Park would gather to jointly evaluate each seminarian on his academic and spiritual life, character, suitability for the priesthood, and so forth, prior to calls to orders.

John usually received very good evaluations in the major seminary. One time, however, John did not fare quite as well. One of his professors viewed the amount of time he spent in the darkroom with suspicion. He found the young seminarian shy and secretive because he was "up in the photography room a great deal," the professor complained, as if he had an agenda all his own. John received a qualified call to orders that year (the only time he did so) and was urged by the faculty to become less solitary and more outgoing.[49]

What can be said about this anonymous professor is that he certainly was observant: John indeed spent many of his free hours in the darkroom running off prints for his classmates. But if he only knew the reason!

In 1962, having dedicated his pontificate to the "new development in the perennial youth of our holy Church," the Holy Father, Pope John XXIII, stunned the world by convening some 2,500 Bishops at an Ecumenical Council to begin debate on developments to keep the Church youthful and strong. The reforms from the Second Vatican Council initiated by Pope

John XXIII and completed by his successor, Pope Paul VI, "have defined the direction of a Church challenged by its own identity in an increasingly eclectic and high-tech age."[50]

Scarcely has there been an event of such monumental importance to the modern Roman Catholic Church as the convocation and deliberations of the Second Vatican Council (popularly known as "Vatican II") in the first half of the 1960s. The worldwide College of Bishops who participated in the gathering addressed and defined nearly every aspect of modern Catholic life and worship, and their pronouncements were set forth in sixteen documents which ultimately emerged from the Council.[51]

The final session of Vatican II ended in December 1965 (after John Wessel was ordained) and the documents weren't widely available until the Council ended, so that for all practical purposes, the Council had little actual impact on seminary life at Roland Park for John and his classmates.[52] Father Raymond Brown recalled:

> My impression is that there was practically no change of seminary life until two or three years after the Council. They'd be getting some idea that changes were abroad, but in point of fact, in terms of Scripture or dogma or systematic theology, there was a fairly open faculty at Roland Park so changes of that sort would not have been new to them anyway.
>
> . . . The rules of seminary life changed drastically, but I don't think that changed till the late sixties.[53]

The liturgical changes were the most significant, of course, simply because to the "people in the pews" they were the most obvious—but again, these came later. The liturgical revisions would involve the structure of the Mass: changing the language from Latin to English (or the vernacular of the country); repositioning the altar so that the priest faced the people; and greater participation by the congregation, just to name a few.[54]

The Roland Park class of 1965 was caught in the middle when everything started to change. The rumor was circulating that everything was going to be in English. Other priests in the seminary cautioned: "Don't bet on the wrong horse. English isn't going to happen!" Up until the last minute they were right, and then suddenly, a year or two later, everything changed.[55]

John seems not to have worried much whether the Mass was in Latin or in English. "He took everything in stride," a fellow seminarian recalled.[56] He displayed a sensible attitude toward change, and a willingness to embrace the end results of the Council positively and with optimism.

A few of John Wessel's professors, including Father Raymond Brown, his Sacred Scripture professor, traveled to Rome and participated in the Vatican II deliberations and brought back news of what was going on. The seminarians were also able to read up on the Council in the Catholic press and periodicals, and visiting theologians would come to Roland Park to address the seminarians on what was happening in Rome. Recalled classmate Wingate:

> We started to see that there was a little more flexibility coming in and as we listened to these people, we'd talk about it and we kind of thought, it does make sense. I think they gradually started to make us aware that the vernacular was going to be helpful. I think John accepted all that in a positive way and I think he thought it was good it was happening.

On June 3, 1964, at the end of his third year of theology, John P. Wessel was ordained a subdeacon by His Excellency, the Most Reverend Lawrence J. Shehan, D.D., Archbishop of Baltimore, in the chapel of St. Mary's Seminary. Upon his return to the seminary in the fall, he was ordained a deacon by the Most Reverend T. Austin Murphy, D.D., Auxiliary to the Archbishop of Baltimore, on September 20, 1964.[57] Prior to this time, he and his classmates had successfully advanced through tonsure and the four minor orders of the clerical state (porter, lector, exorcist and acolyte) while at Roland Park.

In order to appreciate the importance of this event, it is necessary to understand that the subdeaconate was a major step in the pre-Vatican II Church, second only to the Sacrament of Holy Orders itself. It was at that time that the seminarian vowed his life to celibacy and began to read the Divine Office every day.[58]

In our modern, sexually permissive and unrestrained society, the role of celibacy as integral to the priesthood is often misunderstood. Celibacy, properly viewed, is a great and sacrificial gift on the part of the priest to his people, through which he frees himself from any personal or affective needs so that he is truly able to be of service entirely to God, to the Church, and to the Catholic community.

The pledge of celibacy was approached with great faith and trust in God's grace. Even the best prepared and most ardent seminarian could not help but be acutely aware of the sacrifice he was preparing to make for the love of God. John Wessel was no different.

His private views on celibacy may be best exemplified by his very personal notes from a retreat in the seminary:

> Sex is going to be the major sacrifice of your life, but make it a Christian sacrifice "in secret and with joy." Watch the occasions of sin. . . . Don't let yourself drift from your love of God. I love Him above all things. I am His priest. I love His children, His earth because He made it, and they are my job. . . . I'm going to be a priest for the salvation of souls and the Glory of God. "Fear not, little children, for I am always with you."[59]

"In secret and with joy," John came to a decision in the spring of 1964 about the young woman named Laura whom he had met aboard the *U.S.S. America* on his return trip from Germany several years before, and with whom he had kept in touch through a steady correspondence. It is an interesting episode in his life: First, because it shows his humanness and capacity for human love. And second, it was at this time that John (if he had not done so already) decided irrevocably for the priesthood. Yet, it was also the time when, according to his roommate Mike Choma, John came closest to losing his vocation.[60]

John "spent a lot of time with her on the boat and he really liked her," recalled Choma, in whom John confided. "He could've lost his vocation on that trip."[61] She liked him even more.[62] It was his friend's impression that John Wessel struggled with his feelings for the young woman at the time, and it wasn't something easy for him. "He could have left then. That he told me," recalled Mike. "That made him very human. I appreciated that from John, because that just made me realize he's no different than I am."[63]

Among Father Wessel's few earthly possessions was a letter that he had written to Laura in the seminary. He had composed it, but apparently thought better of mailing it, because written boldly across the top were the words "Never Sent."

Dear [Laura],

I better get this off to you before your vacation. I'm sorry but I won't be able to see you. Seminaries are strange places, especially for the students. Visiting is restricted to family and that's it. If you ever wish to see Father Stancs, you don't have to feel chicken. He's a professor, not a student.

In the priesthood there are many paradoxes and that is possibly why it seems so strange to those who look at it from a distance. A priest is to train himself to be as much like Christ as he can and live in a world not at all in His image. You result in misunderstandings and exaggerations on both sides of the fence. One of these is the relationship the priest has with individuals. In the spirit of Christ, all men are free and true but in the spirit of the world, which is certainly good but sometimes misinterpreting, man becomes at this time, a slave. The best thing for us to do is look ahead and not look back and reform our lives constantly in His image as best we can, constantly reforming but never losing our sense of being human and at some time remembering the hope of finding happiness.

Gloomy? Not really but serious. My status? Right now, not much. In a few months, June 3rd, it will change and a year from then, priesthood. My reason for being here? Too difficult to answer. Why be a doctor if you want to heal men you know will eventually die? What will I do? Another mystery. I'm in the diocesan priesthood. That means, under the orders of a Bishop who tells you what he wants done. Parish, Church law, courts, teacher, missionary . . . all are possible. In other words, as Christ obeyed his Father, so much the priest. Sound strange? I'm sure it does, so read it and forget it. You met a strange fellow on the *America*. Pray for me these next few months then forget me. God Bless.

Sincerely, John[64]

At around the same time, John composed another letter. This one he *did* send. He wrote to his Bishop, the Most Reverend George W. Ahr, petitioning to be advanced to the subdeaconate and deaconate. On April 12, 1964, in preparation for the major orders, he solemnly declared,

> upon serious consideration of the matter in the presence
> of God . . . that I am not compelled to by any coercion, force
> or fear to receive these Sacred Orders, but that I desire them of
> my own accord and that I wish to receive them with full and free
> deliberation, as I know and feel that I am called by God.
>
> . . .
>
> In particular, I declare that I clearly know the full meaning
> of the law of celibacy and I firmly declare that, with God's help,
> I will gladly keep it and completely observe it.
>
> . . .
>
> So I promise, vow and swear . . . [65]

Whatever his life might have been with Laura, John Wessel had made his choice for the priesthood. He would remain friendly with the young woman, as befitting an older brother. After this time, John's prayer life seemed to increase and deepen noticeably to his friends in the seminary.[66] "That's when I saw how really great he was—more serious," recalled Choma. "He didn't make a big deal about praying, he just went and did it and he spent time at it."[67]

To the younger theology students at Roland Park, John was a "hero" and a "role model." Father Ronald Bacovin, a year behind him, often observed John quietly praying the breviary.

> I remember . . . when John was ordained a deacon, and that
> year, I was able to observe him. . . . I just noticed John would be
> in the chapel. He wasn't fudging on anything, he wasn't trying
> to impress anybody, but he'd be in the chapel at prayer. And it
> occurred to me he was a very, very good deacon, and kind of
> anxious to get ordained and go about the work.[68]

Although Father Kozak had convinced John Wessel not to run off and join the Maryknolls at the age of thirteen, his interest in the missions remained strong. As a seminarian, it manifested itself principally in his work with the Mission Society. At some point toward the end of his theologate, however, John once again paused to consider the missions as a possible path.

In a private, undated note from around this period entitled, "Thoughts on the Missions," John wrote:

> Emotionally I have always been attracted to their directions—probably from the romantic nature which I seem to possess, especially the love of adventure. Lately, as the time draws near for the final step, and the apparent need to gear oneself for the future, and the desire for a more driving motivation, it seems necessary to once more consider their reality.[69]

There are indications that he talked once again with Father Kozak about his interest in missionary work. Struggling with conflicting emotions and the lure of missionary life, John seems to have come to understand that it was important to be near his mother now that his father had passed away. He came to realize that there could be "a lot of excitement in being a missionary in the United States," observed his sister, and resolved that the diocesan priesthood "was his calling for that time."[70] Maryann privately felt, however, "that John had plans someday of asking leave from the Diocese of Trenton for the life of a missionary."[71]

On March 28, 1965, as his last semester at Roland Park was drawing to a close, John Wessel once again wrote to Bishop Ahr requesting to be advanced to the priesthood.

> I, the undersigned, John Patrick Wessel, a deacon of the diocese of Trenton, do hereby petition that I may be advanced to the priesthood. I do this wholly of my free and spontaneous will, moved thereunder by no consideration other than the glory of God, the service of the Church, and the salvation of my soul.[72]

John Wessel earned his Licentiate in Sacred Theology (S.T.L.), which is equivalent to a Masters Degree in Theology, from St. Mary's Seminary, Roland Park in May 1965. The rector of Roland Park, Father John R. Sullivan, recommended him for the priesthood in these words:

> John P. Wessel is a promising candidate for the priesthood. . . . He is a good, solid, forthright character who

is reliable, responsible and manly. As he acquires confidence in the priesthood he should be more gracious, less self-conscious and better-poised than at present.[73]

The end of the school year brought with it a fond annual custom at Roland Park of sending the graduates off in style as they left for ordination.

Each Bishop set the date for the ordination of priests in his own diocese. The seminarians at Roland Park represented dioceses from Chicago to the East Coast, and from Maine to Florida. By tradition, all the graduates from the same diocese left together at a designated time. The remaining classmates and underclassmen, garbed in their cassocks and collars, gathered on the front steps of the seminary and sang the Latin medieval hymn, *Ecce Quam Bono*—"Behold, how good it is to be friends, and for brothers to dwell together in unity." This was the final tribute of farewell as each group of priests-to-be left to begin work in the mission fields of their own dioceses.[74]

Carl Wingate remembered saying goodbye to John Wessel in the spring of 1965. "We hugged and I grabbed him on the steps there before he got in the car, and just kind of looked at each other. I think we both knew that we might not see each other. He knew I was a 'Sulp' and I knew I was going to California." For Carl Wingate, it was, in fact, the last time he saw John Wessel.[75]

There was a bit of an empty feeling for those who were left behind. But for John, a new beginning. For all the times that he worried that he wouldn't get the call, or that he might not make it, here he was at last—on his way to becoming a priest.

Perhaps John Wessel's true thoughts as he embarked upon his new life as a priest are best captured in a message that he wrote to his mother on the back of a prayer card when he became a subdeacon.[76]

> Mom,
>   Keep me always in your prayers to Our Lady of Lourdes. I'll do my best to do a good job. I know what I must do and with God's grace, it will be done.
>
>   Love, Johnny
>   June 3, 1964

St. Charles

Young seminarian John Wessel gets a haircut at St. Charles. (Photo from Fr. John Wessel's album)

At St. Charles, John Wessel (far left) was President of the Mission Society under the direction of Father Edwin J. "Pop" Schneider. (Reprinted from *The Carolite*, 1959)

Rhets, champs twice over.

John Wessel played team sports at St. Charles. A defensive lineman on the football team, he is pictured in this team photo (bottom row, far right) during his Rhet year. On the gridiron, John was "like a tank," said a classmate. "He played his heart out." (Reprinted from *The Carolite*, 1959)

John (far left), wearing his favorite "Number 35" Notre Dame jersey given to him by his brother Edward, tries to block a kick on the grounds of St. Charles College. (Photo from Fr. John Wessel's album)

After a game of "touch" football, John (second from right) and his seminary classmates often ended up covered in mud. (Photo courtesy of W. Michael Mueller, at far left)

Court champs for '59.

John Wessel (standing, far right) was co-captain of the St. Charles tennis team, along with his lifelong friend James Dubell (kneeling, first row, center). (Reprinted from *The Carolite*, 1959)

The "Carolite" *Chiefs.*

As head photographer of *The Carolite*, John Wessel (standing, far left) was integral to the success of the St. Charles yearbook. (Reprinted from *The Carolite*, 1959)

John Wessel tries on the Roman centurion's costume he and his pals rented for the 1959 yearbook. (Photo from Fr. John Wessel's album)

Nineteen-year-old seminarian John Wessel's graduation portrait from the St. Charles College yearbook. (Reprinted from *The Carolite*, 1959)

Camping/Outdoors

Lake George, summer 1958. The original "canoe catamaran" built by adventurers (l-r) John Wessel, Carl Wingate, Michael Choma and (not pictured) Michael Mueller, out of sapling masts and tent sails. (Photo courtesy of Carl Wingate)

Outdoorsmen John Wessel (left) and Mike Choma enjoy a delicious meal during one of their annual seminary camping trips. (Photo from Fr. John Wessel's album)

John enjoyed hunting, especially the family tradition of an early morning Thanksgiving Day hunt on his grandparents' Mount Holly Farm. (Photo from Fr. John Wessel's album)

John Wessel (right) and fellow seminarian James Roche (left) white water rafting. (Photo from Fr. John Wessel's album)

Shooting rapids on the Penobscot River in Maine, 1964, the last canoe trip before graduation and ordination. John Wessel (right) and James Roche (left) capsized moments after this photo was taken. (Photo from Fr. John Wessel's album)

Trips

John Wessel's 1958 passport photo, at eighteen. (From Wessel family album)

Germany, 1961. John Wessel took this photo of (l-r) his mother, brother Edward, Jr., and sister-in-law Pat Wessel, holding Anne Marie, during his trip to Germany and Scandinavia with his mother in the summer of 1961. Four adults and two children squeezed into the Volkswagen Beetle. (Photo by Fr. John Wessel, supplied courtesy of Kevin Connor)

World traveler John, at 21 (far right), aboard the *U.S.S. America*, his second overseas trip, August 1961. Here John and his mother, Kathleen H. Wessel (far left), are greeted by John's Aunt Clare Hogan and brother-in-law William Beitel upon their return. (Photo supplied courtesy of Kevin Connor)

Paca Street/Roland Park

This photo, probably taken when John Wessel attended St. Mary's Seminary, School of Theology, in the Roland Park section of Baltimore, was made into a Christmas card. (Photo from Wessel family album)

John Wessel (top row, center) is pictured with his class upon his ordination to the subdeaconate, spring 1964. It was at this time the seminarians took a vow of lifelong celibacy. (Photo from Wessel family album)

The priests-to-be received four "minor orders" and two "major orders"—subdeaconate and deaconate—before receiving the Sacrament of Holy Orders in the pre-Vatican II Church. Here, John Wessel (kneeling left) is ordained a deacon at St. Mary's Chapel, Roland Park. (Photo from Wessel family album)

John Wessel with his mother . . .

. . . and family at his ordination to the deaconate at Roland Park, September 1964. (L-r) Kathleen H. Wessel, Maryann, John, and Edward, Jr. (Both photos from Wessel family album)

John P. Wessel (first row, far right) and his ordination class pose for their graduation portrait, spring 1965. John received a Masters Degree in Theology from St. Mary's Seminary. (Photo from Wessel family album)

John Wessel, at 25, upon his graduation and ordination, May 1965. (Photo from Wessel family album)

CHAPTER 17

ORDINATION

It was a glorious day, quite in keeping with the occasion, as seven young seminarians dressed in long white vestments, their hands folded in prayer, made their way in solemn procession to the altar of the stately old Cathedral to receive the Sacrament of Holy Orders.[1]

At 9:30 in the morning on Saturday, May 22, 1965, in St. Mary's Cathedral in Trenton, John P. Wessel was ordained to the Roman Catholic priesthood by the Most Reverend George W. Ahr, Bishop of Trenton, in the presence of his family and friends, invited guests, and fellow priests from the diocese. Around his neck, John wore a delicately embroidered white and gold stole, a special ordination gift handmade by a family friend. His boyhood friend, James Dubell, was among six other newly graduated seminarians ordained at the same time.[2]

The ordination of two native sons was cause for celebration among the small Catholic community of Mount Holly, and had even attracted the attention of the local newspaper. John Wessel and James Dubell were interviewed by the *Mount Holly Herald* shortly before their ordination, and their story and picture were featured in a lengthy article under the headline, "2 Boyhood Friends to Enter Priesthood Together May 22," which began:

> The life-long ambition of two boyhood friends will be
> fulfilled at their ordination to the priesthood on May 22 at St.
> Mary's Cathedral in Trenton.[3]

The ceremony was formal and solemn in character, and family members recall that John was elated on the day of his ordination. "He was very, very happy and it was a sincere happiness," said his cousin, Julian Wessel.[4] For John's family, it was a very joyous but emotional moment. There was great happiness in that the goal for which he had worked so hard had finally been achieved. Family members felt a kind of quiet joy that said, "He made it! The day is finally here."[5] But their happiness was tempered—John's father was not there. Dr. Edward Wessel's presence was missed, but his memory was very much alive in his family's thoughts.[6]

The Sacrament of Holy Orders was conferred in a solemn Mass. The deacons lay prostrate, arms outstretched in the form of a cross, symbolizing the total offering of their lives to Christ and His Holy Church. "Thou art a priest forever according to the order of Melchizedek" (Hebrews 5:6).

Now John Wessel had the special commission of the Church to grow in personal holiness and to share with others God's message of salvation. This was not so much the goal of his life; it was the beginning. For John Wessel, sharing the priesthood of Christ was all.[7]

In a world that was increasingly cynical and rejecting of Christ's message, he was to bravely proclaim "the way, the truth, and the light" of Jesus Christ and His Church.

In a troubled world filled with suffering and pain, he was to lead others to the abundant life that Christ offered to those who would follow Him.

Through his ministry of the Sacraments of Penance and Holy Eucharist, he was to be the channel of God's grace, which liberates the soul from sin and strengthens it on the journey to eternal life.

In a world saturated with all forms of pleasure but so lacking in genuine love, he was to offer the Divine Love of the Son of God who suffered, died, and rose again so that sinful humanity might be redeemed.

In a society increasingly rejecting of the gift of life, he was to celebrate the entry of each new life into this world, comfort the sick and dying on their departure from it into eternal life, and boldly proclaim the dignity of all human life.

And as marriage and family life was under attack and falling apart, he would unite man and woman in the Sacrament of Holy Matrimony, counsel marriages that were in trouble, and unite children and their parents in familial love.

He was to be holy, act courageously, speak truth boldly, witness to God's grace, and proclaim God's power, motivated only by the desire to please and serve Almighty God and to love His earthly children, not to earn the world's good opinion. Indeed, he must expect to suffer even as Christ suffered—to be misunderstood, rejected, criticized, harassed, even put to death.

In short, as John Wessel himself once wrote, the mission of a priest was "to be as much like Christ as he can and live in a world not at all in His image."[8]

Father John P. Wessel celebrated his first solemn Mass the following day, Sunday, May 23, 1965, in Sacred Heart Church, Mount Holly, with friends and family in attendance. Father Joseph V. Kozak, the former Sacred Heart pastor who had persuaded young Johnny to forgo the dream of becoming a missionary priest, preached the sermon. Father Joseph C. Shenrock, a friend of the family, was the deacon. Father Gerald Celentana, the pastor at Sacred Heart Church, was archpriest, and Father Harold L. Hirst, assistant pastor at Sacred Heart, served as subdeacon.[9]

The presence of Father Kozak, who had been so instrumental in John Wessel's vocation, was particularly meaningful for both of them. Months before, John had written to Father Kozak, then pastor at Saints Philip and James Church in Phillipsburg, New Jersey, asking if he would preside at his first Mass. The priest warmly replied:

> It does indeed seem hardly possible that twelve years ago you came into the rectory in Mt. Holly sights set upon being a "Maryknoller." It seems you had read a book entitled "Men of Maryknoll." Their outdoor life seemed inviting and in you they had a willing prospect. But so did the Diocese of Trenton need the priest and today I am happy for having sold you on the idea of becoming a parish priest whose mission field will be Trenton and its environs.[10]

When it came time for the homily, Father Kozak spoke first. Father Kozak was a very good preacher, and was beaming with pride for his former pupil as if he were his very own son. As Father Kozak was speaking on the altar that day, he became so caught up reminiscing that he broke down and cried. He eventually was able to go on, but to those present, it was a very touching moment.[11]

Father Shenrock said a few remarks, and then Father John Wessel delivered his first sermon as a priest.[12]

Father Wessel proved to be an outstanding homilist, which came as a bit of a shock to the rest of his family. They had no idea that he was such a gifted public speaker, and he far exceeded their expectations.[13]

"His first Mass was absolutely gorgeous," Maryann recalled. "He had a beautiful voice. I never knew it, and suddenly this magnificent voice resounded throughout the church. It was indeed a day that I'll never ever forget."[14]

Even though Dr. Edward Wessel was the absent family member at John's ordination, in essence he was truly remembered.

Father Wessel spoke warmly of his father on that day, as he would do on many other occasions. He said, referring to his own father's death, that one can continue to love and grow close to someone even in death as well as in life. One grows close through prayer and through the knowledge of what this journey of life is really all about. If we truly believe what we have been taught, he said, then death is sweet and eternally happy, and not to be feared. And although his father had passed away, he was still present with them in a different way.[15]

Because his father had died when John was just seventeen, he may have felt he did not get to know his dad as well as he would have wanted. This was due, not only to the brevity of his father's life, but because Dr. Wessel was a very hard-working, busy man. Being the youngest in a family of two older siblings also played a part. It is not surprising, therefore, that the theme of "growing closer to someone even in death" was one that Father Wessel often talked about and shared with others.[16] It was a hopeful message for anyone who had ever lost a loved one.

It took John a long time before he was able to speak openly about his father's death. "We were young. We were just in fourth year high school, and his father died of cancer of the stomach, very slowly, very painfully, in the early days when nobody could do anything for it," recalled Monsignor James Dubell. "He saw his father go inch by inch, and he was confused by it all. He took his father's death very hard, but he never really expressed it much. And then later, he talked about it."[17]

To his sister, John was "a private person," and very sensitive to the feelings of his mother and family. "I think John never wanted to upset us," said Maryann, explaining her brother's stoicism.[18] In the eight years since his father had died, however, John Wessel had come to terms with his own grief and, through faith, had gained perspective on life and death.

Father Wessel's words on the day of his first Mass echoed what he had expressed in private many times. Monsignor Dubell recalled:

> He would say that he thought of his father often. He said one time that there was hardly a day went by that he didn't think of his father, and he said that he would think of him at the most unusual times, or just any time at all. . . . And he felt a love and a closeness to his father.[19]

For the first time in his life, Father John Wessel was able to pronounce the words of consecration through which the bread and wine on the altar actually became the Body and Blood of Jesus Christ.

The chalice and paten Father Wessel used to celebrate his first Holy Eucharist that day was a family heirloom rich in symbolism and history. It was known as the "Bordentown chalice" and was a beautiful, ornate masterpiece of gold encrusted with jewels around the base and at mid-stem. But what was surely of greater significance to John, who cared little for material things, was the fact that it had first belonged to his uncles, Father (later Monsignor) Denis J. Duggan and then Father John Duggan. It was engraved with both their names. The chalice was originally a gift from the parishioners of St. Mary's in Bordentown to Father Denis Duggan in honor of the twenty-fifth anniversary of his ordination, which he celebrated there in 1899.

Father Denis Duggan went from Bordentown to Red Bank, New Jersey, where he became a Monsignor and lived to celebrate his fiftieth anniversary as a priest in 1924. He died the following year, on October 25, 1925, and was buried in Red Bank. Upon his death, Father John Duggan, his brother in the Newark diocese, received the chalice and used it until he passed away in 1945. The chalice then left the Duggan family for a period of twenty years. Father John had willed it to his friend, Monsignor John J. Sheerin of Morristown.

When John Wessel was about to be ordained in 1965, his family wrote to Monsignor Sheerin asking for the return of the Bordentown chalice and paten. It was a request the priest was more than happy to grant. The Wessel family engraved the name "John Patrick Wessel" on the chalice next to the names of his two priest uncles, and so it was quite fitting that the Bordentown chalice of Father Denis and Father John Duggan was again used at their grand-nephew's first Mass.[20]

Maryann and Bill Beitel's ordination present to John was also a precious family heirloom. Originally a gold pocket watch given to John's grandmother by her brother, Father Denis, it bore the inscription: "Mary Duggan from her brother Reverend D.J. Duggan, Christmas, 1887." John's sister Maryann had the watch case made into a pix, a small container used to carry the Consecrated Host. Now it contained the additional legend: "Reverend J.P. Wessel, 5/22/65, from your sister M.W.B."[21]

John Wessel's godfather, Julian Wessel, gave him a Hamilton wristwatch engraved, "To John from Uncle Jule and Aunt Helen, 5/22/65." Father John Wessel would wear it constantly from then on.[22]

Many invitations were extended to Father John Wessel's ordination and first Mass. In return, he received numerous congratulatory cards from friends and acquaintances, classmates and former teachers, and encouraging notes from fellow priests warmly welcoming him into the diocese.[23] Father Joseph Shenrock, deacon at Father Wessel's first Mass, had written him some words of encouragement and practical advice: "I suppose these days are filled with fears and doubts but depend more upon God's Grace and less upon yourself and I assure you it will all work out for God's honor and glory."[24]

The Protestant ministers in the town of Mount Holly were friendly with the Wessels and very kind to John, his mother recalled, and some of the ministers and their wives even came to his first Mass at Sacred Heart Church.[25] Among them was Reverend Herbert R. Denton, rector at St. Andrew's Episcopal Church, who promised to remember John at the altar of St. Andrew's on his ordination day, "praying that God's richest blessings may rest upon you as you begin your work as a Priest in His Church."[26] Indeed, it is not too difficult to imagine that in some small way, John Wessel's ordination, along with that of his friend James Dubell, helped unite the Catholic and Protestant communities of Mount Holly in an ecumenical spirit of Christian brotherhood and civic pride in the accomplishments of two of their "favorite sons."

Some of those invited guests who could not attend in person wrote touching notes expressing their joy and pride in his ordination.

John's eighth grade teacher, under whose patient tutelage he had passed his entrance exams for St. Charles College and started on his quest for the priesthood, wrote a heartfelt message:

> Dear Father John,
>
> "And My Joy no man shall take from you." My prayer for you now and always will be the echo of these words of St. John. There is no place I would rather be this Sunday than in Sacred Heart Church participating in your First Mass. Know that I will be with you in spirit sharing the intense joys which will be yours on this truly wonderful day. There are so many things I would like to say and I have whispered them all to Him during these final days of preparation.
>
> . . .
>
> Do enjoy a day replete with His richest graces and blessings and know that you will be in my thoughts and prayers in a very special way during these long awaited days. Thank you so much for remembering one [who] will never forget you. God love you always!
>
> Joyfully,
> Sister M. Espiritu[27]

And John's fourth grade teacher also sent her congratulations from Idaho, recalling the childhood dream which he had confided to her long ago.

> Dear John,
>
> I can't help but shed a few tears as I say congratulations. Tears of joy, knowing another one of our boys is going to the altar of God . . . I have looked forward to this day, John, hearing that you have achieved that little fourth grade boy's desire: "Someday I am going to be a priest and teach Indians. Nobody loves them." I think of you in a special way each time I visit the Indian reservation. Each year Mass is offered at the first Indian Mission Church. It is quite dilapidated but the different tribes

come dressed in Indian fashion and after Mass, they have a pow-wow for the rest of the day on the Church grounds. It is truly edifying to see how reverently they assist at the sacrifice of the Mass. . . .

I will be thinking of you and praying for you. The very best of luck to you John on your journey through your priestly life. . . . May our dear Lord bestow on you and your loved ones his choicest blessing.

Sister M. Christina, I.H.M. [28]

Each year, the members of the Serra Club of Trenton extended an invitation to all newly ordained priests to join them for a dinner in their honor. The Serra Club is a Catholic organization that fosters vocations to the priesthood and religious life. It so happened that at the dinner that year, Father John Wessel and Father James Dubell were seated at a table with Serra Club member James J. Moonan, who was also a trustee of Blessed Sacrament Church in Trenton. In the course of conversation, Moonan said to the two young priests, "Well, I know who is going to be at Blessed Sacrament."

"What's his name?" both of them said. Neither had as yet received his assignment from the Bishop. He didn't know the person's name, Moonan replied, but his pastor, Father Hayes, had told him just the other night that he was mighty pleased with the one assigned since he had the privilege of baptizing him.

"As it turned out, both the priests sitting at the table had been baptized by Father Hayes," Moonan later recalled, "so we were just as much in the dark as ever. We didn't have long to wait though; in a couple of days, Father Wessel came with us."[29]

CHAPTER 18

BLESSED SACRAMENT, TRENTON

A few weeks after his ordination, John Wessel was assigned to Blessed Sacrament parish in Trenton, New Jersey, where Father J. Arthur Hayes, the priest who had baptized him twenty-five years before and predicted he would be a priest, was pastor.

Johnny Wessel, the boy who wanted to be a martyr for Indians, had grown to become Father John Wessel, prepared to realize his dream of bringing people together so they would find the true meaning and value of life. Only instead of a far-off continent, his mission field would be an urban city less than twenty miles from the town where he was born.[1]

The city of Trenton, on the eastern shore of the Delaware River, with a population of over 109,000 in 1965,[2] began as a small outpost for an English Quaker, Mahlon Stacy, around 1679. In 1714, eight hundred acres were sold by Stacy's son to William Trent, a Philadelphia merchant, who in 1719 built a magnificent residence for himself and laid out a small village called "Trent's Town."

Trenton, as it soon became known, has a long and illustrious history in the struggle for American Independence. The city became famous because of the Two Battles of Trenton, which was considered the first turning point of the Revolutionary War. Every student of American history has heard the story of General George Washington's crossing the ice-choked Delaware River from Pennsylvania on Christmas night, 1776, and marching with his troops over eight miles through freezing rain and snow to surprise and defeat the Hessian soldiers garrisoned in Trenton on the morning of December 26th, thus liberating the city from the British. It was this decisive battle, and subsequent victories a few days hence again at Trenton and at neighboring Princeton, that "did so much to bolster confidence in Washington's leadership and ultimate victory."[3]

Trenton was twice the temporary capital of the United States in 1784 and 1799. It was the location where on July 8, 1776, the Declaration of Independence was first read publicly, and was the residence of David Brearly, who aided in the framing of the U.S. Constitution. It also became the State Capital and the Mercer County seat, and its gold-domed capitol building on West State Street remains a recognizable landmark.[4] Woodrow Wilson, the State's most famous governor and former president of Princeton University, served as President of the United States during World War I from 1912 to 1920.[5]

In the 1800s and early 1900s, Trenton rapidly developed as an industrial city, and was at one time the leading manufacturer of iron, steel, pottery and rubber.[6] John A. Roebling, who introduced wire cable into the United States for his suspension bridges, began to manufacture it in Trenton in 1848. Confidently did the bustling city hang its motto over the main highway bridge—"Trenton Makes—The World Takes."[7] In recent times, the city has produced more diversified industries and commodities.

The city was the seat of the Roman Catholic Diocese of Trenton, with a Catholic population in 1965 of over 596,000, or about 33 percent of the total population within the geographic area of the diocese,[8] which stretched across central New Jersey. Its spiritual center, St. Mary's Cathedral, a modified Romanesque structure rebuilt in 1959 after a disastrous fire, stands on land where much of the fighting during the Battle of Trenton took place.

The St. Mary's conflagration in the early morning hours of March 14, 1956 claimed the life of its beloved rector, Monsignor Richard T. Crean, and two women housekeepers in residence. It was later determined that the fire, which had started on the first floor of the rectory and spread with savage intensity, was the work of an arsonist. Monsignor Crean gave his life trying to save the lives of others. Rather than immediately escaping the building, the Monsignor had gone upstairs from his second-floor bedroom to the third floor to warn the others to get out. He was making his way up the staircase and was heard calling out to rouse the sleeping residents when he was overcome by smoke. Four priests staying at the rectory that night managed to escape the blaze, along with the cook.[9] One of the first on the scene, after the police and firemen, was Father (later Bishop) John Reiss, who bravely raced through the burning church to the tabernacle to save the Sacred Hosts from immolation.[10] The rebuilt St. Mary's Cathedral, where Father John Wessel had recently been ordained, was the site of all liturgical functions and celebrations of the diocese.[11]

The Church of the Blessed Sacrament, which would be Father Wessel's home for the next six years, was located at the corner of Bellevue and Hermitage Avenues in the western section of Trenton.

The parish was founded in 1912, and consisted of a large, beautiful, newly constructed sandstone brick church, which was built and dedicated in 1951 under the leadership of Father Hayes. Blessed Sacrament's pastor since the early 1940s, Hayes had come there directly from Sacred Heart in Mount Holly. The parish grounds also included an adjacent elementary school building, a convent for the Sisters of St. Francis who staffed the school, and a rectory which served as the residence and office for the priests.[12]

Blessed Sacrament had long been regarded as a very affluent, social and active parish. Among other parishes in the heart of the city was the consensus that once you had achieved some measure of economic or professional success, you eventually moved to the western section of Trenton and to Blessed Sacrament.[13] At one time, probably three-quarters of the members of Blessed Sacrament were former parishioners of Sacred Heart Church in downtown Trenton. With gentle Irish humor, they used to say that their friends had moved up to "Cracker Hill," because they had to subsist on crackers and milk just so they could afford to live there.[14]

In the mid-1960s, Blessed Sacrament still retained many features of the "elite" parish of Trenton. It had been the home parish of the governor of New Jersey, and its 1,600 families included leaders in State government, city officials, judges, lawyers, doctors, and many of the prominent citizens of Trenton.[15]

But Blessed Sacrament was also being affected by the decline of cities everywhere in the United States in the 1960s: the flight of the middle class to the suburbs of West Trenton and beyond to Lawrenceville and Princeton; changing demographics which brought greater numbers of poor families into the area; and social disorder on the streets and in the schools.[16]

The priests at Blessed Sacrament served a large State mental hospital, which included a medical-surgical facility and a unit for the criminally insane; a correctional institution for delinquent girls; and a sizeable general hospital. These duties, plus administering a parochial school of some five hundred pupils, kept the pastor and his two associates constantly active.[17]

Father J. Arthur Hayes was thrilled and ecstatic that John Wessel was coming to his parish. Proudly, he told just about everyone that he had baptized him, and spoke warmly of John's family, whom he had known in Mount Holly.[18] Father Wessel arrived on June 11, 1965 to join Father Hayes and Father J. William Mickiewicz, an associate a few years his senior.

At that time, Father Hayes was semi-retired and ailing, and rarely ventured out beyond the church grounds. But he was also a bit of a curmudgeon, a bellowing, blustery, authoritarian type of personality who could be intimidating even to those who loved and admired him.[19] "He was very loud and boisterous, and in some ways you would think that he was really a very rough man, but his bark was worse than his bite," recalled Father Mickiewicz. Father Hayes, "as I got to know him, was much different from his reputation."[20] Beneath his gruffness was a very big heart.[21]

Father Wessel was not put off by his new pastor's rough exterior. He loved the elderly priest and they worked together beautifully. Despite the fact that they came from two very different generations, Father Wessel's sister Maryann remembered "John just loving him very much and being very eager to learn from him, and calling him 'a shepherd—an outstanding example of a shepherd, God's shepherd, leading the people.'"[22]

John Wessel, for his part, proved to be "a very great consolation" to Father Hayes.[23]

Father Wessel had a strong sense of obedience to his superiors. He would call each of his pastors by the affectionate yet respectful title, "Boss," which immediately defined their relationship. He earned the reputation among his fellow priests as one who could get along with anyone, whether great or small, and always made it a point of doing so.[24]

As much as Father Hayes clearly loved his new curate, the elderly priest also had a tendency (whether by accident or design) to put his new priests "through the ropes" a bit at first, perhaps as a form of training or testing.[25] John Wessel accepted it with equanimity.

Once, Maryann Beitel attended a Mass at Blessed Sacrament when her brother was reading the Epistle. After he had finished, Father Hayes yelled loudly in front of the entire congregation, "Oh! All right, Father Wessel, do it over again. That was horrible!" It seemed that John Wessel's reading problems would catch up with him every once in a while.

The congregation was stunned and more than a little upset at the embarrassing treatment of the young priest by the pastor. But Father Wessel simply accepted the criticism calmly and read the passage over again without taking any offense. "That was the way he was," said Maryann.

Father Wessel refused to be drawn into any complaint or criticism toward his pastor. He just took the whole episode good-naturedly, providing an example of humility to others.[26]

As the youngest and newest priest, Father Wessel threw himself into parish activities with energy, enthusiasm, and constant devotion to Christian ideals.[27]

He taught Religion to seventh graders at Blessed Sacrament School once a week for several years, and then at St. Mary's Cathedral High School in downtown Trenton three days a week. For the adults of the parish, he conducted a four-part series on the Scriptures that made the journeys of St. Paul come alive.[28]

He visited the sick and the troubled at Trenton State Hospital and at the State Home for Girls where he served as Chaplain to hundreds of Catholic girls over the years. He conducted marriage rehearsals and found it "heartbreaking" that he had to counsel so many parishioners with marital problems.[29]

Along with the other Blessed Sacrament priests, Father Wessel was "on call" at all hours of the day and night for hospital emergencies to anoint the dying and to minister to the sick. As Chaplain to the Mercer Hospital, he was called there so often that the hospital's Intensive Care Unit practically became his second home. He often visited ill parishioners at other Trenton hospitals, St. Francis and Helene Fuld, technically outside the boundaries of Blessed Sacrament parish.[30]

At Masses for Blessed Sacrament School, he drew the children's interest with stories of his personal experiences that held lessons for them.[31] He had charge of the annual Thanksgiving clothing drive, which lasted until the following January. When the schoolchildren brought in clothing for those less fortunate, the young priest packed boxes of clothing until "my hands felt as if they were coming off."[32]

Naturally, there was a certain amount of adjustment for both the new priest and his parishioners. Although Father Wessel had years of study prior to his ordination, and was filled with desire and dedication, he didn't yet have all the answers or know how things were done. In his first days at

Blessed Sacrament, he quickly learned and grew in his priesthood. He also experienced the grammar school youngsters' tendency to try to "put one over on the new guy."

A group of altar boys at Blessed Sacrament School had "funeral duty" just about every Tuesday. The good part of it, from the kids' point of view, was that they got out of school for a while to serve at the funeral Mass in church. And after the Mass was over, the altar boys immediately returned to school. But at John Wessel's first funeral Mass, the altar boys "somehow convinced him that, no, we needed to go to the cemetery to complete the entire ceremony . . . We were getting out of another hour or so of classes, and we went off to the cemetery," recalled Barry Anderson*, who later became very good friends with the new young priest.[33]

Shortly after arriving at Blessed Sacrament, Father Wessel was asked to assist in the Diocesan Vocations Program. He visited Catholic schools in the area and, with zeal and enthusiasm, spoke to young men about the joys and challenges of diocesan priesthood.[34] As a measure of his success, Father Wessel was appointed Mercer County Vocational Director by Bishop Ahr in 1969.

Over the years, he also served as Moderator to various parish organizations to which he provided spiritual guidance—the Holy Name Society, a Catholic men's group, and the Rosary and Altar Society, a Catholic women's group.

He was Spiritual Director to the Sisters of Our Lady of Sorrows for several years, and was Ordinary Confessor for the Sisters of St. Joseph Church in Trenton.[35] He found time to visit a home for unwed mothers in the city and to work with some of the poor families who lived in the "projects" near Blessed Sacrament.[36] He counseled parishioners on a host of personal and spiritual problems, and helped them in countless ways.

And from his very first days at Blessed Sacrament, Father Wessel was Moderator of the parish's Catholic Youth Organization ("CYO"). He cheered for the young boys and girls at their CYO basketball team competitions, and organized the older teenagers of the parish into an active, vibrant Christian community, centered on love for Christ and for each other.

"He made the kids a community and taught them how to take care of one another, and how to lift one another up, and give good example to one another," said a Blessed Sacrament Sister.[37]

In the words of Bishop John Reiss, then a priest in Trenton:

I was aware of the fact that he was doing so much good work with youth, especially with the youth, and that he was a good worker—really going out to people, willing to listen to them at any time and to go out of his way to help them. And that, I think, is basic of what a priest is supposed to do and be: a servant in the image of Christ to other people in good times and bad.[38]

Father Wessel's work with the youth of the parish was his crowning achievement. To be more effective in his youth ministry, he took advanced courses in Juvenile Work at nearby Rider College in the summer of 1968. His efforts were rewarded with an appointment by Bishop Ahr as Mercer County CYO Director in 1970.

The youth of the parish loved him, and the older people loved him, too. Like Saint Paul, Father Wessel could be "all things to all people" for the love of God. Because he was always ready to help others and had great energy and enthusiasm, he was greatly esteemed by the whole parish.[39]

All this was in addition to his liturgical duties at Blessed Sacrament Church, since his first and foremost job was to administer the sacraments. He performed his share of daily and Sunday Masses, confessions on Saturdays and eves of Holy Days, First Fridays, Forty Hours Devotions and Benedictions, marriages, baptisms and funerals. Sometimes the young priest celebrated two or three Masses each day, and spent hours in the confessional.

Father Wessel ministered to the spiritual needs of the parishioners. In the words of his friend, Monsignor James Dubell, "he united man's children to God, their Father, in the Sacrament of Baptism. He brought the healing love and mercy of God to sinners in the Sacrament of Penance. He made Christ the third pastor to bride and groom in Matrimony. He mended man's frail body and soul with the sacred oils in the Anointing of the Sick."[40]

And, "through the Word of Christ and the Bread of Eternal Life, Father Wessel brought his parishioners in a spiritual bond with each other and with God."[41]

Such was Father John Wessel's life as a parish priest. It was no different from that of any other priest in parishes all over the world. What is remembered is the zeal and devotion that Father Wessel brought to his priesthood.

His was a busy, active parish. So much so that Father Wessel jokingly referred to it (in the language of the sixties) as "Parish a Go! Go!"

"We were busy all the time," Father Mickiewicz recalled. And with an elderly pastor, the two younger men "had to do his work, too, plus take care of him."[42]

Father Hayes couldn't run to answer the calls from the institutions under Blessed Sacrament's care, so his two associates ran for him. He used to tell them that "he was the head and we were the feet." And John Wessel certainly ran his legs off for the pastor.[43]

Father Wessel had a great desire to minister to people in ways that were considered new and innovative at the time. When he first came to the parish, the priests generally went to the hospital only when they were called, and in some ways it was ritualistic. Said Father Mickiewicz:

> We didn't have an organized way of working. We didn't visit the hospital, because the pastor didn't like us visiting the hospital. We went and took care of those who were ill. The only organized thing was to hear confessions at the State Hospital during Easter time, because that was our responsibility.[44]

John Wessel envisioned a more systematic kind of ministry—making "rounds" at hospitals, to bring people Holy Communion and pray with them regularly, which was not the way things were done at the time. His fellow associate recognized in him the "initial zeal" of one who "wanted to do things" and "to get it all organized."[45] In many ways, John was ahead of his time.

Father Wessel didn't try to buck the system or change the status quo. He just quietly went about his business doing what he thought needed to be done. He made his hospital rounds as often as he could. Eventually, it seems, he was able to implement some of his ideas on ministry when the parish was assigned a new pastor.

According to his fellow associate, John Wessel was fearless when it came to meeting difficult situations and counseling difficult people. He did not hesitate to go to the criminally insane prisoners in the Vroom Building nor the delinquent girls at the State Home. The young priest was brave in his ministry. He was "fired up" and would "charge in" whereas anyone else might become fearful and withdraw.[46]

Thanks to his athletic, outdoors nature, Father Wessel possessed excellent physical stamina, but he nevertheless worked himself to the point of exhaustion—not only physically but emotionally as well.

In the diary that Father Wessel kept for a few months, his entries reveal the harsh realities of his work and his distress over those who were suffering:

> January 3, 1966:
>
> Today had six anointings at State [Hospital]. One had no face, just a skull—most horrible I've seen. Can't get it out of my mind.

> January 26, 1966:
>
> Call to South Hermitage ... dead for three days, poor woman! Could hardly recognize her as a human being, yet not in records. God help those who die alone.

> February 4, 1966:
>
> Went down to Mercer and St. Francis [Hospitals] in afternoon—many sick. I'm depressed—Cancer is such a hard trial—God have mercy on your people at *finis* ...

> February 8, 1966:
>
> Off for a haircut and then to Girls' Home. [Saw] four of them. Poor *kids*, they were all messed up sexually. Some of them so young you could imagine—11 years old, one was ... looked like any girl on the street.

The demands on Father Wessel's time stemmed from Blessed Sacrament's responsibilities to three large, active institutions: Trenton State Hospital (or simply, "State Hospital"), Mercer Hospital, and the State Home for Girls. Even though the two associates had worked out a "day on/day off" schedule for answering emergency calls, it was grueling for the man who was "on" that day. He might go to one hospital to be with someone who was sick or dying, and no sooner would he come back to the rectory than another call would come in. He could be down at the prison one minute and at the hospital the next. It went on this way all day long and into the night.[47]

Father Wessel was never known to refuse anyone who needed his help.[48] But his diary reveals the grueling pace of answering, at times three, four, or five calls a day:

> January 1, 1966:
> A hectic night with a night call. 1 dead, 2 critical. . . . Said the 11 and 12. Call in between to S.H. [State Hospital] dead. Counted the number of calls. 210 since I came, 130 mine. Dear God, what a mess.

> February 2, 1966:
> Mercer called . . . State called, D.O.A. Get back and Mercer again, D.O.A. The woman should have had me before this. Back in and State called—alive—but I'm getting tired of running. Back home and a call from Mercer—I run. Down there—made the rounds this time. (Communion calls tomorrow).

Although he never complained to others about his routine, Father Wessel often felt extremely tired and exhausted. "I need a shot in the arm," he confided to the privacy of his diary. "I'm so tired I could drop," he wrote on another occasion. "Went to M.A. [Maryann's] for dinner—very good but tired. Must need vitamins," read another entry.[49]

"John would get physically tired," confirmed Monsignor Dubell, due to his exhausting schedule. He was the kind of person who could be on the go for three days straight, and then sleep for a day and a half.[50]

Father Wessel was very close to both his sister, Maryann, and brother, Edward, and their families. Edward had returned from Germany, settled in Newton, in northern New Jersey, and was beginning his career as a surgeon. Maryann and Bill Beitel lived in Morrisville, Pennsylvania, on the other side of the Delaware, just about a ten-minute drive from the parish door across the Calhoun Street Bridge. Both Father Wessel's siblings now had growing families with small children.

Father Wessel became a frequent visitor to the Beitels' home on Crown Street in Morrisville. For him, it was a blessing because he would go there to catch a little sleep and to relax after being on call all night. He often said that if he didn't have a place to sleep before heading back to the parish, where the phone wouldn't stop ringing, he "didn't know what he would do, wouldn't be able to keep it up."[51]

"We used to tease him that we didn't know why he was tired—he only worked one day a week!" said Bill Beitel. It never failed to make John Wessel laugh. His good sense of humor carried him through some of the more difficult situations he encountered in his priesthood.[52]

Being in the company of the Beitels' children was a welcome change of pace for the busy priest who saw so much of human misery. Playing with the happy, innocent little children, his godchild, Beth Ann, then a toddler, and infant Susan, never failed to lift their "Uncle John's" spirits. Soon, another infant girl and two little boys would be added to the Beitel family. "He would come in so depressed, and pretty soon the kids would be playing with him and he'd be relaxed, and then he'd decide he'd had enough. He was always happy to come and happy to go," said Bill Beitel. "We often joked that he'd picked the right vocation because he couldn't take the pressure of all the kids."[53]

In addition to the routine of parish activities, there was always the unexpected moment. Frequently, people who were down on their luck would come to the rectory door looking for handouts. Father Wessel would give them his last dollar. At other times, people would stop by to talk about their marital problems. Father Wessel would take the time to listen to them, and would remark on how very sad it was.[54]

On one occasion, Father Wessel was in the heart of Trenton very late at night when he was accosted by a man who wanted a handout. He took out his wallet and gave the man what little he had, a few dollars at most. Afterward he related the story to his sister. "Aren't you afraid?" Maryann asked him. "No," came the reply. "I really don't ever have any money on me anyway."

Maryann would urge her brother to be more careful, but to no avail. "He never was worried about anything—never," she said. "His whole point to me, when I would caution him the few times when I would see that he was exceedingly exhausted and worry about his driving—and he would always say to me, 'Maryann, don't worry. I am ready whenever God wants me.' He had really total faith in what he was doing."

His total faith in God's love and mercy was such that he was content to leave everything, including his very life, in His hands. At times, his sister found this difficult to accept and would chide him, "God helps those who help themselves, John." And his response? "Well, he would give me one of his looks and consider that rather profound—and do exactly what he intended to do anyway!"[55]

Father Wessel experienced great joy in his priesthood. It was this joy and complete fulfillment in his vocation that made everything else worthwhile.

He once confided to his cousin, Julian Wessel, that becoming a priest "wasn't the easiest thing in the world. It required a lot of work and a lot of dedication—but there was nothing else that he would rather do."[56]

And Maryann well remembered her brother's joy at his first Thanksgiving Mass after his ordination. Father Wessel was just so elated and yet so humbled to be granted the privilege of being a priest that the usually stoical young man was overcome with emotion:

> When he celebrated his first Thanksgiving Day Mass in 1965, he had tears of gratitude in his eyes. He said how happy he was that God had granted him the fulfillment of his goal to enter the religious life.[57]

As he celebrated Mass that day, those who witnessed his sincere and unabashed joy were deeply touched by it. His sister was awed by his "total happiness at what he had chosen to do."[58]

As a servant to others in the image of Christ, the priest is privileged to witness the tangible effects of God's miraculous grace and power in the lives of others. As one who brings the love of God and salvation of Christ to humanity, perhaps the greatest joy for a priest is to bring a lost soul back to God.

On one occasion, Father Wessel was asked to counsel the proverbial "woman caught in adultery." It was a difficult task for the young priest and caused him some degree of apprehension. Praying for guidance from above, he visited the woman and convinced her to stay with her husband, although he was deeply concerned about her moral situation. Some days passed, and the woman apparently asked the priest to visit her again. With some trepidation Father Wessel went. "This is not my cup of tea, but it's God's," he thought to himself.

The unfaithful wife had a change of heart. At her request, Father Wessel heard her confession and granted her absolution. "God certainly acts in strange ways," he commented, as the woman was reconciled with God.[59]

A diary entry for February 15, 1966, illustrates the worth of Father John Wessel's willingness to give an extra measure of devotion and duty:

> Thank God for his miracles and surely this one. 5:45 this morning was called to Helene Fuld [a Trenton hospital outside the parish]. Wasn't going to go but did anyway. Mrs. Johnson, 9 months pregnant, was bleeding like hell. What a mess—nurse said she was very bad so I baptized her—brought her out of shock. The baby was supposed to be dead but was taken alive and she's alright. 2 for one.[60]

After many hours at the hospital with the critically ill mother and her infant, Father Wessel returned to the rectory exhausted but elated that both mother and baby had come through. Truly a miracle![61]

John Wessel had hardly been at Blessed Sacrament six months when Father Hayes became seriously ill and had to be hospitalized. For quite a while he had been a semi-invalid and the two associates had to carry the bulk of the pastoral work. Father Wessel's diary entry for January 6, 1966 indicates the hectic pace:

> Said the eight. Confessions, confessions. Went right down to see Pastor. He's in good spirits but not physically . . . Called the doc when I got through with kids. 5th graders problems with sex—it begins early! Everyone's calling—go—go—hear more confessions and 12. After lunch went box hunting; Art Craft gave them to me . . . Back to the box at 4 to 6; got caught by a drunk—gave him the pledge . . . Calls and back to box at 7:30. No business. Worked until 9:30 and gave up. To bed late—read too long.[62]

The associates now had to take care of administrative and financial matters of the parish for the pastor, in addition to their usual heavy work load. Attending to parish finances and banking each Monday was perhaps Father Wessel's least favorite activity—"Money Monday" he called it.[63]

Father Wessel visited his ailing pastor in the hospital practically "all the time, whenever he had a moment." He prayed for him, and brought other parishioners to the hospital to visit him.[64]

In his diary for January 11, 1966, John Wessel wrote:

> Went down to see Father Hayes in the morning. He seems quite well. Said he was sick after breakfast but kept down the food eaten in the evening. He is a bit worried but a good soldier.

Father Hayes was scheduled for surgery on the morning of Friday, January 14, 1966, for an apparent stomach ailment. The prognosis had been good. John Wessel had visited and talked with him in the hospital the night before. He listened as the elderly priest from a different era reminisced about old times at St. Charles, and serving at the last Mass of the poet-priest Father Tabs.[65]

But Father J. Arthur Hayes died in his sleep in the early morning hours of January 14th—"a real tragedy for me personally but can't let on too much," John Wessel wrote.[66] It was later learned that Father Hayes had died of cancer of the pancreas.

Father Wessel was devastated at his beloved pastor's death, but he tried to contain his emotions and be strong for others. During the wake a few days later, Father Wessel, out of respect for the pastor, asked the men of the parish to take turns standing watch with Father Hayes's body throughout the night.[67] The requiem funeral Mass for Father Hayes was, Father Wessel remarked, "a great tribute to a grand priest."[68]

"He certainly is in Heaven," John said of his late pastor. "My only regret [is] that my days are numbered" at Blessed Sacrament "and I could have learned so much more from him."[69]

After Hayes's death, Father Wessel thought that he might have to leave his present assignment, but he resolved that the matter was "God's will, not mine." A few months later, Blessed Sacrament was finally assigned a new pastor.

In his diary entry for March 15, 1966, Father Wessel wrote:

> Funeral in the morning and normal day somewhat. The new pastor is expected sometime today—of course there are anxieties

attached but encouragement from fellow priests. I hope *I* will be able to adjust well enough—I still, after 9 months, don't have things down. Confession, in particular.[70]

Father Eugene V. Davis assumed charge of Blessed Sacrament on the Feast of St. Joseph (March 19th) 1966, having served as pastor of Sacred Heart Church in New Brunswick for eighteen years.[71] The assignment of Father Davis as pastor eventually relieved the young priests of their extra burdens.[72]

Father Davis recalled his first encounter with Father Mickiewicz and Father Wessel, who both greeted him at the front door of the rectory. "It was a rather formal greeting, and they were both happy to see me." The two associates were both "pleasant, as really they were the whole time we were together. They were two very nice people."

Father Davis was a different personality than the former pastor. He was a quieter man, humble and plain-spoken, with an air of holiness and simplicity. He was a man who loved people, very much like John Wessel himself.

Father Wessel immediately hit it off with his new "Boss," whom he described as a "wonderful man, a bit shy, but I love him very much."[73] Any concern on his part that he might be moved quickly vanished.

Father Davis recalled John Wessel's considerateness. The pace of parish life, especially hospital calls, was as fast and furious as ever, but Father Wessel insisted that pastor Davis should not have to answer the night calls. "Father, we'll take care of that, not you," he said, volunteering himself and the other associate.

"So they took all the night calls," recalled Father Davis. "I would go if there was nobody there, but John . . . said I shouldn't think of it, that they were very able to take care of it. That was John. He was very thoughtful like that."[74]

"I had nobody, my folks were gone," Father Davis said. At Christmas and Easter time, he would stay behind at the parish and send his associate priests home to enjoy the holidays with their loved ones. On these occasions, Father Wessel made sure that his pastor did not spend the holidays alone. He always invited Father Davis to his sister's home in Morrisville, where together they enjoyed a festive dinner with Maryann and Bill and their youngsters.[75] "I remember John passing a few babies around the dining room table, back and forth to Father Davis, as I prepared the holiday meal," said Maryann.

Father Davis's memories of Blessed Sacrament were of "a very happy house." The "house" included not only the pastor and his two associate priests, but Alice, the live-in cook, Catherine, the secretary/receptionist, and Margaret, the cleaning lady. The Sisters of St. Francis resided in the convent nearby and taught in the elementary school. When Father Mickiewicz left for a new assignment in 1967, both priests were "sorry to see him go."[76] Several other associate priests followed and stayed for various lengths of time.

*   *   *

Over the next several years, Father Wessel, now the senior associate, continued to work at a hectic pace and began to distinguish himself in many aspects of his priesthood, but especially in his work with the youth. In the words of Monsignor Dubell:

"He established the C.Y.O. at Blessed Sacrament Parish in Trenton so well that the success of his work attracted the attention and respect of the entire city."[77]

*   *   *

Father Wessel, his older brother, Edward, once observed, "didn't carry his priesthood on his shoulders."[78]

He was unpretentious, quiet, reserved, but with a sense of humor that delighted in pranks and slapstick and often produced laughter that Father Davis described as "a horrible cackle."

Father John Wessel had a lifelong indifference to material goods. His only suit was unpressed and in need of repair. He hardly ever wore his cassock because, as he once explained, "I always trip over the thing."[79]

He drove an old jalopy, and when the pastor once lowered the stipend for the Blessed Sacrament clergymen who served as hospital chaplains, his response was, "but we were too rich."

He was, as his Uncle Michael Hogan said lovingly, "the scruffiest looking priest you ever saw." But he had an interior calm and dignity that shone through his unpolished exterior.

He lived by a favorite Scriptural lesson (Luke 12:22): "Do not be anxious for your life, what you shall eat, nor yet for your body, what you shall put on."

Father Wessel showed ordinary human qualities without pretense. His joy in simple things, in skiing, tennis, and rough outdoor life, was genuine. So were his efforts to curb his sometimes earthy language, which, he once wrote, "as an act of supreme sacrifice . . . I've got it down to damn and hell."

Assigned to an affluent and social parish like Blessed Sacrament "wouldn't mean a hill of beans to someone like John Wessel," said a fellow priest. Unimpressed with wealth and status, he was interested only in going about his work ministering to others.[80]

He shunned the limelight and didn't seek the company of those who could grant him favors and advancement. There was enough to do around the parish, and John Wessel never had to be asked.

*   *   *

Father Wessel and his pastor, Father Davis, worked together for the next five and a half years, until both left the parish at about the same time. Friends recalled that the younger priest "had great admiration for Father Davis."[81]

And of Father Wessel, his former pastor paid him what amounted to the highest compliment: He was "a very, very fine priest."[82]

CHAPTER 19

THE MAN AND THE PRIEST

One of Father Wessel's early assignments was teaching Religion class to seventh graders in Blessed Sacrament School once a week. Sister Bridget, the seventh grade teacher, had these recollections of the young priest:

> [M]y thoughts go back to the time when Reverend John P. Wessel was just a name. Father Hayes told us that his boy "Johnny" was coming to Blessed Sacrament. When he did arrive my first impression was that he was a shy but holy priest. Being holy was proven many times in the next six years but being shy, I have my reservations on that.
>
> The first year at Blessed Sacrament Father was involved in many activities, one in which I had contact was teaching religion to my seventh grade class. He was truly a friend to the children and was always at their call. He helped many a boy, who had a family or social problem, face reality and learn to cope with it. Father always had something positive to say about the way religion had been taught in my classroom. However, when the children did not listen to him, he would leave the room and tell me not to go back until the period was over. This only had to happen once or twice as the children loved Father and did not wish to hurt him.[1]

Many of the Sisters of St. Francis remembered Father Wessel's great concern for the children—not just the children who were in school but those who had graduated, too.

Often Father would stop by Sister Elise Betz' eighth grade classroom after school to discuss certain students he was worried about. He would talk about some of the girls who were in some trouble and ask Sister to speak with them privately. She would do the same with the boys who concerned her, and Father would take them aside. Sometimes it might be a problem in the home or with academics; sometimes a young girl might be "acting fast" or a boy "acting up." There were also the beginnings of some problems with marijuana, petty theft and shoplifting among a few students.[2]

All the Sisters, in fact, would call on Father Wessel when there was a problem with the boys, and he would have a talk with them in the principal's office. Father never seemed to mind. He would always tell the principal, Sister Catherine Georgine Portner, "If you ever have any problems, just call me, Sister." And really, the students never seemed to mind having to go and talk with Father Wessel.[3]

He was "a priest for teenagers," said Sister Catherine Georgine, always trying to help them and see the good in them. He always said that "they weren't bad, if you (the adults) would help them."[4]

The Sisters noted how the young people had the greatest respect for him. They never even called him "Father John," it was always "Father Wessel." It wasn't that he demanded this courtesy, but he was just so good that they immediately recognized that and looked up to him.[5]

Father Wessel seemed quite shy when he first met the Sisters. "There was something very sweet and gentle and naive about him that just immediately won you over to him," recalled a nun. "You just wanted to protect him. He just seemed almost too good to be true."[6]

As they got to know one another, his initial shyness broke down a little. The Sisters soon learned that the young priest had a ready smile and a good sense of humor. According to Sister Bridget,

> Father Wessel's sense of humor was to be found in all he
> did. I often think of the watch with the alarm that went off at

the most unusual times causing embarrassment. Father would say that it was a signal from Father Davis to return to the rectory. This watch was lost in the accident where Father went through the windshield of his car. . . . This did not hold Father down for long as he was back in action in a day or so.[7]

He was quick to laugh and slow to anger.[8] And his walk was memorable. Sister Elise used to call him "Jumpin' John Wessel" because of the very distinctive spring in his gait.

Father Wessel's sense of fun was never more evident than at his "Christmas Eve tradition" of coming over to the convent after Midnight Mass dressed as Santa Claus to wish the Sisters a Merry Christmas. Usually, he had a group of young people from the CYO group in tow.[9]

On one memorable Christmas Eve, there was a terrible snowstorm. It started early on Christmas Eve day, and by midnight the snow was eight or ten inches deep. The Sisters were sitting in their dining room when, all of a sudden, there was a knock at the door. Father Wessel had come over on skis. He brought a Christmas gift for the Sisters, came in and sat down with them. "I remember he brought some type of liqueur, and to be polite, we took it—and I almost choked!" recalled one of the Sisters.[10]

Father Wessel got plenty of use out of his Santa suit—he delighted in playing Santa to his young nieces and nephews. To his niece, Beth Ann Beitel, "He was a real easy person to get along with. We had fun with him. I remember him playing guitar, and dressing up as Santa Claus. And he would never get the beard on right. It would come half off. He didn't do a really effective Santa job, but he tried!"[11]

Despite moments of levity and laughter, Father Wessel always took seriously the most important aspect of his vocation—the sacramental life.

The Holy Sacrifice of the Mass was at the core of Father Wessel's spirituality.[12] He drew his strength from God, and nowhere was God more present than in the Holy Eucharist. He loved celebrating the Mass, and he once told Sister Elise that it was "the high point of his day." To his co-workers, it was obvious that he "really cared about being a priest."[13]

Father Wessel was devoted to the Holy Eucharist. He had no doubt that the Eucharistic Presence of Jesus was an actual reality under the form of bread and wine. His deep and personal devotion was apparent even in his speech. When going to the hospitals on communion calls, he would say that he was bringing "Our Lord" to his sick patients. When the parish had Forty Hours Devotion in progress, he remarked, "Certainly wish I could stay with Our Lord longer."[14]

In his plain-spoken style, he once explained his awe at the mystery of transubstantiation to his cousin, Julian. "It just hit me," he said, after he had been ordained. "You're not doing a milk run on a plywood altar anymore in the seminary. This is the real thing and God is present here!"[15]

Father Wessel had a beautiful way of saying Mass. He was totally absorbed in it. Those who witnessed his liturgies recall him being transformed in mind as he would say the Mass. He was so caught up in the whole spirit of the Holy Sacrifice that people would remark to one another, "Don't you love the way that he says Mass?"[16]

"We all loved to attend Father Wessel's Mass," recalled Sister Bridget, "and felt the reverence by which it was celebrated. His sermons were magnificent and he could hold the second to the eighth grade students spellbound . . ." And it wasn't just children and teenagers who were spellbound. "I knew grown-ups who couldn't wait to hear his homilies," recalled a former parishioner. People would purposely go to his Masses just to hear him give a sermon.[17]

Father Wessel was a good preacher.[18] His sermons, parishioners recall, were uplifting and well thought out.[19] He was able to mesmerize his audience with the wonderful power of his words, and could really zero in on the message of the Gospel.[20]

He could also be hard on himself if he thought his sermons had fallen short. "Preached again but poorly—must get on the ball," he confided in his diary (January 31, 1966). "Shepherd's lost to flock—preached to self, I think" (January 23, 1966). And another time, he remarked that his homily was "pretty good—at least, I *said* what I wanted to say" (February 4, 1966).[21]

About the only aspect of the homily that gave Father real difficulty was in asking his parishioners for money. That was not his forte, necessary as it was, and he was always a little apologetic about it.[22]

Second only in importance to Holy Mass for Father John Wessel was the Sacrament of Penance. Again, he was diligent and zealous in ministering to others as they confessed their sins and received forgiveness.

"He was very wonderful in the confessional," recalled a former parishioner. "You felt the presence of God there." It wasn't just that he would listen to the confession and dispense the penance, but he would also give good advice and helpful words of encouragement to the penitent.[23]

Father Wessel was very earnest about giving the right advice to people in the Sacrament of Confession. In order to help his own understanding of their problems, the young priest sought out the opinions of a few medical professionals to assist him in counseling them. These consultations were done only in generalities, for never would Father reveal the sins of specific individuals. In fact, the priest is prohibited from doing so by virtue of the "seal of confession," by which any sins confessed are held in absolute secrecy.

"He had some problems with some of the contents of the confessions and he wanted it related to medicine, and so we used to talk it over," recalled Dr. Raymond McCormack.

Dr. McCormack and his family were parishioners of Blessed Sacrament and lived across the street from the rectory. He was also a surgeon at Mercer Medical Center and Trenton State Hospital. The McCormack children went to the parish school, and his oldest son was active in the CYO.

One day after Mass, Father Wessel approached Dr. McCormack and asked for his assistance. The two men began to meet regularly on Friday evenings in the rectory. In those sessions, Dr. McCormack advised the young priest on various medical, psychiatric and sexual problems that he encountered in the confessional.

Father Wessel was "one of the nicest priests I ever met," recalled Dr. McCormack. In spite of the seriousness of their subject matter, the doctor's memory was of a priest who was very happy, and very friendly.[24]

Another professional to whom Father Wessel turned was Dr. Julio Del Castillo, a psychiatrist in private practice in Trenton and a clinical psychiatrist at Trenton State Hospital.[25]

He worked in the Forensic Psychiatry Unit of the Hospital, commonly called the Vroom Building, the institution for the criminally insane. Persons who had committed crimes and appeared to be suffering from mental illness were sent to the Vroom Building from jails and penal institutions throughout the State for diagnosis and treatment. Over the years, Dr. Del Castillo had worked with some of the most dangerous and notorious psychotic criminals in New Jersey.

The Del Castillo family were members of Blessed Sacrament Church and deeply involved in parish life. The children attended the parish school. His sons were altar boys, and often Father Wessel would drive them to church and back. His oldest daughter, Ana, a bright and gifted child who excelled in several languages, was a member of the CYO. "My children loved him," Dr. Del Castillo recalled.

Father Wessel consulted with Dr. Del Castillo "on many, many occasions," seeking his advice about psychiatric matters. But where the problems were more complex, such as marital difficulties, serious mental disturbances and substance addictions, Father referred the penitents to the psychiatrist, who would treat them without charge.

The priest and the psychiatrist became good friends. "He was a very courageous man . . . very outgoing and aggressive and wonderful with people," the doctor recalled.

But as a professional psychiatrist, Julio also became concerned that Father Wessel spent a great deal of time in the confessional talking with people, sometimes for hours, giving them advice.

"Father Wessel had the inclination to get too involved with the patients. . . . He wanted an immediate cure," Julio explained. "I advised him not to keep spending time in the confessional giving advice to people" because, for those who are very sick, professional treatment is required, and simple advice won't work. "In many ways, the poor man was wasting his time giving advice to people who wouldn't listen properly," said Julio.

Father Wessel would also visit the homes of people with mental and emotional problems who had asked for his time. This, too, troubled Julio because this was something that a professional would not do.

"I remember talking to him on many occasions," continued Dr. Del Castillo. "I was consistently advising him not to exceed himself in the counseling of people, because he went to the homes of people." The doctor warned Father Wessel not to go to the homes of persons who were troubled, "because there was danger involved" with those who were mentally ill.[26]

A professional person, a psychiatrist, would generally not visit the patient at home, or any place, for that matter, where there was a danger that the patient could attack him. But if on occasion he had to do so, the professional, by virtue of his training, would be alert and suspicious about what could happen, and made sure he was always protected in some way, said Dr. Del Castillo.

"I thought that he was taking too many risks." He was trying to be a psychiatrist, Julio, full of concern, told Father Wessel, and he "shouldn't play at being a psychiatrist" any longer. "The problem was he exceeded himself."[27]

It was probably difficult advice for Father Wessel to heed, because he wanted to do so much for people. Why did Father continue to exceed himself? "Out of kindness," explained Dr. Julio Del Castillo. Father Wessel was "a very kind, good-hearted man" who only wanted to "bring happiness to people."[28]

And so, he continued to exceed himself.

The same zeal that led Father Wessel to expend himself in the confessional also drove him to minister with great devotion to the sick and imprisoned.

In Scripture, the words of Jesus Christ remind us that "For I was . . . ill and you cared for me, in prison and you visited me. . . . Whatever you did for one of these least brothers of mine, you did it for me" (Matthew 25:35-40). This was a lesson that the young priest understood quite well.

"That was one of his special loves—to go to the hospital whenever there was a problem," recalled his sister, Maryann. He never failed to go to the assistance of someone in need.[29]

"I spend more time at [the] Hospital than any other place," Father Wessel once wrote.[30]

Mercer Medical Center, where Father Wessel was chaplain, was his most time-consuming project, although he often visited sick parishioners at other Trenton hospitals.[31] He also ministered to the physically and mentally ill at the Trenton State Hospital, where Blessed Sacrament was under contract to serve as chaplains and was given a stipend for their priests to go regularly.

"He would want to be there when they needed him, and he would cancel his own plans to accommodate them," Monsignor James Dubell recalled.[32]

Father Wessel was deeply concerned about the patients and their illnesses. "Most of the people seem very sick," he remarked sadly after one hospital visit. "Might be losing a few."[33]

Dr. McCormack told of how Father Wessel would go into the chapel at Mercer Hospital, where a record of all the Catholic patients was kept. He would diligently go over the list, note all the room numbers, and visit them. "He was very sincere and hard-working," said the doctor, who saw Father often at the hospital, "sometimes every day."[34]

The story of Donald Matlack is perhaps typical of the measure of Father Wessel's care and concern.[35]

On June 30, 1969, Donald Matlack was severely injured at work on the railroad at a steel company in Roebling when a six-foot steel ingot which was being hoisted on a railroad car came crashing down on him. He jumped just far enough out of the way to avoid what would have been a fatal injury; the steel ingot hit his legs, resulting in the loss of one leg and serious injury to the other foot. Matlack was rushed the twelve miles to Mercer Hospital in Trenton and was prepared for emergency surgery.

Donald asked his wife, Dorothy, to call for a priest. When a priest of their acquaintance at a nearby parish could not be found, the hospital nurse helpfully suggested, "Father Wessel's only a block away, and he's nice. He'll come." They called Father Wessel at Blessed Sacrament and—as Dorothy Matlack told it—no sooner had the nurse hung up the phone than Father came flying through the door. He must have ran all the way over. "I presume I got the Last Rites," said Matlack, who by this time was losing consciousness, slipping into shock.

"So then, while I was in the hospital . . . he came in to visit me many, many times." Matlack had to have seventeen additional surgeries over the next ten weeks. "And I had to go every other day, and every other day he was there to see me. And this I'll never forget."

Donald Matlack was in the hospital for a total of four months. Father Wessel brought him Holy Communion, and stayed to talk and joke with him, at least every other day. Matlack's memories were of a relaxed, happy, smiling priest with a bounding stride. "Every time he walked in that door, he had a smile on his face," recalled Don. "You really looked forward to him coming, and it really gives you a big boost."

Matlack was discharged from Mercer Hospital in the fall, thankful that he was able to walk out on his own with a cane and a prosthetic leg. On the morning he was to leave, Father Wessel came to see him and brought him Holy Communion. At that, the burly steel worker broke down and cried. Matlack had been seriously ill for four months, and the fact that Father Wessel was concerned about him and came to see him all through that time affected him like "no words can express."

To Donald Matlack, Father John Wessel was "irreplaceable."

Trenton State Hospital was a psychiatric hospital founded in 1848. In the mid-1960s, the hospital had a population of approximately 3,200 and contained at least six separate facilities: two semi-autonomous psychiatric hospitals, East Main and West Main; a 400-bed medical-surgical hospital, which functioned as a city general hospital, and also handled physical emergencies from other State institutions; a forensic psychiatric unit, the "Vroom Building," serving the psychiatric needs of New Jersey's criminal population; a children's hospital; and a continued treatment section consisting of four separate buildings, mainly for geriatric patients with varying degrees of physical and psychiatric disability.[36]

When Father Davis came to the parish, he took charge of the State Hospital, and would go once a week to visit the patients and celebrate Mass. But in the case of emergencies or night calls, Father Wessel or another associate priest would respond to the call. Confessions were heard regularly for the psychiatric patients at State Hospital, and Father Wessel assisted his pastor in that, too.[37]

Father Wessel often went voluntarily to the psychiatric hospital to minister to the criminally insane in the Vroom Building, which was in essence a prison, and to the mentally ill in the general population. Perhaps from his Roland Park days visiting the inmates at the Maryland State Penitentiary, Father Wessel had great compassion for those who were in prison. He also seemed to have a special tenderness for the mentally ill, those locked in a "prison" of a different sort.[38]

A letter from Mrs. Kendrick R. Lee, Director of Volunteer Services, Trenton State Psychiatric Hospital provided a clue as to the impact of his ministry to the mentally ill. Mrs. Lee related how she had taken photographs for an open house exhibit at the hospital, which included several pictures of Father Wessel counseling a psychiatric patient:

> The patient in the photograph was discharged shortly after the pictures were taken. . . . [Later] the patient contacted me and asked for copies of the photographs. He said Father Wessel had helped him very much and knew the photographs would be a reminder of their relationship.[39]

Going with Father Wessel to say Mass at the State Hospital was often a daunting experience for his young altar boys. One young man recalled feeling quite intimidated walking into the psychiatric hospital with Father and "practically wanting to hold his hand." But Father always reassured them with his calm and steady manner. He took the time to prepare them for the unfamiliar situation so they would be calm and unafraid, and then talked with them about it afterward.[40] "Maybe he didn't have any fear, or he just didn't show it," another altar boy recalled, "but it sure helped!"[41]

In addition to his emotional strength, the young priest had two other notable qualities which served him well in the psychiatric hospital: the ability to adjust to any situation, and a keen sense of humor. A story recalled by former altar boy, Kevin Gallagher, illustrates both:[42]

One day Father Wessel, with fifteen-year-old Kevin, began Mass in the chapel for the Catholic patients in the general psychiatric ward. Suddenly, just as Father had finished his sermon, a man got out of his seat and came up on the altar.

The patient walked up to Father Wessel and handed him a large, thick envelope addressed to the Pope. "Please, Father," he said, "when you see the Pope you have to give this to him."

And without batting an eye, the priest took the envelope and said gently, "Certainly. Tomorrow when I see him at dinner, I'll hand the letter to him."

Meanwhile, several guards had come up the aisle and took the man by the arm, saying, "Come on, let's go sit down now." At that point, something in the patient snapped. Without warning, he shook off the guards, ran down the aisle, and made a beeline for the door, shouting, "I'll fight for my religion!"

As if on cue, one guard tossed the set of keys to the guard at the back of the room, who quickly locked the doors as the other guards wrestled the patient to the floor in the back of the chapel in an attempt to restrain him. "And next thing you know, behind the pews, periodically, I could see a white-uniformed guard would get thrown up in the air," said Kevin. After about five minutes of struggling, the guards finally subdued the patient. He was placed in a straight jacket, and the liturgy continued.

By this time, Kevin was terrified. Father Wessel must have known it—"it was obvious just looking at me. But he winked at me and said, 'That wasn't so bad now, was it?' and went on with the rest of the Mass."

"The man was a rock," said Kevin Gallagher.

Father had a very special way with the patients. In one sense, he treated them as normally as he treated anyone else. Yet "you could just see that he had . . . an extra reservoir of patience" with them, said Kevin. He was very gentle.

Julian Wessel recalled a conversation with his cousin John while still a seminarian:

"What do you do in the seminary?" Julian had asked.

"Well, we do all kinds of things," John told him. "We just don't sit in the building and pray. We go out, and we go, for instance, to prisons."

John explained about visiting and counseling the inmates in the Maryland State Penitentiary, and playing football with them. "You've really got to take people as you find them," he commented.

"Weren't you scared?" asked his cousin.

"No," John replied. "They're not so tough when you get 'em on a one-to-one basis. 'There is like that of God in every man'," he said, quoting an old Quaker proverb.

For John Wessel, no one was completely evil; some goodness could be found in everyone, even in hardened criminals. It was that goodness that Father Wessel tried to reach with those in the Vroom Building.[43]

One who had a close-up glimpse of Father Wessel's ministry to the criminally insane was Ronald Garrett*, a CYO youth who often accompanied the priest on his visits to the Vroom Building of Trenton State Hospital. Ronald was a youth whom Father had befriended in a special way. As a young man, Ronald had a difficult home life, his father was gone, so Father Wessel became a father figure to him.

Ronald Garrett shared these recollections of the priest he affectionately called "Pop":[44]

Father Wessel constantly went to the prison on his own time. That was not unusual for Father because he went to many other places on his own to try and do some good—like hospitals, soup kitchens, and schools. The criminally insane patients were locked up behind bars, and Father would talk with them through the bars.

Some of the patients were unable to respond. Others sometimes would manage to say "Thank you, Father" or "I'm sorry for what I've done." But with all the inmates, Father Wessel "had the gift of God." He would pray for them, and make the sign of the cross over them and give them his priestly blessing.

After the visit was over, Father asked Ronald what he thought of it. "Pop, I never realized that people were going through that!" the youth exclaimed.

"I don't want you to get upset about it, Ron," the priest replied evenly, "but by the same token I want you to realize what's going on."

Ronald was the only youth that Father ever took on his rounds to "the Tombs," as the Vroom Building was called. And with hindsight, Ronald realized that their visits were probably as much about the priest's desire to help *him* as about helping the inmates. By including him, Father Wessel was trying to show him that there were others worse off than himself and to encourage him to believe that his life would be better one day.

Ronald Garrett never forgot Father Wessel's compassion for the insane prisoners. "Ron, you just need to pray for these people," the priest would often say. "They are God's children."

Father Wessel, in the words of his cousin Julian, "took those people who were the most downtrodden, the most rejected, the bottom of the barrel socially, as we would look at them, and yet found some redeeming features in them."[45]

Another of Father Wessel's great passions was Sacred Scripture. Scripture was a part of everything he did simply because it was God's Word. He lived by its messages, casually interwove it into his speech, and included its verses in his personal correspondence.

When in 1966, grammar school classmate Eileen Egan made her Profession of Final Vows as a Sister, Servant of the Immaculate Heart of Mary, Father Wessel's gift to her was a double volume set of Scripture meditations. "It was so thoughtful of him at the time since we hadn't seen each other since his father's death," said Sister Eileen. "I felt that John knew what I'd appreciate, and it seemed like such a priestly way of deepening our commitment to God's word."[46]

After a few years at Blessed Sacrament, Father Wessel had an opportunity to share his love of Scripture, which developed through his studies at Roland

Park, with the people of the parish. For two years, from spring 1967 to fall 1968, he conducted a four-part series in "The Study of Sacred Scripture" for adults one night a week at the church.

The series that Father Wessel taught at Blessed Sacrament began with a comprehensive treatment of the Old and New Testaments, with special emphasis on the Psalms, the classical prophets, the Catholic Epistles and the Gospel of St. John. The last semester ended with a study of the Apostolic Church through the writings of St. Paul, St. Luke, and the Apocalypse of St. John. According to an article entitled, "Blessed Sacrament, Trenton, Continues Study of Scripture" in *The Monitor*, the Catholic newspaper of the Diocese of Trenton:

> Fr. Wessel notes that no foreknowledge of Scripture is required of those participating, "only the will to learn more of the wonderful works of God in history and His legacy to us in the present day."[47]

The class was a small but very interested group. No one ever wanted to miss a lesson. Using the Jerusalem Bible, they studied the Scriptures from both a religious and historical perspective. "Father Wessel would have us read passages and then open it for class discussion. It certainly produced some lively sessions," said a former student.[48]

Ruth Bacovin, who attended Father Wessel's Scripture classes, recalled "a very bright and energetic young man" who was "wholly committed to his calling." She also remembered her teacher's endearing mannerisms: He had a habit of wiping his shoes on the back of his trousers, and was always pushing his glasses up as they were constantly sliding down his nose.[49]

Many remember his lectures on the Journeys of St. Paul. Father Wessel had great devotion to St. Paul, and under his tutelage, the Epistles of the Apostle to the Gentiles "came alive, as so did all the Scripture around this period."[50] Inspired by Father's enthusiastic teachings on St. Paul, Sister Catherine Georgine embarked upon her own study of the Saint's writings. "I think St. Paul had a great impact on Father Wessel," she said.[51] The adults in the class were very disappointed when Father's pastoral duties prevented him from continuing his Scripture series the following year. But they were grateful for the time they had with him, and for what they were able to learn from him.[52]

Father John Wessel was a man who loved and cared about people. Sometimes he expressed this in ways that seemed quite ordinary, almost inconsequential, except to the person who had experienced it. One such person was Rudy Girandola.

Rudy and his family were parishioners at Blessed Sacrament. Rudy's brother, a priest at the time, was one of the very first to leave the priesthood and marry, and write a book about it. His story, which was almost unheard of in the mid-sixties, made national news. It was quite a shock to everyone in the Catholic community, including Rudy himself.

"This situation was the talk of the parish," Rudy Girandola recalled. "It not only was a condemnation of my brother in the average Catholic's eyes, it spilled over to me and my children in Blessed Sacrament School." One Sunday at Mass, a visiting priest gave "a blistering sermon, condemning my brother's action and the scandal. He urged the parishioners to condemn him, too," all the while Rudy, his ill elderly mother, and his family were sitting in the front pew of Blessed Sacrament Church. They all were left "in the state of shock."

What was memorable to Rudy Girandola, however, is that Father Wessel was the first person from the clergy to call him and offer some kind words. "Considering the situation, Father Wessel's act of reaching out to me immediately becomes more heroic," he said. "Father Wessel helped me to deal with this national attention and place it in its proper perspective." And shortly thereafter, Father Wessel asked him to become a lector at Blessed Sacrament Church. Rudy recalled how Father Wessel would often visit him at home, and how the young priest's empathy and understanding helped him through the situation. "He taught me how to handle it."

Again, Father put himself in the other person's shoes. He anticipated when someone might have felt alone, confused or isolated from the Church community and, without even having to be asked, reached out to make the person feel welcome, loved and needed—because to Father Wessel, he was. Here, too, we see traces of the little fourth grade boy who moved his desk next to another child, to whom his classmates had been unkind, just to make her feel accepted.

Over the years, Rudy Girandola and Father Wessel developed a pleasant friendship through working together at the church. Rudy's recollection was of a "hands-on" priest who was always right in the middle of parish activities, and ever available to those who needed him. He could often be seen walking the streets of the parish talking to people, and even taking care of the church grounds. But his strongest point, said Rudy, was his ability to keep the youth involved in church activities through his "dynamic" approach to young people.

When the Girandolas moved away from the parish in 1968, Father Wessel wrote Rudy a warm and appreciative letter thanking him "for all you have done for me personally, these last three years." Father Wessel's letter continued:

> Rudy, don't lose your generous spirit. In my time here at Blessed Sacrament, this virtue you particularly have shown has made me understand Our Lord's message much better. The big step in the Christian life after "acquiring" this Christ-like way of life, is to keep faith in step with love. Not only divine faith but faith in people.[53]

Rudy reflected that this powerful statement well represented Father Wessel's philosophy of life. He had faith in God, and he never lost faith in people. He would try to help people, no matter what the situation, simply because he *had* faith in people.[54]

Father Hayes had a favorite saying: "God is good and so is His Mother. He never closes one door but He opens another."[55] Perhaps that explains how Father Pat Hannan came to Blessed Sacrament near the end of Father John Wessel's tenure there, at a time when he was sorely needed.

Father Hannan was a priest of the Order of the Holy Ghost Fathers of Ireland, one of three Irish brothers in his family who became priests. He had been a missionary in North Africa, and was believed to have had charge of a school in Kenya until his Order was forced out by the authorities due to political turmoil. Father Hannan returned to his native Ireland.

Father Davis recalled what happened next:

> Pat was over in Ireland and he wanted something to do. So the Chancery called me up and said, "We've got a fellow looking

for work, but you'll have to pay his fare over and back." I said, "It's okay, I'll take him." So that's how we got Pat.

"Pat was a great Irishman. We all got along well there, too," said Father Davis. "I was lucky enough to get him because we needed three men."[56]

Father Hannan was a bit of a shy person, but he had a great gift for working with the sick. The Irish missionary was truly a godsend to the parish because of the several hospitals and the many sick calls that they had to attend to.[57] No doubt, he helped Father Wessel carry the load.

On the cook's day off, Father Hannan prepared dinner for the house. This proved to be an inadvertent source of humor for all, since the former African missionary priest was in the habit of liberally spicing his meals with curry, until he realized that the other two priests couldn't stand such hotly seasoned food. "We both used to howl!" recalled Father Davis. Still, his fellow priests used to get "quite a charge" out of Pat and "that curry business."[58]

Father Hannan was an older man, but he and Father Wessel hit it off immediately and developed a wonderful respect and friendship.[59] Father Hannon considered John Wessel as his "very dear friend" and "one of the most generous hearted and devoted young Priests" with whom he had ever been associated. Perhaps for this reason, Father Hannon counted his days at Blessed Sacrament as among "the happiest 18 months of my Priesthood."[60] Indeed, he wrote, "I would go so far as to say—no Rectory in the U.S. had 3 such differing personalities who formed so strong, sincere and deep a friendship."[61]

From his very first days at Blessed Sacrament, Father Wessel served as chaplain at the State Home for Girls, at that time New Jersey's only correctional institution for delinquent girls. Most were teenagers, but a few were as young as eight or ten.[62]

The State Home for Girls was located on a 183-acre tract of land within fifteen minutes of downtown Trenton. There were ten cottages housing an average of 225 girls. On the grounds were a school, chapel, administration building, infirmary, kitchen and dining room, and other small buildings.[63]

All the girls in the State Home were committed by the New Jersey courts after having been involved in some trouble with the law. The purpose of their stay was for rehabilitation, not for punishment. Each cottage had an adult female "cottage officer" in residence at all times. Educational and vocational training was afforded the girls to prepare them for productive lives after their release. The average length of stay was from twelve to sixteen months.[64]

The residents were predominantly Protestant, although roughly a third of the girls at any one time were Catholic. Protestant and Catholic chaplains were contracted for by the State to provide for the girls' spiritual needs.[65]

Father Wessel visited the State Home every Sunday to celebrate Mass in the small New England-style chapel on the institution grounds. He heard confessions one Saturday a month, and often stopped by during the week to interview the new Catholic girls and see what he could do for them. Moreover, he was available to respond to emergency calls if a staff social worker determined that a girl had a pressing problem involving religion and needed to talk to a priest.[66]

Father Wessel came to know each Catholic girl personally, her name, her family, and her problems. The Superintendent of the State Home, Miss Regina Flynn, estimated that the young priest was a friend to at least two hundred girls there during his years in Trenton. He saw no wrong in any of them.[67]

The girls responded to his genuine concern for them. They liked him very much, "and every one of them, after Mass, would want to stop and talk with him," recalled Miss Flynn. Father would stay and give them as much time as he could, to the point where Miss Flynn would feel compelled to warn him that the girls would keep him there talking all day if he let them. They were hungry for his time and attention because they "just wanted somebody to accept them," noted Regina Flynn.

Father's greatest attribute, and the reason for his success as a counselor and confidant to troubled young girls, according to Miss Flynn, was first, the very fact that he listened, and second, that he did not condemn them.[68]

In 1969, when Patricia,* in the throws of an LSD "flashback," attacked Miss Flynn and threw her to the floor, Father Wessel visited the girl in the psychiatric hospital to which she had been transferred, to reassure her of Miss Flynn's forgiveness and help her regain some emotional balance. Patricia had been consumed with guilt once she realized what she had done. Father's wise suggestion that the girl write an apology letter to Miss Flynn helped relieve her distress.[69]

The young priest was not wholly confident of his ability to deal with delinquent girls. "I hope I do some good out there, but doubt it very much—sometimes I'm the loser," he wrote in his diary. "These kids know more about hell than the devil."[70]

Sadly, some of the girls had been lured into promiscuity as a result of having been molested by older males, often relatives or household members. Father Wessel noted his shock and distress at the plight of a girl at the State Home who "has been seduced sexually to the extent of perversion," he confided in his diary. "The only thing that can save her is a miracle."[71]

The young priest had seen girls as young as eleven who were "all messed up sexually."[72] He prayed for them and tried to counsel them as best as he could.[73] "God enlighten me to be true to the Spirit," was a prayer written in his diary.[74]

Father Wessel sometimes brought members of the parish CYO to the State Home for Girls. One CYO member, Joanne Wesley Gillespie, told of how Father cared deeply for the girls:

> I was there on a few occasions with him with these young girls who were pregnant and not married, or in trouble for whatever reason. His heart would just go out to these girls. And sometimes I remember wondering if he was going to cry, because he appeared to be so touched by their pain or by their isolation . . . He couldn't just witness somebody's pain or somebody's problems and just pass by . . . And that touched us because it was so obvious to us how much he cared. It made us care.[75]

Regina Flynn summarized what she observed of Father Wessel's attitude toward the young girls in her charge: "You have a dignity as a human being no matter who you are, irrespective of what you do." He didn't view them according to the offenses that they may have committed. That was incidental to him. In fact, "he never ever even asked why was a girl there." What was important to him was that this was a child of God, made in His image, with a dignity and worth, who had a right to have somebody listen to her and care about her.[76]

Father's ability to offer these troubled girls unconditional love and acceptance is recalled by Father Wessel's former altar boy, Kevin Gallagher:

One day, fifteen-year-old Kevin accompanied Father as he went to the State Home for Girls to celebrate Mass. They walked past the residence cottages to the building which housed the chapel. "I just remember walking with him and holding his chalice, and listening to them shout out the window at one another." And the things these girls were saying! They "were using words I had *never* heard before," not even "in the locker room with the guys." Kevin was completely shocked at the girls' foul language.

But the truly striking thing to him was Father Wessel's reaction. Unfazed, he walked up to some of the girls who'd participated in these foul-mouthed exchanges only moments before and greeted them as though each girl "was one of the most upstanding women in the parish." Kevin was taken aback at how respectfully Father treated these young ladies and "how calm he seemed to be no matter what the situation."

"Father Wessel always seemed to treat people as he envisioned them," said Kevin, with the hope that perhaps "that's what they would become." Father refused to treat them, as perhaps many others did, as though they were worthless. And if the priest could find some worth and value in these girls, then just maybe they would begin to recognize these qualities in themselves.[77]

There was little that could be done by Father Wessel or anyone else, however, when poor fourteen-year-old Rebecca*, her mother a mentally ill alcoholic constantly in and out of psychiatric hospitals and her father a wandering carnival worker, took her own life at the State Home for Girls.[78]

Rebecca had been admitted to the State Home a few months before. On the night before her suicide, she was the leading lady in the production of a play at the institution. Rebecca was very happy on her way to the play and performed her part very well, but afterward she seemed withdrawn. After getting into a fight with another girl, Rebecca was placed in the detention cottage for the night. She had made no prior statements of suicide.

When the girls put on plays, their families were invited to come and see the performance, but nobody came to see Rebecca on what should have been her special night to shine. In fact, she never had any visitors for the entire time she was at the State Home.

At about eleven o'clock the next morning, a cottage officer discovered that Rebecca had hung herself in the bathroom with a sheet. Desperate attempts to revive her proved futile. In a final, tragic irony, at the same moment she was probably hanging herself, a social worker had been on the phone trying to convince Rebecca's relatives to come and visit her. Perhaps this was "the final blow to her, that really nobody cared for her," observed Miss Flynn sadly.

Father Wessel was called and immediately responded to the institution and gave Rebecca the Last Rites of the Church. He commented that he knew Rebecca as she frequently stopped after Mass on Sundays to talk with him. In fact, he had just talked with her on the previous Sunday.

When Father Wessel came for Mass at the State Home the following Sunday, he devoted his entire sermon to Rebecca, comforting her friends in their shock and sadness while providing a spiritual lesson for them about life and death.

*   *   *

The grim realities of human suffering encountered in his priesthood could not dim Father Wessel's love of life. He still found much joy in simple pleasures, outdoors pastimes, and the company of friends. These moments of relaxation served as a means for him to "recharge his batteries."

In August of 1965, Father Wessel invited three young men from the parish to join him on a two-week camping trip to Quebec and New England. For fellow campers, Ronald Bacovin (then a seminarian in his last year at Roland Park), Ken Kawalek and Bob Ball, it was a memorable experience.

The four adventurers took off in Father Wessel's sturdy green Plymouth for Canada via upstate New York, loaded down with camping paraphernalia. Father "had enough faith in the people he was with that he would let us drive, even though we were only eighteen years old," recalled Ken. So all took turns driving to give the priest a break, and also to allow him time to quietly recite the Divine Office.[79]

"We would be stopping at different campsites along the way to cook our food and camp out," Ken recalled. "So we traveled the first day and we made it to Lake George. . . . Well, that was the afternoon that the whole running joke of the whole trip started. It seemed that every time we stopped to eat or camp, it would start to rain. Matter of fact, it got to be that if it wasn't raining, we weren't eating."

They missed the last ferry of the night across the border from Three Rivers, Canada. Stuck out in the middle of nowhere, they bedded down for the night in a farmer's field. The next morning the happy campers were awakened by a cow.

Once in Canada, the men headed for Quebec and the Shrine of Saint Anne de Beaupré, revered by the French Canadian Catholics as the Mother of the Blessed Virgin Mary and Grandmother of Jesus. Once at the Shrine of St. Anne, they climbed the endless flight of stone steps to the huge Cathedral on hands and knees, like all the other pilgrims, as a sign of penance and piety. It was quite a moving experience for the men.

By this time, the travelers were looking scruffy and disheveled, having been on the road for several days. Father Wessel wanted to look good before they went to the Shrine, so they stopped along the road to shave. They had no water so they used the coffee out of their thermos bottles to shave, recalled Ken.

After a few days camping in Canada, the adventurers were ready to return home. They crossed the border and made their way to the town of Island Pond and spent several days and nights at a little Vermont campground called Brighton State Park, ranging out from there to explore the surrounding area. True to form, every night they camped, it rained; every time they ate, it rained. One night it rained and rained so hard that Bacovin and Wessel's tent filled up with water. Father Bacovin's most enduring memory of that trip was of waking up soaking wet.

Father Wessel's culinary skills with simple ingredients were legend. His friends distinctly recalled the way "Wess" made coffee. He never bothered to use a percolator—he just threw the coffee grounds into a coffee pot and "boiled the hell out of 'em." And how did it taste? "If you didn't mind the grounds, not bad!" said Ken.

Father Bacovin remembered having "one of the best meals in the worst circumstance with John." One night when it was raining terribly, John Wessel made a food concoction just by mixing a bunch of ingredients all together in a pot and cooking it over the fire. "We were drenched but to be under a tent was wonderful and the food tasted very, very good," said Father Bacovin.

While passing through New Hampshire they stopped at Mt. Washington in the White Mountains, the highest mountain peak in the Northeast. After due deliberation, they decided not to drive to the top of Mt. Washington, perhaps fearing that Father Wessel's sedan wouldn't make the climb. But they stopped at a roadside gift shop where Father Wessel bought a Scottish plaid tam-o'-shanter that he liked very much. He had a penchant for berets and tam-o'-shanters and owned several of them.[80]

In no time, the campers were back home in New Jersey. Rain and all, it was still a great trip.[81] For Ken Kawalek the adventure was "probably one of my best memories" of his youth. Father Wessel was "good to be around" in any kind of weather, said Ken. "Whenever you were around him, he treated you like you were his long lost, best ever buddy."

While stationed in Trenton, Father Wessel developed a love of skiing through his friend and mentor, Monsignor Leonard R. Toomey. Monsignor Toomey was Diocesan Director of the CYO and in this capacity their paths often crossed as Father Wessel regularly came to his office to get CYO materials.

Monsignor Toomey recalled being "very impressed" when he first met young Father Wessel. John Wessel was "truly a very spiritual man" and "a thoroughly happy priest" who had great appeal to young people. And "you could sense from being with him, and as one priest to another, that he had a deep-rooted spiritual life and a wonderful sense of priorities. He wasn't concerned with a lot of the trendy things, but was right down to very basic things."[82]

Monsignor Toomey had served in the city of Trenton for many years and in 1966 became pastor of Sacred Heart Church. Father Wessel heard that Monsignor Toomey, being a New Englander from Massachusetts, liked to ski. The elder priest went skiing every week during the winter with a group of men, including a number of priests, both young and old, and several area laymen. The ski areas of Great Gorge in New Jersey, or Camelback or Big Boulder in the Pocono Mountains of Pennsylvania, were frequent destinations.

Monsignor Toomey recounted a conversation in which Father Wessel mentioned that he had never skied but would like to try:

> He said, "Gee, I've always wanted to ski." And I can remember saying to him, "Well then, why don't you join us?" and he said, "Well, could I?" And I said, "Sure, anybody's

welcome . . . the more the merrier." And so he said, "Great," and he started to come with us.[83]

Although he wasn't an expert skier, Father Wessel threw himself into it with gusto, savoring the feeling of exhilaration and freedom flying down the slopes. He didn't mind if he ended up (as was often the case) sprawled out in the wet snow; nor did he mind the amusement of his friends that his pants were usually ripped before the day was out.

When Father Michael Choma came up from Baltimore to visit him the first winter after ordination, John convinced his former seminary classmate to go to Bell Mountain, near Lambertville, New Jersey, to learn the rudiments of skiing.

At that time, Mike didn't know how to ski, but John said, "I'll teach you, no problem. It's easy." At Bell Mountain, they rented skis and boots. John showed him how to put on the equipment, gave him a little ski lesson, and demonstrated for his friend how to grab onto the tow rope and pull himself to the top of the mountain. Mike fell a few times, but learned to ski by the end of the day. "I was beginning to wonder if this was really worth it, and then I just caught on."

A few weeks later, Father Wessel planned a ski trip to Stowe Mountain, Vermont, with Mike Choma and a few of their seminary friends, who were by now all busy parish priests. Without John's knowing it, Mike quietly practiced his skiing, and the next time they got together at Stowe Mountain, John was quite surprised at Mike's improvement.

This was the first of several trips to Stowe Mountain for John Wessel and his former seminary classmates. When they went on these long car trips, Choma recalled how John would always say, "Hey, let's be safe"—meaning, let's get back in one piece and not take any chances. "We always took our time" driving back and forth.[84]

In addition to skiing, John Wessel often played tennis and golf with friends and fellow clergymen. He was one of a group of four priests who would meet regularly to play tennis. In addition to being a very holy priest and an all-around nice guy, John Wessel was "always competitive" and "lots of fun to be with," recalled Monsignor Armand A. Pedata, one of the tennis foursome, which also included then-Father James Dubell, and an older priest, Monsignor Thomas Ryan, who was Father J. Arthur Hayes's good friend.[85]

Father Wessel also had a hunting license and loved to hunt in the woods behind "the Farm" in Mount Holly where his uncle, Dr. James Hogan, now lived with his family.[86]

Marriage and family life are, and always were, matters of central importance for the Church and society, and Father Wessel had a great sense of family. For him, the importance of marriage and family life was not just a matter of teaching and preaching in the abstract, but was evident in the love and commitment he demonstrated to each of the members of his own large, extended family.[87]

Of course, Father Wessel had seen his share of marital problems through his priestly counseling.[88] He knew from the experience of his priesthood, and also from his two older siblings, that marriage was not simply a magical, romantic odyssey of self-fulfillment: It was a godly, mature way of life, filled with joy and happiness, but also demanding tremendous amounts of self-sacrifice and responsibility. "He saw marriage as a serious undertaking, with all of its problems as well as with all of its joys," said Monsignor Dubell. "He was very mature in that sense."[89]

When a young CYO couple turned twenty-one and wanted to marry, Father Wessel was initially concerned that they were too young.[90] Although he did indeed perform their marriage ceremony, he advised and counseled them at length in preparation for marriage. "Now are you very good friends or are you really in love? Is this a serious relationship?" he asked. He wanted to make sure that they were not just mistaking good friendship for the deep love necessary for marriage.[91]

Because Father Wessel had a personal relationship with each of the teenagers in his CYO group, he had insights into what was going on in their homes, and knew what young people needed most in their relationships with their parents.[92]

To parents of the parish, he had some trenchant advice on the subject of raising children: Parents should not try to be "pals" to their children. Don't be afraid to be authority figures. Be firm but loving with them, he told parents.[93]

Father Wessel always seemed to classify himself as an "old timer" and was traditional in his values, recalled Father Davis. He had little patience for the sexual revolution and the hedonistic philosophies that flourished in the sixties.[94] He saw it as the cause of so much of the marital unhappiness and moral confusion that he had observed. He once made a sad but apt commentary on the morality of his times: "Sex is in everything. Publicity has taken the lid off of *sin*."[95]

The young priest was very devoted to his sister, Maryann, and brother, Edward, and to their spouses and children. He was very supportive of them and proud of their accomplishments: Maryann as a devoted mother of five, and Edward, a brilliant, successful surgeon and father of a growing family, which would also eventually include five children.[96]

While still in the seminary, a letter to his brother, Edward, and his wife Pat, shed light on John Wessel's views on parental responsibility. In this passage, which he directed to Edward, he wrote:

> How is your work? I was surprised to hear that you want to go on further. I'm very proud of you, to say the least, but remember your primary responsibilities to your raising those kids of yours. So many times when you have to work so hard for something, that becomes the end all for you.[97]

His sister Maryann was a young mother with five little children during John's years at Blessed Sacrament. Many times she drew upon her brother's support as she and her husband coped with the daunting task of parenting five youngsters.

"John was always full of encouragement" for Maryann in her role as a mother. "When life would get me down and my nerves were frayed, he would listen and console, 'Maryann, you'll be fine. You're doing a beautiful job.'"[98]

Father Wessel also had a strong concept of the role of the father in the family. He felt that the father should be the spiritual head of his household and, in a sense, the "priest" of his own family. He tried to foster this respect for the father as a spiritual leader among his nieces and nephews.[99]

When "Uncle John" joined his brother's family for dinner, the natural tendency was to ask him to say grace. But Father Wessel would demur, saying "I'm not the father in this house. It's the father's position to say grace in this house." And when the children would get a new religious medal and wait for their Uncle John to come and bless it, he would always remind them, "Your father can do that." Father Wessel encouraged the children to look to their own father for moral and spiritual guidance.

Although he was a priest, he never tried to supplant the role of the father in the family, said Pat Wessel. Perhaps he learned this from observing his own father, who was a devout Catholic and an excellent and virtuous role model for his wife and children.[100]

Edward and John Wessel were not only brothers but were very close "buddies." Monsignor Toomey remembered John's admiration when his brother decided to settle in the small town of Newton, New Jersey, and begin a medical career, just like his father had done in Mount Holly, rather than opt for a big-time practice in a large city.[101] When his brother moved to Newton, John pitched right in, helping the young family to unpack boxes and get settled.[102]

Father Wessel loved children and was always solicitous of his young nieces and nephews. When Maryann and Bill Beitel's young daughter, Beth Ann, caught her first big fish, a carp, in the Delaware Canal which was adjacent to the Beitels' backyard, Father Wessel dropped what he was doing at Blessed Sacrament Church, jumped in his car and drove right over with his camera. The child's proud father didn't have film in his camera and wanted a memorial of the occasion, so John happily obliged. The picture that he took of Beth Ann, her dad, and the fish is proudly displayed in the Beitel family's photo album as a permanent reminder of the event.[103]

Father Wessel became a ski instructor to his young nephew, Carlton Wessel, his brother's oldest son. The boy loved visits from his Uncle because he was "a fun guy, upbeat. He never took himself seriously. He would kid around and we always had fun."

In addition, for Carlton it usually meant an afternoon off from school when Father Wessel would come up during the week and take his young nephew skiing in the Poconos, often at the Camelback ski area. "I remember he gave me my first pair of skis and boots and equipment. He would teach me how to ski. As I recall, he was a good skier," said Carlton.

Another of Carlton's memories is of the little plaid tam-o'-shanter that Father Wessel always kept on the dashboard of his car. He told his young nephew it was his "crazy hat." He would put it on "just for a laugh" and "sort of make fun of himself a little bit," said Carlton.[104]

The young priest joyfully participated in the sacramental life of his own family. Father Wessel baptized hundreds of infants as a priest, but surely none so memorable as the baptisms of his own nieces and nephews. "Four months after his ordination John baptized his first Beitel niece in Blessed Sacrament Church," wrote Maryann Beitel.[105] This was the Beitels' second daughter, Susan, who was born in September 1965.

"I remember his joy as he greeted us at the entranceway to the church," said Maryann. Susan's baptism was right after the Vatican Council, and Father Wessel was enthralled and enthusiastic that day as he explained to his family "in great detail the beauty of the new sacramental liturgy of Vatican II."[106]

He gave First Holy Communion to his niece, Anne Marie Wessel. He baptized her baby brother, John Patrick, born in June of 1969, and joked about how great it was to finally have a namesake of his own.[107] He was a consolation to his family when his kindly, gentle, and devout grandmother, Rosalie Wessel, died at the age of ninety-five.[108]

Appropriately enough, the Farm at Mount Holly continued to be an integral part of family life for a new generation of Mary and Patrick Hogan's descendants. "We used to go quite a bit to the Farm, and we loved going over there," his nephew Carlton said. "We loved all the animals." In his free time, Father Wessel also returned to the Farm and could often be found there skeet shooting with his brother Edward and Bill Beitel, or setting off firecrackers on the Fourth of July to the delight of the younger children.[109] He was an enthusiastic participant in family gatherings and traditions—including the annual Thanksgiving Day hunt at the Farm with the men of his family.[110]

And of course, as a devoted son, Father Wessel would visit his mother in Mount Holly as much as he could, often taking her to the movies after dinner.[111]

One of the joint family ventures that brought many hours of happiness for himself and others was the summer house on Long Beach Island, New Jersey, that he purchased with his sister and brother-in-law around 1967. It started out as a "beat-up, dilapidated old wreck," Maryann recalled.

"We bought a handyman's special," said Bill Beitel. "I had a lot of experience with building because of my work, and John was a willing builder. He was one to try anything."[112]

It was a rugged, simple, two-story beach house on Fifth Street in Ship Bottom, with an ample, sandy backyard just perfect for summer barbecues. The two men spent many weekends at the shore fixing up the house. John came down to work on Saturdays and then had to race back to Trenton on Sunday.[113]

Gradually the house came together, and Father John Wessel truly enjoyed it. When he had a day off, he would head down to the shore house and just get away from it all. It was like a quiet retreat for him, and it became one of his greatest satisfactions.[114]

Ship Bottom, right smack in the middle of Long Beach Island, was one of the several shore towns on a long, narrow, barrier island between the Atlantic Ocean and Barnegat Bay. The shore house at 126 East Fifth Street was the scene of many happy hours of summer fun. In the middle of a dead end street, on a simple, unpretentious block, it was but a short walk to the high dunes, reeds and tall grass behind the cyclone fence that marked the entrance to the wide expanse of beach.

There was much to do at the shore during the summer: swimming in the Atlantic Ocean, fishing and sailing on Barnegat Bay. And after a hard day at the beach, there was always miniature golf at Bill Burr's Flamingo Golf Course with its landmark huge pink flamingo.

In the summer of 1968, Father Wessel decided to prepare his Last Will and Testament. For his attorney, he turned to lawyer David Schroth, a Blessed Sacrament parishioner and coach of the CYO boys' basketball team.

There was nothing particularly eventful or even complicated about the preparation of his Will, recalled Schroth, who later became a Judge.[115] Although the young priest's concerning himself about a Will only a few months shy of his twenty-ninth birthday may seem unusual, Monsignor Dubell suggested that perhaps John's acquisition of the house in Ship Bottom with the Beitels convinced him of the necessity of making adequate provisions for its disposition in the event of his untimely demise.[116]

Father Wessel bequeathed his interest in the real estate in Ship Bottom to his mother, or alternatively, to his siblings in equal shares. He made various other small bequests of items of personal property, including a gift of his collection of books to the Mount Holly Library. Not being one to presume his sanctity, Father Wessel prudently gave a small sum of money to his friend, James Dubell, "for the purpose of having Masses said for the repose of my soul." And whatever remained of his meager estate he willed to the Catholic Diocese of Trenton "for use with their Catholic Youth Organization."[117]

Shortly after he had executed his Will, Father Wessel was involved in a car accident. (In fact, he had a few such accidents in his lifetime).[118] It happened that he was returning to Trenton late one night by himself. It was raining heavily. The roads were slippery and covered with wet leaves. Father was saying the Rosary, as he often did while driving, but he was dead tired and fell asleep at the wheel.

Around a sharp curve in Lawrence Township, just outside of Trenton, his car skidded out of control and collided with a huge oak tree. The impact sent Father Wessel flying into the windshield, lacerating his head just above his right eye. He was rushed to Mercer Hospital (in the unfamiliar role of a patient, for a change) where Dr. Raymond McCormack was called upon to sew up his wounds.[119] It was a close call. Father Wessel was shaken up, but fortunately, his head injury was not serious.[120]

"When I saw him the next day, I could've cried," recalled Maryann Beitel. "His face was all swollen and his eyes were bulging out of his head." Her brother had a bad bruise and several stitches on his forehead. He was tired, but he told his sister, "I'm all right. I'm just going to walk it off."

He wouldn't take care of himself, said Maryann, who often urged her brother to watch himself because he wore himself out answering sick calls and running to the aid of people who needed him. "John," she chided him after the accident, "you can't keep up this pace because you're exhausted doing all of these things with helping people!"

"Maryann, you do not have to worry about me," he told her, as he had said on many other occasions: "I am ready whenever the Lord wants me."[121]

But the young clergyman would have yet another dramatic incident involving a car, a dark road, and a brush with death.

Father Wessel was driving down to his old seminary, St. Mary's in Baltimore, when he saw a car stopped on the side of the road. It was pitch dark at night. He had whizzed past it before he thought, "Oh, somebody needs help." He stopped and started to back up to go to the aid of the motorist in distress. But as he was backing up, he saw that someone else behind him on the road had stopped to help the person, so he figured, "Well, it's okay, they're being taken care of." And he went on his way.

The next day Father Wessel saw the headline in the local newspaper: "Good Samaritan Found Murdered." Someone had been murdered on that road, at the exact same place where he would have stopped. Father thought it was the same person who had pulled over to help the disabled vehicle who had been murdered. Had it been Father who had stopped, he would have been killed instead. As best as can be recalled, this happened in the late 1960s, after Father had been at Blessed Sacrament for a few years.[122]

Fellow CYO worker Wes Ritterbusch, an adult counselor, vividly remembers a late night conversation with Father Wessel where the subject turned to weighty matters of life after death. The priest mentioned the story of his almost stopping to help the motorist as an example of how he believed his life had been providentially spared that night. "He was supposed to die but he was spared at that point in time," was how Ritterbusch recalled Father Wessel telling it. "I guess it wasn't my time yet. The Father didn't want me yet," the young priest remarked to his friend. Father Wessel firmly believed that God had a plan for his life.[123]

The brush with death on the road to St. Mary's must have brought home the reality of the words he lived by: "I am ready whenever the Lord wants me."

Father John Wessel did not worry about death, and urged his loved ones not to worry about him either. "Death was, to him, eternal happiness," said his sister, Maryann, "because it was the beginning of eternal life with Christ."

In this, as with all things, he trusted in the Lord's timing.[124]

CHAPTER 20

MISSIONARY TO THE YOUNG

There was no doubt about Father Wessel's ability to reach the teenagers of Blessed Sacrament, to bring them closer to God and to a more mature understanding of themselves and how to live as Christians.

His appeal to youths of high school age was compounded of many things: He treated them as adults. Without descending to immaturity, he talked their language and kept in tune with their concerns about parental relationships, school problems, boy-girl involvements and other "hang-ups." He was ready to "try everything once" and to ignore schedules and routine when something more important appeared. His disdain of status and material goods matched the feelings of young people of that period. His love for them was evident in unstinted giving of his time, his energy, his compassion and his concern.

Above all, in a time when cynicism and negativism were all too prevalent, Father Wessel showed them, by example and precept, a higher and more fulfilling way. He taught them how to pray, to share, to meditate and to worship God.

"When I'm uptight and can't sit still, and the Mass isn't quite enough," he wrote his young friends, "the long, silent and free walk with Him is the most refreshing and loving thing I can do."[1]

From the very first, Father John Wessel instinctively seemed to gravitate to the young people, and they to him. In addition to his many responsibilities at the parish, the hospitals, and the State Home for Girls, he quickly developed a wonderful rapport with the teenagers.

After Mass, the young people would wait for him to emerge from the sacristy. And as soon as he did, they'd all gather around him like bees to honey, calling out, "Father Wessel, Father Wessel." In a large city with not much for teenagers to do, their parents were elated that the young priest was taking the time and effort to get their sons and daughters involved with the CYO.[2]

Father Wessel's primary focus was on teaching and influencing the young. He often said that young people needed direction and stability in their lives, and that it was important that they have someone to pay attention to them and work with them.[3] "If you were to ask me where his biggest love was, it was with the young people in the CYO," said Maryann Beitel.[4]

Father Wessel's approach with young people was as varied as the young persons themselves. He seemed to have an inner sense of how best to reach each one, to help them overcome a problem, or to motivate them to do their best. And more often than not, Father's instincts were right on target.

Joanne Wesley Gillespie described her first meeting with Father in 1965:

> Back in those days, Blessed Sacrament was a very affluent parish. The parish would pay for half of the tuition for all of their students' high school education. I had gone to Cathedral High School for my freshman year, and the summer between each year of high school you had to make an appointment at the rectory for what was called a pastoral approval slip. The pastor or one of the parish priests would sit down with you in an interview and they'd review your records and determine whether or not you were worthy of their sponsoring you in high school.
>
> This particular summer before my sophomore year of high school, I went to the rectory and announced myself and I was told that Father Wessel, who had just arrived recently in the parish, would be interviewing me that particular day. Now, I had never laid eyes on Father Wessel before, and of course, you know, as a teenager you're a little bit nervous . . . walking into the hallowed halls of the rectory.
>
> I waited for a few minutes in the office and he came down the steps and sat me down at the desk, and he very quietly was

going over all of my grammar school records and test scores, and so forth, and then my freshman year of school records. I did extremely poorly in freshman year. I was always an A student all through grammar school, and freshman year I guess I just took off with all the social aspects of high school, and I ended up having to go to summer school. . . . Well, Father Wessel picked right up on that . . . and he said, "Tell me something, Joanne. Why should we waste our money on you? It looks like you're not interested in high school. You did great in grammar school but you're not at all interested in high school. You really messed up here. You're just a dummy. I don't know why we should spend our money on you."

Well, at that, I was so upset! I thought, "Oh my gosh, what if they don't agree to pay half my tuition to high school." I don't know how we ended up smoothing that over. All I can remember is that I was so angry and I thought, "Who is he to tell me that I'm stupid! I'm not stupid! I'll show him!" . . . Well, I got back into high school sophomore year in September and went from . . . bottom of the pile . . . to the top quarter of my class and stayed there for the next three years of high school. . . .

I'm sure that was his intention. He never would have said anything derogatory to anybody. He was a great teaser but he would never even crack the slightest smile so it took a while to get used to his mannerisms. I just remember being very angry . . . but yet, somehow I knew that he didn't mean it personally because I never took it personally. It just somehow shocked something inside of me to realize that, hey, Joanne, you'd better shape up. This is your life you're fooling with here. He made that much of an impression on me.

Around that time, Joanne became involved in the Blessed Sacrament CYO and for the remainder of high school, she served as Secretary of the club and worked on the monthly CYO newsletters. After graduating high school, Joanne remained with the CYO at Father Wessel's request as an adult advisor. Together they ran the youth group for several more years.[5]

John Gummere, quite gifted as an artist, but not especially as an athlete, learned a lesson in self-acceptance:

I . . . remember on the picnic at the end of the year, I guess it was about sixth grade or so, we were having some games—baseball, things like that—and I was one of the most unathletic people . . . but Father Wessel tried to help me to feel okay with that . . . by way of coaching me. I don't remember what he said . . . but he helped me feel more comfortable.

. . . From Father, I learned a certain amount of self-acceptance, and acceptance of other people, and taking a positive approach to life. . . . I think he encouraged each person to be good at the thing they really did well, whatever it was.[6]

There were a number of teens who had lost one of their parents through death or divorce. Father Wessel, because of his own experience, seemed to have a particular affinity for these young people. For many such kids, he gladly became a role model and a substitute father.[7]

"When I think of Father Wessel, I think he was such an ordinary man who accomplished extraordinary things," recalled Suzanne Walsh Walton. "My dad died when I was very young. And there are two people in my life that made a very strong impression on me." Father Wessel was one. "My dad was a priest . . . who had to leave the priesthood because of his illness. And when I met Father Wessel, I kind of connected with him because of that. And then, when I moved into high school, Father Wessel really did a lot for me."

For Karen McGarrity, Father Wessel was a man of unconditional love who just wouldn't give up on her:

When I was in ninth grade, my parents were on the verge of getting a divorce. I really wasn't that interested in the CYO. I had been holding back. Father Wessel would call my mother every time there was a meeting and asked if I wanted to go. And maybe I'd go once and not the next time. And he was very persistent. Whenever he would see me alone, he would talk to me, ask me how I was doing. He made me feel very important. Made me feel as if I could survive this divorce. And as much as I wanted to pull back, he kept pulling me back *in* until I really *was* in. There were so many kids in the CYO. . . . And a lot of kids with problems. My problem was minor compared to a lot of other kids' particular problems . . . And his caring and his love was so unconditional. You could screw up so many times and it just didn't matter. You could not get rid of that man. You really couldn't.[8]

For Christopher Morley, Father Wessel instinctively knew how to make the young man feel he had something important to contribute:

> I was a student in . . . Blessed Sacrament School. My parents . . . divorced when I was in seventh or eighth grade. . . . I got to know Father Wessel, and through his and Father Davis's encouragement, was asked to join the CYO.
>
> . . . As our relationship progressed, Father Wessel was clearly aware of my situation, and how badly, as you might expect, a thirteen-year-old boy really could use a father figure in his life. . . . He picked up very early on that one of the things that really appealed to me was to work hard to help the group. . . . So he asked me to work on all these little work committees. . . . The first job I remember doing for the CYO was setting up and tearing down the kitchen for . . . the Christmas caroling. . . . It wasn't a situation where I'd be a leader, but he'd always put me in a situation where I'd be integral to making things work. . . . Like on the plays, I used to do backstage. On the boat, when he started to build the *Eucharist*, he came to me very early on and said, "I'm doing this, really could use a hand with it." It was never, "Chris, this would be good for you." It was always, "We're doing this, could really use a hand." You could imagine how much self-esteem that built for me personally. . . . I felt like an important support, somebody whose presence mattered even though it may not have been noticed. . . .
>
> What he taught me is that the right solution to adversity is to go outside yourself and to look to your community and how you can improve your community. . . . When things go badly for you, find out how you can go help somebody else. . . .
>
> Just being around him and being near the man made all the difference at a time when I could've easily gone either way.[9]

And for high school freshman Ronald Garrett, Father Wessel was "Pop," not only a father figure but "a savior":

I think that when I was going to church and I saw Father Wessel, I became attached to him because of the things that were going on with my life as far as the abusiveness with my father. My father was an alcoholic and a drug addict, and he beat my mother daily and he beat me daily. . . . This is probably the freshman year which would have been '68. . . . And I was communicating with Pop about it, talking to him about all the things that were going on, and he was very concerned. . . . I can recall one time that he confronted my father face-to-face. . . .

We lived for a while like that and then my father left. He just got up and left, and at that point, I got ahold of Pop and said to him, things were really at a bad, bad way, and he got ahold of my mother. . . . I don't really know what went on when my mother talked to Pop . . . but she says that she really relied on Pop a lot about things and she understood what he was saying. . . . I was fourteen when my father left. . . . I had to go to work to support the family . . .

Father Wessel often told me that there were things that happen that we didn't understand and that there was a reason for them, but he always tried to make the best out of what was going on. . . . I was incredibly involved in the CYO. He just said that was something that I needed to get involved with. . . .

If it wasn't for Pop, I would probably be in prison. When I was about sixteen or seventeen years old, I was living in a world of hell. There was nothing to look forward to at all, okay? . . . And when I met him, he grabbed ahold of me one day and he said, "Ronnie, . . . we can get through this. You know, we can do something about this . . ."

Basically, he was a savior. He was somebody that I could relate to as far as a father figure. Somebody that could lead me out of where I was.[10]

The Catholic Youth Organization was a national Catholic organization with headquarters in Washington, D.C. CYO had a four-fold program:

spiritual, physical, intellectual and athletic. Each parish and each diocese was affiliated with the national office, which in turn would send materials to individual dioceses and parishes. At the parish level, each CYO took and adapted the materials to what they felt would be the most serviceable to the teens in their area. The CYO that Father Wessel moderated at Blessed Sacrament was based on the materials and programs provided through the national or diocesan CYO office, but he quickly put his own distinctive imprint on it.[11]

At the beginning of Father Wessel's tenure at Blessed Sacrament, his diary contained this somewhat tentative note:

> February 16, 1966:
> CYO Meeting of 10 people—? Planning for Dance, etc.

From this inauspicious start came a program for Catholic young people which eventually won the respect of the entire city and the recognition of his Bishop.

Father Wessel took the Blessed Sacrament CYO, which had been little more than a label for a monthly Mass and a boys' and girls' basketball league, and made it into a living, vibrant community of teens, a rewarding center for their activities.[12] What the CYO became under his guidance "says much in itself about Father Wessel's direction."[13]

John Wessel was the type of person who "always wanted to do the best that he could, and wanted to be sure that he was on the right track," recalled Monsignor Toomey, the Diocesan CYO Director. In those early days, Monsignor Toomey occasionally counseled the newly ordained John Wessel to persevere in his work with youth:

> I can remember once encouraging him, "Don't become discouraged because even though you think you're not making progress, they see in you a real role model, and this is a great example. And so often the most valuable thing we can do for them is the example that we give." [14]

Under Father's guidance, the young people themselves ran the CYO club, made the plans, and carried them out, largely through the "Youth Council."[15] In a "recruitment" letter to the high school students of the parish,

Father Wessel described the group's work and rewards in an unpretentious style that teenagers found so attractive:

> CYO and the Youth Council. What's the difference? The Youth Council is a group of kids elected or appointed, or just come, that propose the activities for the kids of the parish and their friends. By the very nature of things, they are also the kids who do most of the work and, also by the nature of things, they are the kids who enjoy the CYO most. If you put something into it, you will get something out of it. All kids have certain things they like to do and friends they like to hang with. Maybe your friends just aren't the type to do this kind of thing. That's fine. You can belong to the CYO general membership. You can take advantage of the activities that are offered one at a time according to your likes and dislikes. If you really want to dedicate your time and reap the rewards of consistent CYO activities, try to get on Youth Council. There are only so many committees and chairmanships available but many a kid comes to a Youth Council Meeting with no particular post. You stick it out and you're in. . . . Take your pick. No one will make a fuss either way, but I think that you know that CYO offers a lot more than anything else you can get involved in in this area of Trenton, but you have to stick with it.[16]

In short order, Blessed Sacrament CYO became a place where the young people wanted to be—to have fun, to enjoy socializing with friends, and because they were drawn to the young priest, not much older than themselves, who was also "a regular guy"—natural, down-to-earth, informal, and approachable.

Father Wessel was "a priest who drew kids to him in a way that I can't really explain," said one CYO youth, Matt Finnegan.[17]

One of those drawn into CYO was Jayne Hartley*, who recalled how Father got her involved in the club:

> When I entered high school I was asked if I wanted to be a part of the "Youth Council," which was the planning group of the C.Y.O. . . . The first meeting I attended was orderly and

mainly business-like, but by no means was the tone or mood somber. Everyone was there because they wanted to be and no one, including Father Wessel, was afraid to take advantage of a funny situation. Father had taken a club which almost did not exist and had given it a structure and a function; that is, to plan and execute activities which would effectively interest the high school youth in the parish.

There were many activities underway when I entered the C.Y.O. To most of the activities Fr. Wessel gave all of himself and without his drive and contributions I am sure many endeavors would have been far less successful.[18]

The mainstays of activity at the Blessed Sacrament CYO were the monthly Youth Masses every third Sunday of the month, followed by breakfast in Casey Hall, the grade school gymnasium and auditorium, and "Activities Nights" after the general meeting on the third Wednesday of the month. In between was a monthly "Youth Council" meeting in the Hunt Room in the basement of Blessed Sacrament Rectory. After a few years, when Saturday evening Masses were allowed to fulfill the Sunday obligation, the monthly CYO Masses were moved to Saturday night. Gathering with their friends to celebrate the liturgy, with snacks and socializing afterward, proved a safe and rewarding way for kids to spend an enjoyable Saturday night out.[19]

In between were a variety of wholesome, fun-filled activities: skiing trips, ice-skating parties, dances, Christmas caroling, interfaith and interracial discussions, hootenannies, movies, communion breakfasts, parties, plays, musicals and comedy shows, barge rides up the Delaware, hay rides, picnics, camping and canoeing trips, crabbing trips and cookouts in the summer, basketball, baseball, and volleyball games. The young people also performed various "good works" around the parish, collecting and packing for clothing drives, visits to Trenton State Hospital and the State Home for Girls, car washes, flower sales, and other fund-raisers for their club.[20]

Everything about Father John Wessel's life experience became a "gift" which he unselfishly shared with "his kids." His knowledge was applied for their benefit; his interests and hobbies became joint activities that all could enjoy; his possessions, though meager, were shared with the group—even down to his old, green Plymouth, which became the principal means to transport kids from one CYO function to another.

In the winter, he took a group of kids to the Poconos and taught them how to ski. To the teens, Father Wessel was a good skier and a daredevil to boot. He would take city kids who had never been on skis before and lead them down the slopes, saying, "Come on, you can do it. Don't be afraid!" By the end of the day, he would have them going down the expert slopes and having fun at it.[21]

The ski trips with Father Wessel had a special meaning for former CYO member Gina Ash Lang:

> I'll never forget the one time where . . . we were getting ready for one of the ski trips. Well, my father had lost his job, so Father Wessel paid for me to go on that ski trip. He would not let me *not* go. I said to him, "I can't really go." I had three sisters . . . And he paid for me to go on that ski trip. It was just something I never forgot. . . . You don't meet people like Father Wessel anymore. . . . He was just so nice. He would do anything for you.[22]

A few weeks before Christmas each year, Father Wessel brought a group of kids to "the Farm" in Mount Holly for the day to cut holly branches to be sold after Mass at Blessed Sacrament Church. It was his big fund-raising event for the CYO.[23]

At Christmas time, Father Wessel gathered the young people to go Christmas caroling in the neighborhood, an activity he had so enjoyed as a young seminarian. As recalled by parishioner Joseph Cappello:

> Each Christmas season, Father Wessel asked me and friends to help him accompany the parish teenagers as they went caroling in the neighborhood. Afterwards, we'd return to the parish hall for hot chocolate and camaraderie. It became something very special to look forward to each year, and I'm sure the teenagers . . . include the experience in their fondest memories.[24]

Father Wessel even involved the CYO in his own ministry to the mentally ill and elderly. He invited a group of teenage boys and girls to sing at the Christmas and Easter Masses he celebrated in Trenton State Hospital.[25] CYO member Jayne Hartley recalled:

It always amazed me how he would talk with the patients
both in his sermons and on a one-to-one basis. He spoke with
them on his own level and with so much love! This was really
inspiring and his kindness and gentleness with the patients who
seemed so strange were real lessons in Christianity.[26]

It was also a remarkable testament to the young priest's charisma that
teenagers were willing to leave their homes and families early on Christmas
and Easter mornings to go with him to the psychiatric hospital. Many fondly
recall Father's sage advice to the group of singers right before Mass: "Just
keep singing. No matter what happens, just keep singing!" And they did.

In summer, Father Wessel, sharing another beloved hobby, took the
CYO boys and girls on camping trips and canoe trips. They could usually
be found on hot summer weekends having cookouts, hot dog roasts and
sing-alongs in nearby Washington Crossing State Park or at Stacy Park, or
sometimes down at Bass River near the Jersey shore.[27]

And when Father Wessel acquired the shore home in Ship Bottom
with his sister and brother-in-law, it soon became yet another site of CYO
activity—the annual summer cookout and beach party.

Every June, at the end of the school year, Father Wessel took about six
or eight cars full of CYO kids to his shore home for a day at the beach. In
the evening, he would celebrate Mass for the young people, followed by a
great big year-end cookout and party. It was a fair exchange, because the
young people cleaned his house and got it ready for the summer season.
Everybody pitched in and worked.[28]

Father "got his house cleaned, and we got a day at the beach" was the
way CYO member Bonnie Lopez* recalled it. "It was great. He always got
us to work, but we got so much fun out of it so we didn't care."[29]

Even Father Wessel's background in music, and his brief stint at acting
in St. Charles Seminary, were put to good use.

After several years as moderator, Father Wessel got the Blessed Sacrament
CYO into the Diocesan One-Act Play Contest. The CYO's first effort
was directed by Father Wessel, as were all the following entries in years to
come. Even entering showed courage, because none of the members knew
anything about staging plays, and John Wessel's first dramatic experience,
as St. Joseph in a kindergarten Nativity play many years ago, had produced
tears of stage fright. But he fearlessly urged the young actors and actresses

on, and their first dramatic effort, *The Hangman*, with eleven cast members, won Second Place in 1968.[30]

In 1969, Blessed Sacrament again took Second Place in the one-act play contest for *Job*, an original play based on the biblical character, co-written by Jayne Hartley and another CYO member. Jeff Callahan, a member of the cast, was named "Best Actor." And in 1971, Blessed Sacrament CYO received recognition for *Little Prince*, a musical with original script, music and lyrics.[31]

"We really put on some serious plays for the budget that we had, which was practically none," recalled Brian Schoeffel. Father "was able to get so much out of kids who never did that before."

"My favorite memories of those times with Father Wessel were the plays—the one-act play competitions that we put on through CYO," said Joanne Gillespie. Mercer County, as well as the Diocese of Trenton, had one-act play competitions once a year for the CYO groups. The winner of the county-wide competition went on to compete with the winners of all the other counties at the diocesan level. "Father Wessel must have had some kind of secret desire for show business because this really got him going. Most times, he would write out the entire script and plan all the music," she recalled.[32]

It was while he was at Blessed Sacrament that Father Wessel taught himself to play the guitar.[33] He would spend time listening to music looking for just the right songs that he could use in his shows or in his contemporary youth liturgies.[34]

The CYO's first offering in the one-act play contest, *The Hangman*, was based on a poem of the same title. One character was "The Narrator" who stood in the foreground reciting the poem, while other characters in the background enacted it.

Mike Ward recalled a humorous incident during a rehearsal for *The Hangman*:

> I was fortunate enough to have the title role of the Hangman . . . because it was really the easiest role of all. I just had to carry a noose around the stage and wear a black cape and look menacing. I didn't have any lines at all. However, one of the young aspiring actresses did . . . And one of the lines that she was supposed to have said was, "And he hung the sign over

the courthouse door." But at this particular practice, she made a little slip of the tongue, and I think it came out as, "And he hung the sign over the *whorehouse* door." . . . Father Wessel just kind of joined in the general hilarity of the moment, and that for me just symbolizes what he was. He was certainly a role model and someone to look up to, but he was also at the same time one of us.[35]

In the spring of 1968, Father Wessel's CYO group presented the entertainment—a combination of music, comedy and pure "ham"—for Blessed Sacrament's annual "Parish Night." This was a largely successful attempt on Father's part to "show off" the talents and personalities of the group and to demonstrate to parents and other adults that the often-criticized teenagers were not as bad as commonly portrayed.[36]

"Parish Night" was a tradition in the parish, a gala social affair and fund-raiser sponsored by the PTA, featuring a card party, raffles, and entertainment. Each year the CYO's entertainment had a theme, and for their first offering, entitled *Noah and the Ark* (inspired by the popular Bill Cosby comedy album), the theme was animals. Father Wessel wrote the script, and he, together with the kids, built all the props. The ark itself was huge and took up the whole stage. To add to the play's authenticity, Father even borrowed his niece Beth Beitel's pet ducks as living props which were incorporated into the production.[37]

Father Wessel usually directed the shows, while CYO Secretary Joanne, with an aptitude for dance, was the choreographer and musical director. "He was so good with the kids," said Joanne. "He sensed who would be good in which roles, and every kid was in it." Father made sure everyone had some role to play, even those with little or no musical or dramatic talent.[38]

As the CYO grew in the following years, and the Parish Night Shows grew along with it, Father jokingly grouped the singers into the "good voices" and the "crows"—because they had such terrible singing voices. "The name was not meant to be derogatory and no one thought it was," recalled Jayne Hartley. "Such antics only added to the fun and probably taught us a lesson about accepting the abilities of others, although at the time the lesson was hidden."[39]

Maria Rodriguez* recalled the Parish Night Shows:

> If you were not a good singer, he'd make you sing anyway and told you you did a good job . . . even when you know it's sounding really horrible. . . . The thing that really sticks out in my mind is that he really made you feel accepted for who you were. And it didn't matter that you couldn't do what everybody else did, or you couldn't play sports as well as other people—you were still "on the team."[40]

The youthful entertainers also performed their shows for the frequently neglected patients in Trenton Psychiatric Hospital, and the young women at the State Home for Girls. Taking their shows "on the road" in this fashion was an activity that usually lasted all summer long.[41]

Father Wessel's mood was generally happy and upbeat. But there could also be a lot of stress, at times, dealing with teenagers, who had a tendency to become loud and boisterous when they got together. "We were a big group and we'd get rowdy and carry on," recalled Bonnie Lopez.[42] When the teenagers got out of line, Father would sometimes show his more "human" side.

A rehearsal for one of the plays in the auditorium provided one such occasion. Father was trying to pull the play together at the last minute but the young people were horsing around—laughing, joking, and being especially obnoxious. They wouldn't pay attention to Father's direction, and nobody was taking the rehearsal seriously. Father Wessel finally blew up at them. "You're just a bunch of prima donnas!" he yelled, and went storming out of the auditorium.[43]

The young people were stunned into silence. They knew Father didn't often get angry, and realized that they'd pushed him too far.[44] Everybody just sat there wondering, Was he going to come back? Father did eventually come back, and sheepishly, he said, "Sorry about that guys, but I couldn't take it anymore. If you want to do this, you're going to have to settle down and listen."[45]

Father Wessel was "very apologetic about his temper," recalled Ronald Garrett. "He thought that was a real weakness. He didn't think that was spiritual."

According to a slogan from a popular movie at the time, "Love means never having to say you're sorry." But Father Wessel's philosophy was the complete opposite. When he lost his temper he did not hesitate to tell the young people he was sorry. His example encouraged them to do likewise to one another.[46]

"Never forget that you are a 'thief of love' and don't be afraid to say 'I'm sorry'," he once told his young friends.[47]

Another facet to Father's scolding was that he didn't keep it up. "When he got mad, he just told us," recalled a CYO member, and that was the end of it.[48] Once he spoke his mind, whatever had provoked his ire was immediately forgotten, and the youths came away knowing that Father still loved and accepted them.

"It made me realize that someone could yell at you and you would care," recalled Matt Finnegan. "You took it seriously and . . . wanted to make the change that he was suggesting . . . and you didn't hate him." And if Father yelled, Matt acknowledged, "we probably had stepped over the line an hour ago."[49]

"He was very honest and was not afraid to give someone 'the devil' if he thought it was necessary," recalled Jayne Hartley. "When he scolded it was with love in his heart and anyone who knew him, knew that and respected and loved him for it. It was one of the countless ways he tried to help other people."[50]

The CYO's dramatic efforts were finally rewarded in 1970 with a First Prize in the Diocesan One-Act Play Contest for a play called *Pinball Wizard*.[51] This original play was based on a popular contemporary music album, the "rock opera" *Tommy* by The Who. The story, told in song, concerned a deaf, dumb and blind young man named Tommy, who had one remarkable ability—playing pinball machines.

Since then, it has been made into a movie and a Broadway musical. But Father Wessel and his CYO thought of it first. Barry Anderson especially loved the album, and one day he and a few other kids were talking with Father Wessel on the back porch of the rectory about ideas for a play, and somehow the suggestion was made, "Let's do something with the music *Tommy* by The Who!" And that was the beginning.

Father Wessel really latched onto the idea, as did all the CYO members. Father wrote the script for a one-act play, following the *Tommy* theme. He chose the music from the album and melded it into a beautiful little story. This was no small accomplishment because the entire story had to be squeezed into a one-act presentation of no more than thirty minutes.[52]

The play used the abilities of some very talented musicians, guitarists Matt Finnegan and Mike Ball, who were able to recreate the original music and lyrics. James Blatchford played the drums.[53] However, they needed a third guitarist, so Barry Anderson was quickly drafted. "That was quite comical because I have absolutely no musical ability whatsoever," Anderson recalled. The two "real" guitarists, Matt and Mike, "were really carrying the weight on the music, but they needed somebody to play the bass, so they taught me how to play the bass—which really came down to, 'Okay, Barry, here are four notes and we're gonna nod when we want you to hit them.'"[54]

Psychedelic lights were quite popular at the time, and Father had a few young men set up a strobe light to give special effects on certain scenes. The strobe light, being homemade, was always breaking, and for the competition, in fact, it didn't work at all.

A few weeks before the competition began, the play was still being written and rehearsed, and didn't even have a name. Nevertheless, by the 25th of April, it all came together. *Pinball Wizard* captured First Prize in the Mercer County One-Act Play Competition, and then, competing against six other CYO winners from each county, took first place in the whole diocese.

There was no other musical in the competition: *Pinball Wizard* was something entirely new. It was such a large undertaking, with all the sound equipment and amplifiers, but that didn't frighten Father nor his enthusiastic group of teens. There was, in fact, no other play in the competition that was not a previously published work.

"It was so innovative," Joanne Gillespie recalled of the play. "In fact, they really didn't know how to judge us because we were so different." The following year, however, the idea of doing an original play really caught on.[55]

A barge ride up the Delaware River canal from New Hope, Pennsylvania, which the CYO had planned for the evening of the diocesan play competition, provided an occasion for the group to celebrate their victory. The majority, if not all, of the cast went on that barge ride, and there was constant celebration and singing the songs from *Tommy* all the way up the canal. At the halfway point, the young people stopped for a cookout of hot dogs and hamburgers, and then turned around and came back down the canal again, singing and celebrating all the way.[56]

It was quite a trip, especially since the barge party was accompanied by two priests—one real, the other fake. A few weeks before, two CYO men, Barry Anderson and Mike Ball, went to New Hope to inquire about the rental of the barge. As Barry recalled it:

> The guy said, "Well, we're just not going to let a bunch of kids go on a barge ride unsupervised." And we said, "Well, we're going to have a priest with us. There shouldn't be a problem." "Naw, that's not good enough." And we said, "Well, then, we'll bring *two* priests. How about that?" And he eventually agreed. Well, the second "priest" was Wes Ritterbusch.[57]

When the CYO finally walked away with First Prize in the One-Act Play Contest, no one was prouder of their achievement than Father Wessel. The show was, in those days, considered quite radical, and there were a few naysayers who told Father that he was crazy to even attempt it. But he pulled it off, and when *Pinball Wizard* was performed in the gym for the whole parish, it was a huge success.[58]

As proud as Father Wessel was of the CYO's victory, he never wanted any recognition for himself. He gave it all to the young people.

"I don't ever remember him being in the limelight . . . or wanting to be," recalled Joanne Gillespie. "Quite the opposite. He put *us* in the limelight. We were always the stars. He was very happy and content to be in the background."[59]

Father Wessel's initial desire to demonstrate to parents and other adults, in his own words—"that every kid in America wasn't a bad kid"—was by all accounts a rousing success.[60] The CYO under Father's guidance continued to put on theatrical and musical productions, including the annual Parish Night entertainment, impressing parents with the talents of their sons and daughters and of their young priest.

After yet another successful Parish Night, in the spring of 1970, Blessed Sacrament trustee James Moonan wrote to Father Wessel:

> For the work you are doing here at Blessed Sacrament Parish you really deserve a great big pat on the back every day of the year. Not just for your priestly duties . . . but particularly

for your work with the young people. To us it is nothing short of sensational.

We can see it all around us—it's particularly pleasing to see the respect and devotion the young people show for you, and their confidence in you as a leader. To mention a few of the things we have observed: the canoe trip with some of the boys not long ago, the ski trips organized in the winter, the hayrides, the CYO car wash, the play which was written, produced and acted in such a professional manner, the entertainment last Friday evening in Casey Auditorium.

. . . If only just a few of the activities that you have developed for the youths of our parish could be seen in TV or even heard on the radio, it would be more representative of our young people as they are today than a lot of the trash that comes into our home, particularly on television.[61]

The play's the thing and so was camping!

Naturally, Father Wessel would also share his lifelong love of camping and rugged outdoors life with his CYO. Each August, Father Wessel led a group of eight or more young men on camping-and-canoeing trips of a week or two, in much the same manner as he had done with his seminary friends—thus providing a new generation of young men with memories of unforgettable outdoors adventures and a new appreciation of the beauty of nature.

These trips included the White Mountains of New Hampshire and Montreal in 1967; the Green Mountains of Vermont in 1968; Little Grand Canyon and Little Pine Creek, Pennsylvania in 1969; and in 1970, the Allagash and Penobscot rivers in Maine, and up to Quebec.[62]

Each trip, of course, had its own joys, challenges, and hilarious moments.

The trip to Little Grand Canyon, outside of Williamsport, Pennsylvania, seemed like a horrible trip at the time, but in retrospect, it was wonderful.

Nine men, including Father Wessel, went on that trip. Along the way, some of the canoes capsized, and since it had been raining, the men looked like "a bunch of drowned water rats," recalled one camper.[63] They found refuge the first night in a hunter's cabin that had been left open for travelers who were just passing through. They were quite exhausted, having been up for about twelve or eighteen hours straight. There were no provisions, but it was at least a roof over their heads, and a place to cook their dinner and rest.

By that time, it was Sunday night, and Father Wessel decided to say Mass. One of the young men, Kevin Gallagher, had fallen sound asleep, exhausted, on a cot underneath the table, which was to be used as the altar for Mass. The other men wondered whether to wake him, but Father Wessel said, "No, he's participating, just at a different level. Leave him alone, he's at peace. He's getting the Word of the Lord one way or the other."[64]

Father Wessel started saying Mass over the table while the young men gathered 'round. It was dark and damp, with lighted candles and camp stoves casting eerie shadows, and suddenly, the fellow who was asleep was startled, woke up, and thought he had died and was witnessing his own funeral.

"And I remember coming to—and vaguely seeing people standing around praying," said Kevin Gallagher. "And I thought, 'Oh my God, I'm dead!' So I just went back to sleep."[65]

It was a very rigorous trip. One problem was that it had been a very dry season, and the river was so low that they actually ended up hiking and dragging the canoes more than paddling them. Father Wessel injured his back because of it, and was in pain for the duration of the trip. But it was also a bonding experience for the young men and the young priest, physically challenging and rugged, testing their strength and survival skills.

The following summer, on a two-week trip to the Allagash Wilderness Waterway in Maine, there were eight men, including Father. It was a much longer drive, with an overnight in Massachusetts, but a much more enjoyable trip, weather-wise.

"The river we were on had water, so it was real canoeing . . . and weather cooperated much more for us. And we finished and went into Canada and just had a wonderful time in Canada, so it was much more pleasant," said Barry Anderson.

The Allagash Wilderness Waterway proved an enjoyable and exciting canoe trip. Late one day, they came upon Long Lake just as a big storm was brewing. The men wanted to get across the lake quickly because they were concerned about the storm and the lightning, so Father Wessel suggested that they lash an Army poncho to two paddles, and had the man in the front of the canoe hold it up like a sail so that it caught the wind. There was quite a breeze, so with their makeshift sails, they were quickly and easily able to cross Long Lake.

There was, of course, the usual high jinx and hilarity that went along with these excursions that would be talked about and laughed about for months and months afterward. There were men who fell in the water and had to be pulled out, men who forgot their gear, or lost it in the water, and practical jokes played all around.[66]

On the Maine trip, Father Wessel and Wes Ritterbusch got even with a couple of guys for an earlier practical joke by sabotaging their canoe. They bent the baffles of the canoe and then poured water into it, so that when the kids hopped into it the next day, they took off with record speed.[67]

About the third or fourth night out on the Allagash trip, the men camped on a high bluff about fifty feet above the river. From their vantage point on the bluff, they could see that it was really wonderful country. The campers joked that they were out in "bear country" because they'd found the carcass of a deer, which they surmised had been killed by a bear. They pitched their tents on the high bluff late in the afternoon, and by nightfall, the possibility of encountering a bear seemed all the more real to many of the campers. There was a lot of nervous joking and some genuine concern about being in "bear country."

It was Sunday evening and Father Wessel decided to celebrate Mass on a picnic table as the makeshift altar. They had just about finished the reading of the Epistle when, all of a sudden, they heard the rustling sounds of something large moving around in the bushes. It had to have been a bear! they thought. At once, everybody reached for their knives and axes and assorted weapons, and asked Father Wessel if they could get his gun. Father's pistol and the other weapons were piled on top of the picnic table/altar, and they then continued with the celebration of the Mass. Fortunately, they heard no more from the bear(?) for the rest of the evening.[68]

On the last day, it rained continuously, but they had a deadline to meet to get to their destination at St. John's, Maine. They broke camp, cooked breakfast in the rain, and paddled all day through the rain. That night in St. John's, everyone was feeling sick, exhausted, and chilled to the bone. Father Wessel was always good for giving out vitamins. "Take some of this," he'd say. "What is it?" "Never mind," he'd say, "it'll make ya better." On this night, though, Father passed around the Old Crow, his favorite Bourbon, so the men could take a few swigs and "take the chill off." Sleeping in their tents was like sleeping in mud puddles, so they slept in their cars and just did the best they could.

The next day, the sun came out, and it was truly a glorious day. The waterlogged campers were able to dry out their clothes and gear and start repacking for the trip into Canada.

After crossing the U.S. - Canada border, it was a day's drive into Canada. At this point, everyone was sufficiently recovered from their illnesses. The men camped for a few more days at a campground outside of a little town called Levis-Lauzon, which was directly across from Quebec City. There was a ferry across the St. Laurence River between Levis-Lauzon and Quebec City, which they took into Quebec for some more exciting adventures.

The last night of each camping trip was always the traditional "potluck dinner"—the so-called "Wessel Special." The recipe changed from time to time, but it was basically anything that was left over. "And we ate it, no matter what it was, and we laughed. And that was what you remember the most—the laughter," recalled Wes Ritterbusch. "We had so many good times. Even when they were *bad* times, they were *good* times."[69]

The spiritual component was incorporated into the trips very naturally, either through Father's celebration of the Mass or informal prayers. "I think that's one of the things that everybody looked forward to so much," recalled Wes Ritterbusch. "We all looked forward to the fun and games and goofing around and everything, but John always brought the spiritual part of it with him, and we learned and grew in that aspect of it."[70]

One of the most beautiful memories for the teenagers of the Blessed Sacrament CYO was of the monthly "Youth Mass," the contemporary Folk Masses that Father Wessel celebrated with them in Casey Hall.

For several years, Youth Masses had been held in the church. When "Folk Masses" came into their own, complete with guitars and contemporary songs, Father Wessel received permission from Father Davis to hold these Masses in the school auditorium. Father Davis wouldn't allow it in the church, as it held little appeal for the more tradition-minded adults, yet both priests recognized its value for teenagers.[71] Father Wessel was always grateful that Father Davis trusted his judgment in implementing programs for the youth, even though some innovations might not have been the older pastor's "cup of tea."

Then too, Bishop Ahr was one of the first Bishops in the United States to grant permission to implement the changes of Vatican II, including Folk Masses, in his diocese.[72]

Father Wessel involved the CYO members in every aspect of the preparations for Mass. Some of the young people would bake the bread that was used for the Consecration from a recipe that Father gave them. Others would help Father choose the songs that were sung, and the passages of Scripture that were read.[73]

Without sacrificing the dignity and holiness of the Mass, Father enthusiastically incorporated those aspects of modern culture and music to make the Youth Mass a more deeply personal, informal, intimate, and joyous experience of worship than the teens had experienced in the more traditional liturgies in Blessed Sacrament Church.

For the liturgical music, they sang contemporary spirituals and popular songs. Instead of the traditional church organ, several gifted young CYO musicians, Mike Ball and Matt Finnegan, played guitars.[74]

In fact, one of Father's favorite songs which was almost always sung at the Youth Mass was the popular ballad, *Bridge Over Troubled Water*.[75] It was a song whose lyrics (whether Paul Simon and Art Garfunkel intended it or not) spoke most eloquently of Christ's unconditional love for each person.

In the counter-cultural age, when many young people were brimming with high idealism, yet looking for something "different" from the older generation, the young appreciated Father Wessel's efforts and responded to him. Father's Youth Masses were always heavily attended by the teenagers of the parish, and more often than not, by a few parents.

When Father Wessel started the guitar Masses, some of the adults of the parish didn't think much of it. Father, on the other hand, thought it would be great for the young people. He liked the concept of it, until he found out that he was the one who was going to have to lead the singing and teach everyone else. But he did, and the kids just loved it.[76]

Yet privately, Father may have been more conservative musically, said Brian Schoeffel.

> I think Father Wessel would rather have *not* had clanging
> and banging and guitar singing and chanting in church. I think
> he went with the flow because that's what was happening back
> then, and that's what his kids were starting to get involved in,

because that's when Folk Masses became popular . . . and that's what we wanted to do, so he did . . . but I think if he had his druthers, he would have been done with it, he wouldn't have had it.[77]

The Youth Mass was intimate and informal. "It was by no means an ordinary Mass," recalled a former CYO member.[78] For one thing, it would go on for hours.

"We would pack kids into that gym for these Masses and they would go on for the longest time and nobody minded," said another. "In fact, to the contrary, you didn't want it to end because it was so moving and so absorbing."[79]

Everyone listened with rapt attention to Father's sermons. He made the Scriptures real to them as he applied their lessons to the contemporary concerns of young people. He showed them, by word and example, how to apply Christ's message to their everyday lives. He taught them how to love and care for one another, as God loved them.[80]

At the Prayer of the Faithful, Father encouraged the teens to offer their own petitions. "Lord, I'm having trouble in school." "Spanish is really giving me a hard time; please get me through this next test." "Lord, I'm worried about my Mom because she's sick in the hospital." The young people often began to share deeply personal concerns during the Prayer of the Faithful. And as one person opened up and bared his heart, it would encourage others to do the same. The sharing that took place during this time was impressive and, although this lengthened the Mass considerably, no one seemed to mind.[81]

The Sign of Peace also went on forever, as the young people greeted each other with a sign of Christ's peace, and offered a handshake or an embrace to each person, since all were true friends in Christ. And at the Our Father, all joined hands for the Lord's Prayer before receiving Him in Holy Communion.[82]

Father Wessel always gave them Holy Communion under the forms of bread and wine. This was a special privilege since in those days it was rare to receive the Holy Eucharist under both species.[83]

Father's Youth Mass in the gym was "a gift to us," recalled Joanne Gillespie. "No one would miss it for anything, which is what Mass should be. You always want it to be that way."[84]

One of Father Wessel's favorite songs was the musical version of the *Prayer of Saint Francis of Assisi*, which was composed by Sebastian Temple. He often asked the young people to sing it as a meditation hymn after the Communion.

Prayer of St. Francis, by Sebastian Temple

Make me a channel of Your peace.
Where there is hatred, let me bring Your love.
Where there is injury, Your pardon, Lord.
And where there's doubt, true faith in You.

Make me a channel of Your peace.
Where there's despair in life, let me bring hope;
Where there is darkness, only light;
And where there's sadness, ever joy.

O, Master, grant that I may never seek,
so much to be consoled as to console;
To be understood as to understand;
To be loved as to love with all my soul.

Make me a channel of Your peace.
It is in pardoning that we are pardoned;
In giving to all men that we receive;
And in dying that we're born to eternal life.

Dedicated to Mrs. Frances Tracy. © 1967, OCP Publications, 5536 NE Hassalo, Portland, OR 97213. All rights reserved. Used with permission.

The *Prayer of St. Francis*, which Father Wessel loved so much, perfectly captured the essence of his faith and spirituality. "The song became more than a hymn to be sung during a liturgy; rather, it became a theme, a petition for help from the Lord, a prayer of thanksgiving."[85]

On November 5, 1970, Father Wessel's success with teenagers was given wider recognition by his appointment as Mercer County CYO Director.

In that position, he was instrumental in organizing the first Diocesan CYO Convention, held around February of 1971.[86] Most of the Blessed Sacrament CYO members were involved either in the overall planning or the workshops, or both.

"At the end of the day when everything had been accomplished, Father started singing the *Prayer of St. Francis*. We all followed in," Jayne Hartley recalled. "It was a very moving moment. The song was a sincere prayer of thanks to the Lord for making the day a success. The song was also a prayer that we might have the strength and the knowledge to become 'Channels of the Lord's Peace.'"

Although a key figure in the planning and success of the day, Father bowed his head and attributed everything to the Lord, taking no credit at all for any of the success. This lesson was an extremely valuable one. "Father Wessel's humility taught us all humility. Through his example Father taught us that it is only through the Lord's help that anything is accomplished. Father lived this belief and the example of his faith had a broad influence on us all."[87]

Teenagers at Blessed Sacrament afflicted with "nothing to do" on a summer or holiday evening usually found Father Wessel ready for spur-of-the-moment activity.[88] For them, the CYO was much more than a club; it was "our second home." They felt so comfortable with Father that they practically lived at the rectory, and would often "hang out" there even when there wasn't a CYO meeting or event going on.[89] Many a time, Father Davis would answer the rectory doorbell, only to be greeted by several happy and high-spirited teenagers asking him excitedly if "Father Wessel could come out and play."

One Fourth of July, several obnoxious and "rowdy" girls and boys visited the rectory and Father enthusiastically suggested seeing the fireworks. Just like that, off they went! recalled Jayne Hartley. Father Wessel "was never afraid to say 'yes' to living and was always ready to get the most from life. He enjoyed the simple things in life, such as those fireworks, and was a terrific lover of nature. He was always indifferent to material goods and through his example, we all learned that one need not have money to be happy," said Jayne.[90]

To CYO member Kevin Connor, Father Wessel taught him, by example, "to live life to the fullest," because this was precisely how Father himself lived. "He just *enjoyed life*, and he was very much at peace with himself," said Connor.[91]

Father Wessel used to say, "Try anything once." By that he didn't mean drugs or anything bad or risky, and the kids all knew that. But because he lived life to the fullest, Father always encouraged the young people to do the same. "Just try it one time," he'd say to them—whether it was skiing or camping in the wilderness or sailing a boat—"who knows, you might like it."[92]

There was always laughter when the teens and Father Wessel got together, and he wouldn't hesitate to join right in the fun. Perhaps for this reason, one CYO girl's mother used to call Father "the Big Kid."

He was not afraid to laugh at the things around him nor would he hesitate to laugh at himself. In fact, making jokes at his own expense was one of the many ways he put people at ease. This trait impressed CYO member Mike Ball one afternoon.

Mike and Father were in the Hunt Room. Father, under a deadline to get some papers printed up, was trying to get the ancient mimeograph machine in the basement to work. He was struggling with the machine as he was cranking it up, trying to figure out how to operate it. All of a sudden, a bunch of papers spewed out of the machine and went flying clear across the room. Mike burst out laughing at the ridiculous sight, but quickly caught himself short.

Embarrassed, he said contritely, "Oh, I'm sorry Father. That wasn't funny."

But Father just looked at him and, laughing himself, said, "Yes, *it is!*"[93]

Beyond all of the laughter, all of the good times, and all of the jokes, John Wessel was a priest and a priestly man. He lived and loved his vocation, and his whole being exuded that. Although he could cut up and joke around with the best of them, Father Wessel had his serious side, and to those who knew him, there was no doubt that his priestly duties came first and foremost.[94]

CHAPTER 21

SEARCH FOR CHRISTIAN MATURITY

The most intense religious experiences for youths under Father Wessel's guidance came in the three "Search" weekends that he organized and led in a rustic basketball camp in the Pocono Mountains of Pennsylvania.[1]

The "Search for Christian Maturity" was a program for high school juniors and seniors encouraged by the National CYO Federation, but the Mercer County weekends had Father Wessel's individual stamp. The first one was held in October of 1970. The second was held in April of 1971. The last one, in October of 1971, came just after he had been transferred from Blessed Sacrament.[2]

The Search program was not a retreat per se, although it had many of the trappings. It was, rather, an attempt to establish a community in Christ, where Christ lives in and through young people. It offered young people an opportunity to give prompt and generous response to the voice of Christ.[3]

"Search is a three day way of life attempting to develop in the teen an insight into Christian life, as a way to a happy and productive life," read the material Father Wessel distributed on the first Search. "It is a search for Christian maturity."[4]

At each, some fifty teenagers from several parishes gathered in a remote setting with two or three priests, a few adult laymen and a dozen or so college-age "leaders" for a concentrated time of prayer, group discussions, meditations, individual counseling and liturgical services.

Father Wessel planned the weekends to be intense. It was an opportunity for young people to break away from their daily routines and to really closely examine their lives. Deep introspection was involved. The youths were asked to look at what their strengths were and at the ways that the Holy Spirit was alive in their lives. They encountered the Person of Jesus Christ—through the Holy Spirit, the Mass and Holy Eucharist, the words of Scripture, the forgiveness of Penance, and the presence of Christ in others.[5]

It was, as one participant said, "a chance to throw off your hang-ups and take up a true Christianity."[6]

The goals of Search, as Father outlined them for the teenagers, were several: to open our hearts to the dimensions of the world around us; to put to purpose youthful energy; to fight the natural enemy of egoism; to curb the natural instinct to violence; to learn how to use our enthusiasm for a better world; to learn how to use generosity, chastity, and sincerity in a productive Christian life; and to meet Christ in a practical way and not theoretically.[7]

"We will in the end become brothers and sisters," Father Wessel's "welcome" to the third Search read, "sharing a feeling beyond anything you could ever dream of. It will not be easy for we will never share each other's love unless we know each other, and we can never know each other unless we suffer with each other. You have begun this beautiful process in your courage to even be here. With all my heart, I ask you to put every effort you can into this weekend. You will never be here again as you are now."[8]

It was completely in character that one of the most profound and elevated spiritual experiences Father Wessel provided to countless teens in the Trenton diocese began in the most ordinary of ways. In fact, it would not be stretching the point to suggest that Father's Search for Christian Maturity weekends really started over a game of poker.

After a few years at Blessed Sacrament, Father Wessel and several of the older CYO fellows and a few adults began to gather on Friday nights at the rectory to play poker. Father Pat Hannon would join them and proved to be a very good card player. Father Wessel, however, was not an especially good poker player and had to dip into a jar of loose change on more than one occasion. This was no high stakes poker match; just a "penny ante" nickel-and-dime game. More than anything, it was an excuse for a "guys' night out,"[9] the lone female exception being Joanne Gillespie, Father Wessel's right hand in CYO work, who occasionally joined them. Father had nicknamed her "Joe" and she became—at least, for the purposes of the card games—"one of the guys."[10]

One night Father Wessel and a few of the young people were indulging in their usual Friday night poker game at the rectory. Father casually asked, "How would you guys like to help me out running this Search for Christian Maturity?"

The "guys" looked at him blankly and asked, What is it? "He was almost afraid to tell us," recalled Kevin Connor. He said, "'It's like a retreat.' And we looked at him and said, 'You've got to be crazy!'" But Father was persistent, and extracted a promise from them to help him run the Search weekend.[11]

Once Father "had his mind set on doing something, that was it," added Joanne. "Nobody could talk him out of it or change his mind." And in the end, he convinced everyone of what a great idea it was to do a Search.[12]

Father Wessel was tireless in planning, arranging, and conducting these weekends. With characteristic humility, he refused all credit for Search, attributing every achievement to God.[13]

"We spent months and months in preparation" for the first Search, recalled Joanne Gillespie, one of the youth counselors. A tremendous amount of effort went into setting up the program and all the details of the weekend.[14]

"We brought in all the food. We did all the cooking, all the clean-ups, and everyone, even the retreatants themselves, was involved in every aspect of the day—setting tables, cooking the food, serving the food, washing dishes afterwards. So it was a real melding of the community, working together. . . . It was just one of the most fabulous experiences of my life," said Joanne.[15]

Father Wessel had everything organized, but each Search team member had his own specific responsibilities. Some team members gave talks, according to the outlines and directions that Father had given them. After each talk, the Search "candidates" broke up into discussion tables, and some team members led the small group discussions, again with Father's guidance and instruction. Other team members were in charge of the liturgy, recreation, and kitchen detail. One older youth served as "young adult director" or overall coordinator of the weekend. Father Wessel was the "spiritual director."[16]

Right before the Search weekend began, Father and a CYO youth made the two-hour drive up to the rustic summer basketball camp in East Stroudsburg, Pennsylvania, to look over the site and make final preparations.[17]

Each of the three Searches was a little different, but all kept to the same basic format. On the first Search, the "Searchers" departed from a central meeting point in Trenton and arrived at their destination in the Poconos on a Friday evening at six o'clock.

Father urged the teenagers to "put away their watches" once they left Trenton and to forget about time and not be concerned about what was coming next. Searchers wouldn't get schedules, they just had to trust. Be open to one another, make friends, he told them. "Learn to know what it means to be free in Christ."[18]

After some welcoming remarks and orientation, dinner was served and the first of the talks began. It asked the Searchers to consider "Who Are You?"—to yourself, to others, to God. It was followed by a talk on "The Joys of a Good Confession." To start the weekend off in the right frame of mind and soul, all the Search candidates went to confession.

Over the weekend, the kids would hear talks on topics such as "Grace," "The Mystical Body," "The Mass," "Commitment," "The Apostolate," "Faith," "Actual Grace," "Matrimony" (given by a married couple), "Challenge," "Baptism, Confirmation and Eucharist," and "Christian Manhood and Womanhood." The speakers were, for the most part, young people like the teenage Searchers themselves.

After one such talk, Father apparently felt that the small group discussions would be hard for the kids. "Very difficult time to get kids through," he instructed his youth counselors. "Give, give, give until you die!"[19]

Although the talks were geared to teenagers, they were conducted at a very elevated level. The information was intellectually challenging and the concepts gave the young listeners much food for thought. None of the presentations consisted of "talking down" to the teens. Consider the outline Father prepared for the talk on "Faith," which was delivered by a young adult. Serious points covered were:

- Definition of faith as absolute trust in God and what He has revealed.

- Problems of trust that lead to doubt (Is faith just kidding yourself?).
- Faith as a perfect act of love.
- Faith as a human virtue absolutely needed for peace.
- Human faith and the unfaithful.
- Faith in a world of the written contract.
- What the world, your world, will be if faith is there.
- Faith is built on prayer.
- Faith makes a man free.[20]

Each evening, Father conducted night prayers, and each morning upon arising, morning prayers. For the remainder of the weekend, there were talks, small group discussions, a film, group sharing, workshops, role playing, communal and private prayer, meditation, silent "faith walks" alone, the Rosary, and visits to the Blessed Sacrament in a makeshift chapel.

During one of the talks on Saturday evening, the Searchers were asked to resolve to do something they had never done before to deepen their contact with Jesus and make it a part of their lives. Three areas of challenge were suggested: the use of the Scriptures; the use of the Sacraments (Holy Eucharist and Penance) and Prayer; and in the Community (the Body of Christ). These "growth resolutions" were written down and offered at Sunday's Mass; they were not read nor revealed by anyone.

Saturday night was a "festive dinner" and community party, a time for the young people to celebrate.

On Sunday morning, the last day of the weekend, Father Wessel celebrated Mass with the group of Searchers. By this time, the young people were no longer feeling strange and fearful as when they had first arrived. They had left behind their shyness and isolation, and had formed a real community based upon love of Jesus and love for each other.

A closing ceremony at three o'clock on Sunday afternoon marked the end of the Search weekend, but the beginning of a new life in mature Christianity for the Searchers themselves.

It was a challenge for young people to see their faith as not just a series of "rules and regulations" observed out of habit, or because their parents did, but as a Christianity freely and maturely chosen and deeply rooted in a commitment to Jesus Christ, in which observances of faith were based on and for the love of God. It was a chance to actually see their Catholic faith as it was, and to say "yes" to Jesus or "no."[21]

Father Wessel had an unwavering faith that, over the weekend, the young person would encounter Jesus Christ through the power and grace of the Holy Spirit. For those who were willing to meet Him, follow Him, and put on an authentic Christianity, this encounter would change their lives. Over these weekends, Father Wessel urged the young people to, in his words, "Say yes to Jesus."[22]

"It was the first time that any of us really experienced our religion the way religion probably was meant to be," said Search team member, Kevin Connor. "Ninety-eight percent of the people came away reborn."[23]

One of the youthful "Searchers" shared these memories of her experience in the Poconos on the first Search weekend, October 16-18, 1970:

> A key to the weekend is that it is youth-to-youth oriented. The group of "Searchers" who were making the "retreat" was broken down into a number of discussion table groups. Each table had about eight high schoolers and two counselors assigned to it. The counselors were for the most part college students not many years older than the Searchers. Through the example of these counselors the Searchers gained a tremendous amount. Here were young people who were just a few years older who were truly living Christian lives. Faith and commitment to Christ were no longer catechism words to be memorized. During the weekend the Searchers saw young people who actually practiced their faith and to whom Christian love was a way of life. One key to the impact of this experience was, perhaps, that the counselors were "normal" kids. They were not "holy-rollers" but merely kids very much like the Searchers. Here were many concrete examples of how, as a twentieth century youth, one could believe in and live a faith in God.
>
> Fr. Wessel was behind this whole weekend. He gave of himself body and soul to the weekend and his own example of living Love was a tremendously powerful one. He was extremely open with all involved and encouraged all on the weekend to trust—to trust in one another and to trust in the Lord.

Father showed many through his example how to pray. This may sound insignificant but it really was of tremendous importance to most of the youth on the weekend.

Father guided the weekend and yet, once again, gave all the credit to the Holy Spirit for any success which was achieved. It is difficult to put into words the size of the effect Father's example had on all there. He was truly living a Christian faith, loving all as brothers and sisters and he willingly gave of himself to everyone. His faith was amazing to see and yet his humility was equally as astounding. Despite all the tremendous realizations he guided the Searchers to, he would deny being of any worth. He *always, always* shrugged off any praise and really disliked being in the "limelight." He believed it was the Lord who made whatever successes Father had and he believed himself to be an "instrument" of the Lord. How much these examples of love, faith, and Christian living influenced us could never be measured nor will they ever be forgotten. Father shared with us all that true peace of Christ which he knew.[24]

The weekend was also profoundly moving for the adult counselors and Search team members as well. Among them was Alice Callery, then a secretary at the Diocesan CYO Office in Trenton, who had these recollections:

To accompany Fr. Wessel on Search was indeed most inspiring. I shared two such experiences with him—two of the most memorable occasions of my life. High on a mountaintop in the Poconos, it is not difficult to imagine you are close to God. With such a program as Search directed by Fr. Wessel, it was even easier to imagine because it was so obvious that the Spirit was working in and through this other man called John.

I remember with real joy a young priest who moved among us dressed in the oldest of old clothes, a cap perched on his head, heavy boots on his feet, and a heart filled with the desire to bring Christ, alive and well to some forty teenagers. Midst uncomfortable odds of very cold weather and unheated cabins on our first Search, Father's unconquerable determination that

Searchers would leave Bob Kennedy's camp more aware of Christ than they had ever been before, remained undaunted.

I doubt that I shall ever forget the tremendous impact Fr. Wessel had on his young charges and, yes, too on we adults privileged to be present those edifying days. Never before, nor since, have I heard a priest pray with such honest-to-goodness downright sincerity as did Father at night prayers. He really talked to God! With his customary humility, he openly admitted he did not know all the answers, that he too knew what temptations were all about, but that together if we trusted in God and called upon Him, he would surely hear us and be with us that night and always. The beautiful thing was that he really meant it and showed it.

I smile when I recall another older team member who was completely taken aback by Father's lack of concern over following a planned schedule—how lunches could be kept waiting indefinitely, dinners be put off an hour or more. This could have been considered the height of inefficiency when, in fact, it was anything but. Father put the emphasis where it rightly belonged and chose the better part. To him, it was much more important that Searchers participate in walks (private moments alone outside to reflect on Christ, etc.) than that the chicken be piping hot; that the Searchers meet Christ in one another than that the bologna lay down and die. The practicality of clocks and all that they impart was left in Trenton, N.J.—that was Christ's time in the mountains to use as He would. The kids sensed this and responded in kind.

I couldn't help but notice and be impressed by the love and devotion that Father brought out in his team members, most of whom were college age youth. Their attitude toward him was so genuine. There was none of the "moldy old yes, Father," routine without sincere meaning, but a true respect which had grown and developed from working with Father and from having seen him in day-to-day living. After all, he was never phoney with them—the example was set, so how could they be otherwise with him? He pretty much treated kids as adults and, although he was more in tune to their vibes than just about anyone I know, he never had to come down to their level to reach them. He rather inspired them to try to reach his by his authentic Christian living.

During my lifetime, I have been fortunate enough to have attended many Masses, some complete with ritual, pomp and ceremony, but never have I been present at any which had the spiritual significance or profound meaning to me as did Father Wessel's Masses in the Poconos. They were offered with the utmost simplicity and in such a beautiful manner and he had an uncanny way of creating a real community. I am the first to admit that there is a degree of emotionality connected with Search and because of this, things look a lot different in the mountains than they might in the local parish church. Nonetheless, I remember commenting when I came home from Search that if Christ wasn't really there at those Masses, it would be tough to convince me He was anywhere. That statement still stands.

All the priests of Search were terrific, especially when it came to hearing confessions in the middle of the night and in devastating cold. I didn't completely agree with Fr. Wessel's conviction that everyone should go to confession until he explained his reasons to me. He was again thinking of the other guy, hoping that some of the troubled teenagers on Search would find in the sacrament at least the opportunity to talk to someone who cared and who was willing to help and guide them in any way possible. Another aside—Father told me he found it a little difficult to hear face-to-face confessions and would prefer "secret." In the end, he heard as many, if not more, face-to-face than the other priests, just another instance of where he gave in to the wishes of others rather then just consider his own feelings.

I think that on Search, as at all other times, Father's biggest appeal lay in the observation that he didn't merely preach but certainly practiced Christ's mission on earth, not in any stuffy, pietistic manner, but in a way that kids could relate to and in an unbelievably trusting and powerful fashion. The kids knew that with Father, they weren't always going to be right by a long shot, but, more importantly, they also knew he was their friend, a friend who recognized no "office hours" or times of day or night, but one who was always available and approachable.[25]

Father Wessel's friend and fellow priest, Father James Dubell, accompanied him on two Search weekends:

> I remember that John had the Search very well organized, in that he had young people in charge of food. He had young people in charge of preparing certain meals. He had young people in charge of giving certain talks. Everybody had a job. It was very well organized.
>
> And he was very much a part of it. He didn't just tell them, "Well, now, you go do it and I'll be over here." He was right with them all the time. They wouldn't go to sleep at night, and he stayed up with them. They roamed around outside, and he went chasing after them. . . . He celebrated the thing with them. When they were sad and they were confused, he was, too. When they were joyful and happy and felt successful, he felt it with them. And you could see it in his face, and . . . in his bodily movements. Even at the liturgy, the young people had a point there where they kind of expressed themselves in a little dance . . . and he joined right in with it.[26]

The Searches also had their unexpected moments that challenged the *pax et bonum*—"peace and good humor"—that Father had asked everyone to bring along with them for the weekends.

On the first Search weekend, it was bitterly cold in the snow-covered mountains overnight. It was so cold in the cabins, in fact, that anybody who could found their way to the kitchen to get warm and sleep on the kitchen floor in their sleeping bags. The bathroom facilities consisted of "all the amenities that cold running water afforded you," recalled one of the Searchers. And miraculously, all survived Saturday night's chicken dinner which, one of the cooks confessed, was "horribly underdone."[27]

The second Search weekend, on April 16-18, 1971, was "every bit as cold as in the fall but no snow," Father Wessel later wrote. "The added attraction was mice. The girls' cabins were filled with them. Although the kids didn't appreciate the difference, the food was much better."[28]

More importantly, the group of Searchers almost lost their spiritual director before the first Search weekend had barely gotten underway!

On that first Search weekend, the young Searchers were sleeping in different cabins while the staff slept in the main building, which consisted of one big room, where they lined up their sleeping bags up and down in rows. Father Wessel had gone upstairs to the attic to change for bed late one night. There was a door that led from the main room to the attic, and since the attic was unfinished, one couldn't walk too far without bumping into wooden planks. There were no lights and no electricity.

The staffers had already bedded down in their sleeping bags for the evening. They were exhausted, having been up since the crack of dawn, running on tight schedules all day. Everyone was trying to get some rest. It was deathly quiet.

"All of a sudden we heard this loud crash," recalled Joanne Gillespie. Father Wessel must have misjudged his distance upstairs or tripped over something. With a great commotion, the priest literally came tumbling down the stairs, barreling through the door, and crash landed in a heap on the floor in the room where the rest of the staff was sleeping. Everyone was jolted awake. "And you should have heard the language that came out of his mouth as he did this! And we started laughing so hard. We couldn't help it. It was so hysterical," said Joanne.

The team members asked him if he was all right, and ascertained that Father wasn't seriously hurt. He was just mad and grumbling to himself as he plopped down in his sleeping bag to go to sleep. They teased him about his earthy language as he fell down the stairs. "Shame on you, Father Wessel. You shouldn't say things like that!"

"That's nothing," he joked, with as much good humor as he could muster under the circumstances. "You should've heard what I was *thinking*!"[29]

Accidents notwithstanding, Father Wessel was always very upbeat on these weekends. He seemed blessed with enormous physical and spiritual energy that carried him and others through the intense three-day Search.

Father Wessel's seminary roommate at St. Charles College, Father (later Monsignor) Eugene Rebeck, helped him on several of the Search weekends. The high school students on the retreats "were always very much in awe of John," observed Monsignor Rebeck, because of his "daringness, his willingness to try things. But yet he always expressed a great spirituality to the kids, which is what they really were there for . . . And they could identify with him because I think they really found him as a person that was very real. But the person who was real was also a person of deep spirituality."[30]

Father's spirituality was evident in every aspect of the weekend, even in the "Community Work Prayer" that he asked the Search team members and Searchers to recite as they worked together and served each other. This little prayer perhaps best reflects the spirituality that Father brought to the weekends:

> Jesus, my Brother, come with me as I do my little share for my friends, and those I do not know. They are Your dear sisters and brothers, too. If I show them my joy, my skill, my smile, my laughter, we are a closer family and You are closer, too. My work is no longer a job but a gift to them and to You.

The Search confessions were always held on Friday nights and seemed to go on until the wee hours of the morning. "Late at night, I'm going to be sitting out in the woods hearing confessions," Father Wessel told the teenagers on the third Search, October 1971. "Come and see me one at a time."

Among the many young people who accepted his invitation was Joseph Parnell*. He went to see Father Wessel alone and they talked. "He was the first person that I remember to actually speak to me about a relationship with God, a relationship with Jesus," recalled Joe. "In other words, going beyond the tenets of the Church that we were all taught, but actually Jesus Himself, to know God in your life."

"He was the first person to give me a hug and call me 'brother'." And the fact that Father, as a priest and authority figure, treated the young man as an equal made a lasting impression. Father Wessel was Joe Parnell's first and deepest influence to go in the direction of serving God and "to the fullness of the life that I have now, knowing Jesus Christ personally."[31]

"Some of the all-time best Masses that we had were in the field," recalled Wes Ritterbusch. The Masses that Father Wessel celebrated on the Search weekends were every bit as beautiful as those CYO "Youth Masses" in Casey

Hall, but with an added attraction: If the weather cooperated, Mass was held out-of-doors. Father would set up a little table for an altar and the young people would sit on the ground all around him in a big semicircle. Celebrating Mass with Father Wessel on a hill high in the mountains, it was easy for the teenagers to imagine being with the Lord and his disciples at the Sermon on the Mount.[32]

Father gave the young people a unique opportunity to participate in the Mass on those weekends. Just as they had done at their Youth Masses back home, the Searchers themselves brought up the gifts, composed the Prayer of the Faithful, and baked all the bread and prepared the wine.[33]

At the Offertory, Father encouraged each person to "offer" something special of themselves to the Lord. One young man, a basketball player, even brought up his basketball during the Offertory procession. At this time, the young people offered the "growth resolutions" they had made and written down from the night before.

The Sign of Peace would take easily twenty minutes, as the Searchers would greet each and every single person who shared the liturgy with a hug or a kiss, and express how they felt about them.[34]

Then, they would pass the Eucharistic Bread from one to the other, taking a small piece while saying, "The Body of Christ. Amen," "The Body of Christ. Amen," For the young high school kids, and even the adults present, "it was so memorable and just so touching. You couldn't get through one of those Masses without crying," said Joanne Gillespie.[35]

Another aspect of the weekend that made it so special was that any teen with a guitar or musical instrument was encouraged to bring it along and play it at the Search Masses. Memorable, too, were the contemporary liturgical songs that were sung. There was Father's special favorite, the *Prayer of St. Francis*, as well as modern spiritual songs such as *Alle, Alle, Good Lady Poverty, Happy the Man, Into Your Hands, Peace, My Friends, There's a New Day, Come Before the Table, The King of Glory, We Are One in the Spirit*, and *Yes to You, My Lord*. A simple but beloved song was *The Love Round*.

Father did not hesitate to use modern rock and soul songs if they expressed a Christian theme: The young people sang everything from Peter Paul & Mary's *All My Trials* and *Blowin' in the Wind*, Simon and Garfunkel's *Bridge Over Troubled Water* and *Sounds of Silence*, the Beatles' *Here Comes the Sun*, James Taylor's *Fire and Rain*, and Bob Dylan's *When the Ship Comes In*, to the *Amen* song from the film, *Lilies of the Field*.

The young people on Search were not only from Blessed Sacrament, but from parishes all over the Diocese of Trenton. And while the Search Masses were moving and very personal for the teenagers, Father Wessel had a very practical concern that the young people who had so enjoyed the guitar Mass, the singing, and the participation in the liturgy would not be disappointed when they returned to their home parishes and found that these "new things" weren't practiced. He encouraged them to work with their own pastors and to share in their own parishes what they had experienced in the mountains, "but most especially that they wouldn't become disenchanted and disheartened and lose their way," recalled Monsignor Dubell.[36]

A closing ceremony at three o'clock Sunday afternoon marked the end of the Search weekend. On the first Search, the ceremony consisted of Exposition of the Blessed Sacrament and Benediction. Father Wessel gave a closing talk to the young Searchers, who were no longer "candidates" but "graduates," urging them to remember and put into practice all they had learned and experienced during the weekend.

Father had gifts for the Search graduates: a small blue pocket New Testament Bible called the "Good News Bible"—the same one that he himself carried at all times—and a simple silver cross and chain. Father blessed the Good News Bible and the Search cross as he presented them to each young person with a special word of love and encouragement just for them.

The conclusion of Search was, for Father Wessel, a moment of great joy. "Even at these times, his pride was always directed towards others' contributions—none of the credit for successes went to him in his own mind," wrote Alice Callery. Father always made a special point to publicly recognize and thank the members of the Search team, and all those who had helped make the weekend a success. "I never once saw him grandstand for the first seat, the most important place," she added. "He was perfectly content to remain out of the limelight. Any other 'M.O.' was completely foreign to him."[37]

The closing ceremony invariably ended with much exuberant singing, dancing, and celebrating. Father Wessel would get so "into the music" that he couldn't stand still. He liked "fast, snappy music, foot-stomping music that would get your soul moving and stir you inside," recalled Joanne Gillespie. He liked whatever the kids liked and made them happy.[38]

"He would always have to stamp his foot and clap his hands and jump around. And he wasn't real coordinated either as a dancer," Joanne continued, "but his enthusiasm was just so catchy that it would just get the kids going, because they would see him being so excited by what was going on that they couldn't help but get involved and be happy about it."

It was characteristic of Father Wessel that his serious religious purpose did not get in the way of his dancing an Irish Jig at the end of the Search weekend.[39]

One time, in fact, Father got so caught up in the celebratory mood that it wouldn't do for him to just remain on the floor and dance. To the delight of the youths, he jumped up on top of a table and danced—until, all of a sudden, the table broke and came crashing down, and Father with it! But he didn't care. No one enjoyed himself more, and nothing could take away from his happiness at the conclusion of the successful weekend.[40]

Father Wessel was right when he promised the teenagers at the beginning of Search: "We will in the end become brothers and sisters, sharing a feeling beyond anything you could ever dream of." By the end of the weekend, there was a lot of tears, crying and hugging, and a newfound religious feeling and spiritual awareness.

"One point which Father stressed during the Search weekend was that living Christian lives was really easy while up on the mountains, but it was when one descended to the valley of everyday living that the real test began," recalled a young participant.[41]

The religious "high" many participants reached would, he cautioned them, be more difficult to sustain once they came down from the mountain. In fact, they could not realistically expect the "summit euphoria" to always continue, but they could take with them a new spiritual awareness that didn't just depend on the fleeting emotions of the moment.[42]

Father compared the spiritual "high" of the weekend to the "mountaintop experience" that Apostles Peter, James and John had with the Lord Jesus during the Transfiguration.[43] Now the Searchers had to take that religious fervor "down from the mountaintop" and back into the "valleys" of their everyday lives, just as the Apostles had done. "You must walk away from the mountain," he told them, "and what do you bring with you? How do you start to think about that?" he asked them.

It was through living a mature, committed Christianity "down in the valley" of everyday life, Father told them, that their faith would grow, be tested, and hopefully persevere. And it was "down in the valley" that the young Searchers needed to be, loving one another and sharing "our Brother, Jesus" with those around them.[44]

The community of Catholic teens that evolved after the "mountaintop experience" of the Search weekend acquired a much deeper level of spirituality than the young people, even in Father Wessel's CYO, had ever experienced.[45]

The CYO became much more than a group of kids who got together mainly to have fun and do things with other teens; for while CYO still had all of these elements, now a real Christian community was taking root in the lives and hearts of the teenagers. Those who had returned from Search were "new people," anxious to share their new awareness of love for each other and faith in God with those around them.

CHAPTER 22

LESSONS AND TEACHINGS

Father Wessel knew how easy it was for the teenagers on Search to lose their way once they "came down from the mountaintop" and returned back "into the valley" they had left behind for one glorious weekend. He knew how easily the Search "euphoria" could be forgotten amid the cares and worries, personal and family problems, fears and inadequacies, that young people experienced in their daily lives. Indeed, one of the talks always given on the Search weekend was the parable of the Sower and the Seed (Matthew 13).

In order to keep the fire of faith alive in the teens, Father, like a modern-day Saint Paul, composed letters which he sent to them after each Search weekend—and indeed, at other times as well—to remind them of what they had learned on Search. His letters were, in the words of one former Searcher, "very much like a little sermon."[1]

As Father Wessel himself wrote to the Searchers:

> The "glow" of meeting Jesus face to face should have worn off a bit by this time and you should be ready to get down to business "in the valley." I would like to remind you and myself of a few things you learned and experienced on Search.[2]

Father's letters were remarkably consistent. With great simplicity and often humor, and yet with deep spirituality, he constantly re-emphasized five basic themes for the young people to remember and put into practice as the key to daily Christian living: Jesus, the Sacraments, Prayer, Scriptures, and Community.

1. Jesus

Each of the five areas Father Wessel enumerated was a necessary ingredient to a mature and vibrant Christian life. All fit together like spokes on a wheel. But first and foremost—at the center of the wheel, so to speak—was Jesus Christ Himself.

There were many ways in which Father Wessel brought the reality of Jesus Christ to his young charges. His own example of Christ-like love and service was a powerful influence. So, too, was the fact that he readily expressed his belief in the Lord. While Father was not recalled as a "preachy" type of person,[3] he often talked about Jesus in his daily conversation in a quite ordinary and natural way, as if he were talking about a good friend. This made a tremendous impression on those around him.

Father Wessel demonstrated an awareness that believing in Jesus Christ, and experiencing His love and salvation, comes mainly through having the Word of God preached by someone else who knows and believes in Him.

As Father himself once wrote:

> Jesus is not inherited. But someone else's faith can help us open to Him.[4]

Secondly, to know and believe in Christ required a personal response. Would the youth choose to love, serve and follow Christ and His message—or not? Endowed with a free will, the young person had the ultimate ability to accept or reject a way of life with Christ as the head.

First and foremost, Father Wessel wanted young people to be committed to Jesus Christ. In Scripture and in Catholic dogma and tradition, images of the Lord Jesus are many: God the Son, the Second Person of the Blessed Trinity, True God and True Man, the Son of God, the Son of Mary, the Savior and Redeemer of the World. And, in the approachable image that Father Wessel often liked to evoke for the teenagers—Our Brother: A God who is yet "one of us" and fully human, who was tempted as are we in all things yet did not sin, a Divine Friend who constantly makes intercession for us before the Father.

As Father urged his young Searchers on the last Search weekend: "Say yes to Jesus."[5]

And a heart that was open to Christ was filled with the Holy Spirit. Father Wessel was "very, very devoted to the Holy Spirit," one CYO youth recalled.[6] "He really believed that the Holy Spirit was a real instrument in delivering the Lord's teachings, and he would always tell us that. He would say that the Holy Spirit is always working; He's always keeping an eye on you."[7]

2. Sacraments

Father stressed the frequent use of the Sacraments of Penance and the Holy Eucharist for all Catholics, especially the young. His own words speak eloquently of the need for young people to remain connected to these sources of grace.

After the first Search weekend in the fall of 1970, Father Wessel wrote the Search graduates:

> We need the Sacraments. How man slips back so quickly to his human instinct of "survival of the fittest." The forgiveness of Jesus that brings peace back into our lives is so wonderful. But, oh, how we neglect it. To say "I'm sorry" and "forget it" seems so difficult some days. ("Seventy times seven.") How we need the Eucharist! Remember how all things were just in there, at Mass? God's words, us, and Jesus. Every time I celebrate the Eucharist and put myself into it, the world is a new place and the people in it are new people. I am a New Man.[8]

And after the Spring Search, 1970, he wrote:

> You need the Sacraments. Christ is ever present and ever loving but needs to be "tuned in." The Eucharist is the most sublime of facts. Don't run away from it. Give yourself and He will give himself back. While we don't run to the Sacrament of

Penance every week, we must be constantly aware of our duty
to do "penance"—share our talent to rebuild the world we have
so much neglected. Never forget that you are a "thief of love"
and don't be afraid to say "I'm sorry."[9]

And again, right before he left Blessed Sacrament, Father Wessel wrote
to the CYO:

You saw the risen Christ on Search. To keep up with His
demands, you must get his energy to love through concentrated,
sincere and wholehearted reception of the Eucharist. You can't
make it alone. Cf., Jn 6.[10]

While Father would encourage young people to receive the sacraments
frequently, he was not afraid to be daring and innovative in trying to make
the sacraments more accessible to young people. Such was the case with
Father's "Youth Masses." Here were liturgies that reached out and drew in
great numbers of enthusiastic young people at a time in society when most
teenagers were often cynical and rebellious toward anything "institutional"
or "authoritarian"—including the Church and traditional religion.

The Sacrament of Confession also could be a daunting prospect to
the teenager, who was often nervous, embarrassed and afraid, but Father
let them know that confession didn't have to be stuffy and formal. "You
can come to me and you can talk to me. If you've got a problem, come see
me," he'd encourage them. And the kids immediately picked up on this
and responded to him.[11]

Confessions with Father were sometimes held in the most unlikely of
places, driving in the car, walking down the street, working on the boat, or
high up in the mountains, recalled Ronald Garrett.[12]

Father Wessel was extremely effective at face-to-face confessions and
was always able to put a young penitent at ease even though, as he once
confided to Alice Callery, he personally preferred "the screen." Father
was keenly aware that in the Sacrament of Confession, the penitent was
literally encountering Christ in the person of the priest. Through Father's
compassionate, Christ-like example, the teenager learned that confessing
one's sins before a loving God was nothing to be afraid of.[13]

3. Prayer

If we love someone, we want to communicate with them. We want to share our hopes and dreams, fears and feelings, with the one we love. We want to listen to what the beloved has to say back to us. Prayer is nothing more than a conversation with God. Any relationship suffers without real communication, and Father Wessel definitely believed in the importance of prayer.[14]

After the first Search weekend, Father Wessel reminded the Search graduates:

> We need real prayer. . . . How long has it been since we prayed for one another as we promised we would do? I did this morning but because I crowded my mind with so many silly things, I did a bad job of it. I get so that Jesus is becoming a brother away in college—spoken *of* but not spoken to.[15]

And after the second Search, spring 1971, he wrote:

> The last time you heard from me was when we were organizing the Spring Search. I thank you for your prayers and any hidden help you gave me. We were running scared at the time and like all "good Christians," we prayed like hell; when we were in trouble He bailed us out.[16]

And yet again, before he left Blessed Sacrament, Father Wessel wrote the CYO:

> I know that with the beginning of school, you are under a certain amount of stress. And I really feel that some solid prayer is in order. It's been a long time, a lot more than a "boat" can get in the way of the real things that count. When I'm uptight and can't sit still, and the Mass isn't quite enough, the "long, alone, silent and free" walk with Him is the most refreshing and loving thing I can do.[17]

Joanne Gillespie recalled how Father made prayer so integral in the lives of the CYO youths:

Always, prayer was so important in everything that we did. And the beautiful thing about it was that he, for the first time in our lives back in those days, introduced us to informal prayer. Up until then, it was always recitation, and all of a sudden, we're discovering, "Hey, you can just talk to God!" And he would, right out loud. . . . He just made God so present in his life publicly that we would look at that and say, "Hey, it's okay to have a relationship with God. God is somebody that we can talk to." Because he made it that way for us.

We would start almost everything with a prayer. Every single endeavor, whether it be a ski trip, a prayer for the road, a prayer before we eat, or a prayer before meeting.[18]

Father Ronald Bacovin also recalled Father John Wessel as a very positive, prayerful person. Once, Father Wessel and his CYO teenagers were at a youth function at Notre Dame High School in Trenton. It was probably a ball game or a sports competition, said Father Bacovin, who was also present.

And while we were there, John gathered all the CYO kids together and they had a little prayer together. He mixed prayers with the youth a lot of times. He was never afraid to pray, never afraid to show that kind of outward expression, and he always brought it in, as far as I'm aware . . . with his kids. He was never without that.

The younger priest "really was impressed when I saw John deal with the kids—getting them all together and saying a prayer. And he was very, very good." Father Wessel wasn't hesitant at all about sharing his faith, "and the kids were very responsive. There were no looks like, 'Oh, what's going on here?' or 'Do we have to do this again?' That was the other thing that kind of caught my eye—how responsive they were to it. Apparently he would do that many times" with them.[19]

That was Father Bacovin's last visual remembrance of Father Wessel—sitting with the teens on the bleachers in Notre Dame High School gymnasium and gathering them all around him to pray. "It might have been some competition and their team might have even lost," added Father Bacovin. "I think part of the prayer was kind of a consolation."

Father Wessel was leading them in giving thanks to God "for the good try" and for "the gift of being together."

4. Scriptures

To Father Wessel, Sacred Scripture was important because it was God's Holy Word. It was Jesus speaking directly to us. At every opportunity, he stressed the importance of reading the Bible regularly. Father Wessel loved all of the Scriptures, especially the New Testament. By giving little New Testaments to each of the Searchers at the conclusion of the weekend, Father sought to enkindle in them a love and thirst for the Word of God.

After the first Search, in October 1970, he asked the Search graduates:

> How long has it been since you pulled out your New Testament and read what Jesus has to say to us?[20]

And after the second Search weekend, in April 1971, Father Wessel reminded them:

> Have you allowed Jesus to speak to you through his Words? Next to the Eucharistic Body of Jesus, the Scriptures are the best gift we have.[21]

It was no secret that Father Wessel's life and direction were very much influenced by the zeal and writings of Saint Paul.[22] One passage that Father Wessel often used to encourage the young Searchers was found in Galatians 5. The passage seems to have held particular meaning for Father, illustrating the difference between a self-centered and a Christ-centered way of life.

> As for you, my brothers and sisters, you were called to be free. But do not let this freedom become an excuse for letting your feelings rule you. Instead, let love make you serve one another. But if you act according to the animal in you, brutes that we all are, hurting and harming one another, then watch out, or you will completely destroy one another. (St. Paul to the Galatians, 5:13-15).[23]

In similar vein, Father exhorted the young people after the second Search:

> Now that you are free men, don't go back to the old
> slavery you once knew. Jesus has made you free. St. Paul to the
> Galatians, 5:1.[24]

To that Father Wessel added his own postscript: "Don't be afraid, don't let the world close you up."[25]

5. Community

Father Wessel constantly stressed the necessity of each person's remaining a part of a larger community of believers in the Body of Christ. Father knew how difficult it was for those who tried to "go it alone." Invariably, they faltered.

For most of the high school age teens, their "community" (apart from their own families) was the CYO, then their parish church, and finally the Roman Catholic Church. Community was necessary to love and serve God and one another. "You need each other," Father told the young people.

Father Wessel's vision of a Christian community was one in which each member was "open, truthful, suffering, and loving" with one another.[26] To illustrate the point, Father once jotted down this phrase:

> "I have a difficulty loving you because I do not know you.
> And I do not know you because we have not as yet suffered
> together."[27]

To bear one another's burdens is a supreme act of love. As Father told the Searchers on the last Search weekend:

> We will never share each other's love unless we know each
> other, and we can never know each other unless we suffer with
> each other.

In such a community of "open, truthful, suffering, and loving" believers, Christ is present. Because, as Jesus Himself assures us, "Where two or three are gathered in my name, there I am in their midst" (Matthew 19:20). And in such a community, all members share Jesus with each other and with those who do not as yet know Him. As Father wrote to his young Searchers: "Share our Brother with all you meet."[28]

After the first Search weekend, Father Wessel reminded the Search graduates of the importance of community:

> We need each other. The community that was established in the Poconos gave to each other the reality of Jesus within the human person. "Rap sessions" are nothing other than the Spirit of Jesus speaking to console, understand, and give courage to the group. St. Paul's understanding of Christ's presence in the community of many parts was not only beautifully put but extremely accurate. Those kids that had to "go it alone after the Search" had a difficult time adjusting to the real world.[29]

And after the Spring Search, 1970, Father's joy at the new additions to the Christian community was evident as he wrote:

> With great joy and thanks to our Lord, we have 47 new brothers and sisters. (Quite a birth rate!) . . . You need each other. It is in each of you—together—that you see Christ most apparent. You have all received some gift—share it. The courage, understanding and guidance that you need will come from Jesus basically through others who have His life within them.[30]

And yet again, right before he left Blessed Sacrament, Father Wessel wrote to the CYO:

> Talk and tears are not enough though, to get ourselves straight sometimes. It seems that if we stop sharing with one another, we stop seeing our Jesus. College will be the "body of Christ" for many of you now. You are beautiful when you are sharing. Share our Brother [Jesus] with all you meet. To be poor through sharing is one of the roads to happiness. Cf., Lk 9:57.[31]

In his end-of-the-school-year message to the Blessed Sacrament CYO in June of 1971, Father Wessel reviewed the group's success in achieving the goals they had set for that year. He revealed something of his vision for a Christian community as he wrote:

> In the best sense of the word Blessed Sacrament CYO became a community whose purpose is "living in Christ Jesus." This community depended not on a few but on each member to contribute and give concrete example of his or her Christ's Life within them. Not an easy job! But, at their very best, they became "beautiful people." And our Lord returned to them a hundred times worth of favors.
> THANK YOU, JESUS![32]

Father Wessel, by his own example, showed the teenagers in the CYO how to become a true community "living in Christ Jesus." First, by caring deeply for each person.

As Joanne Gillespie recalled:

> He felt so deeply about people. There were always some kids who were kind of on the sidelines, the outsiders, kids that he knew of that were having family problems, or had a really bad home life, and you could see that he was just crying inside for those kids. He felt it right to his core for each and every one of them.
>
> He really, sincerely cared. He could somehow see inside of people so easily. . . . He would know everybody's little quirks and idiosyncrasies and he'd make jokes about it and make them laugh at themselves. He would never let you take yourself too seriously.[33]

Father Wessel was "very concerned about everybody," added Ronald Garrett. No matter who you were—whether you did right or did wrong—Father would be concerned about the person because, as he said, "We're all children of God."[34]

Second, Father Wessel went out of his way to make sure that everyone was included in the community, especially those kids who were shy, socially awkward, or just "different." How easy it was for self-absorbed teens to exclude such kids. But by his example, Father taught the CYO youths to extend Christ-like love to all their brothers and sisters, especially those who seemed more difficult to love (and probably needed love most).

Father was tireless in encouraging young people to love and accept one another. He "hated with a passion" anybody making fun of another person, or putting them down, or being unkind—as teenagers sometimes have a tendency to do—and would "teach against that for all he was worth," recalled Wes Ritterbusch.[35]

To Ritterbusch, if there was one lesson Father Wessel would have wanted to impart to people, it was kindness. "Be kind and take care of each other." That was his life, said Wes. "He was a very kindly man."[36]

Perhaps Joanne Gillespie summed it up best, on behalf of many, when she said:

> What Father Wessel brought to us "was a true love of Christ through the love of one another, by caring about one another and sharing with one another. . . . What was so special about association with him was that we learned about the most basic of all human concerns and that is love—love and caring for each other. And this is what Father taught us, and this is the part of him that stayed with us for all these many years since those days."[37]

CHAPTER 23

AN "ALL CHURCH" PRIEST

During the storms of controversy and turmoil that swirled around the Roman Catholic Church, Father Wessel's priesthood was an island of calm devotion to the fundamental tenets of his religion.

He adapted readily to the liturgical changes that came as a result of Vatican II.

The Masses that Father Wessel celebrated in the school gymnasium for CYO members, and sometimes a few parents, created a far different community spirit than would have been possible under the old Latin Mass.

The Scriptural readings were directed to youthful concerns, open discussion of personal feelings about common problems was encouraged, individual intentions marked the Prayer of the Faithful and, during meditation, members of the congregation were free to express their thoughts. The feeling of joy and well-being sometimes led, after Mass, to the young people and their priest singing happy songs, dancing, or just "clowning around."

But for the most part, Father Wessel was neither an aggressive exponent of the changes decreed by Vatican II nor an eager participant in the questioning and rebellion against tradition that followed among some religious and laymen. Not for him were the social causes and political activism that drew some priests of his generation.

He spoke of rebellious priests as "those young kids" and said once that "seminarians must learn to take disappointments without anger and rebellion." To him the priesthood was a full-time job that demanded celibacy and discipline.[1]

Father Wessel, according to Monsignor James Dubell, "had a good deal of common sense and deep devotion to the Magisterium of the Church. In formal and informal discussions on matters of faith and morals, he always showed good balance in distinguishing what was conjecture or opinion and what was official teaching of the Church."[2]

Whatever doubts Father Wessel had were not of Church doctrine or teaching, nor did he ever question becoming a priest. His only doubts were about his own unworthiness.

To Father Davis, John Wessel "looked at things in an old-fashioned way." He respected, and probably agreed with, the older priest's reverence for tradition.

Friend and fellow seminarian Father Samuel J. Lupico may have agreed with Father Davis's assessment. Sam Lupico met John Wessel in the seminary at the age of seventeen. He was ordained with John Wessel and was a priest in Trenton for about seven years, originally assigned to St. Joachim's.

Father Sam was somewhat of a radical. Father John Wessel, he recalled, was slower to make changes, more institutional. For example, when Father Sam tried to organize a "priests' strike" in the 1960s over certain internal diocesan matters, not only did Father Wessel *not* want to join the strike but he was concerned for his friend Sam lest he get himself thrown out of the priesthood.

Father John Wessel was "a very stable guy" and "all priest . . . from the top of his head to the tip of his toes," said Father Lupico.[3]

To Miss Flynn of the State Home for Girls, however, Father Wessel's "new Church" attitude was dramatically illustrated when fourteen-year-old Rebecca took her own life. Her parish priest refused to allow a church burial because of her suicide, but Father Wessel gave her the Last Rites of the Church and reassured Miss Flynn and the girl's friends:

"Don't be upset about her. She's gone straight to Heaven. She's with God. What did this world ever give her?"

Perhaps his lifelong friend, Monsignor Dubell, said it best:

> His approach to the ministry can not be classified as *old* Church—nor can it be classified as *new* Church—Father Wessel was in fact *All* Church. He blended daring innovation with

responsible obedience to his Bishop and Pastor and so put forth
a professional ministry that had both balance and strength.

One significant issue that placed Church teachings squarely at odds with
the popular culture during this time was abortion. Father Wessel loved the
unborn child. Even as a small boy, he understood and valued the precious
gift of life and the dignity of all persons, born and unborn.

Sister M. Christina Murphy recalled an overheard conversation between
fourth graders John Wessel, James Dubell, and another classmate named
Steven. The three boys were talking at the lunch table one day. Steven's
mother was going to have a new baby, and he was telling Jimmy and John
all about it. John looked over at him and said very seriously, "Stevie, do
you know what that means?"

"No," the boy said, perplexed.

John exclaimed, "Just think of the love that baby is getting!"

Steven, somewhat confused, said, "But he's not born yet."

And young Johnny replied, "No, I know he's not born yet, but remember
your mom is carrying that baby under her heart. Just think of the love that
baby is getting, and what love it's going to have when it comes!"

Sister Christina repeated the story to John Wessel's mother, who was
flabbergasted. "Sister," she said, "I don't know where he ever heard anything
like that. We never talked about anything like that!"[4]

When John Wessel was a seminarian at St. Charles and St. Mary's,
it was the beautiful prayer, *O Jesu, vivens en Maria*—"O Jesus, living in
Mary"—composed by Father Jean-Jacques Olier, that he recited daily in
Latin as part of his morning prayers and meditation. Reverence for the
dignity of the unborn child permeated the spirituality of the Sulpician
seminaries, for Father Olier's prayer was, quite literally, a prayer to the
unborn baby Jesus.

The words of the Latin prayer, in English, are as follows:[5]

> O Jesus, living in Mary,
> Come and live in your servants,
> In the spirit of your sanctity,
> In the fullness of your power,
> In the perfection of your ways,
> In the truth of your virtues,

In the communion of your mysteries.
Triumph over all adverse powers
In your Spirit for the glory of the Father,
　　Amen.

John Wessel's understanding hit much closer to home when in 1962, his sister, Maryann, went into premature labor with her first child near the end of her fifth month of pregnancy. A beautiful baby girl was born and lived for a half-hour before dying. The infant was baptized Margaret Mary and was buried in a tiny casket.

John was a support to the grieving parents. He wrote his sister a consoling letter of deep spiritual insight, reminding her that creating a new human life is something wonderful that some people never have the opportunity to do. "You have now a creation by God in your own name" who is "your own special angel to pray to" in Heaven, he said.[6]

During the years of Father John Wessel's priesthood, he witnessed a radical change in American law governing abortion. Colorado was the first State to legalize abortion in 1966. Before this time, the deliberate killing of a child in the womb had uniformly been regarded as a reprehensible act for which criminal sanctions were imposed on the abortionist. Beginning in the early 1960s, however, there was a concerted attempt by a few to de-criminalize abortion laws, fueled by a media all too willing to portray abortion in a favorable light.

The State of New York de-criminalized abortion in 1970. The State legislature twice attempted to repeal the misguided legislation, only to have their efforts twice vetoed by then Governor Nelson Rockefeller, a liberal abortion advocate. Of course, all these efforts culminated in *Roe v. Wade*, the tragic and flawed decision by the U.S. Supreme Court which in 1973 imposed a regime of abortion on demand across the country.

As a priest, Father John Wessel was "adamantly pro-life," said Monsignor Dubell. To John Wessel, there was just no question that abortion was wrong. In discussions with friends, he would often bring up the fact that even Saint Thomas Aquinas spoke against the evil of abortion.[7]

Father Wessel's Bishop, George Ahr of Trenton, a staunch defender of the unborn, was a pioneer in the development of the Respect Life Program in the United States. Monsignor Shenrock's history of the Diocese of Trenton, *Upon This Rock*, describes Bishop Ahr's efforts:

> In the late 1960's, he saw the handwriting on the wall concerning abortion liberalization, and under his guidance the Respect Life Committee was formed in 1968 for the Province of Newark (Archdiocese of Newark and the Dioceses of Camden, Paterson, and Trenton). This led to the formation of the New Jersey Right to Life Committee.
>
> . . .
>
> When the Supreme Court announced its decision legalizing abortion on January 22, 1973, Bishop Ahr was quick to respond with a statement condemning the action. The decision, he said, left unanswered many questions and created more problems than it solved.
>
> "Our principal concern at the moment, however, is not a pastoral one," he declared. "The Supreme Court is not God. It cannot invalidate the moral law. Abortion is still a grave moral evil. Our Catholic people, lay and professional, have an obligation in conscience to accept the teaching of the church on abortion, most recently confirmed by the Second Vatican Council, and to 'obey God rather than men.'"[8]

In a prophetic conversation with his sister in the late sixties, Father John Wessel reiterated that he could never imagine any possible reason for abortion—it was such a horrendous thing. And, he fervently added, he "just hoped and prayed that abortion would never become legal and accepted by anyone."

It was almost as if Father Wessel had a prophetic sense or forewarning of what could (and indeed, what did) happen, said Maryann.[9]

Closely related to the issue of abortion was that of the use of birth control through artificial means. In 1968, Pope Paul VI's encyclical, *Humanae Vitae* ("Of Human Life"), firmly established the moral wrongfulness of not only abortion but of artificial forms of preventing the conception of children by married couples as contrary to the natural and Divine law. Regulation of births by natural means, however, through recourse by the married couple to naturally occurring infecund periods, was not illicit. This was essentially a reiteration of the teachings of an earlier encyclical of Pope Pius XI in 1931 denouncing artificial birth control.[10]

Around the time that *Humanae Vitae* was about to be issued, some Catholics were hoping that the Pope would allow them to use artificial contraception. They were anticipating this "progress" with great expectation, and some were quite disappointed when the Pope condemned it. Of course, the wisdom of *Humanae Vitae* has been confirmed by later experience. There is an intimate connection between the philosophies of abortion and artificial contraception: Both are anti-life and anti-child; one reinforces the other.

The "grave consequences" of artificial birth control enumerated in the Holy Father's 1968 encyclical—that of opening a "wide and easy" road toward "conjugal infidelity and the general lowering of morality," especially among the young, coupled with a loss of respect by the man for the woman—have all sadly come to pass. "Consequently," Pope Paul VI concluded, "if the mission of generating life is not to be exposed to the arbitrary will of men, one must necessarily recognize unsurmountable limits to the possibility of man's domination over his own body and its functions; limits which no man . . . may licitly surpass."[11]

It was sometimes a challenge for the Catholic priest to minister to married couples on the subject of the Church's teaching on artificial birth control. In *Humanae Vitae*, Pope Paul VI himself instructed priests to "expound the Church's teaching on marriage without ambiguity,"[12] but added:

> To diminish in no way the saving teaching of Christ constitutes an eminent form of charity for souls. But this must ever be accompanied by patience and goodness, such as the Lord himself gave example of in dealing with men. Having come not to condemn but to save, He was intransigent with evil, but merciful towards individuals.
>
> In their difficulties, may married couples always find, in the words and in the heart of a priest, the echo of the voice and the love of the Redeemer.[13]

Father Wessel's pastoral ministry in this regard showed a good balance between being "intransigent with evil, but merciful towards individuals."

He firmly preached and defended the Church's teaching on birth control, and fully supported the Church's authority on this topic. He studied the encyclical carefully and carried a copy of it in his back pocket.[14]

But at the same time, he was able to be a gentle and understanding mediator with those persons in the Sacrament of Penance who confessed the sin, and with those married couples he saw in his priestly counseling who were having difficulty with it.[15]

On controversial issues he once said, "I pray that I will always be open to listening."[16]

So just as Father Wessel "upheld the Church's position, he didn't lose anybody in the process," said Monsignor Dubell succinctly.[17]

Father Wessel encouraged people to strive toward the formation of a true and certain conscience, animated and enlightened by the Church's sound teachings on moral and doctrinal issues. In order to illustrate this point, he had a favorite saying: "You can't get the truth from a barstool."

By that, he meant that you can't get your values from the modern culture. The idea being that often we discuss things in the bar, and we often put more stock, he would say, in what "the guy on the barstool" thinks, rather than in what we hear preached from the pulpit in church, or what we hear from the Pope, or the Bishop, or what we read in the Catholic press. And that, not the barstool, is where we are to form our conscience.

In the search for truth and values, "he would use an example like that: You can't get it from a barstool," recalled James Dubell. "You have to be open to what the Church teaches, and get it from the proper source."[18]

Father John Wessel was an obedient son of the Church.[19] He consistently supported the teachings of the Magisterium, and the orders of his superiors; and if perchance he did not agree with something, he would never voice it. With his strong sense of duty and obedience, he "would've made a good Marine," said Wes Ritterbusch.[20]

Father Wessel could get angry at times, although not for inconsequential reasons. One instance which left him furious was that of a young priest who left the priesthood in a very public manner that was destructive to the unity of his parish. To make matters worse, the young priest unfairly blamed his superior, thus causing much unwarranted pain to the older man. John Wessel had known both priests, and was extremely angry at what the rebellious young priest had done. He attributed the young man's actions to the fact that he simply could not take criticism, noting that being able to accept criticism was one of the first things that they learned in the seminary. The incident was the one time Maryann Beitel ever recalled seeing her brother truly angry.[21]

On another occasion, Father Wessel became aware of a priest whom he believed had become improperly involved with a woman in his parish. A friend recalled how very annoyed John Wessel was by it. He was "genuinely concerned for the good of the parish and for the good of the priesthood," said the friend.[22]

Even as a young seminarian, John Wessel was keenly aware that the priest must be an example of Christian virtue. "The eyes of the *world* are upon a priest," he once wrote.[23]

Father Wessel was excited about what was happening in the Catholic Church after Vatican II.[24] He diligently studied the documents of Vatican II and lectured on the Council papers.[25] Embracing the Council's teachings on ecumenism with ease and enthusiasm, he participated in interfaith prayer services which the Catholic Church began to hold jointly with other Christian denominations in the city of Trenton.[26]

Yet, John Wessel was very patient with those who had difficulty accepting the changes mandated by the Second Vatican Council. In his sister's words:

> With [Vatican II] . . . came much criticism of the Church and its priests. I remember John refusing to be drawn into a condemnation of priests who were slow in adjusting to liturgical changes. He encouraged, rather than discouraged, noting that internal and external changes take time.[27]

He was especially kind and patient with older priests who had difficulty adapting to the new formulations, such as the change from Latin to English, and counseled those who would criticize them: "You have to understand, this is what they've known all their lives."[28]

While counseling the progressive-minded to be patient, he also encouraged those fearful and uncomfortable with change to trust. Once, Father Wessel spoke about Vatican II at a meeting of the Christian Family Movement, a lay Catholic organization, during the time when many of the changes were occurring in the Church. He was interrogated at length by some of the more conservative members who were skeptical of the changes in the Mass and so forth, and who asked, "How can we do this? This is not

Catholic. It's not what we're accustomed to." And then there were others who had no patience whatsoever and were on the verge of leaving because they felt change was not occurring fast enough. The questioning jumped from one topic to another as the CFM members really put the young priest under the gun.

"Yes, I'll be the first to admit, it's very, very difficult," he said. Father let them know that he shared their feelings that the Church was going through a confusing time, and so many people had the right to wonder what was happening, but he told them to pray for patience and realize that any change after hundreds of years would take time. "Be open to the Word of God; be open to change; be open to listening."

"Be patient," he said. "It will take time, but it will be for the better. And some of the changes will not occur, because they won't prove the test of time."

"Be patient," he reiterated. "Particularly be patient with the older priests who are just like you, having such a difficult time adjusting to this."

John Wessel tried to reassure them that, indeed, the Church was going through a period of fluctuation, but that what emerged would be even better than before. He was a good and effective speaker, conveying optimism and hope, and the people really listened to him and took his words to heart.[29]

In the years immediately following Vatican II, there was some agitation on the part of Catholics, both conservative and liberal, yet Father Wessel seemed to have a way of calming all who were agitated.[30] Perhaps it stemmed from his unwavering trust in Christ's promise in Scripture to protect and guard His Church, even until the end of time. (Matthew 28:20). If any change is of God, it will last.

The sixties and seventies were also times of great moral and social turmoil in secular society. This turmoil naturally spilled over into the Church. There was much questioning of traditional values and absolute moral precepts. Unchanging principles were replaced by subjective "feelings" as the standard governing behavior in the morally relative culture. Modern society fostered a climate inhospitable to the cultivation of the virtues of chastity, modesty, self-discipline and poverty required of a consecrated religious life.

In the face of such a change in the morality of popular culture, it was inevitable that priestly celibacy would become a topic of conversation and debate, with some arguing that celibacy should be optional for priests.

Father Wessel refused to be drawn into the controversy, and was content to accept the wisdom of the Church on this and other issues. "It wasn't something he was going to fight for, but at the same time, if the Church said that it was good for some, then so be it," was the impression of his friend, Monsignor Dubell.[31]

With typical humor, Father John Wessel loved to quote his pastor, Father Davis, who famously joked, "I hope the Pope never changes the rule about celibacy, because I might be just foolish enough to try it!"[32]

Around this time, some of Father Wessel's good friends in the clergy were leaving the priesthood and getting married. "John was deeply troubled by it and hurt," recalled Monsignor Dubell. He understood it, in the sense of empathizing with human emotions, weaknesses, and needs—after all, he himself struggled to give up the lovely Laura while in the seminary—but Father Wessel remained true to his celibate priesthood, as he did most things, out of strong conviction. He persevered in his vocation "because he believed in it."[33]

As Mercer County Vocational Director, Father Wessel assiduously encouraged young men to consider studying for the priesthood. He once said that the priesthood takes a lot of work and a lot of dedication, but "there was nothing else that he would rather do" in life than to be a priest.[34] In Father Wessel, the young man found a role model of a priest completely satisfied and humbly grateful for his own vocation.

To young seminarians, said Monsignor Dubell, he may have given this advice based on his own experience:

> As a priest, he felt that the best spirituality was that you set realistic goals for yourself that would be helpful to other people . . . Don't be trying to be somebody that you're really not. Be natural. Be yourself . . . and don't be trying to prove something beyond your capabilities or your personality.[35]

"He very definitely believed in the importance of praying every day," Dubell added.[36] And he also knew the importance of learning to take discipline and accept criticism. As Father Wessel once wrote:

> I feel very strongly that the seminarians must learn to take disappointments without anger and rebellion. It's more a matter of pride than conviction but it's difficult to get it across without

experience. God help them if they don't settle this on their minds previous to ordination. Not that it is the end of the world but they will be very unhappy for a while.[37]

Father Wessel's attitude of fidelity to his vocation was best illustrated in a chance reunion in Trenton in 1968 with his grade school classmate, Sister Eileen Egan, who recalled:

I was on the way home for a visit from my teaching assignment at a Catholic school in Providence, Rhode Island, and got off the train in Trenton. There was some free time before my family was to meet me so I went over to Blessed Sacrament to say "hi" to John. He invited me to have a cup of coffee in the kitchen of the rectory. We shared about our apostolates and the impact that the Second Vatican Council was having on the traditional Church.

I asked him how they were working out some of the changes in Blessed Sacrament and how he felt about it, and he told me that "It's just fine, but we just have to keep moving forward and not to be discouraged." (He was a great one for saying, "Don't be discouraged.") And he said that "If it's what God plans, then it's going to happen. We just have to move slowly."

And then he looked at me very seriously and said, "I hope you're being true to your vocation! With all that's changing since Vatican II, the youth need strong and faithful models to bring them through this time. Don't invite them through the front door and then you sneak out the back."

He really laid it on the line about what a religious vocation is all about. He spoke of some people who encourage the kids to be faithful, and then slip out the back door on them for "greener pastures" to find fulfillment in another way of life. He said we must hang in there when it gets rough, because the kids are looking to us for leadership. We shared our hopes and dreams, and they came out to the common denominator of leading others to the love Jesus has for us all.

Even in the midst of our talk, a group of teenagers came in and I wound up in the basement with them before finishing our cup of coffee.

I assured John that I was okay with all the changes, but I knew I'd never forget his observations. He was so strong in his conviction of the need for witnesses to Jesus' mission in the world. It surprised me really, because I just thought we'd just be sharing on a superficial level, apostolates and things, but he became very, very serious. We mutually agreed that we'd be faithful to our vocations.[38]

It would be a promise that both of them would keep. After teaching for some time in various places in the United States, in 1982, Sister Eileen became a missionary Sister among the poor people of Peru and is currently stationed in the village of Sicuani, high in the Andes mountains. Sister Eileen, along with two other members of her religious community, engages in pastoral ministry and education among the natives of about thirty villages.[39]

As Sister Eileen's recollections illustrated, Father Wessel knew how important it was that the clergy and religious provide good role models of fidelity to their vocations, to Christ, and to the Church—as an example for all, but especially the young. He wanted to make sure that young people had no excuse to find fault in the behavior of the Church's chosen representatives.

His message to the high school graduates of the Blessed Sacrament CYO in June 1968, also demonstrated his zealous concern that young people stay committed and involved in the Catholic Church. On behalf of himself and his pastor, Father Wessel wrote:

Our concern, as usual is for your future. Adults and in particular your priests, have a certain sixth sense about the future since we see it sometimes *too* clearly. We have faith in you, but a heart-rending fear along with that faith. We have seen too many young men and women so filled with promise, compromise themselves, worn down and out by sincere fools (mostly adults) who do not or will not obey Christ, our Brother, or His Father. In a year's time, a third of you will leave His people, the Church, without any sense of regret; half of you will no longer want to worship and talk to our Father; and all of you will be confronted with the crossroads of existence, a choice between God and Man, Another or self—this struggle you will face for the first time, ALONE.

Our prayers every day are mingled with the Blood of Christ for you, our Graduates. In the true Christian sense we love you and respect you. This is why you must be free to go your own way. Remember this pledge of Christian love—be loyal to it, and do not add your name to the long list of HEDGERS that make life a cynical joke of compromise.[40]

These words echo what Father Wessel emphasized many times in his CYO: the importance of remaining in the Catholic Church, and of not being led away and astray from Her—no matter what they see, no matter what they hear, and no matter what may be going on in the world around them—or even, for that matter, within the Church.[41]

Indeed, to Monsignor James Dubell, Father Wessel's concern about young people leaving and falling away from the Catholic Church "was really his whole purpose in trying to understand them and work with them: so that they would find a place in the Catholic Church; so that they would feel welcome. . . . He would tell the young people that the Church *needs* them and the Church *wants* them and *loves* them. And that was his whole purpose—to keep them *in* the Catholic Church."[42]

CHAPTER 24

ZEALOUS FOR JUSTICE

Father Wessel was a product of his times. He conducted his priesthood while all around him raged the social and political issues that preoccupied secular society in the decade of the 1960s. It has been called "the most turbulent decade in our history"—the "decade of dissent." It was a decade of great and profound revisions in traditional moral, legal, social, and intellectual norms and beliefs.

Father Wessel cannot easily be classified as liberal or conservative, Democrat or Republican, old-fashioned or new thinker. While, by virtue of his personality and outlook, he seemed to lean more toward the conservative and traditional, yet in other ways he was also quite progressive and daring. Perhaps one of his friends said it best when he observed that "his politics were no politics" at all.[1]

Regardless of his private feelings on many issues, Father Wessel was a parish priest first, and always managed to bring social issues down to a pastoral level, to the level of the individual. He would tend to be more concerned with how a particular societal problem was affecting the person before him who was in need of counseling, or the families in the parish who were struggling and needed help, rather than with a social or political issue in the abstract.[2] "I don't think he really thought on a political plane," said his cousin Julian Wessel.[3]

Father Wessel's non-political outlook also extended to his own ecclesiastical career. He cared not at all about internal politics and the advancement of his own career within the Church hierarchy. He only wanted to do God's work.[4]

John Wessel was basically an optimistic, upbeat, happy person. But he could get "a tad depressed at times" at some of the things that went on in the world,[5] whether it be the loss of life in South Vietnam, or massive protests at home, or the fact that there was widespread poverty and discrimination among some groups of people.

He was gravely concerned about what he termed "man's inhumanity to man."[6] He was very aware of injustice and conscious of social and moral wrongs in the world. When Father contemplated that he was doing the Lord's will, he was happy, said Ronald Garrett, but in terms of what he saw in society as a whole every day, he was not. "He could not believe the cruelty and the inhumanity that went on every single day," said Ronald, and he "couldn't stand the way people were treating one another."[7]

But again, to Father, the solution was to be found within the individual.[8] He usually approached problems by advocating compassion and a change in attitude, rather than engaging in political activism.[9]

He always stressed "solving social problems by setting a good example in your personal life" and "making the difference you could make right where you were now," recalled several of his former students.[10]

Yet, it is perhaps more accurate to say that he was politically aware, but not political. As a lifelong history buff, he was keenly aware of the political situation at home and abroad, and often quite knowledgeable of the historical background and significance of these contemporary political events. One such area of interest for him was Ireland.

"We talked a lot about the Irish people and Irish history—an area of very common interest between the two of us," recalled his cousin Julian. Father John Wessel was very well versed in the history of repression of the Irish Catholics by Great Britain. In eighteenth century Ireland, it was illegal to practice or study Roman Catholicism, Father Wessel once explained to Julian, and future priests had to go to seminaries in France for training and be smuggled back in. Father Wessel bore no bitterness toward the British, but only commented on how rough it was for the Irish Catholics to practice their faith. "How easy we have it here in this country that we can practice our religion!" he exclaimed, and expressed his admiration for the Irish people who persevered in faith despite religious persecution. "They still hold strong to their religion today, and look at what they went through," Father Wessel noted. "Their greatest testament is their faith and their strength."[11]

Perhaps no single event in the decade of the sixties so dominated American life and engendered so much debate as the war in what was then South Vietnam. Involved at first as "advisors," the U.S. military started counting casualties in 1961. The United States assumed a full combat role in Vietnam in 1965, and only stopped fighting, via a peace accord signed in Paris, in 1973. By that time, over 56,000 young Americans had been killed, and over 303,000 wounded.[12]

The conflict in Vietnam affected just about every person and every family across America. Everyone either had a relative or friend who was serving in Southeast Asia, or knew of someone who did. The war even dominated popular culture and music, as expressed in a fatalistic 1967 protest song by Country Joe & the Fish called the *I-Feel-Like-I'm-Fixin'-To-Die Rag.*

During the war years, every young man had to register for the draft upon turning eighteen, and then had to sweat out the draft lottery, which randomly determined who would be called up for military service. Young men of a certain age planned their lives, career choices, and education with reference to the draft. Thousands of young men of their generation lost their lives or were permanently injured in mind and body in combat.

On a pastoral level, perhaps among the saddest duties for the parish priest was to bury a young man who gave his life in Vietnam, and then try to console his grieving parents. A sad entry in Father Wessel's diary on June 29, 1967, read:

> Second Vietnam death, Anthony DiCaesar, 22 year old Marine. Just the week we prayed for their safe return.

Father Wessel's feelings on the war were complex, as perhaps they were for many Americans. As a young man growing up during the Cold War, he was strongly opposed to communism, and the lure of a military career gave his calling to the priesthood some serious competition when he was a boy. Father Wessel probably had little difficulty with the underlying rationale for the combat, that of defending the democratic government in South Vietnam, and hence the rest of Southeast Asia, from falling under the control of the communists—the "domino theory."

Moreover, Father Wessel had a very personal connection to the conflict. His cousin, Colonel Walter Wessel, Jr. (the son of his father's brother, Walter, Sr.), then a First Lieutenant in the 173rd Airborne Brigade in Bien Hoa, had served two tours of duty as a combat infantry officer and paratrooper in Vietnam. He saw major combat action and was highly decorated.[13]

Yet, according to Monsignor James Dubell, Father Wessel was "opposed to the Vietnam War, but he was not willing to demonstrate." He would not join the ranks of anti-war protesters and political agitators, as some among the clergy had done, probably because he thought it was "unpatriotic." It was going against the government, whereas the patriotic thing was to support your country in what its leaders felt was a legitimate fight.

Ronald Garrett talked with Father Wessel about the Vietnam War on many occasions.

> I said, "Well, Pop, what would happen if I was called up [in the draft]?" and he would say, "You'd have to go serve your country." And I asked him about killing people, and he would say, "Well, you've got to stay alive, Ron."[14]

But privately, and as the war continued to escalate, Father Wessel perceived that "it was dragging on, that it was senseless, that a lot of lives were being lost, and that it didn't have a clear purpose and direction," recalled Monsignor Dubell. "And so he was opposed to the Vietnam War, but again, he was not a demonstrator." At that time, too, persons could declare themselves conscientious objectors to the war, and Father Wessel had no problem with that. In fact, he thought it good that people had the right to exercise that option.[15]

When Father Wessel talked about the Vietnam War, his focus was always on the tremendous human cost. "You could see that it would really affect him," recalled Wes Ritterbusch, because "he felt so bad about all of the people that were losing their lives, and then, of course, the protesting here against the military. And that really bugged me big time, being an ex-Marine. We used to talk about these things."[16]

Many have and will debate the merits of the war effort in South Vietnam. For the men and women who bravely served their country in an unpopular war, however, it was an act of great heroism. And in the final analysis, the spread of communism was, in fact, checked and resisted in Southeast Asia. Perhaps this was the real victory of the war.

Despite Father Wessel's personal distaste for public protest against the war, this did not stop him from "going to bat" for a young person who felt and saw things differently. When young Cathedral High School student Karen McGarrity got into trouble with the principal for organizing an anti-war rally (and student walk-out) during school hours, Father Wessel intervened on Karen's behalf and spoke to the principal, ameliorating her punishment.[17] Father respected the idealism of youth. Sometimes, the barely thirty-year-old priest would even remind the adults of the parish in his Sunday homilies to listen to the youth. All the talk about "peace and love" is not really wrong, he'd say, and we, the adults, need to listen to them and think about what they're saying.[18]

Father Wessel had no patience with the sexual revolution. He was a proponent of old-fashioned, traditional moral values.[19] He often preached on the virtue of chastity from the pulpit, particularly to young people, encouraging them to remain true to Christ's teachings about the sacredness of conjugal love and its place in marriage. His private writings revealed a deep concern with the growing immorality of modern culture.[20]

In the course of his ministry, Father Wessel had witnessed enough of the "downside" of the sexual revolution. He had seen firsthand the disastrous effects on people's lives of promiscuity, adultery, out-of-wedlock pregnancy, and abortion.[21]

There was a home for unwed mothers in the parish, off State Street. The Blessed Sacrament priests would call there periodically to minister to the unwed mothers and baptize their babies. "I remember that John was going to that, and I think he may have even had regular hours that he went," Father Mickiewicz recalled.[22]

Sister Nancy Carney, a colleague who later worked with Father Wessel, noted how there was a lot of promiscuity among youths at the time "and he was upset by that." For example, there were always five or six high school kids who never made it home from a Friday night dance. Some adults might dismiss such behavior as "typical of teenagers," but it didn't matter to Father Wessel that there were "only" five or six in a high school of say, five hundred. His point, recalled Sister Nancy, was that "it's not okay to let them get hurt."

"We've got to deal with these kids," he would say, and he had a way of doing that "that wasn't accusatory."[23]

Father was equally upset about "the naiveness of parents," Sister Nancy continued. "Not that parents didn't know the score," but it disturbed him "that they couldn't believe that their kids were exposed to and invited into this kind of lifestyle." Many challenging moral issues daily confronted teenagers that their parents remained unaware of, and consequently, the parents were not able to be the moral supports that their children needed.[24]

When it came to providing moral guidance to young people on everything from promiscuity, to drugs or drinking, certainly one of Father's most persuasive weapons was his own example. "I don't specifically recall him saying, 'Don't do this, don't do that, this is wrong,'" said one high school student. "I think his approach was more that of his living a holy life and it rubbing off" on the young people around him, because actions speak louder than words. "His holiness affected my life," said the student. He had "the right approach," because teenagers could easily get defensive and not listen to someone who was preaching at them or condemning them.[25]

At other times, Father Wessel would not hesitate to take a young person aside and speak to them plainly about sex and chastity, but never with a "holier-than-thou" attitude. He always spoke with patience and love and down-to-earth friendliness.

A young man shared this story of one such talk with Father:

> In high school, I was dating a girl named Annette*. One time, Father came up to me and said, "I know how much you love that little girl, Annette." And I said, "Father, I love her more than anything in the world." So he said, "You know what's going to happen if you go to bed with her?" I said, "Yes, sir." "What's that?" he said. "I'm going to make a baby," I replied. And he asked me, "Are you ready for that?" I had to agree that I wasn't. "Well," he said, "just give her a hug and a kiss and be good to her, okay?"
>
> And I looked at him and I said, "But Father, she's so damn good looking, you know?" And he looked at me and said, "Boy, she really is. She's a nice-looking girl." "What am I supposed to do?" I said. He just rolled his eyes, and pulled his glasses down

on his nose and looked at me over his glasses—and whenever he did that, I knew he wanted to make a point—and he said to me, "Well, maybe you ought to stay out of bed with her, huh?" And I said, "Yeah, I was thinking the same thing."

And you know, I never did go to bed with that girl, because of Father's influence. And because he told me "there's more to love than just getting in the sack." And he was right.[26]

With his common sense approach to teenagers, he helped them realize the consequences of their moral choices, and kept many a young person on the straight and narrow path. This was due, in no small measure, to the fact that the teenagers had so much respect for Father that often only a few choice words, or even a glance, were sufficient.

The Civil Rights movement in America, under the leadership of Dr. Martin Luther King, Jr., sought equality of treatment for Blacks and minorities. Although all peoples were assured of equality under the 14th Amendment to the U.S. Constitution, as a practical matter this had not been achieved. Many States had enacted laws or tolerated customs permitting disparate treatment of persons solely by virtue of their skin color. In other cases, the discrimination was more invidious; while technically equal under law, Blacks were subjected to *de facto* discrimination in many areas of life.

In 1964, the Civil Rights Act eliminated racial discrimination in employment, places of public accommodation, publicly owned facilities, union membership, and federally funded programs. As he signed the Act into law, President Johnson called upon citizens to help "eliminate the last vestiges of injustice in America."[27]

Dr. Martin Luther King firmly believed in non-violence. Through moral and peaceful means, such as peaceful public protests, marches, rallies and prayer vigils, he sought to persuade the conscience of America on the issue of racial discrimination. He dreamed of a color-blind society where people of all races would be judged on "the content of their character" instead of "the color of their skin."

In the middle sixties, however, simmering tensions finally gave rise to the race riots, violence, looting and civil unrest that erupted in many urban areas across the land. All only served to undermine the efforts of Dr. King and others to accomplish peaceful, non-violent change.

Father Wessel greatly admired Dr. Martin Luther King, Jr. and the Civil Rights movement.[28] This, of course, has significance when one considers that it was at a time when many Americans did not fully appreciate what Dr. King was trying to do. In those early years, far from being the revered figure whose birthday is celebrated as a national holiday, Dr. King was a controversial figure—not because of what he actually stood for, but because initially he was perceived as a troublemaker and an agitator by some who resisted change and genuine equality. Yet, Father Wessel instantly grasped his message and its moral imperative.

"I do remember my dad telling me Uncle John was a great admirer of Dr. Martin Luther King," recalled Father Wessel's nephew, Carlton, "and the first time my dad said he realized the significance of what Dr. King was trying to do was when he and John talked about it." Father John Wessel's admiration for Dr. Martin Luther King made a lasting impression on his brother Edward.[29]

Julian Wessel, who often talked with his cousin John about contemporary social issues, recalled that Father Wessel spoke passionately on numerous occasions about how racial discrimination had to change. Not only was it manifestly unjust, he would say, but it was really immoral for it to continue. And it could not continue, even for us to just survive as a nation.[30]

Trenton was not immune from racial tensions and civil unrest. The New Jersey capital was the scene of civil disturbances in the late 1960s and early 1970s (as were other major U.S. cities).[31] During a time of horrible rioting in the cities, Father Wessel remarked to his cousin to the effect that one should not look upon Blacks as they were then being portrayed in the media, but that "they are people with genuine needs that had to be addressed."[32]

Father Wessel, in the words of a CYO youth, "didn't look at people as Black or White or Puerto Rican. He looked at people as God's children."[33]

Father Wessel's concern for injustice led him to become involved in helping the poor in Appalachia. That there was massive poverty among certain groups of people bothered him very deeply.[34] His response was to involve his young people in charitable projects for the poor, thus serving the dual purpose of helping the underprivileged while teaching the youths of the parish to be concerned for others less fortunate than themselves.[35]

Father Wessel's long-range plans were to bring some of the young people from the CYO in Trenton to Appalachia to do volunteer work among the poor in Kentucky, and in fact, he did that for several weeks at a time over a few summers.[36] Father and a number of the older teenagers, juniors and seniors, engaged in service projects in Appalachia, which included building shelters for the residents, while the youths who remained in New Jersey supported them by sponsoring clothing drives and bake sales.[37]

The lesson of sensitivity and caring for the poor was not lost on the young people.

Father Wessel was equally concerned with the welfare of the poor closer to home. "Martin House" was started in Trenton's inner city around 1970 by Father John Wessel's seminary friend, Father Sam Lupico, and two other priests. The House, situated in a poor neighborhood of Trenton, began with the idea that the priests would live in radical solidarity with the poor and minorities, learn about their needs, and help them on their journey through life. The priest-founders were concerned that the Church wasn't doing enough for Trenton's needy at that time.

Father Wessel, although not involved in the founding of Martin House, was very supportive of it and donated money to support their work whenever he could.[38]

The drug subculture exploded on the scene with a vengeance in the 1960s. Its main targets, predictably enough, were the vulnerable teenagers and young adults. Everything from marijuana to LSD and, to a lesser extent, cocaine and heroin, was available to those who cared to flout the law. Of course, prescription drugs—pep pills and tranquilizers—and alcohol were also abused in the wrong hands.

Cultural "role models" often brazenly used, promoted, and glorified in drugs and alcohol. They conveyed it in the manner in which they lived their lives, in their art, films, and music. All things "psychedelic" became quite popular, which was in essence a celebration of the influence of psychotropic, mind-altering drugs. Musicians and artists sometimes even laced their songs with coded references to the wonders of drugs.

It is no wonder then that Father Wessel's love for young people compelled him to squarely confront the drug mentality which was ravaging so many of his generation.

Father Wessel was actively involved in counseling those in the parish community who were addicted to drugs. And as to those teenagers who hadn't yet started the habit, he constantly warned them about the dangers of drugs.[39] "He absolutely, completely couldn't stand drugs," recalled Ronald Garrett. He told the young people that "drugs were killers. Stay away from them."

Father Wessel was a young man himself—very much "in tune" with what was going on in the world, and especially, what was influencing the kids. He was well aware that a frightening number of American teenagers were experimenting with drugs, and a number of popular young rock stars whom the teens looked up to—Janis Joplin, Jimi Hendrix—had died of drug-related causes. Father was "trying very, very hard" to impress upon the youths that "there are other things in life besides drugs," said Ronald.

Although some people found marijuana permissible, and even argued that it was no more dangerous than alcohol, Father Wessel was not among them. One young person who smoked marijuana during that time recalled how Father would always ask him, "Why the hell do you do that? What do you need to do that for?" The youth didn't have an answer for him. For Father Wessel, marijuana was just a temptation to go on to stronger addictive drugs.[40]

A good indication of how seriously Father Wessel viewed the dangers of drugs is an incident recalled by Wes Ritterbusch, in which Father Wessel revealed his involvement in counseling drug addicts and alcoholics:[41]

"He and I were talking with a group of young people," Wes recalled, "and somebody said, 'Oh, so-and-so looks like he's on drugs'—you know, just laughing and goofing around. Later, John and I were talking privately, and he said, 'You know, that stuff is really not funny. I can see where people would say things like that, but I would like another analogy. I don't really appreciate that. I don't think it's that funny.'"[42]

Father Wessel explained "that he didn't appreciate it because he was seeing too much heartbreak and so many people hurt with drugs and alcohol—and how it affected families," Wes continued. "More than anything, that's what really bothered him. What a person chooses to do with himself is one thing, but how they allow that to affect their families was something else."[43]

Father Wessel's deep concern about "the culture of death" overtaking the young people of his generation stemmed from his love of life itself. It was an extension of his personality and how he perceived life. It was evident in his deep concern for those dying in combat, and for those ruining their lives with drugs, alcohol and immorality. It was evident in the way he was adamantly pro-life and in his wanting young people to stay in communion with the Church and the sacraments. It was evident even in his love of the outdoors. All of these qualities were not just accidental; they were all linked together and related.[44]

Because he loved life, he wanted the best in life for others, especially for the young people full of such hope and promise. He lived every moment of his life, in the words of one of his CYO group, "to keep people away from things that were not good for them"[45]—or conversely, to lead them to the things that would bring them abundant, wholesome, happy lives.[46]

What difference did Father Wessel make in the lives of those young people struggling with drug or alcohol addiction? Consider the story of Vincent Thompson*.[47]

Vincent Thompson knew Father Wessel from Blessed Sacrament Church, and from the priest's teaching him in school. Thompson remembered Father Wessel as a real down-to-earth priest and a friend to the youth of the parish. Perhaps because of this, he turned to Father Wessel when he was facing a "moral dilemma."

In about the tenth grade, Vince began using marijuana regularly. By the eleventh grade, he had progressed to using psychedelic drugs about two or three times a week, in addition to marijuana. In the summer after eleventh grade, when Vince Thompson was about seventeen—around June of 1971—he was caught by his high school teachers with psychedelic drugs. It became known that he was using them when a friend overdosed under circumstances that involved Thompson. The school gave the young man an ultimatum: Reveal the person who supplied you with drugs, or else be expelled.

Vince Thompson found himself in a true moral dilemma whether to "give up his source" or not. He decided he would talk it over with Father Wessel (probably, he admitted, to bolster his view that he shouldn't give up his source). Vince's parents, who had no idea of the extent of his drug use, wanted him to turn in the person to school officials. Vince himself, by his own admission, was probably in denial about the extent of his own problem. He thought that he had his drug use "under control" and could quit at any time.

Vince Thompson phoned Father Wessel and asked if he could see him.

"Sure, come on over right now," Father said. So the young man went over to the rectory right after dinner. It was about 7:30 p.m. one evening in June 1971.

Once there, he began to relate to Father the situation he thought was a "moral dilemma"—whether he should turn in the person from whom he had purchased the drugs. Father Wessel listened intently as the young man poured out his story. Then he spoke.

"Your moral dilemma is really *not* a dilemma," Father Wessel said. "It's not really important. It really doesn't matter. What *is* really important is you're doing drugs and doing serious harm to yourself." The priest looked at the young man and continued, "I can tell that you're suffering from the long term effects of psychedelic drugs."

His words caught Vince Thompson by surprise. The youth at first tried to deny that he had a problem at all. "How can you tell that I have a drug problem?" he challenged.

"I can tell by the way you move. By your mannerisms. By your eyes. By the way you're talking," Father Wessel replied evenly. He questioned Vince about what drugs he was using, how much, and how often. Then the priest said, "You're probably a drug addict, and you probably can't stop."

Father Wessel continued to talk to him in this vein. More than anything, Vince Thompson remembered that it was a very caring conversation. Father Wessel didn't lecture or proselytize. He was mainly trying to break through the boy's denial and help him to see that he had a serious drug problem, that he was doing serious harm to himself, and that there was a better way to live. What came through to Vince was how very much Father Wessel cared about him.

Thompson also recalled that as Father Wessel was speaking to him, a very strong feeling came over him. He became aware of a presence of "someone else" in the room—the Holy Spirit. In Father Wessel's presence, the young man felt a strong sense of God, the Holy Spirit, and the message that he could have a better life. He knew it in his soul.

Yet, Vince Thompson did not take the opportunity for a better way of life at that time. He knew on some level that what Father Wessel was saying to him was truth, and that he had to give up drugs—*someday*. But he was not yet ready to give up his way of life. He hadn't hit "rock bottom" yet.

Father Wessel encouraged Vince Thompson to promise that he would get off drugs and get himself clean. Vince said that yes, he would, and yet knew in his heart he wasn't going to do so. Whether Father Wessel also knew or sensed it at the time is unknown, but the priest asked Vince to keep in touch with him and let him know how he was doing. Vince promised he would do that too, but never did.

It may seem as though Father Wessel's efforts with Vince Thompson were a failure at the time. The young man remained on his destructive course of drugs and alcohol for several more years until the circumstances in his life led him to another priest, who also helped him and put him in touch with a psychologist who specialized in substance abuse. Again, Vince Thompson felt the presence of God for the second time. He knew that, once again, he had a choice for a better life, and that he had passed up an earlier opportunity. This time he took it. Finally, he got clean, and has been living in sobriety ever since. The young man went on to further his education and become successful in his field.

Father Wessel laid the foundation for another to build upon. He gave Vincent Thompson a glimpse of a better way of life that was possible with God's help, and opened the young man's eyes to the point where, when confronted with the message a second time, he was ready and willing to accept it. In this way, one might say that Father Wessel's contribution was essential to Vince's eventual recovery from substance abuse.

In the words of a favored motto of the saintly Mother Teresa of Calcutta, "God does not call us to be successful; He calls us to be faithful." Faithfulness, not success, is what God desires of His children.

Father Wessel was faithful in what God gave him to do. He loved and cared for the people who came his way. The final results were up to God, and Father knew that.

CHAPTER 25

THE *EUCHARIST,* PROJECT AND PARABLE

Father Wessel's most ambitious project while at Blessed Sacrament was building an 18-foot catamaran with the CYO in the church basement. Father never attempted an undertaking quite like this before. It was a challenge, and although he had no experience in building a catamaran, it did not deter him in wanting to accomplish this project with the CYO group. He was eager to do it!

Named *Eucharist I,* the catamaran was launched on June 18, 1971, in Barnegat Bay off the New Jersey coast. It was a boat that did not belong to anyone, but welcomed aboard (six or eight at a time) those willing to share the work and the fun.[1]

Father Wessel, conscious of the time, money and effort spent on this "material possession," once jestingly suggested that "Jesus got a little 'mad' because she had been 'demasted twice and sunk twice.'"[2] Nonetheless, sailing the catamaran provided hours of enjoyment for Father and his "city kids" in the CYO during those long, hot, lazy summer days of 1971.

The *Eucharist* is memorable for yet another reason: Finished shortly before his transfer to Toms River, it was Father Wessel's "final project and one of the highlights of his career as the priest leader of the Blessed Sacrament CYO."[3]

Father Wessel kept a detailed ship's log, meticulously documenting the building and launching of the boat, and the sailing done that summer—including destination, crew, passengers, and weather conditions, even down to the knots and direction of the wind—as well as his motivation for embarking upon the project.

Father Wessel's first entry in the Ship's Log on June 19, 1971 began:

> The story of the catamaran *Eucharist* is long and filled with frustration and moments of great satisfaction. I am writing this account the day after launch and trial run. I will begin to recount backwards since these events are freshest in my memory.[4]

This, then, mostly in Father John Wessel's own words, is the story of the *Eucharist*.

> How did the boat begin? I always wanted to sail since high school. The experience of ocean and wind taught me of God and His power and I wanted these city kids to have the same opportunity.
>
> I wrote for catalogs and decided with [CYO members Barry] and Mike to take on the catamaran because of its speed and safety. I also wanted a sail boat that would take a load—no sense in a 2 man'er for a club.
>
> Ship's Log, the *Eucharist*
> Father J.P. Wessel

Indeed, Father Wessel had always wanted to sail. "As we worked on the boat together," recalled Barry Anderson, "he had said that he always had a love of sailing, always wanted a boat."[5] Perhaps Father's thoughts drifted back to his seminary days in the summer of 1958 when he and his three outdoors buddies hastily assembled a makeshift catamaran out of two canoes, some saplings and a pup tent, and went flying down Lake George.

In addition, Father had another reason for wanting to build a boat: The building of a boat, and later the sailing of it, would make a wonderful group endeavor for the CYO.

At that time, there was a little "dissension in the ranks" of the CYO, recalled Wes Ritterbusch. "There were different, fragmented portions to the group." Some young people wanted to do one thing; others wanted to do something else; and the CYO was having difficulty agreeing among themselves on a shared activity. Father Wessel got the kids together one day and said, "Let's do something that's going to draw everyone together for commonality. Let's just get everyone interested in something that we can do together."[6]

That was the basic premise for the boat project, said Wes, plus the fact that Father Wessel had seen plans for the catamaran advertised in a magazine, "and he and I had been talking about what a neat thing it would be to build one of these, anyhow."[7]

In September 1970, Father Wessel sent away for the plans from Clark Craft for the grand sum of $31.50. The boat was called a "Tiger Shark Catamaran" and came from Australia. When Father got the plans back by mail he set right to work.[8]

First, he brought the plans to his brother-in-law. He wanted Bill Beitel to look them over and give him his opinion as to whether this was a possible project for the CYO. Bill had a construction background and owned a company that built exhibits for trade shows.[9]

When John put the plans on the table, Bill exclaimed, "Send them back! Send them back to Australia where they belong!"

The catamaran was a seagoing catamaran, designed for ocean sailing. "It was too much boat for this local area. It didn't make sense," said Bill. It was a very large dual-hulled catamaran, made of marine plywood, and each hull was huge. The boat, in Bill's opinion, would be too large for the inexperienced young sailors to maneuver in the waters around Barnegat Bay.[10]

Nevertheless, something about the seagoing catamaran appealed to Father and the CYO youths, and so, throwing caution to the wind, the project got underway. Despite his initial reservations, Bill Beitel was a great help to his brother-in-law. He was able to obtain materials for him, and to construct certain parts in his shop that were too complicated for the CYO kids to do.[11]

The kit came with plans only; nothing was pre-assembled. They had to buy the plywood and cut out all the pieces from scratch.[12] CYO member Jayne Hartley received a phone call from Father Wessel saying, "Do you know how to sew?" Jayne helped him trace the pattern on the plywood so that he could start cutting the wood.[13]

"I remember the first night we started working on it," said Barry Anderson. He and a few other men were in the basement of Blessed Sacrament Church starting the initial cuts of the wood. Father knew that, down the road, he would get more of the CYO involved in building, but that it would not be practical to do so until it got to a certain point. Initially, he approached a few fellows and asked them if they wanted to help. All responded enthusiastically. Many evenings after school and many Saturdays during that fall and winter, Father Wessel and a few young people could be found in the church basement, cutting out the wood and slowly putting the catamaran together.

It took a long time to build, recalled Father Davis, "because he only did it at night. He wasn't free every night so he would go over there to the basement and sometimes he'd be there till 10:00 or 11:00 at night."[14]

> I received plans in late September and we began to construct frames in first week of October—[Jayne Hartley, Barry], Mike and I. Mr. Ritterbusch helped until we thought we could party—and a hassle began. It became obvious it was a two man job after a hassle with 15 kids. The girls, Sue, [Bonnie, Jayne], Suzanne, helped sand [the] first hull which was finished by Christmas vacation. Work slowed for a time and I worked a great deal alone. It was an *extremely* busy winter with retreats, MC [Mercer County] CYO and club activities. The cost was getting to me and worry about transport and rigging. Fr. Hannon was a great help in encouragement and so was the boss, Fr. Davis.
>
> Ship's Log, the *Eucharist*
> Father J.P. Wessel

Father Wessel, for all his enthusiasm, was not a craftsman. He didn't know a great deal about either construction or sailing, and so it was a monumental task of building for everyone.[15]

"I don't think he knew what he was getting into," added Father Davis. "I think he mentioned that once or twice, but he had gone so far he couldn't stop. He had to go through with it."[16]

It was a big job and it took many, many man hours. But the kids were determined, as was Father Wessel, and they stayed with it. With so many to lend a helping hand, they plodded along and saw real progress as the boat slowly took shape during the early part of 1971.[17]

Bill Beitel and his craftsmen made the wooden mast and other complicated pieces in his shop.[18] Father Wessel was grateful for their help:

> The work of the Beitel Display Company [was] fantastic.
> Mast and center board mast and rudders were occupying a whole
> two days of work for *them*.
>
> Ship's Log, the *Eucharist*
> Father J.P. Wessel

In addition to boat building, which Father Wessel jokingly referred to as "the terror of the year," there were many other events going on that spring which demanded Father's time.

Blessed Sacrament CYO's participation in the Diocesan One-Act Play Contest with *The Little Prince* finished up the month of April, and immediately the CYO began practicing for the Parish Night Show. "These practices went on every other night for three weeks and, to those who saw it, it was worth every minute spent," Father Wessel later remarked.[19]

Another project for the kids of the parish was a day hike to Sunfish Pond at the Delaware Water Gap. Of that event, Father Wessel said, "I had great doubts about the whole affair, and when the club was confronted with 35 kids and 3 cars and 2 VW's to cart them, fear turned to panic. . . . The trip was great and, after the transportation problem was solved—thank God for ex-CYOers—the day was just one great exhilaration."[20]

And meshed in between the practices and the hike was the hugely successful Mercer County Search reunion picnic on May 20th (Ascension Thursday) at Green Grove in Washington Crossing Historic Park, Pennsylvania, the Memorial Day sports races, and the CYO production of *The Little Prince* for Sister Catherine Georgine's grade school and the PTA.[21]

"I went to the church basement many times during the building of the boat," Sister Bridget recalled:

> What precision went into that boat. Many a late night
> call Father Davis received to find out if the kids were still with
> Father [Wessel]. It seems that all trace of time was lost in the
> basement.[22]

It was a secret known only to a few that Father Wessel and the CYO were building the boat in the church basement, recalled Sister Elise. But the "secret" got out unexpectedly one spring day when they resinated and fiberglassed the hull. The fumes from the basement permeated into the circulation system in the church, and everything reeked of the potent aroma of resin for several days.[23] "It was quite an event in the parish," recalled Barry. "And it was probably the beginning of the entire parish—I mean the *entire* parish—knowing what was going on in the basement of their church."[24]

The original plans called for the boat to be constructed entirely out of marine plywood, but someone suggested to Father Wessel that a boat composed entirely of plywood would leak and eventually sink. So Father purchased some fiberglass, and one Saturday, he and a few others began the job of fiberglassing the first of the two hulls.[25]

Neither Father nor the CYO kids knew anything about fiberglassing, but the man who sold Father the fiberglass came to help and supervise the work.

Fiberglassing the hull involved, first, applying a coat of the resin with a brush onto the hull; then taking the fiberglass matte (which looked like mosquito netting) and working it into the resin; and then applying a top coat of resin over that. A catalyst was then applied to the resin which made it dry into a very hard coating, but it was really the fiberglass matting that gave the boat its strength. Ultimately, a pigment was put into the resin for the painting phase of it.

"We started on a Saturday morning," recalled Barry, "and I remember being very concerned about the flammable problem because we were in the church basement and the boilers were there and all your pilot lights and things like that." He put up a "no smoking" sign warning people not to light up around the flammable materials in the basement.

The fumes began just as soon as the first can of resin was opened. But working around it all day, Father and the CYO-ers got used to the fumes and didn't realize what was happening. But when the parishioners gathered for Mass that Saturday night—and indeed, the following Sunday morning—the entire church was permeated with the pungent smell.

"One morning the seven o'clock worshipers were found outside of church thinking that there was a gas leak only to discover that it was the fiberglass that was sprayed on the boat the night before," recalled Sister Bridget.

Father Wessel felt compelled to address it in one of his homilies the next day. Apologetically, he told the parishioners, "If you're wondering why the church stinks, this is why . . ." He briefly explained what had happened, " . . . and now I'm in trouble with the Boss."[26]

Father described these events in the Ship's Log:

> The second hull was complete by Easter and fiberglass net
> on first. We smelled the place up so bad one Saturday we chased
> [everybody] out. "Rosary Altar women did it." Al Polick helped
> us with encouragement and technical help.
>
> [Barry] and I went to the shore to investigate trailers and
> bought first fittings at $19.55. We thought it was exorbitant but
> the worst was yet to come!
>
> We were solving problems, at least in our mind. Search II
> and plays got us [too] involved to really work. We worked Friday
> evening and Saturday after confessions. [Barry] was marvelous
> and so were Joe Minch and [Ronnie Garrett]. They knew tools
> best and as time went on we could direct the work and made
> good time. Mr. Ritterbusch came and helped a great deal with
> wood construction of decks. We completed last fiberglassing net
> on hull # 2 [on] May 23rd. Parish Night was the 25th. . . .
>
> Ship's Log, the Eucharist
Father J.P. Wessel

Even worse was the fact that they had to repeat the fiberglassing several
more times! Now, Father Davis was the most tolerant of men, but he
probably wasn't too thrilled with the idea of his church smelling like a paint
factory. It seemed prudent to move the boat (in large part completed) from
the basement of Blessed Sacrament Church to the Beitel's backyard across
the Delaware River in Morrisville.[27]

Trying to move the dual-hulled catamaran out of the basement of
the church presented an unexpected dilemma. After they'd built it in the
basement, Father and the CYO found that they couldn't get it out. It was
like the proverbial "ship in a bottle." No one took into consideration that
it wouldn't fit through the basement door when they were all done building
it.[28]

It was a strange kind of basement. The late Father Hayes never wanted
to hold any social functions there, so in order to make sure that it would
never happen, he had only one exit leading from the basement in the shape
of an "L". It wasn't a clear doorway out; rather, you walked out a bit and
then turned at a right angle to go up the steps.[29]

"We got it built, and we couldn't get it through the door," recalled Ronald Garrett. Father Wessel looked at the boat and exclaimed, "How are we going to get this damn thing through the door!" After much discussion, they all got together and partially disassembled it and then pulled, pushed, and rolled the large pieces up the stairs "like the Egyptians did with logs," said Ronald.[30] The catamaran was reassembled in the church parking lot and towed over to Morrisville on the trailer which Father had purchased.

Getting the boat out of the basement proved to be the most difficult challenge of the construction project, but a source of endless humor.[31]

> We moved the boat to Morrisville on [May] 29th and then began the deck fiberglass and two first coats of white and blue. This is when real hard work and teamwork began. In two shifts, one in [the] afternoon, the other in [the] evening with stage lights we desperately began the finishing of the boat. The kids were asked for help at [the] Youth Council meeting on June 6 and off we went. Joe Palumbo, Brian Schoeffel and Chris Morley, and at the end Henry Liedtka were the greatest. The girls tried to help but it was in a difficult stage, physically. Joe and I tried to fiberglass by ourselves and that set us back a couple of days sanding.
>
> The glass was terribly irritating but the boys stuck to it. The kids were great and so was Fr. Davis who could have really resented all those sick calls during my absence. The only thing that suffered pastorally was one week—the last week—I did only [the] 8th floor of Mercer Hospital.
>
> Ship's Log, the *Eucharist*
> Father J.P. Wessel

Once the boat was moved to the Beitel's backyard, even more young people got involved in finishing it. At the end, just about everybody had a hand in it, even if it was just sanding a small section of the boat.[32]

Cindy Farrell* recalled the Beitels' incredible patience, even with "hoards of kids in their backyard, in their sheds in the middle of the night, coming and going" during the final stages of boat building.[33]

Father Wessel was under the gun. He was determined to complete the boat in record time, because the launch date was timed to coincide with the annual CYO shore picnic in Ship Bottom on Friday, June 18th,[34] and he wanted to launch the boat from the slip off the causeway in Ship Bottom. Toward the very end, Father was uncharacteristically late or absent for a few parish meetings as he struggled to meet his deadline.[35]

Father and the young people worked round-the-clock for a couple of nights. But the day before the launch, Thursday night, June 17th, was an unforgettable day for all involved. In Father Wessel's words, it was "the most rewarding and frustrating day of all. I knew that we had to work hard to get it out of Morrisville for the launch."[36]

"We worked all night to finish it up in the Beitels' backyard," recalled Barry Anderson. "And there were quite a few kids there . . . working on last minute details."[37] The young people put the hulls together, installed the mast, and got the trailer rigged up and ready to go. They had loads of problems with the electrical wiring on the trailer, but finally they got it done.[38]

The youths worked in the Beitels' garage until the wee hours. They didn't always know what they were doing, but they were having a lot of fun doing it.[39]

"In between the racket of people in and out of the house, we also kept getting phone calls from parents wondering where their children were, because naturally they couldn't understand how anybody could be out this late," Maryann Beitel recalled. "But they always knew their children were okay provided they were with Father Wessel; they just had to check."[40]

Father Wessel described how the day began:

> After grammar school Mass I left with John Cowle, Brian Schoeffel, Jimmy Gerard and Jim Liedtka for Morrisville. I put them to work on the top plate that had dried over the night and I worked on the fitting of the stays on mast. . . . We put in all the stays and worked until 5:45. I came home to eat and went back at 7:15. A group had come to put it on the trailer. Everyone was uptight but soon began to relax. We put the mast in place but had a terrible time getting on the forestay bridle. We worked about an hour on it as Jimmy Blatchford, [Ronnie Garrett], Joe Minch and others held the damn thing up. We almost ruined the boat but luckily for a block of wood and drive we got it in. [Barry] came down and stated he couldn't get lights working. I told him I had my troubles and he was to solve his. Before I

could get to him, Stewart put the side stays about a foot too far back. I could have contradicted him but I didn't. I thought he had taken into consideration the boom swing.

We got the standing rigging up and started on the fittings—they weren't as easily fixed as I thought and it took time.

The boys on the trailer were having a harder time so I didn't worry about it. . . . With incredible drive, the kids went from one job to another. We finished abruptly with half of the tiller put together with a man coming over in pajamas telling us to keep quiet, etc. [Ron] was ready to kill him. We keyed down and began to assemble the boat on the trailer with lights working.

The final problem was the mast since it is 26 feet—the rigging I had designed was never put together. The boys, from Palumbo, Henry Liedtka, [Ron], Stewart, Brian, etc., worked like hell with an impossible amount of rope. At 3:00 a.m. we were ready to move it out of the yard. It was fantastic. [Barry] held the only light out of four that still worked and with grunts and curses we pushed the boat and trailer to the street, hitched it to the car and tested the lights. They worked. I went down to collect tools for the shore. Suzanne came running—"POLICE." I ran contrary to my motives to explain. Heard in boys' squad cars it talked—"they were friendlies"—but we must have created havoc in the neighborhood with radios blaring.

Ship's Log, the *Eucharist*

Father J.P. Wessel

As noted in the Ship's Log, the Morrisville police were unexpected visitors at the Beitels' home on Crown Street that night. With a bunch of young people pulling in and out of the driveway, and all the activity in the backyard through the wee hours of the morning, the neighbors must have thought that they either were partying or were up to no good.[41]

Finally, the police left and the catamaran was ready to go. Father Wessel and a small caravan of cars took off for Long Beach Island in the early morning hours. With him were some of the CYO youths, Kevin Connor, Barry Anderson and Bill Hamilton*, and perhaps one or two others. It was dark when they started out with the 18-foot boat on the trailer attached to the back of Father's old green Plymouth. They had modified the trailer in a great hurry, adding electric lights for the "night run," without being quite sure it was all correct. This, plus the oversized dimensions of the boat, caused some trepidation. Carefully, they proceeded toward the shore as dawn was slowly breaking. Father Wessel recorded their departure from Morrisville:

> With a big hug and kiss from the girls all departed except for Kevin and I who stole into the house to make coffee. [Bill and Barry] returned, drank a quick cup and we departed for Ship Bottom at 3:35 a.m.
>
> Slowly I drove to Yardley in absolute glee—the boat was *beautiful* on the trailer. In the light of street all the dirt vanished, and coated with red of shop lights the white and blue seemed out of this world.
>
> We were afraid to go across Calhoun Street Bridge so the long trip to Scutters [sic] Falls Bridge seemed endless but it was good practice. The boat trailed *very well.* I was able to do 30 m.p.h. on poor roads, 50-55 on good roads.
>
> I had been bumming cigarettes all night so we stopped at "Dunkin' Donuts" for coffee and "breakfast."
>
> [Bill] got hammers out and cursing, started driving nails into support blocks we couldn't put on because of the noise. "They don't make nails like they used to!" as he hit them off one inch. Tired, we continued. Dawn began to show as we left Allentown. The only bad part of the road was near Route 72 where sand covered the road.
>
> Ship's Log, the *Eucharist*
> Father J.P. Wessel

The sun was just rising over the ocean and bay as the happy caravan crossed the Barnegat Bridge and made their way to Father's summer house on Fifth Street in Ship Bottom. They "arrived at half light—yelling and carrying on about 5:35 a.m.," Father wrote.[42]

Before heading off to bed, Father Wessel wanted to celebrate. He passed around the Old Crow and the men drank a toast to their success before falling off to sleep at six o'clock, exhausted from having been up all day and night. They slept for only a few hours.

Father awoke at eight o'clock in the morning and drove back to Trenton with Kevin to pick up the rest of the CYO and bring them down for the picnic and launch. Barry and Bill and a young man named Stewart, who knew about boats, stayed behind and made the boat ready for her inaugural sail.[43]

How did the *Eucharist I* get her name?

The word "Eucharist" has many meanings. First, from the Greek word, *eucharistia*, meaning "thanksgiving." Father once jestingly remarked that the boat was named *Eucharist* "in thanksgiving for its floating." Father Davis thought that perhaps he was simply "thankful" that he got the boat finished in the first place.[44]

The second meaning of Eucharist is Holy Communion, the Lord's Supper. Because the Mass and Holy Eucharist were so important to Father Wessel, many associated the name "Eucharist" with the Body and Blood of Jesus Christ more so than "thanksgiving."[45]

Although the *Eucharist* was exactly the kind of name that Father would have selected, he himself did not name it.

When it came time to name the boat, Father Wessel let the young people name it. All the CYO members were of one mind: They had discussed it among themselves and felt it should be named the "J.P. Wessel." Only Father himself thought otherwise.[46]

Wes Ritterbusch recalled how Father reacted when he heard of the accolade. "Oh, no," he said. "Absolutely not!" Because Father was so self-effacing and so reluctant to take any credit, he went so far as to say, "I would destroy it first. I will not have that. It's not my boat and I don't want it, no."

Even then, Father didn't tell the group what to name the boat. He didn't even give them a hint. He just said, "I think it should be something that we're all interested in, and something that would say what we're really all about." When the kids came back again with the new name "Eucharist," Father heartily approved.

It was a strange and kind of a religious name for a boat. "But the more you thought about it, the better the name sounded, the more you liked it and the concept of it," recalled Wes Ritterbusch.[47] *Eucharist* really did proclaim what they were all about.

Eucharist was launched on [the] 18th of June at 3:00 p.m. from the public dock at Ship Bottom, NJ. . . .

Putting the mast in place was extremely difficult and took about eight of us to do so. [Barry] backed her down the ramp and we filled her up. She ran down well with the exception of her last lunge into the water over the trailer beam. With great cheer she hit the water and the most surprising thing was her good stance in the water. She was beautiful. All ceremonies of christening, etc., were lost in the confusion of setting sail by kids who didn't really know what they were doing. The boat almost took off on its own. I really don't know who was on her first. It ended up that I, Stewart, [Barry, Bill] and Kevin had the first ride.

I took the tiller and we supposedly got organized. We tacked well but in coming about fell dead in the water.

a) Rudder seems to need extending to give push more.
b) You need appreciable speed to make a turn from tack line.
c) She is very, very fast (wind was about 9 m.p.h.)

We would get a good tack line and hold it too long and went aground twice. I pushed off and had a difficult time getting back in. Kevin pushed off once and was dragged behind a very fast moving boat. The boys didn't put in all the screws in the gudgeon and the bottom ones bent loose. We came in to shore, fixed the tiller and I left to get some sleep.

[Barry], Stewart, and [Bill Hamilton] stayed behind to make sure most of the kids got a ride. I think they were all a bit disappointed or let down that she didn't run properly but what can you expect. I was relieved she didn't sink . . .

. . .

Stewart's opinion is she is a boat that knows her own mind and you have to learn her ways. She will be fast but difficult to control. She will go where she wants to go—"some boat."

> I am grateful to God and Jesus for helping us reach this day.
> He helped us enormously, and quietly I "thank Him."
>
> Ship's Log, the *Eucharist*
> Father J.P. Wessel

About thirty or forty young people were present at the public docks at West 10th Street and Shore Avenue, Ship Bottom, for the launch and maiden voyage of the *Eucharist* on Barnegat Bay. Many of the kids were the same ones who had been up late the night before putting the finishing touches on the boat. They were tired, yet the mood was one of elation.

"I remember that we were all so excited," recalled Joanne Gillespie of the launch. And no one was prouder of the boat, and of the CYO kids who built it, than Father Wessel.[48]

Before the launch, everyone climbed on and around the boat, which was sitting on the trailer in the parking lot of the dock, and posed for pictures.

The young people were in high spirits as they all worked together to ready the boat for her maiden voyage. Other people passing by had stopped to see what was going on. And just as they were about to put her in the water, the young people asked, "Are we ready now, Father?" They knew Father wanted to say a prayer before the boat hit the water.

"Let's bless this thing. Let's just have a prayer," he said.

Father bowed his head and gave thanks to God. He spoke of how the young people should take pride in themselves and in what they are and what they can be. Looking at the boat, he reminded them that "there's nothing, but nothing, that we can't do with God's help."[49]

"There was really an austere kind of a feeling about it" was the way one spectator described it. "It was like a hush went over everybody, and you could just feel what everyone else was feeling about this endeavor. The fact that everyone had come together and done this, and this was the result of their labors."[50]

Someone christened the *Eucharist I* with a bottle of inexpensive wine, as into the water she went. A great cheer went up, and then everyone tried to jump on the boat at the same time.[51]

Father was elated as the boat hit the water, and more than a little relieved when it actually stayed afloat. The boat was extremely heavy, and there was some concern that, because of her weight, she would sink to the bottom her first time out.[52]

But as the boat held her own in the water, Father Wessel was "about ten feet tall." He was proud of the young people of the CYO; proud that they all came together as a family; and proud that now they had a beautiful boat which they had built from scratch with their own hands.[53]

His only regret was that not all those who were involved with her building were able to be present for her launching. "But," he added, "I'm sure that it would [have] been impossible at any time."[54]

Father was the captain of the boat that day, and he made sure that everyone got a ride. Since the *Eucharist* held six or eight at a time, this involved taking turns going out for a sail on the bay.[55]

Father Wessel was quite serious about learning the art of sailing. About three or four weeks before the launch, Father had said to two of the young CYO men, Barry Anderson and Kevin Connor, "All right, it's time to learn to sail." So the three of them, casually clad in T-shirts and shorts, went to a marina in Ship Bottom for an hour's sailing lesson. Their instructor was a young fellow in his late teens or early twenties, who couldn't quite figure out why the two teenagers were calling the third young fellow their "father."

As the sailing lesson was getting underway, the young man gave instruction to the three as to where to sit on the boat. "You sit over here, you sit over there," he said to Barry and Kevin. "And your father—or *whoever* he is—you sit over here," pointing to Father Wessel. The trio broke into laughter.[56]

The CYO youths also recalled how Father was great at using nautical terminology. No one really knew how to sail; they were just learning as they went along. But Father had apparently read a book on sailing language, and as the captain of the boat, he would yell out, "Grab the jib!" or "Get on the starboard side!" or "Come about!"—which no one understood.[57] But somehow, despite the confusion and ensuing hilarity, the amateur sailors managed to pilot the boat and to have a great time doing so. Sailing was hard work, recalled one CYO member, but it was exciting and fun.[58]

In many ways, the legendary "boat" was not only a project but a parable—a metaphor for Father's spiritual mission to the young people; an image of what he wanted to do for them; and a legacy of what he hoped to leave with them.

Although it can be found in many places in the Old and New Testament, the image of a boat in Scripture is very often associated with Noah's Ark. Like the Ark, a boat both shelters and protects God's people from the raging and destructive storms, and as a means of passage, safely transports them from one place to another.

A boat is not one's permanent home but a transitory place. Its occupants are a pilgrim people, wayfarers seeking a better place. This serves to remind us that the Church is often called a "pilgrim people on earth" because earthly existence, joyous though it may be, is not our final destination.

For Father J. William Mickiewicz, the building of the boat was a telling reflection of Father Wessel's spirituality. Father Mickiewicz explained:

> It was like something out of the blue, but . . . to me, it became very symbolic. . . . They called the boat, *Eucharist*. If you look at what happened there, you're going to find John's spirituality and his vision, whatever that drove him there. This boat would be to me symbolic of something John innerly wanted to do . . . the exemplification of where his spirituality was.[59]

There were indeed many "storms"—social issues, problems, sufferings, turmoil—around during Father Wessel's day. But he would not necessarily become upset or livid about them, said Father Mickiewicz. Rather, Father Wessel would have responded by focusing on: How does this impact people? How can I be of assistance to people? Father's response to the "storms" of everyday life that were all around in the 1960s and 1970s, and even today, would take the form of the image of the boat: How can we draw people together in this "boat" so that we can help one another, shelter one another, and "weather the storms" together?[60]

The image of a boat could have many other interpretations: Jesus Christ, the Catholic Church, the Christian community (open, truthful, suffering and loving one another), the Mass. Even the Blessed Mother is associated with the metaphor because, as the bearer of Christ into this world, she is called the "New Ark of the Covenant." But it is indeed interesting (and perhaps more than a bit coincidental) that the catamaran was named *Eucharist*, and Father Wessel always held that the Mass was the core of his spiritual life.

The other aspect of the parable of the boat was the building of it. The almost year-long and sometimes tedious work was a group project, a joint endeavor, in which many persons of varying talents and abilities came together. Each person played a part, and each person's individual contribution, whether great or small, was valuable and integral to making the whole come together.

It was "not just a project," said Julian Wessel, but was done "to prove a point"—that young people could work together and build something that was difficult even for adults to do.[61]

*   *   *

Much sailing was done on the *Eucharist I* over that summer. It was a boat that was open to everyone and owned by no one, so any number of CYO teenagers and Father Wessel himself came down to the shore from Trenton and took her out for a sail.

There were, however, a seemingly endless series of problems, and many "highs" and "lows" that were experienced with her, that challenged the group's ingenuity and patience over the summer.

One of the problems that worried Father was the money that he spent on the boat. The day after the launch, he wrote:

> I am personally anxious to get at her again to make alterations and to really sail her. I wish all the bills were paid—that bothers me too but God is awfully good to us and I'll see it through. I do feel that buying a boat would have been easier but I wouldn't have done it. It is exorbitant. I still haven't figured it out yet. I must owe $350.00 at least. It's like a poker game. Once you're in you never can get out.
>
> Ship's Log, the Eucharist
Father J.P. Wessel

It was indeed like a poker game. The costs kept adding up as many unanticipated supplies, equipment and expenses were incurred. By the launching date itself, Father Wessel had spent over a thousand dollars on the boat. Lumber, screws, fittings, sails, and a boating license all added up. Shortly after the launch, Father incurred yet another expense as he hastily purchased insurance against injury to persons and property damage.[62]

Every other day, it seemed, there was some problem with the rudder. As Father noted, the *Eucharist* was demasted twice and sunk twice, and ran aground on several occasions. All the repairs to the boat during the summer added up as well.[63]

After the launching on Friday, June 18th, three of the boys, Bill Hamilton, Kevin Connor and Barry Anderson, stayed behind at the shore for the weekend to rent a slip to dock the boat for the season. As Father Wessel noted, "she is extremely difficult to rig every time she is to be used."[64]

A slip was secured for *Eucharist I* for the summer at Ship Bottom Marina on 19th Street for the grand price of $120.00. The marina itself was like a little island in a lagoon area, and one had to sail out from the lagoon to reach the open bay.[65]

Since the boat didn't have a motor at first, it had to be manually maneuvered in and out of the slip. Brian Schoeffel recalled how, once they unlatched the rope, it often took Father Wessel and his crew "a couple of hours" to get from the marina in the lagoon area to the open bay. "We'd be banging into other boats, banging into pilings. It took forever to get the thing out there. Then once we got it out of there, it was fun."[66]

"We were like the neighborhood spectacle" when it came to docking, recalled a CYO girl. In order to dock, they had to come in under sail, then turn around, drop sail, and throw a rope around the piling and maneuver or paddle the boat into the berth. "Literally, people . . . would send the word that we were coming in and they would get their lawn chairs out and watch this spectacle," she said, "because it really *was* a spectacle!"

It was on Sunday, June 20th, that the tall 26-foot mast on the catamaran broke for the first time. Bill Hamilton, Kevin Connor and Barry Anderson, along with some passengers, had taken her out for a sail. William Beitel, one of the passengers, later recalled, "I went for one ride on the *Eucharist* and almost got killed!" Unfortunately, his early prediction proved uncannily correct: On that day, at least, the seagoing catamaran, tearing along at a good speed in a strong wind, was quite difficult for inexperienced navigators to maneuver in the bay.[67]

Father Wessel was not on board, but an entry in the Ship's Log documents the events leading up to the demasting in excruciating detail:

> After lunch Bill Beitel and Bill Roth came aboard and we took them for a ride. Three Bills on one boat is not too good for communication purposes but that was the least of our worries.
>
> The wind on the bay had increased to about 15 m.p.h. and we shoved off and moved out quick. Time 2:30.
>
> We sailed out about a mile and a half and decided to head north. We came about and sailed down wind. I would estimate that we were making about 6 to 8 knots at top speed. We, at one time, had the right bow completely out of the water. It was beautiful sailing. About ½ mile from the causeway Willie [Bill Hamilton] lost his hat. I turned the boat around and went back for it. This is where all the trouble began.
>
> We couldn't find his hat and had a hell of a time getting back into the wind because the center board was hung up on the bottom. We were pivoting on this because the wind kept blowing.
>
> I saw a small inlet and headed the ship down the mouth of it. What a mistake that was. After about 500 yards into the inlet we found out it led into Beach Haven West. We had to turn around and tack out of the inlet which was only about 100 yards wide. The wind was constantly shifting because of the winding of the channel making it next to impossible for inexperienced sailors to maneuver. For one and a half hours we tried to tack out of there but only lost ground. Finally Kevin and Willie pulled us out and we were once again under way. By now it was about 5:00 and we had to head back. The bay was starting to get rough and tricky to sail on. We headed straight for an island and tacked to the leeward side and sailed south. It was at this point when I noticed the one stern of the boat was out of the water.

Willie was on the jib on the starboard side, myself at the tiller and Kevin and little Bill and big Bill were around someplace. Willie remarked about the tremendous amount of tension on the jib and asked Kevin for help. At this point, all the shit in the world hit a gigantic fan. CRACK! Down went the mast missing Willie's head by inches. What a feeling! The mast did not actually break. It slipped or ripped out of the stip, when the port side stay tightened up it caused a whipping action and then she broke.

We waited for a tow for about 15 minutes and arrived back at the slip around 6:00. Thank God no one was hit by that mast or the sails were not damaged.

Ship's Log, the Eucharist
[Barry Anderson], 6/20/71[68]

Later that night, the young crew members secured the boat in the slip and stripped the mast of rigging. The hulls were loaded with water, so they bailed them out and took the broken mast to Father Wessel's shore house and departed.[69] The only task that was left was considerable: Who was going to tell Father Wessel?

"I remember driving back from the shore that night" with Bill and Kevin, recalled Barry Anderson. Their somber conversation consisted of, "Well, who's going to tell him?" "You tell him." "No, you tell him. I'm not going to tell him, you tell him." They drove back to the Blessed Sacrament Rectory and knocked on the door.

Father Wessel answered, and excitedly asked, "How's everything going? How's the boat? How's—"[70]

"The mast broke," they told him. Father could hardly believe it. "There was one time Father Wessel was pretty mad!" recalled Kevin Connor.[71] Father Wessel gave the three men the responsibility to repair the mast. "It was our fault, so we had to fashion a new mast. He made that clear," said Barry.[72] Another wooden mast was constructed for the boat, and June 29th was "mast installation day."

Sailing resumed as usual, but a few weeks later, the second mast broke again!

Father's entry for July 15th records the second demasting:

"WE TOOK THE DEEP SIX."
Crew: Wessel, Schoeffel, Carson
Passengers: [Farrell], T. Dalrymple, D. Schoeffel
Disembarked under sail 12:30. Demasted—3:40 p.m. Towed
in by 5:30. Mast broke on mid-section near Barnegat Inlet.
Wind—12-20 mph. WHAT A DAY!

Ship's Log, the *Eucharist*
Father J.P. Wessel, 7/15/71

The crew recalled Father Wessel's disappointment after the wooden mast snapped and broke yet again.[73] "He was so broken-hearted because he thought that he had done everything right," added Ronald Garrett.[74] And what a mess when it crashed! The sails and the cabling came tumbling down, and they had to wait until a boat came by and towed them back to shore.[75]

Father Wessel was not one to give up though, after all that work. He was always game to try again. So he bought and installed a mast made of aluminum in mid-July. The cost of the aluminum mast and new rigging came to over $100.00. But this time, it held.[76]

Despite these setbacks, entries in the log reveal many great days of enjoyable and relatively uneventful sailing in the waters around Long Beach Island that summer.

The Ship's Log for Saturday, August 28th read:

[Crew:] Fr. Wessel, [B. Anderson]
Departure 12:00. Return 1:30
Sailed with only 2 and there were small craft warnings but what a sail! Terrific.
Departure 2:00. Return 4:00. More great sailings.

And again, for Thursday, August 31st:

Crew: Wessel, [Garrett, Cindy Farrell, Jayne Hartley, Maria Rodriguez]
Time 12:15-4:00 p.m.
Low tide. Went aground many times. Jib halyard spring off. Ran over channel marker. Lot of laughs. No problem docking.

Occasionally, the *Eucharist* was even amazingly lucky. When Hurricane Doria hit the Jersey shore in late August, nine boats in the marina were sunk, but to everyone's relief, the *Eucharist* stayed afloat.[77]

Even when calamities struck, Father Wessel had a way of making good fun out of them. On more than one occasion, the catamaran sank. One stormy night in the middle of August, Barry Anderson discovered the *Eucharist* was sinking in the marina with a big hole in her side.[78]

Wes Ritterbusch related the story of the late night call:

About two-thirty in the morning, Ritterbusch's phone rang. "There was a storm like you wouldn't believe," he recalled. Barry Anderson was on the other end of the line.

"Mr. Ritterbusch," he said, "Father Wessel said to get hold of you. We've got to go down. The *Eucharist* is sinking in the dock."

Wes said, "You've got to be kidding me!"

"No," Barry replied. "Father says, Can we drive?" Wes had a large station wagon. "Father wants to know if you can come over to the rectory to pick him up before you head down?"

"Sure," Wes said. "What's that noise in the background?"

"That's my father telling me to get the hell off the phone at this hour in the morning," Barry replied.

Wes Ritterbusch hurried over to the rectory in the pouring rain. There were about four or five other fellows already there. Father Wessel came out and started throwing T-shirts at the men. "Now, what the heck is this?" they all thought.

Father said, "Quick, you've got to put it on. We're a team!"

The men looked at the T-shirts. They had the words "All American" emblazoned on the front, and a great big American flag on the back. Everyone quickly donned their T-shirts, and the "All American" team drove down to the shore in Ritterbusch's station wagon to rescue the boat.

The *Eucharist* was sinking fast in the marina at Ship Bottom. "It was taking on water like gangbusters," recalled Wes Ritterbusch. The catamaran was taking a beating, going back and forth in the slip, and a couple of the enclosures for the wells had opened up and the water was pouring in. Together, the men got the heavy boat out of the water and up on land and put on a temporary patch.[79]

CYO member Brian Schoeffel recalled Father Wessel and a few other drenched men from Trenton sitting at Brian's parents' dining room table at their Long Beach Island home near Ship Bottom late one night, blankets wrapped around them, shivering, and eating chicken soup, after rescuing the *Eucharist* from sinking.[80]

A few days later, the boat was permanently patched, cleaned, and waxed. Father and a few CYO kids then went for a sail, and were relieved when the patch held well in the water.[81]

"That boat had caused a lot of happiness" but it also caused "an awful lot of aggravation," said Brian Schoeffel.[82]

The summer of 1971 slowly drew to a close. During the last week of August, Father Wessel and a few of the young men in the CYO returned from a canoe trip to Vermont and immediately went to Long Beach Island to sail the *Eucharist*. The group also helped Father Pat Hannon celebrate his fiftieth birthday at the shore.[83] Much last minute sailing was squeezed in before the end of the summer and the return to the routine of school. It was especially poignant because many of the high school seniors were preparing to leave the CYO and go off to college in September.

With all the time and money that was spent building the boat, and all the incidents that occurred while she was being used—the breaking of the mast, the near-sinking, the repairs, the mechanical problems to be ironed out—Father Wessel would later refer to that summer as "the craziest summer of my priesthood."[84]

*　　*　　*

On Thursday, September 16, 1971, Father Wessel and Wes Ritterbusch went sailing on the *Eucharist*. It was to be their last sail of the season.

In Father Wessel's last entry in the Ship's Log, he wrote in bold script:

> Thursday, September 16, 1971:
> Crew: Fr. Wessel, Mr. Ritterbusch
> 2:30 p.m.-7:00 p.m.
> Light winds—Went crabbing. Beautiful sail. Rudder repaired.
> Wind, S-8 mph.
>
> Ship's Log, the Eucharist
Father J.P. Wessel

"It was a magnificent day," Wes Ritterbusch recalled, "one of those clear sky kind of days. The wind was good, and we did have a good sail." Both he and Father Wessel liked to try to get one sponson out of the water when they sailed.

The catamaran had two sponsons (hulls) on either side of the deck. In order to get one sponson out of the water, somebody had to get up on the elevated side, hold on and lean back over the edge to counterbalance it—a maneuver that was known as "hiking"—so the boat wouldn't flip over. It was hard to do on the *Eucharist* because she was a big, heavy boat, but if there was a really good wind, then "it would just pick you up."

There was a good wind that day. Father John and Wes were able to "hike" one sponson out of the water and have fun with that. "We ran aground at one point in time goofing around," Wes recalled, and even fouled up the rudder.

The two men went crabbing that day, and their conversation turned to a story about crabbing from Wes Ritterbusch's youth.

"I was telling him about my father who had an injury to his hand in World War II. He had his finger crushed and he had no feeling in it." Wes was born and raised in the Baltimore area, and as kids growing up "we used to catch crabs all summer long from the Chesapeake and Back River." Because of his war injury, Ritterbusch's father could pick crabs up with his finger. "He would put his finger in water and crabs would bite him and he would pick 'em up and then drop 'em in the hot water. And everybody who saw him do that would ask, 'Doesn't that hurt?'" and Wes's father would reply, "Nope, nothing to it." So naturally, everyone would try it themselves and cry "Ouch!" when the crab bit them.

"So I was telling him about this," recalled Wes. When they got done sailing, the two men headed back to Father Wessel's shore house in Ship Bottom and cooked up the crabs for dinner. "We had crabs that night," Wes continued, "and we were trying to get somebody else"—it may have been the good-natured Bill Beitel—"to take their finger and pick the crabs up like that."

"We stowed everything after that," Wes continued. "Now this is in September, and you don't do much sailing after that. I can remember we put everything away and we were going to come back one more time to secure it for the winter, to winterize everything." But Ritterbusch never did get to do that with Father Wessel, because soon Father's plans were to be changed.

Like most things involving Father Wessel, the day of the last sail was filled with fun, laughter and genuine enjoyment of each other's company.

Ritterbusch had mentioned to Father Wessel that he regretted that he hadn't been able to get to sail much during the summer because of his work schedule, and the two men were already talking about what they would do differently . . . *next year.*

"Next summer," they resolved, "we'll try to get more weekend sailing in . . ."

. . . *next year.*

Ritterbusch drove back to his home in Trenton that evening. Father Wessel stayed at the shore.

All in all, said Wes, "it was just a good, good day."[85]

Ordination & First Mass

This photo and article appeared in the *Mount Holly Herald* in May 1965, announcing the ordination of lifelong friends John Wessel (right) and James Dubell. Used with permission of *The Burlington County Times*.

Seven priests from the Diocese of Trenton were ordained by Bishop George W. Ahr in St. Mary's Cathedral, Trenton, on May 22, 1965. Father John Wessel is at far left. Used with permission of *The Monitor*, the Catholic newspaper of the Diocese of Trenton.

Father Joseph V. Kozak (left), who helped young John Wessel choose the diocesan priesthood, was beaming with pride as his protege prepared to celebrate his First Mass as a priest. (Photo from Wessel family album)

Scenes from Father John P. Wessel's First Mass . . .

... Sacred Heart Church, Mount Holly, May 23, 1965. Top photo, Father Wessel gives Holy Communion to his mother as family friend, Father Joseph C. Shenrock, serves as deacon. (Photos from Wessel family album)

Blessed Sacrament

Father Wessel and his first pastor, Father J. Arthur Hayes (left), the priest who baptized him, Blessed Sacrament Church, Trenton, June 1965. The photo provides a rare glimpse of Father Wessel wearing his cassock. Father Hayes died about seven months later. (Photo from Wessel family album)

(L-r, center, seated) Father John Wessel, new pastor Father Eugene V. Davis, and Father J. William Mickiewicz, with Blessed Sacrament grammar school class of 1966. (Reprinted from 1972 Blessed Sacrament booklet)

Father Wessel administers the Sacrament of Baptism to his niece Susan Beitel at Blessed Sacrament Church, October 1965. (Photo from Wessel family album)

Father Wessel was known for his compassion for the imprisoned and mentally ill. Here Father is pictured at the Trenton Psychiatric Hospital counseling a patient, who later said that the young priest had helped him very much. (Photo from Wessel family album)

Search

Search for Christian Maturity weekends were held in the Pocono Mountains of Pennsylvania. Teens listen in rapt attention as Father Wessel (standing, far right) speaks, spring 1971. Also pictured (standing l-r) are Father James H. Dubell and Father Eugene M. Rebeck. (Photo from Fr. John Wessel's album)

Blessed Sacrament—Camping

Father Wessel shared his love of the outdoors with the Blessed Sacrament CYO. Here Father (second from left) and the young CYO men enjoyed a rigorous annual canoe-and-camping trip each August. (Photo courtesy of Wes Ritterbusch)

Camping with the Blessed Sacrament CYO, Father Wessel
(seated left) wears his "crazy hat." This photo was probably taken
in Maine. (Photo courtesy of Wes Ritterbusch)

Mountain climbing with the Blessed Sacrament CYO, Father
Wessel (center) reaches the summit . . . (Photo from Fr. John
Wessel's album)

. . . and pauses for a rest. (Photo from Wessel family album)

Eucharist

The launch of the *Eucharist I* in pictures. The Blessed Sacrament CYO members transport their handmade catamaran from Father Wessel's shore home . . .

... to the dock in Ship Bottom, and raise the mast. (Photos courtesy of Wes Ritterbusch)

Father Wessel (standing on deck, right) and the CYO pose for a group photo with the *Eucharist I* just prior to launch. Father was enormously proud of his youth group, who built the boat from scratch. (Photo courtesy of Wes Ritterbusch)

"*Eucharist* was launched on [the] 18th of June [1971] at 3 p.m. from the public dock at Ship Bottom, NJ," wrote Father Wessel. When the boat hit the water, Father was just grateful that she stayed afloat. (Photos courtesy of Wes Ritterbusch)

CHAPTER 26

A NEW ASSIGNMENT

It was in September of 1971, near the end of Father Wessel's "crazy summer"—the summer of launching and sailing (and constantly repairing) the catamaran, *Eucharist I*. In the midst of all his success in youth work, Father Wessel would be transferred to St. Joseph, Toms River.

For some time, Father Wessel knew that a transfer was imminent. A young priest is usually rotated after six or seven years at the same parish, and Father Wessel had been at Blessed Sacrament for slightly over six. And yet, because he loved it so much, he was hoping that it would continue another year. But his time had come to an end at Blessed Sacrament, Trenton.[1]

One day, recalled Maryann, her brother John came over to the Beitels' house. He looked so downcast that his sister jokingly asked if he was leaving the priesthood. "John, you're leaving. You've met a woman and you're leaving!"

"I've been transferred," he said.

"Where are you going to be?" Maryann asked him as he left.

"Oh, here it is," he said. He wrote on a little scrap of paper—a name, address and phone number in Toms River, New Jersey—and handed it to his sister.[2]

Father John Wessel was appointed Associate Pastor of St. Joseph's Church in Toms River by Bishop George Ahr on September 13, 1971. He was instructed to report to the Reverend Lawrence W. Donovan, pastor of St. Joseph's Church, before six o'clock on Friday evening, September 24th. By the time the letter announcing his transfer arrived, there was little time to prepare.[3]

Father Wessel had been given two possible parish assignments, either in Toms River or Moorestown, and had an opportunity to express his preference, although in the final analysis he, like all diocesan priests, would go wherever he was sent.[4]

About two or three weeks before his transfer, his mother, Kathleen Wessel, received an unusual phone call. Her son had always kept his priestly business to himself. He never discussed his decisions with his mother, and she never pried. But this time, he did. "It was the only thing he ever called me about," recalled Mrs. Wessel.[5]

"Mother," he said, "I got a call that I can go to Moorestown." He asked her what she thought about it. Everyone in Burlington County knew of Moorestown. It was the exclusive, wealthy area of the county. In fact, Kathleen Wessel knew many people in Moorestown, since it was close to Mount Holly and many of the Wessels' old friends and neighbors had moved to the affluent town.[6]

"Oh, that's great," she said. "There are a lot of nice people down there." Her son was more hesitant. Although Moorestown was a "plum assignment," something just didn't feel right about it.

"Oh, I don't know," Father Wessel replied. "I don't like to go where I'm known, and I'm known too well around here, around Moorestown, and the name is known. I don't think I want to go there . . . I think I can do a better job somewhere else."

"I agreed with him because he knew so many people" in Moorestown that "it would be hard on him," said his mother. "He was not an extrovert. And he could do well if he didn't know anybody. And I think he was that way with the family, too," she said.[7]

Maryann also recalled her brother saying that he wanted to go to an area where his family was not well known. If that sounds like an unusual concern, it is helpful to recall that the extended Wessel and Hogan families were well known in Burlington County. Father Wessel was also concerned that he may have received a prestigious assignment because of his family, and he thought other priests who had served longer should get the choicer positions over himself.[8]

Another factor, secondary in importance but still a consideration, was that the pastor he would be working with in Moorestown didn't have much of a feel for youth ministry. Working with young people was Father Wessel's gift and he knew it. He was concerned that there would be little opportunity to do youth work in Moorestown, and felt that the pastor in

Toms River would be more to his liking and interests, particularly with regard to young people.[9]

"Well, okay, dear," his mother said. "If that doesn't feel right and you can choose, do it."

"I recall being surprised that he would even ask me," said Kathleen Wessel. It was as though her son had already made up his mind, and just wanted to talk to her about it.[10]

That was how Father Wessel chose to be in Toms River.

When asked some years before by the Diocesan Personnel Office for his parish preferences, Father Wessel demonstrated his willingness to serve wherever he was needed. "No preference," he wrote in 1969, "although I have enjoyed Trenton city very much. No one wants a more difficult time than necessary . . . but if there is a need I'll do my best."[11]

To James Roche, John Wessel's decision reflected a combination of common sense and spirituality. "Because he was selfless in his service as a priest" there was nothing that he wouldn't do for others, asserted Roche, yet John Wessel was also sensible about himself and "was not going to put himself in a spot that he knew would not work. And I ended up giving him credit for being assertive as a man and yet not being a dilettante as a priest."[12]

Father Wessel tried to prepare his friends and parishioners, especially the young people of the CYO, for the day when he would no longer be with them.

Toward the end of the summer, Father gradually began sharing the news of his transfer.

Right before Labor Day, a small group of teenagers and Father Wessel got together and went for ice cream at Buddy Williams, a little drive-in in Lambertville, New Jersey, that was one of their favorite hang-outs.

"Everybody was going away to school and we were together as a group, probably ten of us or so," recalled Barry Anderson—Bonnie Lopez, Cindy Farrell, Jayne Hartley, Maria Rodriguez, Jimmy Egan, Mike Ball, Liz Fadejew, Suzanne Walsh, himself, and a few others. They had wanted to get together one last time before beginning their new ventures in life.

The evening ended in tears, however, for it was then that Father Wessel told them that he, too, was leaving Blessed Sacrament.

"I remember people were pretty upset and disappointed about that," said Cindy Farrell.[13] The youths were dealing with their own emotions about leaving each other and leaving home, and now their friend and mentor, Father Wessel, was leaving, too.[14]

"Father's transfer to Toms River came as a shock and surprise to everyone," recalled another CYO girl. "I think he himself felt very bad about leaving Blessed Sacrament but he knew that it must have been God's will."[15]

Father Wessel put his own emotions aside and tried to reassure everyone that nothing would really change. "This isn't that big a deal," he told them. "We'll still be in touch."[16]

Father Wessel was as kind, compassionate, and empathetic as they come, and his emotions ran deep, but he wasn't the kind of man, or priest, whose emotions spilled over uncontrollably. He did not indulge in public displays of private feelings.[17]

Once, he told a group of girls, tearful and crying at graduation time because they wouldn't see him again, "Don't cry for me, but cry for the people who don't have people to cry for them."[18]

True to character, he was more concerned with helping the kids adjust to his transfer than with his own strong feelings about it.

John Wessel's pastor, Father Eugene Davis, was also being transferred at the same time to St. Alphonsus Church in Hopewell. "It seemed to me he was a little fearful" of his new assignment in Toms River, said Father Davis. The high school would be something entirely new, and he was concerned "that he could handle it."

> I'm quite certain he was very happy where he was [at Blessed Sacrament] and he would like to have stayed there. It was his first move and you're always a little apprehensive. You've gotten used to the people and the people have gotten used to you, and he liked the kids, and the rectory was happy enough, and you don't know what you're going to get into. So I know he would much rather have stayed.[19]

In the fall of 1971, many in the CYO group prepared to leave for college at the same time as Father Wessel was being transferred. One such person was Jayne Hartley, who recalled a conversation with Father around this time.

"Don't be mad at me," Father said to Jayne. "I'm not going to write to you. I'm only writing to the people who really need me." Jayne was very happy and settled at her college, and some of the other young people were not. "Don't feel slighted," he explained, if a mutual friend gets a letter, because she's not happy at school "and I really have to write to her."

The demands on Father Wessel's time were always great, and now he had the added responsibility of a new parish. Jayne understood from that conversation that while Father Wessel was genuinely concerned about everyone, he could only afford to devote special time and attention to those who really and truly needed him.[20]

And indeed, Father did write to the kids who really needed him. His caring and interest made a profound difference in their lives, said a former CYO member:

> An important memory that I have is . . . when I went away to college, I was extremely homesick, and I did write to Father, and have a marvelous letter back from him which basically says "believe in yourself." . . . I drew a lot of strength from that at the time, and really continue to draw strength from that.[21]

It was on Saturday evening, September 18th, at the monthly CYO "Youth Mass"—the Folk Mass in Casey Hall—that Father Wessel officially announced he was leaving Blessed Sacrament.

Father tried to be positive. He had been there for a long time, and had become close to many people, but it was time for him to move on, he said. Their little community had become so tightly knit that it was time for them to open things up with somebody new. Some in the audience even got the impression that Father had sought out his transfer,[22] although this was probably his way of trying to make it easier for them.

Once again, when Father announced that he was going to Toms River, the CYO youths were devastated. Tears flowed.

"We were so heartbroken," Joanne Gillespie recalled. "We thought, What's going to happen to us?"[23]

Father had a strong sense of obedience and he took his vows very seriously. This came through by his example to the young people.[24] He didn't dwell upon his sadness at leaving them—just told them it was his job to go where the Bishop sent him.[25] "The Boss wants me to go," he said. "I have to do this." But he reassured them that "God is going to help us get through it."[26]

"He tried to cheer us up, and we knew that it hurt and bothered him too," said Joanne. Revealing a little of his own struggle to accept the inevitable, he said, "I'm praying over it. I'm praying real hard."[27]

The end of their last Youth Mass became a long goodbye for Father Wessel and the CYO teenagers. At the Sign of Peace, Father gave each person a hug, and a special word, a personal message. This last message was no doubt precious to each young person present, since everyone knew they may never see Father again.[28]

Perhaps no one was more broken-hearted at Father's transfer than Ronald Garrett, the youth for whom he'd become like a father figure. When Father Wessel told Ronald that the Bishop wanted him to go somewhere else, the young man exclaimed, "What do you mean, told you to go somewhere? Can't you tell him to go to hell?"

"No, I can't, Ron," Father said quietly.

"Pop, what are we going to do here without you?" the young man asked.

"You guys will get along," was Father's reply.

He hated to leave, said Ronald. Blessed Sacrament in Trenton was his home, but he knew that he had to go.[29]

Shortly before he left Trenton, Father Wessel was in the basement of the rectory going through his things with Barry Anderson. Father was looking through some old gear, camping equipment mostly, trying to decide what he should take with him. Most things he ended up giving away to Barry. "Here, you can have this. You can have this. You'll need this," he'd say as he handed things to Barry.

A very quick exchange with Father Wessel that day still sticks in Barry's mind. As Father was giving away his camping equipment to Anderson, the young man said, "You seem to be giving away all your material things here." Barry was joking, but half-serious.

And Father said, "Well, I won't need them."

The remark was innocent at the time, but in retrospect, it always struck Barry as odd. Father never explained why he wouldn't be needing his cherished camping gear anymore.

When the parish heard that Father Wessel was to be reassigned, they all wanted to say goodbye. But Father left so fast; it seemed that he told them about it one minute, and the next minute he was gone.[30]

Those who were the recipients of Father Wessel's kindness, however, would not let him go without wishing him well. One such person was Donald Matlack, the steel worker whom Father Wessel had often visited in

Mercer Hospital after his accident, seeing him through his many surgeries and long rehabilitation.

"When I got out of the hospital, I kept in touch with him," said Matlack. Father kept him abreast of the building of the boat and other activities, and then informed him of his transfer to Toms River. Shortly before he left, Donald Matlack went to see Father Wessel at the rectory to say goodbye.

"He was kidding me," recalled Don, who was now able to walk with a cane. Father Wessel met him at the door and said, "Gee, I thought I'd have to come down and carry you up the steps." The two men chatted for a while in Father's office in the rectory.

Father Wessel didn't sit still. He was pacing around the room, "smoking one cigarette after another." Father appeared to be "very concerned about being moved to this new parish in Toms River."

He didn't say what concerned him, but Matlack speculated that it may have been "the size of the parish, compared to where he was," and also that "it must have been very difficult for him to leave. His roots were deep there to a lot of people, and especially to the kids."

The young priest Donald Matlack saw that day was a stark contrast to the relaxed, smiling man who used to come bounding through the door to cheer him when he was in Mercer Hospital.

This time, it was the elder man's turn to cheer the young priest. Watching Father nervously chain-smoking one cigarette after another, Don Matlack reassured him that he didn't have anything to worry about.

"Father, look, when you get there, and you get up on that pulpit, those people will have to look up to you," Matlack told him confidently.[31]

Father Wessel could not leave the young people who had become his close friends over the past six years without one last message. On September 1, 1971, he wrote a letter to his CYO. In this letter, Father Wessel reminded the young people of all that they had learned on Search as they headed off to college, and asked them for prayers for the next Search, which was planned for the coming fall.

The letter was vintage Father John Wessel. He always managed to blend deep spirituality with a little touch of humor to make them laugh.[32] And he wouldn't hesitate to poke fun at himself.

In what was to be his last message to the CYO, he began:

September 1, 1971

Dear brothers and sisters in Jesus,

I know that it's been a long time since you have heard from me, and I suppose that you think I've forgotten you. I haven't! I'm not very pious, but you are in my thoughts like a kid brother I want to see but can't seem to get there. We are united in the Spirit, thank God, and I know that your prayers have gotten me through the craziest summer of my priesthood, e.g., we built a catamaran in the basement of the Church last year and, with many sleepless nights, launched it on Barnegat Bay, June 18. We named it "*Eucharist*" in thanksgiving for its floating. I think Jesus got a little "mad" at that because since, she has been "demasted twice and sunk twice." "Earthly possessions can lead you astray," resounds in my ears every time I think of the time spent on the "thing." When my boss sees me with a long face, he asks, "What happened now?"

I know that with the beginning of school, you are under a certain amount of stress. And, I really feel that some solid prayer is in order. It's been a long time, a lot more than a "boat" can get in the way of the real things that count. When I'm uptight and can't sit still, and the Mass isn't quite enough, the "long, alone, silent and free" walk with Him is the most refreshing and loving thing I can do.

"When you're weary, feeling small, when tears are in your eyes, I'll comfort you, I'm by your side." cf., Lk. 12:22.

Talk and tears are not enough though, to get ourselves straight sometimes. It seems that if we stop sharing with one another, we stop seeing our Jesus. College will be the "body of Christ" for many of you now. You are beautiful when you are sharing. Share our Brother with all you meet. To be poor through sharing is one of the roads to happiness. cf., Lk. 9:57.

"Happy the Man, who wanders with the Lord,
He needs no gold, he wants no fame."

You saw the risen Christ on Search. To keep up with His demands, you must get His energy to love through concentrated, sincere and wholehearted reception of the Eucharist. You can't make it alone. cf., Jn. 6.

I know that we should have had a reunion—but my heart just wasn't in it—but in the real and perfect sense, we share and gain so much from each other in prayer and sacrifice. "You are now in me, remain in my love."

. . .

Pray for the next Search and all your brothers and sisters, *me included.*

With great brotherly affection,
Fr. John P. Wessel[33]

Father John Wessel then packed up all his worldly goods into his old green jalopy and drove off to Toms River, near the Jersey shore, not more than a few miles from the place where the *Eucharist* was launched.

Before he did, however, Father Wessel and Father Davis installed new paneling in Casey Hall, the Blessed Sacrament School auditorium that had been the site of so many memorable CYO Folk Masses Father had celebrated for the youth of the parish. It was also used as a gymnasium, and for basketball games, plays and programs. The paneling had seen its "better days."

"How about we fix up the hall?" John Wessel asked his pastor, who readily agreed. "The two of us paneled the thing where it had been taking a beating," recalled Father Davis. "But he was the one who did most of it and I sort of helped him."[34] It was Father Wessel's last project at Blessed Sacrament.

What were Father Wessel's thoughts as he drove away from Blessed Sacrament? By several accounts, he was nervous and a little fearful about his new assignment. Yet to others, he seemed to be looking forward to the change and ready to tackle the new position. Perhaps his true emotions were a combination of both.

"He looked at Toms River as being a different way of life," said Bill Beitel. He was leaving the city, with its sirens and emergency calls and its never-a-dull-moment pace. St. Joseph's Church had only one hospital under its care, and for Father Wessel, that would be a relief. It was Beitel's impression that he was looking forward to working with the youth of the huge parish high school; at Blessed Sacrament there had been no high school and the young people had to be drawn in.

"He was really eager to get down there," recalled Bill. "He knew it would be a different way of living and a different list of activities."[35]

Some years earlier, Father Wessel was asked by his diocese to evaluate his effectiveness in his present assignment. Of his time at Blessed Sacrament, Father Wessel said:[36]

> Blessed Sacrament has afforded me more experience than I could dream possible in the entire Diocese. I have had experience because of it in education—primary and secondary, adult education; experience in a very specialized sense with delinquent girls, and in a moderate way with the mentally ill and criminally insane. Mercer Hospital was my charge for 3 years and is now my most time consuming project. Youth work through a CYO has been my major accomplishment parochially.
>
> . . .
>
> I feel that I have effectively fulfilled my assignment. I do feel that Blessed Sacrament is an excellent training parish for young priests who are disciplined for professional work within its boundaries.

The only shortcoming Father Wessel noted was that "Blessed Sacrament doesn't afford any time for community involvement." Clearly, he would have liked to have had more time to work with the diverse and racially mixed neighborhood. He then continued:

> I have enjoyed and been somewhat successful in dealing with the youth (14-21). Not in the sense of a "buddy" but in guidance. If I could have my way, and this is almost always impossible, I would like to spend some time (5 years or so) in this specialty.

The new assignment was tailor-made for Father John Wessel, because his greatest aspiration was to continue doing youth work. Secondly, he would have liked to have been a high school chaplain or high school teacher in Religion or guidance.[37]

As the new Associate Pastor at St. Joseph's Church, he would get to do it all.

CHAPTER 27

ST. JOSEPH, TOMS RIVER

The "asides" prior to the arrival of a newly assigned associate were the same at St. Joseph parish as, most likely, they were at any other parish—possibly a bit more so. In the fall of 1971, the priests, nuns, staff and parishioners of St. Joseph were eagerly awaiting the arrival of two new associates, Father John Wessel, from Blessed Sacrament, Trenton, and Father Sean Maguire, newly ordained from Ireland.

There was another new arrival in town. A tormented young man whose troubled life would, before the end of the year, be the cause of sadness in the hearts of many.[1]

On the evening of Friday, September 24th, Father John Wessel arrived at St. Joseph's Rectory on Hooper Avenue, Toms River. Both the pastor, Father Lawrence Donovan, and the other associate priest-in-residence, Father Brendan Gallagher, were having dinner at Citta's Old Time Tavern, a restaurant about a mile away on Route 37, the main highway through Toms River. Mrs. Mary Moser, the housekeeper, told Father Wessel to join them.[2]

Despite any apprehension that Father Wessel may have felt, he was outwardly confident. Brendan Gallagher recalled how at that first meeting with himself and Father Donovan, their new associate "never showed any nervousness—none whatsoever."

At the time, Father Gallagher was CYO Director for Ocean County. Father Wessel held the same position for Mercer County, so both men were acquainted through their work and through monthly Diocesan CYO meetings in Trenton.

As Father Gallagher and Father Donovan were sitting at the table, John Wessel walked in, sat down, and introduced himself. "Don't worry about me," he told them confidently. "I know what to do, and I'll do it." With that, he joined right in and was ready to get to work.[3]

To Father Gallagher, John Wessel "seemed to be very self-sufficient because he came from a parish where he was already a curate for quite some time." He needed no introduction to the parish routine, because "he was well aware of what to do."[4]

The following Sunday, September 26th, Father Wessel celebrated his first Holy Eucharist at St. Joseph Church, and introduced himself to the Toms River congregation.

> Hello, I'm Father Wessel, John Wessel, your new associate. I like people and wish I could say hello to each of you personally, but I know this is impossible. If ever you need me, call the rectory and ask for Father John. You know, I was in the midst of plans for the Youth Program of Mercer County when the Bishop called and said, 'John, I have a new assignment for you'—well, here I am!

These were the words, as memory allows, that the parishioners of St. Joseph's heard from their new associate pastor on that Sunday morning in September.[5]

At St. Joseph in Toms River, Father Wessel continued along the same path he had followed at Blessed Sacrament, and quickly became a part of the parish community.[6] He liked people. He liked youth, and fast became a friend of the students.[7]

Assigned as chaplain of St. Joseph High School, he "changed the whole atmosphere of the school," one student observed. "He brought informality and fun."[8]

"As soon as he got here, he turned this place upside down," a nun commented with approval. "He wasn't flashy. He didn't care whether his shoes were shined—but he got things done."[9]

The unassuming, friendly, deep-thinking young priest, in an unknowing, humble way, represented Christian unity in its truest sense. Soon, Father not only received the respect of his students and parishioners; he also received the respect of the entire Toms River community.[10]

And his fellow priests, his new co-workers? The highest compliment that could be paid is that they considered John Wessel to be "a priest's priest."[11]

Despite his outward enthusiasm and commitment to the duties of his vocation, Father Wessel sorely missed his Blessed Sacrament "family" in those early days in Toms River.

"The men down here are great but it's very lonely not knowing anyone," he confided in a note to Joanne (Wesley) Gillespie shortly after his arrival. "It's going to be a challenge and with all my brothers and sisters to help me I'll make it."[12]

Father Wessel began to get acclimated to the new parish and its people. In addition to the parish church, St. Joseph's encompassed a grammar school, and a high school that drew in students not only from the parish area but from towns all over Ocean County. The Sisters of St. Dominic, who staffed both schools, lived in a convent on parish grounds.

Father Wessel was friendly in a quiet way and got along with everyone, recalled Brendan Gallagher. Father Gallagher's impression was that he was "very easy to talk with" and "very easy to work with," in addition to being "very spiritual" and a "very prayerful, dedicated man." John Wessel was "very conscientious" about his vocation and "tried to follow that as best he could. I think that he kept that in mind at all times," said Gallagher.[13]

Father Wessel developed a good relationship with his pastor, Father Lawrence Donovan, who "loved him like a son."[14]

The silver-haired, gregarious Father Donovan was very outgoing, probably the complete opposite of John Wessel in personality. Father Wessel was on the quieter side. To his new co-workers, he "seemed to think quite a bit. He was never someone that cracked jokes, shook hands, and glad-handed you. He wasn't that type of man," said Brendan Gallagher. If you wanted to speak with him, he was very happy to talk with you, but he didn't go out of his way to start a conversation.

Father Donovan, on the other hand, was very jovial, almost "the life of the party." He liked to make people happy, and loved to crack jokes and make people laugh. Yet, he was also "very conscious of this big undertaking, the parish," recalled Brendan Gallagher. Father Donovan was a builder, having presided over the construction of the parish high school, the ball field, and the cemetery. He seemed to fit in very well with the people of Toms River and was loved by the parishioners, especially the older ones.[15]

According to Sister Julianna Naulty, the grade school principal, the one thing that everyone would remember about Father Donovan over the years was how much he loved the children of the school and the parish.[16]

Father Wessel enjoyed his new pastor very much.[17] In addition to their shared love of young people, they were both "rough diamonds," as one nun put it.[18] "John Wessel was able to deal with him beautifully," recalled Sister Carmella, the high school principal. "They were marvelous together. They were like Bing Crosby and Barry Fitzgerald" in the film, *Going My Way*.

Something about Father Donovan reminded John Wessel of his first pastor, the late Father J. Arthur Hayes.[19] They were both of a similar mold.

Father Donovan for his part had nothing but good things to say about John Wessel.[20]

Father Wessel also enjoyed the company of his fellow priests in the rectory, although he noted a certain amount of "competitiveness" among them.[21] Still, he was a friend to all and never talked ill of anyone. From time to time, Father Wessel became a confidant to the other priests and would try to help them. He could listen and be sympathetic when another priest was having difficulty.[22] Always, he tried to be a peacemaker.

Father Wessel was especially helpful to Father Sean Maguire, the newly ordained Irish priest taking up his first assignment in a strange country.[23]

"There is a uniqueness to my relationship" with John Wessel, recalled Father Maguire. "This was born from the fact that both of us were assigned together to St. Joseph in September, 1971." Father Maguire continued:

> This was my first assignment as a priest and I entered it with unspoken fears: How was I to relate as a priest to the challenges that would confront me? Basically, it was a question of competency. My fears were somewhat compounded due to the fact that I just came from Ireland and had to adjust to a new culture. John responded sympathetically and in many ways exposed me to learning situations. At no time did he present himself as the "expert" with all the canned answers, but shared openly his experiences and his fears. For me, John posed no threat but rather his self-giving and idealism was a maturing agent.
>
> In the rectory, the strength of his own self-identity as a priest was a stabilizing influence. Quiet in disposition, deep in

commitment, he respected his fellow-priests and enjoyed their company. At no time do I remember him as loud or aggressive, although he had strong feelings about many issues. Perhaps the only irritating quality that I remember about him was his periodic silences—when in a bad mood or when upset, he would withdraw into silence and I soon learned to respect this trait.[24]

John Wessel's infectious altruism impressed the young Irish curate. "He taught me more than anyone else that there is no need for competitiveness among priests," said Maguire.[25]

Father Wessel "certainly enjoyed the high school scene," recalled Maryann Beitel. "When he was in Trenton he had so many places he had to be involved with that he wasn't able to." At St. Joseph's, "he enjoyed the fact that he could be in less places and therefore devote a lot more time to this particular love of his, teaching."[26]

One person who was especially pleased with Father Wessel's arrival was St. Joseph High School principal, Sister Carmella V. Di Matteo. This was also her first year at St. Joseph's and her first assignment as a principal. Through her prior teaching experience, she realized what a difference a chaplain could make in a school environment. It was she who had suggested to Father Donovan over the summer that the high school really needed a priest to be assigned as a full-time chaplain, to have an office in the school, and to be available for the students during the day.[27]

Father Donovan was very open to her request. The parish was due for a replacement in September for a priest who was leaving, and he made it known to the Diocesan Personnel Office that he would like someone who could work with the youth of the high school.[28]

"School had started when Father Wessel was assigned," Sister Carmella recalled. The students were already a few weeks into their classes when Father Donovan brought his new associate pastor over to meet the principal in late September. Her first impressions were of a young priest who was very friendly, very quiet, and very serious.

"This is the studious type here," she thought, taking note of the horn-rimmed glasses he wore. But first impressions were misleading. "Well, I think he *may* have been studious," reflected Carmella, but "he had so many wonderful qualities. . . . It was later that I got to know about his tremendously wonderful sense of humor. But my very first impression was . . . of a serious young priest."

Father Wessel came with a reputation. "I had heard through the other priests this is somebody who has done a lot of work with young people and he's leaving a place where young people just adore him," she said.

"I think we both understood his role immediately. I understood his role, because I asked for him," recalled the principal. "He obviously had a great deal of experience with young people, and he knew why he had been requested to be there, so we didn't have a lot of conversation. But I felt very comfortable with him."

Father Wessel had other parish duties in addition to the high school—counseling parishioners, celebrating Masses and funerals, hearing confessions, hospital visits, and emergency calls. "I had been made aware that I couldn't expect to have him there at all hours of the day and night, that he had parish duties," recalled Sister Carmella, but his was such a strong presence that the principal never felt his absence. "I always felt he was there all the time."[29]

Father Wessel had been assigned as the high school's chaplain, but in order to join the Religion department, he had to be interviewed by its head, Sister Nancy Carney. Her most abiding memory of their first meeting was that he "wasn't terribly well turned out for his interview." He looked more like a "scruffy kid that came in off the playground" than a candidate for a teaching position. But he was also "very down-to-earth." He was not about to create an impression or put on airs.

Sister Nancy and Father Wessel got right to work that day, and started to put together a Religion course that they thought would be meaningful for those times. From that day forward, the new high school chaplain was an integral part of the Religion department.[30]

Father Wessel was given a little office in the main corridor of the high school, right near the principal's office. It was a smallish, modest office, with cinder block walls, a desk, phone, and not much else. Father preferred it that way; he didn't want his new colleagues to go overboard with a lot of decorating.[31]

The spiritual program which Father drew up for the student body included a schedule of confessions and monthly Masses, which he usually celebrated in the gym or the cafeteria. He also held monthly "class Masses" for each freshman, sophomore, junior, and senior class.[32]

Father Wessel spent a great deal of time visiting each of the Religion classes. "He was very close to the Religion teachers," recalled Sister Carmella. "He kept an eye on that Religion program." Many fondly recalled how he loved to carry around the polished wooden hatch cover from his boat from Religion class to Religion class and used it as an altar to celebrate Mass for them.[33] "That thing was a devil to carry, 'cause it was heavy," recalled former student Peter Caroselli. But wherever the hatch cover was, that's where he was and that's where the Mass was.[34]

Father was the first to open up a chapel in a little room next to his office. "All of a sudden our senior year the chapel door was open," recalled one high schooler.[35] He would say Mass there some mornings before classes began. Any student who wanted to was free to come into the chapel for Mass. "That chapel originated because of him," recalled Sister Teresa Agnes*, because "he wanted someplace so that he could have devotions with the students."[36]

Father Wessel was the first to introduce the students to the idea of gathering together for "morning prayers" each day at 7:30 a.m., and for after-school Masses every Friday afternoon at 2:15 p.m. Not all students could stay late or come in early, or were inclined to, so participation in these activities was strictly voluntary. As Father diplomatically put it in his invitation—"for all those who wish and can." While no one felt pressured to attend, everyone knew they would always be welcome.[37]

To add to the informality, Father sometimes went out with a group of students for a bite to eat at a local fast-food place after the Friday afternoon Mass. The teenagers thought it was just "neat" that their new young priest would do that with them.[38]

Another of Father Wessel's functions was to be "the legs of the pastor" in the high school. He was available to mediate any problems that arose in the school, to counsel or discipline students, or to meet with parents.[39]

To the students and teachers in the high school, Father John Wessel was like a breath of fresh air. His new colleagues took to him immediately.[40] "He was just fantastic with the kids." "He was a very unusual person." "He came last and everybody else came first." These were typical comments from his co-workers. You never knew what he was doing to help others, recalled a nun, because he was such a private person.[41] "It's almost a consensus of opinion of . . . him as a very quiet man, as a very giving man, and a man who was a friend to everyone."[42]

Father Wessel impressed Sister Julianna Naulty, the grade school principal, with his willingness to help everyone and with his love of poverty. She especially appreciated his assistance at dismissal time as he would help her organize the fifty or so busses that would come onto the playground to pick up the children after school. "He was so genuinely real, and never cared about himself, about what he had, his clothes. He had very little as far as this world's goods, and he said that he didn't want all of that kind of stuff because it was only a burden."[43]

Sister Jorene Cieciuch, the high school music teacher (then known by her religious name, Sister Helen Roberta), remembered Father's "quiet dedication." Both of them had come to St. Joseph's at the same time. "My strong recollection of him was one day I came into the cafeteria, and I was a little discouraged with working with the high school students," she said. "And he was just so kind in listening to me, and very encouraging, saying, 'Stay with it' and 'Don't let this get you down.' And I was very much encouraged by his remarks."

"I had a sense that he was willing to stay with things for the long haul, and not just doing the popular thing to win the students' favor," she added.[44]

Sister Carmella's working relationship with Father Wessel was excellent. "We worked as brother and sister, side by side, under Father Donovan. . . . I was extremely comfortable in confiding in him and sharing with him. I felt that he took a lot of the burden of that school from my shoulders in those first three months."[45]

The principal recalled an early incident in which Father Wessel was very protective of her. It was the occasion of the first PTA meeting of the semester. Sister Carmella was in attendance, as was Father Wessel. "I was the new principal, and I was the speaker and I was very well received by the people," she recalled, "but there was a little flak on the sidelines about who had to get refreshments. All of a sudden, the refreshments became this important item behind the scenes." It appears that the pastor became nervous that the refreshments were not being served fast enough to the nearly five hundred attendees. Although it was really the responsibility of the parents of the PTA, somehow the new principal caught the blame for it.

Father Wessel ran interference between the pastor and the principal. "I remember Father Wessel being very protective of the Sisters and of the faculty at that time. It was just a misunderstanding," said the principal. "I don't remember the words he said, but I just remember being very grateful that he was there."[46]

As fellow priest Sean Maguire observed, John Wessel "would never let anybody trample on you."[47]

While assuming the role of protector, the young priest was always mindful to show great respect for his older pastor. Sister Carmella recalled:

> Father Wessel helped me understand Father Donovan a lot.
> He was very kind to him . . . and I didn't always see that in other
> people. I think that Father Donovan was grossly misunderstood
> by some people, and I think John respected him and he knew
> how to show that respect, and he taught me a lot about a very
> wonderful person. And because of Father Wessel, I was able to
> develop a wonderful friendship with Father Donovan that went
> on for sixteen years.[48]

Father Wessel also worked well with his colleagues in the Religion department. He and Sister Nancy shared similar interests, so "when there was any kind of a discussion, it was almost no discussion," she said, "because we kind of agreed on most of the stuff that he was willing to try. I was just so glad to have a real live chaplain, especially one who wanted to provide liturgies which would be meaningful for the kids."[49]

And how did the students feel about Father Wessel? The comment of one senior girl, Josetta Cascione Burchardt, was typical:

> I liked him right away. I thought he was very honest. . . .
> He was just so casual, friendly, not trying to be cool. He just
> was himself—calm, casual, and relaxed—yet holy and respectful.
> He kind of understood what we were going through. I think
> that's what attracted a lot of people to him; they respected him
> as a priest, and I did too, yet there was almost a "touchability"
> with him, like you could get emotionally close to him and not
> be afraid, or open up and he wouldn't hurt you.[50]

Al Kedz was a parishioner of St. Joseph's Church. As the proprietor of Kedz Funeral Home, then the only Catholic funeral parlor in Toms River, he got to know Father Wessel personally through the funerals that they worked on together. "The man had a magnetism about him," Kedz recalled. "You met him once and you thought you knew him forever." Kedz observed in the priest's demeanor that he "took each family personally. It just wasn't another funeral for him. He was a true priest."[51] But what really impressed

Al Kedz was how much the youths loved Father Wessel. "He was just like a pied piper with kids," recalled Kedz. "You always saw him taking kids somewhere."

The Kedz Funeral Home was located on Hooper Avenue, and Al often saw Father Wessel flying by on Hooper Avenue in his new station wagon, loaded up with kids hanging out of every available window, and piled high with camping equipment. The sight reminded him of one of those hilarious cartoons.

Father Wessel immediately made the rounds of classrooms and introduced himself to the students. But it wouldn't do for him to just sit back and wait for the young people to come to morning prayers, or to drop by to see him in his office. He reached out to connect with them in the way he knew best—by getting a group of a half dozen or so kids together, along with an adult chaperon, for overnight camping trips in the early fall.

The first camping trip was planned to nearby Turkey Swamp Park on Columbus Day weekend, 1971. Father Wessel was supposed to take the group camping, but at the last minute he was unable to go and asked Father Sean Maguire to go in his place.[52] (One cannot help but wonder if this was Father Wessel's way of introducing the young Irish curate to "learning situations.")

Another camping trip later in the fall was to a campground called Pine Woods in Lebanon State Forest, off Route 70, with Father Wessel, another faculty member, and a number of young people. It was very cold that night, and the group spent most of the night shivering and trying to keep warm. The trip didn't have any religious overtones, recalled one of the campers, but it was just something fun and different for the young people to do. It was Father Wessel's way of "trying to get started with us."[53] Through such simple activities, Father got to know the students personally and established a rapport with them.

Father Wessel enthusiastically threw himself into the routines and rituals of high school life. He came to the sporting events, principally the football and basketball games. "He was very supportive. If the kids were there, he was there," said student Dawn Flynn Fowler.[54]

At the football games, Father would usually stand by the fence at one end of the ball field so he could watch the action. People would begin to walk over to say hello to him, and next thing you know, there would be a crowd at the fence. Father was like a "magnet" who drew people to him.

"I got the impression that he liked talking to the young people who would come up to him," recalled Josetta C. Burchardt. "He was really listening, and really seemed to enjoy being with them and they with him."[55]

Father got involved with the athletics department, befriending both the sports coaches and the student athletes. He would come down to the football practices, and after the football games he'd pop into the locker room and joke around with the guys like any "average Joe."[56]

"Once in a while," recalled Father Gallagher, "we'd go over in the ball field and throw [a football] with some of the male teachers from the high school. He liked doing that and he used to fit in very nicely with them."[57]

It was through simple gestures like these that Father Wessel soon earned the respect and affection of his new parish, students and teachers alike.

CHAPTER 28

THE LAST SEARCH

At the time of his transfer from Blessed Sacrament, Father Wessel had been planning to hold a third Search for Christian Maturity weekend in the fall of 1971, so he continued as planned but simply moved his planning headquarters to St. Joseph, Toms River.[1]

He asked a senior girl named Mary, a CYO leader at St. Joseph's High School who had attended a prior Search retreat, to select those among her classmates whom she thought would be good candidates to go on Search. She gave Father a list of names, and encouraged her friends to go and experience it also.[2]

Around the first week in October, the names of about twenty seniors were called over the high school loudspeaker to report to the principal's office. Most of the kids figured that they had all done something wrong. They sat nervously, looking at each other and wondering what was going on, until Father Wessel came in.

"He told us about a program called Search," recalled one of the students. "I don't remember all of what he told us, just the date and time and what we should bring, and that we would be in the same situation with about thirty kids. What I do remember is that he was very secretive about the whole thing, and he said that it would be rough and we would have to be strong."

The kids had no idea what Search was all about. Some thought it was a survival course in the mountains and suggested, "Hey, maybe they're gonna drop us out of a helicopter!" Father gave them as much information about Search as he could (for part of the program's success was not revealing too much in advance), but he did tell them that he had called them there because they were all leaders in their own way. The Search weekend was October 22-24, and each youth was given some time to decide if he or she wanted to go.[3]

"Well, I'd like to go but the Toms River game is that Friday night," someone said. The football game between St. Joseph's and Toms River North was a longstanding high school rivalry in town. That, plus the weekend parties, would be hard for the students to pass up.

One young girl, a cheerleader named Beverly, recalled walking back to Religion class that day with a heavy heart, struggling to decide whether to forego the football game that weekend to go on this unknown Search with Father Wessel. Missing a football game would also mean she might have to give up cheerleading, and all that went with being a part of that elite group. The young people had to consider what was more important to them, but even just doing so was the beginning of their own personal "search for Christian maturity."[4]

In the end, only six seniors accepted Father's invitation to the Search weekend—among them, the young cheerleader Beverly, who later said that "if there was ever one decision I was glad I made, it was to go." For most of them, it would be an experience and a weekend that would change their lives.[5]

Before the Search weekend, Father Wessel returned to Blessed Sacrament in Trenton. The people of the parish, taken by surprise at his sudden departure, quickly organized a "goodbye party" to honor him and Father Eugene Davis on Sunday afternoon, October 17th. Father Joseph C. Shenrock, Blessed Sacrament's new pastor, invited all the parishioners and friends of Fathers Davis and Wessel to the party in Casey Hall from 3 to 7 p.m.[6]

Father Wessel approached the specter of his goodbye party with mixed emotions. He was undoubtedly appreciative of the love of his former parishioners and their efforts to honor him. Yet, humble and self-effacing by nature, Father Wessel "hated any fuss made over him" and, for this reason, he "just dreaded the goodbye party." "If only I could get in the car and drive away, and that's it—and not look back," he told his sister wistfully. Of course, the parishioners would have none of that.[7]

It seemed as if the entire Blessed Sacrament parish—teenagers, parents, families, young and old, sisters and priests—turned out for the occasion. Even Father Wessel's family was there. It was quite a huge gathering; so many people, in fact, that it was hard to get close to the guests of honor or to say more than a few words. Fathers Davis and Wessel were brought up onto the stage, and presentations were made to them by the parish trustees, James J. Moonan and Peter P. Walsh. They tried to make it humorous. Father Wessel was laughing along with them, yet he was also very touched by the outpouring of genuine love for him and appreciation of his work from his former parishioners.[8]

Deeply moved and close to tears, Father Wessel tried to downplay it and reassured his friends, "I'm not that far away, and my door is always open."[9]

With the money he received from his well-wishers, Father Wessel decided to purchase a new car to replace the old clunker he'd been driving. He wanted a station wagon, specifically so that he could "haul kids around." The brand new, beige, four-door 1971 Chevrolet station wagon that he bought also had a pull on the back to tow the *Eucharist*, and he was thrilled to take his new station wagon to Toms River.[10]

"It was really nice and he appreciated it," recalled Wes Ritterbusch of the goodbye party. The two men had a chance to speak after the affair was over. Father Wessel was concerned that the youth ministry continue, and he encouraged Wes to keep the Blessed Sacrament CYO and its activities alive. "Don't let things die off here," he implored. "Keep them going." He knew that whoever would replace him might not be as active in the CYO as he had been, and he felt bad about that. But he was also very realistic. He knew that he had to move on. "I've got things I have to do," he told Wes. "I've got to get on with it. This is what they want."[11]

Father Wessel liked his work in Toms River, and mentioned to his friend that in some respects it was "totally different" from anything he had done before. "But I'm spoiled," he said, "because it's all new people and I'm used to knowing everybody." While Father Wessel would always have a special place in his heart for his first parish, he also liked the idea of having the opportunity for a renewal of his ministry—to try new things with a new group of people and to be able to help more people.[12]

Another who was present at the goodbye party was Blessed Sacrament parishioner Edward C. Fagan:

At that time, or just previous to that time, I had lost my job. The division of RCA that I was with closed, and Father Wessel had been very worried about me . . . At the party he sought me out to ask me, "How are things going?" and said that he was remembering me in his prayers, which I just thought was absolutely wonderful. Here it was his day, coming back and taking all of his credits, but yet taking the time to remember me. And his sincere concern! That stayed with me really forever, that he was so concerned.[13]

One other person who well remembered the goodbye party was Dr. Julio Del Castillo, the Trenton psychiatrist who had befriended Father Wessel at Blessed Sacrament, and who gently advised the young priest not to take so many risks with the mentally ill and to "stop playing psychiatrist." Dr. Del Castillo, his wife and children were among the many parishioners present in Casey Hall that day. There were so many people around Father Wessel, recalled the psychiatrist. And then, the young priest saw his friend Julio and made his way over to him through the crowd.

Father Wessel warmly embraced the doctor. "Julio," he said, mindful of his friend's advice, "I will not play psychiatrist anymore. That I promise you. From now on, I won't be a psychiatrist."[14]

He was crying, but out of happiness, recalled Julio Del Castillo. It was very emotional for him to be back, and the demonstration of love from the people was very touching. "He was very happy that day."

Father Wessel returned to Toms River and put the finishing touches on his plans for the Search weekend.

He had a habit of working in an unlikely place in the rectory, which the other priests found interesting and somewhat unusual. "He liked to work in the kitchen area of the rectory, especially when he was getting ready for the Search retreat," recalled Brendan Gallagher. "And he'd get all his mail there, and he'd stuff his envelopes, and he'd put on his coffee." Indeed, that is how the custom of "coffee-and-tea time" after school began. If anyone wanted a cup of coffee or tea, Father would put the water on for them and have his coffee with them in the kitchen.[15] After a while, it became a habit to get together afternoons for coffee or tea in the kitchen at the end of the school day.

Another interesting habit the priests noticed about their new associate: While he worked in the kitchen, Father Wessel always kept a little blue jar of Vicks VapoRub with him. Like St. Paul himself, John Wessel had his own real life "thorn in the side." He had eczema on his arms and it drove him crazy.

"I remember asking him one time, 'What's all over your arm?'" recalled Joanne Gillespie. A skin problem. "Aw, it's a pain in the neck, Joe," Father replied. Eczema was quite a painful skin condition, but "you'd never hear it from him."[16] Father Wessel would rub the strong-smelling menthol gel on his elbows to keep them moist while he worked.[17]

The two or three weeks wait "seemed like a year" to the kids who were going on Search. "Father was great at keeping secrets," recalled Beverly Choltco Devlin, one of the "Searchers." He still didn't tell them too much about the weekend.[18]

Shortly before the weekend, Father Wessel typed a short note to the high school students, asking them to pray for their classmates who were going on Search. He suggested that their friends send them "Palanca letters"—a term that meant giving people a phone call or a letter to let them know you'll be praying for them while they're on retreat. "Remember each other at least in your prayers," he asked.[19]

Friday, October 22nd, had finally arrived. The night before, Father Wessel attended his first meeting of the Parish Council, where he was introduced as their new Associate Pastor and high school Chaplain. After school on Friday, seven youths from St. Joseph's (six Search candidates and the CYO girl, Mary) together with Father Wessel drove to Trenton. They stopped at the CYO headquarters on Broad Street to join with the rest of the Searchers from other parishes in the diocese. The CYO headquarters in Trenton was a strange building: Once an old movie theater, its interior decor was dark mahogany wood and beveled glass. A movie marquee still stood out front on Broad Street announcing "CYO"—as if that were the feature film playing that evening.

"We had heard so much about it, the CYO, because Father Wessel was always telling us about what the group in Trenton had done," recalled Jill Viggiano Mueller. The kids from Toms River were excited to finally see the place and meet the people that Father had talked about so much, yet were somewhat taken aback at first by the dark, dingy interior.

Many more kids and several priests were assembled at the CYO headquarters. Father Wessel, the spiritual director of the retreat, greeted everyone and made some opening remarks before they all headed off for the Poconos by bus. He told everyone to just "put away your watches" and forget about time over the weekend. And in deference to the realities of the times, he asked, "If anybody's got drugs, just flush 'em down the toilet here, please."

For the third Search, Father had found a new site in the Poconos—the Onawa Lodge in the little town of Mountainhome, Pennsylvania. It was dark by the time the group arrived at the Lodge. Everyone gathered in a large meeting hall before breaking down into tables of smaller groups of six.

The St. Joseph's students were a close-knit group at first, and tended to keep to themselves—all the other kids seemed to know each other. They also wanted to hold close to Father Wessel, but he gently separated himself from them and said, "You have to meet everybody else. You have to mingle."[20]

"Father Wessel floated around among all the groups. He didn't want to be exclusive to us," recalled Ed Staunton. Father emphasized that "there was no exclusivity here" and "we're all here for one reason."[21] Actually, they didn't see that much of Father Wessel throughout the whole weekend. Most of the talks and workshop exercises were conducted by the young adults themselves, and Father stayed mainly in the background.[22]

One other early impression of the weekend: When the group arrived Friday night and gathered in the meeting hall, there was an energy level in the room that was palpable and powerful. The young people could sense that something special was happening and was being experienced by all at the same time. They didn't realize it yet, but it was the work of the Holy Spirit.[23]

The individual's Search for Christian Maturity gradually unfolded over the three-day weekend. As before, the program encouraged deep and earnest introspection. The concentrated weekend gave them a chance to discover who they were, what their faith was all about, what they believed, and what they had to offer the Body of Christ.

The message of Search, as Peter Caroselli expressed it, was that "you're no longer kids now; you're adults. And along with being an adult comes a certain kind of responsibility. You need to be spiritually mature." Everything they learned and experienced over the weekend challenged them "to make choices and to think" about their faith, which was a new concept for many.[24]

The spiritual aspect, they realized, was growing almost from the time they left for the Poconos. The awareness of Christ gradually deepened throughout the weekend, as they participated in workshops and exercises, and even more so when they talked with each other. That was when the real growth happened, in deeply personal interactions among themselves, intimately sharing their faith and what they were experiencing. "That's when I realized that the workshops were a means to an end," said Ed Staunton. The real spiritual growth occurred "when we talked among ourselves."[25]

Nobody slept very well that weekend. They were all excited and anxious to share the experience with their newfound friends. John Gummere from Blessed Sacrament recalled "staying up till three o'clock in the morning" that first night "with a few other kids, people I didn't know before really . . . just getting to know each other and playing music and just chatting."[26]

"We brought sleeping bags, and I don't think they ever even got unrolled," said Beverly C. Devlin.[27]

It was on this Search that Father Wessel first spoke to a Trenton youth named Joe Parnell late at night during confession about having a relationship with Jesus Christ and knowing God in his life. It was on this Search that Father Wessel told all the young Searchers to "Say yes to Jesus."[28]

Father (later Monsignor) Francis Kolby* was one of the priests on that weekend with John Wessel. He had become involved in the Search program because he was stationed at several Trenton high schools and was active in youth ministry.

Monsignor Kolby recalled his fellow priest, John Wessel, was "a down-to-earth person, a holy man. He spoke of the Gospel, but was very much *with* the kids. He would endear himself to every youngster and be concerned about them."

On that third Search, Father Kolby vividly recalled the two of them—John Wessel and himself—hearing confessions around a lake at midnight in the Poconos. It was a chilly night, and one youth came out in the cold to bring Father Wessel a cup of coffee while he was still saying confessions. It greatly impressed Father Kolby that the kids were so thoughtful of Father Wessel and treated him with so much love.[29]

Another priest on this Search weekend was Father Terence McAlinden, who succeeded Monsignor Leonard Toomey as Diocesan CYO Director in 1971. He worked with John Wessel only briefly, but knew that he had a very special gift with young people. Watching Father Wessel in his rugged hiking boots, standing on a hill addressing the kids that weekend, he recalled thinking to himself, "He looks like Jesus."[30]

The Mass and closing ceremony on Sunday was, for the young teens, the culmination of their personal encounter with the Risen Christ in the Poconos. It signified the beginning of a mature spirituality, marked by a deeper relationship with Jesus and a deeper knowledge and commitment to their faith.

Father Wessel, together with the other priests, celebrated the last Mass on Sunday at the conclusion of Search. Before Mass, Father Wessel asked each teenager to write down something that was of great concern to them on a piece of paper and put it into a pot. He picked out a few notes and read them aloud and that became the basis for his sermon.

The Mass was memorable for another reason. Father always encouraged kids to use whatever talent (or lack thereof) God gave them, and he invited any young person with a guitar to come and play it at Mass. For some, it was the first time that they had the courage to play the guitar in front of their peers. The kids from St. Joseph's quickly learned all the catchy folk songs that Father used on Search—*Come Before the Table, We Are One in the Spirit, The Love Round*, and others—and brought them back to their own school liturgies.

As the weekend drew to a close, Father Wessel, as he had done on past Searches, gave each young person mementos of the weekend—a silver Search cross and a small blue pocket New Testament, the Good News Bible.

Father selected a certain quote from Scripture and wrote a personal message in each teenager's Bible. For Beverly Choltco, he chose this verse:

> "I thank my God for you all every time I think of you. And every time I pray for you, I pray with joy because of the way in which you have helped me in the work of the gospel from the very first day until now. And so I am sure of this, that God who began this good work in you will carry it on until it is finished in the days of Christ Jesus." (Philippians 1:3-6)

"Little sister," he wrote—for Father always referred to the young people as his "brothers and sisters"—"Much love, Beve. I will pray for you always because you will need it. You have a beautiful soul. Father Wessel."

Beverly reflected on why Father Wessel selected that particular Scripture verse:

Search, especially, and Father in general just really reaffirmed . . . the importance of the individual, and how they *could* help in Christ. I felt that he was saying that to us—"thank you for helping me spread the Gospel" . . . because that's exactly what that particular passage says. And I said, "Oh, that's a nice passage" when I read it, but it doesn't really sink in until you look at it in retrospect. Spreading the Gospel was what Jesus wanted Father Wessel to do, and I think that's why he *was* a friend to us, because he knew that we all had that potential, and he never saw his potential as any greater than any of ours.[31]

For one girl from St. Joseph's, there was a bit of a disappointment in an otherwise perfect weekend. Father Wessel did not get to write a personal message in her New Testament and give her a Scripture verse at the conclusion of Search. But Father made a promise to Jill Viggiano that he would give her a verse of her very own when they got back to Toms River. He wouldn't forget.[32]

Jayne Hartley, one of the "graduates" from the Blessed Sacrament CYO, returned from college to help Father Wessel as a youth counselor on the third Search. She wrote:

The Search was a good one but the final mood was a little less festive than the previous weekends. Father had told me that he himself had not felt as "high" following that last Search as he had following the previous two. There was a mood of determination to do better. I often think of that lack of much emotional "high" as a foreshadowing of sorts of things to come.[33]

Barry Anderson, another youth counselor on the third Search, also recalled that Father Wessel expressed some concern at the end of the weekend about maintaining the same level of effectiveness of the program. The Search weekends had been such an outstanding success, and so much was being gained from them, that Father didn't want anything to be lost in future Searches.[34]

If Father's last Search was not everything that he hoped or wished it to be, it was not apparent to the youths from St. Joseph's who had experienced

Search for the first time, not to mention their parents and teachers. The kids came back to St. Joseph's "raving about the experience."[35]

It was "the weekend my life changed. My whole life was pre-Search, and now post-Search," was how one young man described it.[36]

In the words of another student, Father Wessel, and Search in particular, "made me feel as if I was a special person." He helped me overcome a lack of self-confidence and self-esteem. Father showed us that there was forgiveness for the mistakes of the past and gave us "a fresh start in life" at a time when it was most needed.[37]

The Search weekend "seemed to be a big success" to Father Brendan Gallagher. "The students came back and were really changed in reference to their families. . . . And Father Wessel was strictly responsible for all that." The parents of several students even remarked to Gallagher what a big change in attitude they saw in their children after they'd come back from the retreat, and what a difference it had made in their children's lives.[38]

How is it that a weekend in the Poconos can "change one's life"? How does one explain an encounter with the Lord Jesus Christ?

As strange as it sounds, Father Wessel's exhortation to "Say yes to Jesus" was a novel concept for many of the high school students, even those in Catholic schools. But it was the basis of a mature adult Catholicism.

For students who attended Catholic school because of their parents' wishes, and not out of strong personal conviction and vibrant living faith, it was possible to "go through the motions" and not even think very much about what they believed and why. This was particularly so if the young person did not see their Catholic faith being practiced and lived out every day in the home. By the time they got to high school, a few rebellious students had all but rejected their faith entirely.

It was also a rebellious age in the '60s and '70s. There was a strong "anti-establishment" feeling in American society, especially among the youth. The term "generation gap" came into vogue to describe the gulf between the values of parents and their children. To some young people, the traditional Church was just another "establishment institution" and its leaders and teachers, the priests and nuns, just more "authority figures" for the young person to rebel against during the angst of teenage years. Rejecting the Church of their Baptism became a form of displaced rebellion against parents, or society, or a misguided attempt to "find oneself."

As one young man on Search put it, prior to that weekend his faith had been merely theoretical and abstract, as was his knowledge of God Himself. "Religion was just another class, like math or gym or English, that we went to. It wasn't something that we had to take personally. It was just another class that you got a grade for."[39]

Father Wessel and the Search experience changed all that. "He was the first person that introduced Jesus to me as a friend," the young man recalled.[40]

Part of Father Wessel's appeal lay in the fact that he related to the youths as someone who was (and wanted to be) their friend—not as their boss, and not as just another authority figure. "It wasn't like he was one of us, so we respected him because he was older and because he was a priest. But he never used that as his trump card." He earned, rather than forced, their respect and because of this, the youths were open to his message: "I'm your friend, and I've got a friend of mine that I want you to meet. And the friend I'd like you to meet is Jesus."

Father Wessel didn't talk about Jesus "as if you were reading about Him from a book," recalled the Searcher. His knowledge of the Lord was based on intimate friendship. "It was the first time that I ever realized that Jesus was a man, and that Jesus was basically the same age as Father Wessel," explained the Searcher. "And it had never occurred to me to accept Jesus as a man or as a friend that you could talk to" or "that He had something personal to say to me. And it was [on] that Search [weekend] that it finally sank in that Father Wessel was bringing us there to introduce us to his friend, Jesus." By taking the students physically away from their normal, everyday surroundings to another place, high up in the mountains, with other young people just like themselves, it was easier for the students to accept and be open to this encounter with Christ than in the usual confines of school, church, or home.[41]

For most after that weekend, their religion became more personal. One girl said, "I think that the gift that I remember Father Wessel giving me is that he made me realize this was a religion that I could make my own. It wasn't just ritual, and answers in books. It was something that I could take inside and . . . find what I needed. It was personal." Because the young people now knew the Lord Jesus and His love and caring for them, the outward expressions of faith really came to life. Through it, they became close to Jesus. And Jesus would meet their needs.[42]

At the end of Search, many of the young people became deeply concerned about having to go back into "the real world" and keep alive the faith that they had nurtured over the weekend. How were they going to share the experience with people who hadn't been there—classmates who'd opted to go to the football game instead—or even parents for whom religion meant a ritualistic observance?

Our faith "was like this wonderful new gift and we didn't want to take it out into the open," recalled Jill. The students worried that they would be misunderstood, laughed at, or thought of as fools or "Jesus freaks." There was a sense of fear and confusion at the retreat's end about having to share so intimate an experience with people that they didn't think would be able to understand.[43]

Father gave them his talk about "coming down off the mountaintop." "Your faith doesn't grow on the mountain," he said. "You have to bring it down into the valley and that's when it really will grow."

"Oh, but how are we going to do this?" they asked him. Father kept referring them to the Acts of the Apostles.

"If you read the Acts of the Apostles," he said, "you'll see. You'll get the courage. And the Holy Spirit will help you do this. You're not going to do it alone."[44]

Some St. Joseph's students recall discussing with Father Wessel their anxieties about sharing the retreat experience with others. He advised them to "be in control of it. It's an amazing power that you don't really have total control of yet," he told them, referring to the power of the Holy Spirit. "Don't let it get out of hand with your enthusiasm, and don't blow people away with it."[45]

In response to the students' concerns, Father Wessel wrote a post-Search letter addressed to the "student body of good will." It was almost a plea for understanding for the kids who went away on Search. He asked the student body to listen to them, and not to laugh at them. He reminded the student body that God speaks through them.

Father wrote, in part:

> The Search week-end for Christian Maturity . . . is an
> attempt to put the Gospel of Jesus the Christ into action as it
> literally exists, and to come to an awareness of things "spooky,"
> about the power of Jesus in us, the Eucharist, Penance, prayer,

and Scripture. The effect is spooky—almost unbelievable. The kids that return to St. Joseph's are changed. Just to look at them you know something is "wrong" or "right" with them. They feel extremely close to you, their classmates and schoolmates, but they don't quite know how to express it.

I write this embarrassing note to those of "good will" for your help for these my brothers and sisters in Jesus. They have fears as I do at times that what we say will be misunderstood and hurt rather than help those we are concerned about.[46]

"I think that letter was as much for us," the Searchers, "as it was for the student body," reflected Ed Staunton.[47]

In order to carry on the Search experience and nurture their faith and newfound sense of community, the students who had been on the retreat decided to meet each morning with Father for prayers before the school day.[48] Many had never attended morning prayers before that weekend, but now, as a result of the retreat, the spiritual life of the school had been turned up a notch.

The site for morning prayers was moved to the "senior lounge" on the third floor, and as time went on, more and more kids started drifting in. This was due, in no small measure, to Father's "advertising." Every chance he got, he reminded the students that they were welcome to come to morning prayers and Masses.

Morning prayers were very simple. The students sat in a semicircle of folding chairs, or sometimes on the carpeted floor. Father would be in the middle, wearing one of those heavy pullover sweaters that he loved so much over his black priests' garb, and would lead the students in prayer.[49] His "prayers" were different than many had ever heard before: He would just talk to the Lord in a very familiar and intimate way. Anyone was free to also pray aloud.

Sometimes Father read from the same Good News Bible that he had given the students on Search, selecting a different reading for each day. At times, a few boys and girls brought their guitars and played them as the students sang contemporary hymns and folk songs. Petitions and prayers were offered for individual intentions. And then, Father and the students would always say, or sing, his favorite prayer which he taught them, the *Prayer of St. Francis.*[50]

Father's whole focus was "to get the students to be more spiritual—without flaunting, without feeling different, without feeling better than anyone else," observed Sister Teresa Agnes. His example gave them "a greater depth to life" and helped them to become more Christ-like.[51]

CHAPTER 29

FATHER JOHN, OUR FRIEND

To the high school students, Father Wessel was "an innovator." Nowhere was that more apparent than in his Eucharistic liturgies. He made the Masses more personal and meaningful to the students than they had ever before experienced.

Father held Mass in places like a cafeteria or a classroom, which was unheard of at the time. "He basically showed you that Mass didn't have to be in a church. You could hold Mass anywhere with a group of people" and it didn't have to be strict or rigid, noted former student John Menter.

Once, Father Wessel was saying Mass for the grade school and needed someone to be a lector. John Menter was nearby. "I remember he just grabbed me and he said, 'Here, you be the lector.' I was never a lector in my life!"

John was supposed to come in at different parts of the Mass with various Scripture readings, but became confused by the format which was different from their high school Masses. While standing at the lectern on the altar trying to read the Scripture, John realized that he made a big mistake, and blurted out, "Oh God, I blew this one, Father!" The nuns in the front row were getting aggravated, and the kids were laughing. He looked over at Father Wessel on the altar.

Father just started laughing and shook his head. To Father, it didn't matter that the youth had made a mistake. It was almost as if he was saying, "Just be yourself, John."

"But," John added, "that was the last time I was pulled out of the blue to be a lector at a grade school Mass!"[1]

In the early 1970s, it was the age of banners and folk music. Father Wessel introduced the idea of having the students make banners with spiritual themes and Scripture verses for the liturgies.[2]

As he had done at Blessed Sacrament, Father incorporated contemporary readings and music—played by the students on guitars—into the youth Masses instead of the traditional organ music and hymns that they were accustomed to.

He used contemporary Christian folk songs, as well as popular music—*The Fool on The Hill,* by the Beatles, *Bridge Over Troubled Water,* by Simon and Garfunkel, and *Michael Row The Boat* and *Suzanne Take Me With You,* by Leonard Cohen—just to name a few. He had the ability, recalled Sister Nancy, "to pull something meaningful" out of the folk music that was popular around that time.[3] The *Prayer of St. Francis* was always the Communion antiphon, or meditation after Communion.[4]

As always, Father encouraged those with "crow's voices" to sing out. "God gives you many talents, and singing is one of them, whether it's a good voice or a bad voice," he told them. One of Father's favorite sayings was "Make a joyful noise." "I remember him encouraging even those with squeaky voices," recalled student Dawn Flynn Fowler. "That's a joyful noise, so go ahead and make it," he'd say.[5]

"His Masses I enjoyed. He was one of the first priests I ever met who got you involved in Mass," explained John Menter. Father Wessel enthusiastically adopted the liturgical changes, already approved by the Church, into his high school Masses. The students brought up the Eucharistic gifts, and other personal "gifts," during the Offertory. They received the Holy Communion under both species of bread and wine.

Father brought "individuality into it" and "he let you express yourself the way you wanted to," Menter recalled. He showed people that worship didn't have to be rigid and could be flexible.[6]

Still, Father lost none of the sacredness of the Mass. "I loved the way he said Mass—very reverently, very holy," Josetta C. Burchardt recalled.[7]

Father had a favorite prayer that he would always say reverently after the Consecration: "Yes to you, my Lord. Yes to me, my Lord. Yes to my brothers free, my Lord."[8]

And when they recited the Our Father, "he would ask everyone to join hands and form a unity bond. And this bond . . . was, as he said, our spiritual link. In that way, we were all not only linked to each other, but linked to those that went before us, those that [will come] behind us, and our spiritual Father," said a student.[9]

His Masses "were different, they were definitely different," explained another, who summed Father Wessel's effect in this way:

> He kind of related to the young people and gave them an opportunity to enjoy the Mass more. Matter of fact, I remember just not liking Mass until . . . he came and . . . started to change things around a little bit and get you more involved.[10]

When the group of seven students returned from Search, they were amazed that, despite their fears, many of their classmates really did listen to them share their experiences. People started coming to Father's Masses and morning prayers, and many more started participating and singing at Mass.

"I remember joking with Father Wessel that he had performed a miracle in getting people to sing at Mass," recalled Beverly C. Devlin, because it was something the other teachers had been trying to do for quite a while and hadn't been successful. Before then, the students hadn't really seemed to care.[11]

At the conclusion of the Mass, the students linked arms with one another, as they had done on Search, as they sang the last song, *The Love Round*. "Love, love, love, love. Christians, this is your call . . ." Amazingly, other people started to follow.

Father Wessel's spiritual influence could be felt on the school in other, more subtle ways. There was not much to be happy about in the larger world in those days. A nun recalled how young people seemed tired of hearing about Vietnam and what they ought to be doing for the poor. Most of the high school youths were either getting ready to go off to Vietnam themselves, or were absorbed in their own personal struggles for self-identity and acceptance, or with academic and career matters. They weren't terribly interested in helping others.

Father Wessel came on the scene and began to make a difference. He opened the eyes of the young and helped them to see that they were not the only ones who were in pain: They were part of a larger group of people whom they needed to love and care about.[12]

The high school scene, like most any high school, was an insular society of many different cliques and factions. And teenagers had the capacity to be extremely cruel and rejecting of one another. Even a Catholic high school was not immune from the worst of human nature.

Father Wessel, through his holy life and quiet example, showed the high school youths what it meant to truly live their faith as Catholic Christians. He began to teach them to love and accept one another, and to share with one another, because all were brothers and sisters in Christ. He was a priest who brought people together. As he interacted with all of them, bridging many different circles in the high school, Father was able to unite many different groups of youngsters who may have thought they had nothing in common with one another.

This was dramatically illustrated one day for a young high school girl who was standing on the sidelines at a teen Mass, even though secretly she wanted to be a part of it. Father looked at her, and without even saying a word, he "grabbed a hold of my hand and pulled me up into a circle" of kids. It was as if he was saying to her—"No one's an outsider. If you're here, you're one of us."[13] Father "was a people person, and he made us accept each other for what we were and who we were," was the way that student, Dawn F. Fowler, put it.[14]

It seemed as though there was more togetherness among the high school students because of the presence of the new young priest. There were less factions and divisions. The whole school environment felt more harmonious when Father Wessel was there.

His great concern for young people was that "he wanted them to be good to each other . . . He wanted them to be kind with each other. He wanted them to get the message and he was very firm about that," said Sister Carmella.[15]

In high school, it was always a matter of "trying to impress people all the time and people having to always be cool," recalled a high school girl. "I think that Father Wessel, if he did anything, he taught me that didn't matter." He gave young people the courage to "really resist peer pressure" and to avoid things that were bad for them but that many were experimenting with at the time.[16]

Father's greatest gift was that "he was able to work with all of us at such an impressionable point and give us each a reason to feel confident," added Jill Viggiano Mueller. "Because I don't ever remember being especially confident, but somehow after Search, and after having time with him and having this gift of faith, I felt somehow like, it's okay, I can make it in life. I'm going to do okay."[17]

Father Wessel was truly a "peacemaker"—a channel of the Lord's peace. He sowed love, peace, pardon and hope, just by his very presence.

* * *

One weekend in the early fall, Father Wessel asked a group of high school youths to help him get the *Eucharist* out of the water. The boat had been berthed in the marina in Ship Bottom since the summer. Father hadn't sailed her since that fine mid-September day with Wes Ritterbusch before his transfer. It was time to pull her out of Barnegat Bay before the water froze for the winter.[18]

It was a cold fall day when Father Wessel and a group of guys and girls drove down to Ship Bottom in Peter Caroselli's car.[19] The group took the catamaran out of the water (by this time, a motor had been added to the *Eucharist* which made its removal easier). They put the boat on a trailer and drove to a nearby car wash to scrape the barnacles off the bottom and get her in shape for the next season.

The huge, 18-foot, dual-hulled, homemade catamaran must have been quite a sight to the motorists on line at the car wash—a bunch of rowdy teenagers and one priest scraping barnacles off the boat and rinsing it down with a little hose, all the while laughing as they worked!

"And of course, we were told the history of the boat," said Peter. It was quite obviously homemade, but it was sturdy. Father's pride was evident as he recounted the efforts of his CYO in Trenton in building the boat from scratch and getting her to sail. "He was telling me the number of buoys that they had run down and broken up, and how they broke two masts while learning how to sail it," Peter added.[20]

They took the *Eucharist* back to Father's summer home for the winter, and spent the rest of the day there, playing football in the street and just relaxing at the shore, now hauntingly desolate and quiet. Toward the end of the day, Father Wessel celebrated a special Mass for the young people. He took the hatch cover from the boat and put it on top of a picnic table as his makeshift altar. He also took out a relic in a small case that he had brought with him and put it on the table, because there had to be a relic, a consecrated religious article, on the altar to celebrate Mass. Later, Father and the youths brought the hatch cover back with them to Toms River.[21]

The teens from St. Joseph's never got to sail the boat. It was too late in the season, although they had high hopes of getting a ride on the *Eucharist* someday. To one young girl, the day was but a metaphor for what life is all about: Although they never achieved their objective of getting to sail, there was such joy in the preparation and in the work that they did together.[22]

Anyone who knew Father Wessel realized that "youth" was an important part of his life. A little house next to the rectory, which had fallen into disuse, was put in order as a place for them to meet and hold after-school activities. They had been meeting in the rectory, but Father Wessel's feeling was that the priests should enjoy the privacy of the rectory—and yet, the youths should also be able to have their privacy. The "little white house" was the answer.[23]

The teenagers and Father held some informal parties in the little white house after the football games. The white house was stocked with snacks and soda, and filled with people talking and sharing and laughing in a very warm and friendly atmosphere.[24]

More and more people would come to these little get-togethers. Toward the end of the season, they had a pizza party at which "a cross section of our class showed up," recalled a senior. It wasn't just the little core group of maybe a dozen or so people who were close to Father anymore, but people from many different peer groups in the high school—"basically everybody at one time or another."[25]

Father Wessel invited some of the kids from Blessed Sacrament to come to the parties, too. Father always wanted to bring people together, and must have been delighted to introduce his new friends from Toms River to his old friends from Trenton. He was very good at integrating the two groups, and wanted them to get to know each other and learn from each other.[26]

After the Search weekend, some St. Joseph's students began going to Trenton to attend the monthly CYO Youth Masses. After Father Wessel had left for Toms River, the Folk Masses that he used to celebrate for the young people in Casey Hall were moved to the CYO headquarters on Broad Street. They were held once a month, in a room they referred to as "the Upper Room." Prayer meetings for the youths were held there also.[27]

The new CYO Director of the Trenton diocese, Father Terence McAlinden, was in charge of the Youth Masses in Trenton and was also the principal celebrant. So when Father returned to attend the Youth Masses with the St. Joseph's students, it was as an old friend and a welcome visitor.[28]

Two high school boys, Peter Caroselli and Thomas Callow, most often drove their peers from St. Joseph's down to Trenton. The trip was not without its risks. Once while driving through Yardville, a little town outside of Trenton and home of the Yardville Prison, something suddenly shattered the rear window of Peter's car. They believed it was either a bullet or a gunshot. Everyone in the car was quite shaken up. If someone had been sitting near the window it could have ended tragically, but mercifully, God protected the young people.[29]

The Upper Room was aptly named. The first impression, according to one of the teenagers, was of the story of Christ's Apostles gathered in the Upper Room in Jerusalem. The room was filled with teenagers and young adults from all around Trenton, several young priests, and a few young men who were studying for the priesthood.

Father McAlinden greeted everyone. He "seemed to be so open that you felt immediately he knew you and you knew him," recalled Dawn F. Fowler. "Father Wessel encouraged us to go there, and he would go with us. And then after you were there at least once, it seemed like people just knew you. . . . You were part of this group."[30]

The Masses in the Upper Room were truly charismatic and spirit filled. "It was like this great big secret had been unlocked," said Dawn, "and it was real electrical. If someone started a song, everybody joined in. It didn't have to be planned." And when it was time to ask for prayers, "we would speak out freely of concerns of ours, and pray for different people." It was a level of spontaneity and sincerity that the young people found impressive.[31] After the Communion, a number of teenagers started to speak in tongues, spontaneously praising the Lord.

"I remember being at this Mass and hearing people start to talk in tongues. I had never heard that before," recalled Ed Staunton. Like most people, he was aware that it existed, having read in Scripture about the Apostles speaking in tongues upon the descent of the Holy Spirit at Pentecost, but had never seen or heard it. They were speaking "in a language I didn't understand," he recalled, "but it wasn't a foreign language" that was recognizable. And they were emphatic about it—standing up and raising their arms, animated in praising the Lord in this strange language of the

Holy Spirit. After a few moments it was over. Ed remembered the feeling of amazement, thinking to himself, "Wow! It really does happen! This really does exist!" The Holy Spirit was moving powerfully among those young people gathered in the Upper Room, just as at that first Pentecost in Jerusalem.

Some of the students from St. Joseph's asked Father Wessel about it afterward. He just told them to "read the Acts of the Apostles" to help them understand what had happened.[32]

During the beginning of the twentieth century, the outpouring of the Holy Spirit began sweeping Christian denominations. It was almost as if, in the last century of the second millennium, there was a return to the early Pentecostal experience of the first disciples and early Christians. This movement was greeted with skepticism by some, but fully supported in Scripture by the experience of the Apostles and in the Epistles of Saint Paul.

The Catholic Church accepts and recognizes the "charismatic movement" as the work of the Holy Spirit. In addition to the gift of tongues, believers experienced the gifts of healing, prophecy, teaching, knowledge—those powers which were an integral part of the early experience of Christian communities. But, as Saint Paul observed in 2 Corinthians, the greatest of these gifts is love.

The origins of the charismatic movement in the Roman Catholic Church can be traced most dramatically to a weekend retreat in 1967 with a group of young Catholics from Duquesne University. From there, the charismatic movement quickly spread like a prairie fire among Catholic communities in colleges, churches, religious societies and retreat houses.[33]

Father Wessel seems to have been personally familiar with the charismatic movement long before that CYO Mass in Trenton. While still at Blessed Sacrament, Father Wessel invited a few CYO youths to accompany him to a charismatic prayer meeting one night at a Catholic campus ministry house at Fairleigh Dickinson University.[34] Surely he welcomed the power of the Holy Spirit, as evidenced by the example of his own life and in his many writings to young people about the work of the Holy Spirit.

As he had done at Blessed Sacrament, Father Wessel loved thinking up "projects" for the kids that he and they could do together. Working together was really a means to an end—of bringing teens together to interact with one another, all the while accomplishing some useful objective. One of the tasks that Father and some of the seniors decided to undertake that year was to redo the little chapel next to his office in the high school. It would be the senior class project.[35]

They had great plans for the chapel. It had been very traditional, but the students were going to make it more contemporary. The plan was to use the hatch cover from Father Wessel's boat for the altar. The teenagers were going to make banners for the chapel, and had talked with Father about the kinds of banners they wanted. They had already decided that one of them would be based on the *Prayer of Saint Francis of Assisi*.[36] Benches would be added on both sides of the chapel and covered with blue carpet for the kids to recline.[37]

Father Wessel began to prepare the wooden hatch cover for the altar, and several high school students helped him with the work. After much sanding and many applications of polyethylene shellac and finally, endless polishing, the hatch cover took on a beautiful mahogany hue, which made the rich wood grain stand out. A very fitting altar indeed![38]

As the Christmas holidays were fast approaching, the students looked forward to continuing the work on their chapel project with Father Wessel. They had barely gotten started, but they had great plans, and Father was going to help them. Of course, they had all year to work on it with him, so there was no hurry, or so they thought.[39]

Although work with young people occupied a major part of Father Wessel's time, he still had his full compliment of parish duties to attend to—counseling, visiting the sick and shut-ins, making hospital rounds. Just as he was always there for the youth, he brought the same zeal and dedication to his work with the rest of his parish community.

Little Kerry Ann Murphy was born in Community Memorial Hospital on November 4, 1971. All was not well with the newborn infant, and Father Wessel quickly came to the hospital and baptized her and visited with her mother. The baby lived only a short time. Again, Father Wessel was there to bury the infant and to comfort her parents, Joan and Bill Murphy.

"I think that he was a very saintly man," said Joan Murphy. "And the thing that I can remember about him the most—he had such piercing eyes. He looked at you so intently."

Father Wessel was a great consolation to Joan and Bill Murphy and their other children. After their daughter had died, Father visited the Murphys at their home on several occasions between November and December just to talk to them and make sure they were all right. "We did get very close to him in just that short period of time. . . . He just kept telling me that I had an angel in Heaven and that I should pray to her," Joan recalled.[40]

Father Wessel was an integral part of the high school Religion department, and he and Sister Nancy Carney worked well together. In addition to being head of the department, she taught five sophomore Religion classes; Father Wessel was responsible for some of the junior and senior classes.[41]

Toward the end of November, Father Wessel and Sister Nancy started an evening Scripture class for adults. The course was well received. For one thing, there was a great interest in the subject matter and people seemed hungry to learn, recalled Sister Nancy. An added benefit was that the adult Scripture class was held every Monday night, the same night as "CCD" (the religious instruction for the public school children) so that parents of public high school kids could come with them and have something to do themselves. "Not that we did it specifically for those parents," said Sister Nancy, "but it made it helpful because then they could drive the kids to CCD. There was a method."[42]

The Scripture course went over so well that there were plans in the works for another adult lecture series to begin the following spring.[43]

In early December, Father Wessel drew up outlines for two new Religion courses for high school juniors and seniors. By mid-December, the courses had already been approved, and he and Sister Nancy were looking forward to incorporating them into the curriculum for the semester beginning in January 1972. One class was in Scripture; the other, called "Discovery," was akin to a clinical pastoral education class.[44]

Father Wessel's course outlines, written in his bold script, portrayed his sense of hope for the Religion program and his optimism in the abilities of the students themselves:

"Discovery: Experiments in Religious Experience and Communications"

Purpose: To deepen awareness of religious facts and train students in communication methods.

Text: Mimeo[graphed] text from "Discovery." Mini-course in "Christian Community" by Lyman Coleman.

Time: 2 class periods a week—one experimental; [the] other analysis of & application of experiment.

"Scripture: The New Covenant"

A New Testament study. This course is prepared and mimeographed. Involves an outline of work to be done and an analysis of students' work.

Scope: New Testament from the standpoint of historical development under Spirit of the early Christian Community.

Time: 2 class periods a week.

Text: Good News for Modern Man ($1.00) or paperback edition of Jerusalem Bible (cost unknown).

"I couldn't attempt to think I could correct papers and type material myself," Father Wessel noted in his course outline, indicating that he would need two student helpers, about four hours per week.

Both courses could hold thirty-eight students, he estimated. "The first course needs team leaders until it gets going. With help it doesn't make much difference how large the classes are!"

"The Discovery course would be invaluable for training juniors for senior year leadership projects!" Father Wessel added enthusiastically.

The "Discovery" course was by far the more experimental of the two. It was similar to a clinical course in that the student would be asked to select a life problem that was personal to him and work it through on day one. The second day would consist of the student's analyzing how well he had worked through the problem. There would also be a free period where the student could come and talk to the teacher for feedback and evaluation of the way he analyzed the situation.

"What we were trying to do was to train the kids to analyze their own behavior and why things happened the way they did," said Sister Nancy.

Father Wessel and Sister Nancy had given the course on a trial basis to a few students that fall and it went well. They were looking forward to offering it to all seniors in January.

Through focusing on working through their own life problems, the young people would also gain the tools to be helpful to others, and this would become the basis for service projects. "We were going to try it on seniors, and then eventually make it a course for juniors where they would learn to be service-oriented for their senior year," Sister Nancy recalled.[45]

Another undertaking that Father Wessel hoped to inaugurate that year was to bring a group of students to work in Appalachia, as he had done with the youths in Trenton. Sister Nancy began to look into some service projects in Lexington, Kentucky. Even as she was doing so, Father found other ways to involve the St. Joseph's students in caring for those who were affected by hunger and poverty.

The students in Toms River held bake sales and collected donations of money and clothing. They then brought the proceeds down to Trenton, to the group that worked directly among the poor in Appalachia. Father stressed to the young people that those in Appalachia "live in utter poverty, and they are our next-door neighbors."[46]

It was around the time that Father Wessel came that the parents of the St. Joseph's teenagers really began to be thoroughly involved in the high school, recalled Sister Nancy. The parents were very impressed by the new, young, zealous priest.

"He would come over for PTA meetings. You never saw a priest there for PTA." But Father Wessel would come and just hang around and talk to people. He had an easy way of bantering and joking back and forth with the parents. "They just watched him, and liked what they saw."

One parent later remarked to Sister Nancy, "We really became Christians, Catholic Christians, when Father Wessel was here."[47]

One of Father's attributes was that he was a person of contrast: a rough exterior, yet a gentle interior. Brian Schoeffel of Blessed Sacrament recalled:

> I think that Father Wessel was a man's man, but he certainly had the sensitivity and compassion that most men wished they had. . . . He was a very adventurous guy. He would love to

be out camping, and he was an outdoors type of a person . . .
which is what I would call "a man's man" . . . But at the same
time, he had so many wonderful qualities within himself of
sensitivity, compassion and caring of people. . . . I was impressed
by that.[48]

One of Father Wessel's favorite "hang-outs," apart from his own office,
was down in the basement office of Coach Steven Gepp, affectionately
known as "the Gepper" to his loyal players.[49] Father would sit, chatting and
joking around, with Coach Gepp and any players who happened to wander
in. To the other fellows, the priest was a regular guy and "a man's man."

Father Wessel was the type of guy to whom you could tell a joke and he'd
kid back with you, and "you could talk to him like another person, not like
a demigod," in the words of varsity football player John Menter. "He wasn't
a phony." He was someone that teenage boys could talk to "man-to-man,"
without putting on any airs."[50]

"He could do just about anything, take anything on, but he was a 'no
bullshit' kind of person," Wes Ritterbusch said. He wasn't above stepping
in and saying, "Hey, come on, let's knock this crap off," when it was
needed.[51]

Father wasn't exactly a "spit-and-polish priest," added John Menter:

> I used to kid him when I'd see him in the morning. His
> hair would be messed up and he'd have shaving cream behind
> his ear, and I'd break his chops about that . . . I respected the
> man . . . but he was one of the guys where you could talk to
> him and not worry about something going back to somebody
> else. You could talk to him in confidence.[52]

Conversely, Father also had a good rapport with women and teenage
girls, and could be attuned to their particular problems and feminine
concerns.

One young girl recalled how Father really listened while she poured
out her frustration at being made to wear a dress to a Youth Mass by her
old-fashioned folks, while the rest of her peers all wore blue jeans. He took
her concerns seriously and helped her sort through her feelings about having
to wear something she was uncomfortable with.[53]

Such a scenario might seem a bit unusual for a priest, except that anytime a youth had a problem, however removed it was from his own life experience, Father took it seriously and dealt with it from his gentle, compassionate heart. If it was important to the youth in need, it was important to him.

Another noted quality Father Wessel possessed was that of being forthright and honest. Father's forthrightness was illustrated after one of the Search retreats. A boy and girl came back from the retreat and began spending a great deal of time together. Father Wessel realized that they were misinterpreting the intense Search experience for an emotional attachment. He took each aside separately and talked to them. "You shouldn't spend all your energy with just one person," he said. "Your reason for being on Search was so that you could come back and share the experience with everyone—not just exclusively with each other, but with other people who hadn't been on the weekend."

"My first reaction," said the young man, even though he loved and respected the priest, "was to tell Father that he was way off base." But in time, it became clear to both young people that Father Wessel was correct, and they learned to respect his honesty and perception.[54]

Father John Wessel was probably one of the most authentic persons around. He didn't seem to care what people thought of him, or whether people liked him or not, recalled fellow associate Sean Maguire. He was not out to impress people.[55]

Perhaps it was because he was so "free" of any concern for others' opinions of him that he was able to be so totally forthcoming, honest, and guileless. It enabled him to be more effective as a leader and role model.[56]

To the high school students, Father was not a "preachy" kind of man, not even in his sermons. His spirituality was always very down-to-earth and real, with his "preaching" done primarily through his own example of daily living out his faith. Yet, he brought all the students closer to their faith because he helped them understand what their faith was really all about.[57]

"He was prayerful, but he wasn't a recluse," added Sister Nancy. "He brought his prayer to the marketplace." To Sister Nancy, Father's spirituality was practical. He emphasized the *quality* of it over the multiplication of it.[58]

"I think he had a deep prayer life" and "a close walk with the Lord," Josetta C. Burchardt also observed. "And because of that he was able to give. And he loved Jesus so much, he imitated Him in his life. His sacrificial giving, love and understanding mirrored Christ's life."[59]

Father was also devoted to the Blessed Mother. He always carried his Rosary beads around with him, recalled Sister Nancy.[60]

When a student was writing a paper on the Blessed Virgin Mary, Father lent her one of his seminary textbooks to help with her research. This student's impression was that Father Wessel "had a deep spiritual relationship with Mary, loved her and prayed to her."[61]

The two primary sources of inspiration that Father Wessel seemed to draw upon for his own vocation, apart from Jesus Christ and the Blessed Mother, were Saint Paul and Saint Francis of Assisi. If Saint Francis explains the young priest's inner life, then Saint Paul explains the drive behind his exterior labors.

Saint Paul and John Wessel "seemed to share a very similar philosophy," in the words of Christopher Morley, a Blessed Sacrament youth.[62] Saint Paul was a "no nonsense" kind of a saint: a builder, a worker, a doer, a man of action. Paul also very much believed in the value of the community, and that the solutions to problems were to be found within the community. Saint Paul journeyed all over the ancient world, preaching and establishing new Christian communities everywhere he went, and then nurtured them through his Epistles and letters.

On a much smaller scale, so did Father Wessel.

In his office in the rectory of Blessed Sacrament, recalled Chris Morley, Father hung a map over his desk of The Journeys of Saint Paul, depicting the Saint's travels through Thessalonica and Corinth, Philippi and Ephesus, Asia Minor and Macedonia, Malta and Rome. No doubt, Father looked at the map and found inspiration in Saint Paul's labors and accomplishments.

"His office was a disaster!" added Morley. But Father had too many other important things to do than to worry about the way things looked.

The young priest also brought this Pauline spirituality to his own priesthood. He approached his vocation as a serious job. He studied for it, believed in it, and worked very hard at it. And although he traveled far less than Saint Paul, everywhere he went he built up little Christian communities of young people.

Father Wessel was "a hands-on guy" who could often be found with his sleeves rolled up, pitching in and working side by side with the youth.[63] "He worked as a blue collar priest, although his education and his background do not suggest anything about blue collar," added Chris Morley.

One of Father Wessel's favorite Scripture passages was found in the Epistle from Saint Paul to Timothy—"I have fought the good fight. I have run the race. I have kept the faith" (2 Timothy 4:7).

"He repeated that several times," recalled Morley. "I think he was attracted to the fighter's analogy" and to the whole Pauline ideal that he had a job to do, which was his vocation. And at the end of the day he could truthfully say, like Saint Paul, he had fought the good fight. That passage "summarized his life as a priest," said Morley.[64]

All who knew Father Wessel also knew of his emulation of Saint Francis and the Franciscan way of life. Nowhere is John Wessel's spirituality summarized more succinctly than in the first few simple lines of the *Prayer of Saint Francis of Assisi*. His motto may well have been—"Let me sow love."

"It seemed to me that whenever he had an opportunity, in conversations or in homilies, his big theme . . . was love and care for one another," said Sister Nancy. To love one another meant "looking at the other person and seeing yourself" and realizing that before you can try to tear somebody else apart, you have to look at yourself and see if maybe you are not quite all you should be.[65]

Another of his big themes was "peace within families, and among students," Sister Nancy continued. He was trying to instill the idea that "if you can bring peace to the family then you will have peace in your own life, and vice versa. The family, in turn, can be there for the individual. And I recall that he talked a lot about that whenever he got a chance."

Underneath these messages "was always the value of laughter and humor," said Sister Nancy. But it took people a while to figure out when they were supposed to be serious and when they were supposed to laugh, because Father's sense of humor was dry.

Sister Carmella also recalled Father Wessel's sense of humor. Father liked to laugh, and his laughter was like a "crazy cackle." "He would tease me often, because . . . I was always so serious about everything . . . and he always managed to make me smile. Always."

She recalled one incident in particular:

> He had such a great sense of humor, and when things got a little bit too much, he'd go for his catamaran, and he'd tell me,

"I'm going down to the beach today. I've got to go to the beach. I've got to get out there. It just does me so much good." . . . One day, I was on a tear about something and he stopped me and he said, "You know what you need? You need a walk on the beach." And I turned to him and I said, "Father, you're not young enough and I'm not old enough for you and me to go walking on the beach together!" Well, his laugh was so sweet and so genuine, and it just echoed off the walls of that corridor. I'll never forget that laugh as long as I live.

It was the laugh of "an innocent heart"—of someone who "knew how loved he was by God," said Carmella. "There was that deep happiness in him that comes when you are totally committed to God and when you are so sure of God's love for you."[66]

Father Wessel's sense of humor was also evident when he remarked to Sister Teresa Agnes about some problem students: "We have some nuts around here, but we'll be able to crack them."[67]

Father Wessel was a man of great and heroic charity, yet such a humble, down-to-earth, ordinary person that the true extent of his virtues often remained secret. Part of his charity was continually "giving"—giving in the material sense, by embracing poverty and giving away almost everything that he had; giving in the emotional sense, by demonstrating love, pouring himself out for others, listening to them, caring for them, and affirming their worth as children of God; and giving in the spiritual sense, by always being available to minister to others, to bring them the sacraments and to counsel them spiritually, and by being a person of deep prayer.

Father zealously embraced the virtue of poverty, which was part of the Franciscan spirituality that he chose to adopt as his own. He was unattached to material possessions—indeed, he owned so few material things to begin with.[68]

"All through his life, John had a genuine sense of the virtue of poverty," Monsignor Dubell observed. "He was completely detached from material goods. He found his treasure in nature and people. Nature, because it was wild and free; people, because they were God's special creatures."[69]

"There wasn't a materialistic bone in his body," said Sister Carmella. "He was very, very unattached to possessions. He was very generous. Whatever he had he gave away" to any student in need. Many times, she recalled, he would even buy food and take it to some people who didn't have much.[70]

At least once, in fact, Father even paid the parochial school tuition, anonymously, for a youth whose family he knew was struggling financially.[71]

What made his attitude all the more impressive was that Father Wessel came from a fine background, blessed with material comforts. He could have had any material thing he wanted, but "nothing like that impressed him," Carmella recalled.[72]

The principal wanted to buy him cufflinks for Christmas, but knowing of his dislike for material things, she used to tease him by asking, "How about some cufflinks?" He looked at her, and let out "one of those maniacal laughs" and said, "You think I'd wear one of those shirts?!"

"He was a very rich person in his poverty," observed Sister Teresa Agnes. Father believed that no matter what you had, it was always more than you really needed, and that was the way he lived.[73]

"Most people at the school didn't realize it," added student Tom Callow, "but he had [only] two pairs of shoes. He lived very modestly." What personal money he had was spent on things that would benefit young people—the boat, camping equipment, or the beige station wagon that he had bought simply to drive kids around.[74]

The students couldn't help noticing Father's lack of material possessions. "He had really beat-up shoes," recalled Jill V. Mueller, and when he knelt down in front of the chapel altar, you couldn't miss the holes in the soles of his shoes.[75]

The students kidded Father affectionately about his shoes. "My God," John Menter exclaimed one day after Mass, "you're going to have to put newspaper in those shoes soon! You're like a hobo priest here."[76]

And somehow, we doubt that Father would have minded being dubbed "the hobo priest."

Another aspect of Father John Wessel's charity was the way in which he "gave of himself" to others, especially to the youth. He gave them his love, his time, his compassion, and his sure belief that each one was loved by and valuable to God. He cared about each person individually.

Sister Teresa Agnes and many others saw in Father Wessel a man of "total dedication to his priesthood." He was truly another Christ, an *alter Christus.* "He would go to anyone who needed him," said the Sister.[77]

Father Wessel always encouraged each young person to develop their God-given talents.

Ed Staunton, now a professional musician, recalled how Father encouraged him to play guitar at the Folk Masses. In those days, Ed didn't own an acoustic guitar, which was the instrument used at Folk Masses. All he had was an electric guitar, and felt a little self-conscious about playing it at the high school Mass. He mentioned this to Father one day.

"Don't worry about it," Father Wessel firmly replied. "The Lord just loves your music. He doesn't care what you play it on, He's happy that you're doing it. Use the talent that you have, that you're developing, and come and play in the Masses with us."[78]

And so he did.

Dawn Flynn Fowler remembered how Father Wessel supported her desire to be a special education teacher even when others had told her that she couldn't do it. "Don't listen to them," he said. "Do what you want. Lead with your heart. You have to decide what you think is best for you."[79]

"We had many conversations about what I wanted to do, and whether I could do it or not," recalled Dawn. Father would say, "Well, if you want something bad enough there are ways around it." His advice to her was to "think with your heart and your mind. And if you have a question, you know who to ask. Get down on your knees and pray. And if not, get on your knees when you're walking. God listens."[80]

Father Wessel was "encouraging, he was patient, he listened. And sometimes, at that stage, you just need someone who is not casting judgment on anything you do or say. And he was that type of person."[81]

Dawn became a special education teacher for learning disabled children in inner-city schools. She attributes her success to people like Father Wessel, one of several significant people in her life who gave encouragement to her vocational goals, and the insight she now uses to work with young people. "And if I did not learn it from people like Father Wessel, I don't think I could do it," she said.[82]

What made a lasting impression was Father's openness and willingness to listen to young people. As Josetta Cascione Burchardt summarized:

> He had a special gift for getting down to the young person's level. He made you feel accepted and there was nothing wrong with you. You're a person and God loves you just the way you are. You can just be yourself. I think he had a way of bringing out the good in people, bringing them out and drawing them out . . .
>
> Even when I would interact with him on a casual level, I sensed that. He had a way of validating you as a person, and treating each person as if they were very important and very unique.[83]

CHAPTER 30

THE CLOSING CIRCLE

As fall turned to winter, it was as though Father Wessel's life was a circle that was being drawn tighter and tighter.

On Wednesday, November 10, 1971, Father Wessel's seminary professor, Scripture scholar Father Raymond E. Brown, S.S., came to St. Joseph's Preparatory Seminary in Princeton, New Jersey, to lecture at the Clergy Conference for the Diocese of Trenton. Father Wessel was among those priests in attendance at the day-long conference listening to his former confessor speak on the topics: "Differing Voices in the New Testament and What They Mean for Us Today," and "The Ecumenical Movement, Insofar as It Affects Priests and Future Priests."[1]

Father Brown was a brilliant and compelling public speaker, much beloved by his present and former students. Priests and seminarians would come from great distances just to hear him speak, so the gathering resembled homecoming day at St. Mary's Seminary, Roland Park, with all the conviviality and camaraderie of an alumni reunion.

Father John Wessel, of course, loved the Scriptures, in no small measure due to the influence of Father Brown, whom the younger priest very much admired.

Monsignor Joseph Shenrock, who had arranged for Father Brown to speak to the clergy in Princeton, recalled that a grateful John Wessel came up to him after the lecture and thanked him for bringing Father Brown to the Diocese of Trenton. He rarely had the opportunity to see his old

Scripture professor since his seminary days, and was no doubt enthralled to hear Father Brown speak once again.[2]

On Thanksgiving Day, 1971, Father Wessel returned home to spend the holiday with his family. "I didn't see John as much as you would think once he was in Toms River," recalled Maryann Beitel, "because he was getting acclimated." So Thanksgiving that year was an especially happy reunion for the Wessels.

It was a long-standing tradition that some of the Hogan and Wessel family members would gather together each year at the Farm in Mount Holly on Thanksgiving morning. There, the men of the family—whoever wanted to join—went hunting for game in the vast fields of the Farm.

The Farm was huge, consisting of several hundred acres, and the land surrounding it was still in its natural and undeveloped state. The men could walk a long distance and enjoy it. John Wessel had always loved the Farm, he loved his family, and he also loved hunting, so the special Thanksgiving tradition combined many of the things that he valued in life.

That Thanksgiving morning was no different from many others. Uncle Michael Hogan, an avid hunter, brought his hunting dogs out to the Farm early Thanksgiving morning. He was very close to all of his nieces and nephews, but he was particularly proud of his nephew "Johnny"—proud that he was a priest and that he was doing such a good job. Father Wessel joined his Uncle Michael and several other men to walk the fields. He wore his plaid tam-o'-shanter and carried his double-barreled shotgun in hand, a beautiful Italian Beretta. They were ostensibly hunting for game—pheasant and quail mostly—but as Bill Beitel observed:

> It was such great fun to get the men of the family together. It was not just he and I. It would be his uncle, cousin-in-law, whoever was around, and we'd all go out for a walk. It wasn't so much to get the game as much as to get out together as men and josh and kid each other.

The men did shoot a couple pheasants and one rabbit that day. One of the young men in the party took care of preparing the game. It was eaten for dinner and didn't go to waste.

The company of men who went hunting that Thanksgiving Day with Father John Wessel included his brother-in-law, Bill Beitel, his Uncle Michael Hogan, Michael's son-in-law, Albert Staebler, a cousin-in-law, Tommy McCarthy, and "Uncle Jack" Crowe, who was not really a relative but a hunting and fishing buddy of Michael Hogan's. Perhaps Father Wessel's Uncle James Hogan joined them too, since he and his family now lived on the Farm.

Bill Beitel recalled that Thanksgiving morning at the Farm with his brother-in-law. They had gone out early to hunt, as light was just breaking.

> The fields were frost covered and we walked through a field that had become overgrown with little bushes and high grass . . . It was the most beautiful sight to walk through this and to see it, because this is a sight you don't see at home, and you don't see it on television, and you don't see it in your garden. It was absolute chaos and weeds, but each one was frosted and crystal. And then the sun came up and we saw it disappear. And if someone had gotten out of bed at 8:00 a.m. instead of 6:00 a.m., you wouldn't see any of this, and it was just a memorable morning . . . because the frost was so beautiful, and then to see it melt from the sun as it came up. . . . That was worth the whole trip, that one little half-hour of beauty.

Several of those on the Thanksgiving Day hunt recall John Wessel remarking that day about how much he loved being in the country, and how he just loved to get out to the Farm. Referring to his work in Trenton, he mentioned how rough things had been in the city, and that he really found respite in the country.

Patty Hogan Staebler, John Wessel's cousin and Albert's wife, had equally strong memories of that Thanksgiving at the Farm. Hunting on Thanksgiving morning had always been a "men only" tradition. The women and girls of the family never went, but for some reason, Patty was invited to join the hunt this time.

"This was the first time I had ever been allowed to go along. I remember it so vividly," said Patty, as she recalled the sight of her cousin Johnny, in

his plaid tam-o'-shanter, walking the fields with his gun. She was struck by
the contrast of "a person that was so gentle, but yet so loved to participate
in the sport of hunting."

"I remember him coming across the field," said Patty. "He was so jaunty
and happy. So happy to be outside. So full of life! . . . He was saying . . .
how much he loved the outdoors."[3]

After spending Thanksgiving dinner with his family, Father Wessel
went to visit some of the teenagers from Trenton who had come home from
college for the holiday. A group of CYO kids had gathered together at Barry
Anderson's house. Father Wessel went over and joined right in.

On the spur of the moment, they decided to go out for a drive in
Father's station wagon. "He took us to Crematory Hill," recalled Cindy
Farrell. "Crematory Hill" was a mythical place of strange gravitational force
where, as the legend goes, if you turned the car engine off, the gravitational
pull would drive the car up the hill by itself.

They spent the evening driving around, and wound up in East Windsor.
"We were out in the woods," recalled Cindy. "And he had, typically, twelve
of us in the car. We were all stuffed in there. And I remember he stopped
the car. There was a building, the remnants of a building, and we all thought
it was the crematory."

Father turned the engine off. Of course, the "gravity" phenomenon
didn't work. The car went no place, but the group didn't care. They were just
having fun and enjoying their get-together. At one point, a couple of people
in the group had to relieve themselves, so Father let them out to go in the
woods. Then he pretended to drive away. The kids started screaming, and
of course, Father turned around again and came back to pick them up.

Before the night was over, the happy group stopped in briefly at
Maryann and Bill Beitel's home in Morrisville. Maryann recalled how her
brother, John, and the young people were laughing hysterically about all
the things that they had done that night, and she thinking to herself, What
in the name of Pete is he doing with all these kids? It was perhaps fitting
that the evening was in keeping with the type of silly, innocent fun that the
young people often enjoyed with their young priest.[4]

After the Thanksgiving holiday, the next item on the school agenda was
a class retreat for the St. Joseph High School seniors. It had been planned
for the first weekend in December at a little monastery in Staten Island.

The students and their teacher chaperons went by bus to the monastery, situated high on a hill. The grounds were quite lovely, but the weather made it difficult to enjoy. For most of the weekend it was damp, misty and rained intermittently.

The retreat had been arranged by the previous principal, Sister Janice, long before Father Wessel had even come to Toms River. As memory allows, the retreat was actually conducted by others, perhaps the retreat directors at the monastery. There were skits and a film, group participation and discussion, and reception of the sacraments.

Still, Father Wessel was an integral part of the weekend. He celebrated Mass for the students and, as usual, his liturgies were intimate and informal, his messages deeply personal, the songs upbeat. The students were in such a celebratory mood at the end of the closing liturgy that they traipsed around the retreat house exuberantly singing and dancing.

At an earlier time over the weekend, students had been asked to come to the chapel for a quiet meditation. This time was probably a prelude to the preparation for confession. All of a sudden, Father Wessel's deep voice could be heard from the back of the dark, silent chapel. He began to speak or recite a prayer of one crying out to the Lord about how alone he felt. Father was talking in the first person, as if it were he crying out to the Lord in pain and isolation. It made such a tremendous impact on those present that some even started to cry in the darkened chapel, including this student:

> I had always tried to be "strong" in the face of life's hurts. As I listened deeply to Father Wessel's voice, something inside of me opened up. I began to feel freely things that I had long ago buried. I think it was at this point that I first began to realize my need before God, or perhaps, my need *for* God. When Father Wessel was speaking this prayer, although he may not have known it, he was speaking for me.[5]

Late in the evening, a few students and Father Wessel were sprawled on the living room floor, still talking when almost everyone else had gone to bed. "We were joking and laughing about a lot of silly little things. Father Wessel was in the middle of it, laughing and enjoying himself, too. He genuinely seemed to enjoy our laughter. Every now and then, he would tell us to quiet down because we were laughing too loudly, making a commotion at that late hour, but that would only make us laugh all the more."[6]

Some students found the weekend moving and spiritually uplifting, and some did not. For the young people who had been on the Search weekend in October, it was somewhat anticlimactic because it did not approximate their Search experience.

Yet, the Holy Spirit moves where He will, and for others the retreat was a catalyst. Beverly recalled a friend coming to her and saying, "Now I know what you experienced" on the Search weekend. When they returned to Toms River, more young people for whom the senior class retreat had been particularly meaningful began coming to morning prayers with Father.

Sometime over the weekend, however, disciplinary problems surfaced. Part of the problem was that every senior was required to go on the retreat. Not every young person was interested in a retreat or approached it with the same level of seriousness and openness to God's grace. Those who put something into it inevitably got something out of it. Yet others just looked upon the weekend as little more than an opportunity to get away from home and party.

A number of students, it was learned, had smuggled alcohol along with them on the retreat, seeking a different kind of "high" than the Holy Spirit would provide. A few were sent home right away, while the remainder were disciplined when they returned that Sunday.

It must have been disappointing to Father Wessel, who had tried to make the retreat worthwhile for the kids. Father was upset when he returned to Toms River on Sunday, December 5th, at the end of the retreat.

"He was furious when he came home," recalled Sister Nancy. "I could get a sense that the alcohol was some of it, but also that that was not all of it." Father Wessel later commented to Sister Nancy, "They shouldn't just be sent. Everybody shouldn't have to go to a retreat. You should *choose* to go."

"He came off one of the buses, and I saw his face," recalled the principal. "It was like a thundercloud."

The next day, Father said to Sister Carmella, referring to the retreat, "I have never been so disappointed."

"What's the matter?" the principal asked, and the priest replied, "I just couldn't believe that, as classmates, they'd be so unkind to each other."

"I never knew what he meant by that. Whether he meant that they had jeopardized the retreat by taking the liquor with them?" Carmella mused. Father never elaborated on what happened, and the principal did not want to pry into the relationship between the chaplain and the students. She just accepted what he told her and didn't inquire further.

Sister Carmella tried to cheer him. "I remember saying to him, 'You know, those of us who love working with teenagers always have to remember that . . . they're not quite developed yet . . . and we just have to be patient with them. They're not perfect children.' And he liked that." It was almost something that he would have said to her if the situation had been reversed.

Father Wessel quickly got over the incident. He went into the Religion classes and made his peace with the students. He said whatever needed to be said, and didn't let it get him down. It was one of those rare times when the principal saw him as anything less than upbeat.

Discipline was dispensed in due course for the wayward seniors. They were given in-school suspension and were made to do physical work, polishing things and cleaning up the school grounds. Father Wessel was always involved if there were disciplinary problems in the high school, and was available to counsel the students.

"He never took sides," recalled Sister Nancy. With the crowd that had been drinking on the retreat, and in other instances as well, Father assisted the principal and Sister Nancy in conferences between the students, the parents, and the teachers. "He was a good balance. He would just kind of balance everybody, and nothing ever got out of hand."

Father had the ability to see the good on all sides. He saw what the teacher had to bring to the situation, what the student had to bring to it, and he never ever left out parents. He'd say to the parents, "Now, this is not all the fault of St. Joe's High School. You sent us a young man or a young woman, and they were already pretty well formed when we got them." And he would do this gently in a way that nobody would become angry, recalled Sister Nancy. When the meeting was over, the parents would be able to better understand their child, their own responsibility for the child's behavior, and what they needed to do.[7]

Father Wessel had a great deal on his mind the weekend of the senior class retreat. If he seemed a little distracted, although no one seemed to notice, it was because that Saturday morning, he had a very important engagement to attend. He was officiating at a wedding in Trenton, and he wouldn't have missed it for the world.

Joanne Wesley, the young girl who helped Father Wessel run the Blessed Sacrament CYO, was marrying her high school sweetheart, James Gillespie, on Saturday, December 4th. Father was close to both young people, especially Joanne. He had great affection for her, as he did for all the CYO kids, so it was only natural that Joanne and James would want Father to marry them.[8]

Theirs was the first marriage among his CYO group. At first, he had a hard time accepting the fact that "his kids" were growing up and getting married and leaving. But, of course, he did. And even though he was stationed in Toms River and had other responsibilities, Father agreed to come back to Blessed Sacrament, after securing the permission of the new pastor, Father Shenrock, to officiate at the wedding of the two young people.

Privately, he recognized that he couldn't do that forever. "I cannot come up anymore," he confided to his sister, Maryann. Joanne and Jim's wedding would be the last he would come back for because, as he said, there was just too much to do in Toms River. "I can just foresee all these kids wanting me to marry them and be their witness," he said. "I have to now concentrate on my own parish." And although he dearly loved all the kids from his CYO in Trenton, he knew it was important to let go and move on.

When James and Joanne were married, it was a very happy time, almost a reunion. "It was a happy occasion," recalled Monsignor Shenrock, who was also on the altar. Father Wessel gave "a very humorous sermon" that left everyone laughing. John Wessel could be very casual and informal at times, and in his opening remarks, he welcomed everyone to "Jimmy and Joe's wedding." But the way he said it made the entire congregation burst out laughing. He quickly apologized and corrected himself—"James and Joanne's wedding."

Father Wessel always tended to look a little disheveled, with his shirts inside out, hair unkempt, and shoes unshined. Before her wedding day, Joanne, knowing of Father's grooming habits, gently reminded him, "Now, Father, I hope you're going to look nice for my wedding?"

"Well, I'll never forget walking down the aisle and looking up at him on the altar," said Joanne. "He was so clean, he looked spit-shined." Father's hair was slicked down and there wasn't a hair out of place. His face was shaved and scrubbed. His collar and cuffs were bright and crisply starched. "I couldn't believe it, and I was just so impressed that he really took care to groom himself for my wedding," said Joanne.

Then Joanne and Jim simultaneously looked down at Father's feet. The shoes he was wearing looked as if he had just trekked through a swamp. You couldn't even tell what color they were. Joanne leaned over to him and jokingly whispered, "Why did you have to stop there? Couldn't you at least have polished your shoes for my wedding?"

And Father Wessel, joking back in the same vein, whispered, "Shut up, Joe, I'm here, aren't I?"[9]

That was just so consistent with his thinking about material things, his clothes, his appearance, reflected Joanne. Those things just didn't matter to him. "I'm here, aren't I?" said it all.

Joanne and Jim's wedding was beautiful, and every bit as memorable as any couple would wish their wedding to be. "I wanted my wedding to be as close to our CYO Masses as I could get it," Joanne recalled.

The members of the CYO had all been invited. They were up in the choir loft looking down, and joined in the singing of the *Prayer of St. Francis.*

The bride and groom read the Prayer of the Faithful. Father had them face the congregation, which was unusual at the time. Traditionally, the bride and groom had their backs to the audience, but Father was so proud of them that he wanted the young couple to be the focal point. "I want everybody to see your faces," he told them.

Father gave Holy Communion under both species at the wedding, which had never been done before at a regular Blessed Sacrament Church Mass. After the bride and groom received Communion, Father gave them each a chalice of the Consecrated Wine to hold. After receiving the Sacred Host, the wedding guests then received the Blood of Jesus from the hands of the newly married couple. The congregation was so touched by that. They had never received the Holy Eucharist that way before, although "we did it all the time at our CYO Masses," recalled Joanne.

Father Wessel's sermon was beautiful as well, said Maryann Beitel, who attended the wedding with her husband, Bill. For many in the audience, thoughts may have wandered back to John Wessel's first days on the altar at Blessed Sacrament as a young and inexperienced priest—his first Mass, his first sermon, his first "dressing down" by old Father Hayes from the altar, his tears of gratitude as he celebrated his first Thanksgiving Mass as a priest.

Maryann, too, reflected upon all these things, and remembered feeling so proud of her younger brother that day as he celebrated his last Mass at Blessed Sacrament.[10]

*   *   *

Father Wessel's earthy yet priestly ways had the natural ability of touching the lives of so many teens: listening to them, advising them, encouraging them—even marrying them! And most importantly, showing them God's love, and inviting them to feel in the depths of their hearts that God, Our Lord, and the Holy Spirit were there for them.

Many teens were renewed in their faith and gained a deeper insight. To some that understanding came gradually; to others quickly, as it did to Josetta Cascione Burchardt:

> I used to like to get together to pray and meditate during the prayer time called morning prayers before homeroom. It was very relaxing and comforting, and one time I remember that really changed my life.
>
> One morning, we were sitting around cross-legged on an old rug on the floor. Father Wessel opened up and was saying how he had a sick call in the middle of the night and he really didn't want to get up to do it. He was exhausted and tired, and he just wasn't in the mood either. He didn't want to get up and get out of bed. He was praying, "My God, I really didn't want to get up in the middle of the night to go out to this person, but thank you for helping me do it." I was really shocked. I had never heard a priest speak like that with such humility and openness in admitting it to us teenagers, and it just struck a chord in me. I just felt so "humbled" by his humility. I thought, A priest said this? A priest thinks like this? I thought they were always one-hundred percent ready to go and help people, and yet, for Father to admit his shortcomings, or really, his humanity, his humanness to us really touched me.

And because of Father's statement, I made a mental prayer. It wasn't even a very noteworthy one, and I didn't really even dwell on it. I just in my mind said, "Oh, Jesus, I wish I knew you better." Just like that. It was almost like a wish when I thought it, and then all of a sudden, within seconds, this feeling came over me that I can hardly describe. It was like a warm rush of love—that's the closest description I can give it. Boy, I felt so loved by God the Father! I sensed it was from the Father. This feeling went through my head to my toes and I felt so happy and full of joy and peace and love. I felt like I was walking on a cloud and I wanted to go and hug everybody. I was ecstatic, and I didn't know what it was. Later, as I became involved in the charismatic renewal, I believe that I experienced what they call the "baptism of the Holy Spirit."

For Josetta, this was the beginning of a spiritual journey and a close relationship with God and Jesus that also brought into her life many wonderful people, experiences and events.

I think I can owe it all to Father Wessel. It was because of what he said that prompted me in my mind to say, "Oh, God, I wish I knew you better." Father's humility stimulated within me a desire to get to know God better. It was almost like he knew God so intimately, like Jesus did the Father, that he was talking to Him as Father. It developed in me a hunger for God.[11]

CHAPTER 31

THE VIETNAM VETERAN

Sometime that fall was the first the rectory heard of a John F. Kelly III, whose parents lived in Toms River and were parishioners of St. Joseph's Church. Then twenty-four years old, John Kelly—"Jack" to his parents—was a Vietnam War veteran who had received the Bronze Star Medal for heroism in battle in the fall of 1968 and suffered serious injuries in a non-combat accident the following year. He returned home, withdrawn and depressed, and was discharged from the service in 1970. The help his parents sought at various agencies and hospitals seemed to bring no permanent improvement in his mental condition.[1]

It was early December 1971, that Father Maguire took a call from John Kelly's mother, Mrs. John F. Kelly, Jr., who asked for help. Her son had left home after a family quarrel.[2]

The Kellys' situation was already familiar to the priests in the rectory. Mrs. Mildred Kelly attended morning Mass at St. Joseph's Church each day before going to her job as the manager of a local bridal shop.[3] Inevitably, observed Sean Maguire, the priests came to know the people who attended daily Mass and became familiar with their problems. Mrs. Kelly had earlier talked to some of the priests about her son. Later, when Jack Kelly moved out of the home, she called the rectory.[4]

Father Maguire brought the problem to Father Wessel's attention, asking for advice as to "how to get this kid back home." Father Maguire remembered distinctly his reaction—he's probably on drugs, he needs a doctor not a priest.

After some time, and considering the alternatives, Father Wessel decided to go to nearby Manasquan, where Jack Kelly was staying in a rented room, to talk with the young man and persuade him to return to his parents.

During this time, Father Wessel began speaking with Mrs. Kelly about the situation with her son.[5]

Behind each request to a parish priest for help is an intricate and at times heartbreaking story of human suffering. Like most stories, the young Vietnam War veteran's was complex in ways that were not then known or readily understood even by those closest to him, much less to Father Wessel.

John F. Kelly III was born in Newark, New Jersey. He, along with a younger sister, was raised in North Jersey, attended Catholic grammar schools, and moved to Brick Town, in Ocean County, at an early age. In 1968, the family moved south to Toms River when his father, John F. Kelly, Jr., found employment as Dover Township plumbing inspector.[6] Jack Kelly received his secondary education at public and parochial schools in Ocean and Monmouth counties, and in 1965 was graduated from Christian Brothers Academy, a Catholic high school in Lincroft.[7]

He was, according to his mother, "a wonderful good boy, loving, kind, generous, no temper whatsoever, just a good child."[8] To his father, "Jack was the last one to be in trouble."[9] Like neighbors and friends, the parents remembered their older child as "outgoing, sociable, and happy."[10] By all accounts, Jack Kelly had a normal childhood.[11] He matured into a tall, handsome, dark-haired young man.

In many ways, Jack Kelly had much in common with Father John Wessel. The young veteran's early environment reveals many influences and personal traits that were strikingly similar to that of the young priest.

Like John Wessel, Jack Kelly came from a devout Irish Catholic family. He loved sports. He played Little League baseball and pitched on his high school varsity baseball team. He was also a very good basketball and football player.[12]

"He was big on physical fitness and loved all sports, including fishing and hunting," his father confirmed, although he probably never shot anything more than a pheasant. His hunting gun, a 12-gauge shotgun, was a gift from his father some years ago when father and son went on annual hunting trips.[13] Jack went horseback riding with his sister and was also an excellent swimmer.[14]

Jack's grades were about average, although (like young John Wessel) he had trouble with high school Latin.[15] He idolized his father's brother, William, a priest in Illinois,[16] and enjoyed a good relationship with his only sister.[17]

"He was a very fine young gentleman," said Brother Stephen, principal of Christian Brothers Academy, of his former pupil. "He was very well liked by his classmates, and respected as a person by his teachers. He was a fairly good student, and an active sort of young man who you always knew was around."[18]

Another teacher at Christian Brothers described John Kelly as "a good student, quiet but not introverted, a boy who got along well with teachers and the other boys—in other words, just a nice, normal kid."[19]

And apparently, Jack Kelly had plans to become a dentist. He briefly attended Quincy College in Quincy, Illinois, majoring in pre-dentistry, before returning home and enrolling at Ocean County College ("OCC"), a two-year community college in Toms River.[20] At OCC, he studied a liberal arts curriculum and joined one of the three off-campus fraternities, Kappa Beta Delta.[21] Criteria for membership in KBD was not scholastic; it was a social fraternity which began when about four or five fellows got together and rented an old farmhouse off Old Freehold Road.[22] The fact that Jack Kelly was accepted into the social fraternity by his peers said something in itself about their regard for him.

A former fraternity brother who knew Jack Kelly casually in college recalled him as a "reserved" fellow who "kept a low profile," but who seemed completely normal and ordinary in every respect. Jack Kelly could sometimes be found tending bar at the fraternity's keg parties.[23]

During the time Kelly attended Ocean County College, the Vietnam War draft was very much on everyone's minds. Just about every young draft-age male was either going to college or trying to get into the National Guard or the Reserves. OCC, and the Toms River area generally, was a fairly conservative environment. The Vietnam War wasn't wildly popular at the college, but neither was it wildly unpopular. A few young men enlisted, but most waited until their number came up and tried their best to stay in school, keep up their grades, and maintain their automatic deferment.

A few of the OCC students were returning Vietnam veterans. They were well treated by their fellow students; no one disparaged them. There were not more than a dozen "hippies" at the college—a handful of kids who played guitars on campus and wore long hair. The "hippie" types really stood out among their more conservative classmates.

It was also recalled that during this time, a young, aspiring musician named Bruce Springsteen attended Ocean County College before fame struck.[24]

After two semesters, Jack Kelly left OCC and got a job working at a local boat basin painting boats.[25] In May 1968, he was drafted into the United States Army, and assigned as a combat engineer to the 65th Engineering Battalion, 9th Infantry, 25th Infantry Division.[26]

After completing basic training, John F. Kelly III was sent into combat in Vietnam in September 1968. His unit arrived at Cu Chi and was transported to Tay Ninh. As a combat engineer, his duties were to sweep roads for mines and to help the infantry build their fortifications.[27] He wrote to his mother often, and sent back photographs to his family.[28]

Killing another human being was the last thing Jack Kelly wanted to do. Before leaving for Vietnam, Jack confided to his mother that he "didn't want to kill."[29] Yet, unlike some of his peers who sought to avoid military service, Jack Kelly did not try to evade the draft nor shrink from serving his country.

He was valorous and brave in combat. A few months after his arrival in Vietnam, Kelly received the Bronze Star Medal for heroism after saving the lives of several wounded men when his unit came under enemy attack.[30]

The citation given to John F. Kelly III accompanying an award of the Bronze Star Medal on April 9, 1968, attested to his bravery:

> For heroism in connection with military operations against a hostile force: Specialist Four Kelly distinguished himself by heroic actions on 22 December 1968, while serving as a demolitions expert attached to the 4th Battalion, 9th Infantry in the Republic of Vietnam. While established at Fire Support Base Sedgwick, elements of the 9th Infantry came under an intense attack from a large enemy force. Immediately, Specialist Kelly began to place devastating fire on the advancing insurgents. As the battle progressed, Specialist Kelly noticed several friendly soldiers, who were in need of assistance. With complete disregard for his own safety, Specialist Kelly exposed himself to the hail

of hostile fire as he helped to evacuate the wounded men to a safe location. His valorous actions contributed immensely to the thwarting of the aggressor force. Specialist Kelly's personal bravery, aggressiveness, and devotion to duty are in keeping with the highest traditions of the military service and reflect great credit upon himself, his unit, the 25th Infantry Division, and the United States Army.[31]

His parents recalled how Jack accepted the medal as a matter of course and didn't even talk about it when he returned home. Although his actions had saved the lives of several of his fellow soldiers, "he didn't want to play the hero act," said his father.[32]

Service in Vietnam was hellish. Jack was affected by the death and destruction all around him. Once he confided to his sister how he'd seen an Army buddy, sleeping just a few feet away from him in the tent, blown to pieces by an enemy grenade, and how greatly it had disturbed him.[33]

In early February 1969, Jack Kelly was severely injured in a non-combat accident in Tay Ninh. The men of his unit were constructing an observation tower out of large timbers, and Jack and a few other soldiers were holding up one side to tack it onto the other side. A helicopter flew by in the distance and created a whirlwind, blowing the tower over. It fell on top of Kelly and two other men, crushing three discs in Kelly's lower back. He was given emergency treatment in a field hospital.[34] It was not until later that the severity of his injuries was fully realized and diagnosed.[35] Jack was transferred to a military hospital in Japan for further medical treatment only after his parents had asked their local congressman to intervene.[36]

Marijuana was plentiful in Vietnam, and like some other soldiers, Jack began to smoke it, at first just a few times a week, and later on, after his back injury, every day. It helped him to forget about his back injury and eased the pain.[37] Everybody in the company smoked, he later said.[38] Once, he took a large amount of speed,[39] and tried opium a few times.[40]

Kelly returned to the United States from Vietnam in October 1969, and was assigned to an Army hospital at Fort Devens, Massachusetts. He was honorably discharged from the Army in May of 1970.[41]

Jack Kelly returned from Vietnam "drastically changed" in ways that soon became obvious to his family and friends. Jack himself felt "unhappy" and "very depressed" and couldn't get along with his parents.[42] To his father, Jack's thoughts and conversations seemed morbid and self-absorbed.[43] His back injury made the young veteran despondent, since he couldn't engage in athletic activities as he had done before,[44] and he frequently complained about his back aching.[45] He became introverted and strange, and began having episodes of bizarre thoughts and behavior.[46]

The change in the once vibrant, happy, athletic young man was painfully evident to his boyhood friend from high school. "We had been like brothers," said Bob Green*, who saw Jack immediately after his release from the Army hospital. "We almost couldn't communicate. It was like his mind had snapped. He no longer seemed to have the faculty to reason in a way that you and I could consider coherent."

"If Vietnam didn't cause all of his problems, it certainly brought them to a head. He'd been able to cope with his life before. When he came back, he simply couldn't."[47]

Jack Kelly's mental condition became progressively sick, disorganized, and out of touch with reality.[48]

Once, Jack knocked his mother to the floor and twisted her arm until she fell to her knees and had to yell for help.[49]

On other occasions, Jack accused his mother of putting magazines under his bed, and placing pennies face up on the floor, with the eyes staring at him.[50] He began to think he heard the voices of people in cars driving by talking about him, even when their car windows were rolled up.[51]

For unknown reasons, he showed up unannounced at the home of a young woman, Deborah Jackson*, who had been a childhood friend, and professed his love for her. He had not seen her for a period of three years. When he refused to leave, she called the police.[52]

With hindsight, it can be said that certain events which occurred to John Kelly in the service, particularly the horror and stress of war, and the injuries to his back, superimposed upon a latent psychotic background, helped to bring about his mental problems which gradually increased in severity upon his return from Vietnam.[53] The use of psychotropic drugs and hallucinogens may have exacerbated his mental condition. Back in the States, Jack took about eight or ten LSD "trips" and smoked marijuana a few times between November 1969 and April 1971.[54]

In February of 1971, Jack threatened his mother with a hunting knife.[55] As a result of this disturbing incident, Mr. and Mrs. Kelly took him to the Veteran's Administration Hospital in East Orange, New Jersey for treatment. His parents had to trick him into going to the hospital voluntarily, ostensibly to receive treatment for his back. He was actually admitted into the psychiatric ward because of his behavior.[56]

Once in the V.A. Hospital, John Kelly was diagnosed as suffering from schizophrenia, paranoid type. A psychiatrist has described paranoid schizophrenia thus:

> Schizophrenia is a general category which is the most severe and significant mental illness. Paranoid describes the variation or the type. Paranoid, particularly or specifically, means that one is suspicious, mistrustful, frequently believing that other people are out to harm one or to do one damage. When people have a condition of paranoid schizophrenia they misinterpret the usual events of life, gestures, remarks, and so forth. People who have paranoid schizophrenia are also considered to be not predictable. Their behavior cannot be depended upon to be the same from minute to minute. They may suddenly become assaultive or dangerous in some other fashion or they may become suddenly withdrawn. They have delusions, which means they have the serious belief that things are other than they really are. They may hear voices. They may see things. They may feel things. These are all symptoms and signs of this very serious illness.[57]

Paranoid schizophrenia is "a very incapacitating mental disease," said another psychiatrist, and the theory is idiopathic, meaning of unknown origin. It is a chemical change, but no one really knows why, although theories about causation now lean more towards it being biological. At one point, it was almost always viewed to be psychodynamic or psychological, with very little to do with genetics, but now the idea is more that it may be even a neurological or physiological disease.

Other factors—environmental triggers or catalysts—can make the condition go from a latent to a more prevalent one, not in terms of causation (since the cause is idiopathic) but in terms of exacerbating it or bringing it out. Drugs, alcohol, physical trauma, and mental trauma all might be what are called "stressors" that bring this type of disease to a more obvious symptomology, but only as a catalyst on an underlying condition. Obviously, wartime combat experience and serious, debilitating injury can act as a significant stressor or catalyst to someone with an underlying, although latent, disease. Alcohol and drugs clearly compound it.

Cases of paranoid schizophrenia, as with any other illness, may differ greatly in degrees of severity. In many cases, it is a malignant mental disease; some other cases are milder. Generally, it is a chronic condition, a sickness for life, and the patient will require psychiatric care and psychotropic medication for the rest of his life. Without medication, he becomes sick again.

A good analogy is to compare schizophrenia with diabetes, which also varies greatly in severity. While both illnesses usually last for life, schizophrenia, like diabetes, can be brought under control. The person can remain symptom free, or at least experience less symptoms, and live with a great deal of functioning, stability and normality. However, treatment must continue, and to the extent that it does, the person remains more intact, symptom free, and better.[58]

The Kellys diligently visited their son once or twice every week in the V.A. Hospital.[59] Jack had been under psychiatric care at the hospital for a period of some two and one-half months when, in late April 1971, he convinced his mother to sign him out of the hospital even though his doctors had recommended that he stay.[60]

Jack had been calling his mother every single day, begging her to take him home, insisting he was feeling fine, and complaining that the drugs he was being given were causing him adverse side effects.[61]

How great this mother's torment must have been! She was not a medical doctor; just a mother who loved her son. Her decision to terminate Jack's hospitalization and relieve his apparent agony was understandable.

The spring and summer of 1971 seemed to bring the troubled young veteran some relief. Jack found work in a construction job for a while and felt all right. His obsessive thoughts that people were talking about him disappeared.[62] In the summer, laid off from his construction job, Jack enjoyed going to the beach every day and to shore dance clubs at night.[63] He dated occasionally during the summer, but not seriously, his mother recalled.[64] He spent many summer hours visiting a young married couple who lived next door.[65]

Jack "loved kids," the wife said. She often noticed him tossing a football around with a group of young boys. He would also stop to play tenderly with her 15-month-old son, and "never behaved in a violent manner," she said.[66]

At summer's end, when everyone was going back to school, Jack decided not to return to college but to take a trip to Europe and visit an Army friend in Naples, Italy. He intended to stay for a few months traveling around Europe, but returned after about a month, very disturbed and nervous.[67]

While in Italy, he began to experience a recurrence of thoughts of a violent and bizarre nature.[68] On one occasion, while panhandling in Italy, somebody gave him thirty cents, or the equivalent of what he thought was "thirty pieces of silver." Because of the incident, Jack Kelly began to imagine he was Judas Iscariot. He became depressed and afraid to go anyplace else, and so on November 1, 1971, Jack returned home to Toms River.[69] He would only tell his parents that the people "weren't very hospitable." He revealed nothing of his bizarre thoughts.[70]

Over a period of the next several weeks, Jack Kelly confided to a friend that he felt he had to do something violent, express himself violently.[71] He said that he thought people were laughing at him and calling him names.[72]

As his illness progressed, Jack came to believe that he was not Judas Iscariot but was, in fact, Jesus Christ. One day he even blurted out to his mother, "I'm Jesus Christ!"

His mother, thinking it was merely a joke, laughed and said, "And I'm the Blessed Virgin Mary."[73]

On Saturday, December 4, 1971—the same day that Father Wessel was marrying the young CYO couple, Joanne Wesley and James Gillespie, at Blessed Sacrament in Trenton—Jack Kelly got into an argument with his parents. The police were called to the Kelly apartment, and Jack was given the choice to either leave the apartment or be arrested. He left with a suitcase and went to a motel for the night.

At seven o'clock the next morning, Jack showed up out of the blue at the home of the same childhood friend, Deborah Jackson, whom he had professed to love. At that time, Jack was seized with the thought that he must marry her, but before he could marry her that he must sexually assault her. He went to see the young woman, intending to force himself upon her—in his delusional state, he believed all this had been pre-arranged—but became frightened and left when she screamed and threatened to tell his mother if he didn't go.[74]

Later that Sunday, Jack Kelly, greatly disturbed, went to the Manasquan home of Mrs. Marian Green*, the mother of his close friend Bob. At that time Mrs. Green, although a lay person, suggested that the young man get psychiatric treatment. Mrs. Green recalled that Jack's conversation that day was strange—sometimes incoherent, or intelligible but bizarre.[75]

The same day, Mrs. Green took Jack to downtown Manasquan and helped him locate a room for rent over a photographer's studio off Main Street. She also made arrangements for him to attend a group therapy session that met in nearby Asbury Park on the following Tuesday. Jack promised her that he would go.[76] He stayed in the rented room for a few days, spending most of his time walking around the town of Manasquan. Once during this time, his mother came to visit him and pleaded for him to return home, but he refused to go with her.[77]

On Tuesday, December 7th, Mrs. Green went to pick Jack Kelly up from the psychotherapy session in Asbury Park that she'd arranged for him to attend. But Jack, apparently afraid of being returned to the V.A. Hospital, never kept the appointment.[78]

Father Wessel had an unusual request of the dozen or so high school students gathered at morning prayers one day in early December. When it came time to offer petitions and prayer requests, Father spoke up and said, "I'd like you to please pray for someone I'm going to see." Of course, the students had no idea who he was talking about but they prayed for the person anyway. Father was asking for prayers because, he said, "I have to take care of someone today."

It is quite possible, indeed probable, that Father Wessel was asking for prayers for John Kelly.

"I remember he said, 'Please pray for me . . . please pray'," added Josetta C. Burchardt. "I remember specifically he had to meet with someone that needed a lot of prayer, and he was very serious about what he said. Very intense." What was striking to her was not only what he said but the manner in which he said it. Usually Father was pretty lighthearted, but at the prayer meeting that day, Josetta sensed "a heaviness in his spirit—a deep sense of concern when he said that."[79]

On Wednesday, December 8th, a cold, wintery, snowy day, Father Wessel set out to see John Kelly in Manasquan, at his mother's request, to persuade the young man to return home.[80]

At first, Father couldn't find Jack's boarding house. He called Mrs. Kelly at her place of work at the bridal shop to say that he was going up and down Main Street looking for the photographer's studio, but couldn't find it. Mrs.

Kelly recalled feeling so sorry for the priest as she thought of him running up and down the street in the snow, trying to locate her son.[81] After some additional directions, Father was able to locate the photographer's studio where Kelly was living upstairs.

Father Wessel talked with the troubled young veteran for about two or three hours. At the end of the conversation, Jack Kelly asked Father Wessel if he would take him back home to his parents. Jack would later remember nothing of his conversation with the priest,[82] except that Father Wessel had told him during the ride home that "sometimes people crack up with too much pressure."[83]

"I like Jack. Jack's a fine boy," Father Wessel told Mrs. Kelly when he brought her son home.[84] Although he recommended professional counseling, he was willing to do what he could to help in the interim.[85]

Later that evening, Father Wessel reported to his fellow priests in the rectory that John Kelly had been returned home.[86]

Sometime after the third Search, Father Francis Kolby, one of the priests on the retreat weekend, received a telephone call from Father Wessel. "Frank," he said. "Can we get together? I'd like to talk to you."

It seemed to Father Kolby that John Wessel had something very specific on his mind. "Sure," Father Kolby said agreeably. But somehow, a date was never set.

Father Francis Kolby was studying for a degree in counseling at the time John Wessel called him. Could the call have been related to someone that Father Wessel was trying to counsel? No one will ever know, because the meeting never took place. Father Kolby never did find out the reason why John Wessel needed to talk with him.[87]

On Friday, December 10th, Father Wessel stopped by at the Kelly home a few days after he had retrieved Jack from Manasquan. No one was home in the Kelly apartment. A neighbor who lived in the apartment next door recalled meeting Father on the porch. He was writing a note and placing it in the Kellys' mailbox: "Jack, you call me, Father Wessel."[88]

Meanwhile, the Kellys continued to try to find professional help for their son, who was becoming increasingly nervous and more withdrawn. Despite their efforts, there seemed to be no place to go and nowhere to turn.

Father Wessel had recommended they take Jack to a private clinic in Princeton, but the Kellys found the facility's fees were beyond their means.[89]

Private psychologists or psychiatrists and private clinics were either too expensive for the middle-income family, or unavailable.

More importantly, the troubled young man practically refused all professional treatment. He only wanted to sit home and watch television and read, his mother said.

Again, Mrs. Kelly re-contacted the Veteran's Administration Hospital in East Orange. Although the facility was affordable, that too was precluded. Jack could not return to the hospital without voluntarily signing himself in, and he wouldn't do that. He would not, or could not, admit that he needed their help.

He did, however, attend some counseling sessions at an "Outreach" center in Toms River.

In desperation, Mrs. Kelly even considered having Jack arrested for a minor charge, something as insignificant as abusive language, "in hopes that he could get help that way."

But Father Wessel, she said, was the only one who ever answered her pleas.

"He was the only one we could ever talk to," said Mr. Kelly.[90]

CHAPTER 32

MISSION OF MERCY

One cannot help but believe that God in His own special way allows His favorite children to know that it is now the time for them to return to Him, with time allowed to put one's house in order.[1] As the month of December moved steadily onward to the celebration of Christmas, Father Wessel's life was mysteriously and inexorably coming full circle.

Josetta Cascione had told her father about Father Wessel—how the students at St. Joseph's were so thrilled to have this young priest who was really interested in them. He would stay after class with them and talk to them in the schoolyard, or help them get their cars started in the parking lot. He was always there and available for them, and was kind and friendly besides.

(John) Harry Cascione was a member of the Holy Name Society of St. Aloysius Church in Jackson, New Jersey. The Holy Name Society met on the second Sunday of each month, and they were always looking for good guest speakers. After hearing about this "Father Wessel" on several occasions from his daughter, it occurred to Cascione that this priest must be something special. "I wonder if I could get him to come up and talk to the Holy Name men?" he thought.

Sometime in November, Harry Cascione telephoned St. Joseph's Rectory and asked Father Wessel if he would come up and give a talk at the next Holy Name meeting on Sunday, December 12th. Father immediately accepted. "I don't recall that there was any hesitation on his part. He seemed more than willing to come," said Cascione. Father just asked about the time of the meeting, and was told that it was after the ten o'clock Mass. "I don't think he was able to make the ten o'clock Mass," recalled Cascione, but "he came at eleven o'clock for our meeting right after Mass."

Sunday morning, December 12th. Father Wessel got in his station wagon and drove north to St. Aloysius Church, about a half-hour from Toms River, for his talk to the Holy Name Society. The pastor of St. Aloysius Church was Father Amedeo L. Morello, the same Father Morello who had been a young pastor at the little church of Our Lady of the Mount in Mount Bethel, New Jersey, where the young seminarian John Wessel began his first parish assignment in the summer of 1960.

"I was very impressed with him," said Harry Cascione, when he finally met Father Wessel on Sunday morning. "He was a fine-looking man, very humble and very straightforward, and he had a great love, I think, for Jesus."

As Father Wessel stood in the front of the meeting hall and looked out at the audience of the Holy Name Society, he probably contemplated what he could tell them that would be most important to them as Catholic men—husbands, fathers, and heads of families.

Father encouraged the men to try to "be like other Christs." To try to help others whenever they could, with whatever gifts they had, and to do whatever they could in this life.

His mood was somewhat intense and slightly serious. "It didn't seem like he was in a joking mood," recalled Cascione. "I remember him being very kind, very polite and nice, but I don't remember any joviality." When he talked, he seemed a little bit serious and "definitely like he had a point to get across to us that he felt was important."

"I just remember that he was really telling us, in as straightforward a manner as he could, to try to be another Jesus. Try to help people. Try to do as much as you can for as many people as you can to help them . . . To give of yourself. To pour out whatever you have for Christ. To help your families, and whoever you come in contact with. Empty yourself, to the extent possible, in doing good works, in performing acts of kindness," said Harry Cascione.

The Holy Name men were greatly impressed with Father Wessel's message that day. It was a short talk, but very much to the point.[2]

On Sunday afternoon, December 12th, both Father Wessel and Father Maguire had a free day—no duty. "It was a bright, brisk day," Father Maguire recalled. Sometime in the afternoon, after the morning Masses were said and Father Wessel had returned from Jackson, "he invited me to go to his home in Ship Bottom." John Wessel told the younger priest that he wanted to "winterize the boat." Father Maguire wasn't quite sure what that meant.[3]

On the way down, the two priests stopped for lunch and then headed on to Father's shore home.

"After showing me around, we went to pick up some rope to tie down a cover on the *Eucharist*," recalled Sean Maguire. "I learned more of his true feelings about his present assignment than ever before."

To his fellow associate, Father Wessel was a serious and quiet man who was not very self-disclosing, "not chatty unless you drew him out." He was "like an older brother" to me, said Sean Maguire, but at the same time, the younger priest felt that he couldn't always tell him everything because John Wessel seemed to have very high standards. On the other hand, noted Maguire, it was precisely because Father Wessel had high standards that he was also a very good and effective leader, and had the ability to raise others up to his level.

The two priests talked generally that afternoon about the people and situations that they'd encountered in the parish, the school, and the rectory. To Sean Maguire, it was basically just that "barriers were removed" in the sense that "he and I could share our feelings."

"He was happy, challenged, and had his plans," recalled Maguire about John Wessel. "We really had a great afternoon."

To complete the day, both Father Wessel and Father Maguire were in agreement to see a movie but on the spur of the moment, decided to go out to dinner instead.

In the course of that week, much shopping was done by Father. Proudly he reported to Mrs. Moser, the housekeeper, "All my Christmas shopping is done, all the presents are wrapped, all my bills are paid, and I even have enough money left to buy a new suit."[4]

Father Wessel had indeed bought a new suit shortly before Christmas at the urging of his mother. Kathleen Wessel, out of motherly concern, was always trying to get her son to "spruce up" a little more. She'd point out if there was a button missing from his jacket, or if his shoes needed repair, and Father Gallagher recalled John Wessel mentioning as much to him.[5] So Father Wessel was quite proud of himself that he had finally gotten around to buying a new suit.

Christmas was coming, and the students wanted to do something special for Father Wessel. Father had a peacoat that needed repair, and some of the kids planned to take it, fix the buttons on it, and have it cleaned for him for Christmas.[6]

Everyone was looking forward to the holidays. For the St. Joseph's students, Christmas break was just a few days away, making it hard to concentrate on classes. The high school basketball and wrestling seasons had just begun, and both varsity teams were off to a fine start.[7]

For Father Wessel, the week's routine went on as usual. Parish duties. Work in the high school. Monday night Scripture class for the adults. Morning prayer meetings at 7:30 a.m. each day for the high school students.

Of all the things that would be recalled about Father Wessel's teachings at morning prayers, one saying stands out. Sharing what was probably the driving principle of his own spiritual life, Father would often tell the students:

"You have to give, give, give, and keep on giving until there's nothing else to give—and then you have to keep on giving."[8]

On Thursday, December 16th, Father Wessel decided to go back to Trenton for no apparent reason, and made a point to stop and visit friends. He had lunch with his longtime friend, Father James Dubell. He may have stopped in at his sister Maryann's, and at Blessed Sacrament.[9]

Maryann Beitel, while unable to pinpoint the precise date, remembered her brother coming to visit her in Morrisville in mid-December. He came to her home briefly, she recalled, to pick up something. Maryann had a strange premonition at the time. It crossed her mind that John would not live to marry her own children. "I remember that feeling, that the way that he led his life, that he just was not going to last long enough to be around to marry our children" or "to enjoy the fruits of a later priesthood."

"I wonder how much longer?" she thought as she saw her brother that day, not really sure of why.[10]

Father Wessel made a stop at the Ave Maria Shop, a large Catholic religious bookstore in Trenton, and ran into someone he knew. He and his friend began talking and reminiscing about their families, and Father made an unusual remark in passing that "the Wessel men don't live to late years."[11]

His remark seemed insignificant at the time. Its full import was not realized until later. According to the friend, "he acted as if he knew his life was going to be over soon. He had a premonition."[12]

Father Wessel never worried about death, and he always told his sister not to worry about him either. But the way Father Wessel lived his life, it was "almost as if he knew that he had to cover all the miles within a short time," reflected his sister.[13]

Indeed, Father John Wessel seemed to have approached his work with a greater sense of urgency and zeal as he progressed in his priesthood, and particularly, at St. Joseph's in Toms River. The effect that he had on the people there in a few short months was nothing short of amazing. This sentiment is echoed by nearly everyone who knew him at St. Joseph.[14]

His impact on St. Joseph's parish, and especially on the students who knew him, was as great, if not greater, than on the people who were with him for six years at Blessed Sacrament. Would this not confirm the sense of Father Wessel's sister that he knew he had a lot to do in a short amount of time?

But if Father Wessel had any sense of foreboding, he kept it well hidden when he met Father James Dubell at lunchtime on Thursday, December 16th. Father Wessel had been shopping and stopped in at the Chancery Office in Trenton, where Father Dubell was then working. They decided to have lunch together at Howard Johnson's Restaurant on Route 1 in Trenton.

"His visit was a surprise," recalled Monsignor James Dubell. "I didn't know he was coming. And the two of us went out for lunch."

"I remember him being on a shopping trip for Christmas gifts for his family, which is unusual. John wasn't really into shopping—that wasn't really his style—but he was concerned about his family. He was concerned that he would have a gift for them," said Monsignor Dubell.

The two men, friends since their earliest grammar school days, settled into the booth at Howard Johnson's and began to catch up on each other's lives.

"I remember that he seemed to be contented with his work. He seemed to be happy," said Dubell. John Wessel was in good spirits. He looked good—trim, in shape, and well rested, his friend recalled.

Their conversation covered a wide range of topics, as would be expected of two old friends who hadn't talked in a while. Father Wessel mentioned a little about the priests, his new co-workers, about his work in Toms River, and some of the things that were going on in the high school. Even after three months, he was still unpacking, he said. But he was pleased that he had just recently purchased a new station wagon.

He talked about his new pastor, Father Donovan. "His pastor was a rough-and-tumble kind of a guy, very much like John," and "they seemed to get along very well."

Mostly, it was a social visit, recalled James Dubell. How are you doing? How are things? There was a lot to talk about. Both men had recently been given new assignments, and it had been about a month since they had last seen each other.

Father Dubell was just beginning to do some graduate work in Education at Rider College. "John thought it was a good idea. He encouraged me to do that," said Dubell, although his friend couldn't resist a little good-natured ribbing. "What are you trying to prove, Dubes? Why do you have to go back to school?" John Wessel kidded.

During lunch, Father Wessel talked in generalities about the different people that he was assisting in his ministry. In passing, he mentioned that he was working with a young man who had been to Vietnam, and whom he had been trying to get to move back to his mother's house. He suspected that the young veteran might be involved with drugs, because he was acting strangely and was kind of incorrigible.

Dubell didn't get the sense that John Wessel thought the situation was dangerous, or that he was at all apprehensive. It was just said more or less in passing.

Building upon the prior conversation, the two men began discussing the use of drugs among the young. In 1971, marijuana, in particular, and LSD, speed, and other addictive substances, were making inroads. Father John Wessel had seen all too much of it.

Father Wessel remarked to his friend that he was kind of disgusted or exhausted with the whole drug mentality. Referring to drug users in general, he said he "didn't see much light at the end of their tunnel." Dubell elaborated:

> The thing that I took from it was he realized that he really didn't have the expertise to really work with these people; that he didn't pretend to know how to deal with them or how to really

help them, other than just simply to listen to them occasionally. And the phrase he used was that he "didn't see much light at the end of their tunnel." In other words, he didn't see much in terms of his being able to help them. That was the way I took it. . . . He felt that drug addicts really needed professional help.

But despite touching on a serious subject, the whole tenor of their lunch meeting was positive and upbeat. When Monsignor Dubell last saw his friend, he was "up, jovial, contented, and happy." As they said their goodbyes and walked away, John Wessel looked like a man who had "springs in his feet."[15]

Father Wessel returned to Toms River sometime after lunch. Later that day, he decided to go to Mount Holly, and Father Maguire went with him. He hadn't been home for a while and he wanted to see his mother.[16]

"The last time I saw him was the Thursday before," recalled Mrs. Kathleen Wessel. "He used to come home on Thursdays when he could."

Kathleen Wessel recalled her son walking through the door with another young, Irish priest. They didn't arrive until quite late in the afternoon. Mrs. Wessel made tea and they sat and talked for a while in the living room. Later, she made dinner for the two men.

There was nothing special or out of the ordinary about the visit, said Mrs. Wessel. It was just a pleasant visit, like one of many over the years. Only one thing stands out. John Wessel didn't care about clothes. He had only one suit to his name. And one of the last times he came home to Mount Holly, his mother had said to him, "John, you've got to get yourself some clothes." So when he came home that Thursday, he proudly said to his mother, "See, Mom, a new suit!"

John Wessel couldn't stay long. All too soon, he and Father Maguire had to leave, and mother and son said their goodbyes.

On the evening of Thursday, December 16th, the Parish Council of St. Joseph's Church had in attendance at their meeting an exhausted Father Wessel. The meeting, in the high school cafeteria, was called to order at 8 p.m. and adjourned at 9:10 p.m. The Council discussions were taken up with the ordinary details of parish life: the parish raffle, the yuletide party, the CYO and CCD programs, the choir, bingo, and plans for the adult lecture series in the spring.[17]

462 NO GREATER LOVE

∗   ∗   ∗

Friday, December 17th. It was a cold, gray day. A dreary, dark, rainy Friday.[18]

The day did not begin well for the Wessel family. Father Wessel's brother and sister-in-law received news that Pat Wessel's mother, ailing with cancer, had passed away in Philadelphia that morning. After securing a baby sitter for their young children, Dr. Edward Wessel and his wife hastened to Philadelphia from their home in Newton to make funeral arrangements. Father Wessel, however, was not yet informed of the death in the family.[19]

Early that morning, Father Wessel saw Sister Nancy Carney in the high school. Every Friday afternoon, because Sister Nancy commuted to Fordham University in the Bronx to attend classes toward a Masters Degree in Theology, the priest substitute taught her seventh-period sophomore Religion class. They had developed a routine to meet every Friday morning and exchange the textbook that he would use later in her class.

Sister Nancy handed the course book to Father Wessel as she headed out the door. "You're on your own, boy," she joked.

And he, joking back, said, "Am I going to survive this?" It was the seventh period of the last day of the week—that in itself presented a challenge to any teacher.

During the lunch hour, Father Gallagher observed John Wessel tossing a football back and forth to some of the grade school boys in the schoolyard.

The sophomore Religion class did not seem to go well for Father Wessel that afternoon. After substitute teaching the class, he returned the course book to Sister Nancy's cubbyhole in the main office. He wrote a note and stuck it in the chapters of the book he covered that day: "I went nowhere. Bummer!!!" In other words, a rotten afternoon.[20]

It was now close to two o'clock. Somewhere between the hours of two and three in the afternoon of Friday, December 17th, a chain of events was set in motion that would decide Father Wessel's ultimate destiny. He had no way of knowing that he was on his way to his last mission of mercy to a youth in trouble.[21]

In the afternoon of December 17th, a call came which John Wessel would have much preferred to have ignored. Mrs. Kelly again telephoned the rectory and requested that Father Wessel visit her son at their home because Jack was "acting up." Father Wessel was not there; Father Gallagher was "on call" that day but because Father Wessel had counseled Jack Kelly before, the young man's mother asked for him.[22]

Usually, Father Wessel celebrated Mass every Friday after school for the students, but there was no Mass this Friday afternoon. Instead, a special Christmas liturgy was being planned for the high school early the following week, just prior to the Christmas break.

After his seventh-period Religion class, Father Wessel met with the principal, Sister Carmella, in her office, for the purpose of planning next week's Christmas liturgy.[23]

It was, coincidentally, the only other time that she recalled seeing Father John Wessel a little "down" in spirits.

This was the way Sister Carmella recalled that Friday afternoon:

> I was with him the last class period of the day. And I'm not sure when school ended at that time. Probably around 2:30. So I was with him from about 1:45 to 2:30, going on to maybe quarter to three, something like that, right through the dismissal.
>
> He had this yellow pad and we were planning the Christmas liturgy, and he was going to plan it with the Religion classes but he needed to have some things set straight with me. We had to plan how we were going to do the gym, where people were going to sit. He wanted music. He just wanted to talk the whole thing over with me, so we spent a good class period together, and I remember hearing the bell ring for dismissal.
>
> I remember hearing dismissal going on, and sometime during the dismissal—there was a lot of noise and confusion—Maureen Ward, the secretary, came in and she said to him—and these are not quite the words but these words have rung in my ears for years, the gist of them at any rate. She said to him, "Father, the rectory just called. Mrs. Kelly needs for you to go to her apartment."

Father Wessel "looked at me and he said, 'Oh!' He kind of threw his pencil down on the yellow pad and he said, 'Oh!'"—long and drawn out, like a sigh. He was "sort of exasperated, but not unkindly," Carmella recalled.

In a few sentences, Father Wessel explained to the principal what the call was all about. Sister Carmella understood that Father was helping a mentally disturbed young man by the name of Kelly who had been in a mental hospital and who needed him. His mother had signed him out of the hospital, and he wasn't well, the principal recalled. "I told her she should have left him in that State Hospital," Father said, finishing up the story. "Now I have to go over there again."

Sister Carmella reflected further:

> He was not unkind about the Kellys. He just was stating a fact that the youngster needed more help, that she should not have taken him out of the hospital. And she apparently had called on him more than once, because he knew exactly where to go and why he was going. . . . So this was nothing new.

"Father, it's okay," Sister Carmella reassured him. "We'll finish this Monday morning. We'll get this done, don't worry about it." The principal fully appreciated that the priests had to be available to counsel parishioners. In addition, she had errands to do herself that afternoon to get ready for the high school faculty Christmas party the following week.

"We'll take care of this Monday morning," she assured him again. And with that, Father Wessel left. Sister Carmella placed the time at between 2:30 and 3:00 p.m.

Father Wessel went back to his office in the high school and returned Mrs. Kelly's call. Father spoke briefly with her since she was calling from work.[24]

"Father Wessel, Jack isn't himself. There is something terribly wrong," said Mrs. Kelly. She related how her husband had come home for lunch earlier that afternoon and called to tell her that Jack was acting strangely. Their son had removed all the windows from his parents' upstairs bedroom, and Mr. Kelly had to replace the windows before he returned to work.[25]

"Well, what's wrong with removing the windows?" Father Wessel asked matter-of-factly. "Maybe he just wants to wash the windows for you."

"Well, I wish you would see Jack and just have a talk with him, Father," she said.

"Mrs. Kelly, your son needs professional help," said the priest, "but I will see what I can do."[26]

Father Wessel left his yellow pad with all his notes for the Christmas liturgy on top of his desk.[27]

Father Wessel was always thinking of what he could do for others, especially for the young people. So it was fitting that his concern for the youths should be the topic of several of his conversations that Friday afternoon.

Just as Father Wessel stepped in early on to smooth over a situation between Sister Carmella and the pastor, he often took on the role of a "buffer" to smooth over misunderstandings between the principal or faculty, on the one hand, and a student or group of students, on the other. With Father's good nature and sound judgment, he had the ability to be a peacemaker and diffuse any number of difficult situations.[28]

One of the youths in need of Father's help that day was John Menter, senior class president and talented football lineman. He had received a number of honors and awards for his athletic abilities, and several college athletic scholarships had been offered to him. John was going through some genuine turmoil his senior year, which began when a faculty member accused him of committing some minor infraction, which had actually been the fault of another boy. The school administration tended to side with the faculty member, Mr. Smith.*

The situation had escalated to the point where young John felt his promising academic career and college athletic scholarships were in jeopardy.[29]

Father Wessel found out about John Menter's problem with the faculty member, and took it upon himself to get involved on his behalf. "I don't know how he found out about it, but he found out about it and got involved with it," said Menter. That Friday afternoon after school, the priest sought him out to talk with him.

Not much more than two hours before he was shot, Father Wessel and John Menter had a major conversation. "We were talking in one of the classrooms . . . down in the 200 corridor." John recalled. "He was helping me through this problem that I was having."

"John, what's happening now is just a little bit of your life," the priest counseled. "When you're seventeen years old, a lot of things seem very important that are not important. . . . Believe me," he said, "this seems very, very monumental to you for now, but it'll pass, along with a lot of other things."

"You have to measure success in different ways," Father Wessel continued.

"Well, how do you?" the young man asked. At seventeen years old, when your whole world is crashing down around you, a teenager doesn't always have the ability to put those kinds of things in perspective.

Father Wessel looked at John and said with sincerity: "A successful person in life is a person who can affect another person, one person, positively."

"If somewhere in your life, you can have a positive influence on one person, you're a success," the priest emphasized. "No matter whatever else happens in life, if you have that positive influence on at least one person, you'll be a success, John. And that's the way to look at it . . ."[30]

John Menter never forgot those words.

"And always keep trying to be a positive influence on somebody," Father concluded.

There was to be a meeting in school on Monday to address John's situation. Father Wessel said, "I promise you, come Monday, this will be straightened out. I give you my word on it . . . I'll be meeting with Father Donovan, Sister Carmella, Mr. Smith, and if need be, you and your parents."

"Well, I appreciate that," John replied.

"But you know," Father Wessel said, changing the subject, "I really have to run."

"Well, that's all right, Father," John said.

"I'll see you tonight at the basketball game," Father Wessel continued. "I want to talk to you at the basketball game. I want to elaborate on what's going to happen a little bit more."

The basketball game was scheduled for seven o'clock that evening in the high school gym. It was the second game of the season, a contest between the varsity basketball team and the returning alumni players—a promise of an exciting match and a good turnout.

"Okay," John said. "Where are you running to?"

"Well, to be honest with you," Father Wessel said, "I'm talking to this gentleman—he has problems."

"I have a problem here with this Vietnam vet," Father explained. He told John that a young man, whom he did not name, had returned from the Vietnam War and was having psychological problems. His mother had contacted the parish church, and that's how he got involved with him.

"But, you know," Father continued, "I can't help him."

"Why not?" John asked.

"Well, he doesn't need a priest. He needs a doctor," Father Wessel replied, with characteristic honesty. "I've been counseling him as a priest but this is a mental thing he has, a psychological thing. I can't help him there."

To Menter, Father seemed a little upset. "I wouldn't say agitated," but he was "very serious. It was a very serious tone he was using, almost like a little bit of frustration . . . from what I remember, it was almost like he had realized that he couldn't help this man with his problem." It had gone beyond the point where a priest could deal with the problem through spiritual counseling alone. "He really needed a doctor to help him, and it was very serious," recalled John Menter.

Father Wessel continued, "I have to tell him today that I can't help him any longer unless he seeks help from a doctor. It's all I can do for him right at this point. He needs a doctor now."

Father Wessel showed no fear or apprehension. He was very matter-of-fact. He had made his decision and was just telling young John about it. "And I guess he was telling me about it almost to kind of say, 'You know, you think *you've* got problems . . . I'm counseling someone over here who has some *real* problems' . . ."

Father did not betray a confidence. He never identified the person he was going to see. But he was trying to help John Menter put his own situation in perspective.

"But we'll talk about it more tonight," Father said, bringing the conversation to a close. "I have to get this straightened out."

John Menter said goodbye to Father, fully expecting that they would pick up the thread of their conversation at the basketball game later that evening.

"See you at the ball game," was the last thing Father Wessel said to John.

"I really can remember that afternoon talking to him," said John Menter, about his turmoil with the faculty member.

> Father Wessel talked to me and he stood up for me is what
> it was. And he didn't know me really per se, except for the little
> bit that we interacted . . . with the Masses for the class, and as
> senior class president, and maybe down on the football field . . .

or down in the locker room, joking around a little bit. But, you know, he came to my aid, and that's what I remember.[31]

After school was over, Father Wessel joined Father Sean Maguire and Jeanne for "coffee-and-tea time" in the kitchen of the rectory. It was about 2:30 in the afternoon. "The whole afternoon tea group felt very harmonious," Maguire recalled of that day. They all had "good feelings about each other."

During this conversation, Father made the unusual statement about his death to his two companions, and added that Mrs. Kelly had called asking him to visit her son Jack, who was acting up again.[32]

When he mentioned Jack Kelly that afternoon, Maguire recalled that John Wessel talked about him as one who was mentally disturbed. His fellow priest didn't get the sense that Father Wessel thought he posed a danger.[33]

It was at this time, too, that Father Wessel confided to Father Maguire—referring to the request to visit Jack Kelly—"I really don't want to go."[34] At that moment, he may have been experiencing the futility of it all, because he had counseled young Kelly before and felt that he could do no more.[35]

Father Maguire then remembered the Christmas party for the grade school faculty scheduled for three o'clock that afternoon. Sister Juliana Naulty, the grade school principal, and her faculty had worked hard on the preparations. All the priests had been invited and were expected to attend.

Assuming that Father Wessel was also going, as he had planned to, Father Maguire went up to his room to get his coat, thinking that Father Wessel would wait for him and that they would go together.

When he came back downstairs, at about 2:50 in the afternoon, Father Wessel was already gone. He assumed that John Wessel had left for the grade school function, and hurried over to meet him there.[36]

Father Wessel's mood was "ponderous when I last left him," Maguire would later recall, like "a man who had to make a choice"—whether to attend the grade school faculty Christmas party that afternoon or to go instead to help Jack Kelly.[37]

But when Father Maguire arrived at the party and didn't see John Wessel, he realized what must have happened. "John Wessel will be delayed a little bit," he said to Sister Julianna. "John went on a sick call. There's a guy that needs some counseling."[38]

If it had been a *high school* function, Sean Maguire speculated, then Father Wessel probably would have chosen to go to it instead, because of his strong sense of duty and responsibility as chaplain of the high school.[39]

Before he left the school grounds, Father Wessel encountered student Peter Caroselli. This was some time after school had ended, Pete recalled, as he was just coming back from the Ocean County Library on Washington Street. Father stopped to talk with the young man briefly.

Father Wessel told Pete that he wanted to get another hatch cover to make into an altar like the one they had done before for the chapel. He asked the youth if he would go with him to Ship Bottom and pick up another hatch cover when they could arrange it. Pete had helped Father Wessel with the preparation of the first hatch cover, and he knew the place that Father had in mind.

"Sure," Pete said. It was now around three o'clock.[40]

Father Wessel then came upon Sister Francis Rita, the elderly mathematics teacher and high school guidance counselor, and exchanged a few words with her on his way to the Kelly apartment. "I must visit someone who is beyond my help," he said.[41]

Then, Father John Wessel got into his station wagon and drove the half mile to the Kelly apartment on Washington Street on his mission of mercy to help the disturbed young veteran.[42]

*   *   *

Unbeknown to Father Wessel, Jack Kelly had been thinking of killing someone.[43] Indeed, in the throes of a severe psychotic episode, he thought of killing his own mother and father on the night of Thursday, December 16th. By the next morning, December 17th, his thoughts of killing had ripened into a plan to kill.

At nine o'clock that Friday morning, Jack Kelly walked from his apartment on Washington Street down to the Sportsman's Guide, a sporting goods shop on Water Street in Toms River. Mumbling and cursing to himself, he went in and out of the store two or three times without making a purchase. His conversations were not that coherent, recalled the clerk. Finally, he purchased a box of shotgun shells and left.

He walked back home with the shotgun shells and sat down, lost in his own little world. On that December 17th, John Kelly was not "one of us." Physically, he was in his apartment on Washington Street, but mentally he was far, far away, in an unreal private world of the paranoid schizophrenic—a world of bizarre thoughts and delusions, and of voices and visions urging him to kill.

The impulse to kill originated in Jack's disturbed mind because he believed that if he killed someone, the police would have to come and kill him, and he wanted to die so he could be reincarnated and come back as "a better person." He thought he would be doing a good thing, and that the person or persons he would kill would be spirits and wouldn't feel any pain.[44]

The day before Father Wessel came to retrieve him in Manasquan, Jack Kelly had found a religious pamphlet lying in a telephone booth as he was walking around town. Jack, still believing he was Jesus Christ, thought the pamphlet contained a message to him that he had to die and be reincarnated. From that point on he became obsessed with the idea.[45]

Back in Toms River, Jack Kelly began making vague attempts to get himself killed by picking fights with strangers.[46] He even went to a local tavern and got into a fight, thinking himself like Jesus Christ throwing the money changers out of the temple. He was hoping that someone would kill him, but instead he was merely removed from the tavern.[47]

On the night of Thursday, December 16th—the day that Father Wessel was visiting friends and family in Trenton and Mount Holly—Jack began running in front of cars along Washington Street, and pulling open the car doors of motorists when they stopped for the traffic light, hoping that someone would take him out of his mental agony and kill him. Then he could come back as a better person. But the motorists, surprised and annoyed, just slammed their doors shut and drove off.[48]

That same night, while eating dinner with his parents, Jack suddenly pounced on his father and poked him sharply in the throat, saying, "You're plotting against me!" As his mother screamed, his father managed to subdue him.[49] In Jack's own mind he didn't think he was hurting anybody. He thought he was doing good. His worried and confused parents had no idea that their son's interior reason for the attack was to try to provoke his own father into killing him.[50]

Jack had been reading a book about Jesus Christ, and with the distorted logic characteristic of his schizophrenic disease, he imagined a passage in the book to imply that Christ's true message was to hate everyone, even to hate his own mother and father.[51] Later, Mrs. Kelly came downstairs at about two or three o'clock in the morning. Jack was wide awake and wanted to discuss the contents of the book, which he found upsetting.

"Look at this, Mother. This book tells you to hate your mother and your father," he said.

"Oh, Jack, you must've read it wrong. It can't say that," his mother replied.

"Well, read it. I want you to read it," her son said.

It was very late. "Jack, can't it wait until morning? I'm tired," his mother said.

But they never did get to talk about it the next morning.[52]

Sometime during the night of December 16th, Jack first thought about shooting his parents.[53] He didn't have to get himself killed, he reasoned with distorted schizophrenic logic. Instead, he would kill his parents, or somebody else, and then the police would have to come and kill him and he would still be able to be reincarnated.[54]

These thoughts, of course, were not the thoughts of the "real" young man of before the war—the happy, athletic fellow who was loving to his parents and sister, was pleasant and kind, and was well liked by his friends and teachers—nor of the brave and heroic soldier who had saved the lives of several comrades in battle. Rather, such thoughts manifested fully the delusional thinking and hallucinations that were characteristic of the acute phase of Jack Kelly's disease.

By the following morning, Friday, December 17th, the plan to kill had been formed in the young veteran's deranged mind. Jack believed he heard voices and saw figures that were saying things to him, encouraging him to go through with his plans.

In his apartment on Washington Street, Jack Kelly loaded the shells he had bought that morning into his 12-gauge shotgun. He was going to start shooting at anyone that went by.[55]

When the landlord, Mr. Brown, came over to the Kelly apartment around midday to fix a leak under the kitchen sink, Jack thought the man was really his father in disguise. As the landlord left and walked back to his own apartment, Jack ran upstairs and aimed the loaded shotgun at him from the second-floor window. For some reason, Jack did not, or could not, pull the trigger. Mr. Brown very nearly became the tragic victim of Jack Kelly's sickness on that day.[56]

Jack went over to the landlord's apartment and asked him to come back. By that time, Mr. Kelly had come home for lunch, and for most of the time, the three men were together in the apartment. The landlord looked at the sink again and left.[57]

Mr. Kelly noticed his son was acting "very nervous" and had removed the second-floor bedroom windows on the cold, wintery day. He thought it strange. The elder Kelly replaced all the windows and called his wife to tell her about Jack's odd behavior before he, too, returned to work.

When he left, his son Jack was alone in the apartment.[58]

Father John Wessel was the next person to come through the door. It was about 3:30 in the afternoon.[59] He went to the Kelly home armed with nothing but his total faith in and surrender to the will of God.

*   *   *

Father Wessel knew that Jack Kelly needed psychiatric help more than spiritual counseling, and a scheduled faculty function offered a convenient reason for avoiding a hopeless mission, "but being the kind of person he was, he couldn't turn his back on someone in trouble," observed Monsignor Joseph C. Shenrock.[60]

Everything happened so quickly in the space of a few hours that afternoon. So quickly that there had been no time for Father to ask the young people in his little morning prayer group to pray for him and for the person who needed his counseling, as he had done before.

Perhaps ringing in Father's memory as he entered the Kelly apartment was the injunction of his friend, Dr. Julio Del Castillo:

"You shouldn't play at being a psychiatrist . . . You take too many risks . . . You mustn't go to the home of persons who are mentally ill because there is danger involved."

But perhaps, drowning out that voice was another one, this in his own voice: "You have to give, give, give, and keep on giving until there's nothing else to give—and then you have to keep on giving."

Like many of their neighbors in those simpler days, the front door of the Kellys' home was left unlocked. Father Wessel was told that he could walk right in, the door was open, and so he did.[61] He sat down in the living room and began to speak to Jack Kelly.

There is no record of what transpired between Father John Wessel and Jack Kelly. Both parents were at work. And Jack Kelly, in the throes of a psychotic episode, later said that he had no recollection of their conversation.[62]

From everything we know of Father Wessel, we can infer what may have transpired:

It is beyond question that Father Wessel would have been patient and kind as he talked with Jack Kelly, as he had been so many times before with the inmates in the Trenton Psychiatric Hospital.

He would have gently told the young veteran what he'd already decided he must: That Jack really needed a doctor, a psychiatrist, to help him. That he couldn't continue to counsel Jack any longer unless he saw a doctor, but would be ready to help him get through this if he was willing to try to help himself. And, Father may have added, Jack's parents were very worried about him.

Perhaps Father Wessel soon realized that his words were not being heard and understood by the unresponsive young man sitting across from him. As the young man's gaze darted around the room, seeing shadows and hearing voices that existed only in his mind, Father may have sensed that Jack, hallucinating and psychotic, was lost in some private and delusional world that he could not enter.

When he saw that he had done as much as he possibly could for the young man, Father Wessel left the apartment.

Father Wessel's words had indeed fallen on deaf ears. When he sat down and began talking, Jack Kelly wasn't listening to anything Father was saying. The disturbed Vietnam veteran imagined that when Father Wessel walked in, the priest had told him that he wanted Jack to shoot him, and Jack was lost in the schizophrenic world of his own thoughts and visions.

With distorted logic, Jack reasoned that since Father Wessel was a priest, maybe the Church was trying to help him because they "knew" he, Jack, was Jesus Christ and they wanted to help him die and be reincarnated as the "true Christ."[63]

As Father Wessel was walking to his car, Jack Kelly ran upstairs to the bedroom. He picked up the loaded shotgun and aimed it from the second-floor window. Again, he could not pull the trigger. He paused for a moment before aiming the shotgun for the second time as Father Wessel walked a little farther down the sidewalk. Jack could feel his hand, his finger, tightening around the trigger. Again, he paused for a moment. From somewhere in his mind he thought, *I don't want to shoot him*, but his finger kept getting tighter and tighter around the trigger until . . .

. . . he pulled the trigger. The gun went off. This time the weapon found its mark. Jack Kelly shot the young priest in the neck and upper back from a distance of about thirty feet.[64]

Father John Wessel collapsed face down on the sidewalk, only a few feet away from the door of his station wagon.

And so, at about 3:45 p.m. on December 17, 1971, Father John Wessel, a priest who was only trying to help the mentally ill young man at the request of his distraught mother, became the victim of John Kelly's sickness.[65]

In the words of Scripture: "No greater love is there than that a man lay down his life for his friends" (John 15:13).

*   *   *

John Kelly remained at the window waiting for the police to arrive. He intended to shoot at them and to keep on shooting until he himself was killed.

Mrs. Cunningham, the Kellys' next-door neighbor, was startled by the sound of the loud shot. She instinctively gathered up her infant son, bolted the front door, closed the curtains, and ran upstairs.

Cautiously, she looked out the window and saw Father Wessel lying face down on the sidewalk. She recognized him as the priest whom she had met on the Kellys' porch only last week. She immediately called her husband at work, and then the police. Then she phoned Mrs. Kelly at work.[66]

During that period of time, while waiting for the police to come for him, Jack Kelly became frightened and went to his own rear bedroom, and put the shotgun and the shells in the closet.

It was at about 3:50 p.m. when the police and first aid squad got the first call about a man lying in the sidewalk near the Washington Street Apartments.[67] An ambulance of the Toms River First Aid Squad raced to the scene and arrived first; immediately thereafter, the Dover Township police. They found Father Wessel lying where he fell, bleeding, unconscious, and gravely wounded. He was rushed by ambulance to Community Memorial Hospital.[68]

After the ambulance and the police arrived, Jack Kelly came out of his apartment. Shortly thereafter, he re-entered it with the police, who found the shotgun and the remainder of the shells in the bedroom closet on the second floor.

The expended shell which had delivered its devastating pellets to the body of the young priest was found outside on the grounds of the apartment.

Later, it was determined that Father Wessel had been struck by ten pellets from the same shotgun shell.

John Kelly was taken into custody and interrogated by the police. At one point during his interrogation, he exclaimed: I confess because I thought I was Jesus Christ. I thought if I killed someone they would kill me and I'd come back to life as a good person. But I didn't think men felt pain . . . I didn't think Father Wessel will feel it . . . "the real me never wanted to hate anyone" . . . I thought everyone died and came back.[69]

When Detective Captain Herbert of the Ocean County Prosecutor's Office first saw John Kelly, it was apparent to him that the young man was not a normal person at the time. The Captain called a local psychiatrist, who interviewed Kelly approximately an hour to an hour and a half after the shooting. The psychiatrist later concluded, "He was sick. He was not responsible."[70]

John Kelly was arraigned for assault and battery with intent to kill. At the police station, he fantasized that one of his lawyers was Father Wessel, reincarnated.[71]

Kelly was immediately taken to the State Psychiatric Hospital—the Vroom Building—the same hospital for the criminally insane in Trenton where Father Wessel had provided spiritual comfort for the mentally disturbed inmates. His treating physician was Dr. Julio Del Castillo, who now had the unbearably painful task of caring for the young man who had just shot his dear friend.

But the psychiatrist was a professional, and immediately felt compassion for the disturbed young veteran.[72] When Dr. Del Castillo, along with other staff psychiatrists, examined Jack Kelly on December 20th, he concluded that Kelly was suffering from acute paranoid schizophrenia—the "most severe type of mental illness"—and was "grossly psychotic and distorted at the time" of the shooting.[73]

CHAPTER 33

NO GREATER LOVE

The devastating news traveled quickly.

Father Wessel's family and close friends were rapidly notified by telephone, and rushed to Community Memorial Hospital in the late afternoon of Friday, December 17th. By early evening, Mrs. Kathleen Wessel, along with her children—Maryann and her husband Bill, Dr. Edward Wessel and his wife Pat—and Father James Dubell, had gathered at the hospital to join Father Donovan and the priests and sisters of St. Joseph's parish. Many of Father Wessel's friends and fellow members of the clergy also came to offer moral support to his family. It was a saddened, numb and devastated group that kept vigil at the hospital that Friday night. As if adding to the misery of those inside was the weather outside—horrible, cold, and raining.

Through frantic telephone calls, Father Wessel's friends, young and old, contacted one another and spread the news from Toms River to Trenton. Several of his friends from the Blessed Sacrament CYO—Wes Ritterbusch, Barry Anderson, and Barry's father—immediately drove to the hospital that evening to offer moral support and to try to donate blood. The latter was of no use.

A doctor at the hospital told Wes Ritterbusch, "I don't see where he has a chance."[1]

Still, people hoped and prayed for a miracle.

It was just about dinner time when the local radio station began reporting that a young man had been shot with a double-barreled shotgun from an apartment window by another young man on Washington Street,

Toms River. The news traveled fast and it wasn't too long before the community at large heard that Father John P. Wessel, an associate priest at St. Joseph, was the "young man" who had been shot.[2]

The basketball game in the high school that night, where John Menter was supposed to meet Father Wessel, went on as planned.[3] When Menter walked in, the game was already in progress. Everything seemed normal. Most of the spectators had not yet heard the news.

"Sister, have you seen Father Wessel? I'm supposed to meet him," he asked one of the nuns. It was then that John Menter learned that Father had been shot as he was leaving the house of a young man named John Kelly, whom he had gone to counsel.[4]

John Menter, upset and shocked, realized that this was the same young Vietnam veteran Father Wessel had talked about just a few hours ago—the young man of whom Father had said, "He doesn't need a priest. He needs a doctor."

When Sister Carmella returned from her shopping expedition Friday evening, she saw the Sisters standing by the office door and became very frightened, thinking that something had happened to her critically ill mother.

"We went into the office, and they said to me, 'Father Wessel was shot this afternoon. We've been looking for you for hours. Everybody's been calling.' I just nearly collapsed. I could not believe it."[5]

Later that evening, the principal called Sister Nancy at her convent in the Bronx to tell her that Father Wessel had been shot. When Sister Nancy returned to Toms River, she found the course book that Father had used to substitute teach her sophomore Religion class, stuck in her mailbox, with his scrawled note to her—"I went nowhere. Bummer!!!"[6]

Sister Teresa Agnes, the high school Biology teacher, had been in the convent alone that dreary, dark Friday afternoon, because the grade school teachers were having their Christmas party. She recalled:

> Monsignor Donovan called and he told me that Father Wessel had been shot. And I remember saying to him, "Has his spinal cord been severed?" He said "Yes." . . . And I said, "Is he going to make it?" And he stopped dead. And after two minutes, he said, "I don't think so."[7]

And when Harry Cascione heard the news, he too was shocked. "Oh my God, the poor man just came to our Holy Name meeting the Sunday before, and now he's shot!"

He immediately remembered Father Wessel's talk that day—how he told the men to pour out everything they had for Christ. He was shot doing "exactly what he had said during the talk," thought Cascione. "He's really poured out everything. He poured out his life's blood . . . trying to help someone."[8]

From the very beginning, the severity of Father Wessel's injuries was such that there was little reason to hope. When Dr. Edward Wessel saw his younger brother that night, he said he was going to die. Through his tears, Ed told his sister, "I know, Maryann, that it's too late." Dr. Wessel sent for his medical partner, another surgeon, to give a second opinion, but even before it came, he knew. "He's gone, Johnny's gone," he said.[9]

Still, Father Wessel continued to cling to life. Still, people hoped and prayed for a miracle.

During the week before Christmas, Father Wessel, comatose and on life supports, was visited daily in the hospital by members of his family, by Father James Dubell, and by his fellow priests from St. Joseph's. Each day they would talk to him, pray and recite the Rosary, read him his mail, and tell him of all the prayers and well wishes sent by his many, many friends.[10] Although Father never gave any outward response, they hoped and believed that somehow he heard what they were telling him.[11]

Dr. Edward Wessel firmly believed that the comatose could still hear, so he would visit and talk to his brother all the time and encourage others to do the same. His older children wrote little notes to their uncle which were read to him.[12]

Bishop George W. Ahr, the Bishop of Trenton, who little more than six years earlier had ordained John Wessel, visited him several times.[13]

Bishop Ahr was "a priest's bishop." He had tremendous respect for priests, and great compassion. His emotions were very deep and not superficial, but self-contained; outwardly, he gave the appearance of being very stoic. Yet, one eyewitness will never forget how the Bishop, upon entering Father Wessel's hospital room, wrapped his arms around the two devastated young associate priests from St. Joseph's who were keeping vigil at Father Wessel's bedside, as if to comfort them as a father would his sons.[14]

As a man of deep compassion, the spiritual leader of the Diocese of Trenton greatly desired to alleviate the suffering occasioned by Father

Wessel's shooting; yet by faith, the Bishop was resigned to it as being a part of God's plan, even though mysterious, recalled a colleague.[15]

During that week, many prayers and Masses were offered in Toms River and in Trenton for Father Wessel's recovery, for the Wessel family, and for Jack Kelly and his family.

At the high school, Christmas festivities were cancelled. What was to have been the Christmas Mass that Father Wessel was planning for the students when he was shot instead became an occasion to urgently petition God for Father Wessel's recovery. Father Lawrence Donovan celebrated the liturgy in his place for the high school teenagers, who were much more reverent and somber than usual.[16]

And in Trenton, when Father Shenrock asked the parishioners of Blessed Sacrament to pray for the Wessel family at Mass on the Sunday following the shooting, everybody—men, women, children—began to weep.[17]

Another congregation brought to tears was at St. Joseph Church the following Sunday. Mrs. Mildred Kelly, racked by despair, got up and spoke to the congregation after the seven o'clock morning Mass and begged forgiveness for her son who, she explained, was not well.

Recounting all the futile attempts she and her husband had made to get some help for Jack, Father Wessel was "her last hope for her son," she told fellow parishioners.[18]

Father Wessel's family publicly extended their forgiveness to John Kelly and their sympathy and prayers to his family. "My family extends our hearts to the young man," said Mrs. Kathleen Wessel. "My son would not want it any other way."[19] Father Shenrock was sent on behalf of the Wessel family to the Vroom building, where Kelly was incarcerated. There he personally assured the troubled young veteran of their forgiveness.[20]

Jack Kelly's uncle, a priest in Illinois whom he idolized, offered a special Mass on Christmas Day for Father Wessel and for his own nephew.[21]

Even now, Father John Wessel was bringing people together.

For John Wessel's family, the week before Christmas was consumed with grieving and praying for his recovery; trying to carry on with Christmas preparations for the children's sake; receiving numerous well-wishers who called to ask what they could do; and responding to endless inquiries from members of the press, who were intensely interested in the story.[22]

The front page headline of the *Trenton Times* on Saturday, "Fr. Wessel Shot on Mission of Mercy," was heart-rending to Maryann Beitel. Each day, the newspapers and radio would chronicle her brother's condition, which was essentially unchanged. Even stoic and seasoned newspaper reporters were affected by the story and expressed genuine sorrow to the Wessel family. "We're so sorry," the reporters told Maryann. "Everywhere we go, people are saying, 'Isn't it just tragic about Father Wessel?'"[23]

As Father Wessel lay fighting for his life, those who knew him, and even those who did not, watched and waited, wept and prayed. They prayed for their priest and friend, and they prayed for his attacker. They tried to make sense out of the senseless. They asked themselves why. They tried to comprehend the larger meaning in the fateful intersection of two young lives which, as one newspaper article observed, represented "the sum total of their times."[24]

The worst of times for Father Wessel's family lay ahead as his loved ones tried to get through Christmas while he was lying comatose in the hospital. Mrs. Kathleen Wessel bravely went ahead with her plans for dinner on Christmas Day, carrying on for her family even though she was bleeding from the heart.[25]

Christmas Day was especially difficult, not the least of which was the poignant memory of how, in happier days, John Wessel would dress up in his red Santa suit and white beard, always slightly askew, and play Santa Claus for his young Beitel nieces and nephews. It had always been an occasion of much fun and laughter in years past.[26]

Now the vibrant, laughing man who so enjoyed life was lying motionless in a hospital room. There were no signs or sounds of life, only the rhythmic motion of the respirator, constantly blowing air in and out of his lungs. His eyes were closed, his mouth was open, and he lay still. Toward the end, his head began to twitch and shake, but it was a nervous reflex not controlled in any way.[27]

What was surprising to those who knew him was the extent to which the assault had so altered his physical appearance. Father Wessel's face was quite swollen almost beyond recognition.[28] The wounded man lying in the hospital bed did not resemble the John Wessel of their hearts and memories.

The young people who had been Father Wessel's close friends gathered together often and prayed during the Christmas holidays. A special CYO Mass was held for Father at the Trenton headquarters of the CYO on Christmas night, Saturday, December 25th, bringing together his young friends from Trenton and Toms River.[29] A number of high school students from Toms River traveled to Trenton for the Mass to the place that Father had introduced them to not long before.

That the young people had no hesitation to leave their homes and families on Christmas night and travel long distances spoke volumes of their love for Father Wessel. As they linked arms and sang the *Prayer of St. Francis* that night, the words of his favorite song had special meaning.[30]

Sunday morning, December 26th. A prayer service was held at the Catholic campus ministry house at Fairleigh Dickinson University, where some of Father's friends from the CYO in Trenton were attending college, and where Father Wessel himself had come for their charismatic prayer meetings. They had gathered together to pray for Father Wessel's recovery and healing.

At the conclusion of the service, they received word that their prayers had been answered, although not in the way they hoped or expected.[31]

Father Wessel was not to have the miraculous healing prayed for. Rumors abounded that Father had opened his eyes, emerged from his coma, and cried when he was read his Christmas cards. Sadly, none were true.[32] There was no realistic chance of recovery, medically speaking, and as the hopelessness of his situation became known and accepted, prayers turned more to asking that "God's will be done."

Father had been on artificial life supports almost from the moment he was brought to the hospital, and those who loved him began to wonder, How long? On Christmas Eve night, December 24th, Father James Dubell had taken Father Wessel's mother to visit him. Probably to spare her, many had urged her not to go, saying, "There's nothing you can do," but she wanted to see him.

But when the grief-stricken mother first beheld her son in his hospital bed, severely injured and hooked up to all the equipment, Kathleen Wessel collapsed and fell to the floor.[33] When she became composed, she blessed her son with Holy Water from the Marian shrine of Knock in Ireland, in the hopes that he would recover.[34]

It was now Christmas night. At the hospital, Dr. Edward Wessel and Father Dubell were struggling with the question of how much longer to prolong John Wessel's life by artificial means. In that situation, Church teaching was clear: Although it was gravely and morally wrong to perform any act or omission that causes death, or to deny a dying patient "ordinary" care, there was no moral obligation to continue "extraordinary" medical procedures to unnaturally prolong life.[35]

But it was a decision no one wanted to make. "Well, let's sleep on it tonight," they decided, and went home.

It was not long after Dr. Edward Wessel and his wife had completed the long drive back to their home in Newton, New Jersey, that the hospital phoned with the news.[36]

Sometime in the early morning hours of Sunday, December 26th, Father John Wessel's great and generous heart took its last beat. He died at 3:25 a.m. in Community Memorial Hospital, Toms River, on the ninth day after receiving his fatal wounds.[37]

"He felt no pain," said Dr. Lucian De Marco, the physician who had treated him since his admission to the hospital. "No, he felt no pain. He was being sedated and taken care of. The spinal cord was transected (severed) by one of the pellets from the gunshot wound in the neck."[38]

Dr. De Marco said there had been no chance of Father Wessel's improving. He never emerged from the coma he slipped into after the shooting.[39] Three of the vertebrae in his neck, from C-3 to C-6, had been transected, and there was hemorrhage of the brain in two different sites.[40]

Dr. Edward Wessel arrived at the Wessel's Mount Holly home in the early morning hours to personally tell his mother and sister that "Johnny's gone." There was, recalled his sister, "a peace that settled in all of us because we realized that he is with God. We could feel his presence."[41]

"I think John held on until the day after Christmas . . . just to get *us* through Christmas," said Maryann.[42]

*   *   *

The long, sorrowful, nine-day vigil was over. Father John P. Wessel had entered into eternal life with Christ on the Lord's Day.

*   *   *

"His death hit me hard," said Michael Choma, his friend from the seminary.

A world away, Father Choma, a military chaplain in Bien Hoa, South Vietnam, attached to the 229th Assault Helicopter Battalion, had finally received a letter from a friend the day after Christmas telling him that John Wessel had been shot in the back and was not expected to live.

"My jaw dropped. It was like a real hurt feeling," Choma recalled. "The first thing that came to mind was what he said to me . . ."[43]

It was the spring of 1971 when Father Michael Choma came to Blessed Sacrament in Trenton to visit with his good friend, John Wessel. Father Choma was headed for Vietnam as a military chaplain. Some years before, he had joined a unit of the National Guard in Baltimore. When his Guard unit went to Vietnam, Father Choma went with it, but before being shipped out, in May of 1971, he was given a thirty-day leave and made the rounds of friends to say goodbyes. Choma recalled sitting with Father Wessel one afternoon in the rectory:

"I went up there to visit John. It was just before I was going over to 'Nam. I don't think he was too happy with me in the military, but he didn't say anything." When Mike told him that he was going to Vietnam, John just said, "Hmmm," nothing more. "So I just got the impression that he didn't agree with what I was doing . . . but he never really expressed it."

They started to talk about many things, and John Wessel mentioned to Michael Choma that he was "counseling some drug addicts." Choma got the impression that it wasn't easy, and that perhaps his friend was working with some tough characters. And then John Wessel made an unusual remark. "I won't be surprised, with what I'm doing, if I get shot in the back someday."

John Wessel was "dead serious" when he said that, recalled Choma. "That was the first time that he said something that serious and really meant it, and it struck home."

Mike was astonished. His first reaction was to say, "You've got to be kidding!"

And John simply said, "No." Just that, "No." His mood was serious—but then, that was the end of it.

Both men did not want to dwell on unpleasant subjects when they got together, and never more so than now. They moved on to more congenial topics before saying their goodbyes.

A week or so later, Father Michael Choma was on his way to Vietnam. Neither could have known that the afternoon they spent at the Blessed Sacrament Rectory in the spring of 1971 would be the last time the two old friends would ever see each other again.[44]

Father Wessel, shot in the back, had died in the precise manner as he had predicted months earlier to Michael Choma during their last conversation.

*   *   *

The next few days would be consumed with the details and rituals of wake, funeral and burial.

A private wake and viewing for Father Wessel's immediate family was held the next night, Monday, December 27th, at St. Joseph's Rectory. By this time, the swelling from his fatal injuries had diminished somewhat, and he was able to have an open casket.[45] Father Wessel's body was then transferred to the church the next day in a solemn procession for public viewing.[46]

Funeral preparations were handled by the Kedz Funeral Home, where Father Wessel himself had come to officiate at the wakes and funerals of several of his parishioners during his three months at St. Joseph's. From the very first moment that Al Kedz received word that he had been chosen by the Wessel family to handle the funeral of the young priest he had befriended, a feeling of awe came over him. It was as if he had been asked "to bury the Pope or a Saint." His staff had the same feeling, working double duty in preparation for Father's funeral without ever having to be asked. It was no small task to prepare for a ceremony of this magnitude in such a short time.

Father Wessel's body was clothed in the new suit he had just bought—and for once, a decent pair of shoes. He was laid out in white vestments trimmed with light blue. Traditionally, a priest is buried in a casket lined with burgundy red velvet, but because of Father Wessel's youth, the funeral director selected a lining of powder blue velvet to match the blue trim of his vestments. A special casket was custom made in less than a day's time. And was it no accident that the color blue was also associated with the Blessed Mother? In his hands, Father Wessel held his black Rosary beads.[47]

When the funeral director first brought the casket carrying Father Wessel's body to the rectory, and before his family arrived, he asked the priests and sisters present, "Is everything okay? Does he look the way that he was?"[48]

The first thing they noticed was that Father's pants were neatly pressed and his shoes were nicely shined—the priests had taken care of that. Sister Carmella remarked about it, and Father Donovan said, "Yeah, well, we weren't going to bury him in those old shoes."[49]

Sister Carmella then said to the pastor, "That isn't the way he combed his hair."

Father Donovan took a little comb out of his pocket and gently said, "Fix it for me." The principal combed and fluffed Father Wessel's hair a bit and tried to get the little wave to come over his forehead like it used to.[50]

Father Wessel's funeral was a shared endeavor in which almost everyone in the community wanted to participate. The bulk of the funeral preparations fell to the priests and nuns of St. Joseph's parish. Father Donovan and the priests, and Sister Carmella and the Sisters of St. Dominic, together with student volunteers, worked round the clock to make Father's last farewell a fitting, meaningful, dignified, and holy tribute to him.

The men of the Knights of Columbus, arrayed in their fine regalia, swords, uniforms and plumed hats, formed a ceremonial honor guard for the funeral in the church.

Students from the high school also formed a young people's guard of honor to stand by his coffin for the public viewing in shifts throughout the night, and for the funeral Mass the following day.[51]

Even the Police Chief had called to ask, "What can we do?" The men of the Dover Township Police Department served as honorary pallbearers as the coffin bearing Father Wessel's body was taken from the funeral parlor to the rectory on Monday, and again when the casket was taken from the rectory to the church the next day.[52]

The police officers were honored to carry Father Wessel's body, and didn't want to offend in any way, even to the point that they were willing to remove their firearms in the church.

"Should we take our guns off and carry Father?" they asked the funeral director.

"No, that's part of your uniform," Kedz replied, "leave them on."[53]

On Tuesday, December 28th, the township closed off Hooper Avenue, the main street, for about an hour, and the whole entourage, priests, sisters, students, and the police pallbearers, walked in solemn procession with the casket from the rectory to St. Joseph's Church.[54]

These were impressive gestures on the township's part.

A three o'clock "Folk Mass" held immediately thereafter filled the church and signaled the beginning of the public viewing.[55]

Father Wessel's body lay in state at St. Joseph's Church from 3 p.m. Tuesday, December 28th, until his Mass of Resurrection the following morning. More than seven thousand mourners, many of them teenagers, filed past the bier during the 19 hours that his body lay in state. The Masses preceding the funeral drew overflow crowds.[56] It was not only the Catholic community in attendance. People of all denominations came to pay their respects.[57]

As soon as Ronald Garrett, the high school boy from Blessed Sacrament parish, heard of Father's death, he drove to Toms River, arriving in time for the wake in the church. He insisted on staying by the coffin all night. "He was like a father, a teacher, a brother to me," the youth said. "He gave me six years of his life, so the least I can do is give him a night of mine."[58]

It was then that the rest of the Blessed Sacrament CYO truly realized how much Father Wessel had meant to Ronald Garrett. His friends from Trenton tried to cajole him to leave, saying, "It's late and we're all tired. We haven't slept or eaten. We really need to go."

But Ronald said to them, "He never left me and I'm not going to leave him. I can't leave him. He was my friend and I'm going to stay here all night with him."[59]

"It was just really touching," recalled a Trenton CYO member. "It said so much for Ronnie to have done that. He was just such a private kid that it just really touched all of us that he would want to be there and not leave."[60]

A newspaper reporter for *The Trenton Times* chronicled the night-long vigil Ronald Garrett kept at Father Wessel's bier:

> Students from St. Joseph's offered [Ronnie] a place to sleep but he refused, insisting on staying with Father Wessel the whole night through.
>
> The St. Joseph students agreed to check on him from time to time and bring him coffee.
>
> [Ronnie] talked about the times when Father Wessel was his religion teacher at Cathedral High in Trenton. "He ran the searches. They're like retreats. I went on two, one as a searcher and one as a helper. I was working in the kitchen and he'd keep going, he never stopped, until [Sunday] night when he used to just collapse from the exhaustion.

"He loved to ski, he was a good skier, taught me to ski. He'd just glide down the hill beautifully. He was really strong—it'd take four of us sometimes just to bring him down when we played football.

"He was human," said [Ronnie], fighting back a choked sound. "It doesn't look like him at all," he said pointing to the coffin at the head of the aisle. "It's not his face—not his body. The only thing that looks real is his hands. They're his hands."

A man at the back of the church explained that he is not a Catholic but he still knew Father Wessel. Father Wessel had been associate pastor at St. Joseph's only since last September, but he quickly became well-known around Toms River, the man explained.

Robin Kerney, "Night-Long Watch Kept At Father Wessel's Bier—Two Congregations Join in Mourning Priest," (December 29, 1971), *The Trenton Times*, Trenton, N.J., 1971. All rights reserved. Reprinted with permission.

There was still a steady stream of mourners on Tuesday night, even into the wee hours of the morning. Many who were coming off shift work would stop in; some would come and return. Throughout the night and into the next morning, there was never a time that the church was empty.[61]

The traditional Mass of Resurrection at 10:30 a.m. on Wednesday morning, December 29th, had perhaps more pomp and ceremony than John Wessel would have liked. Before an altar bright with Christmas wreaths and poinsettias, Bishop George W. Ahr was the principal celebrant of the Mass, which lasted almost two hours. Nearly forty priests of the diocese, including the six members of John Wessel's ordination class, were concelebrants.[62] His young nephew, Carlton Wessel, served as an altar boy.[63] The chalice used during Father Wessel's Mass of Resurrection was the same Bordentown chalice that had belonged to his Irish priest-uncles, Denis and John Duggan.[64]

His funeral was in essence "like a reunion," wrote Father Peter M.J. Stravinskas of Father Wessel in his essay, *Sanctity in a Contemporary Key.* "The Bishop who ordained him was the principal celebrant; Monsignor Foley and Father Kelly who were present at his First Communion were concelebrants as was Father Shenrock who was the deacon at his First Mass; Father Dubell preached the homily; a thousand people whose lives he touched thronged St. Joseph's Church."[65]

Father Wessel had only been in Toms River three short months, and yet, it seemed as though the whole community was packed into St. Joseph's Church that morning, along with most of his Trenton parishioners as well.[66] Both communities were joined in shock and sadness. Whether they realized it or not, their presence was a tremendous support for Father Wessel's mother and family. The funeral ceremonies were difficult, but the family was sustained by the outpouring of love and solidarity from people of all ages.[67]

Among those in the packed congregation was Sister Eileen Egan, Father Wessel's grade school classmate, who shared his youthful desire for the religious life. Sister M. Espiritu Dempsey, Sister M. Raymond Rafferty, and Sister M. Christina Murphy, his grade school teachers, had come from Marywood in Scranton, Pennsylvania. A group of priests who had been his seminary classmates had driven up from Baltimore. Sister Elise Betz, the former eighth grade teacher at Blessed Sacrament School, had come down from New York.

"It was huge and powerful and terribly sad," Sister Elise recalled of the funeral. "All these kids that he had helped and that he loved so much, they were just broken. . . . It was just packed with teenagers, all of them crying."[68]

Father Wessel's family chose as pallbearers for the funeral Mass those who, to their best knowledge, had been among his dearest friends in life. The three young CYO men who were on the boat when the mast broke the first time, several other members of the CYO, and several adults, were honored to serve as lay pallbearers.[69]

The choir of St. Joseph High School sang to the accompaniment of an organ and several guitars in the choir loft. The guitarists included young people from St. Joseph's and Blessed Sacrament who had been among Father Wessel's close friends. They could not help but notice that the songs chosen for the solemn funeral Mass, and accompanied by the deep, resonant church organ, were so much more traditional than the music the teens would have played and sang with Father Wessel at their Youth Masses.[70]

"The funeral was a harder experience for me than I thought it would be," recalled Jayne Hartley, who continued:

I myself received much strength by merely being with my friends; my brothers and sisters who had shared all that I had with Father Wessel. The whole spirit of the day reminded me of Father Wessel. I could not help but think that even in death he was bringing people together, drawing friends closer. The ceremony itself was everything I am sure Father would *not* have wanted. . . . I feel he would have preferred a small, quiet funeral. The nature of the man denied such a quiet funeral, however.[71]

When deacon John Patrick Wessel and his six seminary classmates were ordained by Bishop Ahr in St. Mary's Cathedral, Trenton, on a sunny day in May 1965, the Catholic newspaper, *The Monitor*, contained a prophetic editorial entitled, "Our New Priests."

Ordination is both an end and a beginning. It closes the long years of study and sacrifice that have marked preparation for the priesthood and it marks the entrance upon a new and vital phase of a dedicated life. The service of God and of his creatures on earth becomes the preoccupation of the new priest until his summons by death.

This is not a calling for the weak of heart or those who would cling to the pleasures the world has to offer. Those who follow Him must detach themselves from material interests and strive with a single purpose in view—to do the will of God in all things for His honor and glory and the good of mankind.

This is not an easy decision to make. It calls for a sincere vocation and spiritual courage. The young men who enter the priesthood after the years of trial and endeavor accordingly command our admiration. They stand apart by reason of their superiority in many ways.

The Diocese of Trenton is enriched by the accession of these seven young men to the priesthood. The future holds for them the certainty of noble accomplishments for the progress of the Faith and the welfare of their fellow men.[72]

Six and a half years later, the men of John Wessel's ordination class and the Bishop who ordained them were reunited once again on the altar.

In his remarks at Father Wessel's funeral Mass, Bishop Ahr pointed out that the slain priest had been able to perceive today's problems and cope with them. "It may well be that the Father Wessels, because they have grown up in the midst of the most common problems of our times—the effects of narcotics, the war and tensions—are perhaps more aware of the need for complete dedication than the young priests of another day."[73]

The honor of preaching the eulogy itself fell to Father James Dubell. Putting aside his own shock and sorrow at the violent death of his lifelong friend, Father Dubell stood before the congregation and delivered an eloquent tribute to John Wessel's life.[74]

> *"No greater love is there than that a man lay down his life for his friends."*
>
> Somehow it was appropriate that Father John Patrick Wessel died an extraordinary death because he had lived an extraordinary life. Father Wessel was a Priest of God who loved people. When he was ordained in 1965, he had a dream that he should bring people together to share their successes and their failures, their hopes and their fears so that they could find the true meaning and value of life . . .
>
>   . . .
>
> . . . Bravery and courage were part of everything that Father John Wessel ever did—and so his commitment to the priesthood was *not* a temporary one but a permanent, life-long contract. He gave his all to the people he loved.—Here he gave his life in the line of duty trying to heal a despondent youth, but never let it be forgotten that, like the martyrs of old, Father Wessel gave it willingly and ungrudgingly for the sake of God's Kingdom. . . .
>
> Father Wessel's life and death were a mission of love. And since he believed in our Lord's own words "As long as you did it for one of these the least of my brethren, you did it for Me . . . enter into My Father's Kingdom," Father Wessel has earned eternal Light, Happiness, and Peace.

Boys and girls, Father Wessel has come to that final part of the *Search* program where you all join hands and dance and sing because you have seen the glory of the Lord in His love for you and your love for each other. I call upon all of the youth here present to let Father's life and death be an inspiration for you to always follow the two great commandments that you must love God and love your neighbor.

. . .

. . . The good that John's heroic life and death has done and will continue to do will never be fully known to you—such is the life of a great priest. For the rest, we can say: *"No greater love is there than that a man lay down his life for his friends."* For this we shall remember Father John Wessel always.[75]

At the conclusion of the Mass, as the pallbearers raised the casket above their shoulders for the final procession down the aisle, some of the young people spontaneously burst into the chorus from one of their folk songs, *I Am the Bread of Life*—"And I will raise him up on the last day." The song had not been planned, but the youths just took it out of everyone's hands. At once, the guitarists followed as the whole congregation picked up the refrain, and the church reverberated with their singing:

And I will raise him up,
And I will raise him up,
And I will raise him up on the last day.[76]

*   *   *

After a luncheon reception, the funeral cortege departed St. Joseph's Church at two o'clock on its way to the cemetery in Mount Holly, Father Wessel's hometown. Only a handful of cars was expected to go to the burial, but the funeral procession was enormous. Roughly over one hundred vehicles followed the cortege. So long was the funeral procession that the hearse didn't arrive in Mount Holly until almost 5 p.m. The sun had nearly set and darkness enveloped the late December afternoon.[77]

It took four police cars, spaced out at intervals in the procession, with radio contact, to be sure that all the cars stayed together. Also invaluable was the cooperation of the Dover Township police and Ocean County Sheriff's departments, and the police departments of all the towns that the cortege passed through who stepped in and helped guide the procession.[78]

If anyone had thought to remember, the somber procession of cars that day from east to west into the setting sun might have put one in mind of another caravan that crept across New Jersey from west to east, at sunrise on a day in June nearly six months before, full of joy and hope, trailing the *Eucharist* behind them in preparation for her maiden voyage. It was perhaps another small indication that Father Wessel's life had come full circle, his "mission of love" on earth accomplished.

As the procession drove away down Hooper Avenue and along Route 37, the main road out of Toms River, the people in town came out of their stores and houses and lined the roadsides, some waving, some just standing reverently. A woman with a child stood at the side of Route 37 as the cortege passed. "Silently, with a tear on her cheek, she blew a kiss at the hearse, unknowingly bestowing the town's final farewell," wrote one observer.[79]

As they slowly crept on to Mount Holly, the cortege passed a secluded little house out in the country, way out of town. Suddenly, a young woman came running out of the house to wave goodbye as the funeral procession passed. "I was just so startled by that one woman," recalled Bill Beitel. "I could see downtown, but I couldn't see this."[80]

The Beitels had taken their two older girls, Beth Ann (Father Wessel's godchild), 7 ½, and Susan, 5 ½, to the funeral. "Look at this. This is for your Uncle," Bill Beitel said to his daughters as they passed the people standing on the roadsides. "Look at this and remember this forever, because you will never see anything like this again." He tried to impress upon their young minds how special and beloved their Uncle John was to so many.[81]

The procession continued down Route 37 to Route 70 at Lakehurst, south to Route 73 until the New Lisbon Circle, then west along Route 38 to the cemetery in Mount Holly. All along the route, cars stopped by the sides of the road and clusters of people stood to see the procession go by. As they approached Mount Holly, more and more people began to gather along the way, the clusters of people got thicker, until at last the cortege reached the town of Mount Holly.[82]

Father John Wessel had come home.

Burial was in the family plot in St. Mary's Cemetery. The small Catholic country cemetery is nestled in a grove of pines on the outskirts of Mount

Holly on a rural route called the Marne Highway, named after the First World War. As the cortege drove into St. Mary's Cemetery, the mourners were greeted by the sight of the imposing white marble crucifix in the center. The figure of Christ on the cross seemed to beckon to the weary mourners and promise the departed eternal peace. Father John Wessel's grave was situated, if viewed from the cross, on Christ's right hand.

With a final graveside blessing from his lifelong friend, Father James Dubell, Father John Patrick Wessel was laid to rest next to his beloved father.[83]

He went at a young age to be with the One whose life he constantly strove to emulate.

*   *   *

A poignant newspaper article by Raymond J. Tuers, "Father Wessel Imbued with a Mission in Life," in the *Asbury Park Sunday Press* (January 9, 1972) captured the aftermath of Father Wessel's death and burial:

> His room in the rectory stood as a mute memorial to the man on the day of his funeral. His desk was cluttered. The stereo set was still; the record albums, ranging from Brahms to the Association, were untouched and dusty. In the corner stood a fishing pole and a guitar. On a table was a photo album crammed with pictures of young people. Beneath a family photograph were two boxes of new Christmas cards, unopened.[84]

The Asbury Park Press, © 1972. Used with Permission.

"On a shelf in his room in the rectory," Tuers continued, "he kept books such as, 'The Adolescent: His Search for Understanding,' and through them he polished his methods" of working with teenagers and developing his incredible rapport with them.[85]

Christmas presents were lying in Father Wessel's new station wagon where he left them after a day of shopping the Thursday before he was shot. Later, his family found them and tried to discern for whom they were intended. All the gifts had a certain touch, so they were able to distribute them to the relatives he had in mind. A new FM radio was meant for his mother. Little wind-up toys and things were gifts he loved to buy for his nieces and nephews.[86]

"The scruffiest-looking priest you ever saw!" was the way one relative, his uncle, Michael Hogan, lovingly described Father John Wessel. While engaging in one of his favorite pastimes, camping, he gladly traded in his black clerical garb for slacks, sweaters, hiking boots, and a tam-o'-shanter.

And his older brother, Dr. Edward Wessel, modestly said of the man: "The thing that you remember most about him is that he was a human being . . . he didn't carry his priesthood on his shoulder."

"There was nothing spectacular about him. He just had a job to love people. And he did it."[87]

*   *   *

John Wessel's priesthood was unswervingly dedicated to bringing to those whose lives he touched the unchanging message of Jesus Christ to love God and to love one another.[88]

Encompassed within a small circle, Father Wessel's life repeatedly touched the same people and places. Father Hayes, who baptized him, was the pastor of his first parish as a priest. Monsignor Joseph Shenrock, a longtime family friend who was the deacon at his first Mass, became the pastor at Blessed Sacrament as Father Wessel left. Monsignor James Dubell, his lifelong friend, fellow seminarian and member of his ordination class, was the eulogist at his funeral. His fourth, sixth, and eighth grade teachers, and two priests who assisted at his first Holy Communion, were present at his Mass of Resurrection. The distraught young veteran who fired the fatal shot was confined in the same hospital prison unit where Father Wessel had served as chaplain. The psychiatrist who treated the young man had been a friend and confidant of the slain priest.[89]

The tragic drama of his passing greatly enlarged that circle and brought wider attention to the example of his dedicated life, his "mission of love."[90]

CHAPTER 34

TRIBUTES FAR AND WIDE

The story of Father Wessel's death was reported not only by the local press in New Jersey and Philadelphia, but by newspapers from *The New York Times* on the East Coast to San Francisco papers on the West. The latter prompted a letter from a San Francisco woman to the slain priest's mother inquiring if indeed he was the same young seminarian whom she met traveling with his mother on a pilgrimage to Lourdes and Assisi in 1958.

As evidence of his wide appeal, Mrs. Kathleen Wessel even received a letter of condolence from Sister Lucia, the last surviving visionary of the Blessed Virgin Mary's 1917 apparitions at Fatima.[1]

The Governor of New Jersey, William T. Cahill, also mourned the loss of one "who reached out to the young and devoted his energy to provide counseling and comfort to those most troubled."[2] From his office in Trenton, Governor Cahill issued the following statement on December 27, 1971:

> I am saddened by the tragic violence which abruptly ended the life and vital work of the Reverend John Wessel.
>
> Although only 32 years old, Father Wessel had gained the community's respect and admiration, not only as a priest but as a man who reached out to the young and devoted his energy to provide counseling and comfort to those most troubled.
>
> . . .
>
> Through his work, Father Wessel made a valuable contribution to the betterment of society. He symbolized the

concern and compassionate involvement of men of all faiths with problems affecting the health and welfare of individuals as well as society.

The violence which abruptly ended the life and work of Father Wessel focuses attention on the need for a continuing effort to help the troubled and tormented find new life with meaning and dignity.[3]

And what of the young people whose lives he touched in a special way? The following are some thoughts on Father Wessel's life and death from the adult perspective of just a few of the many young people he befriended during his short public ministry:

Joanne Wesley Gillespie:

> I think because when someone dies, you take them so much deeper into your heart and soul and memorize what they meant to you, and really, really sit and reflect on how important that person was to you, . . . they're even closer to you somehow after they're gone than if they're living . . .
>
>   . . .
>
> I remember kids saying soon after he died, . . . "We'll never be the same people that we were before we met him." I know for a fact that many, many of these kids have gone on to do youth ministry work and have been involved citizens. They're not people that just sit in the background of life and watch things happen. Because of Father Wessel, they care and get involved in what goes on and they've admitted it. We all feel it because of his influence in our lives.[4]

Joseph Parnell:

What Father Wessel taught me and others about love, said Joseph Parnell, prepared us for the time when he would no longer be with us. But "it wasn't just love in the generic sense, but love always based on God's love." Father's time with us "was almost like a rehearsal, so to speak, for when he'd be taken away from us so quickly." When he died, each of us had to ask ourselves, "Are we going to depend now on the person (Father Wessel), or just the basic concept of love, or are we going to depend on God and all the things that Father Wessel taught us?"[5]

Kevin Connor:

Reflecting on the life and death of Father Wessel helped Kevin Connor to a deeper understanding of Jesus Christ. "Very much, I think, in his dying, I've learned very much more about the mystery of the God-Man." The experience that he and his friends had with Father Wessel was "very similar to what . . . [Jesus's] disciples had gone through. Many of us had experienced that type of relationship" with Father Wessel "that maybe the Lord had with His disciples."[6]

Josetta Cascione Burchardt:

Essentially, I think Father Wessel is and was a witness. . . . At the time, I don't think we knew why he was taken from us, but now we can look back and say, this was God's will and it was for a reason. . . . People need to see that there can be selfless and sacrificial dedication to God with the grace to surmount obstacles. . . . Here was a man who was sacrificial and giving and had a deep love of the Lord . . . He was an example of that and how we should be.[7]

Ed Staunton:

I know my life wasn't the same. From that Search weekend on, my life was pre-Search and post-Search, it was that much of a difference. And things that I take for granted about my life and my beliefs and my faith now stem directly from that weekend. . . .

I always said, I remembered the lesson but I forgot the teacher. I had lived the life that he had told me, but I'd forgotten that it was Father Wessel who had taught me this. . . .

. . . And even though he's not here to physically be with us anymore, he is carried on through our actions . . . how we deal with our kids, and our family, strangers, people at work, people that we come in contact with all the time. I could never thank him enough for what he did, but yet, what he would want is by our example. That's our way of thanking him for the brief time that we spent with him.[8]

Beverly Choltco-Devlin:

Oftentimes, it's only because a person dies prematurely, or under tragic circumstances, that they become an important person, but I can honestly say that if Father Wessel had not died . . . he would have had the same profound effect on us. . . . The intensity of the changes that he brought about in my life would still be as intense. . . . This is one case where you can say that a person is not being extolled just because he died young.

What he has done for me? That's not really a tangible thing. . . . The things that are important to me in life are directly related to the things that he taught me . . . He taught me that it's important to be a good person. And that's the most we can ask from ourselves in life. And that's what gives thanks to Jesus, and what reflects so well on Father Wessel is that he's made us all special individuals. And I think that's what he would have wanted.[9]

Peter Caroselli:

The two most outstanding qualities about Father Wessel were his "charity" and his "concern for the kids."

Father Wessel's effect on young people was "definitely positive. He fostered something that I think was there to begin with but probably would have lain quiescent for a long time." He recognized that the students "had the potential to be spiritually mature, and he just brought it out and let it go. . . . Considering the narrow amount of time that he was there, he had a fairly profound effect."

"He wasn't an invasive type of teacher." Some teachers "force-feed you information or ideas or how to think," while others "basically give you the tools or show you the path" and "let you go from there." Father Wessel was "more of a guide than a force-feeder, both personally or in general. Ultimately, I think that works better that way because you can't force anybody to think in a particular way, at least not at that age. By then, your opinions, the way you look at things, are pretty much set . . . And one of the reasons why he was so successful is that he didn't force the kids at all. . . . His influence was entirely positive."[10]

John Menter:

"He was a good man," said the former St. Joseph High School student whom Father John Wessel aided on the day he was shot. "Just a really good person."

> He really showed me not to be a phony . . . What you saw is what you got with him. . . . And that's kind of how I am now and I think that I could probably, looking back now, attribute a little bit of that to him. . . . He showed me to "be yourself" and things will work out well for you, and don't worry about impressing anybody. . . .
>
> And some people are going to like it and some people aren't, but don't lose any sleep over it. Just be honest and don't hurt anybody intentionally. And I kind of live by that rule. He showed me . . . to try to live your life honestly so you can sleep at night and shave in the morning.[11]

Thomas Callow:

Father Wessel's "effect on me was probably nothing he ever even knew about." It was more "who he was and what he made you believe in." Father was the type of man who "sacrificed just about everything, and in the end he *did* sacrifice everything."

"I know he was a decent, good man that looked out for us. . . . All kids were very important to him."[12]

Bonnie Lopez:

> If someone asks me, Who was Father Wessel? I'd want them to know that he was a human being. He was very human. He got mad and he cursed and he yelled and he had a beer and he smoked cigarettes and he cared for people . . . I think he was a real person.

He's certainly one of the most important people I ever met, and . . . one of the most influential in my life . . . because he was a very human person, very genuine . . . very down-to-earth, very real . . . a regular person.[13]

Barry Anderson:

I think he was somebody that was very, very special . . . I haven't seen anyone like him in the past twenty years.[14]

Jayne Hartley:

Father always believed that the Lord knew and did the best and this was the time to remember that. . . . It was with both sadness and probably relief that I learned Father had died the day after Christmas. Of course, I was extremely grieved but I felt that his suffering was at last over and now he had obtained what he deserved—the joy of everlasting happiness.

. . .

Even today I have not fully realized what took place that December and maybe never shall. For a while I totally blocked his death from my mind but then I remembered Father's reflections on his own father's death. I remember he said that even in death you could continue loving someone and that he felt that he had grown closer to his father even after his death. Once more, Father Wessel's example and beliefs helped me to cope with some of the ugliness of life.[15]

"I believe that Father Wessel is in heaven 'pulling' for each and every one of us," concluded Jayne, expressing the thoughts of many. "I am probably a far better person because of Father's influence and feel that even now he will not let us down."[16]

CHAPTER 35

AFTERMATH

When the students at long last returned to St. Joseph High School after Christmas vacation—during which time their priest and friend had died and was buried—it seemed as though a lifetime had come and gone. It was now a new year, 1972. Perhaps there were unspoken fears among those who had been Father Wessel's friends—

What would happen to them now?

What would become of the little community of faith that Father had tried so hard to nurture among them?

What would happen to the sense of love and acceptance of one another that he brought?

Surprising to some, morning prayers in the vacant classroom on the third floor went on as before. Was it imagination, or did even more kids come by for prayers, seeking perhaps a sense of community—to be among friends who would share their faith as well as their loss and pain? All were made to feel welcomed.

In the place where Father Wessel usually sat, a young teenage boy filled his chair and led the other young people in prayers and petitions and songs, just as their priest would have done. Father had brought them together and taught them how to love God and how to love and care for one another. The students would keep his legacy and teachings alive. They would not forget.

And, if perchance the memory of the teacher faded over the years—which Father Wessel wouldn't have minded a bit—then they would not forget the lessons he taught them.

*   *   *

Jill Viggiano was among those young friends of Father Wessel's who continued to gather for morning prayers. Jill had been home alone one day right after Father died. Her parents were very concerned for her because she was grieving, and they asked a neighbor to come over and make sure she was all right.

She was sitting by herself, reading the little Good News Bible that Father Wessel had given her after the Search weekend in the fall of 1971. It was Jill to whom Father had promised he would inscribe her Bible with a special verse just for her, but he had gotten so busy that fall that he never got around to it. In addition to grieving his loss, Jill felt a tinge of regret that she never received a verse from Father as her other friends had done. It would have meant so much to her—and now it was too late, he was gone.

Father always used to say to his young friends, "If you look in the Bible, you will find what you are looking for. When you need an answer, look to your Bible."[1]

Alone and in sorrow, trying to make sense of the death of her friend, Jill said a simple prayer, "Oh, Father Wessel, let me know everything's okay." Then, perhaps remembering Father's advice, she opened her Bible at random. The first thing that caught her eye was a passage from the Book of Revelation.

The first line she read seemed to come alive and jump off the page:

> "I, John, your brother, . . . who share with you the kingdom, and the endurance we have in Jesus . . . was caught up in spirit on the Lord's day . . ." (Rev. 1:9ff)

"I remember getting goose bumps and thinking, 'Thank you. I know that you're with God,'" recalled Jill. "I really felt like he was there and he was telling us it's really okay. And after that I don't remember being as upset anymore . . . I'll always believe that was him speaking to us."[2]

Father Wessel kept his promise. Jill had received her verse.

Perhaps too, the Scripture verse she received brought encouragement to her friends and gave them strength, hope and peace.

* * *

> Much has occurred since the last sailing of the *Eucharist*. Somehow as God would have it, things did seem to work out. December 17th to 26th, 1971 will be days many of us will never forget. However, through all the occurrences, somehow the *Eucharist* with its unusual name makes all the more sense. There is just too, too much to be said and I do not want to start.
>
> Ship's Log, the *Eucharist*
> Kevin Connor, 1972

Initially, out of great loyalty and love, all of Father Wessel's CYO friends said that they would never let go of the boat. It was as though a part of their slain friend was in every board and nail. They were going to cherish it forever and even hand it down to their children.[3]

In April 1972, three of the young CYO men, Barry Anderson, Bill Hamilton and Kevin Connor, purchased the catamaran boat from Father Wessel's estate for $75.00. With great enthusiasm, they made several starts to restore and refurbish the boat and get her ready for summer sailing—scrubbing, sanding, fiberglassing, and sanding again.[4]

They had great plans and high hopes. But despite their good intentions, it was impossible for them to keep up with the work involved in maintaining the large, awkward catamaran in seaworthy condition. For several years, the boat was dry-docked in the backyard of Barry's parents' house until it just began to fall apart, and eventually, was sold at a nominal price.[5]

A story (which may be more apocryphal than real) began when Father Wessel had removed the hatch cover from the *Eucharist* and fashioned it into an altar. Father put the altar to good use bringing it from classroom to classroom to celebrate Mass. His final desire was to make it a permanent fixture in the St. Joseph High School chapel. But first, the chapel needed work and repair.

After Father died, the high school seniors had hidden the hatch cover altar that he made. It only reappeared after the principal assured the class that the school would continue his plans to complete the altar and renovate the chapel, which now would be dedicated in tribute to him.[6]

Today the Alumni Chapel, its location having been moved to a large, comfortable space on the second floor of the high school, now renamed Monsignor Donovan, contains Father Wessel's original hatch cover altar which he sanded and painted with his own hands. On the rugged wooden altar, a little plaque reads simply, "In Memoriam, Rev. John P. Wessel."[7]

The moral of the story of the *Eucharist*, whether literal or symbolic, reminds us of the Gospel story of Martha and Mary, where Jesus speaks of the one who "has chosen the better part" (Luke 10:41-42). The only part of the catamaran *Eucharist* that still remains became the wooden altar upon which the *Holy Eucharist* is consecrated to this day. Out of the remnants of the homemade boat emerged "the better part."

Somehow, we think Father Wessel would have wanted it that way. Somehow, the *Eucharist* with its unusual name still makes all the more sense.

*   *   *

The trial for the murder of Father John P. Wessel was held in Ocean County Criminal Court in Toms River on March 13-19, 1973 before the Honorable William E. O'Connor. John F. Kelly III was represented by Harold C. White, Esq. Assistant Prosecutor Everett T. Denning appeared on behalf of the State of New Jersey.

At that time, Kelly testified that he killed the priest so the police would kill him and he could be reincarnated.[8] He thought that when he shot Father Wessel that he was doing a good thing and that Father Wessel would go to Heaven and become a spirit. Jack testified that he wanted to die so that he could come back as another person, a better person.[9]

All four psychiatrists called as expert witnesses—three for the defense and one for the prosecution—testified that Kelly was acutely paranoid schizophrenic at the time of the shooting of Father Wessel, that he did not know the difference between right and wrong, and did not know the nature and quality of his acts on December 17, 1971.[10]

On March 19, 1973, the jury found John F. Kelly III not guilty of the murder of Father John P. Wessel by reason of legal insanity. He was then committed to a psychiatric hospital for continued treatment.[11]

CHAPTER 36

A CAUSE BEGINS

Many, many honors were bestowed posthumously upon Father John P. Wessel: Scholarships and awards were instituted at the schools where he taught; plaques and memorials were placed at the churches where he served; a Holy Name Society chapter was named after him; a memorial collection of his books is housed at the Mount Holly Library.

His memory also lives on through the several children who were named after him or in honor of him by their parents who, as members of his youth group, had been among his dearest friends in life.

But among the many honors Father John Wessel received after his death, one alone stands out in its uniqueness: Those who knew and loved him hopefully embarked upon the long road to have him canonized a saint of the Roman Catholic Church.

Almost immediately after his death, Father Wessel's special sanctity, virtue and holiness was recognized and acclaimed by those whose lives he touched. It was not simply the fact of his dramatic and heroic death, in and of itself, which attracted such attention, but because the end of his life was fully consistent with the self-giving and self-sacrifice which marked the way he lived each day of his life.

A petition, or Cause, for the canonization of Father John P. Wessel was commenced in 1973 in the Diocese of Trenton. Through this lengthy process, which requires years of investigation, documentation, and miracles attributed to his intercession, friends and supporters of Father Wessel's sanctity seek to have the Roman Catholic Church declare him "Blessed" and eventually one day "Saint"—if it be God's will to accord him such a public honor.

Even today, there are those who continue to report favors received through the intercession of Father John P. Wessel.[1]

Perhaps because of the manner in which he died, and in no small measure aided by the symbolism of his passing away on December 26th, the Feast of St. Stephen, the first Christian martyr, many immediately hailed Father John Wessel as a "martyr."

But he did not die a martyr's death in the strict, doctrinal sense. The distinction of true "martyrdom," according to Church law, is accorded to one who is killed literally "in hatred of the faith." All other candidates for sainthood must demonstrate the practice of the virtues to an extraordinary or "heroic" degree.

While Father Wessel did not die a literal "martyr," his death was surely a "witness" of Christ—which is the actual meaning of the word "martyr" in Greek.

And if his final hours were not a martyrdom in the *technical* sense of dying "in hatred of the faith," then his actions were, at the least, a "martyrdom of charity" in that he died "in the line of duty" as a priest, while performing a mission of mercy for a troubled young veteran, heedless of the risks involved to his own life.

As one who had been consecrated, set apart, to minister to others in the name of Christ, Father Wessel could have chosen no other course. His complete and total dedication to his priestly vocation and his love of Jesus Christ precluded him from refusing anyone in need.

Indeed, there are indications, from the statements that he made to several people shortly before his death, that Father Wessel was consciously willing to offer up his life, if that was God's will, in the pursuit of his priestly work on the day he was shot.

Sister Francis Rita Feigenbutz, the elderly mathematics teacher and guidance counselor at St. Joseph High School, was one of the last persons to speak to Father Wessel that afternoon. Sister Francis Rita was over seventy at the time and is now deceased. Her eyesight, hearing, and voice were fading with advanced years, although she was still an excellent math teacher. Some of the other nuns recalled a story she told them.

Sister Francis Rita encountered Father Wessel on his way to the Kelly apartment in the afternoon of December 17th and exchanged a few words with him. "I must visit someone who is beyond my help," he told her.[2]

The nun then commented to him to the effect that she didn't expect to live much longer. She was not really ill or in chronic pain, just elderly, recalled another Sister.[3] And perhaps because of this, and after a long life of service to God, she may have said something innocuous like, "Oh, Father, I am getting too old. Say a prayer that God takes me!"

Father Wessel's response to her was to quote, or paraphrase, a Scripture passage from Isaiah: "Sometimes it's the young who die."[4]

Sister Francis Rita later wrote, "I think I was the last person (Sister) to speak to him the afternoon he was killed."[5]

Later, with benefit of hindsight, the few words that she exchanged with Father Wessel that afternoon would prompt Sister Francis Rita to remark to her fellow Sisters that the young priest had predicted his own death.[6]

John Wessel was only a young man of thirty-two when he was killed. He was so full of life, and seemingly had so much more to give and to achieve, that his death at first appeared to many of us senseless, confusing, and perhaps even futile. It was only later, upon reflection, that we found meaning in his short life and untimely death: as a hero, as a priest, as a Christian witness, and possibly, as an American saint.

The young boy, Johnny Wessel, who told his fourth grade teacher that his great desire was to become a priest and maybe a martyr some day, had fulfilled his dream. As a thirty-two-year-old priest, he had given his life in the service of Our Lord and His Church while trying to help another human being whose forlorn plight was largely ignored.

For all of these reasons, Father Wessel's life stands as a testament to heroic virtues of charity, trust, faith, and courage—a martyrdom of charity in its truest sense.

The humble and modest John Wessel would be the last person to think of himself as a saint, and would be highly embarrassed at all the attention being paid him.

Yet the attention is well deserved. He was an extraordinary priest. He lived an extraordinary life. He died an extraordinary death. And yet, he did it all in a very "ordinary" way, without fanfare or show, but just by living simply, being faithful to the daily duties of his vocation, and having great love for God and for all his brothers and sisters in his heart.

This is "precisely what should attract the modern mentality," wrote Father Peter M.J. Stravinskas of Father John Wessel in his essay, *Sanctity in a Contemporary Key.* "He did very ordinary things extraordinarily well."[7]

"But what is holiness?" Father Stravinskas continued:

> Holiness consists in doing what must be done as well as possible and as joyfully as possible. Holiness is responding to one's vocation in life with eager enthusiasm. That does not mean that one must smile in the midst of disaster but it does imply being imbued with a spirit of hope which will see one through dark hours.
>
> . . .
>
> John died doing what he had been called to do and therein lies his claim to holiness.[8]

*   *   *

The final disposition of the Cause for Father Wessel's canonization rests in the mysterious will of God. But whatever the final disposition of his Cause, it is clear that the vibrant life and heroic death of Father John P. Wessel, who gave his all to love and care for others, stands as a compelling example for us all.

Now, in churches in Toms River, Trenton, and elsewhere, children and adults join to pray that the beloved Servant of God, Father John P. Wessel, may one day be venerated by the worldwide Church as a twentieth century saint who demonstrated commitment to the Christian ideal and fidelity to his priestly vocation: "The man who holds out to the end . . . is the one who will see salvation" (Matthew 24:13).[9]

Afterword: A Personal Reflection

Was Father John P. Wessel a saint? He does not fit easily into our notions of sainthood, if sainthood is to mean ethereal, otherworldly piety and superhuman perfection. But as the reader was reminded at the start of this journey: "The greatest saints the Church has produced have been, first and foremost, the most human."

Father John Wessel was a very human man, rough around the edges, yet tender at the heart. A man who smoked, enjoyed a drink of bourbon or beer, and occasionally cursed while at the same time admonishing himself for it. A man of good cheer who would sometimes withdraw into moody silences.

Yet he was a man who loved the Lord, and loved people, so much so that the earliest zeal of his boyhood was to offer his life for Christ, and the consuming passion of his priestly ministry was to love all in the name of Christ. By all accounts, he never refused anyone who came to him in need, regardless of the sacrifices to himself. Whenever possible, he anticipated the unspoken needs of others and reached out to them in brotherly compassion. The down and out, the lonely, the despised and the rejected, were all his great friends.

This willingness to love others in the name of Jesus brought him to his own personal Calvary and ultimately to his sacrificial death in the name of charity. It matters very little whether Father John Wessel knew or sensed what would befall him when he answered a mother's distressed plea and went to counsel a disturbed young war hero on that Friday in December 1971. Each day of John Wessel's life was placed at the service of others, and he was always ready to make that ultimate sacrifice if God called him to do so.

As he so often said, "I am ready whenever the Lord wants me!"

"What I just did was to give you an example: as I have done, so you must do" (John 13:15). Our Lord Jesus set the example and many men and women throughout the ages have taken this invitation seriously. Father John Wessel was one who surely did.[10]

The triumph of Father John Wessel's life, then, was that he freely chose to love in a way that virtually paralleled Our Lord's—not because he was perfect, but in spite of his humanness. As the words of Christ to His own echo throughout two thousand years of human history: "This is how all will know you for my disciples; by your love for one another" (John 13:35).

Fulfilling the Lord's command to love one another on that fateful day, Father Wessel responded to the request of a mother he barely knew, but who loved her son and was desperately trying to find someone to help him.

In the futile journey of the Kelly family from the police, to the courts, to the psychologists, to the mental health institutions, all had somehow failed to alleviate their suffering and bring relief to the young war hero's troubled mind. After all the institutions of man-made wisdom had failed her, Jack Kelly's mother turned to her Church. And the Church responded by opening up its arms to her, embracing her pain and that of her son, and giving up the life of one of Her priests.

If there is a moral to the story it is this: When human institutions fail, Christ is there to lay down His life for the least of His brothers and sisters. When human wisdom fails, as it did for Jack Kelly, the Church, which is Christ on earth, was there in the person of Father John Wessel to make the ultimate sacrifice. Just as Jesus carried the cross for suffering humanity and did not recoil from it, so too the Church carries the cross of suffering humanity in the modern world, until it leads to the Resurrection and eternal life.

It should also be recalled that when the Vietnam War veterans returned home, many of their countrymen wanted little to do with them. In a nation trying to forget the unpopular war and its disappointing outcome, the Vietnam soldiers were the "forgotten men." At the time, few wished to become involved with them, or to care about their pain and sickness of mind and soul. But Father Wessel did.

That Father John Wessel would spend his last mission of mercy to try to comfort a mentally ill and troubled young Vietnam War veteran was a witness of his fidelity to Christ's own words: "Whatever you did for one of these least brothers of mine, you did it for me" (Matthew 26:40).

The life of Father John Wessel also provides us with a true illustration of the role and value of the priest in the modern world: a servant in the image of Christ, in the words of Bishop John C. Reiss.[11] The modern world desperately needs more Father Wessels—more good men who are willing to live dedicated, holy, and consecrated lives as priests in service to God and their fellow man.

Surely, Father Wessel embodied the ideal of the priest as an *alter Christus*, "another Christ," by virtue of the grace which he received at his ordination to the Sacrament of Holy Orders.

As Father Andrew Apostoli observes in the Foreword to this book, Father John Wessel was an outstanding example of what Archbishop Fulton J. Sheen called the "Sanctified Priesthood."

As a man and a priest, Father Wessel lived out his consecrated vows in complete openness and obedience to the grace and power of the Holy Spirit. It is for this reason that he was able to accomplish so much, to help so many, and to make such a profound difference in the lives of those he touched. And it is for this reason that he was ready and willing to offer up his life to help another human being for the love of Christ Jesus.

Over the years, much has been written, discussed, and speculated about the life of Father Wessel, and about the way he died—whether it should or should not have happened, and whether it could or could not have been prevented.

But I would modestly suggest that in some mysterious way that will never be truly understood, Father John P. Wessel was chosen to be a contemporary, living witness for us of Jesus Christ, in a very real and tangible way. He experienced the popularity of Christ, and the joy and adulation of having a group of followers who loved and admired him. And he also experienced the desolation of Christ, and ultimately, the laying down of his life. In some mysterious way, God allowed Father Wessel to share intimately in the life and death of Christ, and by faith, the Resurrection of Christ, perhaps as a role model or an example for our modern, often troubled, times.

Although human wisdom would say that Father Wessel's death was a tragedy, in the almighty and infinite wisdom of God, John Wessel's sacrifice was somehow necessary to accomplish some greater purpose. And in this sacrificial event, even Jack Kelly and his family had a part to play, just as surely as did Father John Wessel and his loved ones.

For every act of sacrificial love must have a recipient. Father Wessel did not die in vain or to no purpose: He gave his life trying to help a troubled young man. He gave his life while ministering to him *as a priest*. His doing so gave powerful witness to Our Lord's unmerited, unconditional love for all of humanity, and to His redemptive death on the cross, in atonement for sins, so that all may have eternal life.

Father Apostoli also writes of Archbishop Sheen's powerful insight that every Catholic priest must, like Jesus, be both priest and victim. In a very real way, Father Wessel was, like Jesus, both a priest and a victim of sacrificial love. As a priest, Father Wessel offered himself daily in service and self-sacrifice. As his final act on earth, Father John P. Wessel united himself fully to Jesus Christ, the Eternal Priest-Victim, and willingly offered himself—his body and blood, his very life—as a victim for the pain and suffering of another.

There can be no better example of an imitation of Christ, a Sanctified Priesthood!

Looking at the life of Father John Patrick Wessel is like looking at a prism through which everything is magnified and reflected. The reflection is so beautiful that it compels us to look higher to the source of the Light which illuminated John Wessel's life, that is, to Jesus Christ Himself.

Father John P. Wessel never did anything out of vanity or to gain attention. A man of great modesty, he would never presume to call himself a saint, and would probably not want you to do so either. In the long run, he would probably tell you, my life is not important. Rather, he would point you to the Cross and say, "Behold the Man! Follow Him!"

And that, it would seem to me, is a working definition of sanctity.

Thoughts of Father John P. Wessel By Friends, Family and Co-Workers[12]

His Excellency, Bishop John C. Reiss, Former Bishop of the Diocese of Trenton:

"The message of his life would be one of a Christian servant—willing to help, willing to direct and lead, particularly with youth," and willing "to go out of his own way."

Pointing out that on the day he was shot Father Wessel had something else to do, but put that aside to see somebody who was really in need, Bishop Reiss noted that Father Wessel's generosity provides "a good example for all of us of true Christian living—to be willing to go out of our way to help others, even if it's just a word of consolation."

Maryann Wessel Beitel:

Prayer was very much a part of John's life. John would say the Rosary when we were in the car. In no way was he a "holier-than-thou" person as far as his outward appearance or

socially; he was almost the reversal. It's hard to describe him
because . . . people have a tendency, twenty years later, to look
upon him as "too good" of a person and he wasn't that at all.
He just was doing what he felt he had to do in life and was very
sincere about it. He was certainly a very holy person but he
didn't go out and trailblaze his religion at all. He never made
people feel guilty . . . whether they were Catholic or Jewish or
nothing. He could communicate with them and they respected
him for it.[13]

. . .

I think he'd want to be remembered as a man who loved
Jesus Christ above all else. He lived his life with total, total love
of Jesus Christ in his heart. And he didn't just talk it. In fact,
lots of times he didn't express it in words. But it certainly did
show in the way that he lived.[14]

Monsignor James H. Dubell:

"John fits the category of a saint." In his everyday life, "he was very
honest and sincere." He was "full of good works and genuine piety" and
"lived honestly and faithfully the life of a dedicated priest." John Wessel's
life was "beyond reproach."

He was "a very honest individual, and very intent on helping people, all
kinds of people, and especially the indigent and those that weren't so easy
to care for—like the young people." Because he was young himself, he felt
that he "had a calling toward the young people."

> But I very definitely feel that he was a saint in the technical
> and strict and even in the general sense of the word. . . . He was
> one of us so to speak, and at the same time, he was a few steps
> ahead of all of us in the sense that there was a hundred percent
> integrity there.

Father Wessel was "extraordinary" in that he was "deeply a person of
prayer." He would be "faithful to making a visit to the Blessed Sacrament.
He would be faithful to saying the Office. He would be faithful to trying to

make a meditation every day, . . . not in a fancy way . . . just in a genuine, sincere way."

> He felt a real sense of responsibility, and that came first, almost like he learned from his medical family background—the doctor, the dentist—they were on call for the patient who was needing them at that particular moment. You dropped what you were doing and you went and you took care of the person. . . .
>
> He had an extraordinary sense of dedication and responsibility . . . to the people in the parish, whether it was a sick call or somebody that needed counseling, or whatever it was, he would want to be there when they needed him, and he would cancel his own plans to accommodate them. I think he was extraordinary in that sense.[15]

Sean Maguire:

> A man who sought to realize in his own being the disposition of Christ, his absence has removed from my life a powerful reinforcing influence in my commitment to the priesthood. But then, God is wiser in His ways than man.[16]
>
> Father Wessel had a genuine caring about people and their well-being. This was especially evident toward youth. He was a worker. He invested his drive to do the job of a priest as he understood it. He was not a playboy. He was a humble kind of a guy. He had a good sense of reality and how he fit into the world, into the parish. He was generous in giving his time to others.[17]

Brendan Gallagher:

> He seemed to be very aware of his vocation, and he gave the indication that he would like to stay in the priesthood and give as much as he possibly could in reference to his vocation, and to help people, and to work with people. He was a dedicated man. He really was.

Sister M. Espiritu Dempsey, I.H.M.:

> He was a saint but down-to-earth. He's the kind of saint that would attract people to the Lord because he was so human. He was every bit a human being and yet he had this spiritual life. I guess I kind of think maybe they go together: The closer you are to God, the more of a person you are . . . the more human.

Father J. William Mickiewicz:

"If John had to do it all over again, knowing what would've happened, he would've done it." Father John Wessel "didn't care what people felt about him, he would do what he felt inside was what should be done." He had a quality of "single-mindedness" to him.

> Some people might call it narrow-mindedness, but I think that it's a focusing, a single-mindedness, the kind of thing that I would think Jesus had. Jesus had a very definite single-mindedness—He aimed and drove for it, so when we talk about the cross being Jesus's aim, because that's where it led, I see that almost as a symbol of John's death . . . If John knew he was going to be shot that day, John would've gone to minister to that young man without thinking about . . . his own life or any danger, or whatever else, because you see, there was a call. And that would be the single-mindedness and the purpose to do.

Monsignor Leonard R. Toomey:

> I think that he would like to be remembered as a young priest who was totally committed to serving Almighty God and the people of God . . . He didn't ever think that he was going to do anything unusual, and didn't think that he was unusual—and this is what made him unusual. . . . He didn't think he was special—and that's why he *was* special.

Father Eugene V. Davis:

> As far as I'm concerned, he was a good priest. Now that to
> me, it covers everything. While he was with me, he was a very,
> very fine priest.

Monsignor Joseph C. Shenrock, P.A.:

Father John Wessel had a "great concern for the oppressed and the
needy" and "a great sense of gratitude for anything that people did for
him."

> He was a person who exemplified everything that a priest
> should be in reference to Jesus Christ . . . Surely, he was a
> saintly priest in his own way . . . who did so much goodness in
> his life. . . . I saw in him an example of a good priest—a priest
> who really gave the ultimate example of what a priest should
> be—and therefore becomes a model, so to speak, of what you
> should be.

*Father Joseph J. Procaccini, Former Priest Personnel Director for the Diocese
of Trenton*:

Father John Wessel was "thoroughly priestly." He was "altruistic"
and "not self-centered." At the time he was shot, Father Wessel "was just
developing beautifully as a young priest" and possessed "admirable priestly
qualities."

Christopher Morley:

The "single and foremost" virtue that Father Wessel demonstrated was
"dedication to the vocation." He "constructed everything in his life to follow
his calling," even when this included "doing things that he may not have
been terribly comfortable with, but he knew it was consistent with what
he was called to do." He "worked at it (his vocation). It was a choice and a
calling to serve, and that's what he did."

There were certain duties that "he never said a word about but that he never liked to do"—like interacting with a parish society that "he didn't like at all, because they were always yelling at him about the CYO kids." But it was part of his duties to moderate the group, and he did it. "I don't remember hearing him ever complain about anything."

Father Wessel demonstrated the quality of "saintliness," because of the way he never took his eyes off the prize. He was more than just a "good person," because a mere "good person" can be enticed to take their eyes off the prize by good things, as well as bad. "That ability to shed the human things, both good and bad, to continue to pursue his calling—that's saintliness."

Ronald Garrett:

"He was the voice of Jesus Christ." Now, "every single time . . . that I go up and receive the Eucharist, I look up . . . and I say, 'This is for you, Pop.'"

Carmella V. Di Matteo:

"I really felt such a strong presence from that young priest for myself, my own spirituality, but mostly for the children in that school." Usually, "kids love young people" and they tend to "romanticize them after their death . . . but this was different"—Father Wessel had a following long before his tragic death.

> There was a very strong presence in him that people sensed, whether it was the expression in the eyes, [the] very strong face, the voice, but there was a sense of appropriateness. . . . I think that as much as he had that deep friendship with the kids, he had this sense of what was appropriate. There was something very fine about him . . . I think he was very well raised and I mean you just knew that by the inborn sweet manners. But I think it was more than that. It wasn't just a facade.

"He knew his role. That was one of the things I loved about him." Father Wessel had "a sense of his priesthood" that was "very beautiful."

He knew that he was consecrated but he didn't lord it over everybody. He just shared that. Whatever his priesthood was, it was just shared out with everyone. And I think that he knew that he could communicate with young people, but he wasn't just a pastor for kids. I mean, you will find if you talk to all ages, he touched everybody. He touched older people and he touched middle-aged people, and he touched cranky principals!

Father Wessel was "very spiritual, and in a very sweet . . . and such a spontaneous way." The virtue that "impressed me most about him" was his "deep, deep faith . . . He was very sure of himself, not in an egotistical or arrogant way, just [by] a quiet presence about him. [There was] a strength that exuded from his personality that impressed me."

"I think he was a saint . . . in the way that he affected people, but also in himself. He'd be embarrassed to hear me say this, but there was a holiness about him."

Father Wessel also "reinforced my feelings about the mission of schools, especially of Catholic schools. He showed me what a priest does with kids and what his presence means in a school."

"We may have had a saint in our midst. We certainly had a big sacrifice, that was for sure."

Sister Teresa Agnes:

Father Wessel was a man who was "infinitely patient" and "completely understanding."

I didn't know what his dealings with the students were, but to me he was the type of person that no matter what kind of a problem a kid had, no matter what the kid did, he could go and talk to him about it. . . . They completely trusted him . . . they just loved him. He was here for a very short time, but he left a very, very big impression.

"Holiness to me is what he was—giving, selfless." He "didn't give a hoot" about "the position of the person"—whether they were "one of the biggest donors of the parish, or somebody he saw sitting out on the steps someplace. He'd go up to them and he would talk to them. . . . He'd deal with the person. What they had didn't mean a thing to him . . . If it was a person in need, then he reached out to them."

Sister Julianna Naulty:

Father John Wessel's virtues were most evident in "the way he lived." He was "a real exponent of what the Gospel was all about. . . . In a short time, he did so much."

Sister Nancy Carney:

Father Wessel was "an example of integrity" because he said "whatever was on his mind." He was also "an example of real charity and love, particularly for the kids."

> If being a saint is measured by one's kindness, charity for others, and . . . a powerful desire—and I think John Wessel had this—a powerful desire to pass on philosophy and grass-roots spirituality to the next generation, and if that's what it is, then I would say John Wessel is a saint. He urged people on to become their best, and he didn't get terribly upset if they fell, as long as they picked themselves up. And he would be there to help.

Josetta Cascione Burchardt:

On the seventh anniversary of Father John P. Wessel's death, Josetta Cascione wrote a letter in tribute to him which was published in *The Monitor*, the Catholic newspaper of the Diocese of Trenton:

> It has been said that many people suffer from post-Christmas depression. December 26, 1971, was a day of sadness for myself and others who attended St. Joseph's School in Toms River during that time. It has been seven years since Father John P. Wessel passed away to join Our Lord in heaven. Every time I think of him and how he helped my friends and myself, I thank God for having known him, only if it was for several months. His

spirit of humility and charity, coupled with his friendly ways and down-to-earth attitude will always be cherished in our hearts.

I often wonder why he was taken when he could have contributed so much to those who needed his guidance and support. I feel that God loved him so much, He wanted him for Himself. Also, I feel he has been an example of not only a "real" Christian but a modern-day martyr, who I'm sure asked God to forgive his assailant, just as St. Stephen did for his murderers.

I do not think it is just a coincidence that Father Wessel died on St. Stephen's feast day—I believe it was meant to show us the bond of Christ-like charity that Father Wessel shared in common with our first Christian martyr.

The St. Joseph 1972 high school yearbook had a tribute to Father's memory. His favorite hymn was the Prayer of St. Francis, and every time I sing the beginning line of "Make Me a Channel of Your Peace," it reminds me of Father Wessel, for in his life, he lived the meaning of that verse.[18]

Twenty years later, reflecting on these words and on Father John Wessel's life, she said:

Father Wessel was as close to a saint as I have seen on this earth. I got the deep sense when talking to him that Jesus was right there. It was almost like he was imitating Him so closely. I felt a definite aura of holiness about him that was very powerful. . . . He was very holy, very charitable, and I think in his own way he was kind of prophetic. . . . It wasn't really anything he said as much as the way he re-enacted the Gospel and how he carried that out . . . And in his own way, by his life, imitating Jesus so closely, . . . it brought more people to God.[19]

Dawn Flynn Fowler:

Father Wessel was "someone who touched a great many lives in what some people would take their whole lifetime to do . . . And not just us (the youth), but my parents liked him."

When I think of the word "saint" I think of someone who has led an exemplary life, and they have [taken] what God has given them, whatever talents they are, [and] used them above and beyond the human expectation. . . . Father was able to do so much in so little time, and never really complained about his own life. I knew very little about him himself, other than I knew he had good sense, a good way of judging people, a good feeling about people, a positive attitude, that kind of a thing. But I have never heard him complain. And he led by example. . . . He led his life as if that was what God had given him as a gift. And if the definition of a saint is that, then he has done that.

Carl Wingate:

"John's a saint in my book. He was a neat guy. I would think of him as a saint." As a young seminarian, he "just tried to do the right thing, and usually did an above average job at whatever it was."

Reflecting on John's boyhood desire for martyrdom, and on his passing away on the Feast of St. Stephen, Carl Wingate noted that when they studied high school Latin and Greek, they learned that the word "martyr" really stemmed from the word "witness"—in the true sense, a "living witness"—a witness to the faith, instead of the popular idea of dying for the faith in a particularly violent or gruesome way.

Whether by "a coincidence or divine plan, however you look at what happened, I think John's going to help that young man was a witness of Christ. I think his idea of 'martyr', by the time he was actually 'martyred', was more the 'witness' concept than the idea of dying."

"Being a witness was very important to him."[20]

Michael Choma:

"John was a human being. He never thought of himself as a saint." But there was at least one early indicator of sanctity: As roommates, John Wessel was as sloppy as Mike Choma was neat. "It's been said that it's very difficult to live with a saint—John was difficult to live with!"

Father Samuel J. Lupico:

John Wessel was a "rugged, simple, sturdy individual" who possessed "a rugged honesty about himself and others. He was always there for other people, a very straightforward, good-hearted individual."

He was "all priest . . . from the top of his head to the tip of his toes. It was fitting that he should die the way he died."

"John's dying was part of the whole exposé of the insanity of that Vietnam War and what it did to people." It was a shame that John died, but it would have been "a deeper shame" if thousands had been killed in Vietnam "and no priests had been sacrificed and died in witness of the senselessness of war and the immorality of what was going on in Vietnam."

"In the early days of the Church, if you were a saint in the hearts of people, you were a saint. John is a saint. For those of us who lived with him and worked with him, he was a saint, and we don't need anyone to tell us that."

Father Sam retains "a lasting great deep respect for Wess."

Mrs. Mildred Kelly:

As paradoxical as it sounds with benefit of hindsight, John Kelly's mother barely knew Father Wessel. But "he was a good man," she said, "and he did everything in his power to help Jack."[21]

Wes Ritterbusch:

Father John Wessel best exemplified Jesus Christ by "the very way he lived. He lived everything that he spoke. He really and truly did. He just was that—a good man who wanted to help others."

> Of all the attributes necessary for sainthood . . . it would
> seem to me, John probably met most of them, but I can't see
> John as a saint . . . because John would never see himself that

way . . . But he was a really good man who lived what he spoke. He walked the walk and he talked the talk.

Michael Ward:

Mike Ward related an incident with Father Wessel that, in retrospect, was telling:

> It was during my high school years and the CYO was having an interfaith evening, meeting with some Protestant youth in Casey Auditorium. Father Wessel had asked me to say a few words about what my faith meant to me. Well, it didn't take long before I went completely overboard and, in a lame effort to impress our non-Catholic guests, I was stating how I was ready to lay down my life and become a martyr for my faith.
>
> After the meeting, Father Wessel correctly and gently pointed out to me that the likelihood of anyone being martyred for their faith in this country at this time was rather remote. I was properly chastened.
>
> It wasn't until years later, after I heard of his death that I remembered this incident and I thought that maybe he wasn't completely correct after all.[22]

Brian Schoeffel:

Father Wessel was "a very holy person" and a man of "great faith," but "I think he'd be pleased as punch *not* to be a saint."

> His vocation was being a priest, and sharing his talents with other people, helping people who had problems—and he didn't needed a pat on the back. He didn't need any fanfare . . . He just was very comfortable knowing that he was trying his best . . . in helping spread the Gospel, and spreading his love . . .

to people who needed his help . . . And that, in itself, is good
enough for me, because as far as I am concerned . . . he's a saint
in my book.

James J. Roche:

Several years after John Wessel's death, his seminary friend, Father
James Roche, preached a homily at a Mass in honor of the opening of
Father Wessel's Cause. In his sermon, quoted in an article by Vincent A.
Weiss, "Prayers for Fr. Wessel's Cause Begin," *The Monitor* (January 4,
1974), he said:

> Father Wessel's life and death were "instructive" . . . [H]e
> worked hard, was strong in his faith, was humble, responsible
> and was a man of good judgment, and "he died in a moment
> of routine kindness and self service; he was more and more a
> selfless man."
> That Father Wessel was a holy man there is no doubt . . .
> "It is truly the work of God that John was holy; if it is
> His will, . . . then the cause for John's canonization will go
> forward."[23]

Twenty years later, reflecting on these words and on Father John Wessel's
Cause, his friend said:

> John Wessel was a model of sanctity and virtue "as an
> everyday man and priest." He was "a genuine man" and "a person
> of genuine faith—not a perfect man but a man who is like a
> perfect example of . . . a combination of what comes to him from
> God, the gift of grace, and John's own personal quality, what he
> brings to it . . . I think John demonstrates that to a 'T'."
> He had "a life that was admirable and could be imitated,
> because he's real and a real person of sanctity in service and
> leadership within the Church." Not because he did "great
> things" but because his life was composed of "everyday service
> and solid faith."[24]

Mrs. Kathleen Hogan Wessel:

"On the occasion of his ordination he wrote this message to me.

> Mom,
> Keep me always in your prayers to Our Lady of Lourdes.
> I'll do my best to do a good job. I know what I must do and
> with God's grace, it will be done.
>
> Love, Johnny
> June 3, 1964

"This great desire to serve was carried out in his six years in the priesthood. He spent every waking hour helping the youth, the elderly and those in need. He gave me great peace of mind because I knew he was doing what he wanted to do. And in death he gave me peace of mind because God took him while he was serving others."[25]

St. Joseph

Father Wessel (far right) and Father Eugene Davis (center) are honored at their "goodbye party" at Blessed Sacrament Church, Trenton, Sunday, October 17, 1971. (Photo from Fr. John Wessel's album)

Greeting well-wishers at his goodbye party at Blessed Sacrament. (Photo from Fr. John Wessel's album)

Father Wessel (left) and Father Eugene Davis at their goodbye
party. A "wonderful man, a bit shy, but I love him very much,"
said Father Wessel of his former "Boss." (Photo from Fr. John
Wessel's album)

Father John Wessel's brief tenure at St. Joseph Church, Toms
River, NJ. In his sparse office at the high school; . . .

... enjoying a humorous moment with a fellow high school faculty member; ...

... and preparing to celebrate Mass in a high school classroom. Father Wessel's Masses were informal, yet powerful. (Reprinted from St. Joseph High School yearbook, 1972. Used with permission.)

Father John P. Wessel administers the Sacrament of Holy Matrimony to CYO youths Joanne Wesley and James Gillespie at Blessed Sacrament Church on Saturday, December 4, 1971. He took great care to spruce himself up for their wedding. (Photo from Wessel family album)

Funeral & After

Prayer card from Father John P. Wessel's funeral at St. Joseph Church, Toms River, NJ, December 29, 1971. (Wessel family album)

Bishop George W. Ahr celebrates Mass of Resurrection for Father Wessel as 1,000 mourners join in rites for the slain priest. *The Trenton Times*, Trenton, NJ, 1971. All rights reserved. Reprinted with permission. (Staff photo by John Pietras)

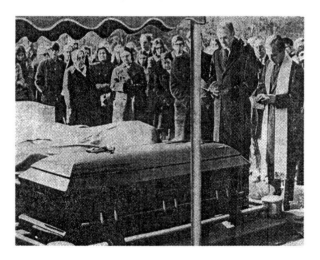

Father James H. Dubell (far right), Father Wessel's lifelong friend, utters the final prayers over the casket as the priest is buried in a family plot in Mount Holly. *The Asbury Park Press*, © 1972. Used with permission. Sister Frances Rita (first row nearest to casket, fifth from right) believed that Father Wessel had predicted his own death.

Mrs. Kathleen H. Wessel reaches out to touch the coffin of her son before it is lowered into the ground in St. Mary's Cemetery, Mount Holly. *The Trenton Times*, Trenton, NJ, 1971. All rights reserved. Reprinted with permission. (Staff photo by John Pietras)

The hatch cover altar Father Wessel built by hand for the students is still used to celebrate Mass at Monsignor Donovan (formerly St. Joseph) High School. (Photo by author)

Rev. John P. Wessel
Born: September 20, 1939
Ordained to the Priesthood: May 22, 1965
Born to Eternal Life: December 26, 1971

Oh God, I adore you. I thank you for all the good things you gave your faithful servant John Wessel. I pray that people everywhere may come to know of him and the way in which he sought to imitate your Son, Jesus Christ. Please grant this favor. Amen

The prayer card prepared for the Cause for Father Wessel's Canonization. (Pen and ink drawing by well-known local artist Peggy Peplow Gummere)

The good that John's heroic life and death has done and will continue to do will never be fully known to you—such is the life of a great priest. For the rest, we can say: "No greater love is there than that a man lay down his life for his friends."

For this we shall remember Father John Wessel always.

Msgr. James H. Dubell's
Eulogy for Father John P. Wessel

The End

PRAYER FOR THE CAUSE

OF FATHER WESSEL

Oh God, I adore you. I thank you for all the
good things you gave your faithful servant
John Wessel. I pray that people everywhere
may come to know of him and the way in
which he sought to imitate your Son,
Jesus Christ. Please grant this favor. Amen.

Kindly acknowledge favors received:

CAUSE OF FATHER JOHN P. WESSEL
Diocese of Trenton
Pastoral Center
Box 5147
701 Lawrenceville Road
Trenton, NJ 08638

ACKNOWLEDGMENTS

AND MESSAGE TO READERS

My Father once said about writing, with wonderfully Irish wisdom, that it is long, hard, tedious work but the end result is very worthwhile: "Never miss out on the joy of completing an 'impossible' task." Nothing could be more true, and I especially realize this as I come to the end of this biography. It has indeed been hard work—much harder than I could possibly have imagined at the start—but it has also been (and I hope you agree) very worthwhile.

Typically, the author's acknowledgments appear at the beginning of a book. On a few occasions I have seen it placed at the end. This is where I think it should be, at least in the case of a good-sized biography such as this. Not because it is of less importance—far from it!—but because the contributions of those who have assisted in this endeavor make so much more sense, and are so much more apparent, after one has read through the finished product.

This biography of Father John P. Wessel has truly been a shared endeavor. I have been blessed with and through the assistance of many persons in bringing this work to fruition. It is difficult to find the right words to express my appreciation and gratitude as they deserve. It is equally difficult to single out only a few for special thanks and praise.

My heartfelt thanks to each and every person who contributed to this effort—whether the contribution was great or small, long or short; whether it took the form of an interview or a telephone conversation, an item of research or information, or ongoing help over the course of many years. I continue to be amazed that so many people, most of whom I had never met before, generously and unhesitatingly opened their hearts and memories to me upon hearing that I was writing a biography of Father John P. Wessel. I have to believe that this response is a reflection of the deep esteem and respect that so many still have for Father Wessel. Whether your name appears in these pages or not, whether you are quoted or not, be assured that all contributions have been invaluable to me, if not in the actual writing of the text itself, then at least for purposes of background and understanding. Each and every contribution is gratefully acknowledged and appreciated and has served to the betterment of this book.

That being said, there are few special people who deserve mention and thanks by name. Without them I would not have been able to write this book, and I would be remiss if I overlooked them—

My heartfelt thanks and gratitude to the members of Father John P. Wessel's family, and especially to the late Mrs. Kathleen H. Wessel and Maryann Wessel Beitel, who were among the first supporters of this work. Father Wessel's mother and his sister, Maryann, together with her husband, William Beitel, were a constant source of assistance, information, encouragement, and patient understanding during the course of this project. My deepest appreciation and thanks to Maryann and Bill Beitel, and also to Beth Ann Beitel, Mrs. Edward J. (Pat) Wessel, Jr., Carlton and Anne Marie Wessel, Julian Wessel, Maureen Hogan, Kathleen Hogan Bradish, and the late Patty Hogan Staebler, for generously opening their hearts and sharing their deeply personal memories of Father John, as well as their private photographs, letters, writings, and family memorabilia, and allowing me access to all of these; and to Father Wessel's Nebraska cousin, Dr. Thomas Ashford Kuhlman, for generously sharing his meticulous research and writings on the Nebraska branch of Father Wessel's ancestral family. I am deeply grateful to all of you for your encouragement and support of my efforts. It has been a joy for me personally to have had this opportunity to get to know you, the family of Father John P. Wessel, and I hope that I have done you and him proud.

I wish to acknowledge, with deep esteem and gratitude, the special contributions of the late Mrs. Kathleen H. Wessel to this endeavor. A woman of great faith and courage who endured the untimely loss of her husband and three of her children, Kathleen Wessel was one of the kindest and most gracious ladies that I have known. My only regret is that this book was not completed in time for me to personally place it in her hands, as Kathleen

Wessel passed away on December, 28, 2001. I have faith that she has been watching over (and probably praying for!) my efforts from Heaven and I hope she is pleased.

I am forever grateful to Monsignor Joseph C. Shenrock, P.A., who was the first person I approached with the idea of writing a biography of Father John Wessel. He could not have been more enthusiastic and supportive, as indeed he has continued to be to this very day, generously sharing with me his own research and materials from the two earlier books that he wrote about Father Wessel, as well as his time, friendship, knowledge, advice, and support. His help and suggestions on every aspect of the biography have made it all possible, and without him it could never have happened. My heartfelt thanks to you, Monsignor, although I could never thank you enough for your assistance, support, and friendship.

I am also deeply grateful to Father Andrew Apostoli, C.F.R., for his generosity of time and spirit in writing the Foreword to this biography despite his very busy and prolific schedule of speaking, writing, and traveling. I am honored that Father Apostoli, an illustrious Catholic writer, speaker, and well-known television communicator, is associated with this project, and I have no doubt that Father Wessel is smiling that the Foreword to his book has been written by a spiritual son of Saint Francis of Assisi.

My thanks also—

To Monsignor James H. Dubell, for sharing his memories of a lifelong friendship, and for his assistance, support, encouragement, and editorial suggestions;

To Joanne Wesley Gillespie, for her generous and invaluable assistance in helping me to find and contact former members of the Blessed Sacrament CYO, as well as providing me with background information on the group and its activities. I know this was a lot of work for you, Joanne, but I could not have done it without you. No wonder Father Wessel considered you such a great help to *him!*

To Father John Bowen, S.S., Sulpician Archivist, Father John McMurray, S.S., and Father Robert Leavitt, S.S., Rector of St. Mary's Seminary in Roland Park, for assisting me in researching John Wessel's seminary years and for providing a wealth of information about St. Charles College, St. Mary's Paca Street, and St. Mary's Roland Park, respectively;

To Sister M. Christina Murphy, I.H.M., and Sister Eileen Egan, I.H.M., for generously assisting me with research, information, and contacts among the Sisters, Servants of the Immaculate Heart of Mary at Marywood;

To Sister Theresa Agnes*, for generously assisting me with research, information, and contacts among her fellow Sisters of St. Dominic and the staff and faculty of St. Joseph/Monsignor Donovan High School. In the same vein, my thanks also to Sister Nancy Carney, Dr. Edward G. Gere, William Vanore, Rita Kearney, and Jill V. Mueller, among others, and to those among my St. Joseph High School classmates, who assisted in some way with my research regarding Father Wessel's brief tenure at St. Joseph/Monsignor Donovan;

To Carl Wingate, Michael Mueller, Kevin Connor, Wes Ritterbusch, and Michael Ball, for sharing their priceless photographs and other personal memorabilia of Father Wessel;

To Michael Choma, for helping me locate members of John Wessel's seminary class;

To Mrs. Mildred Kelly, for graciously providing me with a copy of her son's Bronze Star citation for heroism for use in this biography;

To Bishop John C. Reiss, for his early support of my efforts to honor Father Wessel, and with gratitude to the present Bishop of Trenton, the Most Reverend John M. Smith, J.C.D., and the offices and personnel of the Roman Catholic Diocese of Trenton, for the invaluable assistance and access to information in the diocesan files which was provided to me in the course of my research about Father Wessel;

To my Mother, Rosemarie L. Burke, with love and gratitude, for countless reasons. You were my unofficial co-author and proofreader of sorts, because of all people, you truly "lived" the writing of this book with me. Together we labored over every chapter. On many occasions, I sought the advice of my Mother, a former teacher, when I needed just the right word or proper turn of phrase, and amazingly, she spent an entire summer editing the manuscript from beginning to end as it reached the final stages. I am forever grateful to you, Mother, for your love, help, and support;

To Grace Gargano, a great friend and supporter of this work, without whose contributions this biography would never have been possible, my deepest thanks and appreciation for your generous faith in this story. May the good that you have done here return to you a hundredfold, both on earth and in Heaven;

To Josetta C. Burchardt, for keeping the dream and the memory alive.

My thanks also go to all those special people who helped me with the research and physical preparation of this manuscript, especially—typists Gloria Carlon, Leislene Hendrickson, and Agnes Pompe; researchers Charles Larson and James Colbert; computer expert Lawrence Progel, for his invaluable assistance and technical support; Eileen Monaghan, for her talented editing; Paul Wesley, for his photography; attorney David O. Fuller, Esq., for his wise counsel; the good folks at Xlibris who put it all together;

And special thanks to Robert Henriques for his editorial suggestions, encouragement and support.

Finally, my gratitude and thanks to everyone who has supported me with prayers for the successful completion of this biography.

I'm sure there are many more people who should have been thanked by name. If I have left anyone out, I ask your indulgence and forgiveness, and know that I appreciate everything that everyone has done for me.

Although I hope and trust that those who knew Father Wessel, or are simply interested in his life story, will be pleased that a comprehensive biography of his life is being released at this time, I am sensitive to the fact that there is one family for whom this biography may not be a source of joy but of renewed unhappiness: the family of John F. Kelly III. It is not my intent to cause this family any further pain in the re-telling of this story, but to simply tell an accurate story of Father Wessel's life. So I especially appeal to the readers of this book, and to the community at large, to extend to the Kelly family your love, compassion, and understanding. It should not be forgotten that Jack Kelly was severely ill and not responsible for Father Wessel's death. Please understand that this family has also suffered, and do not treat them with anything less than kindness at this time.

Father Wessel wouldn't have wanted it any other way.

Let us also remember to care for the mentally ill in our midst and not to shun or ostracize them. Every day, progress is being made in the research, understanding, care, and treatment of mental illness, and with new medications and other advances, it is much more possible today for persons suffering from paranoid schizophrenia and other similar mental conditions to live functional and productive lives than before.

It is my hope and prayer that the Cause for the Canonization of Servant of God, Father John P. Wessel, continue, and that (whether I am here to see it or not) he may ultimately be honored by the Roman Catholic Church with the declaration of Sainthood. To this end, it is important to have an accurate record of any miracles or favors received that are attributable to the intercession of Father John P. Wessel. Please, therefore, contact the address noted for his Cause in the Diocese of Trenton to report any favors which you have received, or may yet receive, through his intercession.

Finally, please pray for our Church and for our priests—present and future.

May God bless you. And remember—keep trying to be a positive influence in the life of one other person!

K.M.B.

ENDNOTES

Introduction Notes:

[1] Pope John Paul II, *Pastores Dabo Vobis* ("I Will Give You Shepherds"), Apostolic Exhortation on the Formation of Priests in the Circumstances of the Present Day, promulgated by Pope John Paul II on March 25, 1992.

[2] Statistics derived from *The World Book Encyclopedia*, vol. 15, "Religion," at 216 (Chicago: Field Enterprises Educ. Corp., 1963) (hereinafter *The World Book Encyclopedia*).

[3] Information on Vietnam derived from *Chronicle of the 20th Century*, at 1060 (Liberty, MO: J.L. Int'l Publishing, 1992) (hereinafter *Chronicle of the 20th Century*).

[4] Pope John Paul II, *Pastores Dabo Vobis*.

Chapter 1 Notes:

[1] Information concerning the events of Friday, December 17, 1971 is taken from several main sources:

Document entitled "Toms River, New Jersey, 1971" Report by personnel from St. Joseph Church, Toms River, NJ, author unknown (hereinafter "Toms River Report"), prepared for Rev. Msgr. Joseph C. Shenrock, ed., *No Greater Love: The Story of Father John P. Wessel* (1974) (hereinafter *No Greater Love*); Rev. Msgr. Joseph C. Shenrock, ed., *Three Good Shepherds*, (circa 1973) (hereinafter *Three Good Shepherds*); Interviews with Brendan Gallagher; Sean Maguire*; Sr. M. Juliana Naulty, O.P.; and from various newspaper articles, including Raymond J. Tuers, "Father Wessel Imbued with a Mission in Life," *Asbury Park Sunday Press*, Sun., Jan. 9, 1972, sec. C, at C-1.

Dialogue is substantially accurate, as detailed in the Toms River Report.

[2] Cf., Interview with Al Kedz. Estimated population statistics (for 1970) from State of New Jersey, Dept. of Labor, Div. of Research & Planning.

[3] Rev. Msgr. Joseph C. Shenrock, ed., *Upon This Rock: A New History of the Trenton Diocese*, at 452 (1993) (hereinafter *Upon This Rock*).

[4] Interview with Sean Maguire.

[5] *See* "Priest Remembered," Letters to the Editor, (Letter from "A Former Searcher"), *The Trentonian*, Sat. morn., Dec. 23, 1972. The author of this letter has never been located and so this statement attributed to Father Wessel has not been independently verified.

6   Interviews with Sr. Jorene Cieciuch; Sean Maguire.

7   Toms River Report; Interview with Sean Maguire.

8   Interview with Sean Maguire.

9   *See* Chapter 32, note 66 and text, *infra*.

10   Toms River Report; Interview with Brendan Gallagher.

11   Toms River Report.

12   Toms River Report; Interview with Brendan Gallagher.

13   Id.

Chapter 2 Notes:

1   Material for this chapter is taken mainly from Shenrock, *No Greater Love* and from Interviews with Mrs. Kathleen Hogan Wessel and Mrs. Maryann Wessel Beitel.

      See birth announcement in *The Mount Holly Herald*, undated, circa Sept. 1939, which was in possession of Mrs. Kathleen Wessel.

2   Historical materials derived from *The World Book Encyclopedia*, vol. 19, "World War I," at 365, and "World War II," at 380-388.

3   Shenrock, *No Greater Love*; Interviews with Mrs. Kathleen Wessel and Maryann Beitel.

4   The year was either 1882 or 1883; cf., Interview with Maryann Beitel (#2).

5   Background material and family history for "The Duggans and the Hogans" is taken from Interviews with Mrs. Kathleen Wessel and Maryann Beitel (#1) and (#2).

6   Interview with Julian Wessel.

7   Id.

8   Background material and family history for "The Wessels" is taken from Interviews with Julian Wessel; Maryann Beitel (#2).

Chapter 3 Notes:

1   Interview with Maryann Beitel (#2). Material for this chapter is taken mainly from Shenrock, *No Greater Love* and from recollections of Mrs. Kathleen H. Wessel, Maryann W. Beitel, and Rev. Msgr. James H. Dubell, in personal interviews and written materials. *See* Interviews with Mrs. Kathleen Wessel; Maryann Beitel (#2); and Msgr. James H. Dubell; and document entitled, "A Biography of Father John P. Wessel, 1939-1953," by Maryann Wessel Beitel, dated Aug. 22, 1973 (hereinafter "Written Recollections of Maryann Beitel"), prepared for the *No Greater Love* book by Msgr. Shenrock.

2   Interview with Maryann Beitel (#2).

3   Interview with Julian Wessel.

4   From an original note which was in possession of Mrs. Kathleen Wessel (with appropriate spelling corrections).

5   Interview with Julian Wessel.

6   Information supplied by Maryann Beitel.

7   The survivor quoted was Sgt. Aaron Weber, a radio operator with Cpt. Hogan's unit, the 322nd Fighter Control Sqdn, Air Corp. "No medical officer ever gave more than Hogan did when he gave his life belt to a boy who had been hurt, and had lost his," wrote Maj. William Wilson, who served in a unit attached to Cpt. Hogan's, "because giving away your life belt on a rough sea when the boat is sinking is just sure death. God must have a special place reserved for such people."

      Much of the information about the sinking of *H.M.T. Rohna* remained classified for years due to wartime and national security concerns. *See* The Rohna Survivors Memorial Association, *www. rohna.org.*; *see also www.dvrbs.com/ccwd-WW2/WW2-Rohna-CarltonPHogan.htm* (web site devoted to Dr. Carlton P. Hogan).

[8] Dr. Thomas Ashford Kuhlman's article, "The Capt. Cornelius O'Connor House in Homer: A Symbol for the Dakota County Irish," appeared in *Nebraska History*, a quarterly journal published by The Nebraska State Historical Society, vol. 63, no. 1, at 16-32 (1981) (hereinafter "The Capt. Cornelius O'Connor House").

Assistance and information provided by Dr. Thomas A. Kuhlman pertaining to the Duggan family background in his *Nebraska History* article is most gratefully acknowledged.

[9] Id.

[10] The Winnebago was one of several Indian tribes which inhabited the area of easterly Nebraska.

[11] Kuhlman, "The Capt. Cornelius O'Connor House," 63 *Nebraska History* 1, at 16. Materials from Dr. Kuhlman's *Nebraska History* article and letters from Grandmother Mary Duggan Hogan's cousin Charlotte are in possession of Maryann Beitel. Interview with Maryann Beitel (#2).

[12] *See* Interviews with Mrs. Kathleen Wessel; Maryann Beitel (#2); Shenrock, *No Greater Love.*

Chapter 4 Notes:

[1] Material for this chapter is taken mainly from Shenrock, *No Greater Love* and from recollections of Mrs. Kathleen H. Wessel, Maryann W. Beitel, and Rev. Msgr. James H. Dubell in personal interviews and written materials. *See* Interviews with Mrs. Kathleen Wessel; Maryann Beitel (#2); and Msgr. James H. Dubell; and Written Recollections of Maryann Beitel.

[2] Information derived from *The World Book Encyclopedia*, vol. 19, "World War II," at 398-99, 407-08.

[3] Material on the history and development of Medford Lakes is taken from the 50th anniversary commemorative booklet, H. Harper et al., ed., *The Medford Lakes Story, 1927-1977* (1977) (hereinafter *The Medford Lakes Story*), with special thanks to Mr. Clint Alexander, Medford Lakes Historian, for supplying information about Medford Lakes.

[4] Interviews with Julian Wessel; Maryann Beitel (#2).

[5] Information supplied by Maryann Beitel.

[6] *The Medford Lakes Story*, at 29.

[7] Id.

Chapter 5 Notes:

[1] Material for this chapter is taken mainly from Shenrock, *No Greater Love* and from recollections of Mrs. Kathleen H. Wessel, Maryann W. Beitel, Rev. Msgr. James H. Dubell, and Sr. Mary Christina Murphy, I.H.M., in personal interviews and written materials. *See* Interviews with Mrs. Kathleen Wessel; Maryann Beitel (#2); Msgr. James H. Dubell; and Sr. M. Christina Murphy, I.H.M.; and Written Recollections of Maryann Beitel.

Information on history of Roman Catholic schools is derived from *Collier's Encyclopedia*, "Roman Catholic Religious Education," at 579-580 (New York: Maxwell Macmillian Int'l, 1990).

[2] Material pertaining to the history and development of Mount Holly Regional Catholic/Sacred Heart School is derived from a document entitled "History of Sacred Heart School" (1994), with special thanks to Sr. Jean Louise Bachetti, I.H.M., Principal of Sacred Heart School, who supplied this information.

Chapter 6 Notes:

¹   Material for this chapter is taken mainly from Shenrock, *No Greater Love* and from recollections of Mrs. Kathleen H. Wessel, Maryann W. Beitel, Rev. Msgr. James H. Dubell, Sr. Eileen Egan, I.H.M., and Julian Wessel, in personal interviews and written materials. *See* Interviews with Mrs. Kathleen Wessel; Maryann Beitel (#2); Msgr. James H. Dubell; Sr. Eileen Egan, I.H.M.; and Julian Wessel; and Written Recollections of Maryann Beitel.

Chapter 7 Notes:

¹   Letter from Sr. Eileen Egan, I.H.M., to author (Feb. 15, 1994). Material for this chapter is taken mainly from the recollections of Mrs. Kathleen H. Wessel, Maryann W. Beitel, and Sr. M. Christina Murphy, I.H.M. in personal interviews and written materials. Other information is derived from Shenrock, *No Greater Love* and from the recollections of Sr. M. Raymond Rafferty, I.H.M., Sr. M. Espiritu Demsey, I.H.M., and Sr. Eileen Egan, I.H.M., in personal interviews and written materials.

²   Sr. Carina is now deceased. This story was related to the author by Sr. M. Raymond Rafferty, I.H.M. Other Sisters also confirmed that as a young kindergartner, John would tell Sister Carina, "Someday I'm going to be a priest, Sister." Interview with Sr. M. Christina Murphy, I.H.M.

³   This story is contained in Written Recollections of Maryann Beitel. The fact that John told Sr. Carina that he felt himself unworthy to play St. Joseph was recalled by Sr. M. Christina Murphy.

⁴   Written Recollections of Maryann Beitel; *see also* Interview with Maryann Beitel (#2).

⁵   Written Recollections of Maryann Beitel.

⁶   Id. The bed is still in the possession of the Wessel family. Uncle John's bed has been used successively by a few of Maryann Beitel's children.

⁷   Written Recollections of Maryann Beitel.

⁸   Id.

⁹   Sr. M. Ignatia Murphy is now deceased. Interview with Sr. M. Christina Murphy. I.H.M. The story was related in a letter to Maryann Beitel from Sister Ignatia and is included in Written Recollections of Maryann W. Beitel. (Incidentally, there is no relation between Sr. Ignatia Murphy and Sr. Christina Murphy.)

¹⁰   Interview with Sr. M. Espiritu Dempsey, I.H.M.

¹¹   Letter from Sr. M. Christina Murphy, I.H.M. to Mrs. Kathleen Wessel (circa 1973), original in possession of Maryann Beitel. Interview with Maryann Beitel (#2).

¹²   Id.

¹³   Written Recollections of Maryann Beitel.

¹⁴   Id.

¹⁵   Letter from Sr. M. Christina Murphy, I.H.M. to Mrs. Kathleen Wessel (circa 1973), quoted in Written Recollections of Maryann W. Beitel.

¹⁶   Leonard Foley, O.F.M., ed., "Isaac Jogues and John de Brebéuf and Companions," *Saint of the Day: Lives and Lessons for Saints and Feasts of the New Missal*, at 279 (Cincinnati, OH: St. Anthony Messenger Press, 1990) (hereinafter *Saint of the Day*); *see also* Rosalie Marie Levy, "St. Isaac Jogues and Companions," *Heavenly Friends: A Saint for Each Day*, at 362 (Boston, MA: Daughters of St. Paul, 1984) (hereinafter *Heavenly Friends*).

¹⁷   Foley, *Saint of the Day*, at 279.

18 Levy, *Heavenly Friends*, at 362-363.

19 Foley, *Saint of the Day*, at 279-280.

20 Id.

21 Letter from Sr. Eileen Egan, I.H.M. to Mrs. Kathleen Wessel (circa 1973), quoted in Written Recollections of Maryann Beitel. In addition, Sr. Christina also recalled being told that in one the upper grades John stated publicly that he desired to be a martyr. Interview with Sr. M. Christina Murphy, I.H.M.

22 Cf., Levy, "St. Stephen," *Heavenly Friends*, at 480.

23 Foley, "Stephen," *Saint of the Day*, at 339-340.

24 Cf., Levy, *Heavenly Friends*, at 480.

25 Interview with Sr. M. Christina Murphy, I.H.M.

26 Interview with Mrs. Kathleen Wessel.

27 Interview and Telephone conversation with Sr. M. Christina Murphy, I.H.M. This story was related to the author by Sr. Christina, an eyewitness to the event, and confirmed in essential respects by Sr. Raymond, as told to her by Mother Brigida.

Chapter 8 Notes:

1 Material for this chapter is taken mainly from the recollections of Sr. M. Espiritu Dempsey, I.H.M., and Msgr. James H. Dubell in personal interviews and written materials. Other information is derived from Shenrock, *No Greater Love* and from recollections of Mrs. Kathleen Wessel, Maryann Beitel, and Sr. M. Christina Murphy, I.H.M., in personal interviews and written materials.

2 The poem is reprinted in Written Recollections of Maryann Beitel. The original poem that John Wessel wrote has been revised slightly for grammar and punctuation.

3 John related this conversation with Sr. Espiritu to one other person, Sr. Christina Murphy. His last statement is taken from Sr. Christina's recollection. The remaining dialogue is accurately portrayed from the specific recollections of Sr. Espiritu. Interview with Sr. M. Espiritu Dempsey, I.H.M.

4 Interview with Sr. M. Christina Murphy, I.H.M.

5 Letter from Rev. Joseph V. Kozak, Sacred Heart Church, Mt. Holly, NJ to Rt. Rev. Richard T. Crean, Diocese of Trenton, Trenton, NJ (June 8, 1953). Original contained in Chancery Office Files of Fr. John P. Wessel, Diocese of Trenton, New Jersey (hereinafter "Chancery Files").

6 "Diocese of Trenton, Examination for Entrance to Preparatory Seminary," by John P. Wessel, undated, circa June 5, 1953. Original contained in Chancery Files.

Chapter 9 Notes:

1 Material for this chapter is taken mainly from the recollections of Msgr. James H. Dubell, Carl Wingate, Michael Choma, W. Michael Mueller, and other of John Wessel's seminary classmates in personal interviews and written materials. Other information is derived from Shenrock, *No Greater Love* and from recollections of Mrs. Kathleen H. Wessel, Maryann W. Beitel, Father Raymond E. Brown, S.S., and Rev. Msgr. Joseph C. Shenrock, P.A., in personal interviews and written materials.

Assistance and information provided by Fr. John W. Bowen, S.S., Sulpician Archivist, Catonsville, Maryland, pertaining to background materials on St. Charles College is most gratefully acknowledged.

[2]   Preceding materials taken from St. Charles College High School Catalogue, 1954-1955, at 8-11 (1955) (hereinafter "SCC Catalogue").

[3]   Id. at 8.

[4]   Rev. John J. Tierney, S.S., "Historical Sketch of Saint Charles College," St. Charles College 1848-1948, Commemorating the One Hundredth Anniversary of Its Opening, 1-3 (1948) (hereinafter "SCC 100th Anniversary").

[5]   St. Mary's Seminary and University, Academic Catalogue, 1992-1994, at 6.

[6]   Quoted from the dedication to the 1957 *Carolite* (St. Charles Yearbook), at 2.

[7]   Id.

[8]   Today, St. Charles College, which educated generations of young Catholic men, no longer exists as a minor seminary, although most of its physical buildings still remain on the same site in Catonsville. St. Charles is now "Charlestown," a large retirement community housing some 1200 senior citizens. *See* Rudi E.J. Ruckmann, "A Living Legend Looks Back," *St. Mary's Bicentennial Magazine* at 7 (Oct. 1991) (hereinafter "A Living Legend Looks Back"). The beautiful chapel of Our Lady of the Angels still stands not only as a reminder of a bygone past but now as a haven serving the religious needs of this new community.

[9]   Detailed information about the chapel was provided courtesy of Fr. John W. Bowen.

[10]   SCC Catalogue, at 29; *see also* Telephone conversation with Father John W. Bowen (confirming the "second Sunday" visiting day).

[11]   This paragraph was derived from a document entitled, "Father John Patrick Wessel, The Seminary Years: 1953-1965," by Rev. Msgr. James H. Dubell, undated, circa 1973 (hereinafter "Written Recollections of Msgr. James H. Dubell"), which was prepared for the Shenrock, *No Greater Love* book.

[12]   Interviews with Carl Wingate (#1) and (#2).

[13]   Interview with Michael Choma.

[14]   Written Recollections of Msgr. James H. Dubell.

[15]   Interview with Maryann Beitel.

[16]   Interview with Several Priests of Father Wessel's Ordination Class (Msgr. James H. Dubell) (hereinafter "Interview with Priests").

[17]   Interview with W. Michael Mueller.

[18]   Cf., Written Recollections of Msgr. James H. Dubell.

[19]   Cf., Interviews with Michael Choma; Carl Wingate.

[20]   Written Recollections of Msgr. James H. Dubell.

[21]   Id.

[22]   Id.

[23]   Id.

[24]   1958 *Carolite*, at 3.

Chapter 10 Notes:

[1]   Material for this chapter is taken from the recollections of Mrs. Kathleen H. Wessel, Maryann W. Beitel, William Beitel, Pat Wessel, Julian Wessel, Rev. Msgr. James H. Dubell, Carl Wingate, Sr. Eileen Egan, I.H.M., and Rev. Msgr. Joseph C. Shenrock, P.A., in personal interviews and written materials. Other information is derived from Shenrock, *No Greater Love*.

[2]   Interview with Julian Wessel.

[3]   Interview with Maryann Beitel (#2).

[4]   Interview with Julian Wessel.

[5]   Interview with Maryann Beitel (#2).

6   Written Recollections of Msgr. James H. Dubell.

7   *See* Shenrock, *No Greater Love.*

Chapter 11 Notes:

1   Material for this chapter is taken from the recollections of Mrs. Kathleen H. Wessel, Maryann W. Beitel, William Beitel, Pat Wessel, Julian Wessel, Rev. Msgr. James H. Dubell, Rev. Msgr. Eugene Rebeck, Carl Wingate, and Rev. Msgr. Joseph C. Shenrock, P.A., in personal interviews and written materials. Other information is derived from Shenrock, *No Greater Love.*

2   Written Recollections of Msgr. James H. Dubell.

3   Interview with Julian Wessel.

Chapter 12 Notes:

1   Material for this chapter is taken mainly from the recollections of Mrs. Kathleen H. Wessel. Other information is derived from the recollections of Msgr. James H. Dubell, Carl Wingate, and Maryann W. Beitel in personal interviews and written materials. John P. Wessel's passport provided the dates of travel.

2   By this time, Maryann Wessel was away at graduate school.

3   Copies of this correspondence were found in Chancery Files.

4   John Wessel related this incident to his friend James Dubell upon his return from Europe.

5   Mrs. Wessel believed that one of the young priests was Father John Quinn, the future Archbishop of San Francisco.

6   Information on Lourdes derived from *The World Book Encyclopedia*, vol. 11, "Lourdes," at 437-38.

7   *See* Levy, "St. Francis of Assisi," *Heavenly Friends*, at 374.

8   *See* Omer Englebert, *Saint Francis of Assisi: A Biography*, (Eve Marie Cooper, trans.), at 12 (Ann Arbor: Servant Books, 1979) (hereinafter *Saint Francis of Assisi: A Biography*).

9   Id.

10   Cf., id. at 16-17.

11   Foley, "Francis of Assisi," *Saint of the Day*, at 259.

12   Levy, *Heavenly Friends*, at 375.

13   Cf., id.

14   Id. at 375-376.

15   Id.

16   Foley, *Saint of the Day*, at 260.

17   Id.

18   Levy, *Heavenly Friends*, at 376.

19   Id. at 374.

20   Levy, *Heavenly Friends*, at 376.

21   Foley, *Saint of the Day*, at 260.

22   Id.; *see also* Englebert, *Saint Francis of Assisi: A Biography*, at 268-274.

Chapter 13 Notes:

1   Material for this chapter is taken mainly from the recollections of Rev. Msgr. James H. Dubell, Carl Wingate, Michael Choma, W. Michael Mueller, and other of John Wessel's seminary classmates, in

personal interviews and written materials. Other information is derived from Shenrock, *No Greater Love* and from recollections of Mrs. Kathleen H. Wessel, Maryann W. Beitel, Father Raymond E. Brown, S.S. and Rev. Msgr. Joseph C. Shenrock, P.A., in personal interviews and written materials.

Assistance, information and background materials provided by Fr. John W. Bowen, S.S., Sulpician Archivist, Catonsville, Maryland, pertaining to St. Charles College is most gratefully acknowledged.

2   1959 *Carolite*, at 14.

3   Original retreat notes from John Wessel's "Rhet Retreat" were supplied courtesy of Mrs. Kathleen H. Wessel.

4   Foley, "Theresa of the Child Jesus," *Saint of the Day*, at 236.

5   *See* John Clarke, O.C.D, trans., *Story of a Soul: The Autobiography of St. Therese of Lisieux*, 2d ed., at 197 (Washington, DC: ICS Publications, 1976).

6   *See* 1959 *Carolite*, at pages 60-61 (sports montage).

7   Interview with Michael Choma.

8   1959 *Carolite*, at 3.

9   Cf., *Chronicle of the 20th Century*, at 822-823.

10   Evaluation of John P. Wessel by Very Rev. John F. Linn, S.S. (June 4, 1959), contained in Seminary Files, St. Mary's Seminary & University, Roland Park (hereinafter "Seminary Files").

Chapter 14 Notes:

1   Material for this chapter is taken mainly from the recollections of Rev. Msgr. James H. Dubell, Carl Wingate, Michael Choma, W. Michael Mueller, James Roche, and William Beitel in personal interviews and written materials.

2   Interview with W. Michael Mueller.

3   Interview with Maryann Beitel (#2).

4   Id.

5   Information on Lake George, New York, derived from *The World Book Encyclopedia*, vol.11, "Lake George," at 41.

6   Interview with James Roche.

7   Interview with Carl Wingate (#2).

8   Interview with Michael Choma.

9   Interview with Carl Wingate.

10   Interview with Michael Choma.

11   Interview with James Roche (quotes attributed to John Wessel edited slightly).

12   Interview with Carl Wingate (#2).

13   This story is a composite of Interviews with Carl Wingate (#1) and (#2).

14   The previous year, John Wessel and his friends had gone to the Penobscot River, and so that year, 1964, they were going to the Allagash River. But it was very complicated trying to get on the land, as they needed the permission of the Rangers and the Peabody Lumbering Company that was logging the river at the same time, so they decided to go back to the Penobscot. Interview with James Roche. However, it appears that this is still referred to as "the Allagash trip" (and perhaps they may have even been on the Allagash for some period of time).

15   This story is a composite of recollections of James Roche and Michael Choma. Interviews with James Roche; Michael Choma.

16   Interview with James Roche.

Chapter 15 Notes:

[1] Material for this chapter is taken mainly from the recollections of Rev. Msgr. James H. Dubell, Carl Wingate, Michael Choma, W. Michael Mueller, and other of John Wessel's seminary classmates, in personal interviews and written materials. Other information is derived from Shenrock, *No Greater Love*, and from recollections of Mrs. Kathleen H. Wessel, Maryann W. Beitel, Fr. Raymond E. Brown, S.S. and Rev. Msgr. Joseph C. Shenrock, P.A., in personal interviews and written materials.

The old seminary building on North Paca Street no longer stands. It was demolished in 1975. Only the chapel, the convent, and the Mother Seton House remain. Ruckmann, "A Living Legend Looks Back," at 8. The former seminary at North Paca Street is now the site of St. Mary's Spiritual Center. Id. at 9.

Assistance, information and background materials provided by Fr. John McMurray, S.S., in residence at St. Mary's Spiritual Center, Baltimore, MD, regarding old St. Mary's, Paca Street, is most gratefully acknowledged.

[2] _____, "Old St. Mary's Seminary Chapel," at 1, circa 1970s (hereinafter "St. Mary's Chapel"), copy supplied courtesy of Fr. John McMurray.

[3] Ruckmann, "A Living Legend Looks Back," at 5.

[4] _____, "St. Mary's Seminary Chapel on Paca Street in Baltimore," May 1968 (hereinafter "1968 Chapel Restoration"), a pamphlet prepared for the 1968 chapel restoration and rededication supplied courtesy of Fr. John McMurray.

[5] Ruckmann, "A Living Legend Looks Back," at 6.

[6] Id.

[7] *See* "1968 Chapel Restoration."

[8] Footner, "Old St. Mary's Seminary, Baltimore," *Maryland Main and the Eastern Shore*, date unknown, copy supplied courtesy of Fr. John McMurray.

[9] Interview with Priests (Msgr. Eugene Rebeck).

[10] *See* Ruckmann, "A Living Legend Looks Back," at 9.

[11] *See* "St. Mary's Chapel," at 4-5.

[12] Id. at 1-4.

[13] *See* id.

[14] Id. at 4-5.

[15] *See* "1968 Chapel Restoration"; "St. Mary's Chapel," at 4-5. In 1971, the Chapel of the Presentation of the Blessed Virgin Mary in the Temple at St. Mary's Seminary was declared a National Landmark by the U.S. Department of the Interior. "St. Mary's Chapel," at 5. The Mother Seton House is also a national trust. Since 1985, the old Paca Street buildings which remain have operated as a spirituality center, and today, liturgies are still held in the restored chapel. Ruckmann, "A Living Legend Looks Back," at 9.

[16] Fr. John W. Bowen, S.S., "The Texture of Life at St. Mary's: A Tale of Two Centuries," *St. Mary's Bicentennial Magazine*, at 21 (Oct. 1991) (hereinafter "The Texture of Life at St. Mary's: A Tale of Two Centuries").

[17] Written Recollections of Msgr. James H. Dubell.

[18] Father Walsh was the subject of a 1988 biography by Timothy Leonard, *Geno, A Biography of Eugene Walsh, S.S.*, published by Pastoral Press. Id. at 71.

[19] Written Recollections of Msgr. James H. Dubell.

[20] Letter from Very Rev. William J. Lee, S.S., President, St. Mary's Seminary and University to Rev. Joseph C. Shenrock (Dec. 14, 1973).

[21] Interview with Carl Wingate.

[22] Letter from Fr. Amedeo L. Morello to Bishop of Trenton (Aug. 3, 1960), contained in Chancery Files.

[23] Interview with Mrs. Kathleen Wessel and Maryann Beitel.

[24] Letter from John P. Wessel to Dr. and Mrs. Edward J. Wessel, Jr. (May 13, 1961), copy in possession of Mrs. Pat Wessel. Interview with Pat Wessel.

[25] Recollections of the Scandinavia trip are taken from Interview with Pat Wessel.

[26] *The World Book Encyclopedia*, vol. 13, "Norway," at 418.

[27] Recollections of this story are taken from Interviews with Mrs. Kathleen Wessel; Maryann Beitel (#2); and Michael Choma.

Chapter 16 Notes:

[1] Of the three institutions where John Wessel studied for the priesthood, St. Mary's Seminary at Roland Park is the only one that still exists today as a seminary. *See* Shenrock, *No Greater Love*, at 5.

[2] Cf., St. Mary's Seminary & University, School of Theology, Academic Catalogue (1961-1962), at 12.

[3] Telephone conversation with Fr. John Kselman.

[4] Shenrock, *No Greater Love*, at 5.

[5] *See* Shenrock, *No Greater Love*, at 5; cf., Written Recollections of Msgr. James H. Dubell.

[6] Interviews with Fr. Raymond E. Brown, S.S.; James Roche; cf., St. Mary's Seminary & University, School of Theology, Academic Catalogue (1961-1962), at 17.

[7] Interview with James Roche.

[8] *See* Shenrock, *No Greater Love*, at 5.

[9] Written Recollections of Maryann Beitel; Interview with Maryann Beitel.

[10] Interview with James Roche.

[11] *See* Shenrock, *No Greater Love*, at 5; cf., St. Mary's Seminary & University, School of Theology, Academic Catalogue (1961-1962), at 37. Other materials from Seminary Files.

[12] Interview with Michael Choma.

[13] Interview with Priests; cf., St. Mary's Seminary & University, School of Theology, Academic Catalogue (1961-1962), at 18.

[14] Interview with Mrs. Kathleen Wessel and Maryann Beitel (Maryann Beitel).

[15] Interview with Michael Choma.

[16] Interview with Fr. Ronald Bacovin.

[17] Interview with Msgr. John Kinsella.

[18] Interview with Julian Wessel.

[19] *See* Shenrock, *No Greater Love*, at 5; cf., Written Recollections of Msgr. James H. Dubell.

[20] Quoted statements of Msgr. John Kinsella and Fr. Ronald Bacovin, respectively.

[21] Above statements are taken from Spiral Notebook of Spiritual Notes of John P. Wessel (handwritten, undated, circa 1962), supplied by Maryann Beitel. Some may be thoughts of others, or retreat notes that Father Wessel recorded.

[22] Interview with James Roche.

[23] Evaluations taken from Seminary Files.

[24] Written Recollections of Msgr. James H. Dubell.

[25] *See, e.g.*, Bowen, "The Texture of Life at St. Mary's: A Tale of Two Centuries," at 23.

[26] Interview with Mrs. Kathleen Wessel and Maryann Beitel (Maryann Beitel).

27 Telephone conversation with Fr. John W. Bowen, S.S., Sulpician Archivist.

28 Interview with Carl Wingate.

29 Interview with Msgr. James H. Dubell.

30 *See* Written Recollections of Msgr. James H. Dubell; *see also* Interviews with Msgr. James H. Dubell; Fr. Ronald Bacovin; Carl Wingate.

31 Interview with Fr. Ronald Bacovin.

32 Recollections of John Wessel's visits to the Maryland State Penitentiary are taken from Interview with Carl Wingate.

33 Interview with Msgr. John Kinsella.

34 Interview with James Roche.

35 Recollections on the State Pen Annual Football Game are taken mainly from Interview with Carl Wingate; *see also* Interview with Fr. Ronald Bacovin.

36 Bowen, "The Texture of Life at St. Mary's: A Tale of Two Centuries," at 24.

37 Interview with Priests (Msgr. Eugene Rebeck).

38 Interview with Carl Wingate; *see* Interview with Priests (Msgr. Eugene Rebeck).

39 Bowen, "The Texture of Life at St. Mary's: A Tale of Two Centuries," at 24.

40 Interview with Carl Wingate; *see* Interview with Priests (Msgr. Eugene Rebeck).

41 Interview with Carl Wingate.

42 Id.

43 Spiral Notebook of Spiritual Notes of John P. Wessel (handwritten, undated, circa 1962).

44 Interview with Carl Wingate.

45 Interview with James Roche.

46 Id.

47 Interview with Carl Wingate.

48 Id.

49 Evaluations in this section obtained from Seminary Files.

50 R. Ruckmann, "The New Shepherds," *St. Mary's Alumni Magazine*, 1 (Summer 1993).

51 *See* Lawrence Cardinal Shehan, "Introduction," W.M. Abbott, S.J., ed., *The Documents of Vatican II*, at xv-xvii (New York: Guild Press, America Press, 1966).

52 Interview with Fr. Raymond E. Brown, S.S.

53 Id.

54 Cf., id.

55 Interview with Carl Wingate.

56 Interview with Fr. Ronald Bacovin.

57 Cf., Seminary Files; Chancery Files.

58 After Vatican II, it was no longer obligatory to become a subdeacon in the Roman rite Church, although in the Eastern Church it is still retained. The major step today is the deaconate—and then on to the priesthood. In addition, the institution of the permanent deaconate was also revived in the post-Vatican II Church. Today, a great number of laymen, whether married or single, have become deacons, and are able to preach and perform many of the functions previously done only by the priest, except for those sacramental functions specially reserved to the priesthood by virtue of the Sacrament of Holy Orders. Interviews with Msgr. Joseph C. Shenrock; Carl Wingate.

59 Spiral Notebook of Spiritual Notes of John P. Wessel (handwritten, undated, circa 1962).

60 Interview with Michael Choma.

61 Id.

62 Interview with Mrs. Kathleen Wessel.

63 Interview with Michael Choma.

[64]   Text of this letter provided in Interview with Maryann Beitel.

[65]   Petition, dated April 4, 1964, and Letter, dated March 28, 1964, from John P. Wessel to The Most Reverend George W. Ahr, Bishop of Trenton, contained in Chancery Files; Seminary Files.

[66]   Interview with Michael Choma.

[67]   Id.

[68]   Interview with Fr. Ronald Bacovin.

[69]   Seminary Notes of John P. Wessel (handwritten, undated, circa 1964 or 1965), supplied courtesy of Maryann Beitel.

[70]   Interview with Maryann Beitel.

[71]   Written Recollections of Maryann Beitel.

[72]   Letter from John P. Wessel to The Most Reverend George W. Ahr, Bishop of Trenton (March 28, 1965), contained in Chancery Files; Seminary Files.

[73]   Shenrock, *No Greater Love,* at 6; Letter from Fr. John H. Greenalch, S.S., Rector, St. Mary's Seminary and University, to Fr. Joseph C. Shenrock (Jan. 18, 1974); *see also* Seminary Files.

[74]   Interview with Carl Wingate; cf., Interview with Fr. Ronald Bacovin.

[75]   Interview with Carl Wingate.

[76]   Interview with Mrs. Kathleen Wessel. Original prayer card was in possession of Mrs. Kathleen Wessel.

Chapter 17 Notes:

[1]   Cf., Interview with Msgr. James H. Dubell (#2).

[2]   *See* Interview with Maryann Beitel (#2) (The stole, a gift of Mr. and Mrs. M. Gerald Gleason, was handmade by Mrs. Gleason). For material in the remainder of paragraph, *see* Shenrock, *No Greater Love,* at 6; Written Recollections of Msgr. James H. Dubell.

[3]   Judith A. Walker, "2 Boyhood Friends to Enter Priesthood Together May 22," *The Mount Holly Herald,* (Mt. Holly), May___, 1965, at 1-A, 14-A (hereinafter *Mt. Holly Herald,* "2 Boyhood Friends"). Used with permission of *The Burlington County Times.*

[4]   Interview with Julian Wessel.

[5]   Cf., Interview with Pat Wessel.

[6]   Cf., Interview with Mrs. Kathleen Wessel.

[7]   *See* Shenrock, *No Greater Love,* at 6; *see also* Written Recollections of Msgr. James H. Dubell.

[8]   Cf., Private Note of John P. Wessel, reprinted in Chapter 16, *supra.*

[9]   *Mt. Holly Herald,* "2 Boyhood Friends"; *see* Shenrock, *No Greater Love,* at 6; *see also* Interview with Msgr. Joseph C. Shenrock.

[10]   Letter from Msgr. Joseph V. Kozak to John P. Wessel (Nov. 18, 1964), copy provided courtesy of Mrs. Kathleen Wessel.

[11]   Interview with Maryann Beitel (#2).

[12]   Id.; Interview with Msgr. Joseph C. Shenrock.

[13]   Interview with Maryann Beitel (#2).

[14]   Interview with Mrs. Kathleen Wessel and Maryann Beitel (Maryann Beitel).

[15]   *See* Interview with Maryann Beitel (#2); *see also* Interviews with Msgr. James H. Dubell (#2); Julian Wessel.

[16]   *See* Interview with Msgr. James H. Dubell (#2).

[17]   Id.

[18]   Interview with Maryann Beitel (#2).

[19]   Interview with Msgr. James H. Dubell (#2); cf., Interview with Several Former Members of Blessed Sacrament CYO (Jayne Hartley*) (hereinafter "Interview with CYO").

[20] The material regarding the history of the Bordentown chalice is taken from Interviews with Mrs. Kathleen Wessel and Maryann Beitel; Mrs. Kathleen Wessel (#2); Maryann Beitel (#2); *see also* Shenrock, *Upon This Rock*, at 545.

[21] Interview with Maryann Beitel (#2); cf., Interview with Mrs. Kathleen Wessel and Maryann Beitel (Maryann Beitel).

[22] Interview with Julian Wessel.

[23] Interview with Maryann Beitel (#2).

[24] Letter from Rev. Joseph C. Shenrock to John P. Wessel (circa April 1965), copy supplied courtesy of Mrs. Kathleen Wessel.

[25] Interview with Mrs. Kathleen Wessel (#2).

[26] Letter from Rev. Herbert R. Denton, S.T.M. to John P. Wessel (circa May 1965), copy supplied courtesy of Mrs. Kathleen Wessel.

[27] Letter from Sr. M. Espiritu Dempsey, I.H.M. to John P. Wessel (circa May 1965), copy supplied courtesy of Mrs. Kathleen Wessel.

[28] Letter from Sr. M. Christina Murphy, I.H.M. to John P. Wessel (circa May 1965), in possession of Maryann Beitel; *see* Interview with Maryann Beitel (#2).

[29] Letter from James J. Moonan to Mrs. Kathleen Wessel (March 5, 1973), copy supplied courtesy of Mrs. Kathleen Wessel.

Chapter 18 Notes:

[1] *See* Shenrock, *No Greater Love*, at 6.

[2] Estimated population statistics (for 1965) from State of New Jersey, Dept. of Labor, Div. of Research & Planning.

 Information on the history of Trenton is derived from several sources: _____, *A History of Trenton, 1679-1929* (Princeton Univ. Press: 1929), at 1050-52; Eleanor Nolan Shuman, "Trenton Story," _____ (date unknown), preface (hereinafter "Trenton Story"); "Trenton," *Encyclopedia Americana, Int'l Edition*, (Grolier Inc. 1993), at 87-89; "Trenton," Federal Writers Project (WPA, 1939), at 398-404 (hereinafter "Federal Writers Project").

[3] "Trenton," *Encyclopedia Americana, Int'l Edition*, at 89.

[4] Cf., Shuman, "Trenton Story."

[5] *Chronicle of 20th Century*, at 167, 273.

[6] Shuman, "Trenton Story."

[7] "Trenton," Federal Writers Project, at 398.

[8] Kennedy Directory, 1965.

[9] Shenrock, *Upon This Rock*, at 197-200.

[10] Id. at 198.

[11] Id. at 357-58, 360-61; cf., Interviews with Fr. Eugene V. Davis; Msgr. Leonard R. Toomey.

[12] Shenrock, *Upon This Rock*, at 350.

[13] Interview with Fr. Eugene V. Davis.

[14] Interview with Msgr. Leonard R. Toomey.

[15] *See* Shenrock, *No Greater Love*; Interview with Fr. Eugene V. Davis.

[16] *See* Shenrock, *No Greater Love*.

[17] Id.

[18] Interview with Several Former Blessed Sacrament Nuns (hereinafter "Interview with Nuns"); Interview with Fr. J. William Mickiewicz.

[19] Cf., Interviews with James Roche; Msgr. Joseph C. Shenrock; Maryann Beitel (#1); Interview with Nuns.

[20] Interview with Fr. J. William Mickiewicz.

[21] Interview with Maryann Beitel (#1); Interview with Nuns.

[22] Interview with Maryann Beitel (#1).

[23] Interview with Msgr. Joseph C. Shenrock.

[24] Interview with Mrs. Kathleen Wessel and Maryann Beitel (Maryann Beitel).

[25] Interview with Fr. J. William Mickiewicz.

[26] Interview with Mrs. Kathleen Wessel and Maryann Beitel (Maryann Beitel).

[27] *See* Shenrock, *No Greater Love.*

[28] Id.; *see also*, "Data Requested By Personnel Office of Diocese of Trenton from Associate Pastors and Those in Special Assignments," Priests Personnel Files, Diocese of Trenton (Fr. J.P. Wessel Self-Evaluation), undated, circa Oct. 6, 1969 (hereinafter "Data Request," Priests Personnel Files).

[29] *See* Shenrock, *No Greater Love*; cf., Interviews with Maryann W. Beitel (#1) and (#2).

[30] *See* "Data Request," Priests Personnel Files; cf., Diary of Fr. John P. Wessel (various entries), circa 1966-67 (hereinafter "JPW Diary").

[31] Shenrock, *No Greater Love.*

[32] JPW Diary (Jan. 7, 1966); *See* Shenrock, *No Greater Love.*

[33] Interview with Barry Anderson*.

[34] Cf., Chancery Files.

[35] "Data Request," Priests Personnel Files.

[36] Interview with Fr. J. William Mickiewicz.

[37] Interview with Nuns (Sr. Elise M. Betz).

[38] Interview with Bishop John C. Reiss.

[39] Cf., Interviews with Edward C. Fagan; Wes Ritterbusch.

[40] Shenrock, *No Greater Love.*

[41] *See* id.

[42] Interview with Fr. J. William Mickiewicz.

[43] Id.; Interview with Maryann Beitel (#1).

[44] Interview with Fr. J. William Mickiewicz.

[45] Id.

[46] Id.

[47] Cf., id.; Interview with William Beitel.

[48] Interview with Msgr. James H. Dubell.

[49] JPW Diary (Jan. 3, Feb. 23, and Jan. 9, 1966).

[50] Interview with Msgr. James H. Dubell.

[51] Interview with William Beitel.

[52] Id.

[53] Id.

[54] Interview with Maryann Beitel (#1) and (#2).

[55] Interview with Maryann Beitel (#1).

[56] Interview with Julian Wessel.

[57] Quoted section taken from "John P. Wessel's Specialness As A Priest," by Maryann Wessel Beitel, undated, circa 1973 (hereinafter "Specialness As A Priest"), reprinted in Shenrock, *Three Good Shepherds*, at 27.

[58] Interview with Maryann Beitel (#2).

[59] JPW Diary (various entries).

[60] *See* Shenrock, *No Greater Love*; JPW Diary (Feb. 15, 1966).

[61] Cf., Interview with Maryann Beitel (#2).

62 JPW Diary (Jan. 6, 1966); *see* Shenrock, *No Greater Love.*

63 JPW Diary (various entries).

64 Interview with Maryann Beitel (#1); JPW Diary (Jan. 11, 1966).

65 JPW Diary (Jan. 13, 1966).

66 Id. (Jan. 14, 1966).

67 Interview with Edward C. Fagan.

68 JPW Diary (Jan. 19, 1966).

69 Id. (Jan. 18, 1966).

70 Id. (Mar. 15, 1966).

71 Interview with Fr. Eugene V. Davis.

72 *See* Shenrock, *No Greater Love.*

73 JPW Diary (June 24, 1967).

74 Interview with Fr. Eugene V. Davis.

75 Id.

76 Id.

77 Quoted section taken from "Thoughts of John P. Wessel By A Classmate," by Rev. Msgr. James H. Dubell, undated, circa 1973 (hereinafter "Thoughts By A Classmate"), reprinted in Shenrock, *Three Good Shepherds*, at 25.

78 Most of this section is taken from Shenrock, *No Greater Love*, except as noted.

79 Interview with Ronald Garrett*.

80 Interview with Msgr. Leonard R. Toomey; cf., Interview with Msgr. Joseph C. Shenrock.

81 Interview with Msgr. Joseph C. Shenrock.

82 Interview with Fr. Eugene V. Davis.

Chapter 19 Notes:

1   Written Recollections of Sr. Bridget, Oct. 1973, as edited.

2   Interview with Nuns (Sr. Elise Betz).

3   Interview with Nuns (Sr. Catherine Georgine Portner).

4   Telephone conversation with Sr. Catherine Georgine Portner.

5   Interview with Nuns (Sr. Elise Betz, Sr. William Margaret Romen).

6   Interview with Nuns (Sr. Margaret Bender).

7   Written Recollections of Sr. Bridget, as edited.

8   Interview with Nuns (various).

9   Interview with Nuns (Sr. Catherine Georgine Portner).

10 Interview with Nuns (various).

11 Interview with Beth Ann Beitel.

12 Interview with Fr. J. William Mickiewicz.

13 Letter from Sr. Elise Betz, I.H.M. to Mrs. Kathleen Wessel (Dec. 1971); cf., Interview with Wes Ritterbusch.

14 JPW Diary (Jan. 13, 1966).

15 Interview with Julian Wessel.

16 Interview with Maryann Beitel (#1).

17 Id.; Interview with Wes Ritterbusch; Written Recollections of Sr. Bridget.

18 Interview with Nuns (Sr. Elise Betz).

19 Interview with Edward C. Fagan.

20 Interview with Maryann Beitel (#1).

[21] JPW Diary (dates as indicated in text).

[22] Interview with Wes Ritterbusch.

[23] Interview with Edward C. Fagan.

[24] Interview with Dr. Raymond McCormack.

[25] All material in this section, unless otherwise noted, is taken from Interview and Telephone conversation with Dr. Julio Del Castillo.

[26] Telephone conversation with Dr. Julio Del Castillo.

[27] Interview with Dr. Julio Del Castillo. Preceding paragraph taken from Telephone conversation with Dr. Julio Del Castillo.

[28] Telephone conversation with Dr. Julio Del Castillo.

[29] Interview with Maryann Beitel (#1); *see also* Interview with Msgr. James H. Dubell (#2).

[30] JPW Diary (Jan. 30, 1966).

[31] "Data Request," Priests Personnel Files; cf., JPW Diary (various entries).

[32] Interview with Msgr. James H. Dubell (#2).

[33] JPW Diary (Jan. 7, 1966).

[34] Interview with Dr. Raymond McCormack.

[35] This story taken from Interview with Donald Matlack.

[36] Information on the Trenton State Hospital and the State Home for Girls derived from N.J. Dep't of Institutions & Agencies, "Towards Better Care of New Jersey Citizens," at 28-29, undated, circa 1966 (hereinafter "Towards Better Care"), copy supplied courtesy of Miss Regina Flynn.

[37] Interviews with Msgr. Joseph C. Shenrock; Msgr. James H. Dubell (#2); Fr. Eugene V. Davis.

[38] Cf., Interview with Ronald Garrett.

[39] Letter from Mrs. Kendrick R. Lee, Director of Volunteer Services, Trenton State Psychiatric Hospital, to Fr. Joseph C. Shenrock, Blessed Sacrament Church (June 13, 1973).

[40] Interview with CYO (Matthew Finnegan).

[41] Telephone conversation with Kevin Gallagher.

[42] This story is a composite of Interview with CYO (Kevin Gallagher) and Telephone conversation with Kevin Gallagher.

[43] Interview with Julian Wessel.

[44] This story is a composite of Interview and Telephone conversation with Ronald Garrett.

[45] Interview with Julian Wessel.

[46] Letter from Sr. Eileen Egan, I.H.M. to Mrs. Kathleen Wessel (circa 1973).

[47] "Blessed Sacrament, Trenton, Continues Study of Scripture," *The Monitor*, Oct. 18, 1968, at 3.

[48] *See* Telephone conversation and Written Recollections of Ruth Bacovin (Mar. 27, 1995).

[49] Id.

[50] Written Recollections of Sr. Bridget; *see* Interview with Nuns (Sr. Catherine Georgine Portner).

[51] Interview with Nuns (Sr. Catherine Georgine Portner).

[52] *See* Telephone conversation and Written Recollections of Ruth Bacovin.

[53] Letter from Fr. John P. Wessel to Rudy Girandola (Sept. 28, 1968).

[54] The preceding recollections are taken from Telephone conversation with Rudy Girandola; and Letter from Rudy Girandola to author (Jan. 28, 2003).

[55] Interview with Fr. J. William Mickiewicz.

[56] Interview with Fr. Eugene V. Davis.

[57] Interview with William Beitel (Maryann Beitel).

[58] Interview with Fr. Eugene V. Davis.

[59] Interviews with William Beitel (Maryann Beitel); Barry Anderson.

[60] Letter from Fr. Pat Hannan, C.S.Sp. to Mrs. Kathleen Wessel (Jan. 18, 1972).

[61] Letter from Fr. Pat Hannan, C.S.Sp. to Mr. and Mrs. William Beitel (Jan 18, 1972).

[62] *See* Shenrock, *No Greater Love.* The State Home for Girls, later renamed State Training School for Girls, was closed in 1974. Interview with Regina Flynn.

Assistance, information and background materials on the State Home for Girls provided to the author by Miss Regina Flynn, former Superintendent of the institution, is most gratefully acknowledged.

[63] N.J. Dep't of Institutions & Agencies, "Towards Better Care."

[64] Interview with Regina Flynn; *see also* N.J. Dep't of Institutions & Agencies, "Towards Better Care," at 64-65.

[65] Interview with Regina Flynn.

[66] Id.; cf., Interview with Fr. Eugene V. Davis.

[67] *See* Shenrock, *No Greater Love.*

[68] Interview with Regina Flynn.

[69] Id.; *see* Shenrock, *No Greater Love.*

[70] *See* Shenrock, *No Greater Love*; JPW Diary (Jan. 4, 1966).

[71] JPW Diary (Jan. 29, 1966).

[72] Id. (Feb. 8, 1966).

[73] Interview with Maryann Beitel (#2).

[74] *See* Shenrock, *No Greater Love*; JPW Diary (Jan. 4, 1966).

[75] Interview with Joanne W. Gillespie.

[76] Interview with Regina Flynn.

[77] This story is a composite of Interview with CYO (Kevin Gallagher) and Telephone conversation with Kevin Gallagher.

[78] This incident taken from Interview with Regina Flynn; *see* Shenrock, *No Greater Love.*

[79] Recollections of this trip are taken from Interview and Telephone conversation with Kenneth Kawalek, unless otherwise noted; other recollections taken from Interview with Fr. Ronald J. Bacovin.

[80] Interview with Maryann Beitel (#2).

[81] Interview with Fr. Ronald J. Bacovin.

[82] Interview with Msgr. Leonard R. Toomey.

[83] Id.

[84] Interview and Telephone conversation with Michael Choma.

[85] Interview with Msgr. Armand A. Pedata.

[86] Cf., Interviews with Maryann Beitel (#2); Patricia Hogan Staebler; Pat Wessel.

[87] *See* Interview with Kathleen Hogan Bradish.

[88] Cf., Interview with Fr. J. William Mickiewicz.

[89] Interview with Msgr. James H. Dubell (#1).

[90] Interview with Joanne W. Gillespie.

[91] Interview with Grace Wesley.

[92] Id.

[93] Id.

[94] Interview with Fr. Eugene V. Davis; *see* Interview with Msgr. James H. Dubell (#2).

[95] JPW Diary (Jan. 22, 1966).

[96] Interview with Julian Wessel.

[97] Letter from John Wessel to Dr. and Mrs. Edward J. Wessel, Jr. (May 13, 1961), copy supplied courtesy of Pat Wessel.

[98] "Specialness As A Priest" by Maryann Beitel, reprinted in Shenrock, *Three Good Shepherds*, at 27; *see* Interview with Mrs. Kathleen Wessel and Maryann Beitel (Maryann Beitel).

[99] Interview with Pat Wessel.

[100]　Id.

[101]　Interview with Msgr. Leonard R. Toomey.

[102]　Interview with Pat Wessel.

[103]　Interview with Beth Ann Beitel.

[104]　Recollections taken from Interview with Carlton Wessel.

[105]　"Specialness As A Priest" by Maryann Beitel, reprinted in Shenrock, *Three Good Shepherds*, at 27.

[106]　Id.; Interview with Maryann Beitel (#1).

[107]　Interviews with Pat Wessel and Anne Marie Wessel.

[108]　Interview with Julian Wessel.

[109]　Interviews with Carlton Wessel and Anne Marie Wessel.

[110]　*See* Interviews with Kathleen Hogan Bradish; Carlton Wessel.

[111]　Cf., JPW Diary (various entries).

[112]　Interview with William Beitel.

[113]　Id.; Telephone conversation with Maryann Beitel.

[114]　Interview with William Beitel.

[115]　Interview with David J. Schroth, J.S.C.

[116]　Interview with Msgr. James H. Dubell (#2).

[117]　Last Will and Testament of John P. Wessel (July 25, 1968).

[118]　Interview with Msgr. James H. Dubell (#2).

[119]　Story is composite of recollections taken from Interviews with Msgr. James H. Dubell (#2); Mrs. Kathleen Wessel and Maryann Beitel (Maryann Beitel); Pat Wessel; and Dr. Raymond McCormack, among others. There are some slight discrepancies in these recollections, but Msgr. Dubell pointed out that Father Wessel had a few car accidents.

[120]　Interview with Dr. Raymond McCormack; Interview with Nuns (Sr. Catherine Georgine Portner).

[121]　Interview with Maryann Beitel (#1).

[122]　Interview with Nuns (Sr. Elise Betz, Sr. Margaret Bender, and Sr. William Margaret Romen).

[123]　Interview with Wes Ritterbusch. Father Wessel related the incident in a homily which was recalled by several of the Sisters of Blessed Sacrament. In their recollection, the Good Samaritan was murdered. Mr. Ritterbusch recalled the incident in substance but with some minor differences in detail: He thought that the Good Samaritan of the story was killed by accident, hit by an oncoming car or truck as they were getting out of their own car to help, rather than by being murdered.

[124]　Interview with Maryann Beitel (#1).

Chapter 20 Notes:

[1]　*See* Shenrock, *No Greater Love.*

[2]　Interview with Maryann Beitel (#1); *see also* Interview with Mrs. Kathleen Wessel and Maryann Beitel (Kathleen Wessel).

[3]　Interview with Julian Wessel.

[4]　Interview with Maryann Beitel (#1); *see also* Interview with Mrs. Kathleen Wessel and Maryann Beitel.

[5]　Interview with Joanne W. Gillespie.

[6]　Interview with John Gummere.

[7]　Cf., Interview with CYO (Suzanne W. Walton).

[8]　Interview with CYO (Karen McGarrity).

[9]　Interview with Christopher Morley.

10   Interview with Ronald Garrett.

11   Cf., Interview with Msgr. Leonard R. Toomey.

12   *See* Shenrock, *No Greater Love.*

13   Written Recollections of Jayne Hartley, undated, circa 1973 (hereinafter "Written Recollections of Jayne Hartley"), which was prepared for the Shenrock, *No Greater Love* book.

14   Interview with Msgr. Leonard R. Toomey.

15   Cf., Blessed Sacrament CYO Newsletter, June 1968.

16   Letter from Fr. John P. Wessel to Blessed Sacrament CYO (Summer 1970).

17   Interview with CYO (Matthew Finnegan); cf., id. (Liz F. Walsh).

18   Written Recollections of Jayne Hartley.

19   Cf., Blessed Sacrament CYO Newsletter, Sept. 1967.

20   Cf., Blessed Sacrament CYO Newsletter, June 1968.

21   Interview with Joanne W. Gillespie.

22   Interview with CYO (Gina A. Lang).

23   Interview with Joanne W. Gillespie; *see also* Interview with Ronald Garrett.

24   Letter from Joseph Cappello to author (May 18, 1995).

25   Interview with Joanne W. Gillespie.

26   Written Recollections of Jayne Hartley.

27   Interview with Wes Ritterbusch.

28   Interviews with Joanne W. Gillespie; Bonnie Lopez*.

29   Interview with Bonnie Lopez.

30   *See* Shenrock, *No Greater Love.*

31   Written Recollections of Alice Callery, undated, circa 1973 (hereinafter "Written Recollections of Alice Callery"), which was prepared for the Shenrock, *No Greater Love* book.

32   Interview with Joanne W. Gillespie.

33   Interviews with Mrs. Kathleen Wessel and Maryann Beitel (Kathleen Wessel); Maryann Beitel (#1).

34   *See* JPW Diary (June 27, 1967).

35   Interview with CYO (Michael Ward).

36   *See* Shenrock, *No Greater Love.*; cf., Written Recollections of Jayne Hartley.

37   *See* Interviews with Maryann Beitel (#1); Beth Ann Beitel.

38   Interview with Joanne W. Gillespie.

39   Written Recollections of Jayne Hartley; cf., Interview with Joanne W. Gillespie.

40   Interview with CYO (Maria Rodriguez*).

41   *See* Shenrock, *No Greater Love.*; Interview with Bonnie Lopez.

42   Interview with Bonnie Lopez; cf., Interview with Joanne W. Gillespie.

43   Interview with CYO (Jayne Hartley); Interviews with Bonnie Lopez; Joanne W. Gillespie.

44   Interview with Bonnie Lopez.

45   Interview with Joanne W. Gillespie.

46   Cf., Interview with Ronald Garrett.

47   Letter from Fr. John P. Wessel to CYO (May 1971), after 2nd Search.

48   Interview with Bonnie Lopez; cf., Interview with CYO (William Hamilton*; Gina A. Lang).

49   Interview with CYO (Matthew Finnegan).

50   Written Recollections of Jayne Hartley.

51   *See* Shenrock, *No Greater Love.*

52   Interview with Joanne W. Gillespie.

53   Interview with Barry Anderson; Telephone conversation with James Blatchford.

54   Interview with Barry Anderson.

55   Interview with Joanne W. Gillespie.

56   Interview with Barry Anderson.

57   Id.

58   Interview with Ronald Garrett; cf., Interview with Barry Anderson.

59   Interview with CYO (Joanne W. Gillespie).

60   Cf., Interview with CYO (Jayne Hartley).

61   Letter from James J. Moonan to Fr. John P. Wessel (June 7, 1970).

62   Interviews with Barry Anderson; CYO (Kevin Gallagher); Wes Ritterbusch. Stories of the trips are taken from recollections of Barry Anderson unless noted.

63   Interview with CYO (Kevin Connor).

64   Id.

65   Interview with CYO (Kevin Gallagher).

66   Interview with Wes Ritterbusch.

67   Id.

68   Interview with CYO (Kevin Connor).

69   Interview with Wes Ritterbusch.

70   Id.

71   Interview with Nuns (Sr. Elise Betz).

72   Shenrock, *Upon This Rock*, at 222.

73   Interview with Bonnie Lopez; cf., Interviews with Barry Anderson; Joanne W. Gillespie.

74   Cf., Interview with Bonnie Lopez.

75   Interviews with Bonnie Lopez; Barry Anderson; Wes Ritterbusch.

76   Interview with Wes Ritterbusch.

77   Interview with Brian Schoeffel. *But see* Interview with Joanne W. Gillespie.

78   Interview with Barry Anderson.

79   Interview with Joanne W. Gillespie.

80   Cf., Interview with Bonnie Lopez; Interview with CYO (Joseph Parnell*).

81   Interview with Joanne W. Gillespie; Barry Anderson.

82   Interview with Barry Anderson; Wes Ritterbusch.

83   Interview with Joanne W. Gillespie.

84   Id.

85   Written Recollections of Jayne Hartley.

86   Shenrock, *No Greater Love*.

87   Written Recollections of Jayne Hartley.

88   Shenrock, *No Greater Love*.

89   Cf., Interview with Bonnie Lopez.

90   Written Recollections of Jayne Hartley.

91   Interview with CYO (Kevin Connor).

92   Interview with CYO (Jayne Hartley).

93   Interview with CYO (Michael Ball).

94   Interview with Wes Ritterbusch; cf., Interview with Brian Schoeffel.

Chapter 21 Notes:

1   *See* Shenrock, *No Greater Love*.

2   Id.

3   Search for Christian Maturity Searcher's Manual, National CYO Federation (1966) at 1.

4   Written Search Materials, 1st Search.
5   Written Recollections of Jayne Hartley; cf., Interview with Several Former St. Joseph High School Students (hereinafter "Interview with SJHS") (Jill V. Mueller).
6   *See* Shenrock, *No Greater Love*; Written Recollections of Jayne Hartley.
7   Written Search Materials, 1st Search.
8   *See* Shenrock, *No Greater Love.*
9   Interview with Barry Anderson.
10 Interview with Joanne W. Gillespie.
11 Interview with CYO (Kevin Connor).
12 Interview with CYO (Joanne W. Gillespie).
13 *See* Shenrock, *No Greater Love.*
14 Interview with Joanne W. Gillespie.
15 Id.
16 Cf., id.
17 Interview with CYO (Matthew Finnegan).
18 Mercer County CYO Search Schedule #1, #3; cf., Interview with John Gummere.
19 Mercer County CYO Search Schedule #3.
20 Mercer County CYO Search Schedule #1.
21 Cf., Interview with CYO (Kevin Connor).
22 Interview with CYO (Joseph Parnell).
23 Interview with CYO (Kevin Connor).
24 Written Recollections of Jayne Hartley.
25 Written Recollections of Alice Callery.
26 Interview with Msgr. James H. Dubell (#2).
27 Interview with Barry Anderson.
28 Letter from Fr. John P. Wessel to CYO (May 1971).
29 Interview with Joanne W. Gillespie; *see also* Interview with CYO (Joanne W. Gillespie).
30 Interview with Priests (Msgr. Eugene Rebeck).
31 Interview with CYO (Joseph Parnell).
32 Cf., Interviews with Joanne W. Gillespie; Wes Ritterbusch.
33 Cf., Interviews with Msgr. James H. Dubell (#2); Joanne Gillespie.
34 Interview with Joanne W. Gillespie.
35 Id.
36 Interview with Msgr. James H. Dubell (#2).
37 Written Recollections of Alice Callery; cf., Mercer County CYO Search Schedule #1.
38 Interview with Joanne W. Gillespie.
39 *See* Shenrock, *No Greater Love.*
40 *See* Written Recollections of Alice Callery; Interview with CYO (Joanne W. Gillespie).
41 Written Recollections of Jayne Hartley.
42 *See* Shenrock, *No Greater Love*; Interviews with CYO (various); John Gummere.
43 Interview with SJHS (Jill V. Mueller).
44 *See* id.
45 Cf., Interview with CYO (Jayne Hartley).

Chapter 22 Notes:

1   Interview with Bonnie Lopez.
2   Letter from Fr. John P. Wessel to CYO (May 1971), after 2nd Search.

3   Interviews with Joanne W. Gillespie; Bonnie Lopez.

4   Fr. John P. Wessel's notes in margin of St. Joseph High School religion course book, 1971, copy supplied courtesy of Sr. Nancy Carney.

5   Cf., Interview with CYO (Joseph Parnell).

6   Interview with Ronald Garrett.

7   Id.

8   Letter from Fr. John P. Wessel to CYO (Jan. 28, 1971), after 1st Search.

9   Letter from Fr. John P. Wessel to CYO (May 1971), after 2nd Search.

10 Letter from Fr. John P. Wessel to CYO (Sept. 1, 1971).

11 Cf., Interview with Ronald Garrett.

12 Cf., id.

13 Written Recollections of Alice Callery; see Interviews with Brian Schoeffel; CYO (Kevin Gallagher); Ronald Garrett.

14 See Interview with Msgr. James H. Dubell (#2).

15 Letter from Fr. John P. Wessel to CYO (Jan. 28, 1971), after 1st Search.

16 Letter from Fr. John P. Wessel to CYO (May 1971), after 2nd Search.

17 Letter from Fr. John P. Wessel to CYO (Sept. 1, 1971).

18 Interview with Joanne W. Gillespie.

19 Story is taken from Interview with Fr. Ronald Bacovin.

20 Letter from Fr. John P. Wessel to CYO (Jan. 28, 1971), after 1st Search.

21 Letter from Fr. John P. Wessel to CYO (May 1971), after 2nd Search.

22 Interviews with CYO (Kevin Connor); Ronald Garrett.

23 Letter from Fr. John P. Wessel to St. Joseph High School class (circa Oct. 1971).

24 Letter from Fr. John P. Wessel to CYO (May 1971), after 2nd Search.

25 Id.

26 Cf., Fr. John P. Wessel's notes in margin of SJHS religion course book, 1971.

27 Id.

28 Letter from Fr. John P. Wessel to CYO (Sept. 1971).

29 Letter from Fr. John P. Wessel to CYO (Jan. 28, 1971), after 1st Search.

30 Letter from Fr. John P. Wessel to CYO (May 1971), after 2nd Search.

31 Letter from Fr. John P. Wessel to CYO (Sept. 1, 1971).

32 Blessed Sacrament Church Bulletin, "CYO News," Moderator's Editorial (June 13, 1971) (end-of-year message from Fr. Wessel to CYO).

33 Interview with Joanne W. Gillespie.

34 Interview with Ronald Garrett.

35 Interview with Wes Ritterbusch; cf., Interview with John Gummere.

36 Interview with Wes Ritterbusch.

37 Interview with CYO (Joanne W. Gillespie).

Chapter 23 Notes:

1   See Shenrock, No Greater Love.

2   Id. at 5; cf., Written Recollections of Msgr. James H. Dubell.

3   Interview with Fr. Samuel J. Lupico.

4   Interview with Sr. M. Christina Murphy, I.H.M.

5   A copy of this prayer and its English translation was supplied courtesy of Fr. John W. Bowen, S.S., Sulpician Archivist.

6   Interview with Maryann Beitel (#2); cf., Interview with Mrs. Kathleen Wessel and Maryann Beitel (Maryann Beitel).

7   Interview with Msgr. James H. Dubell (#2).

8   Shenrock, *Upon This Rock*, at 228.

9   Interview with Maryann Beitel (#2); cf., Interview with William Beitel (Maryann Beitel).

10   *Chronicle of the 20th Century*, at 391.

11   *Humanae Vitae* ("Of Human Life") (1968), at 14-15, reprinted in pamphlet form by St. Paul's Book & Media Center.

12   Id. at 21.

13   Id. at 22.

14   Interview with Msgr. James H. Dubell (#2).

15   Id.; cf., Interview with Maryann Beitel (#2).

16   "Specialness As A Priest" by Maryann Beitel, reprinted in Shenrock, *Three Good Shepherds*, at 26.

17   Interview with Msgr. James H. Dubell (#2).

18   Id.

19   Interview with Msgr. Joseph C. Shenrock.

20   Interview with Wes Ritterbusch.

21   Interview with Mrs. Kathleen Wessel and Maryann Beitel; Interview with Mrs. Kathleen Wessel (#2).

22   Interview with [Confidential].

23   Private seminary notes of John P. Wessel, circa early 1960s.

24   Interview with Maryann Beitel (#1).

25   *See* "Alumni in Joint Meeting," *The Monitor*, date unknown (Picture and caption of Fr. John P. Wessel lecturing on Vatican Council II); JPW Diary (various entries).

26   *See* Interview with Fr. Eugene V. Davis.

27   "Specialness As A Priest" by Maryann Beitel, reprinted in Shenrock, *Three Good Shepherds*, at 26.

28   Interview with Mrs. Kathleen Wessel and Maryann Beitel (Maryann Beitel); cf., Interview with Maryann Beitel (#1).

29   Story of this incident is taken from Interviews with Maryann Beitel (#1) and (#2), who was present for this talk.

30   Interview with Maryann Beitel (#1).

31   Interview with Msgr. James H. Dubell (#2).

32   Id.

33   Interview with Msgr. James H. Dubell (#1).

34   Interview with Julian Wessel.

35   Interview with Msgr. James H. Dubell (#2).

36   Id.

37   JPW Diary (Mar. 14, 1966).

38   This story is a composite of Interview with Sr. Eileen Egan, I.H.M.; Letter from Sr. Eileen Egan, I.H.M. to author (Feb. 15, 1994); and Letters from Sr. Eileen Egan, I.H.M. to Mrs. Kathleen Wessel (Dec. 1971, and circa 1973). Sr. Eileen acknowledged that her recollection could be a composite memory of what was actually two separate visits, but the conversation is accurate in substance.

39   *See* Mary Stadnyk, "Peruvian Missionary Is Enriched by the Beautiful People She Meets," *The Monitor*, Aug. 4, 1994, at 3.

40   Blessed Sacrament CYO Newsletter, June 1968, "Moderator's Comments," as edited.

41   Cf., Interview with Wes Ritterbusch.

42   Interview with Msgr. James H. Dubell (#2).

Chapter 24 Notes:

[1] Interview with Wes Ritterbusch.

[2] Interview with SJHS (Ed Staunton, Beverly C. Devlin).

[3] Cf., Interview with Julian Wessel.

[4] Interview with Mrs. Kathleen Wessel and Maryann Beitel.

[5] Interview with Wes Ritterbusch.

[6] Id.; cf., Interview with Julian Wessel.

[7] Interview with Ronald Garrett.

[8] Interview with SJHS (Beverly C. Devlin).

[9] Cf., Interview with Julian Wessel.

[10] Interview with SJHS (Beverly C. Devlin, Jill V. Mueller).

[11] Interview with Julian Wessel.

[12] "U.S. agrees to stop fighting in Vietnam," Jan. 27, 1973, *Chronicle of the 20th Century*, at 1060.

[13] Interview with Julian Wessel.

[14] Interview with Ronald Garrett.

[15] Interview with Msgr. James H. Dubell (#2).

[16] Interview with Wes Ritterbusch.

[17] Interview with CYO (Karen McGarrity).

[18] Interview with Ronald Garrett.

[19] Interview with Msgr. James H. Dubell (#2).

[20] JPW Diary (Jan. 22, 1966).

[21] Cf., JPW Diary (various entries).

[22] Interview with Fr. J. William Mickiewicz. This may have been the Florence Crittenden Home for Unwed Mothers. *See* Interview with Edward C. Fagan.

[23] Interview with Sr. Nancy Carney.

[24] Id.

[25] Interview with Josetta C. Burchardt (#2).

[26] Interview with [Confidential].

[27] "LBJ Signs Civil Rights Act," July 2, 1964, *Chronicle of the 20th Century*, at 918.

[28] Interview with Carlton Wessel.

[29] Id.

[30] Interview with Julian Wessel.

[31] Cf., "Trenton's Pulse Quickens," *Asbury Park Press*, June 7, 1987, at H8.

[32] Cf., Interview with Julian Wessel.

[33] Interview with Ronald Garrett.

[34] Interview with Julian Wessel.

[35] Cf., Interview with Msgr. James H. Dubell (#2).

[36] Interview with Christopher Morley.

[37] Id.; Interview with SJHS (various).

[38] Interview with Fr. Samuel J. Lupico.

[39] Interview with Julian Wessel.

[40] Interview with [Confidential].

[41] Story taken from Interview with Wes Ritterbusch.

[42] Id.

[43] Id.

[44] Cf., Interview with Julian Wessel.

[45] Interview with Ronald Garrett.

[46] Cf., Interview with Sr. Nancy Carney.

[47] Story taken from Interview with Vincent Thompson*.

Chapter 25 Notes:

[1] *See* Shenrock, *No Greater Love.*

[2] Id.

[3] Interview with Maryann Beitel (#1).

[4] Ship's Log, The "Eucharist," 1970-1972 (hereinafter "Eucharist" Log), copy supplied courtesy of Kevin Connor. Entries were written primarily by Father Wessel ("JPW"), but also by some others.

[5] Interview with Barry Anderson.

[6] Interview with Wes Ritterbusch.

[7] Id.

[8] Cf., Interviews with Barry Anderson; Maryann Beitel (#1); William Beitel.

[9] Interview with Maryann Beitel (#1).

[10] Interviews with William Beitel; Maryann Beitel (#1) (William Beitel).

[11] Interview with William Beitel.

[12] Cf., id.; Interview with Maryann Beitel (#1).

[13] Interview with CYO (Jayne Hartley).

[14] Interview with Fr. Eugene V. Davis.

[15] Cf., Interview with Maryann Beitel (#1).

[16] Interview with Fr. Eugene V. Davis.

[17] Cf., Interview with William Beitel.

[18] Id.

[19] Blessed Sacrament CYO Bulletin (June 13, 1971).

[20] Id.

[21] Id.

[22] Written Recollections of Sister Bridget.

[23] Telephone conversation with Sr. Elise Betz.

[24] Interview with Barry Anderson.

[25] Id.

[26] Id.

[27] Interviews with William Beitel; Maryann Beitel (#1).

[28] Interview with Joanne W. Gillespie.

[29] Interview with Fr. Eugene V. Davis.

[30] Interview with Ronald Garrett; cf., Interview with Fr. Eugene V. Davis.

[31] Interviews with Brian Schoeffel; Fr. Eugene V. Davis.

[32] Interview with Barry Anderson.

[33] Interview with CYO (Cindy Farrell*).

[34] Interview with Barry Anderson.

[35] Interview with Maryann Beitel (#1).

[36] "Eucharist" Log (JPW).

[37] Interview with Barry Anderson.

[38] Interviews with CYO (Kevin Connor); Barry Anderson.

[39] Cf., Interview with Bonnie Lopez.

[40] Interview with Maryann Beitel (#1).

[41] Id.; Interview with William Beitel.

[42] "Eucharist" Log (JPW).

[43] Interview with Barry Anderson; cf., "Eucharist" Log (JPW).

[44] Cf., Interview with Fr. Eugene V. Davis.

[45] Cf., Interview with Brian Schoeffel.

[46] Interviews with Barry Anderson; Wes Ritterbusch.

[47] Interview with Wes Ritterbusch.

[48] Cf., Interviews with Joanne W. Gillespie; CYO (Kevin Connor).

[49] Cf., Interview with Wes Ritterbusch.

[50] Id.

[51] Cf., Interviews with Joanne W. Gillespie; Wes Ritterbusch.

[52] Interview with Wes Ritterbusch.

[53] Cf., id.

[54] "Eucharist" Log (JPW).

[55] Interview with Joanne W. Gillespie.

[56] Interview with CYO (Kevin Connor).

[57] Interview with Joanne W. Gillespie; cf., Interview with CYO (Cindy Farrell, others).

[58] Cf., Interview with Joanne W. Gillespie.

[59] Interview with Fr. J. William Mickiewicz.

[60] Cf., id.

[61] Interview with Julian Wessel.

[62] "Eucharist" Log (JPW).

[63] Cf., id.

[64] Id.

[65] Id. (June 19, 1971).

[66] Interview with Brian Schoeffel.

[67] Cf., Interviews with Maryann Beitel (#1) (William Beitel); William Beitel.

[68] "Eucharist" Log, as edited.

[69] Id. (June 20, 1971).

[70] Interview with Barry Anderson.

[71] Interview with CYO (Kevin Connor).

[72] Interview with Barry Anderson.

[73] Interview with Brian Schoeffel.

[74] Interview with Ronald Garrett.

[75] Interview with Brian Schoeffel.

[76] Interview with Maryann Beitel (#1); cf., "Eucharist" Log.

[77] "Eucharist" Log (Aug. 27, 1971).

[78] Id. (Aug. 10, 1971).

[79] Interview with Wes Ritterbusch; cf., "Eucharist" Log (Aug. 10, 1971).

[80] Interview with Brian Schoeffel.

[81] Cf., "Eucharist" Log (Aug. 12, 1971).

[82] Interview with Brian Schoeffel.

83   Cf., "Eucharist" Log (Aug. 26, 1971).

84   Letter from Fr. John P. Wessel to CYO (Sept. 1, 1971).

85   Recollections of this sail taken from Interview with Wes Ritterbusch.

Chapter 26 Notes:

1   Interview with Maryann Beitel (#1).

2   Id.

3   Letter from Bishop George Ahr to Fr. John P. Wessel (Sept. 13, 1971), contained in Chancery Files.

4   Cf., Interview with Msgr. James H. Dubell (#2).

5   Interview with Mrs. Kathleen Wessel (#1).

6   Id.; cf., Interview with Msgr. Joseph C. Shenrock.

7   Recollections of this conversation with her son are taken from Interviews with Mrs. Kathleen Wessel (#1) and (#2); and Telephone conversation with Mrs. Kathleen Wessel.

8   Interview with Maryann Beitel (#2).

9   Interview with Msgr. James H. Dubell (#2); cf., Telephone conversations with Mrs. Kathleen Wessel; Interview with James Roche.

10   Interview with Mrs. Kathleen Wessel (#2).

11   "Data Request," Priests Personnel Files.

12   Interview with James Roche.

13   Interview with CYO (Cindy Farrell).

14   Interviews with Barry Anderson; Bonnie Lopez.

15   Written Recollections of Jayne Hartley.

16   Interview with Barry Anderson.

17   Interviews with John Gummere; Christopher Morley.

18   Interview with Nuns (Sr. Catherine Georgine Portner).

19   Interview with Fr. Eugene V. Davis.

20   Interview with CYO (Jayne Hartley).

21   Interview with [Confidential].

22   Cf., Interview with John Gummere; Barry Anderson.

23   Interview with Joanne W. Gillespie.

24   Id.

25   Interview with Christopher Morley.

26   Interview with Joanne W. Gillespie.

27   Id.

28   Interview with John Gummere.

29   Interview with Ronald Garrett.

30   Cf., Interview with Wes Ritterbusch.

31   Interview with Donald Matlack.

32   Interview with Wes Ritterbusch; cf., Interview with James Roche.

33   Letter from Fr. John P. Wessel to CYO (Sept. 1, 1971).

34   Interview with Fr. Eugene V. Davis.

35   Interview with William Beitel.

36   "Data Request," Priests Personnel Files.

37   Id.

Chapter 27 Notes:

[1] Toms River Report, at 1.

[2] Interview with Brendan Gallagher.

[3] Id.

[4] Id.

[5] Toms River Report.

[6] Cf., Shenrock, *No Greater Love.*

[7] Toms River Report.

[8] Id.; *see also* Shenrock, *No Greater Love*; cf., Interview with John Menter. In August 1983, St. Joseph High School was renamed Monsignor Donovan High School by Bishop John C. Reiss in honor of its founding pastor, Msgr. Lawrence Donovan.

[9] *See* Shenrock, *No Greater Love*; cf., Robin Kerney, "Night-Long Watch Kept At Father Wessel's Bier-Two Congregations Join in Mourning Priest," *Trenton Times,* Wed., Dec. 29, 1971 (hereinafter *Trenton Times,* "Two Congregations").

[10] Toms River Report.

[11] Id.

[12] Letter from Fr. John P. Wessel to Joanne (Wesley) Gillespie, (circa Oct. 1971).

[13] Interview with Brendan Gallagher.

[14] Interviews with Sr. Teresa Agnes*; Sr. Nancy Carney; Carmella V. Di Matteo.

[15] Interview with Brendan Gallagher.

[16] Interview with Sr. Julianna Naulty.

[17] Interview with Maryann Beitel (#1).

[18] Interview with Sr. Nancy Carney.

[19] Interview with Maryann Beitel (#1).

[20] Interview with Carmella V. Di Matteo.

[21] Interview with Maryann Beitel (#1).

[22] Id.; cf., Interview with Sean Maguire.

[23] Shenrock, *No Greater Love.*

[24] Toms River Report.

[25] Shenrock, *No Greater Love.*

[26] Interview with Maryann Beitel (#1).

[27] Interview with Carmella V. Di Matteo.

[28] Id.

[29] Id.

[30] Interview with Sr. Nancy Carney.

[31] Interviews with Carmella V. Di Matteo; Sr. Teresa Agnes.

[32] Interviews with Carmella V. Di Matteo; Sr. Nancy Carney.

[33] Interview with Carmella V. Di Matteo; cf., Interview with Peter Caroselli.

[34] Interview with Peter Caroselli.

[35] Interview with SJHS (Jill V. Mueller).

[36] Interview with Sr. Teresa Agnes.

[37] Interview with SJHS (various); cf., Pre-Search Letter from Fr. John P. Wessel to St. Joseph High School Students (circa Sept. 1971).

[38] Interviews with Josetta C. Burchardt (#1) and (#2).

[39] Interview with Carmella V. Di Matteo.

40 Interview with Sr. Nancy Carney.
41 Telephone conversation with Sr. Teresa Agnes.
42 Interview with Sr. Teresa Agnes.
43 Interview with Sr. Julianna Naulty.
44 Interview with Sr. Jorene Cieciuch.
45 Interview with Carmella V. Di Matteo.
46 Id.
47 Interview with Sean Maguire.
48 Interview with Carmella V. Di Matteo.
49 Interview with Sr. Nancy Carney.
50 Interview with Josetta C. Burchardt (#2).
51 Interview with Al Kedz.
52 Interviews with Peter Caroselli; Sean Maguire; Interview with SJHS (Jill V. Mueller).
53 Interview with Peter Caroselli.
54 Interview with Dawn F. Fowler.
55 Interview with Josetta C. Burchardt (#2).
56 Interview with John Menter.
57 Interview with Brendan Gallagher.

Chapter 28 Notes:

1 Written Recollections of Jayne Hartley.
2 Interview with SJHS (Beverly C. Devlin).
3 Id.
4 Id.
5 Interview with SJHS (Beverly C. Devlin, Ed Staunton).
6 "Frs. Davis, Wessel To Be Honored Sunday Afternoon," *The Monitor*, Oct. 15, 1971.
7 Interview with Maryann Beitel (#1).
8 Id; Interview with Edward C. Fagan.
9 Id.
10 Interview with Maryann Beitel (#1) and (#2).
11 Interview with Wes Ritterbusch.
12 Id.
13 Interview with Edward C. Fagan.
14 Interview with Dr. Julio Del Castillo.
15 Interview with Brendan Gallagher.
16 Interview with Joanne W. Gillespie.
17 Interview with Brendan Gallagher.
18 Interview with SJHS (Beverly C. Devlin); cf., Interview with Peter Caroselli.
19 Pre-Search Letter from Fr. John P. Wessel to SJHS Students; Telephone conversation with Sr. Nancy Carney.
20 Telephone conversation with Ed Staunton.
21 Interview with SJHS (Ed Staunton, Beverly C. Devlin).
22 Id.; Interview with Peter Caroselli.
23 Interview with SJHS (Ed Staunton).
24 Interview with Peter Caroselli.

25	Interview with SJHS (Ed Staunton, Beverly C. Devlin).

26	Interview with John Gummere.

27	Interview with SJHS (Beverly C. Devlin).

28	Interview with CYO (Joseph Parnell).

29	Telephone conversation with Msgr. Francis Kolby*.

30	Telephone conversation with Fr. Terence McAlinden.

31	Interview with SJHS (Beverly C. Devlin).

32	Interview with SJHS (Jill V. Mueller).

33	Written Recollections of Jayne Hartley.

34	Interview with Barry Anderson.

35	Interview with Sr. Nancy Carney.

36	Interview with SJHS (Ed Staunton).

37	Interview with SJHS (Confidential).

38	Interview with Brendan Gallagher.

39	Interview with SJHS (Ed Staunton).

40	Id.

41	Id.

42	Interview with SJHS (Jill V. Mueller).

43	Interview with SJHS (Jill V. Mueller, Ed Staunton).

44	Interview with SJHS (Jill V. Mueller).

45	Telephone conversation with Ed Staunton.

46	Post-Search Letter from Fr. John P. Wessel to SJHS Students (Oct. 1971).

47	Telephone conversation with Ed Staunton.

48	Interview with SJHS (Jill V. Mueller).

49	Cf., Interview with Ronald Garrett.

50	Interview with SJHS (various).

51	Interview with Sr. Teresa Agnes.

Chapter 29 Notes:

1	Interview with John Menter.

2	Interview with Sr. Nancy Carney.

3	Id.; Interview with John and Christine S. Menter.

4	Interview with SJHS (various); Interview with Dawn F. Fowler.

5	Interview with Dawn F. Fowler.

6	Interview with John Menter.

7	Interviews with Josetta C. Burchardt (#1) and (#2).

8	Interview with SJHS (Jill V. Mueller, Beverly C. Devlin).

9	Interview with Dawn F. Fowler.

10	Interview with John Menter.

11	Interview with SJHS (Beverly C. Devlin).

12	Cf., Interview with Sr. Nancy Carney.

13	Interview with Dawn F. Fowler.

14	Id.

15	Interview with Carmella V. Di Matteo.

16	Interview with SHJS (Beverly C. Devlin).

17	Interview with SHJS (Jill V. Mueller).

[18] Interviews with SJHS (Beverly C. Devlin, Jill V. Mueller); Peter Caroselli.

[19] Interview with Peter Caroselli.

[20] Id.

[21] Interview with SJHS (Jill V. Mueller, Beverly C. Devlin).

[22] Interview with SJHS (Beverly C. Devlin).

[23] Cf., Toms River Report.

[24] Interviews with Josetta C. Burchardt (#1) and (#2).

[25] Interview with Peter Caroselli.

[26] Cf., Interviews with SJHS (Ed Staunton); Josetta C. Burchardt (#1) and (#2).

[27] Interview with Barry Anderson.

[28] Interviews with Barry Anderson; John Gummere.

[29] Interview with SJHS (Beverly C. Devlin, Jill V. Mueller); Telephone conversation with Peter Caroselli.

[30] Interview with Dawn F. Fowler.

[31] Id.

[32] Interview and Telephone conversation with Ed Staunton.

[33] That weekend, and the dramatic beginnings of the charismatic renewal in the Catholic Church, have been the subject of much writing over the years, one excellent book on the subject being Patty Gallagher, *As By A New Pentecost* (Franciscan University Press, 1992). Patty Gallagher Mansfield was one of the young Catholic retreatants on the "Duquesne weekend" in 1967.

[34] Interview with Barry Anderson.

[35] Cf., Interview with SJHS (Beverly C. Devlin, Jill V. Mueller, Ed Staunton).

[36] Id.

[37] Cf., Interview with Sr. Teresa Agnes.

[38] Telephone conversation with Sr. Teresa Agnes; Interview with Peter Caroselli.

[39] Cf., Interview with SJHS (various).

[40] Telephone conversation with Joan Murphy.

[41] Interview with Sr. Nancy Carney.

[42] Id.

[43] Telephone conversation with Rita Kearney; St. Joseph's Parish Council Meeting Minutes, Dec. 16, 1971, copy supplied courtesy of Rita Kearney.

[44] Telephone conversation with Sr. Nancy Carney.

[45] Interview with Sr. Nancy Carney. Fr. John P. Wessel's handwritten course outline supplied courtesy of Sr. Nancy Carney.

[46] Interviews with SJHS (various); Dawn F. Fowler.

[47] Interview with Sr. Nancy Carney.

[48] Interview with Brian Schoeffel.

[49] Interview with John Menter.

[50] Id.

[51] Interview with Wes Ritterbusch.

[52] Interview with John Menter.

[53] Interview with Dawn F. Fowler.

[54] Interview with [Confidential].

[55] Interview with Sean Maguire.

[56] Cf., id.

[57] Interview with John Menter.

[58] Interview with Sr. Nancy Carney.

59 Interview with Josetta C. Burchardt (#2).
60 Interview with Sr. Nancy Carney.
61 Interview with Josetta C. Burchardt (#2).
62 Interview with Christopher Morley.
63 Interview with SJHS (Ed Staunton, Jill V. Mueller).
64 Interview with Christopher Morley.
65 Interview with Sr. Nancy Carney.
66 Interview with Carmella V. Di Matteo.
67 Interview with Sr. Teresa Agnes.
68 Cf., Interview with Sr. Nancy Carney.
69 Written recollections of Msgr. James H. Dubell.
70 Interview with Carmella V. Di Matteo.
71 Telephone conversation with [Confidential].
72 Interview with Carmella V. Di Matteo.
73 Interview and Telephone conversation with Sr. Teresa Agnes.
74 Telephone conversation with Thomas Callow; cf., Interview with Peter Caroselli.
75 Interview with SJHS (Jill V. Mueller, others).
76 Interview with John Menter; cf., Interview with SHJS (various).
77 Interview with Sr. Teresa Agnes.
78 Interview with SJHS (Ed Staunton).
79 Interview with Dawn F. Fowler.
80 Id.
81 Id.
82 Id.
83 Interview with Josetta C. Burchardt (#2).

Chapter 30 Notes:

1 See "Clergy Conference to Hear Fr. Brown," *The Monitor,* Oct. 29, 1971, at 1.
2 Interview with Msgr. Joseph C. Shenrock.
3 Recollections of this Thanksgiving at The Farm taken from composite of Interviews with Maryann Beitel (#2); William Beitel; Patricia Hogan Staebler; and Kathleen Hogan Bradish.
4 Recollections of the trip to Crematory Hill taken from Interview with CYO (Cindy Farrell, Maryann Beitel); cf., Interview with Maryann Beitel (#1).
5 Author's recollections.
6 Author's recollections.
7 Recollections of the senior class retreat taken from Interviews with SJHS (Beverly C. Devlin, Jill V. Mueller, others); Carmella V. Di Matteo; Sr. Nancy Carney; and author's recollections.
8 Recollections of the Wesley-Gillespie wedding taken from Interviews with Joanne W. Gillespie; CYO (Joanne and James Gillespie); Msgr. Joseph C. Shenrock; and Maryann Beitel (#2), unless noted.
9 Interview with Joanne W. Gillespie; Interview with CYO (James Gillespie).
10 Interview with Maryann Beitel (#2).
11 Interviews with Josetta C. Burchardt (#1) and (#2).

Chapter 31 Notes:

¹ Toms River Report, as edited; *see* Shenrock, *No Greater Love*. Much of the information pertaining to John F. Kelly III is taken from sworn testimony contained in Transcript of Trial, *State of New Jersey* v. *John Francis Kelly III*, Ocean County, New Jersey Criminal Court, Toms River, NJ, Indictment # 226-71 (March 13-20, 1973) (hereinafter cited as "T.T. at ____"). Other information is derived from contemporaneous newspaper articles; Telephone conversations with Mrs. Mildred Kelly; and from other sources and recollections cited.

² *See* Toms River Report, as edited; Shenrock, *No Greater Love*.

³ Telephone conversation with Mrs. Mildred Kelly.

⁴ Interview with Sean Maguire.

⁵ Telephone conversation with Mrs. Mildred Kelly. Elsewhere, Mrs. Kelly said that she had contacted Fr. Wessel "a few months before". Cf., T.T. at 273.

⁶ T.T. at 192-95, 246-47, 293-94; cf., Prucia Buscell, ". . . Jack Kelly Couldn't Cope with Life's Wounds," *Asbury Park Sunday Press*, Sun., Jan. 9, 1972, sec. C, at C1, C17 (hereinafter *Asbury Park Press*, "Cope").

⁷ T.T. at 195, 295-97; cf., Doris Powell, "Suspect's Family Suffers Too—Father Wessel's Slaying A Double Tragedy," *The Evening Times, Trenton, NJ*, Fri., Jan. 7, 1972, at 1, 28 (hereinafter *Evening Times*, "Double Tragedy").

⁸ T.T. at 247.

⁹ T.T. at 196.

¹⁰ *Evening Times*, "Double Tragedy."

¹¹ T.T. at 295-96.

¹² *Evening Times*, "Double Tragedy"; *Asbury Park Press*, "Cope."

¹³ T.T. at 217; *Evening Times*, "Double Tragedy"; "Priest Slain After Counseling a Veteran is Buried in N.J.," *New York Times*, Thurs., Dec. 30, 1971.

¹⁴ *Evening Times*, "Double Tragedy."

¹⁵ T.T. at 196, 295.

¹⁶ *Asbury Park Press*, "Cope."

¹⁷ T.T. at 302.

¹⁸ *Asbury Park Press*, "Cope."

¹⁹ *Evening Times*, "Double Tragedy," at 28.

²⁰ T.T. at 297-99.

²¹ T.T. at 299-300; cf., Interview with Timothy Long.

²² Interview with Timothy Long.

²³ Id.

²⁴ Id.

²⁵ T.T. at 299, 301.

²⁶ T.T. at 250, 302-03; cf., "Award of the Bronze Star Medal for Heroism" (John F. Kelly), Department of the Army, Headquarters, 25th Infantry Division, G.O. # 5204, TC 320, April 9, 1969. A copy of this citation was supplied courtesy of Mrs. Mildred Kelly.

²⁷ T.T. at 303-04.

²⁸ T.T. at 252; cf., *Asbury Park Press*, "Cope."

²⁹ T.T. at 251.

[30] T.T. at 307.

[31] "Award of the Bronze Star Medal for Heroism" (John F. Kelly), Department of the Army, Headquarters, 25th Infantry Division, G.O. # 5204, TC 320, April 9, 1969.

[32] *Evening Times*, "Double Tragedy."

[33] *Asbury Park Press*, "Cope."

[34] T.T. at 306.

[35] Id.

[36] T.T. at 252-533; *Asbury Park Press*, "Cope," at C1.

[37] T.T. at 304-07.

[38] T.T. at 306.

[39] T.T. at 308.

[40] T.T. at 367.

[41] T.T. at 306, 313.

[42] T.T. at 311.

[43] T.T. at 200-01.

[44] T.T. at 311-12.

[45] T.T. at 259.

[46] T.T. at 254 & ff.

[47] *Asbury Park Press*, "Cope," at C1.

[48] T.T. at 502.

[49] T.T. at 259.

[50] T.T. at 255-56, 329.

[51] T.T. at 206, 317-18.

[52] T.T. at 223-25, 326-28.

[53] T.T. at 11.

[54] T.T. at 309-10.

[55] T.T. at 206, 261-62, 325-26.

[56] T.T. at 208-09, 262, 316-17.

[57] T.T. at 400-401 (Trent).

[58] Preceding four paragraphs taken from Interview with Dr. Julio Del Castillo.

[59] T.T. at 263-64, 319.

[60] T.T. at 320 (J. Kelly III); 264 (Mrs. M. Kelly); 449-50 (Del Castillo); 475-76 (Saexinger); 525 (White (summation)); *see also* T.T. at 392-93 (VA Hospital Records, Exhibit D-2 in Evidence).

[61] T.T. at 215, 263-64, 319-20, 537; cf., *Evening Times*, "Double Tragedy."

[62] T.T. at 264, 321-22.

[63] T.T. at 322.

[64] *Evening Times*, "Double Tragedy."

[65] Id.

[66] Id. at 28.

[67] T.T. at 267-68, 322-23, 369.

[68] T.T. at 323-24.

[69] T.T. at 324-25, 371.

[70] T.T. at 268.

[71] T.T. at 183.

[72] T.T. at 334-35; *Evening Times*, "Double Tragedy."

[73] T.T. at 266-67, 330, 335.

[74] T.T. at 225-27, 330-32, 372-75.

[75] T.T. at 185-90, 333.

[76] T.T. at 190.

[77] T.T. at 333-34, 337.

[78] T.T. at 189-90.

[79] Recollections of this incident taken from Interview with Josetta C. Burchardt (#2).

[80] T.T. at 275.

[81] Telephone conversations with Mrs. Mildred Kelly.

[82] T.T. at 338; cf., 501 (Dr. Motley).

[83] Id.

[84] T.T. at 275-76; Telephone conversations with Mrs. Mildred Kelly.

[85] *Evening Times*, "Double Tragedy."

[86] Toms River Report, as edited; *see* Shenrock, *No Greater Love.*

[87] Telephone conversation with Msgr. Francis Kolby.

[88] T.T. at 28-29, 383-84.

[89] "Priest Dies 9 Days After NJ Shooting," *Philadelphia Bulletin*, Dec. 27, 1971.

[90] Information in preceding paragraphs derived from *Evening Times*, "Double Tragedy," at 28.

Chapter 32 Notes:

[1] Toms River Report.

[2] Recollections of Fr. Wessel's Holy Name Society talk taken from Interview with (John) Harry Cascione.

[3] Recollections of the afternoon of December 12th taken from Toms River Report, as edited, and Interview with Sean Maguire, unless noted.

[4] Toms River Report.

[5] Interview with Brendan Gallagher.

[6] Telephone conversation with Sr. Teresa Agnes.

[7] "CBA Again Rated Parochial Basketball Power," *Asbury Park Press*, circa Dec. 9, 1971.

[8] Interview with Josetta C. Burchardt (#2).

[9] Interview with Joanne W. Gillespie.

[10] Interview with Maryann Beitel (#1).

[11] Id.

[12] Interview with Maryann Beitel (#2). Someone later repeated this incident and conversation to Mrs. Beitel, but she does not now recall who the person was.

[13] Interview with Maryann Beitel (#1).

[14] Interview with Sr. Teresa Agnes; *see also* Interviews with Sr. Julianna Naulty; Sr. Nancy Carney.

[15] Recollections of this lunch on Thursday, December 16th taken from Interviews with Msgr. James H. Dubell (#1) and (#2).

[16] Recollections of Fr. Wessel's visit home to his mother on December 16th taken from Interviews with Mrs. Kathleen Wessel (#1) and (#2); Sean Maguire; and Toms River Report, as edited.

[17] Toms River Report; Telephone conversation with Rita Kearney; St. Joseph Parish Council Meeting Minutes, Dec. 16, 1971.

[18] Interview with Peter Caroselli; Telephone conversation with Sr. Teresa Agnes.

[19] Interview with Pat Wessel.

[20] Interview and Telephone conversation with Sr. Nancy Carney.

[21] Over thirty years later, these are, as best as can be recalled, the events that occurred on the afternoon

of December 17, 1971. Realizing that recollections may be unclear, hazy, or even contradictory after such a span of time, the author leaves it to the reader to sort through any inconsistencies and make his or her own judgment.

22 *See* Shenrock, *No Greater Love*; Interviews with Brendan Gallagher; Carmella V. Di Matteo.

23 Recollections of this meeting taken from Interview with Carmella V. Di Matteo.

24 Cf., Interview with Carmella V. Di Matteo; T.T. at 276.

25 T.T. at 276; cf., T.T. at 216.

26 Recollections of Fr. Wessel's conversation with Mrs. Kelly that afternoon taken from T.T. at 276-77 (Mrs. M. Kelly).

27 Interview with Carmella V. Di Matteo.

28 Cf., Interview with SJHS (various).

29 Interview with John Menter.

30 *See also* Karen Deckelnick, "20 Years Later, Slain Priest Warmly Recalled," *Asbury Park Press*, Fri., Dec. 27, 1991, sec. B, at 1.

31 Recollections of this conversation taken from Interview with John Menter.

32 *See* Chapter 1, *supra*. Material for this section is also taken from Toms River Report and Interview with Sean Maguire, unless noted.

33 Interview with Sean Maguire.

34 Interviews with Sr. Jorene Cieciuch; Sean Maguire.

35 Interview with Sr. Jorene Cieciuch.

36 Toms River Report; Interview with Sean Maguire.

37 Interview with Sean Maguire.

38 Interview with Sr. Julianna Naulty.

39 Interview with Sean Maguire.

40 Interview with Peter Caroselli.

41 *See* "Specialness As A Priest" by Maryann Beitel, reprinted in Shenrock, *Three Good Shepherds*, at 28.

42 *See* Shenrock, *No Greater Love*.

43 Authority and documentation for the remaining materials of this chapter are taken generally from Trial Transcript summations by the Defense, T.T. at 8-11, 523-532 (White), and Prosecution, T.T. at 4-6, 534-538 (Denning). Specific additional cites to the transcript or to other sources are added where appropriate. This chronology represents the best or most plausible approximation of what occurred and as to time, events, etc., based on the information available to the author.

44 Cf., T.T. at 351.

45 T.T. at 337-39, 346.

46 T.T. at 346-49; 502 (Motley).

47 T.T. at 502 (Motley).

48 T.T. at 349.

49 T.T. at 266.

50 T.T. at 349-350.

51 T.T. at 339-40.

52 T.T. at 278-79.

53 T.T. at 350.

54 T.T. at 350-51, 526.

55 T.T. at 352-379.

56 T.T. at 352, 381.

57 T.T. at 381.

[58] Cf., T.T. at 261-17.

[59] T.T. at 352.

[60] Neil A. Sheehan, "Answering The Call-Slain priest remembered two decades after death," *Asbury Park Press*, Thurs., Dec. 26, 1991, A1, B3, at B3.

[61] Telephone conversation with Mrs. Mildred Kelly.

[62] T.T. at 353; *see* Shenrock, *No Greater Love*; *accord* Telephone conversation with Mrs. Mildred Kelly and John F. Kelly III (John F. Kelly III).

[63] T.T. at 353; cf., T.T. at 503 (Motley).

[64] T.T. at 72; cf., T.T. at 354 (J. Kelly III).

[65] T.T. at 30 (P. Cunningham).

[66] T.T. at 30-31 (P. Cunningham).

[67] T.T. at 50 (Lecuyer).

[68] T.T. at 44-48 (Kreger).

[69] T.T. at 243-44 (Herbert). Statements are taken from Det. Cpt. Herbert's testimony and are not verbatim quotes of John F. Kelly III, except for the sentence in quotation marks.

[70] T.T. at 529.

[71] Cf., T.T. at 503 (Motley); 404 (Trent).

[72] Interview with Dr. Julio Del Castillo.

[73] T.T. at 436-37, 438 (Del Castillo); cf., T.T. at 531 (White).

Chapter 33 Notes:

[1] Cf., Interviews with Wes Ritterbusch; Barry Anderson.

[2] Toms River Report.

[3] "St. Joseph's 5 Defeats Alumni," *Asbury Park Press*, Dec. 17, 1971.

[4] Interview with John Menter.

[5] Interview with Carmella V. Di Matteo.

[6] Interview with Sr. Nancy Carney.

[7] Interview with Sr. Teresa Agnes.

[8] Interview with (John) Harry Cascione.

[9] Interview with Maryann Beitel (#1).

[10] Cf., Interviews with Brendan Gallagher; Msgr. James H. Dubell (#2).

[11] Toms River Report; Interview with Msgr. James H. Dubell (#2).

[12] Interview with Pat Wessel.

[13] Interview with William Beitel.

[14] Interviews with Fr. Joseph J. Procaccini; Sr. Julianna Naulty.

[15] Interview with Fr. Joseph J. Procaccini.

[16] Interview with Sr. Jorene Cieciuch.

[17] Interview with Maryann Beitel (#1).

[18] Stuart Rose, "Suspect's Mother Begs Forgiveness in Shooting," *The Trentonian*, Mon., Dec. 28, 1971.

[19] Quoted in Carlo M. Sardella and Kathy Begley, "One Entered Seminary, One Went to War; Now Priest is Slain and Vet is Accused," *Philadelphia Inquirer*, Sun., Jan. 9, 1972, at 19-A (hereinafter *Phila. Inquirer*, "One Entered Seminary").

[20] Interview with Msgr. Joseph C. Shenrock.

[21] "Priest Dies 9 Days After NJ Shooting," *Philadelphia Bulletin*, Dec. 27, 1971.

22   Interview with Maryann Beitel (#1).

23   Id.

24   *Phila. Inquirer,* "One Entered Seminary."

25   Interview with Maryann Beitel (#1).

26   Id.; Interview with William Beitel.

27   Interview with Msgr. James H. Dubell (#2); cf., Interviews with Brendan Gallagher; William Beitel.

28   Interview with Al Kedz.

29   Interview with Dawn F. Fowler.

30   Cf., Interview with Peter Caroselli.

31   Interview with Bonnie Lopez.

32   Interview with Nuns (various).

33   Interview with Msgr. James H. Dubell (#2).

34   Interview with Brendan Gallagher.

35   "Here one does not will to cause death; one's inability to impede it is merely accepted." *Catechism of the Catholic Church,* § 2278 (New York: Catholic Book Pub. Co., 1994).

36   Interview with Pat Wessel; cf., Interview with Msgr. James H. Dubell (#2).

37   *See* Shenrock, *No Greater Love;* Interview with Al Kedz.

38   Dr. De Marco was quoted in, "Mass of Resurrection Offered for Fr. Wessel," *The Monitor,* Fri., Dec. 31, 1971, at 1 (hereinafter *Monitor,* "Mass of Resurrection"). An identical article of the same title appears in, "Mass of Resurrection Offered for Fr. Wessel," *Burlington County Herald,* Mt. Holly, NJ, Thurs., Jan. 6, 1972, sec. B, at 12.

39   *Monitor,* "Mass of Resurrection."

40   Interview with Al Kedz.

41   Interview with Maryann Beitel (#1).

42   Id.

43   Interview with Michael Choma.

44   Interview and Telephone conversation with Michael Choma.

45   Interview with Al Kedz.

46   Cf., Interview with Maryann Beitel (#1).

47   Interview with Al Kedz.

48   Interview with Brendan Gallagher.

49   Interview with Carmella V. Di Matteo.

50   Id.

51   Id.; Interview with John Menter.

52   Interview with Al Kedz.

53   Id.

54   Id.

55   *Trenton Times,* "Two Congregations."

56   *See* Shenrock, *No Greater Love;* cf., "Many Mourn Slain Priest; Burial Held at Mount Holly," *Burlington County (NJ) Times,* Thurs., Dec. 30, 1971; Interview with Al Kedz.

57   Interview with Al Kedz.

58   *See* Shenrock, *No Greater Love;* cf., Interview with Ronald Garrett.

59   Interview with Joanne W. Gillespie.

60   Id.

61   Interview with Al Kedz.

62   *See* Shenrock, *No Greater Love;* cf., Interview with Al Kedz.

[63] Interview with Carlton Wessel.

[64] Cf., Interview with Carmella V. Di Matteo.

[65] Fr. Peter M.J. Stravinskas, "Sanctity in a Contemporary Key," (unpublished essay), undated, circa 1974, at 6 (hereinafter "Sanctity in a Contemporary Key").

[66] Interview with Al Kedz.

[67] Interviews with Maryann Beitel (#1); Pat Wessel.

[68] Interview with Nuns (Sr. Elise Betz).

[69] Interview with Maryann Beitel (#1).

[70] See Shenrock, No Greater Love; Interviews with SJHS (Beverly C. Devlin); Sr. Nancy Carney.

[71] Written Recollections of Jayne Hartley.

[72] Editorial, "Our New Priests," The Monitor, May 28, 1965, at 4.

[73] Phila. Inquirer, "One Entered Seminary."

[74] Cf., Interview with Msgr. James H. Dubell (#2).

[75] Fr. Dubell's eulogy of Fr. John P. Wessel was reprinted in St. Mary's Bulletin, vol. 2, no. 4 (Winter 1972), at 1-2.

[76] Interview with Sr. Nancy Carney. Cf., Sr. Suzanne Toolan, I Am the Bread of Life © 1971, 1982, 1986 GIA Publications, Inc. In some versions of the song, the verse is alternatively, "And I will raise you up."

[77] Cf., Interviews with William Beitel; Al Kedz.

[78] Interview with Al Kedz.

[79] Raymond J. Tuers, "Father Wessel Imbued with a Mission in Life," Asbury Park Sunday Press, Sun., Jan. 9, 1972, sec. C, at C-1, The Asbury Park Press, © 1972. Used with Permission.

[80] Interview with William Beitel.

[81] Interviews with Maryann Beitel (#1); William Beitel (Maryann Beitel).

[82] Interview with Al Kedz.

[83] See Shenrock, No Greater Love.

[84] Raymond J. Tuers, "Father Wessel Imbued with a Mission in Life," Asbury Park Sunday Press, Sun., Jan. 9, 1972, sec. C, at C-1 (hereinafter Asbury Park Press, "Mission in Life"). The Asbury Park Press, © 1972. Used with Permission.

[85] Quoted section taken from Asbury Park Press, "Mission in Life."

[86] Interview with Maryann Beitel (#1).

[87] Shenrock, No Greater Love; cf., Interview with Maryann Beitel (#2). Preceding three paragraphs taken, in part, from Asbury Park Press, "Mission in Life."

[88] Shenrock, No Greater Love.

[89] See id.

[90] Id.

Chapter 34 Notes:

[1] Interview with Mrs. Kathleen Wessel and Maryann Beitel (Mrs. Kathleen Wessel).

[2] Shenrock, No Greater Love.

[3] Letter from New Jersey Governor William T. Cahill, Dec. 27, 1971, copy supplied courtesy of Mrs. Kathleen Wessel. (The original proclamation incorrectly listed Fr. Wessel's age as 33).

[4] Interview with Joanne W. Gillespie.

[5] Interview with CYO (Joseph Parnell).

[6] Interview with CYO (Kevin Connor).

[7]   Interviews with Josetta C. Burchardt (#1) and (#2).

[8]   Interview with SJHS (Ed Staunton).

[9]   Interview with SJHS (Beverly C. Devlin).

[10] Interview with Peter Caroselli.

[11] Interview with John Menter.

[12] Telephone conversation with Thomas Callow.

[13] Interview with Bonnie Lopez.

[14] Interview with Barry Anderson.

[15] Written Recollections of Jayne Hartley.

[16] Id.

Chapter 35 Notes:

[1]   Interview with Dawn F. Fowler.

[2]   Interview with SJHS (Jill V. Mueller).

[3]   Interview with Maryann Beitel (#1).

[4]   "Eucharist" Log (undated, circa June 1972).

[5]   Interview with Maryann Beitel (#1); cf., Interview with Barry Anderson.

[6]   Interviews with Sr. Teresa Agnes; Carmella V. Di Matteo.

[7]   Personal observations of the author.

[8]   Shenrock, *No Greater Love*.

[9]   T.T. at 526-28.

[10] T.T. at 400, 416-17 (Trent), T.T. at 436-37, 441-42 (Del Castillo), T.T. at 469-70, 474 (Saexinger), T.T. at 496-97 (Motley); cf., T.T. at 529-30 (White); T.T. at 537 (Denning).

[11] Shenrock, *No Greater Love*; *see also* T.T. at 571-573.

Chapter 36 Notes:

[1]   Letter from Sr. M. Christina Murphy, I.H.M., to author (March 3, 1996).

[2]   *See* "Specialness As A Priest" by Maryann Beitel, reprinted in Shenrock, *Three Good Shepherds*, at 28.

[3]   Interview with Sr. Nancy Carney.

[4]   Interview and Telephone conversation with Sr. Nancy Carney. Cf., Isaiah 9:16 (". . . the Lord does not spare their young men . . .").

[5]   Letter from Sr. M. Francis Rita to Diocese of Trenton (Dec. 1980), original contained in Chancery Files.

[6]   Sr. Francis Rita is now deceased. Recollections of this encounter are taken from the memories of a number of her fellow Sisters with whom she spoke at the time, and from a handwritten note that Sr. Francis Rita left. Interview and Telephone conversation with Sr. Nancy Carney. *See also* Interview with Carmella V. Di Matteo; "Specialness As A Priest" by Maryann Beitel, reprinted in Shenrock, *Three Good Shepherds*, at 28; Letter from Sr. M. Francis Rita to Diocese of Trenton (Dec. 1980), original in Chancery Files. Sr. Nancy thought this conversation took place on the morning of December 17th, but according to Sr. Francis Rita's handwritten note, it had to have occurred in the afternoon.

[7]   Cf., Stravinskas, "Sanctity in a Contemporary Key," at 6.

[8]   Id. at 1, 6.

9   Shenrock, *No Greater Love*; *see also*, Stravinskas, "Sanctity in a Contemporary Key," at 7.

10   Cf., Stravinskas, "Sanctity in a Contemporary Key," at 6.

11   Interview with Bishop John C. Reiss.

12   Materials and quotes in this section, unless otherwise noted, are taken from the author's interview with the named persons. The quote will not be otherwise cited, except for clarity, or where the author interviewed the person more than once.

13   Interview with Maryann Beitel (#1).

14   Id.

15   Interview with Msgr. James H. Dubell (#2).

16   Sean Maguire was quoted in, Toms River Report.

17   Interview with Sean Maguire.

18   "Tribute to Fr. Wessel," by Josetta Cascione, Letters to the Editor, *The Monitor*, Jan. 4, 1979, at 7.

19   Interview with Josetta C. Burchardt (#2).

20   Interview with Carl Wingate (#1).

21   Telephone conversation with Mrs. Mildred Kelly.

22   Letter from Dr. Michael J. Ward to author (Jan. 24, 2003).

23   Vincent A. Weiss, "Prayers for Fr. Wessel's Cause Begin," *The Monitor*, Fri., Jan. 4, 1974, at 1, 2 (quote at 2).

24   Interview with James Roche.

25   "Mrs. Wessel's Reflections on her Son's Letter and Life," reprinted in Shenrock, *Three Good Shepherds*, at 23-24, as edited.

Printed in the United States
104192LV00002B/52/A